- 176 -

JUVENILE DELINQUENCY

A Systems Approach

Curt R. Bartol
Castleton State College

Anne M. Bartol
Castleton State College

PRENTICE HALL, Englewood Cliffs, New Jersey 07632

Library of Congress Cataloging-in-Publication Data

Bartol, Curt R.
    Juvenile delinquency : a systems approach / Curt R. Bartol, Anne
M. Bartol.
        p.   cm.
    Bibliography: p.
    Includes index.
    ISBN 0-13-514431-0
    1. Juvenile delinquency. 2. Juvenile delinquency--United States.
3. Social systems.   I. Bartol, Anne M.   II. Title.
    HV9069.B35 1989
    364.3'6'0973--dc19   88-28948
                                                                 CIP

Editorial/production supervision
  and interior design: *Carol L. Atkins*
Cover design: *Joel Mitnick Design, Inc.*
Manufacturing buyer: *Robert Anderson*

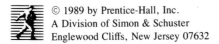 © 1989 by Prentice-Hall, Inc.
A Division of Simon & Schuster
Englewood Cliffs, New Jersey 07632

Printed in the United States of America
10 9 8 7 6 5 4 3 2 1

ISBN   0-13-514431-0

Prentice-Hall International (UK) Limited, *London*
Prentice-Hall of Australia Pty. Limited, *Sydney*
Prentice-Hall Canada Inc., *Toronto*
Prentice-Hall Hispanoamericana, S.A., *Mexico*
Prentice-Hall of India Private Limited, *New Delhi*
Prentice-Hall of Japan, Inc., *Tokyo*
Simon & Schuster Asia Pte. Ltd., *Singapore*
Editora Prentice-Hall do Brasil, Ltda., *Rio de Janeiro*

Contents

LIST OF TABLES

LIST OF FIGURES

Preface

This book is the result of a combined 25 years of college and university teaching. It is primarily directed at upper-level undergraduate students taking a first course in juvenile delinquency. The material is intended to be challenging, balanced, and accurate. Much of the text has been carefully read and critiqued by students majoring in criminal justice, psychology, sociology, or history.

We have not followed either of the two dominant approaches to organizing a juvenile delinquency text. We eschew not only the format in which theories and their various versions are presented sequentially, but also the topical approach which deals with such areas as delinquency and family, peers, and school. The voluminous research literature defies efforts to tame it into the strict theoretical structure demanded by the first approach. The second approach, though seemingly offering more organization, often becomes detached from necessary theoretical moorings. Instead, we have used a social systems approach—to be explained shortly—to coordinate the rich and complicated study of juvenile delinquency.

Five key words or concepts best characterize the book. They are

1. history
2. interdisciplinary approach
3. social systems
4. theory
5. research

To appreciate fully contemporary thought about juvenile delinquency, one must have a solid sense of history. Students of crime and delinquency sometimes consider classical theories hardly relevant to current problems. However, if we approach theories of delinquency as reflections of different versions of social and cultural phenomena constructed at different times and in different places, we will be less inclined to dismiss them as dated or misguided versions and will be more willing to seek the meaning, lessons, and wisdom potentially inherent in each.

Our position in this book is that there are many "right" but conflicting theories or explanations of delinquency, even within the same era. They are "right" given the time and context within which they were developed and debated. It is instructive to follow not only the theories themselves but also judicial, legislative, and other developments along an historical course. This allows us to assess both the relative merits of what has been tried and what is being tried now and to speculate about future effective and creative approaches to the problem of delinquency.

The term "interdisciplinary" often brings a mixture of reactions from professionals and scholars in the field of crime and delinquency. Some are convinced it is foolhardy to even attempt to bring different disciplines under the same roof; others may feel the idea has merit, but is unattainable. Nonetheless, we have tried to present classical and contemporary literature from the two major fields of sociology and psychology, along with a smattering of anthropology. We have tried to coordinate the extensive theory and research into a coherent structure that will allow the student to see how each of these disciplines fits into the overall study of delinquency. The structure we have found most useful is social systems theory.

Social systems theory—the theoretical framework for this text—allows us to examine the vast amount of theoretical and empirical work in juvenile delinquency with some thematic orientation. Social systems theory facilitates a synthesis of what we know across disciplines and viewpoints. To understand delinquency, we must study not only delinquents themselves but also their families, peers, schools, neighborhoods, communities, and cultures. A social systems approach enables us to do this with organization.

Theory and research, the essentials of science, are also the hallmarks of criminology. Most students of crime and delinquency would not disagree with this statement. It is crucial, therefore, that anyone carefully educated about delinquency understand the nature of the scientific enterprise, including its strengths and limitations, frustrations and excitements, and mysteries and complexities. We have devoted an early chapter to science to set the tone for the remainder of the book.

The book does not attempt a comprehensive treatment of juvenile justice. Our primary goal is to stimulate and cultivate an interest in and understanding of delinquent behavior. How this understanding is to be applied involves complex administrative and legal strategies and policies that we believe are best left to a separate text. This is not to say that juvenile justice is ignored. Chapters 3 and 12 cover the history of juvenile justice and recent developments relating to the prevention and control of delinquency.

Finally, there is no separate chapter on female delinquency for two main reasons. First, such a chapter would not fit into the social systems structure of the text. Instead, sex as a structure variable is considered as a subsection of Chapter 10, as are age and social class. Second, research on female delinquency is incorporated throughout the book. We believe it is important for authors to cease treating the burgeoning literature on female crime and delinquency as an afterthought and begin integrating it into the criminological literature as a matter of course. We have attempted to do this throughout the text.

Many individuals contributed to various aspects of the book. We would especially like to thank the anonymous reviewers and Professor George T. Bergen who offered invaluable advice and commentary. Special thanks are also due the enthusiastic and knowledgable students who read and commented upon various drafts. They are: Kate Barber, Richard Curtiss, Diane Fitzgerald, Cindy Lack, Gina Menagh, Virginia Philo, Paul-André Richard, Jane Roies, and Wendy Swanson. Finally, the Prentice Hall staff has offered encouragement, patience, and competent support throughout all phases of the book, especially editors Paul Corey and Matt McNearney and production editor Carol L. Atkins.

Curt R. Bartol
Anne M. Bartol

Defining and Measuring Delinquency

1 CHAPTER

Near the brink of the twentieth century, the French social psychologist Gabriel Tarde and the American developmental psychologist James Mark Baldwin separately published their theories of imitation. Apparently, neither man was aware of the other's work, although Tarde's ideas were published five years earlier than Baldwin's. They reached a similar conclusion: All human behavior can be explained by an imitation process. Their perspectives, however, were dissimilar. Tarde, more a sociologist than a psychologist, studied sociological phenomena associated with crowds, crazes, fads, fashions, customs, and crime. Baldwin relied on ''individual psychology,'' studying the mental development of the child, primarily that of his own two daughters. The idea of imitation as the root of behavior did not originate with Baldwin or Tarde. Philosophers David Hume, Walter Bagehot, and the psychologist William James, among others, had alluded to it previously. Tarde and Baldwin, however, formulated and developed their theories more clearly and systematically than anyone had before.

Tarde, who published his theory in *Les Lois de l'Imitation* (1890) and *Les Lois Sociales* (1898), asserted that all activities of human societies are, in one way or another, outcomes of the process of imitation. Society itself is, in effect, the end product of imitation: Its members copy each others' behavior, attitudes, and emotions. This process occurs selectively rather than automatically, since individuals imitate only those they respect or otherwise find worthy of emulation. Imitation also can occur as a group process. Tarde was so convinced of the "truth" of his observations that he considered his theoretical formulation another basic "law" of the universe. He proclaimed that there were three separate laws of imitation, and that they were to sociology ". . . what the laws of habit and heredity are to biology, the laws of gravitation to astronomy, and of vibration to physics" (Tarde, 1890, p. 18).

The essence of his three laws is as follows:

1. Humans imitate one another in direct proportion to the amount of close contact they have with one another; the more they see or interact with one another, the more likely they are to imitate.

2. The superior are imitated by the inferior. People who are in positions of royalty, power, or authority, or who are deeply respected, are far more likely to be imitated than peasants or those who are powerless. This holds for groups as well as individuals. Fad-setting cities (e.g., Paris), are more likely to be imitated than rural towns.

3. When two mutually exclusive fashions compete, an "average" of the two occurs.

James Mark Baldwin published his theory of imitation in *The Mental Development in the Child and the Race* (1894) and *Social and Ethical Interpretations in Mental Measurement* (1897). Initially a firm believer of Darwin's concept of evolution, Baldwin apparently altered his thoughts about human instincts and evolutionary theory shortly after the birth in 1893 of his first child, Helen. After observing her early development, Helen's father posited that " . . . the prime and essential method of his [the child's] learning is by imitative absorption of the actions, thoughts, expressions of other persons" (Baldwin, 1897, p. 581). Therefore, children develop intellectually and morally by *imitating* the thoughts and actions of significant others around them. This flew in the face of Darwinian theory, which contended that development unfolded according to the laws of nature. The Darwinians gave little credit to the role played by others or the social environment. A parent's efforts to enrich a child's environment could not overcome the genetic determinants of moral and intellectual development. Moral development, for example, depended upon a time sequence programmed into the child's biological makeup; when the time came, the child "naturally" acquired the necessary moral reasoning. "Timing" was determined solely by the child's ancestry. Similarly, environmental enrichment could do little to change a genetically determined level of intelligence.

For reasons which will be discussed shortly, the theory of imitation did not reappear in sociological or psychological literature until nearly fifty years later. Baldwin, considered one of the most eminent psychologists of his time (Broughton, 1981), abruptly left academe and the United States for Mexico in 1909; shortly thereafter he moved to Paris, where he lived until his death in 1934. Only recently have we learned that he was forced to resign his position at Johns Hopkins University and was blackballed by the psychological "establishment" after being caught in a police raid on a Baltimore brothel. We will return to Baldwin's work later in the book, since he laid some of the foundation both for Jean Piaget's cognitive development theory and for contemporary social learning theory.

At this juncture, the reader may be thinking that the preceding paragraphs are an unusual way to begin a text on delinquency. A major objective of this text is to cultivate in readers a patience to see the world from multiple perspectives and to provide the necessary concepts with which to refine these perspectives. This will require an examination of history and an appreciation of science, theoretical development, and the philosophies of human nature held by individuals and social groups at any one time. Perspectives on behavior, including delinquent behavior, are strongly influenced by the political, economic, and social climates and by the dominant thinking of the time. Even in a pluralistic society, it is possible to identify social moods or trends which bear heavily on explanations of behavior.

When Baldwin and Tarde proposed their separate theories, Darwinism and biological determinism dominated American and European perspectives of human nature and society. Interestingly, sociologists as well as psychologists adhered to this view. Biological determinism argued that behavior was determined largely by heredity and instincts. Furthermore, mental development was believed to be limited, controlled, and modified by a series of instinctive impulses which are relatively fixed in the individual through a process of evolution by natural selection. Against this backdrop, the "radical" ideas of Baldwin and Tarde were not well received. The sociologist Charles A. Ellwood (1901) took Baldwin's theory of imitation to task, implying that it was sacrilegious to question mainstream thought about evolution and human instincts. Ellwood scolded Baldwin for theorizing about some "absolute gulf between man and the animal world." This violated the doctrine of development "which since Darwin has been the major premise of all scientific thought about man" (Ellwood, 1901, p. 728). Humans, Ellwood said, represent but a small gradient of development in the evolutionary chain along which all living creatures are positioned. Any imitation that occurs, he argued, actually is a feature of animal instinct, nothing else. "Accordingly, we find Professor Baldwin, almost alone among eminent modern psychologists, refusing to recognize the importance of the innate or instinctive in mental development" (Ellwood, 1901, p. 733). Interestingly, in spite of Ellwood's assertions, Darwin's theory was losing popularity among *biologists* around the turn of the century because they were unable to identify any biological mechanism which could support it satisfactorily.

The traditional Darwinian view espoused by Ellwood and other social scientists was devastating to any notion of equality among human beings, since it allowed for the possibility that some races or ethnic groups were less developed than others. Note Ellwood's comments:

> . . . the negro child, even when reared in a white family under the most favorable conditions, fails to take on the mental and moral characteristics of the Caucasian race. His mental attitudes toward persons and things, toward organized society, toward life, and toward religion never become quite the same as those of the white. (p. 735) [Similarly,] . . . the "instinctive criminal" and the "hereditary pauper" are such, not because of the contagion

of vice, crime, and shiftlessness which certain models in society may furnish, but because *inborn tendencies lead them to seek such models for imitation rather than others;* because they naturally gravitate to a life of crime and pauperism (p. 736, italics added).

In a footnote attached to the last statement, Ellwood wrote: "It is unnecessary to point out that this is practically the unanimous conclusion of all experts engaged in the study of these classes." Today, we find Ellwood's views outrageous. Nevertheless, we must keep in mind the social context in which they were expressed.

In 1870, approximately 20 years before Baldwin's and Tarde's theories were published, the behavior of animals began to be viewed within the context of a widely recognized theory of evolution. Charles Darwin's *Origin of Species* had been published in 1859 and Thomas Huxley's *Evidence as to Man's Place in Nature* in 1862. In 1864, Alfred Wallace published a paper that applied the theory of natural selection to human evolution. In the United States, Herbert Spencer was talking about the "survival of the fittest" and arguing for the evolution of the mind. Darwin's controversial *Descent of Man* was published in 1871 and soon became widely cited.

During that same year, the Italian physician-anthropologist Cesare Lombroso noticed that the skull of one notorious criminal—a murderer named Vilella—was significantly different from other human skulls. Specifically, Vilella's skull had depressions where others had crests. These intriguing cranial depressions led Lombroso to examine and measure skulls of other criminals, living and deceased. For example, he performed autopsies on the bodies of 66 male criminals obtained from anthropological museums throughout Italy. He also made various physical measurements of 832 living Italian criminals (both males and females) who were "among the most notorious and depraved" (Beirne, 1987, p. 791). Lombroso was convinced that the anatomical features that he found " . . . were similar to insane persons examined in his clinic, to the American black, to the Mongolian races, and, above all, to prehistoric man" (Beirne, 1987, p. 791). From these observations, he formulated his theory of the "atavistic" nature of the criminal. Loosely defined, an atavism is a "throwback" to an earlier time.

Lombroso was greatly influenced by the views expounded upon by Darwin in the *Descent of Man*, especially the notion that some people are genetically closer to their primitive ancestry than others. Lombroso's basic premise, published in *L'Uomo Delinquente* [Criminal Man] in 1876, was that these individuals—atavists—were born with strong, instinctive predispositions to behave antisocially. The criminal, he believed, represented this "left-behind" species that had not yet evolved sufficiently toward the more "advanced," civilized *homo sapiens*. Criminals, therefore, were genetically somewhere between modern humans and their primitive origins in both physical and psychological makeup.

Lombroso's "born criminal" concept generated much interest in Europe, perhaps because the study of crime and delinquency on that continent was dominated by physicians and psychiatrists. As late as the mid-1930s, Lombroso's concepts were still embraced by most Italian criminologists (Monachesi, 1936). Physicians, psychiatrists, and anthropologists joined to form the Crimino-Biology Association, which was devoted to the biological study of crime. Crimino-biologists were interested in all potential biological features that would provide an index of "criminal degeneracy." The physician Louis Vervaeck, for example, collected physical data on 30,000 inmates from prisons throughout Belgium. Vervaeck believed that he had discovered a very reliable index of criminal tendencies with a physical measurement he called the "grand stretch." Extend your two arms horizontally and to the sides. Measure the distance between the index finger on your right hand and the index finger on your left. Now measure your height. The grand stretch is the ratio of the one to the other. Vervaeck would say that if that distance between your fingertips is unusually long compared to your height, you are predisposed to a life of crime! In his view, a short youth with long arms should be watched very closely.

In France, Gabriel Tarde argued forcefully against any notion of a born criminal. He attacked the many flaws in Lombroso's methods of measurement as well as the bases for his conclusions. Crime, Tarde maintained, is a social phenomenon that follows the laws of imitation (Beirne, 1987). In fact, Tarde believed that most crime originated in the higher social classes and descended to the lower classes. After all, one of his laws of imitation predicted that the inferior copied the superior. "Drunkenness, smoking, moral offenses, political assassination, arson, and even vagabondage . . . were crimes that originated with feudal nobility and were transmitted to the masses through imitation" (Beirne, 1987, p. 800). He also asserted that the city, where greed was predominant and traditional values were weakened, was a primary breeding ground for crime. "The prolonged effect of large cities upon criminality is manifested, it seems to us, in the slow substitution, not exactly of guile for violence, but of greedy, crafty, and voluptuous violence for vindictive and brutal violence" (quote from Tarde's *Penal Philosophy* cited by Beirne, 1987, p. 802).

However, Tarde was largely unsuccessful in shifting criminologists away from biological determinism and toward social influences. Biological determinism was deeply entrenched in Europe, and Tarde's radical viewpoint received the same reception as Baldwin's did in the United States. In the United States, however, Lombroso and his successors, referred to as the "Italian School of Criminology," were greeted skeptically, criticized, and generally shunned. Darwin's views on natural evolution, on the other hand, *did* have great impact on perspectives of human nature, as illustrated by the comments of Charles Ellwood noted earlier. It was not until the 1930s that Darwinism began to lose favor in sociological theory. Although most psychologists continued to accept it, sociologists were rejecting individual explanations of behavior for those rooted in the structure of society.

In addition to providing a sense of history, the foregoing material reveals some characteristics about the nature of science and the development of theory, topics to which we will return in the next chapter. Each scientific discipline, it seems, is dominated by one or more theories during certain epochs. At certain times, for example, the theories of Freud, Lombroso, and Darwin dominated the field of psychology, sometimes all at once. Today they do not. Philosophers and historians of science warn us that at any given moment scientists and laypersons alike are trapped in the framework of their theories and their language. It is difficult to step outside this conceptual framework, because we are convinced that we have finally discovered (or are approaching) the "truth" or absolute facts about a phenomenon. Ellwood's condemnation of the theory of imitation underscores this point. Ellwood was prisoner of the Darwinian viewpoint. Tarde, however, appeared to be equally a prisoner of his "laws" of imitation. Consider the following words, written over fifty years ago:

> The progress of science is often portrayed as a majestic and inevitable evolution of ideas in a logical sequence of successively closer approximations to the truth . . . (T)his conception does not apply to criminology wherein myth and fashion and social conditions have often exercised an influence quite unrelated to the soundness of theories or to the implications of accumulated evidence. One of the sources of protection against invasion by fads, and against these extra theoretical influences, of which criminology of today has not availed itself, is a sound appreciation of its own past. (Lindesmith and Levin, 1937, p. 671)

In recent years, philosophers and historians of science have come to appreciate the wisdom of the Lindesmith-Levin statement. Some even believe that empirical research plays a surprisingly minor role in the development and survival of any theory (Lakatos, 1970). Instead, the life span of a theory, particularly a social science theory, often depends upon two things: first, how the theory fits into the other interests of the community of scientists; second, the ability of the theory to fulfill the needs of a society at a particular time in history (Cole, 1975). A theory survives as long as it fits into the social, economic, and political scheme of things, despite the amount of evidence that seems to refute it (Kuhn, 1970). At the turn of the century, in both Europe and the United States, the social science community believed strongly, not only in evolution, but also in biological and genetic determinism and the strong role of instinct in human behavior. Accordingly, human behavior was believed to be controlled and dictated by biological factors beyond individual control. The environment was believed to play only a secondary role in influencing individual actions.

The life of a theory also may depend upon the presence or absence of scientific technology available to detect or identify phenomena. Later, elements previously "missed" or "misidentified" may emerge. Lombroso's theory and its offshoots "lived" partly because science had no alternative explanation for the research findings. Today, we can speculate that if physical differences really were found, the Italian School might have been identifying biological afflictions or genotypes rather than "evolutionary throwbacks." For example, many individuals who have an extra Y (male) chromosome (called the XYY chromosomal anomaly) have above average height, above average arm length, protruding nose and jaw, and an over-extended brow. Similar characteristics are associated with the pituitary dysfunction "acromegaly" (gigantism), also unknown during Lombroso's time. Persons with these characteristics are believed, even today, to be more involved in criminal activity than the chromosomally normal population (Jarvik, Klodin, and Matsuyama, 1973), although their crimes are generally property offenses rather than violent ones (Price and Whatmore, 1967). Viewed from this perspective, modern criminologists could explain the behavior of Lombroso's "born criminals" in a variety of ways. Some, for example, would say that a society fearful of someone who looked unusual may have imprisoned that person without cause. Others would suggest that, because of their size, parents of these individuals exerted less control over their behavior. Still others—a minority—would argue that the hormonal imbalances facilitated or even produced aggressive tendencies.

It is important that all theories of crime and delinquency be placed in their historical context rather than dismissed prematurely as "wrong," "misguided," or just plain "dumb." Past theories of delinquency were not necessarily "wrong" considering the time and place in which they were developed. As the American philosopher Nelson Goodman (1978) observed, theories may be the right version of the world given from where they take their start.

It often happens, also, that we prefer contemporary, "new" theories to classic, "old" ones. We will find throughout the book, however, that many old theories anticipated the newer versions in many ways. Furthermore, while the newer versions may account for contemporary phenomena quite well, they would not necessarily account for what was happening at the turn of the century. Criminologist Travis Hirschi (1987) observes that theories of crime and delinquency often have been developed specifically to *oppose* an existing theory of crime or delinquency. He suggests that many of the current criminological theories were constructed precisely to be incompatible with and different from other theories. "Oppositional theory building" gives the impression of adherence to scientific objectives, but theorists may be simply constructing models that deliberately make statements challenging established perspectives. Hirschi's observations suggest that while many theories of crime and delinquency *are* different, the newer are not necessarily better.

If we approach theories of delinquency as reflecting different versions of a social and cultural phenomenon, constructed at different times and in different places, it will be easier for us to understand that the scientific study of delinquency does not proceed in a straight line, getting closer and closer to an ultimate "truth." Rather, it has taken many twists and turns. All science seems to proceed in this way. Feyerabend (1970) commented that in following the progress of all science, we must consider accidents, prejudices, equipment, new methods, oversight, superficiality, pride, and many other factors in order to get a complete picture.

Even the whole issue of what is "truth" is highly debatable, especially for the social sciences. Criminologists have widely differing opinions about the causes of delinquency. One set of opinions may be as near the "truth" as many other versions, for there may be no one correct way of viewing delinquency. Each of us has what we believe are "correct" versions of the world, "correct" versions of human nature, and "correct" versions of the causes of crime. These personal versions are constructed from learning experiences garnered during our lifetimes. Many are as "correct" as any other, even if they differ dramatically. Research data may lean toward supporting one version over the other, but even that empirical support is based upon one person's interpretation of the data. There are, however, many possible interpretations to any set of data. This point will become clearer as we move through the text.

We must also appreciate that all explanations of crime and delinquency are based on some philosophical underpinning or perspective of human nature. This philosophy may be implicit (not stated by the theorist) or it may be explicit (stated for all to examine). No theory of delinquency is constructed within a social vacuum, nor is it constructed with total objectivity. All theorists have pre-existing cognitions or constructs about how the world is or should be ordered. As Jerome Bruner (1986) observes, it is far more important for appreciating the human condition to understand the way human beings construct their worlds than it is to examine the products of these processes.

The preceding themes will be developed throughout the book, but most specifically in chapter 2. At this point, it is important to give more attention to both the subject matter and the goals of the text.

DEFINITIONS OF JUVENILE DELINQUENCY

Stephen Toulmin (1961), the distinguished philosopher of science, drew an analogy between definitions and belts. The shorter the belt, the more elastic it needs to be to accommodate all customers. Similarly, a short definition, when applied to a wide assortment of cases, must be expanded and contracted, qualified and reinterpreted to fit every case. So it is here. We may start by defining juvenile delinquency briefly and concisely, but we will have to make adjustments as we go along. At first, one sentence, a simple *legal* definition, *seems* to suffice. Delinquency is behavior against the criminal code committed by an individual who has not reached adulthood, as defined by state or federal law.

Legal definitions at first blush appear to offer the best avenue for defining clearly what delinquency is and is not. Upon closer examination, however, they are often imperfect. The definition of delinquency just cited is incomplete, since offenses such as running away from home or being truant (status offenses) are not against the criminal code but are nonetheless considered delinquent actions in most states. Moreover, we soon confront the familiar cross-jurisdictional quagmire of inconsistent and contradictory provisions. State statutes vary widely, and federal statutes are different still. In addition, these statutes are periodically changed by legislatures or interpreted by courts. Defining delinquency, then, is problematic; we must remind ourselves that the "belt" will need constant adjustment.

Even age is not a simple issue. Although no state considers anyone above 18 a delinquent, some have provisions for "youthful offenders," who are older, and many use 16 as the cut-off age. At this writing, four states give criminal courts, rather than juvenile courts, automatic jurisdiction over juveniles at age 16, and eight states at age 17. Several other states are considering changes. Furthermore, *all* states allow juveniles—some as young as age 10—to be tried as adults in criminal courts under certain conditions and for certain offenses. Under federal law, juveniles may be prosecuted under the criminal law at age 15.

State statutes relevant to age often are changed by legislatures in reaction to a particularly heinous crime. In 1980, two Vermont youths, aged 17 and 15, accosted two 11-year-old girls on their way home from school. The girls were tortured and raped, and one was killed. At the time there was no provision in Vermont law for adult criminal prosecution of youths under age 16. The 17-year-old was tried as an adult and convicted of murder and is now serving a 30-year to life sentence. The 15-year-old was detained in a juvenile facility until he turned 18, when state law mandated his release. A shocked and outraged state legislature lowered the minimum age for adult criminal prosecution, but the delinquent in question was not, of course, affected.

It will become obvious as we proceed through this chapter and others in the text that the measurement of delinquency and the determination of who is delinquent are extremely problematic. Delinquency is not a distinct entity easily located and studied. Whether defined legally or socially, delinquency is an idea that is ever-changing and conceptually slippery. It is an imprecise, nebulous label for a wide variety of law- and norm-violating behaviors. Furthermore, the concept ''delinquent'' changes from society to society, culture to culture, and jurisdiction to jurisdiction. The two youths just mentioned would qualify as delinquents in some states, but not in others. In addition, society might resist calling a brutal killer a ''delinquent.'' In general, however, legal definitions rest on social definitions of delinquents and delinquency. Laws are made in response to societal values and demands. This legislative response is often a very gradual and conservative process, but it is almost invariably strongly influenced by society's perception. Traditionally, for example, society considered acting out behavior on the part of girls as more unacceptable than the same behavior on the part of boys. These value judgments were reflected in statutes which allowed longer detention of girls than of boys for offenses such as running away from home. Today, such laws are considered unconstitutional, but in pockets of society the attitudes persist.

Finally, we must be careful to distinguish between a delinquent and one delinquent *act*. The act is the behavior which violates the criminal code, whereas ''delinquent'' is the label we assign to a youngster who deviates from the prescribed norms. A youth who commits a legally defined delinquent act is not automatically a delinquent. A broken window or a stolen tape deck does not a delinquent make. Usually, society reserves its judgment until there are a number of such acts over time. In general, we are inclined to consider a minor delinquent act here or there as a teenage prank or mischief which is a part of the rites of passage into adulthood.

It is much easier, although still not easy, to measure delinquency than to identify the delinquent. Given figures on crimes and status offenses committed by juveniles, we can separate also the mild from the serious offenses, the violent from the nonviolent. These aggregate figures allow us to see trends in offending and to identify types of offending in relation to time and place. Identifying the delinquent becomes much more difficult, particularly if we resist using a strictly legal definition. Joseph Weis and John Sederstrom (1981) recommend that the most useful empirical distinction of the juvenile offender is between the serious and less serious (or petty) offender. Recently, Delbert S. Elliott and his associates (1987) have developed a more refined classification system of juvenile offenders based on both the seriousness of the offenses and the frequency of offending. We will return to the Elliott work later in the chapter.

Official Statistics and the Definition of Delinquency

Official statistics, which among other things give information about those who have been apprehended by police, do not end the search for an appropriate definition of either delinquency or the delinquent. It is widely acknowledged that many crimes—adult or juvenile—are not reported to the police. If reported, they are not necessarily *recorded*. And if recorded, there may be no arrest made. Therefore, although statistics suggest that roughly 1.8 to 2.2 million juvenile arrests are made each year (FBI, 1987), we must keep in mind that the figure underestimates juvenile offending. Only about half of those arrested are referred to juvenile court; the others are not charged, or the charges against them are dropped. Another 250,000 youths are not arrested, but are referred to juvenile courts by parents, citizens, social agencies, or probation departments. Of the total number of cases referred to juvenile court (approximately 1,450,000), about half (46 percent) subsequently involve a delinquency hearing. And, of the total cases certified for hearing, about three out of four result in the child being adjudicated—in some fashion—"delinquent." Roughly, then, about 500,000 young people each year are relegated to delinquency status. They may then be institutionalized, placed on probation, made to pay fines or make restitution, ordered to undergo counseling or to enroll in specified programs, or any combination of these (U.S. Department of Justice, 1983).

Many researchers argue that we lose valuable clues about delinquency if we define the delinquent population strictly according to legal rules, and they are, of course, correct. After all, only about 20 percent of those arrested ever are assigned delinquency status and, as with adult crime, there is a "dark figure" representing young lawbreakers who never come to official attention at all. Research by Elliott et al. (1987) suggests that as many as 86 percent of American juvenile offenders escape detection, including the more serious and repeat offenders. The nonrandom sample designated "delinquent" severely misrepresents the population of true delinquents for other reasons as well. Due to widespread prosecutorial and judicial discretion, juveniles who have engaged in similar conduct will not necessarily be treated similarly. Furthermore, some juveniles may have been diverted from the court either by specific programs intended for that very purpose, by the discretion of a police officer, or by the intervention of parents or guardians. In short, official arrest figures based on legal definitions represent a special population of people under special circumstances, not the whole population of the individuals about whom we are concerned. It is primarily for this reason that legal definitions or official figures alone should be used with caution.

Status Offenses

Recognizing the inadequacy of legal definitions and official statistics, it is nonetheless important to understand what they represent. Unlawful acts committed by delinquents are generally divided into five major categories for statistical purposes:

1. those against persons;
2. those against property;

3. drug offenses;
4. offenses against the public order; and
5. status offenses.

The first four categories are comparable to crimes committed by adults. Status offenses, alluded to earlier, are acts which only juveniles are prohibited from committing. The same act committed by an adult incurs no sanctions. Typical status offenses range from specific misbehaviors such as violating town or city-established curfews, running away from home, and truancy, to loosely defined offenses such as unruliness and unmanageability, which are responded to with wide discretion.

Historically, much of the discretion has been based on gender differences. Law enforcement officials as well as representatives of the judicial system have treated male and female offenders, particularly status offenders, differently. Adolescent girls have often been detained for incorrigibility or running away from home, when the same behavior in adolescent boys has been ignored or tolerated. Generally, about three times as many girls are held for status offenses as boys (U.S. Department of Justice, 1983). In recent years, as a result of suits brought on behalf of juvenile girls, many courts have put authorities on notice that this discriminatory approach is unwarranted, and overtly the practice appears to be diminishing. Moreover, under the federal law, juveniles are no longer punished for status violations. Nevertheless, some research suggests that officials circumvent the rules by reaching for ways to bring adolescents, particularly girls, under the aegis of juvenile courts (Chesney-Lind, 1986).

Furthermore, though some *states* have removed status offenses from the jurisdiction of the courts, many have also replaced or supplemented these offenses with statutes allowing the detention and/or supervision of youngsters who are presumably in need of protection, either from their own rash behavior or the behavior of others. These statutes are usually referred to as PINS, CHINS, MINS, or YINS laws (person, child, minor, or youth in need of supervision). Under these laws, runaways or "incorrigible" youngsters are subject to juvenile court jurisdiction, often at the instigation of their parents, and even though they may not have violated a criminal code.

Should we be concerned about the status offender or the "incorrigible" adolescent? For our purposes, only if these youths are also involved in conduct which would be criminal if displayed by an adult. This is not to say that society should not be concerned, for status offenders and children in need of supervision often have been and continue to be abused, emotionally and physically. Humane intervention may be required, but it should not be accomplished through the use of criminal sanctions or without regard to the rights of the juveniles or their families. Ironically, officially labeled juvenile delinquents have been given a greater measure of constitutional protection than have children determined to be "in need of supervision."

The foregoing comments relate to important issues in the area of juvenile justice, which is only peripherally related to the subject of this text. The major goal of the book is to draw together and evaluate the extensive research on the explanations and causes of juvenile delinquency. Much less attention will be given to the process and procedures of the juvenile justice system. Although chapter 3 will be devoted to tracing the history and development of the juvenile justice system, this will be done as a backdrop for the theory and research which are the focus of the text. Our immediate attention, then, remains with the problem of determining the nature and extent of delinquent behavior.

THE MEASUREMENT OF DELINQUENCY

In light of the discussion of the previous pages, we might ask, how does one obtain a "true" picture of delinquency? To some extent, the answer depends upon whether we decide to accept a strictly legal criterion, broaden it to include undetected violations of the criminal code, or narrow it to exclude status offenses. A similar dilemma faces researchers interested in the study of crime in general. Should crime consist only of what legislatures have decreed it to be, or should it include offenses against humanity, such as pollution of the environment? Should some "crime" not be considered crime at all? In this section, we will discuss the various methods through which delinquency is measured, focusing upon the type and amount of behavior identified by each. The methods may be divided into two major categories: official and unofficial. Official statistics refer to recorded data published or supervised by governmental agencies. Unofficial statistics refer to data published by private organizations or independent researchers. It is important to note that some types of measurement may fall into both categories. There are official as well as unofficial victimization studies, for example. For that reason, criminologists often prefer to classify delinquency data according to their source: criminal justice personnel, victims, or offenders themselves.

Surprisingly, *comprehensive national* data on youth crime and its control do not exist (Krisberg & Schwartz, 1983). Although a variety of sources may be consulted, none gives us the total official picture. The two major sources of official information are the FBI's *Uniform Crime Reports* and the National Crime Survey. The primary source of data on juvenile corrections is a biennial census published as *Children in Custody*. Each is reviewed next.

The Uniform Crime Reports

The Federal Bureau of Investigation's *Uniform Crime Reports* (UCR), compiled since 1930, is the most cited source of U.S. crime statistics. The UCR is an annual document (released to the public anytime between late July and early September) containing information received on a voluntary basis from law enforcement agencies throughout the country. While the first UCR was published with data from fewer than 1,000 law enforcement agencies, the 1986 UCR data collection was based on nearly 10,743 agencies, representing about 97 percent of the total U.S. population (FBI, 1987). The UCR represents the only major data source permitting a comparison of national aggregate data broken down in a number of ways. It divides crimes according to whether they are reported, recorded, or cleared by arrest and region of the country. Crimes are also categorized according to seriousness. Serious crimes are referred to as index crimes, non-serious as non-index crimes. Table 1-1 contains definitions of some of the crimes reported in the UCR, specifically those which will be discussed in the text.

To be recorded in the UCR, a crime must (at a minimum)

1. be perceived by the victim or by someone else;

2. be defined as a crime by the victim or the observer;

3. in some way become known to a law enforcement agency;

4. be defined by that law enforcement agency as a crime;

5. be accurately recorded by the law enforcement agency; and

6. be reported to the FBI compilation center.

The UCR divides offenders by age, sex, and race, but not by social class or socioeconomic status. As you can see from Figure 1-1, based on 1986 UCR data, arrest rates for serious *property* crimes peak at around age 16. With increasing age, and particularly after age 20, the property arrest rate shows a continual, gradual decline. The *violent* crime arrest rate peaks at about age 18 and shows a more gradual decline with age. Notice also that the violent crime arrest rates are substantially lower than property arrest rates during the adolescent years. The relationship between age and crime has been observed as far back as any crime statistics have been kept. Some criminologists have suggested that this relationship is invariant, holding across cultures and nations as well as history (Hirschi and Gottfredson, 1983; Gottfredson and Hirschi, 1987). This suggestion, rejected by other criminologists (e.g., Greenberg, 1985; Farrington, Ohlin, and Wilson, 1986), is the root of one of the current controversies in the field, which will be discussed in chapter 10.

Note also that Figure 1-1 illustrates arrest *rates*—the number of arrests made for every 100,000 persons within a specified age group. Arrest *rates* adjust for changes in population across age groups. The 14- to 16-year-old population may be much larger in one five-year-period than in another. If there were no adjustment for these differences, an increase in the number of arrests would be misleading. Although it would simply reflect the fact that there is a larger population, the increase might be interpreted as an upward shift in the prevalence of offending. In the early 1960s, for example, the baby boom generation reached adolescence. In 1960, the total population of adolescents (ages 14 to 17) in the United States was about 11 million. In 1970, it jumped to 16 million, and in 1975 the total population of adolescents peaked at about 17 million. Since that time, the adolescent population has steadily decreased every year. Failure to take into consideration these fluctuations might lead us to conclude that the juvenile crime rate has similarly decreased since 1975.

Table 1-2 lists the offenses for which juveniles are most often arrested, in descending order. As you can readily see, larceny-theft tops the list by a wide margin, and

TABLE 1-1   DEFINITIONS OF OFFENSES IN UNIFORM CRIME REPORTING

Index crimes	Definitions
Criminal homicide	Divided into two parts: (a) Murder and nonnegligent manslaughter refers to the willful (nonnegligent) killing of one human being by another; and (b) manslaughter by negligence refers to the killing of another person through gross negligence (traffic fatalities are excluded).
Forcible rape	The carnal knowledge of a female forcibly and against her will. Included are rapes by force and attempts or assaults to rape. Statutory offenses (no force used—victim under age of consent) are excluded.
Robbery	The taking or attempting to take anything of value from the care, custody, or control of a person or persons by force or threat of force or violence and/or by putting the victim in fear.
Aggravated assault	An unlawful attack by one person upon another for the purpose of inflicting severe or aggravated bodily injury. This type of assault usually is accompanied by the use of a weapon or by means likely to produce death or great bodily harm. Simple assaults are excluded.
Burglary-breaking or entering	The unlawful entry of a structure to commit a felony or a theft. Attempted forcible entry is included.
Larceny-theft	The unlawful taking, carrying, leading, or riding away of property from the possession or constructive possession of another. Examples are thefts of bicycles or automobile accessories, shoplifting, pocket-picking, or the stealing of any property or articles which are not taken by force and violence or by fraud. Attempted larcenies are included.
Motor vehicle theft	The theft or attempted theft of a motor vehicle. A motor vehicle is self-propelled and runs on the surface and not on rails. Specifically excluded from this category are motorboats, construction equipment, airplanes, and farming equipment.
Arson	Any willfull or malicious burning or attempt to burn, with or without intent to defraud, a dwelling house, public building, motor vehicle or aircraft, personal property of another, etc.

Common non-index crimes of juveniles	Definitions
Other assaults	Assaults and attempted assaults where no weapon is used and which do not result in serious or aggravated injury to victim.
Stolen property; buying, receiving, possessing	Buying, receiving, and possessing stolen property, including attempts.
Vandalism	Willful or malicious destruction, injury, disfigurement, or defacement of any public or private property, real or personal, without the consent of the owner or persons having custody or control.
Weapons; carrying, possessing, etc.	All violations of regulations or statutes controlling the carrying, using, possessing, furnishing, and manufacturing of deadly weapons or silencers. Included are attempts.
Sex Offenses (except forcible rape, prostitution, and commercialized vice)	Statutory rape and offenses against chastity, common decency, morals, and the like. Attempts are included.

TABLE 1-1   (CONT.)

Common non-index crimes of juveniles	Definitions
Driving Under the Influence (DUI)	Driving or operating any vehicle or common carrier while drunk or under the influence of liquor or narcotics.
Liquor laws	State or local liquor law violations, except "drunkenness" and "driving under the influence." Federal violations are excluded.
Drunkenness	Offenses relating to drunkenness or intoxication. Excluded is "driving under the influence."
Disorderly conduct	Breach of the peace.
Curfew and loitering laws	(Restricted to persons under age 18). Offenses relating to violations of local curfews or loitering ordinances where such laws exist.
Runaways	(Restricted to persons under age 18). Limited to juveniles taken into protective custody under provisions of local statutes.

Source: Adapted from FBI Uniform Crime Reports (1987), pp. 331–332.

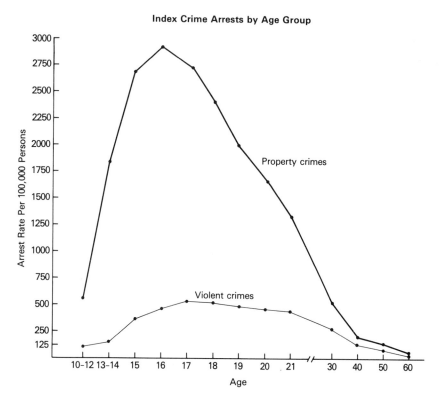

Figure 1-1 Index crime arrests by age group. (Based on data from FBI *UNIFORM CRIME REPORTS*, 3-year average, 1983–1985.)

TABLE 1-2   TOTAL ARRESTS FOR JUVENILES IN 1986 [IN 1000s]

Larceny/theft (378)
Runaways (138)
Burglary (135)
Liquor laws (132)
Vandalism (96)
Disorderly conduct (83)
Curfew/loitering (73)
Drug abuse (68)
Motor vehicle theft (50)
Aggravated assault (38)
Stolen property (29)
Robbery (28)
Drunkenness (26)
Weapons violations (25)
DUI (23)
Fraud (18)
Sex offenses (14)
Forgery (7)
Arson (6)
Forcible rape (5)
Vagrancy (2)
Prostitution/vice (2)
Homicide (1)

Source: FBI *UNIFORM CRIME REPORTS*, 1987, p. 174.

violent offenses are comparatively low. The table represents arrest *rates* (per 1000 juveniles ages 10–17) for all juveniles in 1986.

Two other observations based on information from the UCR are worth noting. First, girls are arrested proportionately less than boys (see Table 1-3). Second, blacks are arrested proportionately more than whites. In 1986, boys outnumbered girls 8 to 1 in arrests for violent offenses and approximately 4 to 1 in arrests for property crimes. These ratios closely parallel the ratios in *adult* male and female offending. The most common arrest for girls was for larceny-theft, followed by the status offense of running away. Violations of liquor laws was a distant third. Arrests for all other offenses were negligible. Judging from these figures, girls are not violent compared to boys. Furthermore, in only one offense were girls arrested at a higher rate than boys: running away. This difference may be due in part to the traditional view among police and in society that we should be more concerned about unsupervised girls than unsupervised boys (Empey, 1982), a topic to which we will return in chapter 9.

The black juvenile population (10 to 17) in the United States in 1986 numbered just over four million (4,065,000) and the white juvenile population over 27 million (27,421,000). Blacks were overrepresented in the UCR statistics, particularly in arrests for violent crimes, where about 37,000 black juveniles were arrested compared to approximately 33,000 white juveniles. White outnumbered black arrests for property crimes—410,000 to 145,000—a ratio of roughly 3 to 1. We would expect a ratio of 7 to 1 if the arrest rates were to be in line with juvenile population figures. Like the ratios of males to females, those of blacks to whites parallel UCR data on adult offenders. The

TABLE 1-3 TOTAL JUVENILE
ARRESTS BY SEX IN 1986 (in 1000s)*

Male	Offense	Female
278	Larceny	101
125	Burglary	10
98	Liquor laws	34
87	Vandalism	9
68	Disorderly conduct	16
59	Drug abuse	10
59	Runaways	80
54	Curfew/loitering	19
45	Motor vehicle theft	5
32	Aggravated assault	6
26	Robbery	2
23	Drunkenness	4
20	DUI	3
13	Fraud	4
12	Sex offenses	1
5	Arson	0.50
4	Forgery	2
4	Forcible rape	0.07
2	Vagrancy	4
1	Homicide	0.09
0.72	Prostitution	1

*Adapted from FBI *UNIFORM CRIME REPORTS*, 1987, p. 169.

race classification is a troubling one, however, because it is so confounded with other variables such as geographical area, social class, education, occupational opportunity, and discrimination. A classification based on ethnic or racial origin and nothing else evokes confusion and controversy and provides little insight into the causes of crime. In this text, we will look to factors such as level of education, place of residence, or parental styles of discipline as more fruitful potential predictors of delinquency than race.

Once again, it is important to stress the need to treat UCR data very gingerly. For a host of reasons, including possibly inaccurate reporting by local and state agencies and the fact that the data do not consider early decision-making by law enforcement officers, UCR data are misleading. Bernard Cohen (1981) has pleaded for a more accurate and precise indicator of the extent of national crime.

(This) is essential for the following reasons:

1. UCR crime rates are frequently used as an indicator of basic social problems;
2. they are the most influential of noneconomic indicators;
3. they are, probably more than any other noneconomic indicator, subject to public and official attention;

4. they are frequently cited by the press;

5. they are used extensively for scholarly research; and

6. they form the basis for far-reaching legislative proposals and decisions (Cohen, 1981, p. 86).

National Crime Survey

Another source of official statistics on delinquency is the National Crime Survey (NCS). The Bureau of Census interviews, on a staggered schedule, a large national sample of households (approximately 60,000) representing 136,000 persons over the age of 12. The households sampled are asked about crimes experienced during the previous six months. Thus, the procedure is a *victimization* survey. Victimization surveys do not always fall under the official statistics category, however. As will be noted soon, questionnaires and surveys designed to measure the extent to which people have been victims of crime are often administered and conducted by private organizations or independent researchers.

NCS researchers use a *panel design*, a method which involves examining the same selected sample or group repeatedly over a certain length of time. In this case, each household is contacted twice a year for three years. The interviewers return to *addresses* (place of residence) rather than to individuals. That is, they contact (in person or by phone) the same housing unit every six months. If the family contacted during the last interview cycle has moved, the new occupants are interviewed. Housing units in the panel are visited a maximum of seven times, after which new units are selected.

The original impetus for the NCS came from the President's Commission on Law Enforcement and Administration of Justice, which in 1966 commissioned the first national victimization survey. The Commission wanted to supplement the annual UCR compiled by the FBI, because of widespread dissatisfaction and distrust with the accuracy of this source. After considerable experimentation and a variety of pilot projects to test the method and its feasibility, the NCS was fully implemented in 1973. The survey is currently designed to measure the extent to which persons and households are victims of rape, robbery, assault, burglary, motor vehicle theft, and larceny.

When respondents indicate they have been recent victims of a crime, they are asked a series of detailed questions relating to the offense, including the offender's approximate age. Specifically, the NCS interviewer wants to know:

1. exactly what happened;

2. when and where the offense occurred;

3. whether any injury or loss was suffered;

4. whether the crime was reported to the police; and

5. the victim's perceptions of the offender's sex, race and—most important for us— age.

These data, as estimates of juvenile crime, are dependent upon:

1. the victim actually seeing the offender; and
2. the victim's correct perceptions of the age of the offender.

Unfortunately, these important potential shortcomings undermine the accuracy of the NCS data to some extent.

Juvenile delinquency researchers have analyzed NCS data in a variety of ways. We will refer to these studies throughout the book when relevant. For the present, it is instructive to make note of a study by John H. Laub (1983a), who wished to evaluate whether public and government alarm about the "exploding" rates of juvenile crime was justified. He examined NCS data obtained between 1973 and 1980. Contrary to claims of dramatic increases in juvenile crime, especially serious crime, Laub found that the NCS data did not support any increase in juvenile offending over those years. In fact, the data revealed that the rate of juvenile offending in personal crimes (rape, robbery, assault, and larceny) actually decreased across the country during the 1973 to 1980 period. Furthermore, Laub noted that data from the National Juvenile Justice Assessment Center and the National Center for Juvenile Justice corroborated this trend.

Probation and Parole Statistics

Juvenile *probation* refers to the conditional freedom granted by the court to a juvenile offender in place of incarceration, as long as he or she meets certain conditions of behavior. *Parole* is a status granted an offender upon release from a correctional facility if his or her sentence has not expired. It is a release conditioned upon the person's meeting standards of conduct imposed by a parole board. *Parolees* are placed under the supervision of a parole agency until their sentence has expired, at which time they are free.

National data on probation and parole of juvenile offenders are especially difficult to obtain. The U.S. Bureau of the Census (1978) collected a one-day count of the number of juveniles on probation and parole on September 1, 1976, but since then little has been done on a national basis. According to the Census Bureau's survey, 328,854 juveniles were on probation and 53,347 were on parole on that date. However, data on individual characteristics, on the conditions of supervision, and the nature of the supervising agencies are extremely limited (Krisberg and Schwartz, 1983). Barry Krisberg and Ira Schwartz (1983) found this lack of data especially troubling because studies continually show that probation is the most common decision made by the juvenile court. "Without more current and comprehensive data on community supervision for juveniles, a major dimension of the juvenile corrections system remains obscured" (Krisberg & Schwartz, 1983, p. 339).

Children in Custody

The principal source of data on incarcerated juveniles is the biennial census on children in both public and private juvenile correctional facilities, including detention centers, throughout the 50 states and the District of Columbia. It is known as *Children in Custody* (CIC). In 1977 the Office of Juvenile Justice and Delinquency Prevention assumed sponsorship of the census, although the data are collected by the U.S. Bureau of Census and are now analyzed by the Bureau of Justice Statistics. Mail questionnaires are sent to all institutions and agencies dealing with the incarceration of juveniles. Response rate usually ranges between 96 and 100 percent. The CIC questionnaire requests data from facility administrators on the number of youths admitted, their demographic characteristics, and pertinent budgeting information. A one-day count of inmates also is sought.

The first two censuses in 1971 and 1973 were limited to gathering data only from public residential correctional facilities, but all subsequent censuses have included private facilities. The private and public facilities included in the tabulation are:

1. "short-term" facilities like shelters, detention centers, and reception or diagnostic centers; and
2. "long-term" facilities such as training schools, ranches, forestry camps, farms, and halfway houses.

Generally, short-term facilities are for pre-adjudicated youth (before a court decision is reached) and long-term facilities are for those who have been adjudicated delinquent. It is not unusual, however, for nondelinquent youths to be housed with juvenile offenders, particularly in private institutions.

A 20-year-old college student who spent a year in such a private facility believes it saved him from becoming criminal. "I hated my homelife; the cops were getting to know me; it was either the Home, a jail cell, or the streets. Some of the guys in the Home had been through the system, though. One had almost killed his sister's kid. I was 17 and could take care of myself, but I always felt sorry for the little guys who couldn't do that. I don't think 13- or 14-year-olds who run away from their foster homes should be forced to live with 16- or 17-year-old delinquents."

Excluded from the CIC census are juveniles in federal correctional institutions, foster homes, nonresidential facilities, and facilities designated exclusively for drug abusers, alcoholics, unwed mothers, the emotionally disturbed, and dependent or neglected children. Data and trends reported in the CIC will be analyzed and commented upon in the final chapter of the text.

Offender Self-report Methods

It is doubtful any researcher believes that official statistics reveal an accurate picture of crime and juvenile delinquency. As we noted earlier, a vast majority of adult and juvenile offending, for a variety of reasons, goes undetected or hidden from the official figures reported in the UCR. Victimization studies, both official and unofficial, offer additional information, but they are limited in a number of ways, including the willingness of victims to reveal what happened to them. Some researchers maintain that a third procedure for estimating the "true" delinquency rate is even better. It involves having juveniles in the general population simply reveal the extent of their own misconduct. Instead of relying on biased or incomplete official records, researchers obtain information from a random sample of youths who report their norm or law violations themselves. This procedure, called the *self-report* method (hereafter abbreviated SR), is extremely important in the measurement (and definition) of delinquency. Currently, the SR method is the dominant method of measurement in studies focusing on the extent and cause of delinquency (Hindelang et al., 1981). It is also used almost exclusively with juveniles, rarely with adults. We will encounter the ongoing debate among researchers over the relative advantages and disadvantages of self-report and other procedures frequently throughout the course of the text.

SR information is most often acquired either through interviews (personal or telephone) or questionnaires. Although the victimization surveys just discussed may be considered self-report, researchers reporting on SR data are generally referring to behavior admitted by individuals as perpetrators. The usual procedure is to prepare a list of questions asking about specific law-breaking activities. The list is then presented to youths, most often in questionnaire form, but occasionally in an interview setting. Very often, the youths are "captive" subjects in schools or detention facilities. (We will learn later, however, that certain SR methods, such as those used in ethnographic studies, are less restrictive.) In SR measures, subjects usually are asked to indicate whether they have engaged in any of the specified activities and, if so, how frequently. Some studies ask whether the activities resulted in police contacts. In most cases, anonymity is guaranteed. Interestingly, Michael Hindelang and his colleagues (1981) found in their research that anonymity did not significantly increase the quality of the responses.

Gwynn Nettler (1984) noted that the numerous international studies employing the SR procedure have consistently drawn the following three conclusions:

1. almost everyone, by his or her own admission, has violated some criminal law;
2. the amount of "hidden crime" is enormous; and more importantly
3. most of the infractions are minor.

On the basis of these findings, Nettler suggested that those who commit crimes or delinquent acts are better described as existing on a continuum than as being "criminal" or "noncriminal," "delinquent" or "nondelinquent." Very few people commit many offenses or serious ones. The question remains, of course, to what extent do SR studies provide a "true" picture?

SR studies also continually show that the proportions of respondents involved in *serious* crimes are relatively small, but that those juveniles who commit serious crimes are quite busy (Weis and Sederstrom, 1981). Carl F. Jesness (1987) suggests that offenders must be working overtime to accumulate the large numbers of offenses they report. In short, he finds some self-reports very hard to believe and recommends that criminologists be cautious about accepting the validity of SR questionnaires. It does appear, however, that most serious juvenile crime is committed by a small portion of the juvenile population. Furthermore, contrary to common belief, the SR investigations indicate that there is *not* "offense specialization" among delinquents. That is, active juvenile offenders do not concentrate upon a specific criminal activity, such as robbery; they show considerable versatility in criminal involvement, committing a wide variety of offenses, violent as well as non-violent.

SR data also underscore the observation that serious juvenile delinquency is not evenly distributed across the country, nor across cities or communities (Weis & Sederstrom, 1981). Youthful offenders are more prevalent in some communities and neighborhoods than others. Certain communities, sectors of cities, and neighborhoods tend to have criminal careers of their own, even with turnovers of population. By inference, then, if we are to accept the information gleaned from SR studies, some neighborhoods and communities may play a key role in the development of crime and delinquency.

Although advocates of the SR method believe that SR measures are more accurate indices of delinquency than other methods, caution is urged about accepting this claim. Psychologists and sociologists for many years have wrestled with the troubling problems of SR questionnaires. For at least a hundred years, for instance, psychologists attempting to measure personality via SR methods have continually encountered a myriad of problems. For one thing, individuals attach a wide range of interpretations to the wording of questions. For another, they enter a test situation displaying widely different attitudes about answering questions. These pretest attitudes are called "response sets." An offender, then, may

1. misinterpret a question
2. approach the questionnaire or the interview with suspicion, determined not to be honest.

Sociologists, too, have recognized these dilemmas. They have examined the many pitfalls in survey research in general, realizing that the quality of this research depends on many things, including the content of the questions and the manner in which they are asked. Thus, images of delinquent conduct drawn from SR studies vary according to who is drawing them, with which methods, and to which population they apply (Nettler, 1984).

IDENTIFYING THE SERIOUS DELIQUENT

There appear to be two very broad categories of juvenile offenders—the serious and the nonserious. Finer distinctions are desirable, but are very difficult to make. Later in the chapter we will discuss the impressive attempt of Delbert Elliott and his colleagues (1987) to develop and refine an elaborate juvenile offender classification system. Additional theory and research on the serious delinquent is reviewed throughout the text. At this point it will be beneficial to describe two important "cohort" studies which provide a beginning thumbnail sketch of serious and nonserious delinquents. One study, a classic in the field of criminology, was conducted some years ago by Marvin E. Wolfgang and his associates; the other, a more recent project, was conducted by Donna Martin Hamparian and her associates.

Cohort Studies

Wolfgang and his colleagues (Wolfgang, Figlio, and Sellin, 1972; Wolfgang, 1983) actually carried out two massive cohort studies. The term "cohort" refers to a group of subjects having one or more characteristics in common. In the two Wolfgang projects, the subjects were born in the *same year*. The first birth cohort consisted of 9,945 males born in 1945 who resided in Philadelphia from their 10th to their 18th birthday. The second birth cohort consisted of 13,160 males *and* 14,000 females born in 1958 who also lived in Philadelphia from their 10th to their 18th birthday. Essentially, the 1958 project was a "replication" of the 1945 one. In the social sciences, a replication occurs when researchers "copy" the procedure and methodology of a previous study as closely as possible to see if they can obtain similar results.

Wolfgang followed the members of these cohorts through their adolescent years to discover who became delinquent and who did not, or more specifically, who had official contacts with police. He collected data about their personal backgrounds and delinquency history from three sources: schools, police, and juvenile courts. Background data pertaining to race, sex, date of birth, and residential history were obtained from school records. Delinquency involvement was checked through the records of the Juvenile Aid Division of the Philadelphia Police Department. These data consisted of all *recorded police contacts*, whether or not the contact resulted in an official arrest. In Philadelphia, as in most jurisdictions, when a police officer has contact with a juvenile, he or she has the option of handling the offender informally or making an arrest. Delinquency, in the Wolfgang studies, was defined exclusively by the number of police contacts. The records of the Juvenile Court Division of the Court of Common Pleas for Philadelphia were also examined to determine how a case was handled.

Of the 13,160 males in the 1958 cohort, 4,315 or 33 percent had at least one police contact before reaching their 18th birthday, a ratio very close to the 1945 cohort of 34 percent. Females were not included in the 1945 cohort analysis, but the 1958 data revealed that male adolescents were two-and-one-half times more likely to have a police contact than female adolescents. Of the 14,000 females, 1,972 or about 14 percent had at least one police contact.

In both studies, Wolfgang differentiated three groups of offenders based on the frequency of police contacts: one-time offenders, nonchronic recidivists (two to four police contacts), and chronic recidivists (five or more police contacts). Since a "recidivist" is technically a person who re-offends after being *convicted* of one or more crimes, Wolfgang took some liberty with the term. Subsequent researchers must be careful to recognize this small but important deviation in terminology. Wolfgang's "recidivists" did not necessarily have prior juvenile records.

In the 1958 cohort, the distribution of delinquents—those with police contacts—was 42 percent one-time offenders, 35 percent nonchronic recidivists, and 23 percent chronic recidivists. In the 1945 cohort, 46 percent were one-time offenders, 35 percent nonchronic recidivists, and 18 percent chronic recidivists. Thus, in both studies, the distributions were similar. Female delinquents in the 1958 cohort were 60 percent one-time offenders, 33 percent nonchronic recidivists, and 7 percent chronic recidivists.

One of the most important findings of both cohort studies pertains to the chronic recidivists, a group which qualifies as serious delinquents on the basis of their offenses. In the 1945 cohort analysis, male chronic recidivists constituted only 18 percent of the delinquent sample, yet they were responsible for over 52 percent of *all* juvenile offenses. Even more striking, these chronic offenders accounted for 71 percent of the homicides, 73 percent of the rapes, 82 percent of the robberies, and 69 percent of the aggravated assaults. Similar statistics were found for the 1958 cohort. While 1958 male chronics constituted only 23 percent of the delinquent group, they were responsible for 61 percent of all juvenile offenses. They were also involved in 61 percent of the juvenile homicides, 75 percent of the rapes, 65 percent of the aggravated assaults, and 73 percent of the robberies. In sum, a relatively small number of males seemed to be responsible for the bulk of the serious, violent delinquency. This finding, you will recall, has also been consistently reported in SR studies.

Donna M. Hamparian and her colleagues (1978, 1985) conducted a longitudinal cohort analysis of 1,222 males and females born between the years 1956 and 1960 and arrested, as juveniles, for at least one violent offense. They found that violent offenders accounted for just over 30 percent of all the juvenile arrests. However, nearly one-third of the cohort qualified as chronic offenders (five or more *arrests*). Furthermore, these chronic offenders accounted for two-thirds of all reported juvenile arrests in the birth cohort.

Like the SR data discussed earlier, the Hamparian project also found that the subjects did not specialize in the types of crimes they committed. Few of the violent offenders became repeat *violent* offenders, for example. Rather, multiple offenders engaged in a *variety* of illegal acts, ranging from violence to petty larceny.

The researchers tracked the offenders into their adult years to determine whether they had continued their criminal activity. They learned that approximately 60 percent of the males and fewer than one-third of the females were arrested for felonies as adults. Those who went on to be arrested as adults tended to have more arrests as juveniles, to have begun their delinquent careers at an earlier age, and to have been involved in the more serious types of violent offenses as juveniles. Significantly, three-fourths of those juveniles who had qualified as chronic offenders continued their criminal activity into adulthood. Thus, there appears to be a clear continuity between juvenile and adult criminal careers.

Following Juveniles over Time: Longitudinal Studies

The Wolfgang and Hamparian projects both were *longitudinal studies*, studies which involve repeated measures or continual follow-up of the same individuals or groups over a specific length of time. Typically, investigators conducting longitudinal studies follow a group of youths over a number of developmental milestones in an effort to identify features which explain eventual delinquency. Since we will encounter the longitudinal method frequently in the pages ahead, it is important to review some of its major characteristics.

There are two major types of longitudinal methods, *retrospective* and *prospective*. In retrospective investigations, individuals are identified after the events of interest have already taken place. For example, juveniles who are delinquent might be compared with nondelinquents. When the retrospective procedure involves some self-report, as it often does, individuals are asked to remember events (e.g., delinquent offending) that occurred earlier in their lifetimes, often covering a span of many years. Accuracy of recall, of course, becomes a critical factor in this method. While human memory has incredibly extensive storage capacity, it is also replete with distortions, misrepresentations, and biases. This is particularly true of memory about one's childhood. In prospective studies, on the other hand, subjects are identified before the event of interest occurs, and data are collected as relevant incidents are happening. For example, researchers might select 500 newborns in a community and follow them through high school graduation to see who becomes involved in delinquency. The prospective approach is often preferred over the retrospective because of its reliance on recent memory and events in contrast to ''old'' memory or records, but it is also far more expensive and time-consuming.

Both approaches have advantages and disadvantages. David Magnusson and Vernon Allen (1983, p. 379) assert: ''Both approaches are valuable and should be used; the one cannot replace the other.'' Their respective value depends on the issue being examined, the nature of the data, and the resources available. The simultaneous application of both prospective and retrospective longitudinal studies may be necessary in some cases.

Some writers (e.g., Gottfredson & Hirschi, 1987) subsume retrospective studies into the same category as cross-sectional studies, which gather information about subjects at one point in time. A researcher using a cross-sectional procedure might select groups of 10, 14, and 18 year-old delinquents and compare them with groups of same-aged nondelinquents to see if there are any discernible differences in their backgrounds. In effect, this method cuts a ''cross section'' through time. For organizational purposes we will treat retrospective studies as variants of the longitudinal method, because they generally look back at more than one point in time. The Hirschi-Gottfredson position will be discussed again later in the book, however.

Desirable Features of Longitudinal Studies

David P. Farrington, Lloyd E. Ohlin, and James Q. Wilson (1986) recommend four features that should be part of any longitudinal design. First, they argue that ideally the study should be prospective. Suppose we wished to design a longitudinal study to explore the effects of parental abuse on serious delinquency. Obviously, we would want to sample subjects randomly, without exercising too much bias in the selection process. We would hope, then, to select our subjects before there was evidence of child abuse or before they demonstrated delinquent or nondelinquent patterns. Furthermore, we would want to keep close tabs on the subjects as they grow up. In short, we would want a prospective design.

Farrington, Ohlin, and Wilson also recommend that the longitudinal investigation collect data from a number of sources, such as self-report questionnaires, court or police records, and interviews with teachers, peers, and parents. Material from different sources provides checks on the accuracy of the information and helps fill gaps in information. A high agreement among various sources offers *consensual validation* of the data.

A third desirable feature is that the sample size (the number of subjects in the study) be large—at least 100. In our proposed study, if we were to select only 50 youths, we might find ourselves with very few serious delinquents—perhaps none. Similarly, we might also find little evidence of child abuse. Our research, then, would run the risk of having limited applicability to the study of delinquency. When a study can be generalized to other similar populations (e.g., serious delinquents) researchers say it has high *external validity*. Low external validity indicates that the data are not representative. Consequently, a longitudinal design should include as large a percentage of the relevant youth population as time and money will allow.

A fourth desirable feature is that the longitudinal project cover a significant amount of time in the life course of the subjects—the longer the better. Farrington, Ohlin, and Wilson recommend that the project cover at least five years of development. Presumably, short longitudinal studies do not allow researchers to discover satisfactorily what is contributing to delinquency. David Magnusson and Vernon Allen (1983) believe that for any longitudinal study to be effective it must:

1. cover the total critical periods of development for the behaviors of concern (in this case, delinquency); and
2. include observations made frequently enough so as not to miss any of these critical periods of development.

In essence, this means that longitudinal studies continue over rather long periods of time. It is not very meaningful, for example, to begin examining the effects of child abuse during early adolescence without knowing how much earlier in the child's development the abuse began, and how it affected that development.

Examples of Longitudinal Studies

Farrington, Ohlin, and Wilson were able to identify only eleven American studies on crime and delinquency which met the four desirable features just outlined. The Wolfgang and Hamparian projects were not among them, since they relied primarily on written records. Several of the eleven studies are classics in the study of delinquency and will be discussed in detail in chapter 8. Three were conducted by Sheldon and Eleanor Glueck (1930, 1934, 1937, 1943, 1950, 1968). Although Farrington, Ohlin and Wilson classify the Glueck studies as prospective, they are, strictly speaking, both prospective and retrospective, since the Gluecks selected their subjects *after* they were labeled "delinquent" and then carried out extensive follow-ups. The longest-lasting American longitudinal study, also a classic, was the Cambridge-Somerville Youth Study, designed by Robert C. Cabot and carried on by Edwin Powers and Helen Witmer (1951). It is called ". . . one of the most famous criminological experiments of all time" (Farrington et al., 1986, p. 65). Joan and William McCord (1959) achieved fame in the field of criminology by reviewing and analyzing its results. The Cambridge-Somerville boys and their offspring are followed even today (McCord, 1986).

Two other longitudinal studies were conducted by psychologist Starke Hathaway and sociologist Elio Monachesi (1957, 1963), who assessed the personalities of predelinquent boys. Personalities were measured by an extensive inventory, the Minnesota Multiphasic Personality Inventory (MMPI), which Hathaway helped develop. The researchers administered the MMPI to nearly 2,000 ninth-grade boys in Minneapolis public schools and then followed them and their official delinquency records throughout high school. In a second study, the research team tested another 5,700 ninth-grade boys, using the same basic procedure. They discovered ultimately, however, that their personality measures were not reliable predictors of delinquency. Another longitudinal project was conducted by Emmy Werner and her colleagues (1971, 1977, 1982, 1987) on nearly 700 Hawaiian children. This research will be reviewed in chapter 6. Other longitudinal designs include the work of Langner et al. (1977), Lefkowitz et al. (1977), and Kellam et al. (1981).

The preeminent contemporary longitudinal study is the well-executed and informative National Youth Survey (NYS) (Elliott and Huizinga, 1983, 1984; Ageton, 1983), which also is one of the best SR surveys undertaken to date. The NYS is based on SR and official data collected on 1,725 youths who were between the ages of 11 and 17 when the project began in 1977. The survey involves a *panel design* in which the same youths are sampled repeatedly over several years. The NYS self-report questions were constructed to address many of the major criticisms usually directed at SR measures of delinquency. For example, critics often complain that self-report questionnaires ask about status or trivial offenses such as running away, violations of sexual mores, acting out in school, occasional drinking of alcohol, or disobeying parents. Others complain that questions are ambiguous or that the choices are unclear or inappropriate.

Another ambitious longitudinal study sponsored by the National Institute of Juvenile Justice and Delinquency Prevention began in 1988. Substantial grants were awarded to the State University of New York at Albany, the University of Pittsburgh, and the University of Colorado to track 7th and 8th graders (ages 11 to 13) in three American cities over a period of four years. Researchers interview the children twice a year and the parents once. Additional data are gathered from a variety of psychological, social and community resources. The objective is to identify the causes of delinquency and nondelinquency in city children and recommend effective strategies for intervention and prevention. In the next few years, we will be learning more about the results of this investigation.

Although we have discussed only American studies up to this point, the reader should be aware that longitudinal research is a hallmark of criminology in Great Britain and the Scandinavian countries. Among the best known British studies are those directed by Donald West and David Farrington (1973, 1977) and the National Survey of Health and Development, formulated by Douglas, Ross, and Simpson (1968) and carried on by M. E. J. Wadsworth (1975, 1979). We will encounter material from these investigations periodically in the course of the book.

A cautionary note is necessary before we proceed. While most criminologists endorse the prospective longitudinal method, some are very critical. Michael Gottfredson and Travis Hirschi (1987), for example, argue that longitudinal research is not a necessary or even a valuable procedure to use in the study of crime and delinquency. They are convinced that cross-sectional procedures are more efficient and equally effective in gathering data about crime and delinquency. Other criminologists accept the value of longitudinal research but do not agree with the Farrington, Ohlin, and Wilson requirements for data collection and quantification. Instead, they believe that verbal descriptions and other "qualitative" data offer as many insights about delinquency as numerical data. In other words, they contend that research designs which allow researchers to talk informally with and perhaps even live among their subjects over a period of time without collecting extensive numerical data also supply valuable material. We will return to these important issues in Chapters 2 and 10.

Summing Up the Findings of Longitudinal Studies

At this point, we should assess what existing longitudinal studies tell us about delinquency. According to Farrington and his colleagues, longitudinal research indicates that juveniles involved in a high rate of offending represent a small proportion of the entire juvenile population. Furthermore, frequent offenders do not seem to specialize in any one particular kind of offending, such as theft or larceny. Instead, they tend to be involved in a wide assortment of offenses, ranging from minor property crimes to serious violent actions. Each of these points was stressed earlier in the chapter. Longitudinal research suggests also that these offenders are unusually troublesome in school, earn poor grades, and have inadequate or inappropriate social skills. Moreover, these troublesome behaviors began at an early age, and the more serious the offender, the earlier the childhood patterns appeared. The patterns of going "against the environment" extend into adolescence, frequently resulting in the youth dropping out of school and being unable to maintain steady employment. Serious offenders very often use drugs and alcohol regularly. In sum, serious delinquents have frequently and persistently been in conflict with their environment.

The Serious Juvenile Offender over Time:
The "Career Criminal"

Up to this point, we have used the term "serious" rather loosely, with no attempt to define it carefully. Who, precisely, is the serious offender? Is he the 13-year-old who holds up the local grocer at the point of a realistic toy gun? Is he the high-school junior who has built an impressive rock-music collection from shoplifted tapes? Is she the gang member who has been arrested four times for simple assault? Law enforcement officers, the public, victims, and researchers might all differ in their responses. Yet criminologists invariably express concern about the serious delinquent and draw conclusions about his or her background. For example, some believe that serious delinquents tend to come from families characterized by marital conflict, divorce, or poor parental supervision, or that gangs are prominent in their lives. Others observe that serious delinquents come from high crime communities with ineffective informal social control and support systems. It will be important, when we assess these contributions to the criminological literature, to recognize how seriousness is being defined.

The Wolfgang and Hamparian studies discussed earlier emphasized *frequency* of offending as an adequate feature of the serious delinquent. More recently, Delbert S. Elliott, Franklin W. Dunford, and David Huizinga (1987) have argued that both frequency and type of offense (index or non-index) are better measures. Furthermore, they introduce the element of *persistence* and recommend that juveniles committing a number of delinquent acts over several years be designated "career offenders."

As a first step in identifying the juvenile career offender, Elliott et al. developed classifications based on the *frequency* and *type* of offenses committed within one year. Using the SR data from the National Youth Survey, they divided juvenile offenders into four classifications. The researchers believed that since a great majority of all youths, particularly males, report an occasional non-index delinquent act, it is reasonable to classify those who commit three or less non-index offenses in any given year *nonoffenders*. Those youths who commit four to eleven such offenses but no more than one index crime in any given year are classified *exploratory offenders*. A third category, *patterned nonserious offenders*, refers to those who are steadily engaged in primarily non-index illegal behavior within any given year (12 or more offenses and no more than two index crimes). A fourth category, *serious patterned offenders*, includes those youths committing three or more index offenses in any given year, regardless of the total number of non-index offenses.

As a second step, the researchers introduced the element of time, or persistence. This time factor enabled them to identify the "career offender" along with the "serious offender." The final categories obtained by the researchers are summarized in Table 1-4. *Serious career offenders* are those youths who qualify as "serious patterned offenders" for two or more consecutive years. *Nonserious career offenders* are youths classified as "nonserious patterned offenders," again for two or more consecutive years. *Noncareer offenders* are those juveniles who demonstrated a sporadic pattern of offend-

TABLE 1-4   THE ELLIOTT ET AL. CLASSIFICATION SYSTEM OF DELINQUENCY*

Offender classification	SR offenses	Index crimes	Time (in years)
Nonoffenders	0–3	0	1
Exploratory	4–11	1 or less	1
Nonserious patterned	12 or more	2 or less	1
Serious patterned	NA	3 or more	1
CAREER OFFENDERS			
Nonoffender	0–3	0	Classified as nonoffender through adolescent years
Noncareer	Generally, any combination of above categories, but with some exceptions	Generally, any combination of above categories, but with some exceptions	No two consecutive years
Nonserious career	12 or more	2 or more	2 or more consecutive
Serious career	NA	3 or more	2 or more consecutive

*Table adapted from Elliott et al. (1987).

ing over the years, but did not sustain a minimum of 12 total or three index offenses per year for any two consecutive years. *Nonoffenders* are those juveniles classified as non-offenders for five consecutive years.

Elliott, Dunford, and Huizinga found that about 19 percent of the National Youth Survey sample met the criteria of career offenders—13 percent nonserious, 6 percent serious career offenders. Furthermore, these self-reported career offenders were dispro-portionately older, urban, and male, a finding consistent with research based upon offi-cial statistics. Contrary to expectation, there was no relationship between race and career offending status.

Other findings of this research are worth noting. Serious career offenders reported a higher rate of offending on *all* categories of offenses, not just index crimes. Further-more, career offenders, particularly the serious ones, accounted for a large portion of all SR offenses. While nonserious career offenders contributed approximately three times their proportionate share of offenses, serious career offenders contributed over *ten times* their proportionate share. Most significantly, only 14 percent of those classified as career offenders had been arrested during a five-year period, *suggesting that a vast majority (86 percent) of career offenders are unknown to the police.*

GOALS OF BOOK

As scientific knowledge on juvenile delinquency accumulates, it is increasingly difficult to select and organize this knowledge into a coherent theoretical framework and present a comprehensive, carefully documented synthesis of the field. This task is especially difficult if we wish to coordinate relevant scientific knowledge from several disciplines and perspectives, particularly sociology and psychology.

In his well-received book, *General Social Systems*, biologist Ludwig von Bertalanffy (1968, p. 195) stated, "Social science is the science of social systems." In recent years, social systems theory has captured the interest of a number of researchers and other scholars in the social sciences, but it has yet to be tried as an organizational platform for surveying the theory and research on crime and delinquency.

A system is an arrangement of things that are related to one another. The concept of "system" is a human creation which is used to describe regularities or consistencies found in our world. A system is a conceptual tool used, for convenience, to put order into an otherwise chaotic mass of data and theory. Social systems theory, the theoretical framework for this text, will allow us to examine the vast amount of theoretical and empirical work in juvenile delinquency with some thematic orientation; it offers a tentative structure for our topics.

Currently, the social world, as compartmentalized by the various social science disciplines, exists at different levels and is seen from different perspectives. A social systems approach facilitates a synthesis of what we know across disciplines and viewpoints, whether we are talking about social class, neighborhood, community, culture, or individual. The social systems framework will accommodate all. Furthermore, this approach urges us to realize that research concerned with aggregate data at the community or national level is not superior to research at the family or individual level. Rather, each research project or theoretical endeavor is at a *different* level of study and explanation, and each has merit. Superiority based on level of study is not tenable in this scheme.

Social systems theory also assumes that, while it is helpful to study social structures (social class, family size, number of single family dwellings, etc.), social relationships, or individual personality characteristics, it is far more effective to study these variables in *relationship* to one another. That is, rather than study isolated hierarchies, we need to study dynamic interplays. To understand delinquency, we must study not only delinquents themselves but also their families, peers, schools, neighborhoods, and cultures, all in relationship to one another. A delinquent is part of a system that cannot be studied in isolation. The delinquent affects the systems, and the systems affect him or her in complex ways.

It may not be apparent to the reader precisely how this systems framework will be achieved until the second part of the text. The theme will be discussed again in more detail beginning with Chapter 6. The following few chapters offer crucial background information for contemporary theory and research in juvenile delinquency. Chapter 2 discusses scientific knowledge and assesses why it is often so inconclusive. It attempts to cultivate some appreciation for the scientific endeavor from the social science viewpoint, and more specifically, from a criminological perspective.

Still another goal of the book is to place the study of crime and delinquency in historical perspective. As noted earlier, theories and practices are to a great extent dependent upon the spirit of their times. History provides clues about what we have done and tried, where we are, and where we may be going. To appreciate the complexity of the study of juvenile delinquency, it is crucial that we follow the historical evolution of its concepts, theories, and methods. .

For the first half of the book, therefore, developments in criminology, including important developments in the juvenile justice system, will be introduced roughly according to the historical sequence in which they occurred. A comprehensive treatment of juvenile *justice*, however, requires a separate text in itself and thus is beyond the scope of this book. Although the book can give only summary attention to juvenile justice, it is important to recognize that historical and current developments in the judicial and legislative realm affect and are affected by theory and research in delinquency. This will be evident in chapter 3 and in the book's concluding chapter. Chapters 4 and 5 will describe some of the early work in criminology, consider how these theories were devised, how bias might have occurred, and how discoveries were made. The second half of the book introduces the "knowledge explosion" that occurred during the 1950s and 1960s. Because theory and research at that time were going in such diverse directions, social systems theory will be introduced to provide the framework for a bewildering array of information.

The Study of Delinquency as a Science

2
CHAPTER

The study of crime and delinquency is foremost a scientific enterprise, an enterprise called "criminology." Therefore, before we can proceed, it is important to know what science is, what it does, and how it affects our knowledge about delinquency. Otherwise, discussions and debates concerning the research and theory on delinquency will appear as an uncoordinated mass of contradictions or a chaotic list of seemingly unrelated facts. It will be hard to know which presumed fact to believe or which statement is most "accurate." For example, we may read in a newspaper that a famous researcher claims that the principal cause of delinquency is parental abuse. In that same article, we read that another equally famous researcher strongly disagrees with the conclusions of the first, maintaining that dire economic conditions are chiefly to blame. As we read further, police sergeant Jones contends that lack of parental supervision is the most important contributing factor. In Jones' 35 years of police experience, he has continually found that parents of delinquents seldom know their whereabouts. And yet, parole officer Jackson is convinced that drug abuse is the main culprit. Who is right? And how do we go about disentangling this thicket of expert opinion? One place to begin is the writings of Charles Sanders Peirce (1839–1914), the American philosopher, physicist, and mathematician who described four methods by which we gain knowledge and eliminate doubt about our world. Peirce considered doubt an unpleasant, uncomfortable feeling which all of us wish to minimize or eliminate. He believed we do this through one or more of four methods: the methods of tenacity, authority, *a priori* logic, or science.

METHODS OF KNOWING AND ELIMINATING DOUBT

The most simple and direct method is what Peirce called the *method of tenacity*. Positing that most people want calm and complacent lives, Peirce suggested that once we reach this comfortable mental state, ". . . we cling tenaciously, not merely to believing, but to believing just what we do believe" (Peirce, 1877/1955, p. 10). Most of us tend to avoid contrary opinions and beliefs by closing our minds to new and different information, Peirce said. We isolate ourselves, become dogmatic in expressing our opinions, and generally resist change, because change would upset the equilibrium we have established for ourselves. The tendency to do this becomes especially apparent with advancing age. The method of tenacity was demonstrated by colleagues of Galileo, who refused to look through his telescope to observe contradictory facts about their universe. They refused, thinking it was unnecessary to look. They *knew* the facts; there was simply no point in observing anything contradictory. The criminal justice scholars Michael Tonry and Norval Morris (1983) have remarked that most people think they know why crime occurs and what to do about it.

> . . . (P)eople are born experts on the causes and control of crimes; they sense the solutions in their bones. Those solutions differ dramatically from person to person, but each one knows, and knows deeply and emotionally, that his perspective is the way of truth. (p. vii)

Some individuals "know" better than others what works or doesn't work, how to treat adult criminals, what juvenile offenders need, why prisons are not effective—and they may refuse to look through the telescopes of researchers and other scholars who suggest creative solutions or who have uncovered contradictory information. The major problem with the method of tenacity, therefore, is the absolute refusal to look at other points of view.

The second method, the *method of authority*, is encouraged primarily by governmental and religious institutions, but it can be found operating in numerous other settings, including families, the educational system, the media, social service groups, the corporate world, and, of course, the criminal justice system. According to Peirce, the method of authority is especially prevalent where the objective is "to keep correct doctrines before the attention of the people, to reiterate them perpetually, and to teach them to the young" (Peirce, 1955, p. 13). To achieve these objectives, those in authority sometimes keep others ignorant. Otherwise, people lower in status may learn of some reason to think differently from the established beliefs.

The motives of those in authority may be benevolent—"we really know what's best for you"—patronizing, selfish, or corrupt. Regardless of the motives, however, several messages are conveyed, either implicitly or explicitly. First, those who reject the established beliefs should be silenced by social pressure and rejection. Second, something is true because the authority or expert says it is true. The authority leads others to believe that it possesses knowledge and experience unavailable to them but that, if they did possess it, they would reach the same conclusions. A third message is that those who trust and accept the established belief system will be free of doubt. Under these conditions, knowledge advances only within the prescribed and narrow limits set by the authoritative institution or persons.

By no means are we saying that the method of authority is all negative. In fact, this book is using the method of authority to convey what we know about delinquency. No one acquires knowledge in isolation, independent of the input of other more experienced or knowledgeable individuals. We all must rely on what experts and authorities tell us about their research findings, about their experiences and techniques for handling seemingly incorrigible delinquents, about their theories and conclusions about how the world works. We rely on the media to keep us informed about events and trends. Certainly these sources are all very valuable. The point is this: We should not unquestionably accept the conclusions of someone in authority without including our own critical thinking about an issue, seeking additional information, and remaining constantly open to other points of view. After all, it is highly doubtful that any one mortal, authority figure is "*the* ultimate bearer of the truth."

Peirce's third method, the *a priori* method, relies on reasoning and logic to reduce personal doubt. One follows either the organized logic developed by others—such as philosophers or legal scholars—or one's own tenets derived from reasoning and critical analysis, or some combination of both. New information will be incorporated into the belief system, but only if it fits into the already accepted logical order. The *a priori* method or rationale is more intellectually taxing than the first two methods. In the case of delinquents, for example, one must systematically construct a logical, consistent rationale for why delinquency occurs. In large part, scientists use the *a priori* method in developing a hypothesis or a theory.

The *a priori* method is less likely than the first two methods to eliminate doubt, since a person still may not be certain of his or her own conclusions. For example, consider the thought processes involved in trying to answer, in a logical manner, "What is justice?" or, "What rights do or should children have?" Logic must be used, but the final answer will very likely still include elements of doubt. Suppose you had the final say in deciding the fate of a serious juvenile offender. You may know that he is an urban male, age 17, who has been involved in a number of criminal acts—the most recent being aggravated assault. On what would you base your final decision? Although you may want to know more about his circumstances, your decision is apt to be based on rational thinking (within the broad sweep of the pertinent law).

Rational thinking is fine for most situations, but at times it may have to be mingled with research (empirical) evidence. This fourth method, the *method of science*, is perhaps the least successful at reducing doubt but most productive in advancing knowledge. To Peirce, the method of science allows us to discover ". . . 'real' things, whose characters are entirely independent of our opinions about them . . ." (Peirce, 1955, p. 18). The method of science tries to discover these "real things" through systematic observation, measurement, and explicit statement. Ideally, the method of science reduces the subjectivity inherent in the way the other methods perceive "reality." Thus, according to Peirce, the method of science permits every person, through the careful use of his or her senses, to arrive at the same ultimate conclusions. This view is very similar to that expressed by the sociologists Auguste Comte and Emile Durkheim who held that the highest form of intellectual knowledge is the description of facts based on direct experience *independent* of preconceived or philosophical notions. This scientific viewpoint, called "positivism," argues that scientific knowledge should be based solely on observable, scientific facts and their relations to each other.

Today, positivism is often seen as too restrictive in its stringent demand for direct experience of the phenomenon and concrete definitions of everything examined. For example, the eminent philosopher of science Stephen Toulman (1961, p. 108) writes ". . . the business of science involves more than the mere assembly of facts: it demands also intellectual architecture and construction." Toulman argues that science must be rational as well as positivistic. We need both the logic and empirical testing of the phenomenon. We need both the theory and the data.

QUANTITATIVE AND QUALITATIVE METHODS IN CRIMINOLOGY

For scientific knowledge to advance, various strategies and methods are necessary, not just highly controlled and precise measurement of phenomena. The use of a variety of methods and strategies is especially important for the social sciences. Howard Schwartz and Jerry Jacobs (1979) have outlined some of the differences between the various scientific methods used in the social sciences. One of the most relevant distinctions is that between *quantitative* and *qualitative* methods. Quantitative methods assign numbers to observations which allow researchers to analyze data systematically and to detect patterns and differences. Typically, quantitative methods collect measurements on variables and apply various statistical techniques to these measurements. Researchers using quantitative approaches might collect arrest and victimization data describing the distribution of delinquency in a particular city. Armed with these data, the researchers might do a statistical analysis to discover where delinquency is most heavily concentrated, what types of crimes are being committed, and whether the perpetrators are male or female.

Qualitative methods are quite different. Researchers using the qualitative approach seldom make counts or assign numbers to their observations. Rather, "Qualitative methodology refers to those research strategies, such as participant observation, in-depth interviewing, total participation in the activity being investigated, field work, etc., which allow the researcher to obtain first-hand knowledge about the empirical social world in question" (Filstead, 1970, p. 6). Researchers using qualitative methods most generally describe their observations in the "natural language" at hand. For example, some researchers try to gain the trust of a group of youths by interacting with their gang, hoping to acquire an "inside" view of how these youths perceive and construct their world. In this case, "natural language" would include the jargon, speech patterns, and symbols of the youths themselves, instead of the artificial categories and concepts imposed on them by the researcher. From this qualitative perspective, if we want to understand delinquents, it is important to know what they know, to see what they see, and to understand what they understand.

A good illustration of the qualitative approach is the research conducted by Anne Campbell (1984) on the role of girls in New York street gangs. She writes, "I wanted to observe and interact with girl gang members and to represent their own views of their situations'' (p. 1). After researching the nearly 400 known gangs in New York City, she selected three which seemed to represent the diversity of gang life: a street gang, a biker gang, and a religio-cultural gang. One was racially mixed, one was Puerto Rican, and one was black. She was introduced to the gangs by a police officer who knew them well or by agencies and youth project members who worked with them. She spent several months with gang members, getting to know them and building their trust. She did not disguise her identity or purpose to the gang members, and data collection was through either field note taking or a tape recorder. Much of her book, *The Girls in the Gang*, is written in the girls' ''own words.''

Campbell found some very interesting things about contemporary gang members. She found them conservative in their attitudes, structure, and philosophy: pro-America, pro-capitalism, pro-education, pro-mainstream values. ''The girls especially are subject to the dictates of fashion and consumer fetishism: substantial sums are spent on the 'right' jeans, hair perms—even cigarettes'' (p. 241). They believe in American society and what it stands for. The girls accept the same roles within the gang as they probably would in the larger society, with males being the central, pivotal figures, and females supporting, nurturing, and sustaining them. The girls follow soap operas closely, with little apparent concern about the vast economic and social disparities between themselves and TV dramas. Campbell concludes:

> While some writers have argued for the existence of a set of focal concerns specific to lower-class male life, this should not be parodied into a simplistic belief that gang members are isolated from society at large or hermetically sealed in an alien set of norms. As much as anyone, they are exposed through the media to the images of a life lived with limitless luxury, in which everyone is beautiful and relationships are passionate, stormy, superficial, and ultimately selfish. They subscribe to this as the natural order. (Campbell, 1984, p. 242)

We will return to Campbell's important study in chapter 9 when we talk about peer groups, but at this point we wish to emphasize that both methods—qualitative and quantitative—are highly useful methods for the science of delinquency. According to Schwartz and Jacobs (1979, p. 5) ''. . . quantitative methods are best for conducting a 'positive science'; that is, they allow for the clear, rigorous, and reliable collection of data and permit the testing of empirical hypotheses in a logically consistent manner.'' On the other hand, ''. . . qualitative methods, which use natural language, are best at gaining access to the life-world of other individuals in a short time'' (Schwartz & Jacobs, 1979, p. 5). Qualitative methods allow us to examine the motives, meanings, emotions, and other subjective aspects in the lives of delinquents. In short, they add life to our knowledge.

It is also important to realize that one method does not necessarily have to be chosen over the other. David Silverman (1985, p. 17) asserts: ''. . . it is not simply a choice between polar opposites that face us, but a decision about balance and intellectual breadth and rigour.'' In the pages ahead, we will encounter studies using one or the other method, and, in some cases, a combination of both. At this juncture, it is necessary to describe more carefully what is meant by the terms "scientific law," "theory," and "hypothesis." From there, we will move to Bronowski's three central features of all science: order, cause, and chance.

SCIENTIFIC LAWS, THEORIES, AND HYPOTHESES

Three concepts that are most commonly used in any discussions of science are law, theory, and hypothesis. Before we can proceed with our discussion of the nature of science, it will be worthwhile to examine these terms, both from the traditional scientific frame of reference and from a contemporary perspective.

The search for natural laws has long been seen as the central task of science, at least since the time of Isaac Newton. A *law* is an "if A then B" statement. Given conditions A, B will follow. In the physical sciences, a lawful relationship is established if, whenever condition "A" occurs, condition "B" is sure to follow. For example, conditions A may be a mixture of specified chemicals under a specified temperature and specified pressure. Conditions B are the chemical reactions obtained as a result of conditions A. Not only must it be demonstrated that B *always* follows A, however; it also must be established that A and not some other factor (C) is contributing directly to B. The chemical combinations under a specified temperature and pressure (condition A) must directly cause B; no other extraneous factor can be responsible. Finally, the if-A-then-B relationship must hold across time and place. The relationship must be assumed to have existed 100 years ago and presumed to continue to exist everywhere for another 100 years. If the relationship is valid for all times and all places, we have a *universal* law, and our ability to forecast with precision is fully established. The extent to which such laws exist in the physical and social sciences will be discussed shortly.

A *hypothesis* is a hunch or speculative statement about a lawful relationship. A scientist makes observations that suggest there may be a lawful relationship between two conditions or variables. On the basis of a hypothesis, the scientist teases out lawful relationships by preparing a carefully controlled experiment or study and taking meticulously measured observations of the phenomenona he or she is studying. The social scientist is less likely to conduct a laboratory experiment than one in the field, such as a survey, a systematic study based on interviews or observations, a study based on aggregate data already available, or a "quasi-experiment," which allows some manipulation on the variables of interest. Each of these techniques will be illustrated in later chapters. The scientist records the findings, interprets them, and determines whether the results support or disconfirm the hypothesis. If the hypothesis is not supported, an alternative may be suggested. If the hypothesis is supported, the scientist may well be on the road to establishing another scientific law which will unlock more of the secrets of nature.

A *theory* is a statement that integrates and simplifies a cluster of scientific laws. Ideally, before we can have theory we must have scientific laws. Theory is not, however, simply a collection of these laws; it is a conceptual arrangement of the world constructed by human thought. It is a creative statement or group of statements, based upon scientific laws, that explains past events and can predict future events and relationships.

The preceding descriptions of law, hypothesis, and theory represent the *ideal* toward which science should be striving. In social science we have a long road ahead, for we have no laws, as we defined them here. Social scientists have not yet found highly consistent relationships between any two events that would follow the traditional definition of a scientific law. Technically, and in accordance with the foregoing definition, we cannot have a theory. This is why some social scientists prefer to refer to lawlike propositions rather than universal laws. According to sociologist Herbert M. Blalock, Jr., a theory "must contain lawlike propositions that interrelate the concepts or variables two or more at a time" (1969, p. 2). Blalock notes that the social scientist, because of the enormous complexity of social phenomena, must do a balancing act between scientific rigor and social reality. Because social phenomena do not remain the same over time and place, the best a social scientist can hope for is an *approximation* of a law— "lawlikeness."

Blalock's conception of theory may needlessly be promoting a physical-social science gulf, however. If we examine the theories of many of the physical sciences (e.g., chemistry, physics, geology), we find that they, too, fail to meet rigid criteria. If the requirements of theory were rigidly observed, for example, Newton's laws of motion and gravitation and Kepler's law of planetary motion would not qualify as laws. According to current knowledge, they hold only *approximately.* Even physical scientists, therefore, use "law" and "theory" somewhat liberally, applying the terms generally to certain statements that are known to hold only *approximately* (99.99 percent of time) and with certain qualifications (Bronowski, 1978). The point made here is not that the physical and social sciences are identical. Indeed, there are important distinctions that will be recognized shortly. It is a mistake, however, to think of the physical and social sciences as qualitatively different. The physical sciences are not "better" by virtue of having laws whereas the social sciences have only lawlike propositions. To reinforce this point, we will use the term "law" in the pages ahead. For our purposes, we will distinguish three types of scientific laws:

1. *universal*
2. *statistical* and
3. *non-universal*

Universal laws refer to highly consistent relationships that seem to hold across time and place as long as the essentials of condition A remain the same. The major feature of a universal law is that it appears to hold for centuries, across all cultural contexts, and in any geographical area. For example, Gabriel Tarde believed that all humans imitate others they respect, regardless of the cultural context, generation after generation. Cesare Lombroso, during his early thinking, was convinced that violent crime was committed exclusively by biologically inferior humans, a propensity that existed across all cultures. Both are classic examples of ill-fated attempts at universal laws.

Statistical laws refer to statements about mathematical probabilities. A statistical law might predict that out of a sample of ten parolees, three will commit another offense within one year of release from prison. This estimate is reached on the basis of empirical data. A statistical law cannot tell us which *particular* individual will conform to it, only that a certain percentage will. In addition, a statistical law may be able to *predict* with a high degree of accuracy, but it cannot *explain*. In the preceding example, we might predict that three out of ten parolees will engage in illegal activity, but we do not know *why*. Today, social science statisticians are keenly attuned to the desirability of explaining events. As a result, they have devised sophisticated techniques which have brought them closer to this goal. We will refer to some of these techniques in the following pages.

Non-universal laws allow far more exceptions than universal laws, but they have valuable explanatory power. In non-universal laws, the 'if A than B' conditions are not absolute, but they are consistent enough to warrant some degree of lawfulness. As Hans Reichenbach (1947) suggested, if-A-then-B laws in the social sciences should read: If A, then B *with a certain probability*. Moreover, non-universal laws *do* hold explanatory power for a particular set of circumstances at a particular time. However, while they may be well-confirmed for now, for this culture, and with some exceptions, they may not generalize to other cultures, or even to the same culture after the passage of some time. For example, school failure seems to be associated with delinquency in American society, but we cannot state with certainty that this relation will exist 20 or 30 years from now. Therefore, theories developed from non-universal laws are necessarily limited.

Non-universal and statistical laws are most applicable to the study of crime and delinquency. The theoretical statements advanced in criminology are highly unlikely to be based on universal laws; indeed, the criminologist who searches for universal application may be merely tilting at windmills. It is more likely that theories of juvenile delinquency and criminal behavior cannot be generalized across time and space.

Now, let us shift our attention from some of the terminology of science to its characteristics. The scientist Jacob Bronowski (1978) wrote that three central features of science are *order*, *cause*, and *chance*. Next, we will consider how these relate to the science of crime and delinquency.

Order

During the last 20 years of his life, Albert Einstein wrestled with the question, "Does God play dice with the universe?" It was a question he never answered. Einstein was wondering whether random events are truly random or are simply our way of perceiving the world. This has continued to intrigue other scientists. In recent years, a new discipline interested in studying chaos and unpredictability in nature has emerged as a viable avenue for understanding the universe (Gleick, 1987).

Science always has assumed that the world is orderly or at least can be sensibly ordered by human thought. During science's infancy, within the religious and cultural climate of the times, order and lawfulness were assumed to exist independently and to be external to the perceiver. Nature was orderly (and thus lawful) because it represented a divine plan or creative arrangement. Later, when Darwinian theory gained favor, the role of a divinity was de-emphasized, but the belief in universal order remained a central theme.

Today most scientists believe that order is partly within nature itself and partly within human intellectual arrangement. Some scientists and philosophers of science are now postulating, in fact, that the order of the universe is a human invention subject to constant revision; that is, order exists primarily in the human mind. This especially seems to be the case when we try to put order in the social environment. *We* order the events and objects of our known universe; there may be no "naturally occurring" order at all. This human ordering process is desirable, for with ingenious thinking and theory building, it can produce useful frames of reference for our knowledge. Order in our social world, then, may be not so much discovered as it is created, through the systematic, verifiable (or falsifiable) observations that characterize scientific research.

Anytime we label others, we are trying to put order in the social environment. Calling someone "hostile" or "friendly" is ordering behavioral patterns through labeling and classifying. The criminal justice field offers numerous examples of attempts to order. Herbert Quay (1987) is well known for his research on patterns of delinquent behavior in which he divides delinquents into three or four groups—those with undersocialized aggression, socialized aggression, attention deficit, and anxiety. We will cover this and other classification systems in more detail in chapter 7. Recent research by Cornell, Benedek, and Benedek (1987) concludes that juvenile murderers fall into three categories: the criminal, the conflictful, and the psychotic. The researchers examined 72 juvenile murderers and found the largest group was the criminal. Members of the criminal group were those youths who committed murder in the course of some other criminal activity, such as robbery or rape. The second largest group—the conflictful type—murdered in the course of "resolving" a family quarrel, such as that brought about by an abusive parent or stepparent. The psychotic adolescent as murderer was the smallest group (about 7 percent). Classification systems in juvenile institutions, where youths are categorized according to dangerousness, rehabilitative potential, or types of offenses are other examples. Putting order into behavioral patterns simplifies an otherwise chaotic mass of behavior so research, treatment, and policy planning can take place. The thing we need to keep in mind is that this "order" is human made and is not necessarily something that exists "out there," independent of human cognitive construction.

Cause

Some perspectives of the scientific endeavor maintain that the ultimate purpose of all scientific inquiry in the social sciences is to gain some understanding of the causes of social phenomena and human behavior. Once we understand, or at least can identify, the causal agents we should be in a good position to remedy, modify, or control. But identifying cause is rarely easy. In fact, it is a great challenge to all science. Bronowski asserts that the cause-and-effect relationship has been the "natural way" of looking at all problems since the triumph of gravitation and Newtonian physics. Gravity *causes* objects to fall, and *causes* the orbit of planets. Flipping a switch *causes* a light to go on. Likewise, until recently, even physical science assumed that a given cause produces an *inevitable* effect, which can therefore be predicted once the cause is determined. This is referred to as the *mechanistic* perspective of science. Today, science is shifting from a firm belief in inevitable effect to a more tentative belief in probable effect.

The causality problem is more troublesome for the social sciences than for the physical sciences, partly because of the great complexity and dynamic quality of the objects of study. Some criminologists argue that we can be reasonably certain we are on the right path to explanation, however, if we can meet three fundamental criteria. First, there must be a demonstrable, *consistent* relationship between each of the relevant variables. It is not necessary that this relationship be inevitable. A researcher might demonstrate that lower socioeconomic status (SES) and delinquency are consistently related, thereby meeting the first criterion. Second, it must be clear that the assumed causal variable *precedes* the effect variable. Our researcher must be able to say with objective confidence and supportive evidence that SES characteristics existed *before* the criminal activity of the members of the group he or she is studying. If criminal activity preceded lower socioeconomic status, the latter could not, of course, cause crime. Third, it must be established that lower SES and not some other variable is *directly* responsible for criminal activity. In other words, a researcher must eliminate rival causal factors, such as level of education or birth order, from the relationship. Generally, it is with this third step in the process that studies in criminal justice have had greatest difficulty (Hagan, 1982).

The foregoing three criteria for establishing a causal relationship are fine for determining a *single* cause that moves in one direction, from the antecedent A to the consistently caused B. It is highly unlikely that delinquency is caused by any one factor, however. Single-parent homes are not *the* cause of delinquency; neither is intelligence, nor birth order. Delinquency is caused by many factors, and these *may* be among them.

But identifying the multiple factors at work is only one of the troubling concerns in our search for the causes of delinquency. Another is *reciprocity*. Reciprocity refers to the process whereby the individual and social environments mutually influence one another in an ongoing process. For example, peers may be a contributing "cause" to delinquency, but it is equally plausible that delinquent behavior "causes" certain individuals to seek each other out. In other words, delinquency-prone adolescents may look for the company of other delinquency-prone adolescents, and when they get together, their delinquent behavior may increase. Or, the child's family may influence his or her relationships with peers and peers may, in turn, influence the relationships with family. Steven Burkett and Bruce Warren (1987) illustrate this reciprocity. These researchers found that, among high school students, marijuana use increases associations with delinquent peers, while associations with delinquent peers reduce religious commitment and belief. This reciprocity of influence results in deeper involvement with marijuana-using peers and less association with family and non-marijuana-using peers. In the Burkett and Warren research, the trend was especially apparent for youths with low religious commitment to begin with. On the other hand, if the youth's religious commitment was strong, he or she would more likely seek out companions with similar religious commitment and attitudes, and most probably reject those who use marijuana. ''For these youth, the adolescent peer group would seem . . . to serve as an effective moral community which supports beliefs which inhibit the use of marijuana'' (Burkett and Warren, 1987, p. 127).

The concept of reciprocity signifies that the causes of delinquency are unlikely to be in one direction (unidirectional) from a simple antecedent to a consequence (if A, then B). Rather, the causes of delinquency are apt to be operating in a two-directional (bidirectional) fashion. ''A'' influences ''B'' and vice versa. Level of parental supervision influences delinquency, and delinquency influences parental supervision. In some respects, causation may operate in several directions (multidirectional). ''A'' and ''C'' cause ''B,'' and ''B,'' in turn, causes ''A'' and ''C.'' Drug use and faulty parental supervision lead to delinquency, and delinquency increases drug use and a reduction in supervision by frustrated parents. The contemporary school of thought that subscribes most clearly to causal reciprocity is called *interactionism*. We will return to this very important topic in chapter 9.

Chance

In many areas of science, scientists are reluctant to predict with any kind of certainty what will happen in the future. The social sciences must worry about chance factors even more than the physical sciences, just as they can rely on even less man-made order and less demonstrable cause and effect. For example, if a social scientist understands condition A, he or she can predict the resultant behavior *across groups of people* with some statistical probability. The group aspect is important. If we are to predict the behavioral pattern of a group in an ''if-then'' relationship, we must understand all the relevant variables in condition ''A.'' However, social scientists readily admit they seldom understand all—or even most—of the relevant variables in situation ''A.'' Therefore, they must rely on statistical probabilities to predict behavior (statistical laws) and non-universal laws to explain it. To a great extent, then, contemporary criminology is partly a science of behavior patterns, tendencies, and *probabilities* that vary from time to time and place to place.

Scientific knowledge, whether physical or social, has numerous limitations and is continually susceptible to revision. This premise especially underlies applications of scientific knowledge about human behavior. Before knowledge about human behavior can be applied, theory must be monitored and tested constantly to determine whether it produces and explains the desired or expected results. If the knowledge clearly fails to account for some phenomenon or observation, it needs to be revised, reorganized, or discarded in favor of better theory or explanation. And then the *new* theory must be tested.

TESTABLE THEORY

Many scientists believe that the paramount goal of all science is to develop reliable theory. As we have seen, theory is not developed merely by systematically tying together existing events or "facts"; it is an intellectual construction based on the perceptions of someone trying to understand the world. According to the philosopher of science Karl R. Popper (1968), theories are like conceptual nets that are thrown out over what we call the world. The task is to make the mesh of the net ever finer and finer, each time trying to capture more of the essence of the world.

There are no established techniques or strategies for weaving the conceptual nets. They may be constructed spontaneously, in an academic tower, at a party, at the kitchen sink, or on the golf course. Only an educated and prepared mind, attuned to potential discoveries, will recognize a conceptual net, however. On the other hand, the existence of the net could elude that same mind. Edwin H. Sutherland, known for his work on white collar crime and his theory of differential association (see chapter 5), was said not to have recognized he *had* a theory until this fact was pointed out to him by a colleague.

The scientist's next step is to formulate a *testable* statement or series of statements about the potential discovery. These statements must be capable of being examined through systematic observation and experiment. They must be worded in such a way that subsequent researchers can clearly understand what is being said about the events or relationships to be observed. Furthermore, they must be accompanied by an outline of conditions under which the events can be reproduced. Scientists call this feature *replicability*. If all the statements are replicable, the theory may be said to be verified. Sutherland's differential association theory of crime and delinquency has often been criticized on this basis, because the various propositions he formulated seem to defy testing.

Verifiability and Falsifiability

In his classic work, *The Logic of Scientific Discovery*, Karl Popper (1968) contends that a truly scientific statement not only is capable of being verified or shown to be correct for the time being, but also is capable of being *falsified* or shown to be incorrect. In fact, Popper argues that one criterion of a scientific statement is its vulnerability to being refuted by common or special experience. The scientist must ask, "Is it conceivable to set up conditions where the statements accounting for the observed phenomena could be shown to be incorrect?" If such conceivable conditions cannot be proposed, the statement is not scientific. A truly scientific statement, then, according to Popper, is constantly at risk of being shown faulty in accounting for observations and experience.

To describe the differences between verifiability and falsifiability, Popper uses the scientific statement, "All swans are white." No matter how many times we may observe white swans, our observations do not justify the conclusion that *all* swans are white. Verification is forever inconclusive. If, after one million observations (verifications), a black swan is seen, the statement "all swans are white" has become incorrect. In a sense, we have learned much more about our statement by this one falsification than by many verifications. One falsification has forced a revision of our thinking about swans, rendering the original statement non-universal. Now we must try to develop a better scientific statement, such as "*Most* swans are white" or "All young swans are white." It is important to note, though, that the falsification must itself be replicated. Others also must see the same black swan, or another one like it, and establish authenticity. In effect, two falsifications are desirable in order to falsify a statement.

The strength and power of one replicated falsification in contrast to many verifications is what Popper calls the *asymmetry* of scientific discovery. Millions of verifications can be quickly undermined by just one falsification. The statements, "Most child molesters were sexually abused as children" and "Every 20-year-old, at some time in his or her life, has committed a criminal act" are subject to falsification. On the other hand, how could we conceivably falsify the statement, "Most youngsters who set fires are acting out their sexual urges"?

Falsifiability means that every scientific statement remains tentative forever, because it is only a human interpretation of the known universe and is always subject to revision. Hence, scientific knowledge is not a system of certain, well-established statements, nor is it necessarily a system that steadily advances toward finality or "ultimate truths." Scientific knowledge is an open system that is tentative, fallible, and developing.

Popper's ideas certainly are not embraced unquestioningly by the scientific community. Experimental data, particularly in the social sciences, are rarely clear or convincing enough to warrant either confirmation or falsification of a lawful relationship or a theory. As Manicas and Secord note (1983, p. 405), most events of the world ". . . cannot be explained as the simple manifestation of some single law or principle." Often, the data are open to multiple interpretations and subject to varying explanations. In the social sciences, other criteria determine whether a theory will be embraced, discarded, or simply ignored. According to Stephen Cole,

> . . . the acceptance or rejection of a theory is not primarily dependent on empirical evidence. It is dependent on the way the theory fits in with the other interests of the community of scientists and the ability of the theory to fulfill what might be called its "functional requirements." (Cole, 1975, p. 212)

In other words, if a theory serves a useful function for the community of scientists or for makers of public policy, it is retained and cited, regardless of whether it has been submitted to empirical verification.

Nevertheless, Popper's point about falsification should not be dismissed. Its value lies in reminding ourselves about how observable or testable a particular statement is.

Just because a statement has been falsified, this does not mean it should be discarded, however. It may still be relevant to evaluating scientific statements and theory in criminology. Social science theory may be replete with apparent exceptions, but falsification should not be taken to mean that a theory is useless in helping us understand crime and delinquency. Formulating theoretical statements that are clear enough to be forever susceptible to falsification through well-designed research is one ultimate goal in explaining delinquency. Popper's emphasis on falsification encourages a critical appraisal of popular, expert, or scientific statements. If they are not susceptible to being shown wrong, they should be viewed with caution, although not necessarily discarded. If they are convincingly falsified, we must look for a better explanation.

Some scientists say, in fact, that the "truthfulness" or "untruthfulness" of a law or a theory is an illusion. It is the *usefulness* of a lawful statement or theory that is being confirmed or disconfirmed (Cook and Campbell, 1979). If a theory seems to account for the observations and predicts them with reasonable probability, then it is useful for the time being, but certainly not correct or truthful for all time. This point is an important one, for it underscores the dynamic ever-changing quality of all testable theory, whether it is based upon universal, statistical, or non-universal laws.

Science as well as the world in general is stratified, an assumption which accounts for the tenuous nature of any scientific statement (Manicas and Secord, 1983). The "things" in our world are complex composites defined by many—perhaps infinite—layers. Manicas and Secord (1983, p. 401) illustrate this as follows:

> Ordinary table salt is not, usually, *just* NaCl, since the purest of it contains other "things." But more important, at another *level* the compound NaCl is a complex of elements, Na and Cl. Sodium and chlorine each have causal properties, and NaCl has causal properties that are not true of either sodium or of chlorine. But at still another level, sodium and chlorine are themselves complexes of electrons, quarks, and so on.

Most people, if asked "What do you see right now?" name objects in their immediate environment—a foreign car, a bowl of strawberries, a Jack Russell terrier. They do not "see" the molecules, electrons, and ultra-violet light before them. Neither do they "see" the state they are in, the country, the planet, the political system that runs the city. Yet these are all assumed to exist at different layers of description and explanation. With each technological advance in our power to observe, we find the world has more layers of description than we previously thought. Frequently, new advances demand different explanations which do not always fit neatly into a mechanistic perspective of the world. We will return to this "system phenomenon" throughout the course of the book in our quest for an understanding of delinquency, since our social systems analysis will be used to organize relevant research and theory.

The method of science can help us obtain information about the central issues of human nature. However, we must be careful to distinguish between the *methods* used by social scientists and the potentially contaminating influence of their *philosophical perspectives*. If a scientist believes strongly that humans differ only in degree from animals or that everything in our world is material, he or she may devise experiments, collect data, and interpret data in accordance with those beliefs. The method of science holds great promise of answering, "What factors contribute to criminal or antisocial behavior?" but it is by no means foolproof.

But to what extent should the science of criminology pattern itself after the physical sciences? The goal to establish testable theory *may* be the same, and the scientific methods used *may* have many similarities, but the subject matter is decidedly different. In the following section, we will address that question.

THE PHYSICAL AND SOCIAL SCIENCES: A COMPARISON

We have developed the argument that the basic aim of science is to develop testable theory, but this task appears to be more difficult for the social sciences. Physical science is in quest of abstract, generalizable theories which, as much as possible, seem to be independent of the political, moral, social, economic, and psychological context within which they are formulated. The physical sciences are subjected to outside influences, but perhaps less so than the social sciences. The physical sciences seem to perform their role quite well; testable explanations of natural events are advanced and predictions offered with some regularity. To many, the social sciences are "inexact" sciences, hardly capable of being useful for "scientific" explanation or prediction. In fact, many feel that even the term "science" should *not* be used when speaking of psychology, sociology, or criminology. We can isolate at least five factors to explain this attitude toward the social sciences.

Stability of Objects and Events

It is much easier for physical scientists than social scientists to develop testable theories, because many of the objects and events studied in the physical sciences have general stability in the world of nature. The laws of the physical sciences appear to have universality. Objects falling in a vacuum almost always fall at the same speed. (Although recent data suggest this is not correct because of "antigravity" inherent in each object, depending upon its density.) Chemical mixtures under similar conditions almost always produce the same anticipated reaction. Falling bodies and chemical reactions will most probably remain stable today and perhaps tomorrow. If not, the physical sciences would be seriously limited in their quest for universal testable theories. Universal laws of science would not have been formulated, and technology would not exist as it does today.

The subject matter of the social sciences is quite different. Ideally, science should develop testable theories that traverse time and history, explain phenomena, and predict future events. As we have discussed, this search may not be a feasible goal for criminology. The criminologist is confronted with an organism—the human being (or groups of human beings)—which is both sensitive to wide-ranging influences and capable of immense variation in its own behavior. Furthermore, unlike the objects in the material world of the physical scientist, those in the world of the social scientist have purpose.

Behavior, whether within one individual, among groups, or across generations, is any-thing but stable, highly replicable, or predictable.

The goal of developing transhistorical theories of human behavior or society may be unrealistic, therefore, since human behavior often changes across generations. Even a cursory review of history reveals changes in human attitudes, motivations, values, and satisfactions. Child rearing practices provide a good illustration. Between the 15th and 17th centuries, the child was perceived as an adult in miniature, with fully developed mental capacities and lacking only experience (Gergen, 1978; Van den Berg, 1961). "Thus, a child in the wealthy classes might be expected to master four separate lan-guages, to translate Plato from the original, and to hold serious discussions on death, sex, and ethics before the 7th year" (Gergen, 1978, p. 1353). Contrast that with the coddled child of the 1950s, whose parents wanted childhood to be a happy, carefree time. Contrast that again with today's children, who often lack the protective and shel-tered upbringing that was common during America's postwar years. Instead, the children of the '80s are thrust into roles demanding emotional maturity and adult decision-making that are beyond their capabilities. They may be expected to be advisors to their parents—as in divorce situations—or may be confronted prematurely with sexual dilemmas. To what extent can we compare the 16th century child to the child of the 1950s, or the 1950s child to the child of the '80s?

Historical changes are extremely relevant to the study of crime and delinquency. Even some theories of criminal behavior formulated only a decade ago may have ques-tionable relevance to contemporary problems. Theories in criminology, whether "clas-sical" or current, need to be constantly tested and updated. It is in this context that the chronic clamor in the literature for more research should be heeded.

Subjectivity

As we just noted, when a human researcher studies other humans, the researcher's value systems and implicit theories about human behavior may strongly influence interpreta-tions of the data. Physical scientists, too, are prone to subjectivity, but when the subject of study is human behavior, the tendency to humanize the data increases.

Robert K. Merton (1957) and more recently Edward Sampson (1978) have co-gently addressed the pitfalls of scientific objectivity. They note that when modern sci-entific methods were beginning to emerge in the 17th century, the Puritan Protestantism which dominated the era strongly influenced scientific thinking. According to Merton,

> Even a cursory examination of the writings suffices to disclose one outstanding fact: Certain elements of the Protestant ethic had pervaded the realm of scientific endeavor and had left their indelible stamp upon the attitudes of scientists toward their work. (Merton, 1957, p. 575)

Later, Merton added: "It has become manifest that in each age there is a system of science which rests upon a set of assumptions, usually implicit and seldom questioned by the scientists of the time" (1957, p. 581).

Sampson (1978, p. 1338) made similar observations of the social scientific enterprise: "In essence, if we argue that facts are part of the natural order and thus not historically generated, we have a kind of built-in blindness to the bias of our own sociohistorical position." He suggested that the social and behavioral sciences are so dominated by the white male perspective that they are often blind to minority or female perspectives. The example he used was Lawrence Kohlberg's theory of cognitive moral development. It was devised by a white middle class male who argued that he had "discovered" a universal law of morality, not realizing that what he had discovered was his *own* definition of morality. Carol Gilligan (1977, 1982), Norma Haan (1978), and C. B. Holstein (1976) found empirical support for the idea that, to use Gilligan's terminology, women approach morality in a "different voice." American female moral development *may* follow a decidedly different course than the moral development of American males.

If scientists studying the physical world are susceptible to cultural and moral influences, so too are those studying human behavior. The dispassionate approach expected of all scientists is contaminated at times by their preconceptions and theoretical notions. For the social scientist, this may mean yielding to the temptation to fill gaps in knowledge with personal bias. Although the intention to remain objective may be present, subjectivity almost inevitably asserts itself. Even the most objective scientist is seldom completely so. A person's sensations, perceptions, and thoughts are always susceptible to bias and error. As David Silverman (1985, p. 178) notes, "Weber pointed out in the early years of this century, all research is contaminated to some extent by the values of the researcher." The method of science *at the least* helps us be aware of the possible contamination and encourages us to keep subjectivity to a minimum.

Laboratory Artificiality

Physical science usually studies phenomena within the confines of a laboratory setting, often with considerable control over irrelevant or extraneous variables. The same strategy for the social scientist is questionable procedure. In the past, psychologists moved into the experimental laboratory to observe selected populations of people under special circumstances. Typically, the experimental methodology involved holding a large number of variables constant while systematically changing others. This approach assumed that when subjects are exposed to conditions that are approximately identical, comparisons of their behavior are possible. For the first 60 years of this century, much research in psychology followed this line of reasoning. For example, human subjects were often brought into a situation set up and controlled by the researcher. The situation was often drastically removed from anything that happened or would happen in the daily life of the subjects. Furthermore, the subjects were constantly aware that the situation was an "experiment" and remained wary of the intentions of the researcher. Some recent research (see, for example, Magnusson, 1981; Magnusson and Allen, 1983) suggests that studying human subjects in their natural habitats without researcher interference or manipulation is more realistic.

It has become apparent, however, that human beings not only respond to environments, they also *create* the environments to which they respond. Moreover, this dynamic interaction is continual. By holding situations constant, or by "setting up" situations that are out of the ordinary, researchers create artificial conditions which are independent of the subject's usual methods of responding. Generalizations based on an experiment's results may not extend to the natural environment outside the laboratory or to the natural situation free of the researcher's influence. In essence, both experimental and quasi-experimental procedures may bleach human behavior of the very properties that are of interest.

One of the advantages of qualitative research is that the subjects are functioning in their natural environments in the course of their daily lives. *Systematic observations* and *descriptions* in real-life situations are important methods for data collection. David Magnusson and Vernon Allen (1983, p. 381) write:

> The lack of generalizability and the inconsistency of results of much research in psychology can be explained by the fact that it has been conducted by experiments in laboratory settings without preceding systematic observation of the phenomena under consideration in real-life situations.

The degree of generalizability from the laboratory or from the experimental condition to the world outside the laboratory is an issue involving *external validity*. If the results of an experiment have limited resemblance to what could occur without the researcher's intervention, the results have no external validity. An example is the use of some "behavior modification" techniques in juvenile correctional facilities. Behavior modification was developed in the psychological laboratory—primarily on pigeons and rats—under highly controlled, artificial conditions. The success rate of getting an organism to do something that the experimenter wanted was impressive. It still is. Behavior modification also has had impressive success in getting people in institutions to perform "appropriate" and "desirable" behaviors. However, failure often occurs when the once institutionalized person changes his or her social context, such as returning to the community. What often happens is that the person reverts to his or her old ways, supported and encouraged by the original social environment. Thus, behavior modification techniques usually have limited "external validity" or power to generalize to all situations.

Defining Terms and Concepts

A fourth impediment to formulating universal theories about human behavior is the intractable problem of defining the terms or concepts under study. Often, the stuff of crime and delinquency is remote from its measurement. Therefore, there must be some agreement within the social science community that a researcher's definition meets certain explicit or implicit standards. As Gergen noted (1978, p. 1350):

> The fact that a given stimulus pattern falls into the category of "humor," "aggression," "dominance," or "manipulativeness" . . . depends not on the intrinsic properties of the

relevant pattern but on the development of a community of agreement. As a result, the labeling of any given action is forever open to negotiation among the interested parties, and the legitimacy of any observation statement is continuously open to challenge.

Any observed behavior may be defined in a number of ways, and any observed behavior may be an objective indication of some directly unobservable personality trait or hypothetical construct. For example, playground fighting may be linked to low self-esteem. As long as some segment of the scientific community accepts that supposition, it maintains life; if no one accepts it, it most likely will fall into oblivion. Moreover, a supposition or definition may lose favor when it is challenged by a large segment of the scientific community. The conceptual foundation of any theory is vulnerable. However, in the physical sciences, most theoretical terms relate to specific empirical operations or *measurements*, and this problem is less likely to occur.

Behavioral Effects of Enlightenment

Charles Kingsley in 1860 said "Man has the mysterious power of breaking the laws of his own being" (Carr, 1962, p. 121). Once people know and understand the theory about their behavior, they may feel obligated to alter it. Gergen (1973) refers to this as the "enlightenment effect." In the early 1970s, social psychologists conducted a series of "bystander apathy" studies, in which they found that under certain conditions individuals would not go to the aid of someone in trouble (Latané & Darley, 1970). Reports of the studies were invariably included in introductory psychology textbooks, and since then half a generation of college students have been shocked at the lack of good samaritans in the world. Consequently, if the same experiments were conducted today with a population familiar with bystander apathy, researchers *might* find different results.

A biologist's understanding of a snail apparently does not change the snail's behavior. An astronomer's discoveries about a planetary orbit do not change that orbit. But if we theorize that introverts conform to the demands of authority, they may retaliate with noncomformity. If we predict what individuals will do in a situation, and those individuals are aware of the prediction, there is apt to be no predicting what they will do! Carr (1962, p. 90) notes that one reason why history rarely repeats itself among historically cautious people is that the "dramatis personae are aware at the second performance of the dénouement of the first, and their action is affected by that knowledge." Under these conditions, a theory will not be confirmed or verified; it will most likely be falsified.

These, then, are several of the major reasons why the social sciences do not have the impressive track record of the physical sciences. As we have noted, many have even questioned whether the social sciences, including criminology and its subfield of juvenile delinquency, can legitimately be called "sciences." Some have recommended that there be two classes of sciences—the exact and the inexact—with the social sciences considered members of the second class. However, any attempt to divide the physical and social sciences into some dichotomy based on "exactness" represents a misunderstanding of the methods of science. The social sciences cannot be judged by the standards advocated by the physical sciences because they are concerned with substantially different objects of study.

SUMMARY AND CONCLUSIONS

In this chapter we described the science of crime and delinquency and compared it to science as it is traditionally understood. We began by outlining Peirce's four methods of knowing and eliminating doubt and the importance of identifying the source of one's knowledge. We then defined theory, law, and hypothesis the traditional way and found that these ideal definitions do not dovetail into the reality of much of the scientific enterprise. Distinctions were also made between universal, statistical, and non-universal laws of science, and we concluded that non-universal laws are most apropos to the study of delinquency, although this is not to deny that statistical laws have considerable value.

We also discussed the nature of science, framing the presentation around Jacob Bronowski's three central ideas of order, cause, and chance and related these concepts to the study of delinquency. We then focused on what is meant by testable theory, verification, and falsification, and how they related to the advancement of our knowledge about delinquency.

The chapter ends with comparisons between the physical and social sciences, emphasizing that the nature of the phenomena studied are quite different. The physical sciences generally study objects while the social sciences study people. This section—and the chapter in general—is motivated in part by the critical comment made by David Matza in his book *Becoming Delinquent*. Matza (1969, p. 8) asserted: "He who says 'that the only difference between physical science and social science is a billion man-hours of work' simply continues to miss the fundamental point made by Weber, Mead, and MacIver." Matza was emphasizing that the *nature* of the scientific enterprise is basically different for the physical and social sciences, not that one is more rigorous or better than the other. In one sense, human beings study other human beings; in the other, human beings study other things.

While the first chapter began to define juvenile delinquency and provide an historical overview of the system, this chapter tried to set the tone for the remainder of the book. The text will not simply offer a collection of observations and facts about delinquency. As Hermann Mannheim (1965) noted, facts and data about crime and delinquency have no meaning without interpretation, evaluation, and general understanding. All of these processes require a clear understanding of science. We must also be cautious about what we mean by cause and be mindful that the order and classification schemes we place on criminal and delinquent phenomena are largely *our* rendition of order, not the way things necessarily are. In short, students of criminology must learn to have a high tolerance for ambiguity and multiple interpretations and a respect and appreciation for the method of science.

Origins
of Juvenile
Justice

3

CHAPTER

"Juvenile justice" was officially ushered into the United States on the last day of the 1899 session of the Illinois legislature, when that body passed the seminal Juvenile Court Act. This comprehensive child welfare law created a juvenile court in Illinois and gave it jurisdiction over delinquent, dependent, or neglected children. For our purposes, we discuss only the sections of the statute which pertained to delinquents, originally defined as children under the age of 16 who violated a state criminal law or any village or city ordinance. The law was soon revised (in 1905) to specify a delinquent as any boy under 17 or girl under 18 who violated any criminal law of the state. This differential age criterion for males and females remained in the statute for over 50 years.

Although other states had adopted various procedures and regulations to deal with their "wayward" and neglected youth, the Illinois Juvenile Statute of 1899 represented the first comprehensive attempt at codification. The statute did *not* create a new or separate court system within the Illinois court system. Rather, it established a special division within the existing courts of general jurisdiction. The first entirely *separate* juvenile court was established in Indianapolis in 1903.

The Illinois juvenile statute had *four* essential features, which will be discussed in detail next. Briefly, the statute:

1. refined the definition of delinquency;
2. removed the jurisdiction of juvenile cases from the adult criminal court;

3. authorized the placement of juveniles in separate facilities, away from adult offenders and for limited time periods; and

4. provided for a system of probation, allowing the state to supervise the child outside the confines of an institution.

The first feature made delinquency an offense, distinct from the terms "neglect" and "dependency." In previous legislation, "delinquency" had been used as a catch-all term, often overlapping with dependency or even indistinguishable from it. This is not to say that the new statute specified precisely what courts should do about delinquency. In fact, it remained so vague in this respect that, for all practical purposes, it placed no limits on the court's decision-making latitude.

The second feature of the Juvenile Court Act was its provision for a separate hearing of children's cases in a chancery court rather than one of criminal jurisdiction. Until the enactment of the Illinois statute, young people were subject to all the criminal processes applicable to adults—including arrest, detention, and trial—and could be housed with adult offenders in a house of correction or county jail at the discretion of the court. For serious offenses, youths were usually committed to state reformatories, or more commonly, "houses of refuge," which will be discussed shortly.

The Illinois juvenile statute circumvented the usual formalities of the criminal process. It provided for non-adversarial proceedings which focused more on the child and his or her protection than on the nature of the offense. The proceedings were to be conducted informally, whereby an intimate, friendly relationship presumably would be established between the judge and the child. Even the physical layout of the court reflected a benevolent philosophy. Hearings were usually conducted in a small, private room, often in the judge's chambers, with a simple table arranged so that the judge would appear less intimidating and authoritative. Uniformed officers were excluded from the hearings, and no record was kept of the proceedings or of the disposition of the cases.

The statute also encouraged the court to try to *understand* and help the child rather than to blame or condemn. With the help of probation officers, courts investigated the social background, psychological makeup, and level of maturity of the child, and prescribed strategies to draw the child away from his or her misguided ways. Children were to remain with their parents if at all possible; in some cases, parental surrogates who maintained contact with the courts were assigned as guardians. Thus, the juvenile courts under this statute were able to use their authority to reach into homes they considered undesirable and intervene before children developed a hopelessly errant lifestyle. The court hearing and all collateral investigations were meant to focus upon the needs of the child, not upon guilt or innocence. Ostensibly, the court's purpose was not to punish but to "save." In short, the apparent underlying intent of legislators was to encourage the juvenile court to function as the primary institution for the resocialization of the wayward child.

The third feature of the statute was its authorization of temporary detention separate from adult offenders, reflecting a belief that young, malleable minds were corruptible. Illinois legislators believed that when immature and highly impressionable offenders were exposed to hardened adult criminals, they would easily learn to be deviant and antisocial. Furthermore, the adults might prey upon and victimize the children. When institutionalization was deemed necessary, therefore, it was crucial that the facilities be separate from those of adults. Even so, institutionalization was meant to be only temporary, until the natural home situation improved or an alternate home could be found. The proponents of the act were opposed to long-term placement in "houses of refuge" or reform schools. This was for good reason, as will be apparent as we consider the dismal history of these institutions.

The first house of refuge for children in the United States had opened its doors in New York City to "six unhappy, wretched girls and three boys, clothed in rags, and with squalid countenances" on the first day of January, 1825 (Peirce, 1869, p. 78). The following year (1826), the Boston House of Reformation opened, followed by the Philadelphia House of Refuge in 1828. Not surprisingly, the institutions were all racially segregated. Philadelphia, for example, opened a separate House of Refuge for Colored Juvenile Delinquents in 1849. The "houses" received all varieties of impoverished and "criminal" children who had been sentenced for indeterminate terms. The children could be released only at the managers' discretion, or when they reached 21.

The houses of refuge were strongly influenced by Quaker reformers. They were originally intended to be *schools* to salvage children who might go, or who were going, astray. In reality, they were far from being solely, or even predominantly, educational enterprises. Children spent only four hours a day in the classroom: two for moral indoctrination and two for "mental improvement." The remainder of the day (eight hours) typically was spent at labor for industries and factories to which the "house" had subcontracted the children's services. Emphasis was on order, firm discipline, punishment, and carefully constructed and scrupulously observed daily work schedules.

Although these institutions were intended to reform erring children, they soon earned reputations for being both cruel and ineffective. Some superintendents blamed their lack of success on the presence of older children who were "seriously prejudicial" to the young boys and girls. The managers of the Philadelphia Refuge, for example, concluded that "experience has shown that after the child has reached fifteen or sixteen years [of age] there is little hope of reformation" (Peirce, 1869, p. 165). Supporters of the New York Refuge expressed similar sentiments and recommended that older children not be placed in their institution. Hence, those who could not be "rescued" would be prevented from contaminating the process of saving the youths for whom prognosis was better. As a result, it was not unusual for a 16-year-old waif to be housed in an adult prison. The juvenile court movement was directed at redressing these unacceptable practices.

As will be noted shortly, some writers have questioned the motives of the proponents of the juvenile court, and today, nearly a century later, judicial treatment of juvenile offenders remains controversial. Nevertheless, it is clear that the framers of the Illinois Juvenile Act at the least were conscious of the abuses prevailing in houses of refuge and believed it was undesirable to house young people with adult criminals. In short, they wished to avoid past mistakes in the institutionalization of children.

Thus far we have discussed three features of the Illinois statute: it circumvented the formality of the criminal process, it encouraged courts to understand and help children, and it sought both to keep erring youth separate from older offenders and out of houses of refuge. The fourth feature of the Illinois statute was its provision for a system of probation so that the child and his or her parents would receive the proper supervision and training necessary to prevent future delinquent behavior. Courts had been experimenting with adult probation in some form for a number of years. Probation is the system of keeping convicted offenders under the supervision of the court but outside of an institution. A prison sentence is suspended, or not imposed, conditioned upon the individual meeting court-imposed standards of behavior. The probationer, for example, usually must be home by a certain time each evening, may not use alcohol, and must report weekly to a probation officer. In the United States, probation probably began "unofficially" in Massachusetts in 1841 when John Augustus, a bootmaker living in Boston, *volunteered* to become the first probation officer (Cromwell et al., 1985). For this reason, Augustus is regarded by many as the "father of probation." In 1878, 20 years after his death, the citizens of Boston authorized their mayor to appoint a member of the police force to serve as a paid probation officer (Cromwell et al., 1985). Statewide probation was developed in Massachusetts in 1890, but the law specified that the officer could not be a member of any regular police force. By 1925 probation was authorized by statutes in all 48 states. During that same year, Congress enacted the National Probation Act, which authorized the federal district courts, except in the District of Columbia, to appoint salaried probation officers.

Juvenile probation developed later than adult probation, becoming officially recognized by six states by 1899. Massachusetts and Vermont had enacted adult and juvenile probation statutes in 1898, and Rhode Island did the same a year later. Colorado, Minnesota, and, of course, Illinois enacted statutes that specifically recognized juvenile probation. According to the provisions of the Illinois Juvenile Court Act, probation officers (initially unpaid volunteers) were to provide judges with all the appropriate information to help them understand the personality and social environment of the youths who appeared in court. The probation agents were encouraged to become surrogate parents as well as instructors in parenting. They had the authority to go into homes, investigate circumstances, and offer to parents suggestions on how to fulfill their responsibilities.

We have spent some time examining the Illinois statute because it rapidly became the model for juvenile justice. By 1911, 22 states had adopted similar measures. By 1925, all but two states (Maine and Wyoming) had established juvenile courts (Tappan, 1949). Wyoming was the last to capitulate, enacting a juvenile court law in 1945. The first juvenile court within the Federal court system was created in 1906 in the District of Columbia, with jurisdiction over delinquent, dependent, incorrigible, and truant children. Other federal jurisdictions followed suit. In 1938 the Federal system developed a nationwide juvenile court law.

The movement to pass the juvenile act in Chicago not only influenced lawmakers in this country but also extended to many parts of the world. Juvenile courts were officially established in Canada in 1909, the first in Winnipeg in accordance with the National Juvenile Delinquents' Law passed in 1908 (Lou, 1927). Juvenile court legislation spread throughout the rest of the world in the following order, beginning in Great Britain in 1908; Geneva (Switzerland) in 1910; France, Austria and Belgium in 1912; Hungary in 1913; Croatia in 1918; Argentina and Austria in 1919.

In chapter 1, the importance of evaluating any theory or movement within the context of its times was emphasized. Let us examine in more detail, therefore, the philosophical justification for the juvenile court and for the "invention" of juvenile delinquency.

THE SOCIAL FOUNDATIONS OF JUVENILE JUSTICE

The Juvenile Court Act culminated many years of discussions and experiments on the part of public and private organizations, in conjunction with legislative and judicial officials. The initial impetus for the statute, however, came from prominent women's clubs in the Chicago area, especially the Chicago Women's Club and National Congress of Mothers (forerunner to the PTA). But the sustaining impetus came from Ben Lindsey, a Denver judge who lobbied state legislatures, and spoke and wrote extensively and cogently throughout the early part of the 20th century about the merits of the juvenile court.

The motivations and the precise influence of the women's groups on the Juvenile Act are obscure and debatable. Despite encouragement from and consultation with the Chicago Bar Association, there is little evidence that they clearly understood the legal system or were able to specify how the juvenile court should be structured (Sutton, 1985). But this was not their goal. Their main purpose was to guarantee that wayward children would receive an approximation of the care, custody, and discipline given by loving parents. The reformers were critical of existing criminal law for failing to distinguish between young offenders and adult criminals and for considering the two moral and psychological equals (Ryerson, 1978). They hoped that the court could become a benevolent surrogate for ineffective parents and corrupt subcultures. The purpose of the juvenile court should be "child-saving" and not "criminalizing."

We should realize that this was during the child-oriented "Progressive Era," a time when reformers were instrumental in establishing child labor legislation, compulsory education laws, kindergartens, playgrounds, and municipal bureaus of child health and hygiene (Rothman, 1980). Within this social context, the arguments advanced by the Chicago women's groups were not all that controversial and therefore met with little opposition. Nevertheless, the bill passed the Illinois legislature only after considerable cutting of costly items.

In hindsight, the motives behind the reforms have been questioned. Anthony Platt (1969) asserted that the child-saving movement which led to the juvenile court was not simply a humanistic enterprise on behalf of the lower classes. On the contrary, its proponents were those of the middle and upper classes who were seeking new forms of social control to protect their privileged positions in American society against crime. The child-saving movement did attract women from a variety of political and class backgrounds, but it was dominated by daughters of the old landed gentry and wives of the upper-class nouveau riche. True, many may have been genuinely concerned about alleviating human misery and improving the lives of the poor, but, Platt insisted, the child savers and other progressive reformers were predominantly concerned that crime, rising from the "lowest orders," was threatening to engulf respectable society like a virulent disease.

The motives and philosophy of Judge Ben Lindsey and other juvenile judges of that era have also been questioned. Lindsey—the "kid's judge" as some have called him—was one of the foremost sustaining forces behind the juvenile justice movement. Schlossman (1977, p. 56) wrote:

> Lindsey stood in relation to the court movement much as John Dewey did to progressive education and Jane Addams did to social settlements. All were popularly acknowledged as leaders of their respective institutions, yet all differed considerably from the rank and file of reformers who identified with them. Just as Dewey's grasp of the educational needs of an industrial democracy and Addams's insight into the psychological and cultural mainstreams of immigrant behavior far surpassed their followers' understanding of the issues in both sensitivity and sophistication, so Lindsey's understanding of the possibilities and limitations of the court was more profound than that of most partisans.

Tireless and energetic, Lindsey spoke to various charitable groups and organizations across the country, lobbied legislatures in several states, and wrote voluminously about the advantages of the juvenile court. He believed that individuals were not by nature bad or corrupt, but that the environment was the main determinant of human behavior. David Rothman (1980) refers to his activity pejoratively as a "one-man traveling road show" (p. 215). Sutton (1985) calls him the "most active evangelist" of the juvenile court movement during the early 20th century.

Lindsey's exploits also extended into the courtroom. He independently organized a personalized juvenile court in 1899 under the so-called "school law" in Denver. The school law supposedly gave the court limited jurisdiction over delinquent children of school age. Lindsey managed to expand it (at least in his own courtroom) to include any child he believed was moving along the "wrong path." Lindsey single-handedly created a juvenile court in Denver in 1901, without statutory authorization. At this time, he may or may not have been aware of the similar court established in Chicago two years previously. Rothman (1980) notes that Lindsey's flamboyant personality dominated, indeed monopolized, the juvenile court's proceedings. His courtroom was his stage from which he performed various dramatics and gave powerful speeches and pleading sermons to groups of offending youths. In addition to his flair for oratory, he had a great sense of humor and an ability to empathize. He was small of physical stature and had a very youthful face. Although his court took on an arbitrary quality, many historical accounts conclude that he was quite effective in positively changing the life course of many children.

It is difficult to estimate how many states would have adopted juvenile court laws—or at least how long it would have taken them—without Lindsey's influence. After all, it *was* the Progressive Era, and the time was right for codification of juvenile justice and the legal separation of child transgressions from adult crime. But there is little doubt that Judge Lindsey had a strong impact on the overall movement at the turn of the century.

John Sutton (1985), another critic of juvenile court philosophy, contends that the establishment of the juvenile court allowed the legal system to *appear* responsive to the demands for individualized, therapeutic justice without any real alteration in routine decision-making practices. Furthermore, it allowed juvenile justice agencies to maintain their ideology and discretionary authority. In other words, the creation of the juvenile court may have changed procedures, but it was not truly a substantive reform.

Sanford Fox (1970), kinder but still critical, insisted that the primary motivating force for the Juvenile Act was a genuine desire to change institutional conditions for predelinquent children. Given this assumption, the reformers' trek to the Illinois capital in the spring of 1899 was a colossal failure, since institutional conditions hardly changed as a result of the legislation. Moreover, nothing was done about children in poor houses or local jails, both of which often housed youths as well as adults. The only change was the provision that children under 12 were not to be detained in a jail or police station. Furthermore, the statute did not provide funds for leasing, building, or otherwise finding suitable places even for temporary detention. According to Fox, the Juvenile Act passed by the rural and conservative Illinois legislature represented a victory for private enterprise and sectarianism.

It is important not to lose sight of the fact, however, that the turn of the century reform represented a marked change from viewing children as nonentities or even chattel in the legal system to acknowledging that they had a measure of legal rights. As one scholar noted, "While the legal reforms may now seem in the light of revisionist histories, to have been catalyzed by questionable motives, they did give children certain legally enforceable rights not previously held" (Rodham, 1973, p. 495). These did not include, however, rights to an adversary hearing or lawyer. Rodham made the important point that "Whenever reforms have been enacted—the rights they provide are those which the state decides are in the best interests of the public and the child" (p. 496). This "best interest" philosophy, derived from the legal doctrine of *parens patriae*, is the foundation of the juvenile justice system. Since it is encountered frequently in discussions of juvenile delinquency, it is important to give some attention to its development and implications. This will lead us directly to developments in juvenile justice up to the present.

THE LEGAL FOUNDATIONS OF JUVENILE JUSTICE

From the early development of the juvenile court, disparities in the treatment of children and adults have been tolerated and often encouraged. Although the differences were justified in the child's best interest, they were also founded on a belief that children below a certain age have substantially different constitutional rights than adults. The U.S. Supreme Court articulated this succinctly in 1967 when it said that a child, unlike an adult, has a right "not to liberty but to custody" (387 U.S. 1 at 17). This means that if parents or guardians default in their care-giving duties, the child has a constitutional right to receive proper care, and the State may intervene to insure this right. The legal rationale most often cited for this power of intervention rests with the doctrine *parens patriae*.

The Latin phrase, *parens patriae* (literally, "parent of the country"), has had a long and ambiguous history, dating as far back as ancient Roman law, where it was applied loosely to situations where the State considered the head of the family incompetent and in danger of wasting his estate. The State was then vested with the power to declare him *non compos mentis* and commit him and the estate to the care of curators or tutors designated by the praetor. *Parens patriae* was a doctrine particularly applicable to persons with valuable property holdings and wealth rather than to the general population.

The concept was later adopted from Roman law in the 11th century by the Anglo-Saxon King Athelred II and further developed and expanded during the early years of Edward I's reign (1272–1307) (Kittrie, 1971). The doctrine was first codified in 1324 during the reign of Edward II in the statute *Prerogativa Regis*, which gave the King the power to protect the lands and profits of "idiots" and "lunatics" until their mental restoration (Cogan, 1970). While the main focus on the statute was on idiots and lunatics, it included a wide range of "unables," such as the poor, and incapacitating behaviors, such as card playing.

At the time the colonies were being settled, English law still empowered the King to act as the general guardian of "infants, idiots, and lunatics," and those individuals "incompetent" to take care of themselves (Developments in the Law, 1974). After the American Revolution, the *parens patriae* power was imbued in the state legislatures which, in turn, delegated the principal authority to the state courts.

Although *parens patriae* has been used in various contexts in American law, it has generally referred to the role of the state as the sovereign guardian of persons under some form of "legal disability." It authorizes the state to substitute and enforce its decisions about what it believes to be in the best interest of persons who presumably cannot or will not take care of themselves. Therefore, the *parens patriae* doctrine is used as the basis of state laws protecting the interests of minors, establishing guardianships, and providing for the involuntary commitment of the mentally ill. Throughout its early history, *parens patriae* was used in the service of *dependent* persons, usually with propertied status. It was not, however, generally used to "protect" or take control over persons who had violated the norms of society.

This changed in 1838 when a Pennsylvania court ruled in *Ex parte Crouse* that the *parens patriae* doctrine could justify detaining young persons for reform or rehabilitation purposes. From all accounts, *Crouse* was the first legal decision incorporating the power of *parens patriae* into American juvenile law (Schlossman, 1977). Mary Ann Crouse was committed to the Philadelphia House of Refuge upon her mother's complaint and without her father's knowledge. The mother alleged "that the said infant by reason of vicious conduct, had rendered her control beyond the power of the said complaint, and made it manifestly requisite that in regard to the moral and future welfare of the said infant she should be placed under the guardianship of the managers of the House of Refuge'' (Curtis, 1976, p. 901).

When the father became aware of the mother's actions, Mary Ann was already incarcerated. He promptly filed a habeas corpus petition on her behalf, charging that she had been deprived of the right to trial by jury guaranteed to criminal defendants by the state constitution. The petition was denied. Mr. Crouse then challenged the confinement on federal constitutional grounds, specifically charging that the Sixth Amendment of the U.S. Constitution prohibited the state from incarcerating Mary Ann without trial. In rebuttal, the managers of the House of Refuge denied that the Bill of Rights applied to children. The court accepted their arguments and unanimously approved of Mary Ann's continued detention until the age of 21. Basing its argument largely on the *parens patriae* doctrine, the Pennsylvania court insisted that children had no rights guaranteed by the Constitution. The objective of the House of Refuge, the court said, was to train children for citizenship and furnish them with a means to earn a living—much like any school. This was to be accomplished through work and moral and religious training, away from the corrupting influence of improper associates. "To this end, may not the natural parents, when unequal to the task of education, or unworthy of it, be superseded by the *parens patriae*, or common guardian of the community?" (4 Wharton 9 (Pa, 1838), p. 11).

Thus, *Crouse* represents "the first explicit judicial resort to *parens patriae* as justification for seeking to instill virtue in children who would otherwise be doomed to a life of depravity" (Fox, 1970, p. 1206). Through the remainder of the 19th century and well into the 20th, *Crouse* was the leading authority for the right of the state, under the power invested in it by *parens patriae*, to confine children against their or their parents' wishes (Fox, 1970).

The proponents of the first juvenile courts would have disagreed vehemently with the long-term institutionalization of Mary Ann Crouse, yet they would have accepted the court's rationale that it acted in the best interest of the child. In their zeal to remove offending youth from what they saw as rigidities, technicalities, and harshness of criminal law, they ignored or deprived children of rights that were due adults. Sanford Fox (1970) suggested that this was because early reformers melded, in their own minds, the terms "dependency," "neglect," and "delinquency." That is, they did not believe the labels could be separated on the basis of personal responsibility. A child was dependent, neglected, or delinquent as a result of poverty, dire home conditions, or faulty parenting—all conditions over which the child had no personal control. Thus, "delinquent" children were not criminal; they were misguided and unsocialized. Since they could not be held responsible for their predicament, criminal procedure, determinations of responsibility, sentencing, and punishment were simply not appropriate.

The reformers tried to make the court a benevolent parent intent on care and welfare rather than a forum for procedures, due process, fairness, and resolution. But this presumably *benevolent* role invited arbitrary behavior by those who assumed it. The capricious actions engaged in by many juvenile courts were not curbed until the 1960s, when the U.S. Supreme Court stepped in. As the Court recognized in 1966,

Juvenile Court history has again demonstrated that unbridled discretion, however benevo-
lently motivated, is frequently a poor substitute for principle and procedure . . . the absence
of substantive standards has not necessarily meant that children receive careful, compassionate, individualized treatment. The absence of procedural rules based upon Constitutional principle has not always produced fair, efficient, and effective procedures. (*In re
Gault*, 387 U.S. at 17 (1967))

CURRENT TRENDS IN AMERICAN JUVENILE JUSTICE

The philosophy and procedures of the juvenile justice system remained largely unchanged until the second half of the 20th century. The juvenile court and its ancillary
institutions became firmly established. Juvenile judges, probation officers, correctional
workers, and police officers working with juveniles increased in number and acquired
considerable prestige and power. At the same time, those working in the juvenile justice
system and those who were asked to rehabilitate young offenders worked closely together. Most programs directed at preventing or treating juvenile delinquency were created and managed by psychiatrists, psychologists, or social workers, who promoted extensive testing, individual counseling, and therapy for youthful offenders. The courts,
trusting that these approaches were beneficial, responded favorably. Illinois remained
the pioneer in this area, having the first clinic to provide psychiatric diagnoses to juvenile
courts, the Juvenile Psychopathic Institute. The clinic and the philosophy of its founder,
William Healy, will be discussed in detail in Chapter 4.

In 1930, the approach to the prevention of juvenile offending took a dramatic turn
when University of Chicago sociologists collaborated with researchers at the Institute
for Juvenile Research (formerly Healy's diagnostic clinic) on the Chicago Area Project,
a monumental effort to involve communities in the solution of their delinquency problems. The project paved the way for reassessment of the existing programs based on
individual treatment. It also represented the first systematic challenge by sociologists to
the domination of psychologists and psychiatrists in both private and public juvenile
programs (Schlossman and Sedlak, 1983).

The Project, which lasted 30 years, has been amply described, lauded, and criticized in the sociological and criminal justice literature. Essentially, it immersed researchers and volunteers, including erudite sociologists from the Chicago School, in
communities with higher than average rates of delinquency. The researchers obtained
oral histories and accounts of juvenile activities, organized recreational programs, offered "curbstone counseling," and mediated with police and juvenile justice agencies
on behalf of community youth. The Project de-emphasized the "individual casework"
approach and drew attention to the role of the community as an agent of informal social
control to prevent delinquency. We will cover the Chicago Area Project in greater detail
in the next chapter.

By the early 1960s, serious juvenile crime was an issue of major public concern.
At the same time, there began to emerge a focus on the plight of abused and neglected
children and on children's constitutional rights. This was a logical extension of changes

wrought by the various civil rights movements of the late 50s and 60s, by controversies over the effectiveness of social welfare programs, and later—at least where female delinquents were concerned—by the resurgence of the women's movement.

The academic community, which had long contributed to the intellectual climate assessing the juvenile justice system, was experiencing its own transformation. Alongside the traditional research on the control, prevention, and cure of juvenile delinquency, research focusing on the shortcomings of the system made its appearance. The juvenile court was not only criticized as ineffective in preventing delinquency; it was also accused of fostering juvenile crime through its labeling or stigmatizing of young norm-violators as ''delinquents.'' In short, the juvenile system was itself becoming viewed as harmful to the juvenile.

Some warned that the extensive criticism of the court should not result in its demise, however. The legal scholar Francis A. Allen, for example, advocated a reassessment of the court's function in society. ''. . . (T)he tendency to describe the court only by reference to its therapeutic or rehabilitative potential creates the peril of unrealistic and unrealizable expectations'' (Allen, 1964, p. 56). Allen noted that the court had a role in protecting the community from the violent or predatory acts of some children for whom rehabilitation was not realistic. In such cases, the primary function was the temporary incapacitation of children. He added, however, that this should be done only if they were given the same procedural safeguards as were adults accused of criminal acts. Allen's philosophy was reflected in some measure in subsequent decisions of the U.S. Supreme Court, to which we now turn.

Landmark U.S. Supreme Court Decisions

Arguments questioning the proceedings of juvenile courts gained legal support with the Supreme Court decisions of *Kent* (1966), *In re Gault* (1967), and *In re Winship* (1970). Other decisions, such as *McKeiver v. Pennsylvania* (1970), *Fare v. Michael C.* (1979), and *Schall v. Martin* (1984), however, made it clear that juvenile offenders remained in a separate category. For our purposes, we will discuss only three major juvenile decisions of the U.S. Supreme court. Readers should keep in mind, however, that lower appellate courts, state and federal, frequently rule on juvenile matters and that cases involving the custodial interrogation of juveniles and conditions of institutionalization are often settled in these lower courts. With the exception of *Schall v. Martin* and *Fare v. Michael C.*, to be discussed soon, the U.S. Supreme Court has spoken primarily to the *proceedings in juvenile courts*, not to the many other issues which may be raised with reference to juveniles. As this book goes to press, the U.S. Supreme Court is scheduled to rule on whether capital punishment may be imposed on a person who committed his or her crime before reaching adulthood.

Kent was the first delinquency case in which the U.S. Supreme Court extended limited due process guarantees to juveniles. Morris A. Kent Jr. was a 16-year-old charged with housebreaking, robbery, and rape while on probation under the jurisdiction of the District of Columbia Juvenile Court. When arrested, Kent admitted committing the offenses and was placed in a receiving home for children. The Juvenile Court transferred

Kent's case to adult criminal court over the objections of Kent's lawyer, who argued that the boy had rehabilitative potential. The lawyer also requested that the court review his client's social service records, a request the court denied. In adult court, Kent was found not guilty by reason of insanity on the rape charge but guilty of housebreaking and robbery. He was sentenced to 30 to 90 years and transferred to St. Elizabeth's Hospital for the mentally ill.

In reviewing Kent's appeal, the U.S. Supreme Court first recognized that there was no constitutional requirement for a separate juvenile court system. When such a system does exist, however, a juvenile court may not waive jurisdiction over a juvenile without a hearing and accompanying safeguards. "There is no place in our legal system for reaching a verdict of such serious consequences without a hearing, without effective assistance of counsel, and without a statement of the reasons" (383 U.S. at 554). The Court's opinion, written by Justice Abe Fortas, strongly criticized, not the philosophy of the juvenile court, but its operation. The case foreshadowed the decision the following year which extended broad procedural safeguards to juveniles charged with criminal conduct and which would have a profound impact on the structure of juvenile courts.

This second decision, *In re Gault*, involved a 15-year-old Arizona boy, Gerald Gault, who was accused of making an "obscene" phone call to a neighbor. The Supreme Court later referred to the telephone remarks as "of the irritatingly offensive, adolescent, sex variety," Gerald Gault was taken into police custody at about 10 a.m. without his parents' knowledge and placed in a children's detention home. When his mother arrived home that evening, she dispatched her older son to search for Gerald and soon learned of his whereabouts. The mother and older brother went to the detention home and were informed that a hearing was scheduled for the following afternoon.

Gault, his mother, his older brother, and two probation officers appeared before the juvenile judge in chambers. The father was working out of town and could not attend. The complaining neighbor was not in attendance. Gerald had no attorney. The judge questioned the boy, but there was no transcript or recording made of the hearing. Later, there was conflicting information about what was said. A week later, at a second hearing, Gerald was declared a "delinquent" and committed to the State Industrial School until he reached the age of 21. At that time, it was a misdemeanor to make lewd or obscene phone calls in the State of Arizona. Had Gerald been an adult and been convicted, his maximum penalty would have been $50 or two months' imprisonment.

When the U.S. Supreme Court ruled on the Gault case, it held that juveniles appearing before a juvenile court have the following constitutional rights:

1. to adequate written notice of the charges against them in order to afford them a reasonable opportunity to prepare a defense;
2. to the assistance of counsel, and if indigent, to the appointment of counsel;
3. to invoke the privilege against self-incrimination; and
4. to confront and cross examine witnesses.

Gault had received none of those protections at his hearing.

In 1970, the Court in *In re Winship* held that before a juvenile may be adjudicated a delinquent there must be proof beyond a reasonable doubt of every fact necessary to constitute the offense with which he or she is charged. Until the *Winship* ruling, juvenile courts routinely found delinquency on the basis of less stringent standards. The Court found unpersuasive the argument that juvenile proceedings were noncriminal and were intended to benefit the child.

It is clear that before these decisions juveniles could be confined to institutions for long periods of time at the discretion of the court, for minor offenses, and without procedural protections. The three landmark decisions dramatically altered the legal system's processing of juvenile offenders. By conveying to juveniles many of the constitutional safeguards provided adult offenders, these and related decisions severely undercut the juvenile court's emphasis on informal "humanitarian" proceedings (Mennel, 1983).

Nevertheless, juveniles do not enjoy all of the constitutional protections extended to adults. In *McKeiver v. Pennsylvania*, for example, the Supreme Court rejected the contentions of juveniles in two states that they were entitled to a jury trial just as were their adult counterparts. Pennsylvania juveniles had argued that the juvenile proceedings in that state were virtually identical to those of adults. They were detained before their hearings in buildings similar to adult prisons, plea bargaining was allowed, and the proceedings were open to the press and public. In North Carolina, juveniles argued that the adjudication of facts was indistinguishable from a criminal trial, and that a jury would provide a protective factor. The Supreme Court, however, believed juries would substantially change the nature of juvenile hearings and refused to impose that requirement on states, although they were free to offer juries if they wished.

On a different issue, it is clear that police must inform a juvenile in custody of Miranda rights, and that the juvenile may not be interrogated if he or she indicates he or she wishes to remain silent or wishes to consult an attorney. In *Fare v. Michael C.*, however, the Supreme Court rejected the notion that a juvenile's request to see his probation officer was comparable to a request for an attorney. In a 1984 case, *Schall v. Martin*, the Court supported the preventive detention of juveniles before their scheduled hearings for up to 18 days when charged with serious crime or a maximum of six days otherwise. If there was any doubt that the *parens patriae* doctrine still lives, it could be laid to rest with the *Schall* decision. The juveniles' interest in freedom was "qualified," the Court said, "by the recognition that juveniles, unlike adults, are always in some form of custody." If their parents faltered in controlling them, government could appropriate that role.

We conclude this section with the important caveat that this brief review of cases is meant only to give some flavor of judicial interpreting of the rights of juveniles. Again, there is considerable activity in state court and lower federal courts with respect to other issues dealing with delinquents. Can they be kept in solitary confinement and, if so, for how long and under what conditions? Can they be administered drug therapy? Can status offenders be housed with juveniles who have committed serious crimes? These are among the numerous issues addressed by lower courts, but which are beyond the scope of the present text.

Recent Shifts in Federal Policy

Along with judicial decisions, changes in public attitudes and social policy also have undermined the presumption that juvenile courts exist primarily as benevolent authorities. These shifts have been reflected in state and federal statutes taking power away from those charged with dealing with delinquents. One example is the revision of many statutes that had specifically allowed girls to be institutionalized longer than boys for the same offense. Another is the removal of status offenses, such as running away from home, from the list of criminal offenses. As we will note toward the end of this book, these "decriminalization" strategies have not always had the intended effect. Still another example is the removal of "defective delinquent" statutes, laws which allowed the indefinite confinement of those who had been persistently antisocial or criminal and had intellectual or emotional deficiencies. The final chapter of the book will discuss in more detail the significance of some of these changes.

Lloyd Ohlin (1983b), traces three major shifts in *federal* policy regarding youth offending during the past two decades. It is instructive to review these, since changes in the federal law are often precursors of changes in state laws. This is not to say that state laws parallel the federal, however. It is not unusual, for example, for states to change their statutes in apparent *resistance* to the changes on the federal level. Furthermore, some states have provided their citizens with more protections under their state *constitutions* than the U.S. Supreme Court has provided under the federal constitution (Wilkes, 1974).

In the early 1960s, Ohlin notes, largely because of the history of the Chicago Area Project and others like it, federal policymakers drew upon community organization strategies to foster community responsibility for juvenile misbehavior. A variety of social programs toward that end were funded. The programs in general were not successful, however, partly due to naiveté and partly to the massive social changes in society that were occurring during the 1960s. "We are much more aware today that juvenile justice depends on the successful operation of a *broad formal and informal* network of social relationships that guide youth development" (italics added) (Ohlin, 1983b, p. 464). Ohlin notes that "the growing gap between expectation and achievable results fostered disillusionment, alienation, social unrest, and ultimately, abandonment of the programs themselves" (Ohlin, 1983b, p. 464). He also suggests, however, that we can learn valuable lessons from the failure of those early community programs.

The second shift in social policy was spearheaded by a series of Presidential Commissions studying the broad problems of crime and violence. In 1967 the first of these Commissions, the President's Commission on Law Enforcement and Administration of Justice, set the tone. Its primary task was to recommend ways to identify and control delinquents and status offenders. The Commission recommended six major strategies:

1. *decriminalization* of status offenses (such as running away from home);
2. *diversion* of youth from court procedures into public and private treatment programs;

3. extension of *due process* rights to juveniles in the same spirit as they had been extended to adult offenders;

4. *deinstitutionalization*, whereby delinquents would be cared for in families, group homes, or small treatment centers instead of the traditional large institutions, "reform" schools, or training schools;

5. *diversification* of services; and

6. *decentralization* of control of juvenile proceedings and care.

Implicit in these recommendations is a pervasive distrust of institutions and an assumption that delinquents are not as much guilty of crimes as they are victims of social and economic deprivation. The fundamental premise was that families, group homes, and peer groups would provide suitable alternatives to the discredited courts and institutions. Ohlin notes that, although the Commission's recommendations were well received, implementation of the strategies has been "spotty" and their effectiveness difficult to assess.

In addition, implementation has been somewhat overshadowed by a third change in social policy, which began in the mid-1970s with a nationwide shift toward a "law-and-order" commitment. Apparently in response to a rapidly growing fear of crime and allegedly serious juvenile delinquency, the public began to demand quicker punishments and mandatory sentencing procedures, first for adults and eventually for juveniles. Ohlin notes that this new focus reflects in part a strong conservative reaction to the liberal policies advocated by the National Crime Commissions of the '60s. He writes (1983b, p. 467),

> We are now in one of those periods of conservative reaction where the prevailing views about crime express beliefs about retribution, deterrence, and incapacitation that are deeply rooted in our religious and cultural heritage . . . . Our policies are now being developed by those who believe that the traditional system of punishment can be fine-tuned to control offenders by increasing the predictability and certainty of punishment.

In recent years, those calling for reform of the juvenile justice system have suggested it in three areas. Many states have lowered the age whereby youths may be tried as adult offenders for serious violent offenses like rape or murder. This reflects a greater concern about chronic, violent offenders, who actually comprise a very small proportion of the juvenile offender population. Some, a minority, have also called for the abolition of the juvenile court altogether (Schichor, 1983), arguing that, since the U.S. Supreme Court has established similar procedures in juvenile court to those in adult criminal courts, it does not make much sense to keep two separate systems. Criminal offenders, no matter what age, should be tried by the criminal court, while status offenders and neglected children should be handled by the family courts. A third recommendation for a change in policy is that for the public's protection, society must punish and confine dangerous young offenders. Any notions of rehabilitation or therapy should be discarded, because approaches along those lines have failed. Society should be more concerned with establishing procedures for deterrence and increased respect for authority.

Together, the three suggested areas of reform may be subsumed under what Geoffrey Hazard (1976) called the contemporary "hard-line" approach to juvenile justice. It embraces attitudes that emphasize family structure, early subjection to strict discipline, and respect for authority symbols and institutions. In reference to the courtroom, the hard-line approach is that a no-nonsense procedure—stripped of the delays and quibblings inherent in elaborate procedural protections—will instill a healthy respect for authority that will carry over to the offender's behavior out of court.

Not to be confused with the hard-line approach is the "due process" orientation, which criticizes the juvenile justice system not because rehabilitation doesn't work, but because the truly humane way to treat offenders is to assure that their constitutional rights are not abrogated. This approach assumes that *parens patriae* restricts the juvenile's freedom disproportionately to what he or she did. Juveniles, like adults, should get their "just deserts"—no more, no less. The surest way to provide fair treatment to juvenile offenders is to offer them procedural safeguards comparable to those offered adults.

SUMMARY AND CONCLUSIONS

In this chapter, we traced the legislative and judicial origins of contemporary juvenile justice and the early formulation of the term "juvenile delinquency." A more comprehensive update will be provided in the final chapter of the book. Most of this chapter was devoted to historical background. While the book is primarily intended to review and evaluate theoretical and empirical explanations of delinquency, it is impossible to understand the field adequately without referring to its history. And, because the study of delinquency cannot be separated from its legal context, we must give some attention to the status of juvenile justice.

The watershed year for juvenile justice was 1899, when the Illinois legislature passed a state law which represented the first comprehensive attempt to define juvenile delinquency and provide for the care of the offender. The statute emphasized the need to separate adult from child offenders for purposes of definition, processing, and treatment. It was followed by similar statutes, many establishing juvenile and family courts, throughout the nation.

Social and political factors significant to the evolution of the Illinois statute were summarized. The motives of those who prompted and sustained reforms in the treatment of juveniles have been dissected elsewhere (e.g., Platt, 1969; Rothman, 1980). Were the reformers truly well-meaning individuals responding to appalling conditions in institutions which housed juveniles, or were they righteous members of the privileged classes intent upon protecting themselves against crime? Even if well-meaning, did their reforms harm more than help juveniles? Whatever the answer, reformers received legal support in the doctrine of *parens patriae*, the care-giving principle that continues to pervade legal opinions in cases involving juveniles.

In the 1960s, scholars, courts, and legislatures began to reflect a growing disenchantment and discomfort with the system of juvenile justice. The U.S. Supreme Court began to extend due process guarantees to juveniles. Although these protections are now firmly in place, more recent decisions have signalled that the Court does not intend to extend to juveniles the full panoply of protections given to adults. Observers have remarked upon discernible shifts, not only in judicial, but also in legislative and social policy with reference to juveniles. These shifts, including the 1974 Juvenile Justice and Delinquency Prevention Act and its amendments, will be discussed again in the final chapter of the book.

At this point, we will set aside the legal events that have shaped and continue to shape decisions about juvenile delinquents and direct attention to the search for causes and explanations of delinquency. Discovery of causes would enable us to formulate systematic policy directed at the prevention and control of delinquency. Again, we will begin by examining history. A review of the theoretical developments, research, and dominant scientific ideology of the early 20th century will contribute to an appreciation of where we are today and where we may be heading in our goal to understand delinquency.

Early American Criminology

4

CHAPTER

Any comprehensive presentation of delinquency must consider events occurring in Chicago at the turn of the 20th century. As we have seen, the city was the site of the first formal juvenile court in the United States and of the earliest clinic specifically established for research on juvenile delinquency, the Institute for Juvenile Research. Furthermore, Chicago during these years offered an environment uniquely conducive to extensive research into the effects of rapid growth and industrialization on a variety of social problems, including delinquency. This feature did not escape the energetic faculty of the University of Chicago's Department of Sociology, who precipitated the emergence of modern American criminology.

Chicago had developed from a central trading station in 1830 to a congested and sprawling metropolis by 1890. Between 1870 and 1900 its population increased by 468 percent (Walker, 1949). By the end of the 19th century, over 70 percent of the city's inhabitants were foreign born, and most of the remainder were the first-generation offspring of foreign born people (Linn, 1935). The immigrants had arrived primarily from eastern and central Europe and were often from peasant backgrounds. They found urban, industrialized Chicago confusing and overwhelming and a threat to their traditional, old-world values.

Industrialists soon grasped the potential of an uneducated labor force supplied by a steady influx of immigrants willing to work for low wages. In the decade from 1880 to 1890, the number of factories nearly tripled. Chicago quickly became the business center for the entire Mississippi valley and Rocky Mountain region. Its central location on the Great Lakes made it the hub of all transportation systems (primarily the railroad) linking the two coasts. If industry prospered, the workers did not, however. They lived in substandard tenements and often worked for a pittance in factories which operated under minimal standards of safety. It is within this environmental context that the scientific study of crime and delinquency in the United States began.

As mentioned earlier, two important events marked the beginning of scholarly attempts to study and explain juvenile delinquency. One was the establishment of the Institute for Juvenile Research headed by the influential psychiatrist, William Healy. For three decades the Institute would have a significant impact on the direction of delinquency research and data collection. It would also serve as a model for the clinical treatment of juvenile delinquency that continues to be followed today. The second event was the creation of the first sociology department in the United States at the University of Chicago, a department often referred to as the "Chicago School."

WILLIAM HEALY AND THE INSTITUTE FOR JUVENILE RESEARCH

In 1909 William Healy established the first psychiatric clinic specifically targeted to study and to a lesser extent diagnose delinquents. It was initially named the Juvenile Psychopathic Institute. Years later Healy admitted that the name was inappropriate, since a majority of the youth he saw were by no means "psychopathic," nor did they have anything "wrong" with them emotionally (Snodgrass, 1984). In the early 20th century, however, 88.3 percent of all adult inmates in Illinois were classified as "psychopathic personalities" (Bennett, 1981), a classification which reflects the dominant belief of the time that most criminals were insensitive, cruel, and biologically inferior creatures. In 1920, three years after Healy had moved to another setting, the clinic was renamed the Institute for Juvenile Research, which better reflected its original purpose.

The Institute was established with the help of Chicago philanthropist Ethel S. Dummer, who donated sufficient funds to guarantee the first five years of its operation. The Institute's primary purpose was to study the "causes" of delinquency and to suggest strategies for its prevention. Its secondary role was to provide diagnostic services for the newly established Juvenile Court of Cook County. Although Healy was convinced that psychological treatment for misbehaving youths could be effective, treatment was not a priority. It was done only on a limited basis and primarily under the direction of Grace M. Fernald, who had received her doctorate in psychology from the University of Chicago in 1907 and helped Healy establish the Institute. Fernald was one of the earliest psychologists to specialize in the diagnosis and treatment of delinquency and very probably was the first clinical psychologist to work under the supervision of a psychiatrist.

Healy's All-encompassing Search for the Causes of Delinquency

Healy was a physician by training, having received his medical degree from the University of Chicago. Before attending medical school, however, he had worked as an undergraduate at Harvard with psychologist William James, who is now considered "the father" of American psychology. Consequently, Healy had been indoctrinated into a strong empirical approach to social problems. Although he first specialized in gynecology, he soon became interested in "mental diseases." At a 1908 conference held at Hull House, Healy cogently argued that delinquency could not be treated effectively without prior identification of its causes. Ethel Dummer, who was in the audience, was apparently so impressed that she provided Healy with the necessary funds to put his ideas into action. Healy eagerly launched his search for causal factors, an odyssey that was to capture his time and interest through many years and result in a lengthy list of possible causes. Throughout his career, Healy was convinced that a detailed and close examination of the delinquent's background and unique way of looking at the world were prerequisite to understanding why he or she was delinquent.

At first, Healy relied on whatever information he could find, including Freudian concepts. Although these were useful, he was not committed to them exclusively, however. In fact, during the early stages of his professional development, Healy tried to reject any preconceived theoretical framework. His overriding ambition was to discover the cause of delinquency in the most objective way possible, and he did not care whether it was found in a youth's biological makeup, family background, living situation, mental state, or some combination of these factors.

Eventually, however, Healy began to favor Freud's psychoanalytic approach, commenting that his interest in it was fueled "by the common-sense explanations and therapeutic results it has given us" (Healy, 1915, p. 85). The two aspects of psychoanalysis that Healy found most compatible were:

1. the powerful effects that early, traumatic events have on a child's later life and ways of viewing the world; and
2. the major role played by the unconscious in daily behavior.

Healy believed that delinquents often did not know why they misbehaved; they were surprised and accepting when the unconscious reasons for their conduct were revealed to them.

When Healy began using some Freudian concepts, Sigmund Freud was virtually unknown in the United States. Freud and his then associate, Carl Jung, were invited to lecture at Clark University in the Autumn of 1909 during that institution's 20th anniversary celebration, and it is likely—though not certain—that Healy was in attendance. Historian David Rothman, one of the foremost contemporary critics of the social policy during the Progressive era, maintains that Healy "was an early reader of Freud, but his grasp of Freudian principles was weak'' (Rothman, 1980, p. 54). This seems a harsh assessment, considering the complex nature of Freudian theory and the fact that Freud himself was revising his theory extensively during its formative years. In 1929, Healy trained briefly under the direction of the well-known Neo-Freudian Helene Deutsch, and in 1930 he underwent a brief analysis with Franz Alexander, with whom he later wrote *The Roots of Crime* (Bennett, 1981). In an effort to clarify and popularize Freudian theory, Healy, along with Augusta Bronner and Anna Mae Bowers, produced *The Structure and Meaning of Psychoanalysis* in 1930.

Although Healy eventually favored Freudian concepts, it would be misleading to suggest that Healy ever rejected social factors in his explanations of delinquency. He was impressed about the impact the environment—including the current environment—had on the mental life of a person. Still, he suspected that certain early traumatic experiences were far more prevalent in the lives of delinquents than nondelinquents. In addition, he attributed delinquency ultimately to the internal psychological conflicts within the child, not to the conditions of society.

In his first major publication, *The Individual Delinquent*, Healy reported the results of meticulous examinations of over 800 delinquent cases brought before the Juvenile Court of Cook County during the five-year period 1909 to 1914. The ratio of males to females was about 3 to 1. Each case had been studied by a psychiatrist, a physician, a psychologist, and a social worker. The psychiatrist headed the team and often elicited from the youth his or her ''own story,'' a method which will be explained shortly; the psychologist administered tests; the social worker interviewed and gathered a social history; and the physician reported on the physical exam. The ''team'' then conferred and decided what factors contributed to that delinquent's behavior. This team approach was to provide the model for clinics designed to diagnose and establish treatment plans for decades to come.

The Individual Delinquent was intended to be an exhaustive study of ''. . . all the available facts by combination of all the methods which bid fair to offer explanatory results'' (Healy, 1915, p. 18). Healy reported 11 major causes of delinquency, which he subdivided into 138 specific major and minor factors! The list included ''direct'' causes such as love of adventure, social suggestibility, mental conflict, natural adolescent impulses, school dissatisfaction, and an ''excessive street life.'' A year later, Healy and newly appointed psychologist Augusta F. Bronner published a follow-up paper to the 1915 book (Healy & Bronner, 1916). They reiterated the case study findings of *The Individual Delinquent*, namely that delinquency is caused by a complicated combination of dispositional and environmental factors, with family dynamics and the degree of supervision the child received being especially significant. Shortly thereafter, in 1917, Healy became Director of the Judge Baker Foundation in Boston, now the Judge Baker Guidance Center. Bronner was appointed Assistant Director.

Some writers have concluded that Healy, especially in his initial work, was propounding a ''multiple causation theory'' of delinquency. However, Healy at first resisted any one *theoretical* explanation for delinquency, including an eclectic one. He thought he was searching for cause on the basis of careful study of each case and in the most objective manner possible. It was not until 1925, at a symposium marking the 15th anniversary of the founding of the Juvenile Research Institute, that Healy finally presented a paper in which he issued a theoretical statement.

The paper, titled "The Psychology of the Situation," summarized Healy's clinical and research experiences. He affirmed that after 15 years of studying delinquents he was convinced that one must look at the entire situation, which included the mutual interaction of the person and the environment. "Circumstances *and* the person, the person *and* circumstances, all interweaving, form the warp and woof of any good biography, including that of a delinquent (Healy, 1925, p. 41). Healy also wrote, "the environment plays upon and modifies the individual and, what is usually not observed or set forth, the individual plays upon and modifies the environment" (p. 41). Healy called this process the "circular response." The term anticipated interactionism, one of the basic tenets of modern social learning theory. Healy's 1925 paper also anticipated the "labeling" theory which emerged 13 years later in the works of Frank Tannenbaum. "By our methods, general or personal, we play our part in creating the psychology of the situation. Take your delinquent, arrest him, detain him, let him go, be severe or be lenient, educate him or neglect him, study him . . . in any case we are part of the psychology of the situation that goes on in the making of him" (Healy, 1925, pp. 42–43).

To Healy, then, the "real" situation was not merely what an observer could see, but also how the individual interpreted it. This depended substantially upon a person's previous experiences in similar situations. "Perhaps it might be said of everybody that the conduct of today is made by the experience of yesterday" (Healy, 1925, p. 41). Two important points are implicit in this observation. First, the meaning a person attaches to a situation can only be determined by that person and not any outside observer, including a social or behavioral scientist. Therefore, the best way to understand behavior is not by formulating generalizations that presumably hold for everyone, but rather by case study of the person's unique mental representations. The psychologist Jerome Bruner (1986) has recently said something very similar: to appreciate the human condition, it is far more important to understand the ways human beings construct their worlds than it is to examine their behavior alone. Second, Healy emphasized the critical role of learning from past experience in any kind of human behavior, including delinquency. Instincts, indicating biological determinism, were secondary.

The method of research Healy relied most heavily upon in his search for the causes of delinquency was the life history record, or what he called obtaining the youth's "own story." Prior to Healy's work, offenders had either been classified as "types" or "statistics." Tarde, for example, decided that all criminals could be classified under five types: criminal lunatics, criminals born incorrigible, habitual criminals or criminals from acquired habits, occasional criminals, and emotional criminals. Lombroso divided the criminal population into seven types based on observation. William A. Bonger, a Dutch socialist, sought to explain crime through Marxian economics and statistical distributions. He put together large aggregates of statistics to demonstrate that in a capitalistic society, members of the proletariat class were forced into crime either as victims of the economic and political order or as rebels against it.

Ernest Burgess (1923, p. 661) thought that Healy's life history method "wrought a revolution in criminology." Another writer proclaimed: "This method and this concept stand out so boldly in contrast to the studies of the preceding hundred years that they may be said to signalize (sic) a new approach to the study of the individual offender in the United States" (Fink, 1938, p. ix). Healy's procedure was also used extensively by the Chicago School of Sociology. It was adopted by Burgess, W. I. Thomas (primarily through the use of personal letters and autobiographical documents to reconstruct Polish life), and most extensively by Clifford Shaw in his work with delinquent boys. These pioneering sociologists will be discussed shortly under the "Chicago School." Eventually, however, many sociologists viewed the "own story" or life history approach as having limited value and rejected it in favor of quantitative methods. As Schwartz and Jacobs (1979, p. 69) note, ". . . the whole notion that one's personal circumstances would be useful in explaining individual or group behavior was discredited by Durkheim and mainstream sociology." As we pointed out in Chapter 2, however, qualitative sociology (and psychology in general) continues to rely on the life history method as an invaluable procedure for reconstructing people's realities, and we will encounter illustrations of its use throughout the text.

Healy's Swing toward the Freudian Viewpoint

The "own story" method consisted primarily of encouraging the youth to tell about his or her life as completely as possible in writing, orally, or both. The Healy research teams believed they could gain considerable information and diagnostic clues about each person through this procedure. Eventually, on the basis of hundreds of "own stories," Healy increasingly became bolder and more willing to advance and display a theoretical bias. In 1936, Healy and Bronner, now husband and wife, published the often cited monograph, *New Light on Delinquency and Its Treatment*. Interestingly, the "new light" was decidedly dispositional and sympathetic to the Freudian viewpoint and has had a substantial impact on the "dynamic" viewpoint of delinquency. Healy and Bronner concluded that delinquency "appears to be a reaction to emotional disturbances and discomforts" (Healy and Bronner, 1936, p. 132). In line with Freudian doctrine, and in contradiction to Healy's earlier position, they apparently did not consider immediate circumstances to be terribly significant. Individual urges, desires, and wishes reigned supreme; social forces, peer pressures, and social attitudes were secondary. Because "discomfort" was far more common in delinquent stories than in nondelinquent ones, Healy and Bronner maintained that delinquents, compared to nondelinquents, felt deprived, inadequate, and misunderstood. Whereas Healy earlier would have attributed this to the individual's interaction with the environment or the way he or she interpreted a situation, he and Bronner now pointed to the Freudian "hydraulic model of forces" and instincts as probable culprits in the development of delinquency.

Still, they were not wholeheartedly Freudian. Delinquency, they said, was caused by the "blockage" or "damming up of fundamental wishes" that somehow must be released. A staunch Freudian would call these forces sexual (libido), or possibly aggressive, springing from the deep, instinctive underworld of the Id. To Healy and Bronner the fundamental wishes were nearer to what psychologist Abraham Maslow (1954) would later call secondary common human needs. Blocked were "the desire for feeling secure in family and other social relationships, for feeling accepted by some person or group, for recognition as having standing as a personality, for feeling adequate somehow or somewhere" (Healy and Bronner, 1936, p. 133). Anything that interfered with the satisfaction of these wishes resulted in frustration and a drive to get them satisfied. Delinquency, of course, offered youth an avenue for getting these needs met.

Essentially, therefore, delinquency was a substitute activity for obtaining thwarted or frustrated fundamental wishes for security and social significances. If the child or adolescent had a satisfactory relation with parents or with significant others who provided "good" role models, delinquency probably would not occur. Repeatedly we get the message in Healy's later writings with Bronner that social and parental relationships are critical predictors of delinquency in any given youth. "The feeling tone about right conduct derives *most powerfully* from the emotional side of human relationships" (Healy and Bronner, 1936, p. 11, italics added). Yet at the base is the hydraulic model of urges that must be satisfied. In the Healy-Bronner scheme, the parental role was one of oiling the machinery of human need. By implication, there were deficits in the relationships between delinquents and their parents; if these relationships were not supplanted by other acceptable social relationships, the youth would surely be driven to delinquency.

The Freudian influence appears again when Healy and Bronner describe the delinquent's own explanations for his or her behavior. "Usually the act is engaged in by the delinquent without verbalizing to himself, indeed, without conscious awareness that he is engaging in an evasive, substitute, or compensatory form of behavior" (Healy and Bronner, 1936, p. 135). A basic tenet of Freudian thought is that *all* human behavior has a purpose, a doctrine referred to as "psychic determinism." According to this position, much human conduct occurs without our awareness of our own specific intent. We are unaware or unconscious of the significant meaning of forgetting a name, an object, a date, and of our "slips of the tongue." It is the role of the analyst to guide us toward uncovering these unconscious meanings or purposes. Again, it is important to note that these treatment methods were not applied extensively in Healy's clinics. The emphasis was on gathering information in an attempt to uncover *causes* of delinquency.

Healy's work undoubtedly has had substantial influence on the psychiatric treatment of delinquents, however. He was heavily cited for over four decades and was a "guru" to many clinicians (Meltzer, 1967). Many psychiatrists, psychologists, and social workers still follow his and Bronner's lead in emphasizing dispositional more than social and environmental factors in the treatment and prevention of delinquency. For example, psychiatrist Hervey Cleckley (1976) credits Healy as having an incalculable effect on modern psychiatric thinking about crime and delinquency. It is sometimes forgotten, however, that during a brief period Healy argued that the interaction between the individual and his or her immediate environment was a crucial factor in delinquency. In doing this, Healy may have stepped onto a theoretical continuum that eventually led to the current, promising explanations of delinquency which will be discussed later in this book.

For 32 years William Healy and Augusta Bronner worked as an inseparable team assisting the courts, publishing numerous papers and books, and researching the causes of delinquency. They were married in 1932, after the death of Healy's first wife, Mary Tenney. In 1949, they retired to Clearwater Beach, Florida, where he died in March 1963 and she four years later.

THE ECOLOGICAL APPROACH TO DELINQUENCY: THE CHICAGO SCHOOL

Late one rainy and bleak afternoon in 1890, Albion W. Small, president of Colby College in Waterville, Maine, met with the newly appointed president of the University of Chicago, William Rainey Harper. Harper was a man of leadership, inventiveness, and daring. He was also the close personal friend of John D. Rockefeller. The latter, already in possession of his Standard Oil fortune, wanted to build and endow a small college to provide moral training in the Baptist tradition (Faris, 1967). Harper, a Yale professor of Greek and Hebrew, had agreed to administer the project, but he had a vision much greater than that of Rockefeller. Harper immediately began to scour the country for bright, energetic faculty, with the goal of building a great university.

The main topic of discussion between Small and Harper that afternoon was a faculty position for Small when the new university opened its doors, the projected date being fall of 1892. Small was interested only on one condition, to which Harper readily agreed: the university *must* include a department of sociology. The first department of sociology in the United States thus was established at the University of Chicago, with Small as Head Professor. Several other universities quickly followed suit, but the Chicago department was to dominate the intellectual and professional development of sociology for almost half a century. It became known as the "Chicago School of Sociology."

An Early Psychosocial View of Delinquency: W. I. Thomas

The four best known sociologists during the school's very early years were Small, George Vincent, Charles Henderson, and William I. Thomas. Of these, the work of Thomas is most relevant to the study of crime and delinquency. All four had theology backgrounds, but they soon directed their energies toward the more secular goal of building a new science of social behavior (Faris, 1967). They, their students, and the prolific and energetic faculty who would join them, created and promoted a scientific discipline based on direct observation. As Head Professor, Small stressed the importance of theory and research to both faculty and students, and he strongly encouraged them to venture outside the confines of the department. The city of Chicago should be their laboratory.

Thomas was the youngest member of the department. He received his Ph.D. from the school in 1896 and immediately joined the faculty, where he remained until his forced resignation amidst scandal in 1918 after being discovered in one of Chicago's brothels during a police raid. Finestone (1976a) notes that this unfortunate event even cost Thomas a publication, since a book he wrote, *Old World Traits Transplanted*, appeared under the name of his Chicago colleagues, Robert E. Park and Herbert A. Miller (1921). Because of the scandal, Thomas was not credited.

Thomas initially was interested in folk sociology and ethnology. During the early stages of his professional development, and in line with the dominant scholarly thought of the time, he preferred biological explanations of individual behavior. He considered humans creatures of instinct whose most natural behaviors were roving, fighting, and hunting. The needs for food and sex were their chief motivating forces, as they were for all animals. Emphasis on these biological needs would be untenable for contemporary sociologists, but we should keep in mind that in their infancy, sociology, psychology, and psychiatry all were responsive to the dominant, Darwinian perspective. Consequently, representatives of these three disciplines were sometimes indistinguishable. It was not until the early 1930s that sociology began to break away from an individual perspective and emphasize the importance of the social environment and the structure of society.

Eventually, Thomas abandoned his food and sex theory of motivation and replaced it with his "four wishes theory," similar to the wishes which Healy and Bronner (1936) later identified. In fact, Thomas may well have influenced Healy, both in this aspect and in Healy's discussions of the psychological situation, as we will note shortly. The new wishes, or innate needs, according to Thomas, were for recognition, response, new experience, and security (Thomas, 1931). *Recognition* was the general need for individuals to struggle for positions of status within their social group. This struggle added significantly to the development of personality. *Response* referred primarily to the innate desire for sex and love, a combination of physiological and emotional needs. *New experience* was a need to obtain exciting and adventurous events from one's environment. *Security* was the need for a stable, predictable environment where one could develop regular habits and a systematic work routine. Thomas thought that all human action, including delinquency, could be accounted for by these four wishes. The wishes had a biological basis, but they could be modified by the social environment.

One controversial aspect of his work was his emphasis on sex differences in human needs. He has been criticized extensively for drawing a sharp distinction between male and female "needs" and applying this to juvenile delinquency, which he believed was predominately a male endeavor (Chesney-Lind, 1986; Leonard, 1982; Klein, 1973). Boys, Thomas said, naturally crave excitement and adventure, and under the right conditions, they might disregard the prevailing social standards to get these needs met. In contrast, Thomas noted in his *Unadjusted Girl* that the beginning of delinquency in girls was usually the result of an impulse to get amusement, pretty clothes, favorable notice, distinction, freedom in the larger world which presents so many allurements. Sexual passion, according to Thomas, did not play a role in the delinquent behavior of girls— only in that of boys.

The Concept of "Social Disorganization"

In his later writings, Thomas began to give credit to the role played by the environment, leaning toward a more solid sociological perspective. In his classic book *The Polish Peasant in Europe and America* (Thomas and Znaniecki, 1927), Thomas described the concept of *social disorganization*, which became central to much of the work of the Chicago School, despite the fact that Thomas had by then moved on. Social disorganization was and continues to be a nebulous concept that was never clearly defined by the Chicago group, however (Carey, 1975). Despite this ambiguity, it has been used extensively in the formulation of many theories of juvenile delinquency, often being cited as an implicit or explicit cause of delinquency.

To Thomas, social disorganization was a breakdown in the influence of existing rules of conduct on individual members of a group. It was caused by erosion of standards and values as a particular subculture encountered an alien environment to which it was ill-adapted. With reference to the Polish culture which Thomas studied, social disorganization reflected the disrupting influence of an urban, industrial environment. Children were deprived of an effective guide to behavior as the amount of control the nuclear family had over its members was greatly reduced. Thus, delinquency was the result of ineffective socialization by the conventional institution of the family. It was random and "wild" behavior without parental or social control. It was also behavior instigated by temperamental tendencies and swayed by momentary moods (Finestone, 1976a). Thus, Thomas had not lost his psychological perspective, nor had he apparently modified his belief in the influence of the four wishes.

Disorganization was a temporary state occurring within cycles of organization, disorganization, and reorganization, and it was commonly found in societies facing rapid change. Although Thomas applied his concept primarily to a subculture within the larger society (viz., the Polish immigrants within the United States), he also used it to explain what happened in smaller groups—such as the family—within those subcultures. *Individual* disorganization, however, had no invariable connection with social disorganization (Elliott and Merrill, 1934). Under certain social conditions, disorganization in the family would be followed by reorganization. If the family could satisfactorily meet the wishes of the child, some degree of control was reinstated. For example, a Polish family trying to adapt to urban life might be disorganized for lack of sufficient income. Its influence on individual members might cease temporarily, leaving them susceptible to delinquency. If the family's financial status improved, it could move to a "better" neighborhood where it could reassert its social control, and where other controlling forces—schools, churches, and other community members—made it likely that delinquency would be lower. The family, then, could become reorganized.

Thomas observed in the Polish peasant family—as well as in other families he studied—that social disorganization in the broader subculture led to decreased control of the family unit over the children's behavior. However, disorganization was not inevitable when old-world values clashed with those of the new world; it occurred only if the old-world subculture lost its force with exposure to the American urban environment. Delinquency was one by-product of this decrease in social control.

Ecological Foundations of Delinquency: Burgess and Park

Two individuals who more than any others in the early Chicago group laid the groundwork for the sociological study of crime and delinquency were Ernest W. Burgess and Robert E. Park. Park joined the faculty in 1914, under the strong recommendation of W. I. Thomas. This was a year after Burgess had received his degree from the school. Burgess taught at other colleges for three years, then returned to his alma mater as a professor in the department of sociology. The two men were office mates, with little in common other than their love of sociology and their workaholic habits, which led them to collaborate on one of the most influential sociological textbooks ever written, *Introduction to the Science of Sociology* (1921), a hefty, green-covered volume which sociology students for decades have called the "green bible."

Burgess, 22 years younger than Park, was a slight man who rarely left the office. He was so caught up with his work, to the exclusion of everything else, that he continually looked pale, worn, and harried. A lifelong bachelor, he lived with his father and sister. Finestone (1976a) notes that Burgess once joked that his unmarried status lent objectivity to his studies of the family, since he could not generalize from one case and assume that all, or even most, families operated as his did.

Park, a former newspaper reporter, led a sedentary life, chronically thinking about and planning research (Faris, 1967). He was the prototypical absent-minded professor. His unruly white hair was long and wild-looking. At times he appeared before his classes with traces of shaving soap on his face and with his clothes terribly wrinkled and disheveled. Faris (1967) repeats an anecdote in which Park continued to lecture without breaking stride while a student walked to the front of the room and tied and adjusted the professor's necktie, which had been dangling loose from his collar. The students were both amused and impressed.

During his 12 years as a newspaper reporter, Park became intrigued by the city of Chicago, particularly its structure. He sincerely wanted to improve the city, but believed his newspaper work was not the way to do it. Publicity, he concluded, aroused interest and stirred the emotions of the public, but it rarely led directly to constructive action. Park enrolled at Harvard University, studying psychology and philosophy, then went to Germany (Berlin and Heidelberg), where he studied sociology and completed a doctoral dissertation on "The Crowd and the Public."

Park was fascinated with theories of plant ecology and their possible application to humans. Ecology is the study of the relationship between living organisms and their natural habitats. Park hoped to apply this study to urban life. He believed, for example, that the process of invasion, dominance, and succession demonstrated by plant species in taking over regions of the world might have relevance for the growth of populations in urban regions. Eventually, he framed a theory of "human ecology," speculating that the city was a super-organism, with its physical structure, people, and institutions comprising separate, interlocking parts.

Sociological (and ecological) studies of Chicago began with Park's article, "The City: Suggestions for the Investigation of Human Behavior in the Urban Environment." It was published in the *American Journal of Sociology* in 1916, the year Burgess was welcomed back to the University of Chicago as a member of its faculty. Burgess was intrigued with Park's theory. In an effort to test it, the two soon set out to gather as much information as they could about the city, using the student power at their disposal to do so. They demanded high quality term papers, encouraging students to focus on information about Chicago. "Students made spot maps, rate maps, conducted interviews, attended meetings, and in various ways observed and systematically recorded phenomena of the city" (Faris, 1967, p. 54). Within a short period of time, many of these students were enrolled in the graduate program at the university, and the department was accumulating large sets of data, both quantified and descriptive. The Chicago School became well known internationally for its "urban ecological" focus. Although the interests of its members were broad and diversified, it was the ecological orientation that led to sociology's dominance in the field of crime and delinquency.

Researchers at the Chicago School began to discover that extremes in poverty, illness, and crime were found disproportionately in particular parts of the city. According to the maps, both male and female juvenile delinquents lived and operated in certain locations and were less conspicuous in others. At first, Juvenile Court officials and youth workers in other cities were skeptical about these findings (Burgess & Bogue, 1967). They maintained that while these strange patterns might be characteristic of Chicago, delinquency in *their* cities was distributed evenly. Studies of these other cities, however, revealed the same disproportionate patterning (Morris, 1957). In urban areas, delinquency seemed to be concentrated where buildings deteriorated, poverty was widespread, and the population was in transition. It was almost nonexistent in the "better" residential neighborhoods. Moreover, delinquency seemed to fit neatly into a pattern of circular zones around the centermost part of the city, called in Chicago the "Loop."

Burgess, then, began to fine tune the ecological theory and propose his "Concentric Circle Theory" (also called the "zonal hypothesis"): American cities expand radially outward from their center in five discernible circular patterns. Each circle represents a zone with distinct demographic and physical characteristics. The first zone, where businesses are most concentrated, is the core. The second zone, which circles the core, is the "area of transition." It is a place of high mobility, constantly being invaded by small businesses and light manufacturing. The third zone houses the working class who have escaped the area of transition but work in industries located within that second zone. Zone four, the "residential zone," consists of high-class apartment buildings and single-family dwelling units. Zone five is the commuters' region.

In Chicago, the area of transition (zone 2) was where delinquency, youth gangs, crime, poverty, spousal desertion, abandoned infants, and serious health problems seemed most concentrated. A contact with a juvenile court was used as the measure of delinquency. Even when the population density of the districts in relation to the number of juvenile court cases was taken into account, delinquency was higher in zone 2 than in other zones. This ratio—the rate of delinquency—was a new statistical concept that Burgess considered invaluable in promoting sociology as an empirical science.

Boy Scouts and Gangs: Thrasher

Inevitably, the Chicago group was to give some systematic attention to delinquency as a gang activity. The faculty member who specialized in this area was Frederic Thrasher. A former newspaper reporter like Park, Thrasher enrolled as a graduate student at Chicago and wrote a Master's thesis on "The Boy Scout Movement as a Socializing Agency." The study whetted his appetite for more study of group activity among boys, and he undertook a seven-year project examining the numerous gangs that had been identified in the city. The massive study was completed in 1926 and served as his doctoral dissertation. It was published a year later in book form under the title *The Gang: A Study of 1,313 Gangs in Chicago*. It remains a classic in the field of criminology.

Thrasher wrote that gangs represented the spontaneous effort of young people to create a society for themselves that offered excitement and adventure in the company of peers. Gangs provided the medium for stimulation, thrills, and togetherness that many low income families living in impoverished neighborhoods did not offer. Since a majority of the Chicago gangs engaged in unconventional and delinquent behavior, Thrasher's gangs were an appropriate unit for the study of delinquency as group behavior. Of the 1,313 gangs he studied, 530 could be classified as delinquent, and another 609 as "often delinquent." Unfortunately, he did not explain the criteria for these classifications.

In line with the Chicago School's emphasis on urban ecology, Thrasher observed that gangs were concentrated in the *interstitial* zones of the city. In the natural world, Thrasher noted, matter collects in every crack, crevice and cranny—in other words, in all interstitial areas. Similarly, Thrasher assumed that there were fissures and breaks in the structure of social organizations. Accordingly, he considered the gang the interstitial matter filtering into the framework of society; the areas where they developed were interstitial regions in the layout of the city. These regions were found primarily between the business and industrial districts and the better residential areas. In short, gangs were found principally in Burgess' zone of transition, concentrated near the center of the American city.

Gangs were interstitial in time as well as in geographical location. The gang, Thrasher said, was an adolescent phenomenon, "an interstitial group, a manifestation of the period of readjustment between childhood and maturity" (quoted by Finestone, 1976a, p. 160). Gang members, then, were psychologically normal, whether or not they engaged in antisocial or illegal behavior. When delinquency was prevalent, Thrasher concluded that community forces countering illegal behavior were weak or inoperative. The usually influential, controlling institutions of family, church, and school had "broken down" and become ineffective socializing mediums. Given these "social control voids," the most influential "organizations" were the youth gangs located in various areas of the transition zone. Gangs took up the socializing slack that the conventional institutions could not or would not provide. Like Thomas, Thrasher believed the children of immigrants not experienced in American traditions were especially vulnerable. They lacked parental control, because their parents were not versed in the American lifestyle and were probably overwhelmed with the day-to-day struggle to make ends meet.

Thrasher, much like Thomas, *described* what he observed, and he interpreted what he saw largely in the Chicago School's ecological tradition. His descriptions of gangs of young people are rich with detail, but he did not develop a theory of delinquency. It is important to note his and Thomas's emphasis on lack of *social control* as one explanation for delinquency, however. The concept was later used by Travis Hirschi (1969) as the cornerstone in the formation of his social control or bonding theory.

The Major Force in Early Studies on Delinquency: Shaw and McKay

While Thrasher was observing youth gangs, researchers at the Chicago Institute for Juvenile Research were working on a systematic project covering 20 years of study on the ecological distribution of delinquency. Clifford R. Shaw and Henry D. McKay were the leaders of this group. Shaw, a former probation and parole officer who developed strong compassion for the powerless and poor, became a research associate at the Institute while still a graduate student at the University of Chicago. In 1926 he was appointed director of the new sociology research section, which was created after a group of private citizens raised money to fund research into the causes and cures of delinquency. As a result, Shaw became the link which connected the Chicago School with the Institute. The close working relationship that developed between these two institutions was to last for nearly three decades.

Under Burgess's tutelage, Shaw became keenly interested in the ecological distribution of delinquency. He and his colleague, Henry D. McKay, embarked upon a project which probably did more to transmit the essence of American social ecological research than any other project to date. As Shaw freely acknowledged, however, it was not the *first* geographical study of its type.

Geographical or ecological studies of crime and delinquency had been conducted in Europe at least as early as the first half of the 19th century. These studies reported on crime distributions city by city or province by province, but they did not focus on areas and regions within a city. In the United States, Sophonisba Breckenridge and Edith Abbott of the Chicago School of Civics and Philanthropy (later the School of Social Service Administration), published in 1912 a report illustrating the geographic distribution of juvenile delinquency within the city of Chicago. The Breckenridge-Abbott article ''The Delinquent Child and the Home'' was significant because it underscored the city's zonal patterns much as did the urban ecological studies of the Chicago School. Breckenridge and Abbott used all the cases which came to the attention of the juvenile court of Cook county during the years 1899 to 1909 as their index of delinquency. They constructed a map pinpointing the homes of the children and illustrating the fact that a disproportionately large number of the juveniles were from impoverished areas of the city where housing was inadequate. For example, 76 percent of the delinquent boys and 89 percent of delinquent girls came from homes where the family's financial status was described by Breckenridge and Abbott as "poor" or "very poor."

The Breckenridge-Abbott maps depicted only the *absolute* numbers of cases in the various districts, however. *Rates* of delinquency (number of cases in relation to the population density) were not calculated. It was not possible to conclude whether the observed concentrations of delinquent cases were due to anything other than high population density compared to other areas. Shaw and his associates intended to analyze delinquency rates throughout Chicago, as had Park and Burgess. However, their study would go beyond statistical analysis and would attempt to interpret the information they obtained and offer recommendations for society's response to what they saw as a mounting delinquency problem.

In a report written for the 1929 *Illinois Crime Survey*, Shaw, McKay, and their colleagues offered a comprehensive interpretation of the nature of the delinquency problem, its causes, and the shortcomings of existing treatment methods. Delinquency, they declared, was clearly a product of the social situation; its roots could be found in community characteristics, the family situation, and peer companionship, including gang membership.

Using an elaborate system for plotting the home addresses of over 100,000 juveniles processed by the Juvenile Court of Cook County between 1900 and 1927, the Shaw group had found that the regions having the highest rates of delinquency corresponded roughly to Burgess's concentric zones theory. Specifically, areas of high delinquency were characterized by deteriorating buildings, widespread poverty, and residences interspersed with industry and commerce. These areas not only had the highest rates of delinquency, but the highest rates of adult crime as well. Shaw and his colleagues posited that criminal adults were deviant models for the young.

In addition, delinquency was especially high in areas with high concentrations of *recent* immigrants. As the economic status of these immigrants improved, they often moved to more attractive outlying regions. The "hot beds" of delinquency—areas of high poverty—remained the same. Once a family moved to better surroundings, the children apparently did not continue their previous behavior, since rates of delinquency in the new areas were not high. This recurring pattern of high delinquency even in areas of high resident mobility suggested to the Shaw-McKay group that delinquency was not due primarily to cultural or ethnic background but to a "delinquency tradition" transmitted from older to younger youths within a specific geographical area, year after year.

The Continuance of the Life-history Method

Shaw and McKay compared features of two living areas: the better residential areas and rent areas where residential mobility was high. In the better residential neighborhoods, they found attitude similarities among families. They adopted conventional values, such as the desirability of a general health program, education, and the promotion of constructive use of leisure time. There were also subtle pressures throughout the community to keep the children engaged in conventional activities, as well as some not-so-subtle condemnation directed at those who violated the community's standards of conduct. By contrast, in sections with high delinquency rates, attitudes and values varied widely. Families were so mobile and hard-pressed economically that they paid little attention to what others did or thought. Furthermore, in the better residential areas, the youth were on the whole insulated from direct contact with deviant forms of behavior engaged in by older models. In other words, the "delinquency tradition" was absent.

Shaw and McKay believed that many of the relationships between delinquency and social factors were too complex to be unraveled strictly by statistical data. Clearly, not all youths living in delinquency-prone areas became delinquent; moreover, for those who did, the sequence of influences were not always the same. Thus, Shaw in particular became an advocate of the "life history" method, to which he had been introduced by his mentor, Burgess. In addition to compiling maps and official data, Shaw and his colleagues asked some youths to tell about various experiences of their lives. The information was recorded, often in their own words, and often written as autobiography, as a diary, or presented in the format of an interview. According to Shaw (1945), the life history or own story method revealed important information on three aspects of delinquent behavior:

1. the point of view of the delinquent;
2. the social and cultural situation within which he lives; and
3. the relevant experiences in his life that had an extended impact on his point of view.

Three classic books by Shaw illustrate the life history method: *The Jack Roller: A Delinquent Boy's Own Story* (1930), *The Natural History of a Delinquent Career* (1931), and *Brothers in Crime* (1938), the last written with McKay and James F. McDonald.

The Jack-Roller is perhaps the best known qualitative case study in the field of juvenile delinquency. (A "Jack-roller" is one who robs drunk persons or individuals sleeping on city streets.) The book is a biography of "Stanley," an adolescent boy who grew up in a poor neighborhood near the Chicago stockyards. Stanley's story is continued in the book *The Jack-Roller at Seventy*, written by Jon Snodgrass (1982).

Some writers (e.g., Bennett, 1981; Geis, 1982) have alleged that Shaw's case history books appear to be more directed at convincing his audience of the community theme than providing new, scientific data. The life history method was an effective medium through which to communicate Shaws's solution to the delinquency problem and improve the community (Bennett, 1981). Shaw also believed that delinquents were essentially alike; they were good kids striving to acquire what people in society typically acquired. Bennett (1981) suspects that Shaw selected and edited those materials that best built his case.

Another perspective is offered by Harold Finestone (1976b, p. 116) who wrote about Shaw:

> As long as he lived, his sense of justice was continually outraged by the treatment that the existing correctional system and other social agencies accorded the delinquent. It was, how-

ever, an outrage that he scrupulously sought to harness within the impersonal disciplines of
social science and rational analysis. It was this fundamental ambiguity, this ceaseless tension between his heart and his head, his moral judgment, and his striving for the objectivity
of the scientist, that rendered him so complex and vital a person.

Finestone would disagree with Bennett's suggestion that Shaw's work was deliberately
selective.

The life history approach easily falls prey to criticisms about objectivity. The work
of the Chicago School, for example, did not include middle or upper class delinquents.
Shaw did not do case studies of delinquents outside of areas characterized by social
disorganization. Nor did he include life histories of youths who did not become delinquent but yet were exposed to many of the same life events. Despite questions about its
ability to produce generalizable data, the life history can provide valuable insights into
how particular individuals perceive and mentally construct their worlds. Consider the
following.

A 17-year-old boy was recently arrested and charged with the murder of a pregnant
woman and her two children in a small New England town. The boy allegedly raped the
mother and shot her through the head. Next, he drowned her 5-year-old son in a bathtub.
He then waited for her 7-year-old daughter to come home from school and drowned her
in a separate bathtub.

For sometime, residents of the upper-middle-class neighborhood had been concerned about the boy's behavior. Approximately a year before the triple murder, he took
a family of four hostage, surprising them when they arrived home by jumping out of a
closet, wearing a black ninja mask, an Indian headdress, and waving a hatchet. He stuck
knives into the woodwork and smeared mayonnaise and ketchup on the walls. Eventually, the terrifed family managed to barricade themselves in a bedroom and were able
to escape. The boy was awaiting trial on the earlier incident when he allegedly murdered
the mother and the children.

This case is clearly atypical. Most delinquents, even serious delinquents, do not
commit such bizarre or brutal crimes. A life history approach, however, would be extremely valuable in reconstructing how this youth arrived at his version of the world.
How much influence might be attributed to television, parenting, temperament, peers,
or the community? As Solomon Kobrin (1982, p. 153) points out, the life history method
''. . . can serve as a test of the adequacy of the theory purporting to explain delinquency
. . . and suggest neglected variables in theory building. These are typically the more
elusive elements of deviant behavior that are often difficult to capture in quantifiable
variables . . .''

Conclusions from Shaw and McKay

The extensive and carefully accumulated Shaw and McKay data supported Park and
Burgess's earlier conclusions that the distribution of juvenile delinquency corresponded
to the physical layout and social organization of the American city. Delinquency, the

researchers found, was concentrated near the center of the city where physical deterioration and social disorganization were most in evidence. Dilapidated housing, proximity to railroad yards, crowded neighborhoods, and industry represented the physical structure. Adult crime, poverty, disease, suicide, mental disorders, and family instability represented the social disorganization element. As one moved away from the city's core, the rate of delinquency decreased until it almost vanished in the residential areas with better physical environments and less social disorganization.

The Shaw-McKay research also supported Thrasher's contention that delinquency is principally a group activity, since 82 percent of the juveniles brought before the juvenile court had committed their offenses in the company of others. Shaw and McKay (1931) noted, however, that delinquent acts typically were committed with a few partners who were members of the same gang, but not by the gang as a whole. Furthermore, like Thrasher, they were careful to say that gangs did not "cause" illegal actions, but rather facilitated them. Traditions of delinquency are *transmitted* through successive generations in much the same way that language, social roles, and attitudes are transmitted. Shaw and McKay did not specify the *process* of becoming a delinquent, however. This was left to later theorists, including Edwin Sutherland (1939) and his theory of differential association, to be discussed in Chapter 5.

Members of a gang helped and encouraged one another to engage in unconventional actions, but a major factor contributing to delinquency was lack of parental control. According to Shaw and McKay, when parental influence and control over children were weakened or hampered, delinquent behavior increased dramatically. For example, newly arrived immigrants would find themselves living partly in their own old-world traditions and partly in the new-world expectations. Many children, sensing the confusion, were drawn more to their peer world and less to the traditional lifestyle, which peers rejected. Under these conditions, parents lost much of their influence over their children. The youths also had little respect for the parentally supported conventional institutions such as the church or the school.

Shaw and McKay observed that many of the alienated youths developed their own splintered "subcultures" where certain forms of conduct were expected and particular symbols took on group-specific meanings. Thus, while Thomas believed delinquency could be explained by a lack of socialization, Shaw and McKay saw it as the result of an *alternate mode of socialization* into a deviant subculture. Both the Thomas and Shaw-McKay perspectives, however, posited that the seeds of delinquency were lack of parental and social control. Shaw and McKay stressed that the deviant subcultures were not independent of the ethnic cultural context in which they developed, nor were they autonomous from mainstream American society. Rather, these youth subcultures *interacted* with several cultural and social contexts simultaneously, adopting some aspects of one, some of another. In short, they saw the deviant subculture as one system within many systems.

Shaw and McKay's theoretical orientation shifted over the years as they continued to accumulate massive amounts of data. Whereas their early writings reflect the strong influence of Thomas and his concepts of social disorganization and social control, their later writings lean toward a strain perspective. The most notable shift can be detected in their 1942 publication, *Juvenile Delinquency and Urban Areas*. Here, rather than emphasizing the impact of severed traditional family ties on juvenile conduct, they highlighted a discrepancy between delinquent areas and mainstream society in the achievement of goals. Furthermore, whereas Thomas had focused on the effects of social control (or lack of it) on individuals, Shaw and McKay now began to develop interest in the discrepancies between subgroups and mainstream society.

Shaw and McKay found that most delinquents they studied had internalized the central values of mainstream society but had difficulty reconciling them with their present predicament. Youths in deprived areas wanted what society apparently advocated everyone should have, including material goods, education, and prestige. Yet, these youth did not have the legitimate avenues to obtain what society valued. Delinquency provided a means of securing some of these valued aspects of mainstream society.

> Groups in areas of lowest economic status find themselves at a disadvantage in the struggle to achieve the goals idealized in our civilization. Those persons who occupy a disadvantageous position are involved in a conflict between the goals assumed to be attainable in a free society and those actually attainable for a large proportion of the population. It is understandable, then, that the economic position of persons living in the areas of least opportunity should be translated at times into unconventional conduct. (Shaw and McKay, 1942, p. 233)

In short, youths living in delinquency-prone areas are pulled toward the things society advocates, but they have no legitimate way to obtain them. This creates a conflict or a *strain* in the youth, who may turn to illegitimate activities in order to ease it. This perspective anticipates the strain theory that will be discussed in the next chapter. In fact, it is possible that, by 1942, Shaw and McKay had been exposed to Robert Merton's seminal 1938 article, which introduced what was to become known as "strain theory" in criminology. The Thomas perspective, on the other hand, viewed delinquency as the result of a "push" toward deviant groups because conventional groups were ineffective in promoting a reasonable quality of life.

One last point about the Shaw and McKay research should be noted. Female delinquents were generally not included in their investigations. This was not unusual. Many contemporary theorists and researchers have remarked that early criminologists gave scant attention to female offenders and that the classic theories were formulated on males (Leonard, 1982; Chesney-Lind, 1986; Klein, 1973). Martin Gold (1987) suggests that, because male offenders accounted for the vast majority of the official data on delinquency, Shaw and McKay may have been drawn to what appeared to be the more pressing social problem of male offending. Gold also cites evidence, however, that shows Shaw and McKay did *not* believe that their ecological theory applied equally to all delinquency. He speculates that they ". . . probably believed that the offenses of most female delinquents, with whom they had little personal experience, were of a different nature" (Gold, 1987, p. 71). That, of course, is no excuse for ignoring female delinquency. It is likely that its nature *was* very different, just as female delinquency today is quite different from male delinquency. The Shaw-McKay data do not recognize the differences, much less suggest an explanation.

The Chicago Area Project

Shaw had found repeatedly that areas with high delinquency rates lacked adequate neighborhood organizations or any community life. This, in addition to his experiences in probation and parole, convinced him that the most effective way of reducing rates of delinquency was to improve the community and give its members a sense of control over their fate. This led to the famous Chicago Area Project (CAP), which Shaw as director consistently and vigorously propelled forward. The fact that Shaw never completed his Ph.D. work at the University of Chicago suggests that the project may have consumed his career. His initiative and the CAP itself account for sociology's success at challenging and countering the powerful stronghold that psychiatry and psychology had on the treatment of delinquency.

The Chicago Area Project (CAP) was an experimental program to test various methods of preventing delinquency. According to one of its participants, Shaw wished to apply information derived from ecological and socio-psychological research in delinquency (Kobrin, 1959). It is important to note that Shaw considered the CAP a social experiment and never made extravagant claims about its capacity to prevent delinquency. The project was initiated in 1932, incorporated in 1934, and essentially terminated with Shaw's death 25 years later, although its actual lifespan was 30 years. It had four goals:

1. to provide less formal treatment of delinquents;
2. to emphasize that juvenile offenders needed understanding, not punishment;
3. to demonstrate the Chicago School's belief that environmental influences were far more critical than individual factors; and
4. to show that working with the delinquent within his own community is a more effective strategy than institutional confinement (Bennett, 1981).

The project has been described as a combination of recreation, communal self-renewal, and mediation. Shaw and his associates hypothesized that a significant amount of delinquency could be prevented if residents of disadvantaged areas could be persuaded to get involved and to form or strengthen community groups designed for collective action and willing to take communal responsibility for delinquency prevention.

The Chicago Area Project has been referred to extensively in criminology literature, but is rarely described in detail. Noting this, two scholars, relying on archival data, have recently provided an excellent description of the day-to-day activities in the South Chicago neighborhood of Russell Square (Schlossman & Sedlak, 1983). The CAP took 15 months to become fully operational. It began with an initial identification of natural juvenile leaders and the formation of a basketball league. Shortly after this, "street workers'' were dispatched to ''hang out'' with youth, help structure recreation, and offer problem solving advice—a feature of the project referred to as ''curbstone counseling.'' The street workers took copious notes and elicited life stories of local youths. Because Shaw was intent upon keeping youths away from juvenile courts, it was not unusual for the CAP street workers to mediate with police, schools, and police departments. ''On the other hand, CAP workers tried to persuade local youth—in a low-keyed, tolerant, nonabusive manner—why it was both morally right and ultimately in their best interest to conform to the values and expectations of conventional society'' (Schlossman and Sedlak, 1983, p. 48). Eventually, adults in the community were persuaded to take some control.

The CAP developed a number of subsidiary programs and projects, including a school guidance clinic staffed by a social worker, psychologist, and psychiatrists, a camping program, and a parole program, which indicates that the project did not shy away from serious offenders. The probation program was, in fact, one of its most often cited successes (Schlossman and Sedlak, 1983). The Schlossman and Sedlak article also details the political intrigues that were associated with the CAP and the frustration and incremental victories experienced by the community and the researchers.

For a variety of reasons, it is difficult to evaluate the overall ''success'' of the project. Shaw himself welcomed impartial measurements of the results, yet he doubted that these could be obtained (Bennett, 1981). Many criticisms of the program came from adults in the community, including school officials or mental health workers who believed their roles were being appropriated. Community organizer Sol Alinsky, an early CAP worker, eventually concluded that its mediation tactics were ineffective in comparison to confrontational styles (Bennett, 1981). The CAP was most successful in those communities with some effective conventional institutions already in place, including churches, schools, or kinship groups, or even cohesive youth gangs. It was less effective in communities lacking these fundamental structures. Since delinquency is most prevalent in disorganized communities, CAP's success was limited in the communities where it was most needed. The apparent low impact on high delinquency areas may account for why the project was not repeated in other cities (Finestone, 1976b). Schlossman and Sedlak, however, believe the project itself had merit.

> In a field where a quest for perfect knowledge has proved so frustrating and where there is no consensus on appropriate designs for research or evaluation, the numerous distinctive features that separated the Chicago Area Project from virtually all other experiments in delinquency prevention would appear to warrant serious study and reconsideration. (p. 461)

SUMMARY AND CONCLUSIONS

The ecological research of the Chicago School revolutionalized the study of crime and delinquency. In effect, it can be considered the beginning of American criminology. Prior to the ''Chicago School,'' explanations of delinquency were dominated by a biologically based social science which asserted that delinquency was due to individual deficiencies. "Poverty, crime, suicide, mental abnormality, and other behavioral defects of slum dwellers were seen as inborn legacies from their defective ancestors who had been reproducing at a higher rate than the normal population" (Faris, 1967, p. 62). As we shall learn in the next chapter, one proposed remedy was to prevent deficient members of society from reproducing, a remedy which included forced sterilization. This assumed biological deficit doctrine even received support from Supreme Court Justice Oliver Wendell Holmes, who proclaimed in an often cited decision: "Three generations of imbeciles is enough."

The ecological research of the Chicago School shifted attention away from the Darwinian approach toward social factors as causal agents of crime and delinquency. It emphasized the effects of social disorganization and deteriorating physical environments, and it rejected notions of genetic and biological inferiority. In other words, the ecological orientation reversed the causal equation to read: Social disorganization and inadequate living conditions cause people to act like "animals," not "animal-like creatures live in social disorganization and commit crime because they do not know any better." Once policy makers and the public began to understand that crime and delinquency were not inevitable biological aftermaths of genetic coding or defective evolutionary development, more attention could be directed at the social, emotional, and physical environment as a powerful factor in the development of delinquency.

On the other hand, the contributions of the psychiatrist William Healy continued to be influential. Healy increasingly moved away from environmental influences and toward more psychoanalytical, individual determinants of delinquent behavior. He was increasingly convinced that the causes of delinquency reside within the individual, while the ecological perspective was equally convinced that the causes existed within the environment. These two parallel approaches had their respective adherents and represented competing views and policies, which, we could argue, have not yet been merged to produce comprehensive responses to juvenile delinquency.

Today, the ecological perspective has found new life—as we shall see—and represents the higher or more abstract levels of our social systems' approach mentioned in Chapter 1. The *strictly* individual approach, on the other hand, is waning as a cogent explanation of delinquent behavior. However, the individual approach is highly relevant if linked to the other systems that interact in our lives. This will be the theme of Chapters 6 and 7.

Two names that should be highlighted at this point in our historical review are Clifford R. Shaw and Henry D. McKay—two of the most influential researchers in criminology during the twentieth century. They are known not so much for any specific theory (primarily because they kept changing their explanations with each new set of data), but more for their painstaking descriptions and geographical mapping of crime and delinquency in various urban areas. They were also pioneers in attempts to prevent delinquency by involving the community and its existing social networks. Their preventive strategy was epitomized by the Chicago Area Project, an approach that lasted for three decades.

Shaw also emphasized that delinquency is largely a group activity rather than an individual one. Furthermore, he was instrumental in bringing the life history or case study method to sociological research on delinquency, although the overall value of the method as a scientific tool remains much debated (see Geis, 1982; Short, 1982). Questions center around two issues:

1. the extent to which we may generalize to all delinquents on the basis of one individual's version of the world; and
2. the extent to which an investigator unknowingly slants or biases the questions, procedure, and data selection to his or her own version of the world.

There are other significant names as well. William I. Thomas is best known for his elaboration of the concept of "social disorganization." He also added invaluable insights into "symbolic interactionism" characterized by his oft-cited dictum, "If men define situations as real, they are real in their consequences" (Thomas and Thomas, 1928, p. 572). This quote suggests that the key to evaluating behavior is to understand how a person perceives and construes a situation. For Thomas, all human behavior was situationally oriented, and personal constructions of that situation dictated behavior. Thomas is less admired for his work on the female delinquent, *The Unadjusted Girl*, primarily because of its strong individual, psychological leaning and unwarranted assumptions supported by little empirical documentation.

The careful reader may wonder how Thomas, an integral member of the Chicago School, could have been toying with individual factors when we have just emphasized that the ecological perspective was the Chicago hallmark. The Chicago School, however, did *not* represent a unified system of thought. The term "Chicago School" was not even used until the 1950s. Lee Harvey (1987, p. 255) notes, "There are virtually no references to the 'Chicago School of Sociology' in the published literature during the first half of the century." Furthermore, interviews with the early Chicagoans reveal that they hardly considered themselves a "school of thought" during the first 30 years after the founding of the sociology department (Kurtz, 1984; Harvey, 1987). Instead, they remember the University of Chicago as vibrant, full of energy, and a collection of people with wide interests. Thus, it is wiser to use the "Chicago School" loosely, to represent those divergent and influential thinkers associated with the University of Chicago's department of sociology who were keenly interested in crime and other social problems.

Thomas was an integral part of that "school" and from many accounts was the "sparkplug" for much of its activity (Harvey, 1987). If Thomas was the inspirational leader, Ernest W. Burgess and Robert E. Park were the early leaders in the theoretical development of the ecological perspective. They provided much of the conceptual framework for the Shaw-McKay investigations. Shaw, after all, became interested in juvenile delinquency after taking courses from Burgess (Bennett, 1981).

Frederick Thrasher is best known for his pioneering work in juvenile gangs, particularly as they existed in Chicago's "slum" communities. While Thrasher did not develop a theory of gang delinquency, he did provide a vivid tapestry of descriptions of juvenile life. According to James F. Short, Jr. (1963, pp. xv–xvi), Thrasher's work stands "after more than three and a half decades as the most comprehensive study of the phenomenon of adolescent gangs ever undertaken.'' This statement still holds today. But Thrasher's work does have its problems. James Bennett (1981, p. 161) agrees that the work offers rich descriptions, but he also identifies many flaws: ''. . . not much information is given about any one gang; there is too little detail about episodes to permit group-process analysis; the study lacks analytic sophistication in holding variables constant; it does not set out to test hypotheses; age differences are not related to other variables; . . . some of the writing has a naïve quality.'' Bennett finds the statistical analyses crude and notes that interpretations of the data do not support Thrasher's causal conclusions. In fact, ''We do not even know how he collected his material; how he chose his informants, or how representative they were'' (Bennett, 1981, p. 161).

Shaw and McKay's contributions may have been outstanding, but each of the other theorists reviewed also offered much-needed incentives for the study of delinquency. In the next chapter, we will continue the historical venture into an era characterized by general, universal *theory* building on crime and delinquency.

The Era of Grand Theory Building

5
CHAPTER

The popular physicist Freeman Dyson (1988) observes that scientists may be divided into two camps: unifiers and diversifiers. Unifiers seek grand, unified models that reduce nature to a finite set of equations or propositions. Examples of unifiers include Einstein, Newton, and Darwin, whose "driving passion was to find general principles which will explain everything. They are happy if they can leave the universe looking a little simpler than they found it" (pp. 44–45). Diversifiers, on the other hand, enjoy exploring details and relish the heterogeneity and diversity of nature. They are happy if they leave the universe a little more complicated than they found it. They believe that the universe is immeasurably complex and forever mysterious. Examples include the British physicist Ernest Rutherford and the mathematician Kurt Gödel.

The same observations may be made about criminologists. Some believe that eventually we will discover or formulate theories so powerful that they explain all deviant or criminal behavior. Others believe that nothing stays the same, that human behavior is resistant to any notion of universal laws and that explanations are inexhaustible. Criminology needs both viewpoints; one balances the other. One overemphasizes unity and abstract structure, foregoing diversity; the other overemphasizes difference and richness of detail to the exclusion of unifying, theoretical structure.

In this chapter we examine the early attempts at formulating universal theories to explain crime and delinquency. The theory building during this era was directed at discovering the universal principles that would explain crime for all persons, independent of cultures and time. In short, this chapter is about the early unifiers involved in the study of delinquency. During this era (1910 to 1940), "proper" science was independent of historical events and social context. In an effort to be "proper," psychology and sociology sought to "discover" abstract, general, and universal principles of behavior. The word "discover" is in quotes because it implies that universal truths exist in nature, waiting to be uncovered. In Chapter 2, we questioned this perspective.

The chapter focuses on the work of Henry H. Goddard, Robert K. Merton, and Edwin H. Sutherland, and, briefly that of Frank Tannenbaum. As we shall see, Goddard was convinced that intellectual deficiency causes crime and delinquency. Merton thought that "strain" between the culture and social structure of a society causes crime and delinquency. Sutherland thought, at first, that crime could be universally explained through conflicts between the values of mainstream society and its subcultures. His theory gradually moved toward a learning perspective, stating that almost all criminal behavior is learned according to the universal principles outlined in his theory of differential association. We begin with the eugenics movement spearheaded—during this era—by Henry H. Goddard.

PSYCHOLOGY AND THE EUGENICS MOVEMENT

During the years 1910 to 1940, most academic psychologists were preoccupied in their laboratories with studying memory, perception, attention, sensory discrimination, association, and learning. They were, in effect, trying to model the well-publicized successes of the physical sciences, believing that the methods that had led to remarkable progress in the physical sciences could be emulated. Furthermore, most experimental-academic psychologists were not interested in the application of psychology to social problems, such as crime and delinquency. They believed that psychology was not advanced enough in its quest for general, universal laws of human behavior to be "given away" to the public. In due time, they reasoned, the fruits of their research would make social contributions, but not until the researchers discovered some basic principles of behavior. Scientific psychology, then, had little to say about contemporary social problems.

Meanwhile, the applied fields of educational, industrial, and clinical psychology were struggling. The small market for psychological services was dominated by psychiatrists and, unfortunately, by charlatans with little or no training. Clinical psychologists with valid credentials and with knowledge to apply were in the minority. Most worked in clinics under the supervisory thumb of psychiatrists. Nearly 80 percent of these clinical psychologists refused or saw no need to join their national professional organization, the American Psychological Association (Napoli, 1981). Moreover, the number of individuals interested in clinical psychology as a field of study was disappointingly small. Henry H. Goddard, writing in 1917, lamented that "Clinical psychology has so far proved of interest to only a very small percentage of the students and teachers of psychology and what is still more to the point, very few of those who are interested in clinical psychology take it seriously" (cited in Napoli, 1981, p. 56).

Finally, academic psychologists considered clinical work menial, done in a subservient role, and most often by women (Napoli, 1981). A 1932 survey revealed that 63 percent of all clinical psychologists in the United States were women. Napoli (1981) speculates about the extent to which academic psychologists did not take clinical psychology seriously because they did not take women seriously.

Thus, the one area where psychology could have made significant contributions to the social problems of crime and delinquency—clinical psychology—was small, unorganized, and under the rule and theoretical leanings of psychiatry. Clinical psychologists were used either as "social workers" or "mental testers," and their opportunities for leadership were limited. Meanwhile, their academic colleagues were in laboratories searching for universal laws of behavior that might be applied to all social problems. It is no wonder, then, that criminologists writing about the early "psychological" perspective see little need to distinguish between psychiatry and psychology. Nor is it surprising that sociologists were able to pry the study of crime from the control of these disciplines.

Goddard: Early Mental Testing and Delinquency

The mainstay of applied psychology during the first few decades of the twentieth century was mental testing. Aptitude and intelligence tests did not suddenly arrive on the scene at the turn of the century, however. We know, for example, that the Chinese used an elaborate system of competitive, civil service exams at least as far back as 3,000 years ago (Dubois, 1970). Still, the development and use of intelligence and aptitude tests became more widespread in this country during the first half of the 20th century than at any other time in human history, and perhaps any time since. Not surprisingly, some of the earliest psychologists were conducting studies and drawing conclusions about delinquent children on the basis of intelligence tests they had administered to them.

The most notable work in this field began in 1905 with the establishment of a research center at the Training School for the Feeble-Minded at Vineland, New Jersey. Henry H. Goddard, a psychologist trained by G. Stanley Hall, was appointed director of the center in 1906. Goddard would soon become the foremost intelligence tester in the United States. The research center, supported by special funding provided by Samuel Fels (a Philadelphia soap merchant and philanthropist) was established specifically to investigate the causes of mental retardation. Under Goddard's zealous leadership, it expanded rapidly to a staff of nine, who tested, observed, and crudely classified the mentally retarded children at Vineland.

Meanwhile, in France, the physician Alfred Binet and his colleague Victor Henri were concentrating upon measuring the "higher psychological processes" they called "intelligence." Binet had been asked by the French Ministry of Public Education to develop a method for identifying children most likely to benefit from public school instruction. In 1905, in collaboration with his colleague Theodore Simon, Binet published the first intelligence test, a scale of 30 items presented in order of increasing difficulty. In 1908 a revised form of the test appeared. It was here that the concept of "mental age" was first introduced. Mental age allows a comparison of each child's test performance to that of other children within his or her particular age group. The mental age and chronological age were then used to compute an intelligence quotient, or IQ.

In 1908 Goddard read a report on the Binet scale and became enthusiastic about its potential for classifying the mentally deficient. He immediately translated the test into English and began to use it at Vineland. He was impressed with its usefulness in diagnosing the intellectual level of the mentally deficient. Soon he began classifying the population at Vineland into three categories, idiots, imbeciles, and morons, based on their intelligence quotients. "Idiots" were those evaluated as unable to develop full speech and with mental ages below what a normal three-year-old can do mentally. Parenthetically, the concept "mental age" was developed by test designers (beginning with Binet) as a standard for interpreting test scores. Originally, it was intended to be a standard of comparison between the test performance of a particular child and the performance of normal children his or her age. However, this approach became confusing, and mental age has come to represent an index of mental performance, calculated by simply adding up the number of items passed, each having a certain number of months' credit. The Vineland label "imbecile" designated those who were unable to master written language and had a mental age between three and seven years. The word "moron" was derived from the Greek word foolish and was reserved for "high-grade defectives." Morons were those who could be trained to function in society and had mental ages between eight and twelve. Americans began calling them "feebleminded" to imply the weakness of their intellect. It is important to note that Goddard always believed that IQ scores reflected a single, innate attribute which could be used as a causal explanation for many of society's woes, including, of course delinquency and crime. Binet never accepted this conceptualization. Goddard thus became a zealous proponent of IQ testing, convinced that he had found the *one* attribute which could help rid society of most of its undesirables.

Genetics, Feeblemindedness and Deviance

Goddard's testing program drew favorable attention, and eventually he turned the Vineland summer school for teachers into a training center for Binet testing. Unfortunately, the graduates of Goddard's summer program had little psychological background and virtually no familiarity with measurement or statistical concepts. The brief and hurried "workshops" failed to equip participants with the necessary caution, knowledge, and professionalism (Dahlstrom, 1985). In a few years, therefore, hundreds of "mental testers" with great enthusiasm but little testing competence were launched toward many facets of American life and numerous institutions.

As these quasi-qualified examiners invaded sectors of society—particularly industry, schools, prisons, and juvenile homes—estimates of the number of feebleminded Americans began to dominate the popular literature. By early 1913, an alarming 283,000 such Americans were said to be "running around freely" without proper supervision (Town, 1913). The fact that many of them were children presented two problems: They were considered prime candidates for delinquency, and they would most likely perpetuate the feebleminded strain well into the future. The examiners did not blame Lombrosian born-criminal proclivities, but rather an inherited mental weakness that rendered feebleminded children highly susceptible to social influences, both good and bad. One of the testers proclaimed, for example, "It cannot be said that such children are vicious or immoral; they are simply an easy prey to any influence in the environment" (Town, 1913, p. 87).

When the testers examined inmates of children's reformatories, they found, probably as they expected, that most delinquents were mentally deficient. For example, 59 percent of the inmates housed in the Girls Industrial Home of Ohio were found to be "feebleminded"; 46 percent of the inmates at the Boys Industrial school were so classified. Similar studies in Illinois, California, and Massachusetts yielded similar results. In Albany, New York, a team of intrepid testers examined local prostitutes and discovered that 54 percent were feebleminded. Statistics like the latter confirmed to the testers that there was a clear link between morality and mental defect.

In 1914 Goddard published *Feeblemindedness: Its Causes and Consequences*, in which he discussed the many studies being conducted on the relationship between intelligence and delinquency. He found the percentages of feebleminded inmates ranged from 28 to 89 percent. He concluded that, overall, about 70 percent of the inmates in reformatories, jails, and prisons across the country were mentally deficient.

Re-examination of the research focusing on the link between mental deficiency and delinquency reveals numerous and significant flaws, something which Goddard himself later acknowledged. L. D. Zeleny, in a sophisticated and penetrating review published in 1933, analyzed 163 separate studies on criminal intelligence which were conducted between 1910 and 1930. A total of 62,000 adult and juvenile offenders had been tested; fully 30 percent had qualified as feebleminded ("morons") or lower. Across the research sample, the figures varied dramatically, ranging from 5.5 percent in a Missouri workhouse to 100 percent in a New York state institution housing women. Zeleny attributed the variations in feeblemindedness to a variability in:

1. standards for what constitutes a feebleminded person; and
2. the kinds of IQ tests used.

Zeleny criticized both Goddard and Lewis Terman for using biased samples of subjects as representatives of the general population. For example, Terman used 1,000 "native" white, California children from city schools in communities of average social status for his standard of the "average" American population. Obviously, comparing these white, urban middle class children with institutionalized delinquent youth is stacking the cards against the latter. It is not surprising that researchers found delinquents tested below the average for the American population in IQ. Later, both Goddard and Terman abandoned their faulty standards of comparison for slightly better ones, but testers and researchers continued to use the old standards. Also, Zeleny found comparisons were often made using different IQ tests and recommended that some IQ test be standardized to be used in the measurement of "criminal intelligence."

Goddard generated even more controversy, however, in his study of hereditary generacy, *The Kallikak Family*, published in book form in 1912. Here, Goddard discussed the family of one of the inmates at Vineland. Goddard had uncovered two distinct branches, each originally sired by a soldier during the Revolutionary War whom he called "Martin Kallikak" (The pseudonym Kallikak was derived from the Greek words for beauty (kallos) and evil (kakos).) One branch was originally germinated from a purportedly feebleminded barmaid whom Kallikak had met in a tavern. The woman eventually gave birth to a son, whom she named Martin Kallikak, Jr. After the war, Martin, Sr. left the army, became a respected and wealthy citizen, and entered into a "suitable" marriage with a woman from a solid Quaker family.

According to Goddard, the marriage between the Quaker woman and Martin, Sr. produced respected, upstanding citizens, who in turn bred and produced more of the same. Martin Sr.'s earlier liaison, however, made him the progenitor of six generations of alcoholics, prostitutes, and others who came into conflict with society's norms. Specifically, in the illegitimate feebleminded line, 143 were regarded feebleminded, 33 were sexual immorals or prostitutes, 24 were alcoholics, 8 were brothel keepers, and 3 were criminals. The union with the Quaker woman, on the other hand, resulted in 496 descendants; only one was mentally deficient, two were alcoholics, and none were criminal. Goddard believed that the explanation for these dramatically opposite features could only be a hereditary one: an innate mental defect had been passed from the barmaid to the first child and continued to be transmitted through the generations.

Goddard was certainly not the first to study the backgrounds of offenders and to conclude that criminality and feeblemindedness were inherited. Dugdale (1877), a member of the New York State prison commission who visited and inspected county jails in that state, was impressed by the fact that six inmates in one county jail were related to each other. He traced the lineage of this family, found more criminals, and determined that they had all descended from six sisters. He estimated that the descendants of this family, whom he called the Jukes, had cost New York state in excess of one million dollars for institutional care.

Goddard's conclusion that feeblemindedness is clearly inherited and was the basic cause of immorality and crime was quoted widely. Everyone with less talent has less virtue, Goddard claimed, and many psychologists and psychiatrists were persuaded. The psychiatrist Walter Fernald (1919) asserted that feeblemindedness was the most important cause of crime, degeneracy, and pauperism. The well-known psychologist Louis Terman argued that the feebleminded were incapable of moral judgments and therefore must be viewed as potential criminals. ". . . all feeble-minded are at least potential criminals. That every feeble-minded woman is a potential prostitute would hardly be disputed by anyone. Moral judgment, like business judgment, social judgment or any kind of higher thought process, is a function of intelligence" (Terman, 1916, p. 11).

Goddard apparently felt he had a mission to protect the American citizenry from contamination. He argued that all feebleminded Americans should be prevented from reproducing so that their weak genes would not be passed on to future generations. Thus, they should be educated to the limits of their capacity and segregated during their reproductive period. Better yet, they should be sterilized. He fervently advocated sterilization laws and was effective in getting them passed in 24 states. Generally, the laws provided for the compulsory sterilization of inmates of taxpayer-supported institutions—mental and correctional—before their release. They gave institution managers the power to sterilize, at their discretion, delinquents, habitual criminals, or anyone guilty of certain offenses, such as rape (Kelves, 1984).

By no means can blame for the sterilization movement be placed squarely on Goddard, however. Eugenics was an extremely popular movement during the first third of the 20th century, both in this country and in Great Britain. Eugenics, a term coined in 1883 by the English scientist Francis Galton (a cousin to Charles Darwin), was a "scientific" enterprise designed to improve the human "stock," primarily by limiting human reproduction of the genetically inferior while encouraging the reproduction of the genetically superior. Proponents of eugenics were instrumental in getting the first sterilization law in the United States passed in 1907 in Indiana. A physician at the Indiana State Reformatory, Harry C. Sharp, had been experimenting with sterilization at least as early as 1899. By 1907, Sharp had performed a total of 465 "voluntary" vasectomies on delinquent boys (Kelves, 1984). Sharp, a strong advocate of sterilization laws, was convinced (and equally convincing to legislators) not only that vasectomies would reduce "sexual overexcitation" in delinquent boys, but quite possibly that salpingectomy might serve the same purpose for delinquent girls.

Between 1907 and 1917, sterilization laws modeled on the Indiana law were enacted in 16 states. The eugenics movement received a boost from the U.S. Supreme Court in 1927, when it supported—with only one Justice dissenting—the sterilization of an allegedly mentally retarded young mother who was herself the daughter of an allegedly mentally retarded woman. "It is better for all the world, if instead of waiting to execute degenerate offspring for crime or let them starve for their imbecility, society can prevent those who are manifestly unfit from continuing their kind . . . . Three generations of imbeciles are enough" (*Buck v. Bell*, 274 U.S.). By 1930, the number of states with sterilization laws had increased to 24. Between 1907 and 1928, about 9,000 individuals had been forcibly sterilized in the United States, and by the late 1930s, lawful sterilizations had increased to nearly 20,000. By 1964, the number of forced, legal sterilizations had burgeoned to well over 60,000 (Lombardo, 1985).

Goddard's views on the damaging effect of feeblemindedness also had an influence on United States immigration policy. Prior to World War I, there were no numerical limitations or geographical restrictions on immigrations to the United States. In 1912 the U.S. Public Health Service invited Goddard to Ellis Island, the central processing place for immigrants, to apply the new mental tests to arriving immigrants. He reported (1913) that based upon his examination, 83 percent of the adult Jews, 80 percent of the Hungarians, 79 percent of the Italians, and 87 percent of the Russians were "feebleminded," with a mental age of 12 or lower, and he recommended that they not be allowed into this country. In 1917 Goddard proudly announced that substantial numbers of feebleminded aliens had been deported on the basis of low intelligence.

In most recent years, critics have strongly questioned the objectivity of Goddard's research. Gould (1981) notes that Goddard's faith in visual identification and diagnosis was virtually unbounded. His method of research rested upon the training of "intuitive women" to recognize the feebleminded by sight. During his study of immigrants, for example, Goddard sent two women to Ellis Island. They were instructed to pick out the feebleminded by sight. Goddard preferred women for this task because he believed they possessed an innate superiority of intuition. For two-and-one-half months, these two women observed and classified immigrants the instant they got off the boat. After this visual classification, they tested with the Binet Scale those whom they suspected were defective. They tested a total of 35 Jews, 22 Hungarians, 50 Italians, and 45 Russians and found feeblemindedness in over three-fourths of them, a figure that surprised even Goddard. Gould urges us to picture

> a group of frightened men and women who speak no English and who have just endured an oceanic voyage in steerage. Most are poor and have never gone to school; many have never held a pencil or pen in their hand. They march off the boat; one of Goddard's intuitive women takes them aside shortly thereafter, sits them down, hands them a pencil, and asks them to reproduce on paper a figure shown to them a moment ago, but now withdrawn from their sight. (Gould, 1981, p. 166)

Could their low scores be due to factors other than innate ability?

A similar procedure had been used in Goddard's Kallikak study. "Intuitive" women, fully aware of the hereditary-immorality hypothesis, visited the families in an effort to reconstruct the lineage. Critics are skeptical about the accuracy of these reconstructions and diagnoses of the mental attributes of both the living and the dead. Moreover, there is little documentation to support the claim that the younger Martin was progenitor of all the offspring of the deviant Kallikak line. If his paternity is not adequately demonstrated, of course, the whole study becomes suspect. Above all, Goddard ignored the possibility that differences in environment might have created some of the disparity between the two Kallikak lineages. What, for example, were the social opportunities of a presumably (but not necessarily) mentally handicapped tavern maid at the turn of the eighteenth century? Under what environmental conditions would her children and their children be raised?

Perhaps most damaging to Goddard's contention of objectivity, however, is the evidence revealed by Gould (1981) of possible "doctoring" of the photographs of members of the Kallikak family. According to Gould, someone (perhaps Goddard himself) had inserted dark lines on the faces of the family members to give them a "depraved look." For example, the Kallikak mouths were made to look sinister, their eyes appear as heavy dark slits, and their general countenance is irregular and bizarre. Gould notes that dark ink was used to achieve these effects. Considering the state of photography at the turn of the century, a bit of ink would not be discernible. Over 70 years later, however, the ink has faded and the retouching is apparent, even to the untrained eye.

Raymond Fancher (1987) disagrees with Gould's interpretation, however. He suggests that these pictures were retouched principally to improve their reproducibility for publication in the book, not to make them look sinister. An alternative explanation, also proposed by Fancher, is that the photographs were altered to protect the privacy of the Kallikaks by disguising their appearance.

Goddard's contributions to the field are looked upon now with both appreciation and embarrassment. On the one hand, he was instrumental in developing a psychological instrument which, properly used, can yield valuable information. On the other hand, his links with the eugenics movement and his crabbed view of social policy are disturbing. Furthermore, if Goddard did support his claims about the Kallikaks with doctored photos, we are led to wonder about other misrepresentations in his data. There is no clear evidence that his intentions were to mislead, however.

Fortunately, psychology has progressed in social and empirical sophistication since the Goddard "theory" about feeblemindedness and crime. Currently, intelligence testing and the concept of IQ are by no means approached in such a simplistic fashion. First, both must be approached with extreme caution, since psychologists are far more conscious of the social, political, and emotional dangers of poorly conceived classification procedures. Second, few psychologists would accept that, even given a valid test, any relationship that might emerge between crime and intelligence is significant without attention to numerous other factors. Finally, many psychologists no longer view intelligence as a static entity, or even a stable personality trait that generalizes across situations. Intelligence is more frequently viewed as a complicated cognitive process dependent upon an array of experience and personal development. It is probably better conceived of as an individualized construct system and personal style strongly influenced by a wide range of factors, especially social ones. We shall return to the topic of intelligence and delinquency in Chapter 7.

A Significant By-product of Eugenics: Statistical Correlation

One of the major contributions of scientists to the study of crime and delinquency was the development of statistical methods to evaluate and make inferences from data. The necessity of making comparisons of physical features of populations and of psychological attributes among various groups led to the advancement of mathematical tools for the social sciences. Increasingly, the study of crime and delinquency has relied on the statistical methods invented and refined by researchers during the first third of the 20th century.

Most influential of this group was Francis Galton, a leader of the eugenics movement in England and well-acknowledged contributor to the mental testing movement. The Belgian astronomer Adolphe Quetelet and others antedated Galton in the application of quasi-statistical procedures, but it was Galton who popularized and improved contemporary statistical methods. Until his contributions, *stat*istics referred specifically to numbers collected by the *state*, such as tabulations of the population, births, marriages, deaths, and trade—numbers governments used to make policy decisions. And it was Galton who developed the most important statistic for criminology: the correlation. The correlation is important because it allows the researcher to look for *relationships* in data instead of cause-and-effect events. Nineteenth century science was in hot pursuit of causal relations (If, then statements) and had little use for statistical probabilities. Furthermore, 19th century scientists focused on one-to-one relationships: Does "A" *cause* "B"? Galton introduced a method for stating the degree to which two variables are *related*, without having to determine that one caused the other. Scientists should now ask, "Are A and B related?"

Galton, a British scientist and statistician, was interested primarily in meteorology (he created the modern technique of weather mapping) and in the study of evolution and genetics. Galton was conducting intensive investigations of heredity, where many attributes were related or connected. For example, the height and body structure of sons appeared to be closely related to those of their fathers, yet father's height and body structure did not "cause" the son's. Galton set out to measure the extent of this relationship in a given sample. At first Galton arranged the heights of fathers and sons on a square chart, with father's on the *x*-axis and son's on the *y*-axis. He then stretched a silk thread diagonally across the center of the chart until he thought the position of thread approximated the middle point of all the data points (Hull, 1928). He would measure the angle by which the thread deviated from the vertical and then look up the tangent of this angle in a table. Since the tangent of a zero angle (angle showing no relationship) is zero, and since the tangent of the angle showing a perfect relationship is 1.00, these numbers made a decent index (or coefficient) of the extent of the relationship.

Galton's concept was promising but his method was awkward. Galton did manage to find "co-relations" between the heights. Moreover, he noted that inherited characteristics tended to *regress* toward the average of the distribution. That is, he observed that tall men are, on the average, not as tall as their fathers, and that sons of very short men are, on the average, taller than their fathers. Put differently, children of extremely tall or short parents *tend* to be closer to the norm of these characteristics than their parent.

Karl Pearson, Galton's promising student and subsequent close friend and colleague, believed his mentor was making things unduly difficult for himself. There should be no need to "eyeball" data and roughly calculate the co-relations. Pearson proceeded to develop the still-used mathematical formula for calculating the correlation coefficient, known as the Pearson product-moment coefficient of correlation or Pearson's *r*. The symbol "*r*" was a tribute to Galton's original discovery of the tendency for "regression" toward the average.

Most of the research studies to be reviewed in this book are correlational. Therefore, it is important that the concept of correlation be clearly understood. A correlation is a statistical term for a relationship between two variables. A variable is essentially anything that can be measured. A correlation tells us two important things about a relationship:

1. the *magnitude* of the relationship; and
2. the *direction* of that relationship.

The more closely related two variables are, the greater the magnitude of the relationship. This magnitude is expressed statistically in numbers. For example, the relationship between juvenile delinquency and IQ might be .25, while the relationship between juvenile delinquency and socioeconomic class (SES) might be .50. Thus, the relationship between SES and delinquency is greater than the one between delinquency and IQ, indicating that SES is a better predictor than IQ. The numbers are obtained through mathematical calculations according to a formula which compares the two variables. Due to the nature of the statistical formula for the correlation, the magnitude will never be larger than 1.00.

Correlation also tells us something about the direction of the relationship. Direction informs us what one variable does if the other variable changes. If the length of the average prison sentence in any given year is increased, does the crime rate decrease? Or does it stay the same, or even increase? Direction is expressed either by a positive (+) sign or a negative (−) sign. If one variable changes and the other changes in the same direction, we have a positive relationship. For example, if length of sentencing decreased and the crime rate also decreased, we would have a positive relationship. However, if length of sentencing increased and crime decreased, this would be a negative relationship. In a negative relationship, as one variable changes, the other variable changes in the opposite direction. When both change in the same direction, whether there is an increase or a decrease, the relationship is positive.

Thus, one relationship might be expressed as −.50 and another one as −.25. The first tells us that the variables are more closely related than the variables in the second relationship (.50 is closer to "perfect" relationship of 1.00 than .30). In both cases, the negative sign informs us that as one variable increases the other decreases. If the sign were positive, we would know that the variables both increased or both decreased. One more thing needs to be mentioned. The correlation of .50 is *not* twice that of .25 in magnitude. The way to determine how much larger one correlation is compared to another is to square both. Thus, the correlation of .50 squared equals .25, while the correlation of .25 squared equals .0625. In this case, the correlation of .50 is *four* times larger than the correlation of .25. The number obtained as a result of this squaring procedure is called the coefficient of determination.

So far we have only talked about the correlation between two variables (e.g., IQ and delinquency). This basic correlation is called a "bivariate correlation," but, with new developments in statistical techniques spurred on by the computer, correlations can be used to measure much more complex relationships, as we shall learn later in the text. There is one crucial point that must be understood about a bivariate correlation. It can help us predict something about one variable if we know the nature of the other one, but it cannot tell us what is causing what. Simply because we know that a low IQ may be related to a high incidence of delinquency, we cannot conclude that low IQ causes delinquency, or that delinquency causes low IQ. A correlation *cannot* provide a cause, although it may suggest one.

Pearson was later to establish the theory of multiple correlation and regression. Factor analysis was soon developed by Godfrey H. Thomson in 1925, refined by Charles Spearman in 1927, and further refined by L. L. Thurstone in 1935, in their search for the many components of intelligence. However, outside of the field of mental testing, these multivariate statistical methods did not find their way into the study of delinquency until Lander's controversial "ecological" investigation of 1954, which will be covered in Chapter 10.

EDWIN H. SUTHERLAND: THE INFLUENCE OF THE WRONG CROWD

Edwin H. Sutherland is regarded by many scholars and students as one of the masters of theory in American criminology. His major contributions include the earliest published research on white collar crime and a comprehensive statement on the etiology of crime known as *differential association theory*. With the publication of the theory, Sutherland opened a new era in American criminology, since his was one of the earliest systematic statements specifically directed at crime (Finestone, 1976a). Shaw and McKay certainly had toyed with a theory, and they are *sometimes* credited with one (e.g., Kobrin, 1959), but they did not formulate a theory that explained or predicted criminal events in any broad or systematic fashion. Other Chicago School sociologists were mainly interested in *descriptions* of ecological factors as they related to crime rates. Psychologists at this time (1930s and 1940s) were occupied with looking for universal principles that would hold for *all* behavior across *all* situations—and they had not found any. Thus, criminal behavior merely represented one of the many human behaviors that needed to be explained.

Sutherland's Personal Background

Sutherland was a graduate of the University of Chicago who had worked primarily with Charles Henderson, Albion Small, and W. I. Thomas of the Chicago School. He received his Ph.D. in 1913 (completing a dissertation on unemployment), and thereafter took a number of teaching jobs at several universities before returning to the University of Chicago in 1929. During these early years, his accomplishments in criminology were unremarkable. At the persistent urging of one his chairmen, he wrote the first edition of the now famous textbook, *Principles of Criminology* (also known as simply *Criminology*) in 1924. This early text did not advance any particular theory, but was instead a compendium of research studies reported by other criminologists throughout the world. In fact, no complete or systematic formulation of Sutherland's theory was ever published while he was alive. His views appeared only in part in a number of scattered papers, book reviews, and in his text *Criminology* (Vold, 1951).

Students who took college courses from Sutherland report that he certainly did not possess a "silver tongue." He was drab and boring as a lecturer (Schuessler, 1973) and would mumble and stare pensively out the window as he talked (Cressey, 1983). At the same time, he was a gentle person who had a knack for pushing students to their intellectual limits. Students found him at his best in small, informal groups in his office, where he sat in his favorite wicker rocking chair. In this environment, he was thoughtful and logical. He was unpretentious, honest, ethical, and loyal to friends, colleagues, and students.

In 1935 Sutherland left Chicago to succeed U. G. Weatherly as head of the department of sociology at Indiana University, a position he held until 1949. During that year, he turned over his administrative duties to conserve his waning energies for writing. He died of a heart attack at age 67 on October 11, 1950.

Sutherland as a Theorist

Sutherland stated his own general theory in a series of propositions that presumably had universal application. He differed from psychologists in his theory-building approach in that he tried to explain criminal behavior, not behavior in general. It should be noted, however, that Sutherland did not believe it was useful to distinguish between juvenile and adult criminal conduct; in his opinion, they followed the same principles of development. Both juvenile and adult criminal behavior were learned by exposure to events and persons conducive to the development of antisocial action.

The year Sutherland returned to Chicago, 1929, he published an article on "Crime and the Conflict Process." The paper is significant because it shows how the issue of "normative conflict" entered into Sutherland's early thinking on the causes of crime. Sutherland observed that modern societies rarely have a clear consensus about what should be the desirable goals of human endeavors or even an agreed-upon means for reaching these goals. Instead, modern societies comprise a wide assortment of social groups with different goals and various strategies for reaching these goals. Thus, a person may find that behavior which is "right" or "proper" in one group may be "wrong" and "improper" in another. These conflicting attitudes and strategies among subcultures are what is meant by "normative conflict." With reference to crime and delinquency, a hodgepodge of norms in a given society increases the likelihood that there will be groups with criminal ideas and strategies. On the other hand, societies that encourage conformity to a limited number of attitudes and beliefs and are not tolerant of "different" ones will have less criminal activity. Thus, Sutherland originally used the concept of normative conflict to account for the different crime rates throughout American society as well as why the United States has such high crime rates compared to other countries of the world.

In 1932, Sutherland, being strongly influenced by the Chicago School, took a closer look at the subcultural concept. He believed that the high crime rates observed by Shaw and McKay and others in the Chicago School could be explained by the overriding impact of America's "public culture" on the newly arriving immigrants. Public culture, he posited, was the conspicuous consumption of material goods and the apparent rapid accumulation of wealth portrayed by the American media. If the advertising media could be believed, most Americans wanted a luxurious standard of life. However, this public culture did not dovetail into reality, or the way most Americans were living. That was what Sutherland called the "private culture." Immigrants, however, did not realize this, because most were physically and socially isolated from the private culture of the settled, traditional areas of the city and its surrounding areas. They saw only what was printed in the newspapers or aired on the radio. This might be news of politicians cheating, gangsters running amok, or images of material goods, excessive competition, and a general disregard for the welfare of human beings. Sutherland reasoned that these American "standards" were in *conflict* with the immigrants' native standards of hard work, honesty, and thrift. The conflict between a family's own values and lifestyle and the "idealized" life portrayed by the media was found to be especially difficult for children of immigrant parents. Delinquency and crime, Sutherland believed, were the products of the pursuit of the elusive American dream of wealth and comfort.

Sutherland's continuing emphasis on culture conflict is reflected in his 1934 (2nd) edition of *Criminology*. He later admitted, however, that he did not realize he had the makings of a theory until his colleague Henry McKay, in a conversation, referred to the "theory" in 1935. Sutherland sheepishly asked McKay what the "Sutherland theory" was. Chuckling, McKay suggested that he read pages 51 and 52 of the 1934 edition. Sutherland hurriedly located the pages and was surprised to find the statement: "The conflict of cultures is the fundamental principle in explanations of crime." McKay's prompt stimulated the evolution of one of the best known (as well as controversial) theories in the field of criminology.

Sutherland had a strong bias against psychiatry, especially the notion that criminal behavior is some form of emotional disturbance or mental illness. He particularly did not like Healy and Bronner's final contention that emotional disturbance is at the root of *most* delinquency. In contrast, Sutherland pushed the idea that criminal behavior is learned, not inherited, and not due to some mental illness. Criminal behavior is learned, as is all social behavior, in interactions with other persons. He also did not take a particular liking to the psychologist John B. Watson's brand of Behaviorism (neither did most psychologists). However, like Watson who perceived the human organism as a passive recipient of the controlling influences of stimuli, Sutherland saw the person as a passive recipient of cultural influences. The social influences of associations with others dictate what one believes and does, according to Sutherland. The decision-making ability, thoughts, and unique cognitive features of an individual were irrelevant to Sutherland as they had been to Watson. "If a person is self-determinative, science is impossible and criminal behavior cannot be explained" (Sutherland, 1973, p. 43).

By the third edition of *Criminology* (1939), Sutherland was well in command of his theory, which he called Differential Association. It was set forth in seven propositions. By 1947 (4th edition), he had refined and extended it to nine propositions, with the core being proposition six: "*A person becomes delinquent because of an excess of definitions favorable to violations of law over definitions unfavorable to violation of law. This is the principle of differential association*" (Sutherland & Cressey, 1974). The term "association" signifies the critical importance that close contacts with others have in determining one's behavior. The term "differential" was introduced to emphasize the importance of a *ratio*, specifically of favorable to unfavorable definitions or contacts. The theory explains that adolescents become delinquents or adults become criminals because their associations with criminal behavior patterns outnumber associations with anti-criminal patterns. Sutherland did *not* postulate that persons engage in criminal conduct because they are simply exposed to criminal behavior patterns. Rather, they become criminals because of an *overabundance* of such associations, in comparison with non-criminal behavior patterns. In other words, the critical aspect of Sutherland's theory is that a higher *ratio* of associations with criminal behavior patterns promotes criminal activity in people. If the association ratio is in reverse (the ratio is in favor of noncriminal patterns over criminal patterns), the person will not be criminal. Thus, criminal behavior depends upon a differential (a ratio) of associations. Furthermore, Sutherland did *not* say that persons become delinquent *only* because of an excess of associations with delinquents. The critical aspect lies in the associations one has with *patterns of behavior*, regardless of the *character* of the person presenting them. Adolescents can learn anti-social conduct from persons who are not criminals or delinquents (even from well-meaning parents) and can likewise learn anti-criminal patterns from criminals and "hard-core" delinquents. A father, for example, may verbalize that it is wrong to break the law, but may display a reckless disregard for the property of others or regularly beat his wife. On the other hand, an individual labeled "delinquent" may demonstrate honesty and integrity in most situations and generally be a "good" model except for rare transgressions.

Sutherland, continually refining his theory, found it necessary to qualify the term "association," since it was excessively broad and vague. A simple, differential ratio of criminal associations over anti-criminal associations is not enough to explain criminal conduct. Therefore, Sutherland proposed that associations vary in their frequency, duration, priority, and intensity. Frequency and duration are self-explanatory, though still not easy to measure. Intensity refers to the prestige and significance of the models with which one associates. The behavior patterns of respected models have more influence (and thus are more "intense" in impact) than those of less respected models. Priority refers to Sutherland's belief that behavior learned in early childhood has more impact on a person's overall conduct than behavior learned later in life.

Let us stop at this point to illustrate the complexity of Sutherland's theory. Consider the case of 6-year-old Preston, who had an excess of associations with the firesetting behavior of his 8-year-old neighbor. Presumably, he would learn from these associations more than from associations with firefighters the following year. On the other hand, we could easily complicate this scenario by supposing that his uncle, to whom he has recently been introduced and whom he idolizes, happens to be a firefighter. Can this new intense association with noncriminal behavior patterns outweigh the earlier frequent associations? What appeared to be intuitively sensible has now become a Gordian knot.

Critics have identified a variety of similar problems of vagueness in Sutherland's theory. In answer, he noted that criminal or delinquent behavior is not always a result of excessive associations with criminal patterns; it may also be influenced by "opportunity." There are unexpected times when a person may be pushed toward criminal action, even without a high ratio of criminal to anti-criminal associations. Jock, a "good" 14-year-old with nary a police contact, visits his cousin Jay for a week. One evening, along with a group of Jay's cohorts, the cousins notice that a store is unattended. Jock steals a $622 Walkman and ends up in juvenile court. On the other hand, a delinquent with a strong propensity toward criminal action as a result of numerous associations with criminal patterns may not have the opportunity to engage in criminal conduct. Thus, in some cases, differential association is not a "sufficient" explanation for criminal behavior.

In keeping with the Zeitgeist ("spirit of the time" or fad) of grand theory building, Sutherland had ambitions to develop this theory of associative ratios into a mathematical model or formula that would allow precise prediction (Sutherland, 1956). In this vein, he was thinking along the same lines as the pioneering psychologists Clark L. Hull and Kurt Lewin who, during these same years, were convinced that, with enough research data, they would soon discover the universal mathematical laws that bind humans to the rest of the universe. However, the ambitious search for mathematical models and grand, universal theories of human conduct lost popularity and really never got off the ground. But Sutherland throughout his professional career continued to search for the universal principles behind criminal behavior.

Differential Association Theory has been criticized most often for its overall vagueness and its use of unclearly defined terms and concepts. Even the current spokesperson for the theory, Donald R. Cressey, once admitted (1960, p. 3): "The current statement of the theory of differential association is neither precise nor clear." The theory's lack of clarity and precision makes empirical investigations nearly impossible to carry out, although researchers have attempted to test it. Although the proposition that criminal behavior is learned has appeal, researchers have found it difficult to measure frequency, duration, intensity, and priority of associations. We are not even certain precisely what "intensity" or "priority" means. Still, differential association theory continues to hold much interest and prominence among students of crime and delinquency.

ROBERT K. MERTON: STRAIN AND ANOMIE

Robert K. Merton was one of the earliest American sociologists *not* affiliated with the Chicago School to make major contributions to the field of crime and delinquency. Merton received his Ph.D. from Harvard in 1936 and spend most of his professional career on the faculty of Columbia University. His contributions to sociology were multiple and diverse and hardly restricted to the sociology of deviance. In some circles, Merton is regarded as the father of modern sociology, because of his pioneering work on the relationship between empirical evidence and theory. His early work on science in 17th century England—the topic of his Ph.D. dissertation—was well received and helped earn him a position at Columbia in 1941, where he remained until his retirement in 1979. Merton was instrumental in making Columbia's sociology department one of the best known in the country and sociology a more scientific and thoughtful discipline. For our purposes, we are most concerned with a paper published in 1938, "Social Structure and Anomie," which was to become the most cited (and reprinted) article in the sociology of deviance.

Merton was born in 1910 and grew up in a South Philadelphia slum. His parents were immigrants from Eastern Europe, not unlike those immigrants who were subjected to intense scrutiny by early sociologists of the Chicago School. His father barely made a living by alternating between carpentry and truck driving. Merton, the younger of two children, was an immigrant child; he was also a faithful gang member. Had the family lived in Chicago, Merton may well have qualified as a "juvenile delinquent" in the Shaw and McKay descriptions being published around that same time. Nevertheless, he was different from his peers in one important aspect: he was an avid reader. As early as age 8, he was a regular visitor to the neighborhood public library. He eventually developed an interest in philosophy and matriculated at Temple University, where he was strongly influenced by the sociologist George E. Simpson. Merton decided to pursue a graduate degree and make sociology his career.

Merton was in graduate school during the American Depression. Because of his background, he was a sensitive observer of the plight of the disadvantaged during these years. He noted a wide discrepancy between the ''American dream'' and the realistic opportunity for the disadvantaged to reach that dream. Since he was well read and acquainted with the work of European social theorists, it was not surprising that Merton looked there for some guidance in explaining what was happening to American society.

Merton as a Theorist

Merton was drawn to the concept of ''anomie'' described by the French sociologist Emile Durkheim. Like the Austrian psychiatrist Sigmund Freud, Durkheim believed that humans are born with intense, biological desires which must be held in check by society. He was convinced that people are incapable of controlling or limiting their biological needs without society's help and controls. Without social controls, an individual's desires expand until he or she aspires to everything and is satisfied with nothing. Thus, when social controls are weak or non-existent, individual needs run rampant, and chaos and normlessness result. Durkheim labeled this state of affairs ''anomie.''

While Merton liked some of the ingredients in the concept of anomie, he rejected Durkheim's view of human nature. He did not believe that people are driven by innate impulses and desires. He believed that one's wants and goals in life are acquired as a result of living in a given society. Culture, not biology, determines an individual's behavior. Culture sets the individual's goals and designates the appropriate means of achieving them. Thus, while Durkheim's positions viewed humans as driven by innately programmed, physiological needs, Merton's suggested that humans follow the values and opportunities set forth by a given society. In other words, Durkheim thought humans had a propensity to ''sin''; Merton identified society as the facilitator of ''sin.'' Furthermore, Merton's theory was proposed primarily as an explanation of *utilitarian, profit-oriented* crime and delinquency. It did *not* purport to explain violent crime, sexual crime, or other crimes such as drug abuse, although it can account for these crimes to some extent. In addition, the theory tried to account for deviant behavior at the larger cultural or societal level and not at the individual or family level. In this sense, Merton's theory is more concerned with predicting and explaining delinquency *rates* and *distributions* than with why certain individuals engage in criminal conduct. The theory's strength lies in its ability to explain why utilitarian crime rates are so high in one society (e.g., the United States) and so low in another (e.g., England), not why John burglarizes and Tom does not.

Merton posited that deviance (including crime and delinquency) occurred when there was a discrepancy between the values and goals cherished and held in high esteem by a society and the availability of the legitimate means for reaching these cultural goals. If, for instance, a society communicated to its members that the accumulation of wealth was paramount, but offered few acceptable ways for everyone to do so, "strain" would develop. Groups experiencing this strain would be inclined to violate norms and thus contribute to anomie.

Merton—probably ever mindful of his childhood experiences—was disenchanted with American culture, its emphasis on the goals of economic success, and its persuasive communication that all the symbols representing wealth should be valued. Merton believed that while American society myopically and fanatically pushed economic success, it failed to provide means for everyone to reach these goals. Good jobs and education, for example, simply were not available to everyone. For many who were economically disadvantaged, the only means to success was illegitimate conduct.

Merton's "strain" theory was formulated when he was only 26. Believing that his youth would be a liability in getting his ideas accepted by the academic community, he waited two years, until 1938, before publishing his theory. He chose to do so through the vehicle of a short essay in the *American Sociological Review*. While it received considerable immediate attention, it was not an instant success. First, Merton was an unknown in the field of sociology. Second, the theory seemed too neat and simple to have much validity. Thus, the paper that eventually would be a classic in the field was ignored or dismissed upon its first publication.

Merton's strain theory would remain dormant until he published a revision of it in 1949, at which point it received much attention. A number of explanations for this delayed influence have been offered. Cole (1975) remarked that the later version was better developed and more clearly written. Therefore, many sociologists and criminologists may have found it more convincing and exciting than its precursor. Cole believes that the primary reason for the theory's rejuvenation, however, was the intellectual climate in the 1930s and 1940s, which was not ripe for a full-blown theoretical explanation of crime that blamed the cultural fabric of American society. In the 1950s, juvenile delinquency suddenly emerged as a pressing problem and answers were sought from all quarters. In a sense, Merton's strain theory was rediscovered.

The theory became more polished and refined with time, but the original essay continues to reflect the essence of Merton's concept of strain. Nonetheless, Merton did change his approach, and it is of some importance that we note the differences in the two publications. While the discrepancy between cultural goals and means for achieving them accounted for strain in the 1938 version, Merton (1957) in his later work clearly distinguished between *culture* and *social structure*, culture being the goals and values taught by society and social structure being the norms, resources, and social networks that regulate our behavior. In other words, culture refers to what we believe is important and desirable, while structure refers to the opportunity to act on it. According to Merton, members of the lower class had acquired the beliefs, but were not provided with legitimate opportunities. The important aspect, then, is the interaction between culture and structure. For example, a society may overemphasize the goal of wealth (culture), but limit its attainment (structure). If the social structure of the society allows people to strive legitimately toward the cultural goals, strain will be unlikely. However, social structure offers differential access to opportunities for the legitimate pursuit of culturally prescribed goals. The various positions in a social structure carry distinct sets of activities, roles, resources, and links to other positions. A lower position may preclude attainment of these goals. The appetites are culturally induced, but social structure either acts as a barrier or as an open door. If it is a barrier, it engenders strain and ultimately produces deviance and delinquency. All of the foregoing was at least implicit in Merton's first paper (as suggested by its title).

Thomas Bernard (1987a) recently wrote an interesting commentary concerning the culture and structure distinction inherent in Merton's theory. He posits that the *cultural* aspect focuses upon both the value of monetary success and the importance of using legitimate means in pursuing that value. A society that overemphasizes monetary success while underemphasizing legitimate ways of achieving this success, is more likely to have higher rates of profit-oriented crime than one that emphasizes both. In other words, a society that greatly values material attainment while "looking the other way" when its members obtain it through illegal ways obviously is bound to have a very high incidence of utilitarian crime. The second component in the theory, of course, is the *structure* of a particular society, or the available opportunity to acquire material success. According to Bernard, "strain" is most likely to occur, therefore, when a society or culture is characterized by three things:

1. overemphasis on monetary success;
2. underemphasis on adhering to legitimate means of acquisition;
3. uneven or "unfair" distribution of legitimate opportunities.

In 1949, Merton also refined the concept of expectations. Crime and delinquency are not generated simply by a lack of opportunity or by an exaggerated emphasis on economic success. Groups must expect or hope to improve their status and achieve cultural goals; if not, there is no strain. Thus, in rigidly stratified societies where one's status was clearly delineated and etched in stone, there was little if any strain, no hope for change, and consequently little crime or delinquency. In open class societies, on the other hand, where there was hope to change one's status and wealth level, strain was a fact of life. Furthermore, socioeconomic classes differed in the degree of strain: Upper and middle classes normally showed little strain, but lower classes, where there was hope and expectation of wealth attainment, exhibited considerable strain. In sum, strain occurs when there is a discrepancy between socially induced aspiration level and expectations.

One of the more interesting and most commented upon aspects of Merton's strain theory was his suggestion that individuals differed in their acceptance of society's view of goals and means. According to Merton, there were five possible strategies or modes of adaptation: conformity, retreatism, ritualism, rebellion, and innovation. The five forms appeared in both his 1938 paper and his later work.

Merton believed that most individuals accept, and therefore conform to, both the goals advocated by society and the means to achieve them. He suggested that if this conformity did not occur, the stability and continuity of society would be threatened. *Conformity*, then, is the rule rather than the exception. *Retreatism*, the rejection of both goals and means, is the least common strategy. Individuals who rely on this form of adaptation are considered aliens within a given society. Merton gave as examples the emotionally disturbed, vagrants, vagabonds, tramps, alcoholics, and drug addicts. *Ritualism* occurs when a person accepts the means but rejects the goals because they are beyond reach. In Merton's view, many law-abiding citizens go through the motions: They work hard but believe that certain goal attainment is impossible. *Rebellion* occurs when a person rejects both the means and the goals of the social mainstream and replaces them with new ones. "Rebels" deviate from the social mainstream perspective and try to introduce a "new social order."

The fifth mode of adaptation, *innovation*, was to Merton the most relevant to the study of crime and delinquency, since innovative persons very often engage in criminal conduct. They have accepted the cultural emphasis on success, but not the prescribed norms for reaching it. The innovative person rejects institutional or approved practices, but retains the culturally induced goals. This is most likely to occur when the person has little access to conventional means for attaining such success. Innovative individuals, therefore, adopt unapproved means, such as theft or burglary.

Violence occurs as a result of anger and frustration over lack of opportunity to fulfill the American dream. Such people are angry about being blocked from attaining widely prized aspirations by the existing structure of society. In effect, angry, frustrated individuals can adopt any of the five modes of adaption outlined by Merton.

Strain theory is a comprehensive statement intended to explain most profit-oriented crime at the culture or societal level. The strongest challenges to Merton's position revolve around frequent research findings that there are no significant differences in rates of deviant behavior between lower class and middle class people (Cole, 1975). Merton's theory is essentially a class-based theory of crime. He assumed that official crime statistics accurately portrayed the amount and class distribution of criminal offenses, and, since the lower socioeconomic class was greatly overrepresented in these official statistics, it experienced the greatest pressure toward anomie. According to Stephan Cole (1975), had Merton looked upon anomie as a feature of the entire society, creating high rates of deviance across society, most of the criticisms directed at his theory would have been avoided.

Merton's anomie theory has not been tested adequately. Cole (1975) carefully examined the available sociological research and found exceedingly few investigations that actually test the Merton theory. If anything, researchers and authors use Merton's theory to support their own version of research data or to legitimize their own work. Researchers today too often collect data first and then find a theory that fits it. Ironically, Merton himself strongly advocated that theory and hypotheses come first, and that they then be tested through data collection.

Thomas Bernard (1987a) agrees that Merton's theory has not been adequately examined, but for different reasons. Bernard contends that the few investigators testing the theory have examined the individual variables of "frustration" when they should have been focusing upon cultural and societal variables. As you recall, Merton's theory was specifically developed to account for differences in profit crime between groups, cultures, and societies. Individuals who participate in profit crimes, Bernard tells us, are not necessarily frustrated or thwarted in their attempts to reach material success. "... (P)eople in Merton's theory who are deprived of legitimate opportunities would resort to illegitimate opportunities *even if they were not frustrated*" (Bernard, 1987b, p. 219).

Robert Agnew (1987) disagrees with this interpretation, however. He argues that Merton's strain theory, as all strain theories, is built upon the basic assumption that individual frustration is the main reason for profit crime and delinquency. "These theories, in particular, all assert that social conditions in the United States prevent many individuals from achieving their goals. This goal blockage is frustrating, and, this frustration, in turn, plays a central role in the generation of delinquency rates and/or delinquent subcultures" (Agnew, 1987, p. 281). Thus, testing Merton's strain theory with individual variable measures is, according to Agnew, legitimate.

The debate underscores the importance of understanding what level of explanation one is aiming at. Are we trying to explain cultural differences in delinquency rates or to explain why a particular individual vandalizes and another does not? We will return to this issue in later chapters. We will also return to different versions of strain theory later, especially in Chapter 9, where we discuss Albert Cohen's theory, Richard Cloward and Lloyd Ohlin's theory, and the influence of peer groups in general.

FRANK TANNENBAUM: RUDIMENTS OF LABELING THEORY

In 1938, the same year that Merton published his theory on anomie and deviance, Frank Tannenbaum, a history professor also at Columbia University, published *Crime and the Community*. This book set the stage for contemporary labeling or social reaction perspective, which will be discussed in detail in Chapter 7. Tannenbaum, a colorful character who once crossed Mexico on a burro, received a Ph.D. in economics from the Brookings Institute in 1927 with a dissertation on Mexican land reform. Although he was soon to become a leading expert on Latin American history and politics, his scholarly interests were diversified and multidisciplinary.

Tannenbaum had a deep and enduring interest in criminology and criminal justice and was a compassionate proponent of prison reform, a fact which might be traced to a personal experience. In 1914, at the age of 21, he was convicted of disturbing the peace following an act of civil disobedience. Tannenbaum had led a group of homeless and hungry men into several churches for shelter (and public attention). He spent one year in a prison on Blackwell's Island, New York, where he befriended a number of inmates. The experience attuned him to the injustices of the criminal justice system. Throughout his professional career, he spoke and wrote often about the need for prison reform. He was especially concerned about conditions of prisons in the U.S. South and the treatment administered by prison officials therein. He had a lifelong concern for the plight of the American black and the very poor white. In 1947, he wrote a powerful book, *Slave and Citizen, The Negro in the Americas*. Interestingly, Branch Rickey, manager of the then Brooklyn Dodgers, once commented that Tannenbaum's book was influential in his decision to hire Jackie Robinson as the first black to play major league baseball.

It was Tannenbaum's 1938 book, *Crime and the Community*, which contained the seeds of the labeling perspective. In it, he argued that the proper study of crime and delinquency was not the behavior itself but society's reaction to it. He maintained that once individuals were "tagged" or labeled deviants or delinquents, others began to see them as such and treat them accordingly. The reactions of these others became the primary source of the individual's conduct. "The process of making the criminal, therefore, is a process of tagging, defining, identifying, segregating, describing, emphasizing, making conscious and self-conscious; it becomes a way of stimulating, suggesting, emphasizing, and evoking the very traits that are complained of . . . the person becomes the thing he is described as being" (Tannenbaum, 1938, p. 19–20). Tannenbaum believed that initially, children were involved merely in mischief, but that some were labeled "bad" as a result. These children then came to see themselves as bad and to take on the role behaviors associated with "badness."

This process, which he called "the dramatization of evil," was a slow and gradual one, and represented the transformation of an offender's self-identity as a doer of mischief (typical of many adolescents) to a doer of evil. As the community's definition of a person changed from one who occasionally misbehaved to one who was a delinquent, so the person's own definition changed. Eventually, he or she came to believe that he or she was basically an evil person, quite possibly beyond salvation. Furthermore, all behavior came under suspicion. The child became defiant and escaped the community, physically or psychologically, often joining a youth gang.

Tannenbaum also believed that the motives of the taggers were irrelevant. In a slap at the benevolent reformers of the day, he noted that those who wanted to reform were just as dangerous as those who wanted to punish. His solution was to refuse to dramatize the evil of the one person, whom Tannenbaum argued was responding normally to the demands of a group. The solution was to change the habits, interests, attitudes, and ideals of the group. "The first dramatization of 'evil' which separates the child out of his group for specialized treatment plays a greater role in making the criminal than perhaps any other experience" (Tannenbaum, 1938, p. 19).

Again, a more systematic presentation of the labeling perspective will appear in Chapter 7. It is important to note that during this era of grand theory building, Tannenbaum laid the cornerstone for contemporary approaches.

SUMMARY AND CONCLUSIONS

In this chapter we reviewed the major attempts to formulate universal, "grand" theories of crime and delinquency that were tried during the period 1910 to 1940. Goddard and the eugenics movement argued that genetic transmission of inferior human qualities was the root of our crime problem. Sterilization and birth control was the advocated solution. This "inferior genes" hypothesis, although very popular during the first third of the 20th century, has lost its following in modern times.

Sutherland's theory of differential association and Merton's strain theory are two of the most often cited and debated theories in criminology today. Both were attempts to construct a universal theory of criminal or deviant behavior. Both theories perceive humans as passive pawns, manipulated and controlled by culture. Merton presupposes that cultures dictate what is important in life and humans dutifully try to follow, even when the means to reach these social goals are unavailable. Sutherland presupposes that humans follow the dicta of their association ratios, like computerized robots. If your associations with others result in an "excess" of messages favorable to criminal behaviors over noncriminal behaviors, you are destined for criminal activity.

General, universal theories of human activity are, by necessity, highly abstract because they try to account for so many social phenomena. With abstraction comes vagueness and confusion. Both theories have been bombarded with heavy criticism for their lack of clarity in their terms and concepts, and ambiguity in their hypotheses (see Kornhauser, 1978; Davis, 1975). Attempts at direct empirical tests of these theories have been unsuccessful, primarily because of their susceptibility to multiple interpretations. We will continue to refer to the Merton and Sutherland theories throughout the book. Goddard will receive only passing comment. Tannenbaum will be discussed in conjunction with labeling theory in Chapter 7.

There is serious question whether it is even possible to construct universal theories of human behavior. If there is a single invariant law of social science, "it would be that human nature and customs (society) change, not all at once but by degrees and over a long period of time. People change, societies change, ideas and language change, so that everything is ultimately in flux" (Rosnow, 1978, p. 1323). "Change" is what is meant by the term "process" in the social sciences and is an integral part of the entire enterprise. Universal theories of human behavior must account for changes across time or else they are not meaningful outside their own historical context. The Merton, Goddard, Tannenbaum, and Sutherland theories of human behavior may be prisoners of their own time, useful for understanding the social context in which they were developed but limited for understanding crime in other times and places. Theories of criminology and delinquency may be human constructions of events occurring at one point in time within a particular culture.

Beyond the historical and cultural questions that universal theories of human behavior must answer, they must also account for the different systems that are in constant interaction. Beginning in the next chapter, we shall look at what social systems are and how they can help us understand delinquent behavior.

Social Systems and Delinquency

6
CHAPTER

The previous three chapters summarized the major developments in delinquency theory and research until just past the middle of the 20th century, at which point academic interest in the study of crime and delinquency intensified. The task of the remainder of the book is to gather together this contemporary work and to organize it in some meaningful fashion. Accordingly, the text will now reflect much more clearly the social systems approach alluded to in Chapter 1, since social systems theory provides a useful framework for organizing the mass of available data.

SOCIAL SYSTEMS THEORY

Systems theory has adherents in a variety of disciplines spanning the natural and social sciences. As noted earlier, the biologist Ludwig von Bertalanffy (1968) is credited with developing the most comprehensive systems approach. Currently, social systems theory is particularly well articulated by the developmental psychologist Urie Bronfenbrenner. It is Bronfenbrenner's approach, slightly modified to include an individual perspective, that will be used throughout the remainder of the text. We chose the Bronfenbrenner model because it is based on human development, and juvenile delinquency is, after all, at least in part, a developmental problem. Second, the model is highly compatible with interactionism, a perspective that describes the mutual and ongoing influence of the environment on the individual and the individual on the environment. We will refer to interactionism frequently throughout the remainder of the book.

It is important to recognize that there are many formulations and variants of systems theory, however. Sociologists are displaying one variant when they refer to micro- and macroanalyses. Microanalysis focuses on explanations of behavior at the individual or psychological level. Motivation, socialization, attachment, and learning are all concepts that involve microanalysis. Macroanalysis concentrates on collective behavior, the patterns of large groups, or social institutions. *Social structure* is a key concept in this approach. Studies examining social class, socioeconomic status, anomie, value conflict, social disorganization, and social ecology are examples of macroanalysis. While microanalysis might focus on the individual attributes of delinquents, macroanalysis is more concerned with the big picture—the time, space, and social context of delinquent behavior. To understand crime and delinquency, is it more helpful to develop theory at the micro level or the macro level? Criminologists differ in their response. Furthermore, there is current debate over whether theories developed at the two levels can be combined. There are those who argue that they should be (e.g., Elliott, Ageton, and Canter, 1979; Elliott, 1985; Pearson and Weiner, 1985). Others insist that cross-level integration is not possible (e.g., Hirschi, 1979, 1987; Short, 1979). This text adopts the view that, at least for the present, information obtained from research at different levels of analysis cannot be integrated into one grand theory of delinquency. However, delinquency can and should be researched at different levels, and the resultant knowledge applied to an overall understanding. Furthermore, relationships among the different levels are a promising area of exploration, as will be noted soon.

Psychologist Urie Bronfenbrenner (1979, 1986b) has outlined a social systems theory which has considerable relevance for the study of delinquency. Bronfenbrenner specifically applied his ideas to research in child development. Those psychological explanations which view delinquency within a developmental context, then, such as the moral development theories that will be discussed in Chapter 7, seem most obviously in tune with Bronfenbrenner. However, his theory is also relevant to all human behavior within any social environment as well as to the social environments themselves. Systems theory can comfortably accommodate a wide range of perspectives, from those which argue that delinquency is a result of unique, individual factors to those which indict the structure of society as a whole.

Microsystems

Bronfenbrenner's view of the social environment is more complex than the view of those who discuss the relative merits of micro- and macroanalysis. He conceives of society as a set of nested structures, which are called ''systems'' because they involve interrelationships and mutual, ongoing influences. The nested systems exist at different levels of abstraction, from the concrete to the general. Each requires a different level of analysis. Families, schools, neighborhoods, cities, nations, and the world all exist at increasingly larger or more abstract *levels of description*. The immediate setting, which contains the person, is called a *microsystem*. It is, to Bronfenbrenner, the smallest unit for social analysis. Microsystems are patterns of activities, roles, and interpersonal relations that take place within settings *directly* experienced by an individual. Each person is an active participant in his or her microsystems, which include his family, her anthropology class, her juvenile gang, his poker group. The microsystem consists of how the person acts and reacts to others within these groups. The microsystems also contain "subsystems," such as how Lucia reacts to her twin brother or Larson to his bridge partner.

An important phrase contained in the definition of microsystem is "experienced by an individual." Bronfenbrenner (1979, p. 22) states:

> The term [experienced] is used to indicate that the scientifically relevant features of any environment include not only its objective properties but also the way in which these properties are perceived by the persons in that environment . . . Very few of the external influences significantly affecting human behavior and development can be described solely in terms of objective physical conditions and events; the aspects of environment that are most powerful in shaping the course of psychological growth are overwhelmingly those that have meaning to the person in a given situation.

By implication, if we are to understand delinquent behavior, or any human behavior, we must appreciate how different people perceive, interpret, and reconstruct their environments. While social pressures and influences are critically important, so too are the personal interpretations of those pressures and influences.

Mesosystems

Also important in Bronfenbrenner's scheme are interrelationships among microsystems. The child does not remain within the family microsystem; he or she goes to school, to the homes of relatives and friends, to grocery stores, to amusement parks. Each of these settings influences the child, and they in turn are influenced by him or her. Bronfenbrenner calls these *interrelationships* between microsystems *mesosystems*.

Thus, a wider social environment must always be kept in mind when considering the child and his or her family, since what goes on beyond its immediate boundaries invariably affects and is affected by what transpires within it. Consider, for example, how the safety of a neighborhood playground can influence the freedom parents grant their children in playing there, away from their careful supervision. Child rearing practices, in turn, affect how the child approaches other children in the neighborhood playground.

Mesosystem models, then, take into account the joint effects of processes occurring within and between two or more settings, in each of which the developing person is an active participant (Bronfenbrenner, 1986b). In essence, a mesosystem is a system of microsystems, or a network of relationships among our microsystems. Bronfenbrenner argues that for too long researchers interested in child development have concentrated upon microsystems without commenting on the relationships among them.

Exosystems

He introduces still another concept, that of *exosystems*. These are systems beyond the micro- and mesosystems that affect one's development, feelings, thoughts, and actions, even though one may not directly participate in them. Exosystems include a least one setting that does not directly involve the person as an active participant. For example, what happens at the parent's place of work has considerable impact on the child at home, even if the child never visits that workplace or has direct contact with it. Research by Melvin L. Kohn (1977) illustrates this point very well. It indicates that the type of work engaged in by the father may strongly influence the development of everyone within the home (e.g., Kohn, 1977). For instance, Kohn found that occupations allowing considerable freedom and personal autonomy seem to have a significantly different impact on parenting styles than occupations requiring conformity and personal constraints. Specifically, working class men whose jobs involved compliance with authority tended to demand unquestioning obedience on the part of their children. On the other hand, middle class fathers who held jobs encouraging self-direction and independence expected similar behaviors in their children. This is a good illustration of the influence of an exosystem on lower level systems, particularly the family. Of course, the fathers may have done some self-selection of their own by choosing the nature of the work, independent of any major influences of the job on the father's personality or family style. More likely, though, the situation is likely to be bidirectional. The father does some selecting and influencing, and the work system influences the father and his role at home.

The amount of outside social supports (such as friends, relatives, adequate health care, social guidance) the family receives strongly influences the home microsystem. A child may never meet the members of his parent's alcoholics anonymous group, but what happens to the parent there ultimately affects the parent-child relationship. James Garbarino (1976) suggested an association between maternal child abuse and the degree to which mothers receive adequate social support in parenting—the less adequate the social support, the higher the probability of abuse. The Garbarino research is intriguing to those who believe that child abuse is a predictor of delinquency and crime.

Neighborhoods also qualify as exosystems (as well as a microsystem) according to Bronfenbrenner's scheme. The neighborhood as a whole, with its many clusters of groups, represents the larger exosystem. However, peer groups or gangs within a neighborhood—say the youth corps or the Sharks or the Jets—represent microsystems if one is a direct participant in them. Although the person is not an active participant in all their settings, what happens in them inevitably affects his or her life. Ever since the pioneering work of Burgess and Shaw and McKay, criminologists have recognized the importance of the neighborhood in the development of crime and delinquency. The ecological perspective to this day points to the robust relationship between deteriorated residential areas and rates of delinquency. The neighborhood, therefore, represents another level of analysis in the systems approach that cannot be neglected in any explanation of delinquency.

Social environments do not allow for neat, distinct boundaries. They often merge and overlap. As we mentioned previously, a neighborhood is a microsystem to the extent that it constitutes our immediate environment. A neighborhood may also constitute an exosystem to the extent that it does not make up our immediate environment and we do not interact directly with it. Yet, the neighborhood as a *whole* may affect our lives, such as by defining the value of our property or the degree to which we feel safe from crime.

Macrosystems

At an even higher level of analysis, Bronfenbrenner suggests clusters of interrelated exosystems that form *macrosystems*. In Bronfenbrenner's scheme, macrosystems are the social institutions and associated ideologies that pervade major segments of society or permeate the society as a whole. They are the belief and value systems of the larger society. Boys are supposed to do this, and girls are supposed to do that. Little boys are not masculine in pink. Little girls should not punch and fight. Hence, sex differences in behavior, as an aggregate variable across American culture, represent a component of the macrosystem. Social class is also a component of the macrosystem. However, sex and social class data are useful but hardly sufficient. By themselves, they only provide hints at the underlying *processes* operating among people. The limitations of ''social structure variables'' will become obvious as we move along in the text. The macrosystem is not a static system as portrayed by social structure conceptualizations, but is a dynamic system susceptible to significant and novel transformations.

It will be necessary in the course of the material on delinquency to divide the macrosystem into additional categories because we will encounter different geographical and social systems beyond the level of the local community. That is, the delinquency pattern found within a particular city may represent one level of analysis (intracity), while intercity comparisons may require another level of analysis. Comparing state or country patterns represents yet another level of analysis.

Chronosystems

Bronfenbrenner (1986a) revised his model to add another system, the *chronosystem*. He found this necessary to account for the obvious changes that occur in *time* across all four systems just outlined. Historically, developmental psychologists have treated the passage of time as synonymous with chronological age. In current research designs, time appears not merely as an attribute of the developing person but also as a property of the surrounding environment (Bronfenbrenner, 1986b). Neighborhoods change, communities change, cities change, and cultures change. The school environment is different in September than it is in June. First borns experience a different home environment when later children are born. A child's adjustment to school, for example, is affected by events that occur on an apprehensive first day (microsystem), the death of his mother (mesosystem, representing the relationship between home and school), the fact that his father suddenly becomes unemployed (exosystem), or the society that becomes torn by racial hatred (macrosystem). Each person's life course involves numerous transitions that accumulate and interact to have an impact on his or her emotions, cognitions, behaviors, and overall perceptions of the social world at any given point in time. Bronfenbrenner distinguishes between two types of chronosystems: those that most people experience (normative) and those that are unexpected (non-normative). Normative chronosystems include school entry, puberty, entering the labor force, marriage, retirement. Examples of non-normative chronosystems include a death, a severe illness in the family, divorce, moving, and winning the sweepstakes. Non-normative events may have decidedly different effects on one's life and the people within that life than normative events.

It is important to keep in mind that some of the controversy in theory and empirical research we shall review may stem from the confusion surrounding what system is being defined or explained. Delinquency patterns gleaned from large collections of aggregate data across nations—macrosystems—are apt to provide a different picture than delinquency patterns gathered at the neighborhood or exosystem level. Macrosystem analysis offers different clues about delinquency than microsystem analysis. For example, part of the controversy between the strengths and weaknesses of the SR method and official statistics is that SR data are gathered at the individual level by asking individuals their *perceptions* about their involvement in crime. Official statistics are collected from agencies and large organizations across a wide cross section of society. These methods approach the issue from two different levels, requiring different perspectives. In this sense, whether self-report data support official data may not be all that important.

Individual Systems

Bronfenbrenner's basic framework does not conceptualize the individual as a system within him or herself. This is a significant omission. We have adjusted his theory, therefore, and added an *infrasystem*, where personal constructs, beliefs, or schema interact with temperament and genes to form a "personality." "Whatever else personality may be, it has the properties of a system" (Allport, 1961, p. 109). The personal system changes and continually interacts with higher level systems, particularly the microsystems and mesosystems. It is sometimes tempting to conclude that social environments dictate who we are or what we do. Yet it is not wise to overlook the fact that each person has a personal version of the world, conceptualized and organized in a unique way. The environment provides us with information and experience, but how these are integrated and stored is itself a system. It is premature then, to attribute most behavior to either social or individual factors. Failure to recognize either component or a tendency to assume that one overrides the other leaves an incomplete picture of delinquency and how it develops.

If we are to understand juvenile delinquency and construct and implement effective policy to deal with it, we must approach its study in a way that recognizes the multiple social systems impinging on each human life. Sociologist Albert J. Reiss, Jr. writes: "If our understanding of crime and criminal behavior and its control is to advance, governmental data collection and scholarly research must be designed to collect individual, organizational, and community-level information" (1986, p. 27). Elsewhere, Charles

Wellford (1987, p. 7) asserts: ''. . . (W)e must develop theories of criminal behavior that take seriously the notion that there are biophysical effects on criminal behavior, psychological effects, social effects, cultural effects or any other organized effects that we wish to identify through our specification of the appropriate categories or levels of analysis.''

The remainder of this chapter, as well as the next, will concentrate on the individual or infrasystem. Biopsychological and genetic factors that contribute to the individual system will be introduced here. We will ask, for example, how important is body structure or temperament in the development of delinquency? The focus of Chapter 7 is on mental and cognitive components of the individual system. Do intelligence and moral development matter? And if they do, to what extent? Following that, the book proceeds to increasingly higher levels of analysis, moving from the family, school, and peer group microsystems and the relationships among them (mesosystems) to the neighborhood and community exosystems, and on to the broader macrosystem level: cities, the nation, the world.

TEMPERAMENT

Temperament—defined very loosely for the moment as a ''natural'' mood disposition—may offer important clues about delinquency. It is, of course, a psychological construct, and as such may be rejected by some schools of thought as having no relevance to delinquency. But there is no question that how we approach and interact with our social environment influences how that environment will interact with us. This is true even of children. Parents, teachers, physicians, and caretakers know very well that infants and young children differ in activity, emotionality, and general sensitivity to stimuli. A smiling, relaxed, interactive child is apt to initiate and maintain a different social response than a fussy, tense, and withdrawn one. A consistently ill-tempered child, or one who never sits still, may become so frustrating to parents that they feel overwhelmed and helpless in dealing with him or her. Their own resulting irritability may feed into the behavior of the child in a reciprocal fashion, producing a serious disruption in parent-child relationships. Disruption may progress into physical or emotional abuse or neglect by the parent. Research has suggested with some regularity that poor parent-child relationships and a conflictful home are common, although not inevitable ingredients in delinquency. It is suggested here only that temperament *may* increase or decrease the probability of delinquency, *not* that it determines whether an individual will or will not be delinquent. Nor should it be assumed that *poor* temperament is a necessary condition of a delinquent. As Robert Hogan and Warren Jones (1983, pp. 6–7) write: ''It is easy to imagine that a child who is very emotional, active, unsociable, and impulsive might be constantly in trouble with his or her adult caretakers and perhaps predisposed to delinquency.'' The temperament model ''. . . is interactional in the best sense of the word; it does not maintain that certain temperaments cause delinquency, but rather that the concurrence of these temperaments *and* certain kinds of family environments may lead to delinquent outcomes.''

As currently used in the research, ''temperament'' is assumed to:

1. have a constitutional or biological basis;
2. appear in infancy and continue throughout life; and
3. be influenced by the environment (Bates, 1980).

Most experts today believe that temperament has biological underpinnings that are best discerned at birth (Goldsmith et al., 1987). Most of the contemporary research on temperament, therefore, focuses on the the infant, because the connection between temperament and behavior seems uncomplicated at this stage and becomes more complex as the child matures.

Among researchers, there is no universally accepted definition of temperament. Most define it operationally by identifying the behaviors commonly associated with it. There is little disagreement that *activity* and *emotionality* are two of those behaviors. Activity, the most widely studied, refers to gross motor movement across a variety of settings and times, such as the movement of arms and legs, squirming, and crawling or walking. Children who exhibit an inordinate amount of movement compared to their peers may be labeled ''hyperactive.'' Emotionality refers to such features as irritability, sensitivity, soothability, and general intensity of emotional reactions. However, researchers disagree as to what other behaviors should be included in descriptions of temperament, and some argue that temperament should not be defined accordiing to demonstrated behaviors in the first place. This disagreement has splintered current psychological reseach into four somewhat overlapping schools of thought.

The Thomas and Chess Perspective: Innate Readiness to Respond

One of the most influential perspectives has been advanced by Alexander Thomas and Stella Chess (1977). They define temperament as a behavioral *tendency* rather than a concept measured by a cluster of behavioral *acts*. To Thomas and Chess, temperament is an *innate readiness to respond* across a variety of situations. It is continually evolving along with other psychological attributes (cognitive and emotional). During its maturation, temperament is strongly influenced by the intra- and extrafamilial environment.

Thomas and Chess asked parents to report on nine characteristics of their infant children:

1. rhythmicity of biological functions, such as the regularity of bowel movements, sleep cycles, and feeding times;
2. activity level;
3. approach to or withdrawal from new stimuli;
4. adaptability;

5. sensory threshold;
6. predominant quality of mood;
7. intensity of mood expression;
8. distractibility; and
9. attention span or persistence.

It is important to note that the researchers assumed that these were temperamental predispositions. They then classified infant temperament into three personality styles:

1. The *easy* child,
2. the *difficult* child, and
3. the *slow-to-warm-up* child.

Table 6-1 summarizes the characteristics of each style. The easy child is characterized by rhythmicity, positive moods, high approach, rapid adaptability, and low intensity. The difficult child shows the opposite patterns: irregular biological functioning, initial aversion and slow adaptability to environmental changes, high intensity in emotional expression, and more generally a negative mood (Bates, 1980). The slow-to-warm-up child displays rhythmicity, withdrawal, slow adaptability, negative mood, and low intensity.

"Difficult children," according to the Thomas-Chess viewpoint, represent a specific cluster of inborn temperamental attributes which make child rearing more difficult for most, though not all, of their parents. Such children are at higher risks for developing behavior problems, particularly delinquency.

The research support for the Thomas and Chess typology is mixed (Campos et al., 1983). The existence of the "difficult child" syndrome is a matter of considerable debate, for example. Bates (1980) reports that factor analysis does reveal that soothability, fussiness, and intensity of protest do emerge with some consistency and are statistically significant. Furthermore, he notes that no matter what a parent considers as "being difficult," frequent fussing and crying continually crop up as the repetitive theme. However, Bates emphasizes that the parent-child relationship is an interactive one, strongly influenced by the parent's perception of *why* the child is fussy. Some parents see fussi-

TABLE 6-1 THOMAS-CHESS CATEGORIES OF CHILD TEMPERAMENTS

	Easy child	Difficult child	Slow-to-warm child
Rhythmicity	Regular	Irregular	Regular
Moods	Positive	Negative	Negative
Approach to others	High	Low	Low
Adaptability	Rapid	Slow	Slow
Intensity	Low	High	Low

ness as a normal developmental stage or a result of environmental changes, and therefore something that will pass or can be moderated. Others ascribe it to native, enduring tendencies. According to Bates, the parent's explanations relate to how he or she reacts. Thus, the parent's own temperament is also a factor. Depending upon the parent's own temperament, parental style, and beliefs, whether or not the child is "difficult" may not be an issue. The existence of the "difficult child syndrome," therefore, may hinge more on the subjective interpretations of each parent than on objective, measurable features in the child. What one parent considers a passing stage falling within the normal realm of infant behavior, another may consider an abnormal disposition or simply sheer nastiness. This possibility may account for why the research on "difficult child syndrome" is highly inconclusive and controversial, particularly since it generally gathers data from parental reports.

The Buss and Plomin Perspective: The Inherited Triad

A second school of thought is represented by Arnold Buss and Robert Plomin (1975, 1984). They postulate there are *three* basic dimensions of temperament: emotionality, activity, and sociability. Each is conceptualized as existing on a continuum. *Emotionality* ranges from a stoic, almost total lack of reaction to intense emotional reactions that are out of control. At the higher levels of emotionality, a child demonstrates frequent crying and tantrums, may have breath-holding spells, and cannot be easily soothed. The child at the lower end of the spectrum is very quiet, easy to sooth, and rarely shows anger. The *activity* continuum ranges from lethargy to extremely energetic behavior. The best measures of activity are the amplitude of speech and the rate of motion, displacement of body movements, and the duration of energetic behavior. *Sociability* refers to the extent an individual likes to be with others. Individuals at one extreme of the continuum seek to share activities with others, to receive attention, and to be involved in the back-and-forth responsivity that characterizes social interaction. Typical measures of sociability are the frequency of attempts to initiate social contacts, number of affiliations, the amount of time spent with others, and reactions to isolation.

According to Buss and Plomin, these three dimensions, which characterize temperament types, are *inheritable* personality traits. In fact, they may be observed in animals and in older children and adults as well as in infants. The traits may change somewhat over the course of childhood, however. For example, as the individual grows in size, strength, and endurance, activity is apt to increase. As a child grows older, he or she also tends to have more opportunities to seek out others, and thus sociability increases. In other words, microsystems increase in variety and number. Finally, as the nervous system matures and socialization practices have an effect, emotionality becomes less intense. Despite these changes in development and experience, however, Buss and Plomin maintain that the basic personality core remains stable. The most outgoing child in kindergarten is expected to have a wide circle of friends in high school.

Sociability, however, is of little relevance to Buss and Plomin's conception of the "difficult child." For them, that child is one who is highly emotional and active. Emotional children are problematic because they have frequent temper tantrums and are difficult to handle and socialize. Children high in activity are problematic because they continually press against limits, become easily bored, and may wear out parents with their energy. A reasonable prediction is that the active child will be a risk taker, one who likes excitement, takes chances, and pulls pranks. Perhaps it is this child who is *prone* to engage in minor, mischievous kinds of delinquency. On the other hand, it is reasonable to suppose that the nasty, emotional, impulsive child will be more *inclined* toward violent or serious delinquency.

Buss and Plomin go far beyond outlining behavioral descriptions which accompany various temperaments. They see a major role for temperament, arguing that it *interacts* with the social environment in a dynamic and *bi-directional* way. Temperament continually influences the environment and the environment continually influences temperament in a reciprocal fashion. Thus, a child elicits certain types of parental behaviors, and the parent elicits certain behaviors in the child. Furthermore, the impact of such parental behaviors varies as a function of the child's temperament. And how well things work out over the long haul is a function of a good match in the temperament and behavioral styles between parents and the child. For example, a parent with low tolerance for a hyperactive child would be a poor match compared to a more tolerant and patient one.

In many ways the Buss and Plomin position is similar to that advocated by Sandra Scarr and Kathleen McCartney (1983). They say genes (including temperament) play a substantial role in directing development and experiences. Individuals with certain temperaments will receive certain kinds of parenting, evoke certain responses from others, and select certain aspects from the available environments. True, the environment and its experiences strongly influence human development, but the genetic makeup of the individual in part determines which environment that individual will be exposed to. According to Scarr and McCartney, genes organize and direct one's development and experiences. Babies and children with high needs for stimulation, for example, seek out and create environments that best meet those needs. Others may prefer to play by themselves, be aloof toward parents, and seek out quiet, sedentary activities.

The Rothbart Perspective: Differences in Reactivity

A third major perspective on temperament is represented by psychologist Mary Klevjord Rothbart (Rothbart and Derryberry, 1982; Rothbart, 1986). She defines temperament as a relatively stable, constitutionally based construct representing individual differences in

1. reactivity of the nervous system and
2. self-regulation of that reactivity.

The term "constitutional" emphasizes the enduring biological makeup of the individual, influenced over time by heredity, maturation, and experience. Reactivity of the nervous system refers to the innate arousability or excitability of the nervous system to stimuli. It is similar to a concept used in the theory of Hans J. Eysenck, which will be discussed in the next section. Self-regulation refers to processes, such as attention, approach, avoidance, and inhibition, that enhance or inhibit reactivity.

Like Thomas and Chess, Rothbart developed her theory primarily on the basis of parents' reports. According to Rothbart, temperament can be observed in all age groups as individual differences in patterns of emotionality, activity, and attention. The behavioral expression and personal experience of temperament will be influenced by the degree of stimulation and regulation provided by that environment. For example, a young child who is highly reactive with few self-regulative controls must rely heavily on the parent as an outside source of regulation until self-control is established. If those external controls are not introduced or do not succeed in modifying the child's high reactivity, the result may be a lifelong pattern of inadequate control of impulses or temperament. This might be illustrated by "impulsive" violent delinquent behavior.

Rothbart also introduces the concept of "niche picking." Temperament will influence the circumstances under which individuals feel comfortable and happy, and thus will influence the situation—or niches—they choose to enter or avoid. Temperaments are strongly influential in one's choice of friends. "Niche-picking" will be relevant in the discussion of the microsystem of peer groups and its influence on delinquency.

The Goldsmith and Campos Perspective: Differences in Emotionality

In a fourth school of thought, Hill Goldsmith and Joseph Campos (1982) consider temperament to be emotionality—nothing more. Temperament refers to individual differences in the expression of primary emotions—anger, sadness, fear, joy, pleasure, disgust, interest, and surprise—and in the experience of emotional arousability. Emotionality lays the foundation for personality characteristics. For example, temperamental proneness to anger influences the development of aggression; temperamental persistence affects the motivation to achieve; fear may affect one's willingness to take risks, make career moves, or even move to another part of the country.

Research by Olweus (1980) lends support to Goldsmith and Campos' perspective. In his investigation of the determinants of aggressive behavior in adolescent boys, Olweus had parents rate (retrospectively) the childhood temperaments of their offspring as "hot-headed" or "calm." The hot-headed ratings predicted later aggression. Moreover, early activity and emotionality indirectly predicted aggression through their tendency to encourage parents to become permissive of aggressive behavior. Thus, individual differences in children produced differences in parental behavior which, in turn, affected later development. A major difficulty with the Olweus research design, as with many studies of temperament, was its reliance on parental reports of their children's behavior. Retrospective reports based on parental recall of such developmental milestones as a child's first steps or first sentence are notoriously inaccurate.

Neither Goldsmith and Campos nor Rothbart saw any need to consider the "difficult child" pattern as a meaningful concept. Rothbart believed there were serious problems in defining it. Goldsmith and Campos argued that there was little value in discussing such a pattern independent of the context in which it occurs.

McCall (cited in a symposium reported by Goldsmith et al., 1987) summarizes the concept of temperament very well. He states that at the least it consists of relatively consistent, basic dispositions inherent in the person and that these dispositions underlie and modulate the expressions of activity, reactivity, emotionality, and sociability. The biological elements of temperament are strongest early in life, but as development proceeds, the expressions of temperament are influenced increasingly by experience and context.

Temperament and Delinquency

Although temperament has captured the attention of a good number of researchers, they have been unable to agree upon a common definition of the concept. However, Robert McCall (Goldsmith et al., 1987) makes the point that definitions should not be simply valid or invalid, confirmable or refutable. Instead, they are more or less useful. For our purposes the concept of temperament is of use in that it encourages us to consider the possibility that individual differences *may* be critical in the early formation of delinquency and crime. In other words, temperament is a viable causal agent in the delinquency complex. ''Difficult children''—even if this label comes strictly from subjective parental perceptions—may be at higher risk to engage in delinquency than ''easy'' children. Temperamentally emotional and hyperactive adolescents *may* present handling problems for caretakers and the social environment, whereas adolescents at the lower end of these dimensions may not. Interactions between the person and his or her environment merit consideration in any comprehensive attempt to explain delinquency.

It is likely, therefore, that certain temperamental dispositions of activity, reactivity, emotionality, and sociability that exist at an early age render certain high risks to engage in behaviors that run counter to society's expectations and regulations. Highly active children move into (and often against) their environments at a higher pace and perhaps more impulsively than less active children. Because of their high activity levels, the probability is greater that they will collide with the wishes of parents and society. Furthermore, children with highly irritable, nasty temperaments and children with relaxed, pleasant ones are apt to create environments and to influence parenting in significantly different ways. Failure to acknowledge these dispositional variables at the individual systems level may leave us with an incomplete picture of the etiology of delinquency. Likewise, the temperament of parents must also be considered as a possible component in the development of the delinquent child.

Longitudinal Studies Connecting Temperament
with Delinquency

Emmy Werner and her collaborators (Werner, Bierman, and French, 1971; Werner and Smith, 1977, 1982; Werner, 1987) followed a cohort of 698 children living on the Hawaiian island of Kauai from birth to adulthood. This perspective longitudinal study spans the years 1954–1986 and uses the measures and observations of pediatricians, psychologists, public health personnel, and social workers. The project identified a number of personality, constitutional, and environmental variables which presumably distinguish children who become delinquent from those who do not. Problems arise, however, when we look at the Werner measure of delinquency. One hundred and two of the 698 children were labeled "delinquent" based on official records or police and family court files. However, a vast majority of the 102 "juvenile offenders" (of both sexes) committed relatively minor violations (traffic violations, running away). With this important caution in mind, Werner (1987) states that a combination of about a dozen variables provides the best prediction for eventual delinquency. For example, children with a history of a difficult temperament, hyperactivity, substandard living conditions, low IQ, and an unstable conflictful home life were more likely to be delinquent than children without these background variables. However, a significant number of these children (total of 72) with four or more of these features in their backgrounds did *not* become delinquent, indicating that predicting delinquency on the basis of background variables is risky business.

Werner divides those children with four or more high risk variables into a "resilient" group (those who did not become delinquent) and a "vulnerable" group (those who became delinquent). She reports that one of the strongest differences between the two groups was the perceptions of the mothers concerning the child's temperament. Specifically, mothers of the resilient children perceived them as affectionate, cuddly, good-natured, and easy to deal with. The children seemed to have a positive social orientation toward others. Furthermore, the families of the resilient children had fairly extensive social support systems. That is, they had supportive adults and caretakers available to them if problems arose. On the other hand, mothers of vulnerable children perceived them as being difficult to handle and as exhibiting more temper tantrums, eating and sleeping problems. Moreover, the children's orientation toward others was negative and aggressive. In addition, families of vulnerable children seemed to have meager support systems.

Another perspective longitudinal study by George Spivack and Norma Cianci (1987), using a cohort of 660 kindergarten children, analyzed the extent to which behavioral patterns observed in kindergarten were predictive of later delinquency. Delinquency was defined as a "police contact" with the Philadelphia Police Department before age 17. Each offense was coded for seriousness using the Sellin-Wolfgang scoring method. Overall, statistical correlations between police contact or seriousness of these offenses and early classroom behavior were low, ranging from .13 to .26 and averaging in the mid-teens. Therefore, relationships were weak and intrepretations must be made with caution.

Spivack and Cianci found that excessive aggressive and antisocial behavior at an early age is a modest predictor of the same behavior at a later age. The most relevant finding to our present topic, however, was that delinquency-prone children were more likely to exhibit a "difficult temperament," as reflected in their impatience, impulsiveness, annoying interpersonal behavior, poor adaptability, and moodiness.

In conclusion, Spivack and Cianci recommend that future research focus upon ". . . the issue of 'match' between parental child rearing styles and child temperament, hypothesizing that the high-risk pattern will emerge with greatest frequency when children with a 'difficult' temperament have parents who perceive such behavior in a negative light . . . and thus respond to the child impatiently, punitively, and without understanding of the child's needs and feelings'' (1987, p. 69). In addition, both the Kauai and the Spivack-Cianci studies emphasize the bidirectionality (reciprocity) of the child influencing the parents and the parents influencing the child.

The Caspi Study: The Long-term Fate of Ill-tempered People

Avshalom Caspi, Glen Elder, and Daryl Bem (1987) distinguish between two kinds of person-environment interactions. One is reciprocal and dynamic: The person acts, the environment reacts, and the person reacts back, and so forth, in kind of a causal loop. For example, a child's temper tantrums may coerce others into offering short-term pay-offs as temporary appeasement. However, this immediate appeasement precludes the learning of more controlled behaviors that would, in the long run, be more effective. Caspi, Elder, and Bem are suggesting that temper tantrums reflect on *interactional style* that evokes reciprocal, reinforcing responses from others. The explosive, undercontrolled style that appears as temper tantrums in early childhood may later manifest itself in undercontrolled rages when the individual again confronts frustration or controlling authority in adulthood, such as in the work setting or the marital relationship.

The second type of interaction between the person and the environment relates to the stability of temperament. Here, the individual's innate dispositions systematically select environments that reinforce and sustain them. For example, ill-tempered or anti-social dispositions may deliberately select environments that condone and immediately reinforce antisocial approaches to the world. The ill-tempered boy drops out of school and associates with boys who do not challenge or care about this ill temper, or who display the same feature. In this sense, ill-tempered children represent high risk candidates for delinquency; their behavior increasingly channels them into environments that facilitate antisocial conduct.

Caspi, Elder, and Bem followed the life course of 87 boys and 95 girls in a project initiated in 1928 by the Institute of Human Development of the University of California, Berkeley. Most subjects were white, Protestant, middle-class children when the project began. A major finding of this longitudinal study was that ill-tempered children became ill-tempered adults. Whatever had been involved in childhood patterns of temper tantrums or uncontrolled behavior had carried over into adulthood. The uncontrolled behavior was evoked in adult roles and settings, especially those requiring a high degree of subordination (e.g., military and employment settings) and those requiring negotiation of interpersonal conflicts (e.g., marital and parenthood settings).

The researchers found some sex differences in their results. Ill-tempered compared to even-tempered boys were substantially less likely to complete a formal education, to maintain a job for any length of time, or to remain married. Their lives reflected erratic work habits and little persistence on tasks. They preferred to ''resolve'' interpersonal conflicts with demonstrations of anger and aggression. The Caspi group also discovered a progressive deterioration in SES for ill-tempered boys. As a group, they showed *downward* class mobility; most came from midde class families, but by age 40 they had fallen to working class status. Part of this downward mobility could be attributed to their lack of formal education and their inability to maintain steady employment. Ill-tempered men were significantly more likely to be unemployed, to hold a variety of short-term jobs, and to express less satisfaction with their careers and their supervisors than even-tempered men. On the other hand, recent evidence (Snarey and Vaillant, 1985) suggests that working class even-tempered boys tend to move *upward* in SES over the years. In the study by Caspi and his colleagues, ill-tempered men were twice as likely to have been divorced by age 40 and were more likely to be judged inadequate parents by their spouses.

The pattern for women was similar to that for men, but there were some differences. Movement on the SES scale was confounded by the cultural and social forces which dictated different proper roles for women than for men during the years covered in the study. For women, movement along the social class spectrum hinged primarily on the jobs and social class of their husbands. Women were expected to move up by marrying higher social class men, not through their own efforts, and they were expected to maintain the proper model home. Caspi and his colleagues did discover that 40 percent of girls with frequent childhood tantrums eventually married down (as measured by occupational status of husbands), compared to only 24 percent of their even-tempered peers. It seems, therefore, that insufficient self-control consigns women to marriages "below their station." Other trends emerged from the data. Ill-tempered girls grew up to be ill-tempered women. The relationship between temper tantrums and achievement in later life, however, was not nearly as strong as that found for men. However, like ill-tempered men, ill-tempered women experienced deterioration in marital and personal relationships. Twenty-six percent of ill-tempered women were divorced by age 40, compared to only 12 percent of even-tempered women. Furthermore, the ill-tempered group reported more marital conflicts and were generally more dissatisfied with their marriages. By their own reports, they were more likely to be ill-tempered parents.

Although the Caspi-Elder-Bem investigation did not directly examine the amount of delinquency and criminal conduct in their sample, some inferences may be drawn based on their findings. The evidence certainly indicates that ill-tempered people are in store for a life of unnecessary strife and general dissatisfaction. Ill-tempered, irritable youngsters characterized by temper tantrums and "poor impulse control" would appear to be prime candidates for serious delinquency. We can anticipate further that ill-tempered people, because of the tendency to react to things with explosive tirades and temper tantrums, will be more involved in violent "solutions" to frustrations. Sheldon and Eleanor Glueck (1950), for example, found that serious delinquents were nearly six times more likely to exhibit "temper tantrums" than nondelinquent peers. D. Zillman (1979, 1983) hypothesizes that individuals prone toward temper tantrums temporarily suspend their rational thinking processes and do things they would normally not do.

Compounding the problem is the finding by the Caspi group that ill-tempered people fail at educational and occupational endeavors, a feature that occurs all too often in the backgrounds of adult criminals. Delinquents have a higher rate of school failure as reflected by poor grades, truancy, conduct problems, and dropping out completely. The issue of temperament, temper tantrums, and poor impulse control leads us to the biosocial theory of Hans J. Eysenck.

EYSENCK'S THEORY OF CRIMINALITY

In 1977, the British psychologist Hans J. Eysenck proposed a theory of crime and delinquency which clearly fits into the individual system category of social systems theory. It is a temperament perspective built upon a genetic-biological platform: Innate temperamental traits influence in part all personality and behavior patterns. We should note that Eysenck prefers the term "antisocial behavior" to the terms "crime" and "delinquency," because antisocial behavior covers a broader realm of human activity. Although criminal conduct is always antisocial, antisocial behavior is not always criminal. A consistently disruptive student may be considered antisocial but not criminal. In addition, Eysenck feels that using the term "antisocial behavior" releases us from relying on official statistics for measuring crime.

According to Eysenck, antisocial behavior is the result of an interaction between certain environmental conditions and *inherited* personality traits. He believes that any comprehensive theory of criminality must advocate a careful examination of both the biological makeup and the socialization history of each individual. Since we clearly inherit morphological, physiological, and biochemical properties through genes, there is no reason not to believe that we also inherit personality traits or temperamental predispositions to antisocial behavior (Eysenck, 1983). He asserts: "No serious student can doubt the relevance of both the *biological* and the *social* aspects of an individual's behaviour" (Eysenck, 1984, p. 90).

People differ in the degree to which they indulge in antisocial conduct, from those who never do so to the habitual criminal who continually and frequently displays such conduct. Most people, according to Eysenck, lie somewhere between these extremes; the majority occasionally indulge in such conduct, but only to a minor degree and when chances of detection are minuscule. While he admits that the causes of antisocial behavior may be multiple, Eysenck contends that a classical error in sociological and economic theories of crime is the rejection of individual differences (especially temperamental ones) and the assumption that nonpsychological factors (e.g., crowded living conditions, injustice in society) account for antisocial behavior. He considers this view seriously misleading.

Main Reason for Delinquency: Lack of Proper Conditioning

Eysenck believes that most people do not participate regularly in antisocial behavior because, after several experiences in which some form of punishment followed their misconduct, they rapidly made strong connections between their behavior and its aversive consequences. On the other hand, those persons who did not make these connections are at high risk to engage in antisocial conduct. The development of "connections" between stimuli and certain consequences is called classical conditioning. In Pavlov's classical conditioning experiment, a stimulus (such as food) that normally evokes a particular response (such as salivation) was repeatedly paired with another stimulus that does not normally evoke the response (for example, a bell). Eventually, the subject was conditioned to salivate to the sound of the bell. It is this process that forms the fundamental premise upon which Eysenck's theory of criminality is built. Antisocial behavior is the conditioned stimulus and pain/fear/anxiety/shame is the conditioned response. By consistently punishing antisocial behavior, parents or other caretakers, teachers, and even peers perform the role of the Pavlovian experimenter. Gradually, the child acquires a conditioned response of pain/fear/anxiety/shame to the conditioned stimulus of misconduct—even the *contemplation* of misconduct. Eysenck's is essentially a deterrence theory of punishment.

Eysenck maintains, however, that not everyone adapts to this conditioning process. People differ considerably in the speed with which they form conditioned responses and in the strength of these conditioned responses. Those individuals who are genetically predisposed to condition quickly, easily, and strongly are likely to become law-abiding citizens; those who develop conditioned responses slowly, weakly, and only with difficulty are liable to lack the "conscience" which will preclude them from engaging in antisocial conduct. "Conditionability," then, is the underpinning for the construct typically called "conscience." Moreover, Eysenck contends that conditionability is the reason why individuals with similar backgrounds act differently in similar situations. Eysenck admonishes that he is not suggesting that *all* human behavior is caused or determined by conditioning (Eysenck, 1983). He leaves little doubt, however, that conditionability is the primary factor in determining who engages in *antisocial* conduct and who does not.

According to Eysenck, the "conditioned conscience" has two effects on behavior: It may prevent us from engaging in forbidden activities, or it may make us feel guilty after we commit them. The conditioned conscience inhibits most people from repetitive, antisocial conduct by its association with prior adverse consequences. In addition, once we have committed an antisocial act, we tend to feel uncomfortable about our transgression. Eysenck (1983) supposes the difference rests in the timing of the aversive consequences. Scolding a child *before* or *during* an act would produce different effects than scolding a child *after* the act. The former situation would result in feelings of discomfort before the act (or while committing it); whereas the latter would produce discomfort (guilt) after the act. Furthermore, caretakers and parents are probably the best agents to carry out the conditioning process.

Eysenck (1983) attributes supposedly rising crime and delinquency rates to increased permissiveness in homes, schools, and judicial processes. The issue of social and parental permissiveness as a major factor in delinquency, of course, has been addressed many times before (e.g., Toennies, 1957; 1971; Simmel, 1950; Tarde, 1897/1969). The explanations for this permissiveness, however, have differed. Gabriel Tarde, for instance, was more inclined to blame the judicial process of France and other countries. He wrote (1897, p. 270): ". . . it is natural that with the progress of judiciary indulgence—and there is abundant proof of indulgence of judges and juries alike—youthful criminality grows even faster than that of adults." For Eysenck, permissiveness means less conditioning. The children of today, he says, are exposed to fewer conditioning experiences. As a result, children grow up with weaker consciences and freely engage in antisocial behavior. He believes that antisocial behavior is an instinctive proclivity, ". . . a natural type of behaviour for all animals and infants" (Eysenck, 1984,

p. 92). Furthermore, "Socialized behaviour, which often goes against the interest of the individual, although it is line with the best interests of society, . . . is, in a very real sense, 'unnatural'!'' (Eysenck, 1984, p. 92). It is also unlikely that socialized behavior can be acquired through rational means. That is, reasoning with the child would not have the effect that an aversive stimulus would. Instead, it must be instilled through classical conditioning. According to Eysenck, if children are exposed to a stricter regimen of conditioning, they will likely grow up to be respectable and law-abiding citizens. Nevertheless, there will always be some children who engage in antisocial behavior in spite of a strict conditioning regimen.

It must be stressed that Eysenck is *not* advocating that some individuals are *born* criminals. Rather, some people are born with nervous sytem characteristics that:

1. are significantly different from the general population; and
2. affect their ability to conform to social expectations and rules.

With an effective conditioning schedule, just about any person, regardless of nervous system characteristics, can be made to conform to societal needs. It will take longer and require more intense conditioning for those who demonstrate poor conditionability—but it can be done. Furthermore, there are no sex differences in conditionability. Male and female conditionabilities are evenly distributed within the general population. What makes the differences between male and female offending rates revolves around what the "conditioners" consider appropriate behavior. Since "boys will be boys," violations by boys are not as severely punished by parents and authorities as violations by girls.

Eysenck's theory is similar in many ways to the theoretical concepts of temperament discussed previously. Eysenck believes that nervous systems differ in their reactivity, sensitivity, and excitability. It is these features that predispose a person to act antisocially. But it isn't the temperamental characteristics of the nervous system working in isolation that dictate antisocial action. Innate features of the nervous system, influenced by experience and the social environment, render certain persons more at risk for delinquent and criminal action than others.

Three Personality Dimensions and Their Role in Antisocial Behavior

Research by Eysenck and his colleagues has delineated three major biological components of personality: extraversion, neuroticism, and psychoticism. Extraversion is the dimension that dictates conditionability and therefore is the principal factor in antisocial behavior. Although these components do not account for all our personality characteristics, Eysenck believes they form the basic structure from which much of our behavior originates. Extraversion represents a central nervous system tendency that determines needs for stimulation and excitement. It exists on a continuum, ranging from very high needs for stimulation and excitement (extraverts) to very low needs for stimulation and excitement (introverts). A majority of the population (about 67 percent) fall somewhere between these two extremes (ambiverts).

Neuroticism reflects an innate biological predisposition to react physiologically to stressful or upsetting events. Basically, neuroticism represents emotionality. Persons high on neuroticism react intensely and lastingly to stress and are generally moody, touchy, sensitive to slights, and anxious or nervous. People at the lower end of the continuum are emotionally stable, calm, and even-tempered.

Psychoticism is characterized by cold cruelty, social insensitivity, disregard for danger, troublesome behavior, dislike of others, and an attraction toward the unusual. The individual high on psychoticism tends to be an impulsive, aggressive individual without appreciable conscience or concern for others (Pulkkinen, 1986). In many ways, the descriptors for psychoticism follow those of the classical "psychopath," or, more commonly, the "sociopath." The biological mechanism responsible for psychoticism has yet to be identified, but it continues to emerge as a third factor in factor analytical studies, statistically unrelated to extraversion and neuroticism.

As just mentioned, the extraversion personality dimension plays the greatest role in crime and delinquency. Extraverts not only have high needs for stimulation but they also do not condition easily. They frequently seek stimulation, excitement, and thrills, all of which can get them into trouble; they are also less able to make the connection between antisocial conduct and aversive consequences. Introverts, on the other hand, condition readily and have less need for thrills and excitement. Because they easily make connections between behavior and consequences, they are much less prone toward antisocial conduct.

Eysenck (1983) postulates that the extraversion factor is particularly crucial in dealing with young children when socialized conduct either is or is not acquired through the proper development of the conditioned conscience. Extraversion is slightly less important as the child gets older, becoming even less a factor in adolescence, and much less a factor in the case of criminal adults.

Neuroticism or emotional instability acts like an amplifier of an already existing habit, good or bad. In effect, high levels of neuroticism enhance whatever habits the individual has previously acquired. If a child fails to acquire socialized habits and consequently behaves antisocially, high neuroticism (or drive) will multiply this conduct and produce an even stronger tendency toward continued antisocial behavior. Eysenck believes neuroticism is most important in understanding some adult criminals, less important in understanding adolescents and even less young children.

The psychoticism dimension is hypothesized to be linked with crimes of violence, and appears to be equally important across all stages of development, from childhood through adolescence to adulthood.

Eysenck's theory sensitizes us to the possible role of biological and genetic factors in the etiology of delinquency. The concept of temperament does the same. But let us be clear about what is being said here. Certain persons may be "wired up" in such a way as to increase the *probability* that they will engage in frequent misconduct, depending upon their experiences with the social environment. In other words, it is unlikely that human beings are neutral, passive pawns waiting for social forces to shape them. Rather human beings come into the world with predispositions that do resist some of the shaping. Some are full of energy and activity and mood shifts. Some are, very early in life, pleasant, while others are irritable. Their pleasantness or irritability and needs for stimulation affect those caregivers around them, setting up a dynamic, interactive chain of events. The etiology of delinquency may be here, but the social environment plays the major role in its overall development. Eysenck agrees, of course, that the social environment does play a role in the formation of behavior, but he believes conditioning and aspects of the human nervous system are more important. To Eysenck, what passes as social learning or socialization is really a conditioning process.

Research Support for Eysenck's Theory

Eysenck's theory of criminality has received mixed reviews. He and his followers (1977, 1983, 1984) claim empirical support for the theory with minor revisions. Others (e.g., Passingham, 1972; Farrington, Biron, and LeBlanc, 1982) report only very limited support. Typically, the research procedure for testing the theory has involved an administration of an Eysenck personality scale (there are several) to institutionalized delinquents and a control group. The two groups' scores on the scale are then compared.

R. E. Passingham (1972) reviewed much of the pre-1972 research literature and found serious flaws in the basic experimental designs of most of the studies, rendering any conclusions suspect. However, even if the studies were flawless, there would be little support for the Eysenckian theory. "Even when the inadequacy of the studies is taken into account, this review indicates that evidence on Eysenck's theory is only partially confirmatory, suggesting that the theory applies only, if at all, to a subgroup of offenders" (Passingham, 1972, p. 365). David P. Farrington's more recent review (Farrington, Biron, and LeBlanc, 1982) is even less heartening. Farrington and his colleagues state ". . .the usefulness of the Eysenck theory in relation to crime and delinquency has not been demonstrated" (p. 166). In their own empirical test of the theory, the researchers compared London adolescents to Montreal adolescents and found no significant relationship between official delinquency and any of the Eysenck personality dimensions. They did, however, find a significant relationship between self-report delinquency and extraversion. SR delinquency correlated positively with extraversion scores (the higher the delinquency, the higher the extraversion score). However, the researchers attributed this finding to a "self-report bias." That is, extraverts have a greater tendency to admit socially disapproved behavior than other personality groups. In summary, they write, "Our conclusion is that, at the present time, it seems unlikely that the Eysenck theory, the Eysenck scale, or the Eysenck items are of much use in the explanation of delinquency" (p. 196).

The basic fatal flaw of the Eysenckian position is his attempt to construct a universal theory for all people, for all criminals, for all delinquents, for all cultures, for all time, based on the relatively simple process of conditioning. Delinquent behavior is determined by a constellation of factors, including the interplay of various systems. Conditioning may be a factor, but it is highly unlikely to be the only—or even the major—factor. The search for the universal, all-encompassing theory of crime and delinquency is an illusion, an unattainable goal if our present knowledge is any indication. One strength of the Eysenckian theory that should not be overlooked, however, is that much of it is stated in terms that are reasonably testable; thus it is susceptible to falsification. This is one reason why it has drawn so much "falsifying" research.

WILSON AND HERRNSTEIN: AN OLD STORY IN A NEW PACKAGE?

In 1985 James Q. Wilson and Richard J. Herrnstein, professors of public policy and psychology, respectively, at Harvard University, produced a mass market volume, *Crime and Human Nature*, in which they outlined an all-encompassing, eclectic theory to explain crime. They did this after asserting that the criminological theories proposed thus far were inadequate and incomplete, each representing special cases of a general theoretical position. The Wilson-Herrnstein master theory supposedly embraces a wide variety of positions, be they sociological, psychiatric, psychological, biological, or economic.

Wilson and Herrnstein's theory rests solidly on the proposition that individual constitutional factors interact with social factors to account for human behavior, including criminal behavior. Included in the list of constitutional factors are personality traits, such as intelligence or impulsivity, sex, body type, race, and age. Wilson and Herrnstein maintain that we must understand how these factors interact with familial, economic, peer group, or other social experiences to create the forces that propel individuals toward crime.

Like Eysenck, Wilson and Herrnstein are quick to disassociate themselves from the born-criminal theory of Cesare Lombroso or the notion that we are at the mercy of biology or genetic makeup. Individuals, they say, *choose* to commit crime, by balancing the net value of crime against the net value of noncrime. By net value, they mean "the sum of all the reinforcements, positive and negative, less the punishments, associated with either crime or noncrime, as expressed in the strength of the competing behaviors" (p. 50). These reinforcers, or rewards, may be either primary or secondary, and the two categories may explain one criminal incident. According to the theory, for example, a child molestation may be simply the result of the drive to satisfy the primary sex drive, or it may include a need for human closeness. The child molester, therefore, has balanced the net gains of committing his or her crime against the gains of noncrime (which are almost invariably more remote in time) and has concluded that the gains from the criminal offense are greater. Even crimes that are bizarre and incomprehensible can be explained by this balancing of rewards and punishments. Thus, people are continually calculating the rewards over the costs of all behavior.

Wilson and Herrnstein are careful to present their theory as one which takes into account social and constitutional factors, and they emphasize that the extent of influence of constitutional factors is "unknown, but not trivial." Nevertheless, they subtly give inordinate weight to the latter. Moreover, the "choice" between crime and noncrime seems at least partially illusory. In discussing intelligence, for example, they note that persons of higher intelligence can better perform the balancing function, appreciating the delayed rewards of noncrime. In a chapter titled "Gender," they maintain that only constitutional factors can account for the well-recognized gender gap in violent crime. Males consistently are more antisocially aggressive because they lack the female hormone of estrogen which appears to water down aggressive tendencies. In support of this emphasis on hormones, they discuss the alleged propensity of women to commit more violent crime during their premenstrual cycle, when estrogen levels are low. Socialization as explanation for the gender gap in violent crime is relegated to a secondary role as Wilson and Herrnstein remark that aggression, and perhaps other primary drives, "flows into the definition of sex roles" (p. 124).

Criticisms

Crime and Human Nature has been alternately lauded and condemned since its publication. While some criminologists were aghast that two contemporary writers of considerable professional stature would conclude that factors such as intelligence, race, and body structure play a notable role in criminality, others commended the authors for daring to treat sensitive topics and for drawing together a wide array of interdisciplinary research. A primary criticism is that the book does little more than rehash a very old question concerning the determinants of crime and delinquency. In short, the book offers nothing new in the debate. Like it or not, the book is impossible to ignore and, according to one critic, "seems destined to be one of the most influential works on crime and delinquency produced in the 1980s" (Gibbons, 1986, p. 189). Nevertheless, Gibbons (1986) challenges Wilson and Herrnstein's assertion that their theory can explain all crime, noting that they give scant attention to those types of crime which are either invisible in official statistics, such as white-collar crime, or are not of the street-crime or violent or larcenous variety.

Critics also note that the authors of *Crime and Human Nature* glibly assert "facts" in criminology that are not at all well-established. Wilson and Herrnstein cite uncritically the Danish adoption studies, which they find in basic support of their thesis. They also insist that "there is at least a statistical association between the menstrual cycle and female crime" (p. 121), but are able to cite only one study to support this contention. The alleged association has been widely rebutted in the literature.

In a well-reasoned, extensive critique of the book, Christopher Jencks (1987) faults the authors for perpetuating misunderstanding about the role of genes in crime. Jencks argues forcefully that constitutional factors matter, but their influence is less deterministic than Wilson and Herrnstein would have us believe. Jencks believes that if society would recognize the influence of IQ and heredity, rather than deny it, it could take steps to alter their effects, just as it attempts to alter the effects of poverty. *Crime and Human Nature*, he maintains, is disappointing because it fails to suggest realistic policy responses.

The policy implications that Wilson and Herrnstein do suggest are in line with those of conservative criminologists, who argue that society must make detection and punishment more certain, swift, and severe. In Wilson and Herrnstein's schema, this would increase the gains of noncrime, and make criminal behavior a less attractive choice.

BODY BUILD AND DELINQUENCY

The belief that personality or temperament is somehow closely related to bodily appearance has been expressed in a variety of forums for at least 2,000 years (Montemayor, 1978). In criminology, the view is associated primarily with W. H. Sheldon, a physician who theorized that body structure and delinquency were closely related. Sheldon developed a classification system based on the shape of the body and related these "body types" directly to a genetic propensity to engage in delinquency. After extensively and painstakingly collecting physical measurements and documenting them with photographs, Sheldon delineated three basic body builds in both males and females: ectomorphic (thin and fragile), mesomorphic (muscular and hard), and endomorphic (fat and soft). The reader with some background in embryology will recognize that the terms refer to layers of the embryo. The ectodermal layer evolves into the nervous system. The ectomorph, therefore, has a well-developed brain and central nervous system compared to the rest of his or her tall and thin body. The mesodermal layer of the embryo develops into muscle and, therefore, the muscular body that is tough and well-equipped for strenuous activity is labeled the mesomorph. The endodermal embryonic layer develops primarily into the digestive tract, and thus individuals who are flabby and fat (endomorphs) are associated with the digestive system.

Somatotypes: Indexing Body Shapes

Sheldon did not make sharp, abrupt distinctions between the body types (which he called "somatotypes"). Rarely did a person's body structure fall exclusively into one of the three "pure" somatotypes just described. Rather, most individuals had features of all three to varying degrees. Sheldon ranked his subjects on a 7-point scale, with 7 representing maximum features of the body type and 1, the minimum. A "pure" mesomorph would have a somatotype of 1-7-1. A 3-2-5 person would be primarily endomorphic (5), but have some features of ectomorphy (3) and mesomorphy (2). Notice that the first score reflects ectomorphy, the second, mesomorphy, and the third, endomorphy. Sheldon assigned a 4-4-4 to the average body. This indicated constitutional "balance." Furthermore, while we used whole numbers in the examples, the actual indexes usually contained decimals, such as 3.6-4.8-5.5.

Sheldon claimed that he discovered a strong correlation between personality (or what he termed "temperament") and somatotype, and he proceeded to describe personality types which were linked with body types: cerebrotonia to the ectomorphic, somatotonia to the mesomorphic, and viscertonia to the endomorphic. In Sheldon's theory, the cerebrotonic person is inhibited, reserved, self-conscious, and afraid of people. A somatotonic person ordinarily needs muscular and vigorous physical activity, risk, and adventure. A person with this temperament is likely to be aggressive, ruthless, and callous in relationships with others, and to be relatively indifferent to pain. Mesomorphs are associated with these features. The third personality, the viscertonic, loves comfort, food, affection, and people. This type of person, according to Sheldon, is usually even-tempered and easy to get along with, traits that describe the endomorph.

Testing the Theory

Sheldon began to test his theory of delinquency in 1939 by exploring the relationship between delinquency and body type. He published the results in 1949, in his book *Varieties of Delinquent Youth*. He had classified the body structures of 200 "more-or-less delinquent boys" from the Hayden Goodwill Inn, a Boston rehabilitation home for the "incorrigible" and the "disappointing." Each boy was assigned an index. Results were compared to indexes of 4,000 male college students. As predicted, Sheldon found a preponderance of mesomorphs and very few ectomorphs in his delinquent sample compared to his normal college sample. The average somatotype of the 200 "delinquents" was 3.5-4.6-2.7, compared to an average somatotype of 3.2-3.7-3.5 for college males. Sheldon identified a special group of boys as definite "criminals;" their average somatotype was 3.4-5.4-1.8.

"Whatever else may be true of the delinquency I saw in Boston, it is mainly in the germ plasm," Sheldon concluded (1949, p. 872). He was convinced that genetics, as reflected in body structure, was the primary causal factor of delinquency and a life of crime. He discussed the desirability of "thoroughbredness in the human stock" and recommended that serious consideration be given to selective breeding. We should keep in mind, as always, the tenor of Sheldon's times. However, Sheldon seemed out of step with his time, since the eugenics movement was losing steam in 1949, and biological causation was certainly not popular at that time.

As you would expect, Sheldon's work was widely criticized. Sutherland (1956a) asserted that Sheldon's conclusions were unwarranted on the basis of the data. He called *Varieties of Delinquent Youth* "useless." "This book fails completely to add anything to scientific knowledge except the evidence from which the conclusion can be drawn that in this particular group of 200 youth, variations in civil delinquency are not related to variations in the basic indices of Sheldon's constitutional psychology" (Sutherland, 1956a, p. 289). Other critics pointed to the numerous flaws in the project, such as the subjective and unreliable criteria for determining delinquency. Sheldon did not merely select youths who "violated the law;" he preferred his own subjective method and vague criteria for selecting the "delinquent" sample. At one point, Sheldon had arbitrarily eliminated 200 other Hayden Inn residents because their records were "less than complete."

Also contaminating his results was the fact that his subjects, being early to mid-adolescent males, were most likely experiencing dramatic growth spurts and undergoing other physical changes. This could be said of any research on the body appearance of juveniles. Finally, the college males in Sheldon's control group were older than the delinquent boys, making comparisons, at best, difficult (Montemayor, 1978). In sum, Sheldon's method of somatotyping was so confusing and subjective that his measures of body type lacked both validity and reliability. Even researchers sympathetic to Sheldon's approach resorted to other measures or variations of his procedure.

Shortly after Sheldon's work was published, Sheldon Glueck and Eleanor Glueck (1950, 1956) reported on their own scheme for somatotyping applied in their classic and extensive study of delinquent boys, which we cover in some detail in Chapter 9. The

Gluecks classified 60 percent of their delinquent sample as mesomorphs compared to 30 percent of the control group. Other researchers followed suit. Gibbens (1963) studied English borstal boys and discovered an unexpectedly large percentage of mesomorphs, but he was unable to somatotype his control sample for comparison purposes. Cortes and Gatti (1972) reported that delinquents (100 boys adjudicated by juvenile court) were preponderantly more mesomorphic than nondelinquents (100 male high school seniors). They classified 57 percent of the delinquent group as mesomorphic compared to 19 percent of the nondelinquents. Epps and Parnell (1952) compared the physiques of 177 female delinquents to those of 123 Oxford undergraduates and found the delinquents to be shorter, heavier, more muscular or fat, suggesting mesomorphy *and* endomorphy.

Later, more sophisticated research reached very different results. McCandless, Persons, and Roberts (1972) found physique unrelated to either self-reported delinquency or the seriousness of criminal offenses. Wadsworth (1979), using data from the British National Survey, reported that delinquents, especially those who committed serious offenses, were generally *smaller* in stature and appeared to reach puberty later than their nondelinquent peers. While no somatotyping was done, the results suggest that the delinquents were not mesomorphs, since mesomorphs reportedly reach puberty before the other body types (Rutter and Giller, 1984). Finally, in their longitudinal study of working class boys in London, West and Farrington (1973) reported little association between delinquency and either height-weight ratios or physical strength.

Conclusions

James Q. Wilson and Richard J. Herrnstein (1985, p. 90), in their recent and controversial book *Crime and Human Nature*, concluded that, ". . . the evidence leaves no doubt that constitutional traits correlate with criminal behavior." While the evidence we have reviewed so far hardly justifies a "no-doubt" conclusion, it does *suggest*—on the basis of small but significant correlations—that there may be a link between body build—specifically mesomorphy—and a tendency to be delinquent. Studies in this area do not invariably yield significant correlations, however. The next and most difficult question is, "How do we explain the relationship if it does exist?"

Nigel Walker (1968, p. 47) offered a sensible hypothesis. He suggested that when we think of a mesomorph, we imagine "a muscular, athletic boy," and when we think of a juvenile delinquent we imagine a "large boy who fights, robs, and steals." It is easy to see, Walker commented, how the mesomorph's physique is well-suited to do the sorts of things a delinquent does: assault others, climb walls, run away from police. In addition, children begin to learn at an early age what they are physically able to do and do well. Youths who get their way more readily by physical threats and blows tend more often than not to be large, muscular, and active.

Certainly, individuals of different body structures engage in different types of activities, which in turn affects the reactions of others toward them. These reactions in turn affect the self-image as to whether one is physically robust or threatening to others. The body structure-delinquency connection may also reflect social stereotypes of the ways in which people with particular body types are expected to behave. A large, muscular 13-year-old often is expected to be aggressive. Consider the following comment made by a father about his 5′3″ 115 lb. 17-year-old son: "Take a good look at him. Is he the type who's going to make trouble?" How an individual acts, especially during adolescence, is in large measure determined by how others react to him.

The delinquency-physique connection is clearly not the most fruitful area to pursue in a study of the causes of delinquency, however. Delinquents may be disproportionately mesomorphic, but it would be folly to conclude that mesomorphic body types are heading for delinquency.

GENETICS: THE SCIENCE OF ALREADY DIFFERING INDIVIDUALS

Social scientists, especially criminologists, support a long-standing tradition of animosity toward biological-genetic explanations of human behavior (Rowe and Osgood, 1984). Moreover, "Most sociological texts on crime and delinquency discuss genetic explanations only as bad examples, the reprehensible products of a less-enlightened era" (Rowe and Osgood, 1984, p. 526). What is not often recognized or emphasized is that the assumptions and contentions of Lombroso, Goddard, and Sheldon are also *not* acceptable to most biologists, psychobiologists, or psychologists today. Contemporary scientists find the assumptions made by these early writers untenable and their research methods crude. Genes influence human behavior, but the influence is modified by, even buried under, environmental influences. Still, we must be ever mindful that genetics and biological factors do play some role in the formation of behavior. Earlier in the chapter, we discussed the role of temperament, which is believed by some researchers to be an inherited personality trait. In the following pages, we will consider briefly twin and adoption studies and delinquency.

Attempts to Disentangle the Genetic-Environmental Thicket: Twin Studies

If genetics play a substantial role in behavior, that role should be clearly outlined in the conduct of identical and fraternal twins. That assumption underlies the work of researchers who have conducted empirical research on crime and delinquency among twins. Fraternal twins (also called dizygotic twins) develop from two different fertilized eggs and are not more *genetically* alike than ordinary siblings. Identical twins (or monozygotic twins) develop from a single egg; they are always the same sex and share the same genes. Presumably, then, if genes are determinative, identical twins should display highly similar behavior.

Twin researchers report their results in concordance terms. Concordance, in genetics, is the degree to which pairs of related subjects exhibit a particular behavior or condition. It is usually expressed in percentages. For example, assume we wish to determine the concordance of intelligence between 20 pairs of fraternal twins and 20 pairs of identical twins. If 10 pairs of the identical twins obtained approximately the same IQ score, but only 5 pairs of the fraternal twins obtained the same score, the concordance for identicals would be 50 percent and for fraternals, 25 percent. The concordance for identicals would be twice that for fraternals, *suggesting* that hereditary factors play a role in the formation of intelligence. If, however, the concordance for identicals was about the same as that for fraternals, genetic factors could be presumed unimportant, at least as represented by that sample and measured by our methodology.

One of the earliest twin-criminality studies was conducted by the German psychiatrist Johannes Lange in 1929 on inmates in Bavarian prisons. He discovered a 77 percent concordance for criminality for identical twins and a 12 percent concordance for fraternals. Many subsequent twin studies have confirmed Lange's findings (Bartol and Bartol, 1986). On the average, investigations reported a concordance rate of 60 percent for identicals and about 30 percent for fraternals (Mednick et al., 1986).

In spite of this, researchers are hesitant to accept the genetic implications of twin research. Most twin studies have lacked rigid sampling or testing procedures, leaving their results questionable. Gordon Trasler (1987) observes that the more carefully designed a twin study is, the less pronounced the concordance differences in offending between monozygotic and dizygotic twins. For example, early investigations—such as the one by Lange—were handicapped by unreliable methods of determining whether twin pairs were monozygotic or dizygotic. Now, with increased sophistication in blood and serum testing, the large differences reported in the earlier studies have dropped substantially. For instance, Dalgard and Kringlen (1976), in contrast to Lange, report an offending concordance rate of only 26 percent for monozygotic twin pairs compared to 15 percent for dizygotic twin pairs.

The twin method assumes that the environment exerts a similar influence on each member of the set, whether the twins are identical or fraternal. Differences, then, must be due to genetic factors. Many critics have noted, however, that identical twins are so alike physically that it is very likely they elicit *more similar* social responses than fraternal twins. Similar behavior, then, could just as easily be due to environmental influences. For example, when Dalgard and Kringlen adjusted their data to take into account the effects of the social environment (whether they were treated alike, dressed alike, and so forth), the concordance differences in offending disappeared. Their conclusion: "These findings support the view that *hereditary factors are of no significant importance in the etiology of common crime*" (1976, p. 231). Overall, because of these questions about the twin method and the failure of the studies to separate decisively genetic from environmental effects, many if not most criminologists are suspicious about the genetic implications of twin research.

Further Attempts to Disentangle: Adoption Studies

Another method used to identify relevant variables in the interaction between heredity and environment is the adoption study, which assumes that, if siblings are raised apart, similarities in their behavior may be due to genetic influences. Theoretically, adoption studies should be especially useful for determining what kinds of environments are most conducive to criminality. Unfortunately, the few investigations of criminality among adopted children have been fraught with methodological difficulties.

Crowe (1974) followed 52 persons relinquished for early adoption by female offenders. Ninety percent of the biological mothers were felons at the time of the adoptive placement, their most common offenses being forgery and passing bad checks. Twenty-five of the 52 adoptees were female, and all were white. Another 52 white adoptees with no evidence of criminal family background were selected as a control group and matched with the index group for age, sex, and race at the time of adoption.

In the follow-up study, Crowe selected the 37 index and control subjects who had by then reached age eighteen. Of the 37 index adoptees born of female offenders, seven had arrest records as adults, all seven had a least one conviction, and four had multiple arrests, two had multiple convictions, and three were "felons." Of the 37 matching controls, two had adult arrest records and only one of these resulted in a conviction.

Crowe's study found a positive correlation between the tendency of the index group to be antisocial and two other variables: the child's age at the time of adoptive placement and the length of time the child had spent in temporary care (institutions and foster homes) prior to that placement. The older the child of an offender upon adoptive placement plus the longer the temporary placement, the more likely that child would grow up to be antisocial. The control group apparently was not affected by these conditions. This suggests that the early, disruptive environment may have facilitated antisocial behavior, but it is unclear what processes are operating.

Like Crowe, Barry Hutchings and Sarnoff Mednick (1975) reasoned that if there is a genetic basis for criminality, then there should be a significant relationship between the criminal behavior of biological parents and that of their children who were adopted by someone else. In 1971 Hutchings and Mednick identified 1,145 male adoptees from Copenhagen adoption files. At the time of the study these adoptees were between the ages of 30 and 44. The adoptees were matched for sex, age, occupational status of fathers, and residence to an equal number of non-adoptee controls.

The researchers were able to determine that 185 of the adoptees (16.2 percent) had criminal records, compared to 105 non-adoptees (8.9 percent). The biological fathers of the adoptees were nearly three times more likely to be involved in criminal activity than either the adoptee's adoptive fathers or the fathers of the non-adopted controls. Furthermore, there was a significant relationship between the criminality of the sons and that of their natural fathers. If the biological father had a criminal record while the adoptive father had a clean record, a significant number of adoptees still became criminal (22 percent); but if the biological father had a clean record and the adoptive father had a criminal record, the number of adoptees who pursued criminal activities was less (11.5 percent). If both the biological and adoptive fathers were criminal, the chances were much greater that the adoptee would be criminal than if only one of the fathers was criminal. Hutchins and Mednick (1977) concluded that genetic factors exerted strong influences in the tendency toward criminality, even though environmental factors also played important roles.

One serious limitation to the Hutchings-Mednick data is that Danish agencies—

perhaps more so than those in the United States—attempt to match the adopted child with the adoptive family on the basis of the child's biological and socioeconomic background. The Danish adoption agency used in the Hutchings-Mednick project confirmed that this was done.

Mednick and his associates recently described a similar ongoing adoptive study being conducted on a cohort of 14,427 Danish adoptees (Mednick et al., 1986). Conviction rates of male adoptees and their biological fathers continue to be considerably higher than the rates for adoptive fathers. This is especially true of repeat offenders. That is, the genetic connection seems to be stronger for chronic offenders (with three or more *convictions*) than for occasional offenders. Note that the Mednick group defined the chronic offender differently than did Wolfgang in his birth cohort study discussed in Chapter 1. Wolfgang (Wolfgang, Figlio, and Sellin, 1972) defined the chronic offender as one with five or more *police contacts*. Mednick preferred to count *convictions*. According to the Mednick data, chronic offenders are far more likely to have criminal biological fathers than occasional offenders or nonoffenders. In fact, Mednick's chronic offenders, while constituting only four percent of the male adoptee cohort, accounted for 69 percent of all the court convictions for all the male adoptees, a finding similar to the Wolfgang cohort studies in Philadelphia.

The Mednick group also report that the biological mothers of convicted female adoptees show higher levels of criminality than their adoptive mothers. Both adoptive fathers and adoptive mothers exhibited average criminality for the country. Furthermore, there were a number of instances where biological mothers and/or biological fathers contributed more than their fair share to the adoptee population. Therefore, while some of the children are full siblings, others are half-siblings. The Mednick group predicted that full siblings would have higher concordance rates for criminal convictions than the half-siblings. As predicted, the results revealed that as the degree of the genetic relationship increases, the level of concordance also increases.

The Mednick Theory

Mednick and his associates propose that this genetic-crime relationship can be explained, at least in part, by Mednick's (1977) theory of individual differences in the reactivity of the autonomic nervous system. Mednick contends that law-abiding behavior must be learned, and that this learning requires both environmental conditions and individual abilities. He believes that there are, in everyone, strong impulses that "society must channel and inhibit to maintain even the poor semblance of civilization we see around us" (1977, p. 3). He emphasizes that his theory pertains primarily to a small active group of chronic offenders, who have not been normally socialized because of defective characteristics of their nervous systems. Specifically, Mednick proposes that chronic offenders have a sluggish autonomic nervous system that prevents them from inhibiting their impulses.

The Mednick theory assumes that the reduction of fear is the most powerful, naturally occurring reinforcement for the human being. Mednick supposes that *fast* dissipation of fear is a more powerful reinforcer than slow dissipation, since research has shown that the speed and amount of reinforcement determine its effectiveness. The faster the reduction in fear, the more effective and lasting the reinforcement. Consider the following sequence of events:

When Harris is aggressive toward Zeek, Harris is punished on the spot by his mother.

After a number of such punishments, just the thought of the aggression should be enough to produce some anticipatory fear in Harris. If he reacts like the normal child, he will begin to inhibit his aggressive impulses.

When he inhibits the aggressive response, fear is reduced.

Each time an aggressive impulse arises and is inhibited, the inhibition will be strengthened by the reinforcement of fear reduction.

Mednick believes that the fear response is largely controlled by the autonomic nervous system. He reminds us that individuals differ in the activity of this system. If Harris has a normal autonomic nervous system, he will recover from fear very rapidly, but he will also receive immediate, strong reinforcement and learn inhibition quickly. On the other hand, if Harris has a "sluggish" autonomic nervous system that reacts slowly to fear, he will receive a slow, weak reinforcement and learn to inhibit aggression very slowly, if at all. The slower the autonomic nervous system, the more serious and repetitive the delinquent behavior predicted. Therefore, delinquents, and presumably adult criminals, have some defect in their nervous system that interferes with their ability to refrain from antisocial behavior. Correspondingly, serious delinquents have a more pronounced defect than nondelinquents. The Mednick model shows promise and should stimulate considerable research in the future, particularly since researchers and clinicians often observe that many serious delinquents and repetitive adult offenders appear to lack an appreciation for the consequences of their actions (Trasler, 1987).

SUMMARY AND CONCLUSIONS

In this chapter we have reviewed the individual or infrasystem based on the biological and genetic factors. There is some evidence that biological and genetic components play a role in the equation, but much of the theory and research in the area suffers from being either too broad or too specific. Eysenck's search for the universal theory of criminality built upon conditioning has received only weak support. Body-type theory is no more promising. Wilson and Herrnstein also propose a universal theory of constitutional factors interacting with environmental factors, with the view that people are ultimately "cost accountants" concerned with maximizing personal profit. The Wilson-Herrnstein proposal is too new to have drawn any empirical research. However, it seems broad and vague and is at high risk to suffer the same fate as other universal theories discussed in Chapter 5. As noted by Hubert M. Blalock, Jr. (1970, p. 79): ". . . the grand theorists have provided us with relatively few specific *propositions* that are sufficiently precise to yield testable hypothesis."

While it is correct that Eysenck and Wilson-Herrnstein recognize the influence of social factors, their emphasis is clearly upon the single-level and individual factor of genetic determination, or—put more cautiously—"predisposition." The problem is not so much their emphasis on the genetic-biological components of the infrasystem; rather, they contend tht delinquency is a phenomenon caused primarily by individual level influences. However, the social phenomenon of delinquency cannot be explained solely in terms of knowledge about individuals. We need explanations at other levels as well. Individual level explanations are invaluable for understanding *that* particular individual, but when we are trying to understand the behavior of thousands of juveniles, we also need some explanation at the macrosystem level. And if we want to understand the delinquents within a certain neighborhood, then we need to focus at that exosystematic level, while simultaneously considering other systems.

Twin and adoption studies do offer *some* support to the genetic influence on criminal behavior, especially the Mednick work. Still, the research is basically correlational without consideration of other influences and higher levels of explanations. The research is "correlational" in that it searches for relationships between behavior and biological parents' behavior. In sum, genetic research does not lead beyond the conclusion that "genetics may predispose some people toward delinquency."

One important point about the relative effects of genetic versus environmental factors needs to be emphasized. Human behavioral patterns are partially influenced by millions of genes having a very small effect (Trasler, 1987). Thus, we are *not* talking about one single gene or a small number of genes having significant effects on human conduct. We are talking about an incalculable number of genes and their combinations possibly having some small effect on behavior against a backdrop of enormous environmental influences. Attempts to group people on the basis of genetic differences are, at best, risky and full of error. "The potential for genetic differences between individuals is staggering, even within a family. The numbers of genetically different types of sperm and egg which any one individual could in principle produce is many millionfold more than the number of humans who have ever lived. This extraordinary genetic uniqueness of the individual must apply to all his attributes. . ." (W. Bodmer, cited by Trasler, 1987, p. 106). Gordon Trasler (1987, p. 106) concludes: "We might venture the comment that social scientists often think in excessively simple terms about the respective influences of genetic and environmental factors in controlling the delinquent."

The most promising genetic-biological work is contemporary research on temperament. It not only recognizes the bidirectional, reciprocal influences between child and parent, but it is beginning to explore other influences as well, such as the self-selection of social environments by the participants themselves. The study of temperament has become popular in developmental psychology in recent years, and it is hoped that some attention will be directed at delinquency in the future. Still, it is important to be ever mindful that when it comes to human behavior, cognitive or mental factors take precedence over genetic-biological or neurological ones.

The next chapter will continue to focus on the individual system or infrasystem, but instead of the genetic-biological component of explanation, we will shift to the mental-cognitive component.

Learning, Cognitive Development, and Construct Systems

CHAPTER 7

George A. Kelly (1963) theorized that humans look at their worlds through mental images similar to transparent patterns or templates. We create these templates and try to fit them over the reality of the world. Often the fit is not very good. Yet, without our templates, the world would appear chaotic, unpredictable, and fragmented. Without them, we would have little to anchor down our senses and perceptions. Thus, even a "poor fit" is more helpful than none at all. Kelly called these cognitive templates "constructs." They enable us ". . . to chart a course of behavior, explicitly formulated or implicitly acted out, verbally expressed or utterly inarticulate, consistent with other courses of behavior or inconsistent with them, intellectually reasoned or vegetatively sensed" (Kelly, 1963, p. 9).

Constructs, then, are mental representations of the environment. They are our mental shorthand or summaries of what we know about the world. They make us liberal or conservative, optimistic or pessimistic, jaded or naive, for whatever those labels are worth. The constructs are dynamic and interrelated and are, therefore, cognitive systems. This chapter will be concerned with their description and development.

More than the individual genetic or constitutional systems of the preceding chapter, construct systems provide a solid framework from which to build a social systems approach to the study of delinquency. Just as important, however, they have considerable unexamined influence over what theories criminologists find attractive, their feelings about data and facts, and how amenable they are to various explanations of behavior.

We begin the chapter with attention to basic principles of learning and to the specific area of social learning, illustrated by theories of both psychologists and sociologists. Following that we move to moral development, I-theory, and the labeling perspective. What these seemingly diverse views have in common is a foundation in the internal construct systems of the individual, even though the experiences offered by society play a crucial role.

SOCIAL LEARNING AND DELINQUENCY

Although there are variants of social learning theory, they can be generally divided into two categories:

1. those based on social reinforcement, derived from principles articulated by B. F. Skinner; and
2. those based on social imitation.

Both positions have their roots in behaviorism and the Skinnerian concept of operant conditioning, and each has something to say about the development of delinquency.

Social learning theory can be traced at least as far back as the late 19th century to the writings of child psychologist James Mark Baldwin and social psychologist Gabriel Tarde, who were discussed briefly in Chapter 1. Theories based on social reinforcement and imitation were stated most explicitly by psychologists during the early 1960s (Cairns, 1983), but they were also implicit in the work of the sociologist Edwin Sutherland. Today, no single discipline can claim exclusive guardianship of the basic ideas of social learning. Theorists in both psychology and sociology, for example, have tried to reformulate or expand various aspects of earlier approaches.

Gewirtz (1961) and Bijou and Bair (1961) adapted B. F. Skinner's operant conditioning to emphasize *social reinforcement* in child development, especially concerning prosocial and deviant behavior. The *social imitation* school of thought was led by Albert Bandura and Richard Walters (1963) who emphasized—as Baldwin had earlier—the important element of *modeling* the behavior of significant others in the social environments. Because there is so much confusion and misunderstanding among students of crime and delinquency about Skinner, operant conditioning, and behaviorism in general, it will be worthwhile to begin this section by addressing these topics.

Behaviorism

Behaviorism ''officially'' began in 1913 with the publication of a landmark paper by John B. Watson, ''Psychology as the Behaviorist Views It.'' The paper, which appeared in *Psychology Review*, is considered the first definitive statement on behaviorism, and Watson is thus acknowledged as the school's founder.

In this paper and in subsequent writings and public appearances, Watson continually declared that psychology is the *science* of behavior. He argued that psychologists should eliminate the "mind" and all of its related "vague" concepts from scientific consideration, because they could not be observed directly or measured. He was convinced that the fundamental goal of psychology was to understand, predict, and control human behavior; only a rigorous scientific approach could reach this goal. He was convinced, also, that psychology must closely mimic the physical sciences if it was to accomplish the extensive explanation and control achieved by those sciences.

Greatly influenced by Ivan Pavlov's research on classical conditioning, Watson thought psychology should focus exclusively on the relationship between stimulus and response. A stimulus is any object or event that elicits behavior. A response is the elicited behavior. Watson was convinced that all behavior—both animal and human—was controlled by the external environment in a way similar to that described by Pavlov in his initial study—a stimulus produces response (sometimes called S-R psychology). Therefore, for Watson, classical (or Pavlovian) conditioning was the key to understanding, predicting, and controlling behavior, and its practical applicability was unlimited.

Today, the chief spokesperson for behaviorism is B. F. Skinner, who has been one of the most influential American psychologists of the 20th century. For many years, the Skinnerian perspective dominated the application of "behavior modification" in the correctional system and in institutions for the mentally handicapped or disturbed. Eventually, practices associated with behavior modification were strongly challenged and very often curtailed. Some recent theories about delinquency (e.g., Akers, 1977, 1985) have tried to integrate Skinnerian behaviorism with sociological perspectives.

Like Watson, Skinner believes that the primary goal of psychology is the prediction and control of behavior. And like Watson, he believes that environmental or external stimuli are the primary—if not the sole—determinants of all behavior, both animal and human. Environmental stimuli are called independent variables, and the behaviors they elicit are dependent variables. You will recall that in our discussion of science in Chapter 2, we noted that consistent relationships between independent and dependent variables (stimulus and response) are scientific laws. Thus, according to Skinner, psychology's main goal is to uncover these laws, making possible the prediction and control of human behavior.

Unlike Watson, Skinner does not deny the existence and sometime usefulness of "private" mental events or internal stimuli. He emphasizes, however, that these stimuli are not needed by a science of behavior, since the products of mental activity can be explained in ways that do not require allusion to unobserved internal states. Specifically, mental activity can be explained by observing what a person does, and it is what a person does that counts.

Skinner is a strong *situationist*. He believes that all behavior is at the mercy of stimuli in the environment and that individuals have no control or self-determination. Independent thought and free will are myths that humans use to delude themselves that they are under their own control. Animals and humans alike react, like complicated robots, to their environments. For Skinner, crime and delinquency are exclusively the result of the environment and are not due to any predisposition or personality trait.

Skinner accepts the basic tenets of classical conditioning but asserts that we need an additional type of conditioning to account more fully for all forms of behavior. Ivan Pavlov had conducted experiments with hungry dogs who learned to salivate at the sound of a bell. The bell was usually followed by food, but sometimes by electric shock. Regardless of the outcome, the dogs salivated, because they had been conditioned by the bell. The dogs did not "operate" on their environments to receive rewards (or punishments); the event (food or shock) occurred independently of what they did. Skinner calls this "responding conditioning" and contrasts it to a situation in which a subject "does" something that affects the situation. In other words, subjects behave in such a way as to expect reinforcement. To uncover this "operant conditioning" principle, Skinner established an association between behavior and its consequences. He trained pigeons to peck at telegraph-like keys or push levers for food. The pecking or pushing were "operations" on the environment. The operation or *operant behavior* should not be construed to imply any notion of free will, however. The operant behavior was simply a *reaction* to stimuli (the telegraph key) in order to receive a certain consequence or reward.

Skinner was by no means the first to draw attention to the simple principle that people do things to get rewards and avoid things when punishment is involved. In the early 19th century the philosopher Jeremy Bentham observed that human conduct seemed to be controlled by the seeking of pleasure and the avoidance of pain. In essence, this is what is meant by operant conditioning. People do things solely to receive rewards and to avoid punishment. The rewards may be physical (e.g., material goods, money), psychological (e.g., feelings of competence), or social (e.g., improved status, acceptance by peers).

Skinner refers to rewards as *reinforcements*, defined as anything that increases the probability of future responding. Reinforcement could be either positive or negative. In *positive reinforcement* one gains something desired as a consequence of certain behavior. Nicole disciplines herself to train faithfully for the track team and is rewarded with a varsity position. In *negative reinforcement*, one *avoids* an unpleasant event or stimulus as a consequence of certain behavior. Densmore successfully avoids what he anticipates will be an unpleasant day at school by feigning illness. The behaviors of both students were reinforced, and are thus likely to be used again—in the one case to gain rewards, in the other to avoid events that are anticipated to be unpleasant or painful. Both positive and negative reinforcement can *increase* the likelihood of a particular behavior.

Negative reinforcement must be distinguished from "punishment" and "extinction." In punishment, a person receives noxious or painful stimuli as a consequence of something he or she did. In extinction, a person receives nothing, neither reinforcement nor pain. Skinner argues that punishment is an ineffective way to eliminate or change behavior, because it merely suppresses it temporarily. At a later time, under the right context, the response is likely to occur again. Extinction, he believes, is a far better procedure for the elimination or alteration of behavior. Once the person learns that a particular behavior brings no reinforcement, it will eventually drop out of the repertoire of possible responses for that set of circumstances. For example, once 6-year-old Scott realizes that temper tantrums at the checkout counter of the local supermarket will not gain the anticipated gum, the behavior should drop out of his response pattern.

The premise that operant conditioning is the basis for the origins of delinquent behavior is deceptively simple: Delinquent behavior is learned behavior. It is behavior that is learned through the principles of operant conditioning. It is behavior that brings rewards for the respondent. According to Skinner, human beings are born neutral—neither bad nor good. Culture, society, peers, parents and the whole social environment reward and shape behavior. Delinquent behavior, then, is a result of rewards received from the social environment.

Delinquent behavior, according to Skinner, is a social problem, not an individual one. He is convinced that searches for individual dispositions or personalities that lead to misbehavior will be fruitless because people are completely determined by the environment in which they live. He does not entirely discount the role of genetics in the formation of human behavior, but sees it as a very minor one. According to Skinner and his followers, if we wish to eliminate delinquency and crime, we must change society through behavioral engineering based on a "scientific conception of man." Skinner says we must design a society in which members learn very early that reinforcement will not occur if they violate prescribed rules and regulations, but will occur if they abide by them.

Contemporary psychology has grown cool toward the Skinnerian perspective as an explanation of human behavior. It is, in the eyes of many theorists and practitioners, too narrow and restrictive in explanation to account adequately for the constellation of factors that are characteristic of human behavior. Skinner's brand of behaviorism tends to see humans as robots. It should be noted that when Skinnerian theory was introduced, Ludwig von Bertalanffy, the founder of general systems theory, argued vehemently against it. "The organism is not a passive but an intrinsically active system," he wrote (1968, p. 208). "The robot model . . . only partly covers animal behavior and does not cover an essential portion of human behavior at all" (1968, p. 209).

Not all behaviorists, of course, are Skinnerians. Many of them also find the Skinnerian brand of behaviorism too limiting (e.g., Bandura, 1978, 1983). While they agree that a stimulus can elicit a reflexive response (classical conditioning) and that behavior obviously produces consequences that influence subsequent responding (operant conditioning), they are also convinced that additional factors must be introduced to explain human behavior. Still, the call for the study of behavior as the proper object of study remains respected. Classification and diagnostic systems based on behavioral observations continue to be highly popular among clinicians and practitioners. It will be worthwhile, therefore, to become familiar with the popular Quay classification systems of delinquent behavior before we move into the social learning perspective.

Typologies and Classification Systems: Putting Order into Delinquent Behavior

A typology is the study of types. In fact, the origin of the word "typology" can be traced back to the study of printing "types." In contemporary psychology, however, the term refers to a particular system for classifying personality or behavioral patterns. Usually, the typology is used to classify a wide assortment of behaviors into a more manageable set of brief descriptions. In recent years, Herbert C. Quay (1987) has been the leading spokesperson for a behavioral typology for delinquency.

Quay envisions a classification scheme that includes *four* types of delinquents. One type is labeled the *undersocialized* or *unsocialized delinquent*, a classification first used by Hewitt and Jenkins (1946) and Jenkins and Glickman (1947). The major characteristics are aggression, negativism, resistance, and lack of concern for others. In general, the undersocialized delinquent is at odds with everyone in the environment and does not seem to fit in anywhere. Moreover, he or she demonstrates very little guilt, no matter how damaging or hurtful the offense. Quay feels that youths in this group closely follow the characteristics of adult psychopaths.

According to Quay, youths institutionalized for repetitive, serious offenses tend to be of the undersocialized variety. As the label implies, they have not become adequately socialized to mainstream social values and standards. These delinquents are often associated with disciplinary problems and are substantially less likely to respond to various institutional, rehabilitative programs.

A second type of behavioral pattern is designated the *socialized delinquent* or the socialized aggressive type. While the interpersonal relationships of the undersocialized delinquent are poor, the peer relationships of the socialized delinquent are generally positive. In fact, the quality of the relationships with peers is considered the precipitating force for involvement in such acts as stealing, truancy, and drug use. Many of the illegal acts of the socialized delinquent would qualify as ''gang delinquency,'' the focus of so much contemporary concern. Gang delinquents have become ''socialized'' to the norms and values of the delinquent subculture.

Quay's third category falls under the rubric of *attention deficit disorder* (ADD), previously called learning disability or dyslexia. This behavioral pattern has also been referred to as immaturity and hyperactivity. The common ingredients in the pattern are: difficulty staying on task and remaining cognitively organized, impulsivity, and difficulty sustaining academic achievement in the school setting. It seems that the schema or cognitive constructs of ADD children have been hampered or delayed in their development. ADD youths do not seem to possess effective strategies and cognitive organization to deal with the daily demands of both school and work requiring abstract thinking. Moreover, they do not possess organized constructs or schema for dealing with new knowledge and thus seem destined to fail in the academic environment. And the intense and continual frustrations of failure may ultimately lead to deviance and delinquent activity.

The fourth of Quay's categories carries the intimidating clinical label, *anxiety withdrawal dysphoria delinquent*. Youths in this category are described as neurotic, overinhibited, anxious, and socially withdrawn. They do not deal completely with the social environment and generally prefer to avoid it by withdrawing from social interactions. Delinquent or deviant acts in this category are motivated by a need to escape or avoid stressful situations. Truancy from school and home, or the theft of a motor vehicle to get away for awhile, may be examples of delinquent actions motivated by anxiety withdrawal.

According to Quay (1987, p. 123), "Each individual, delinquent or not, has a place on each of these dimensions and that place can be determined only by assessing the degree to which the individual manifests the characteristics subsumed by the dimensions." Determining the category into which a person falls can be done in various ways, including behavioral ratings, analysis of life histories, and self-report questionnaires. The emphasis, however, is clearly on behavior and not attitudes or features of an individual's cognitive processes.

Placing individuals into behavioral categories, however, is based on the fundamental assumption that behavior is consistent across time and place. In other words, behavioral typologies are generally constructed on the premise that human behavior is largely the same from situation to situation. Typologies assume that the way a person acts at home is pretty much the same way he or she acts in the classroom, in the college dormitory, at work, and on the street. However, the validity of this assumption is very much open to debate. For example, some writers (e.g., Mischel, 1968; Mischel and Peake, 1982) argue that human behavior across *different* situations is inconsistent and that notions of stable behavioral dispositions or personality traits are largely unsupported. On the other hand, consistency across time, called "temporal consistency," is acknowledged. As long as situations are similar, people will likely respond the same way over their lifespans. But when situations change, behavior is apt to change. Walter Mischel and Philip Peake (1982) conclude, on the basis of their research findings, that behavior is highly dependent upon the nature of the situation, and that humans discriminate between situations and respond accordingly. Can we expect a socially withdrawn child to be withdrawn on all occasions—even with family? In any event, cross-situational consistency is a critical issue in the formulation of any classification system or typology. A reasonable answer to the riddle may lie in the research findings of Bem and Allen (1974) and Kenrick and Springfield (1980). That is, *some* behaviors are consistent across both time and place, but *most* are not. Perhaps the best source of information about a person is the person him or herself.

This brings us to the topic of mental states and cognitive processes, which Skinner urges us to shun. In recent years, many psychologists have been examining the roles played by self-reinforcement, anticipatory reinforcement, vicarious reinforcement, and all the symbolic processes that occur within the human "mind." Social learning theorists led the way.

Social Learning versus Behaviorism

In contrast to Skinnerian behaviorism, social learning theorists see humans as active problem solvers who perceive, encode, interpret, and make decisions on the basis of what their environment has to offer. To understand delinquency, social learning theorists tell us we must examine perceptions, thoughts, expectancies, competencies, and values. Viewing humans as reinforcement maximizers who consider only the ratio of rewards to punishments before making decisions is overly simplistic and not in line with present research on cognitive processes.

To explain human behavior, social learning theorists emphasize cognitive variables, such as the internal processes we commonly call thinking and remembering. They note that classical and operant conditioning perspectives ignore what transpires between the time the person perceives a stimulus and the time he or she responds or reacts to it.

The term "social learning" reflects the theory's strong assumption that we learn primarily by observing and listening to people around us—the *social* environment. In fact, social learning theorists believe that the social environment is the most important factor in the *acquisition* of most behavior. They do accept the necessity of reinforcement for the *maintenance* of behavior, however. Delinquent behavior, for example, may be *initially* acquired through association and through observation, but whether or not it is maintained will depend primarily upon reinforcement (operant conditioning). We will elaborate on this process when we discuss the imitational aspects of social learning soon.

Expectancy Theory

Julian Rotter is best known for drawing attention to the importance of expectations (cognitions) about the consequences (outcome) of behavior, including the reinforcement that will be gained from it. In other words, before doing anything, we ask, "What has happened to me before in this situation, and what will I gain this time?" According to Rotter, whether a specific pattern of behavior occurs will depend upon our expectancies and how much we value the outcomes. That is, Rotter puts considerable emphasis on *social reinforcement* as opposed to *social imitation*. To predict whether someone will behave a certain way, we must estimate that person's expectancies and the importance he or she places on the rewards gained by behavior. Often, the person will develop "generalized expectations" that are stable and consistent across relatively similar situations. For example, Luke has learned to expect that passivity and silence bring the best outcomes while in the presence of dominating, talkative men. On the other hand, Luke expects confrontation to bring negative outcomes, such as physical altercations.

The hypothesis that people enter situations with generalized expectancies about the outcome of their behavior may be important in the study of delinquency. Juveniles, according to Rotter's perspective, engage in misconduct because they expect to gain something in the form of status, power, affection, material goods, or living conditions. The social reinforcement perspective sees delinquent behavior as a situation where the individual has learned to value goals or reinforcements that, while bringing the disapproval of the larger society, lead to approval and acceptance of those in the delinquent's reference group (Phares, 1972). "Thus, quite simply, he engages in such activity because of the expectancy that it will lead to the rewards of approval and recognition from those people who are particularly reinforcing for him. In short, the principles by which he becomes a criminal are the same as those that turn someone else into a social conformist. He is not deviant in terms of his own subculture" (Phares, 1972, p. 648). The Rotterian version of social learning, therefore, reflects a *cultural deviance orientation*, a position that we will talk about throughout the text.

Imitational Aspects of Social Learning

According to Albert Bandura (1973), an individual may acquire behavior simply by watching others in action; direct reinforcement is not necessary. Bandura calls this process observational learning or modeling. Thus, Bandura subscribes to the social imitations brand of social learning. Bandura contends that much of our behavior is *initially* acquired by watching others, who are labeled *models*. For example, a child may learn how to shoot a gun by imitating TV characters. He or she then rehearses and fine tunes this behavioral pattern by practicing with toy guns, and then watches the models again for confirmation. The behavior is likely to be *maintained* if peers also play with guns and reinforce one another for doing so. Even if the children have not pulled the triggers on real firearms, they have acquired a close approximation of "shooting someone." It is likely that just about every adult in the U.S. "knows" how to shoot a gun, even if they have never actually done so. Of course, shooting safely and accurately are much more complicated, but the rudimentary know-how has been acquired through *imitational or observational learning*. The behavioral pattern exists in our repertoires, even if we have never received direct reinforcement for acquiring it, a point with which Skinner would disagree.

According to Bandura, the more significant and respected the models, the greater their impact on one's behavior. Relevant models include parents, teachers, siblings, friends, and peers, as well as symbolic models like literary characters or, more likely, media heroes. Rock stars and athletes are modeled by many young people, which is one reason why our society is exposed to so many public figures touting everything from cosmetics to a drug-free life.

Reinforcement has its place in Bandura's version of social learning, however. The observed behavior of the model is more likely to be imitated if the observer thinks the model is rewarded for the behavior. Conversely, a model is less likely to be imitated if that model is punished. Bandura believes—much like Rotter—that once a person has made the decision to use a newly acquired behavior, whether he or she actually performs it and maintains it will depend on the situation and the expectancies for potential gain (reinforcement). This "potential gain" may come from outside in the form of praise from others or financial profit or from within in the form of self-satisfaction.

Bandura, like most other social learning theorists in psychology, did not discuss crime and delinquency specifically. Much of his research was directed at the learning of aggressive and violent behavior, however, and the experimental literature offers impressive support for his views. In his classic Bobo experiment, preschool children who watched a film of an adult assaulting an inflated plastic rubber doll were significantly more likely to imitate that behavior than were a comparable group who viewed more passive behavior (Bandura & Huston, 1961; Bandura, Ross, and Ross, 1963). Many studies employing variations of this basic procedure report similar results, strengthening the hypothesis that observing aggression increases the likelihood that the observers— either children or adults—will engage in aggressive action.

The theories of Bandura and Rotter "humanized" the Skinnerian viewpoint, since they provided clues about what transpires inside the human brain or mind. They drew attention to the cognitive, mediational aspects of behavior, while classical and operant conditioning had focused exclusively upon what happens outside the individual. Social learning theorists use "environment" in the social sense, to include the internal as well as the external environment. Skinnerians prefer to limit relevant stimuli to physical surroundings.

Differential Association-Reinforcement Theory

When psychologists discuss social learning theory, they invariably cite Bandura and Rotter. When sociologists discuss social learning theory, they invariably cite Ronald Akers (1977, 1985); Burgess and Akers (1966). Akers proposed a social learning theory of deviance that tries to integrate core ingredients of Skinnerian behaviorism, the social learning theory as outlined by Bandura, and the differential association theory of Edwin Sutherland. Akers call his theory *differential association-reinforcement* (DAR). It postulates that people learn to commit deviant acts through experiences with their social environment.

As you will recall, Sutherland believed that criminal or deviant behavior is learned the same way all behavior is learned. The crucial factors are:

1. with whom a person associates;
2. for how long;
3. how frequently;
4. how personally meaningful the associations are; and
5. how early these social experiences occur in an individual's development.

According to Sutherland, people observe, imitate, internalize, and manifest the needs and values of the subgroups with which they associate; a process, you will recall, he called "Differential Association." If the attitudes and values learned are socially undesirable and if the behaviors are unlawful, and if these values and behaviors outweigh desirable and lawful attitudes and behaviors, the individual is likely to engage in unlawful activities. Note that deviant or delinquent behavior does not invariably develop out of association or contacts with "bad companions" or a criminal element. The ratio factor is crucial. Contacts with unlawful or deviant patterns must *outweigh* contacts with lawful patterns of behavior.

Sutherland's theory, although intuitively appealing, was widely criticized by criminologists who found it vague and impossible to submit to empirical falsification. Burgess and Akers (1966) and ultimately Akers alone (1977, 1985) tried to correct some of these problems by reformulating differential association theory. He proposed that most deviant behavior is learned according to principles outlined in Skinner's operant conditioning, with classical conditioning playing a secondary role. Furthermore, the strength of the deviant behavior is a direct function of the amount, frequency, and probability of reinforcement the individual has experienced by performing the behavior in the past. The reinforcement may be positive or negative, in the Skinnerian meanings of the terms. In Sutherland's perspective, reinforcement had no explicit role.

Critical to the Akers position is the role played by *social* reinforcement, in contrast to other forms of reinforcement. "[M]ost of the learning relevant to deviant behavior is the result of social interactions or exchanges in which the words, responses, presence, and behavior of other persons make reinforcers available, and provide the setting for reinforcement . . ." (Akers, 1977, p. 47). It is also important to note that most of these social reinforcements are symbolic and verbal rewards for participating or for agreeing with group norms and expectations. For example, Erik longs for acceptance by his "deviant peers." He burglarizes his neighbor's home, a behavior in accordance with their norms, and is rewarded by their admiration and by entry into their social circle.

Deviant behavior, then, is most likely to develop as a result of social reinforcements given by significant others, usually within one's peer group. The group first adopts *normative definitions* about what conduct is good or bad, right or wrong, justified or unjustified. These normative definitions become internal, cognitive guides to what is appropriate and will most likely be reinforced by the group. In this sense, normative definitions operate as *discriminative stimuli*—social signals transmitted by subcultural or peer groups to indicate whether certain kinds of behavior will be rewarded or punished within a particular social context.

According to Akers, two classes of discriminative stimuli operate in promoting deviant behavior. First, "positive" discriminative stimuli are the signals (verbal and nonverbal) that communicate that certain behaviors are encouraged by the subgroup. Not surprisingly, they follow the principle of positive reinforcement: The individual engaging in them gains social rewards from the group, as did Erik. A second type of social cues, "neutralizing" or "justifying" discriminative stimuli, neutralizes the warnings communicated by society at large that certain behaviors are inappropriate or unlawful. According to Akers, they "make the behavior, which others condemn and which the person himself may initially define as bad, seem all right, justified, excusable, necessary, the lesser of two evils, or not "really" deviant after all" (Akers, 1977, p. 521). Statements like "Society gave us a bum rap," "Cops are on the take; we just want our fair share," or "She deserved it" reflect the influence of neutralizing stimuli.

The more people define their behavior as positive or at least justified, the more likely they are to engage in it. If the deviant activity (as defined by society at large) has been reinforced more than conforming behavior (also defined by society) and if it has been justified, it is likely that deviant behavior will be maintained. In essence, behavior is guided by the norms the individual has internalized and for which he or she expects to be socially reinforced by significant others. Akers agrees with Bandura that modeling is a crucial factor in the initial acquisition of deviant behavior. Its continuation, however, will depend greatly upon the frequency and personal significance of social reinforcement, which comes from association with others.

Akers's theory has received its share of criticism. Some sociologists consider it tautological: Behavior occurs because it is reinforced, but it is reinforced because it occurs. Taylor, Walton, and Young (1973) accused Burgess and Akers of theoretical illiteracy. Kornhauser (1978) declared that there was not empirical support for the theory. Akers himself stressed the need for longitudinal research to test the theory and began to do so himself in a series of studies of drug use among adolescents, which will be discussed in Chapter 9.

COGNITIVE AND MORAL DEVELOPMENT

In 1983 Albert Bandura added a significant clarification to his social learning theory. He emphasized that individuals are able to exercise cognitive control over their behavior. In other words, the fact that behavior has been learned by imitation and maintained by reinforcement does not guarantee that it will be performed. This is not a new position taken by Bandura; it was in his earlier versions of the theory. However, it was an aspect that was frequently misunderstood.

From the social learning perspective, cognitive processes enable the individual to transcend the present and think about the future as well as the past, even in the absence of immediate environmental stimuli. This conceptual thinking ability allows the individual to guide his or her behavior by thinking about its possible outcomes. Nevertheless, circumstances do sometimes weaken cognitive control and facilitate "impulsive" actions. This self-regulatory process presumes the development and refinement of cognitive structures, to which we now turn.

Moral Development

How people acquire, internalize, and develop personal values are key concerns in the study of the delinquent. Some philosophers and social scientists argue that we develop our morality and belief system, our concepts of right and wrong, through a series of cognitive stages, with the highest levels being reached through lifelong periods of logic and self-discovery. They contend that through the principles of logic and continual learning, humans can discover and cognitively construct ethical and moral principles of fairness, responsibility, and empathy toward others.

The most widely cited early research on moral character was conducted in 1924 by Hugh Hartshorne, Professor of Religious Education at the University of Southern California, and Mark A. May, Professor of Psychology at Columbia University. They examined the qualities of honesty, generosity, and self-control in children. To their surprise, they discovered that these moral traits were not consistent across situations. Instead, they found that a child may conduct him or herself in a moral fashion in one situation but did not necessary act commendably in a different situation. Hartshorne and May concluded that no one is basically honest or dishonest, generous or selfish, self-controlled or impulsive. Instead, conduct is largely controlled by the situation.

The disappointing conclusion that the setting determines moral behavior temporarily slowed efforts to delineate a personality theory of morality. For many years, the Hartshorne-May data were used to support assumptions that behavior is situational. Later statistical analyses of the Hartshorne-May data revealed that the researchers' original conclusion of situation specificity may have been unjustified, however (Burton, 1963, 1976; Eysenck, 1977). The current research suggests that while the situation plays an extremely powerful role in determining what individuals do, personality components also play a crucial role. The question becomes, does one outweigh the other?

Subsequent investigations of moral development focused on moral judgment and reasoning. The Swiss psychologist Jean Piaget (1948) was a pioneer in studying how we symbolize and organize social rules and make judgments based on that organization. He hypothesized that morality develops in a series of steps or stages, each one depending upon the completion of previous steps and upon the intellectual equipment and social experiences of the individual. Much of Piaget's thinking was strongly influenced by the forgotten James Mark Baldwin, whom he freely acknowledged throughout his works. The developmental psychologist Lawrence Kohlberg (1976) revised Piaget's theory and revived research in moral development. Like Piaget, Kohlberg postulated that moral development evolves in sequential stages. The sequence is invariant, with each stage following another in an orderly fashion. The individual must develop the features and skills of a lower moral stage before attaining a higher one.

Kohlberg identified three primary stages: *preconventional*, *conventional*, and *postconventional*. Each primary stage comprises two substages, which we will refer to here as "early" and "late." During the *early preconventional* stage, the child acts only to obtain rewards and avoid punishment. In essence, the child has not developed any moral reasoning and is basically amoral. According to Kohlberg, this amoral orientation characterizes children below age seven, but may be seen at any age in some individuals. During the *late preconventional* stage, the right action is that which satisfies one's own needs. This stage reflects a selfish orientation which considers the needs of others only to the extent that favors will be returned. In other words, the individual will only be helpful or ostensibly "moral" to others when it clearly serves his or her personal interests. According to Kohlberg (1976, 1977) human relationships at this stage are viewed as in a marketplace, not with loyalty, gratitude, or justice, but with the goal of using others to obtain something.

The *early conventional* stage is referred to as the "good boy" or "good girl" orientation. The individual's behavior is directed toward gaining social approval and acceptance, especially from peers, and he or she conforms to a stereotyped image of what the majority of the peer group regards as acceptable behavior. To obtain social rewards and avoid punishment, a person at this stage believes he or she must conform precisely to what is expected. The conscience, or the ability to feel guilty, begins to emerge. At the *late conventional* stage the person does things out of duty and respect for the authority of others. Certain rules and regulations are acknowledged as necessary to ensure the smooth functioning of society; if one is derelict in performing his or her duty, dishonor and blame will result. This late conventional stage is often labeled "law and order" morality, because of its strong emphasis on unquestioning respect for authority, conventionalism, and rigid rules of conduct.

The final and highest primary stage of moral development—the postconventional—is, in Kohlberg's estimation, reached by few people. To reach these stages one must have the cognitive ability to abstract and to perceive issues in "gray shades" rather than in a strict "black and white" dichotomy. During the *early postconventional* stage, correct action is determined by principles which reflect an appreciation for the general rights of individuals as well as the standards which have been critically examined and agreed upon by society. Note that there is a strong assumption running throughout Kohlberg's theory that there *is* consensus in society about what is right and wrong.

Kohlberg believed individuals at the early postconventional stage had achieved a mature balancing of individual and societal rights. In addition to taking into consideration what is democratically agreed upon, the early postconventional person relies on personal values to consider the rightness and wrongness of behavior. These personal values may not be in agreement with those of society. Kohlberg believes that this stage reflects considerable emphasis upon the "legal" point of view, but with the personal conviction that unjust laws can be changed.

The *late postconventional* person demonstrates an orientation "toward the decisions of conscience and toward self-chosen ethical principles appealing to logical comprehensiveness, universality, and consistency" (Kohlberg, 1977, p. 63). The moral principles are highly abstract and ethical, and they reflect universal principles of justice and the reciprocity and equality of human rights. The person relies on his or her own *personally* developed ethical principles and shows respect for the dignity of human beings as individual persons.

According to Kohlberg, people go through the stages at different rates and thus reach them at different ages of their lives. Some never go beyond the preconventional stage, and most never reach the postconventional. The development of moral judgment depends upon the intellectual capacity and life experiences. Thus, someone may possess the cognitive ability to develop high stages of moral development but lack sufficient social experiences. On the other hand, despite adequate moral upbringing, the individual may lack the cognitive ability to abstract and generalize the moral principles involved at the higher stages. What constitutes "adequate" moral upbringing or "adequate" life experiences is unclear. Kohlberg contends, however, that the judgment of a large majority of juvenile delinquents is at the preconventional stage (Kohlberg & Freundlich, 1973).

It is important to realize that Kohlberg's theory is specifically related to moral *judgment* and the person's rationale for his or her behavior. What may appear to the observer to be unethical or clearly immoral conduct may, in fact, have a morally sound reason to it from the actor's perspective. Therefore, Kohlberg argues that we must try to understand *intentions* before we draw conclusions about another's *actions*.

Kohlberg measured moral development by presenting his subjects with dilemmas and asking them to choose solutions. One item on the test reads:

> In Europe, a woman was near death from a special kind of cancer. There was one drug that the doctors thought might save her. It was a form of radium that a druggist in the same town had recently discovered. The drug was expensive to make, but the druggist was charging 10 times what the drug costs him to make. He paid $200 for the radium and charged $2000 for a small dose of the drug. The sick woman's husband, Heinz, went to everyone he knew to borrow the money, but he could only get together about $1000, which is half

of what it cost. He told the druggist that his wife was dying and asked him to sell it cheaper or let him pay him later. But the druggist said, "No, I discovered the drug and I'm going to make money from it." So Heinz gets desperate and considers breaking into the man's store to steal the drug for his wife. (Colby et al., 1983, p. 75)

The subject is then asked such questions as: "Should Heinz steal the drug?" "Why or why not?"

For his doctoral dissertation completed in 1958, Kohlberg administered his moral development test to boys in custody awaiting juvenile hearings. He found that they were at lower levels of moral development than their "nondelinquent" peers. A "higher percentage" of the boys in detention, who were charged with repetitive car theft, burglary, and assault and robbery, were functioning at the preconventional stage. Later, Kohlberg (1973) elaborated on the delinquency, nondelinquency, and moral development relationship. Preconventional judgment, he explained, does not lead to delinquency. Rather, it is more correct to say that the *conventional* stage *insulates* the adolescent against social pressures toward delinquency. In other words, at the conventional stage the adolescent's cognitive development has matured to a point where internal reasoning overrides outside influence. Adolescents with more principled normative reasoning are better able to think through their own options for each situation, relatively independent of social pressures.

Research support for Kohlberg's theory has depended upon the sample of adolescents used. Studies of institutionalized or officially labeled delinquents support it, while studies using self-report data do not. Hudgins and Prentice (1973) discovered that boys with official delinquency records (such as repetitive auto theft or burglary) exhibited lower moral development than those boys with no official records. Interestingly, while mothers of both groups scored higher than their sons on a moral development scale, the mothers of delinquent sons scored lower than the mothers of nondelinquent sons. Campagna and Harter (1975) compared the moral development of institutionalized delinquent boys who had the temperamental and behavioral characteristics of psychopathy (impulsivity, hyperactivity, pathological lying) to nondelinquent boys. They found that the delinquent boys were significantly lower in moral reasoning than their matched peers. Moreover, the delinquent boys, compared to their matched peers, scored significantly lower in all verbal sections of an IQ test (Wechsler Intelligence Scale for Children), suggesting that they had less adequate language skills and vocabulary. (Recall that one of Kohlberg's requirements for moral development is good abstract ability.) Jurkovic and Prentice (1977), using 120 institutionalized delinquent boys, found that psychopathic delinquents lagged considerably behind both nonpsychopathic delinquent boys and nondelinquent peers in moral reasoning.

All the studies just mentioned used subjects who had committed official and serious offenses. Merry Morash (1981) went a step further. She studied 201 youths charged with committing *misdemeanors* or minor juvenile offenses. All were white males, 14 to 16 years of age. Morash administered Kohlberg's moral development scale as well as a self-report survey developed by Elliott and Voss (1974) to measure the extent of the boys' prior delinquent behavior. When the results of the self-report questionnaire were taken into account, Morash found that most of the boys (78 percent) were functioning at the conventional stage of moral development rather than the preconventional stage, in contrast to what Kohlberg would have predicted.

Delorto and Cullen (1985), tested moral development theory on a sample of 109 high school students from a rural Illinois community. They measured delinquency with the self-report scale developed by Elliott and Ageton (1980) and moral reasoning with Rest's Defining Issues Test (DIT) (Rest, 1979). The DIT consists of six hypothetical scenarios of moral dilemmas (similar to the druggist example described earlier). Respondents read stories and then answered 12 questions. On the self-report survey, students were asked if they had committed any of 45 listed offenses within the last year, running from very minor offenses to serious ones. The delinquency score was compiled in relation to the number of different offenses in which they had participated. In line with Elliott and Ageton, the researchers grouped the overall delinquency measures into six subscales. One subcategory related to "predatory" crimes against persons, and another involved "hard drug" use. Both subcategories represent serious offenses. The other four subcategories consisted almost exclusively of minor offenses. Most of the Elliott-Ageton scale (both versions) taps minor delinquency, a point we should very much keep in mind. Unfortunately, Delorto and Cullen did not ask the subjects how *often* they engaged in the listed offenses.

In any event, the Delorto and Cullen data did *not* reveal any association between self-report delinquency and moral reasoning, a finding which held for both minor and serious offenses. This is not surprising since, as noted in Chapter 1, self-report measures of delinquency suggest that a very large proportion of the adolescent population commit acts which may be defined as "minor delinquent." A delinquency-moral development connection is more likely to surface in self-report studies that measure *chronic* or *repetitive* serious offenses. Delorto and Cullen did not measure this aspect of juvenile offending. However, the research that has concentrated on repetitive serious offenders has found signs that moral reasoning is linked to delinquency (see Jennings et al., 1983). In short, serious offenders seem to have a different construct system from youths who engage in mischievous or nonrepetitive lawbreaking.

Criticisms of Kohlberg's Theory

Albert Bandura (1977) and other social learning theorists question Kohlberg's contention that moral development follows a universal and invariant stage sequence of cognitive construction. Bandura argues that moral judgment can be acquired and modified through imitative and observational learning processes, including the powerful influence of peer models. While he admits that personal experiences and changing social demands produce cognitive development with age, he considers "universal" stage development of morality farfetched. Moral reasoning is highly dependent on culture and the social milieu, and it is surely unique for each individual. The stages of morality constructed by Kohlberg, if anything, reflected *his* personal construct systems and beliefs. They represent what he as a theorist conceived of as the correct way of dealing with certain issues. It is unlikely that the Kohlberg stages represent universal, transcultural, and transtemporal principles that reside in nature as a given form of "natural justice."

Others have proposed theories of moral reasoning and judgment not dependent on universal stages. For example, researchers Carol Gilligan (1982), Norma Haan (1977, 1978), and Merry Morash (1983) have all theorized that an additional, "other-oriented" dimension is needed to explain moral conduct. Gilligan calls this dimension "contextual relativisim," Haan calls it "interpersonal morality," and Morash prefers "other-oriented reasoning." Regardless of the label used, each dimension focuses upon the extent to which a person has developed responsibility, concern, and care for *others*.

Researchers studying the other-oriented dimension have reported intriguing findings, particularly with respect to sex differences. They contend, for example, that boys develop an ethic of care for others at a later time than girls, usually sometime after adolescence (Morash, 1983). Research by Hoffman (1977) indicates that empathy is better developed in females than males at all ages, although Eisenberg and Lennon (1983) point out that this finding may be attributed to Hoffman's method of measurement. More specifically, self-report questionnaires consistently revealed that females were more empathetic than males, but behavioral observations showed few sex differences. Males may be more reluctant to admit that they care. Sex differences, if supported, could shed light on the consistent finding that males commit proportionately more violent crime than females.

Morash (1983) notes that the family is especially important in developing concern, empathy, and an other-oriented perspective in children. Interestingly, Kohlberg (1969) emphasized the substantial importance of inductive reasoning as a stimulus for moral development while insisting that family life in general had minimal or no importance (Morash, 1983). We will discuss family influences on delinquency in considerable detail in the next chapter.

Interpersonal-Maturity Theory

Related to moral development is still another theory, first proposed by Sullivan, Grant, and Grant in 1957 and developed by Marguerite Q. Warren (formerly Grant) (1983). Called *interpersonal-maturity* theory, or more generally "I-theory," it separates personality development into seven stages. I-theory became the main treatment planning and evaluation tool of the California Youth Authority from 1961 to 1975 (Harris, 1988).

According to I-theory research, most delinquents are clustered around three of the seven stages: stages (maturity levels) I-2, I-3, and I-4. People at maturity level I-2 demand that the world take care of them; they see others primarily as givers and withholders of punishments and rewards. They also seem to have limited skills for explaining, understanding, or predicting the conduct or reactions of others. They are not interested in things outside of themselves, except as a source of supply. People at maturity level I-3 see the world in an oversimplified fashion. They cannot understand the needs, feelings, and motives of others or why these should be different from their own. They perceive the social environment only as an arena in which they manipulate others for personal gain. Moreover, everyone is out to manipulate everyone else. At the I-4 level, people are primarily concerned about status and are strongly influenced by those they admire. Hence, they are especially susceptible to the influences of models. They see things as either good or bad, with no in between. Because of their rigidity, they are most susceptible to guilt and self-criticism when they feel they have failed to meet their rigid standards of conduct. Warren suggested that very few delinquents—fewer than one percent—progress beyond maturity level I-3.

Based on I-level theory, Warren was able to disentangle nine delinquent substages (Warren, 1969). Subsequent research by Palmer (1974) reduced the list to three broader subtypes: the passive conformist, the power-oriented, and the neurotic. According to Palmer, the neurotic type is by far the most common among delinquents. Carl Jesness (1988) has developed a more quantified measure of I-levels, the Jesness Inventory Classification System. More research is necessary before the instrument can be evaluated, however.

Like Kohlberg's theory, I-theory sees cognitive development as the result of an interaction between the cognitive ability with which one is born and one's experiences with the social environment. From this interaction, a person develops a relatively consistent set of expectations—an implicit philosophy of life—that constitutes a large segment of the mental component of personality. In this sense, interpersonal maturity theory is grounded on how the individual perceives the world and those within it (Quay, 1987). Although I-theory continues to be used in treatment planning by many juvenile agencies and correctional facilities, it appears to have limited value beyond providing a rough estimate of maturity (Harris, 1988).

CONSTRUCT SYSTEMS

Several decades ago, psychologist George A. Kelly (1955), introduced at the beginning of this chapter, began to write about personal constructs, which he conceived of as basic mental building blocks that represent individualized versions of the world. He suggested that all of one's present interpretations of the universe and social world are forever subject to revision or replacement. Objective reality or absolute truth are figments of the imagination. Each of us acquires new experiences that lead us to restructure and reinterpret our environment. This process of experiencing, interpreting, and structuring is "construing." Those constructs that seem to make sense of the world, we keep; those that do not, we discard.

Nelson Goodman (1978) explained human thought in similar fashion when he referred to "world-making." Each person constructs a world on the basis of personal experience and unique mental structure. Goodman suggests that worlds are made as they are found. There are many world versions, and it is foolhardy to presume that they can be reduced to a single base.

Edward Sapir (1921), trained by the anthropologist Franz Boas, hypothesized that a person's thinking processes are structured, if not controlled, by the properties of the language he or she speaks. The language habits of our community, culture, or subculture predispose us to what we see, hear, or otherwise experience. Sapir's student, Benjamin Lee Whorf (1956) developed his mentor's ideas further by hypothesizing that no individual is free to describe nature with absolute impartiality; rather, we are all constrained to certain modes of interpretation by the properties of our language and our habitual ways of thinking. In short, Sapir and Whorf believe that the language used by a group is a principal determinant of the belief structures and the ways of thinking of that population. One's language is the guide to social reality.

Children's construct systems vary with age. As experiences with the environment accumulate, the number, quality and organization of these constructs likewise change. Over the course of development, interpersonal construct systems should become:

1. increasingly differentiated (contain a greater number of constructs);
2. increasingly abstract (contain constructs pertaining to the more psychological, subtle aspects of other persons and their motives;
3. increasingly organized (contain constructs that are more interconnected with one another); and
4. increasingly perspectivistic (contain constructs less directed at self-involvement and self-reference). (Werner, 1957; Applegate et al., 1985)

Research in cognitive psychology has provided consistent support for these theoretical propositions (Applegate et al., 1985). This maturation phenomenon may account, at least in part, for the empirical observation that for most offenders involvement in crime peaks at an early age (16 to 18) and declines or disappears thereafter.

Furthermore, some people seem to possess more structure about the world than others—another way of saying some people are more ''cognitively complex.'' People with many sophisticated structures can evaluate behavior and world events in more complex ways than can people with a few, crude structures. Nevertheless, one's language, cultural background, cognitive sophistication, and, more generally, one's versions of the world are all likely to have an extremely important connection to delinquency. For example, several years ago Charles King (1975) conducted a qualitative study of ten adolescent murderers. Nine were boys and one was a girl. Their murders were unusually brutal (e.g., a machete dismembering, a gasoline burning) and, to the outsider, they seemed senseless. The average age of these violent teenagers at the time of the murder was 14. To the consternation of authorities, none had expressed any guilt or remorse. Their families, while intact, were characterized by turmoil, conflict, and excessive drinking. Parents exhibited unpredictable mood swings and physical violence, especially when drinking.

On the basis of interview data, King determined that these youngsters were ''confused'' about their environment, viewing it as chronically hostile and largely unpredictable. Most surprisingly, however, were the psychological evaluations. While these adolescents had average IQ scores, ''. . . every youth was most severely retarded in reading, and drastically stunted in language skills'' (p. 136). This finding led King to conclude that lack of language skills and cognitive constructs may have interfered with the youths' ability to interpret and interface adequately with the world. Such cognitive deficits, he believed, contributed to poor judgment and little realization of the consequences for their actions. Furthermore, these youngsters seemed to be unable to conceptualize their victims as persons. To the offenders, the victims were merely nonperson objects or targets. In short, King maintained that the poverty of language may have directly contributed to their actions. Their versions of the world seemed to be simplistic, black-and-white conceptions where hostility reigned and compassion was for "suckers."

This study illustrates the potential value of studying language development and the construct systems of serious delinquents. Far-reaching generalizations from a single study are, of course, unwarranted. Furthermore, we are not implying that "intelligent people" do not commit crimes. Rather, individuals with limited cognitive constructs and language skills may be less able to mediate and get along in their social worlds, compared to others with a richer cognitive structure and process. This brings us to the next topic: the relationship between intelligence measures and delinquency.

IQ AND DELINQUENCY

In 1977 criminologists Travis Hirschi and Michael Hindelang took the sociological perspective on delinquency to task for ignoring a persistent and statistically significant negative correlation between IQ scores and delinquency. After reviewing major official and self-report studies (e.g., Wolfgang et al., 1972; Reiss and Rhodes, 1961; West, 1973; Hirschi, 1969), Hirschi and Hindelang concluded that IQ was at least as strong a predictor of delinquency as social class and race. Specifically, they continually uncovered in their literature search the negative correlation: The lower the IQ, the higher the incidence of delinquency, whether official or self-reported. In that article, Hirschi and Hindelang hypothesized that an *indirect causal* relationship exists between IQ and delinquency. By "indirect" the writers meant that a low IQ leads to poor performance and attitudes toward school, which in turn leads to delinquency. A high IQ leads to good performance and attitudes toward school, which in turn leads to conformity (or at least nondelinquency). Thus, Hirschi and Hindelang saw school performance and attitudes as "intervening variables" that mediate between IQ and delinquency. Furthermore, they asserted that in spite of vehement denials of an IQ-delinquency relationship, most mainstream criminological theories implicitly assume that it exists.

With the publication of the Hirschi and Hindelang article, a controversy again surfaced that had been dormant since Sutherland authoritatively declared that mental tests were irrelevant to sociology (Sutherland, 1931). (Sutherland's assertion was made at a time when Henry Goddard's crusade against "mental undesirables" contaminating society was most zealous. Sutherland's indignation was well founded for that particular era.) The Hirschi-Hindelang paper touched nerves in two respects: First, they publicly challenged the firm sociological resistance to allowing individual differences any role in the etiology of crime—a resistance Hirschi and Hindelang attributed to a "moral commitment" that everyone is as good as everyone else. This does not necessarily mean everyone is *the same as* everyone else, they said. Second, they elicited some of the traditional interdisciplinary hostility among sociology, psychology, and behavioral genetics. At best, they were seen as gadflies whose conclusion could be dismissed for lack of relevance (e.g., Johnson, 1979). At worst, they were severely criticized for flirting with racism and for setting criminology back to its unpalatable positivist origins (e.g., Simons, 1978).

The Hirschi-Hindelang paper is one of the most challenging in the modern literature on the relationship between IQ and delinquency. It is also one that is frequently misunderstood. Ronald Simons (1978) accused the authors of disinterring the connection between "genetic IQ" and delinquency and chastised them for concluding that IQ is a stable ability that is largely independent of cultural and social influences. However, careful reading of the article reveals that Hirschi and Hindelang did *not* conclude that IQ is inherited or independent of cultural or social influences. If anything, their paper "pointedly ignores" heritability (Hirschi and Hindelang, 1978). The principle point that Hirschi and Hindelang made was that the inverse relationship between IQ score and delinquency continues to be substantiated in the research, *for whatever reason*. They urged criminologists to address the relationship and try to explain it rather than deny it exists. Interestingly, current research continues to support Hirschi and Hindelang's observation. The important question is, how should this persistent relationship be interpreted?

Unquestionably, we must focus first on the meaning of "IQ." The term is an abbreviation of the "intelligence quotient" derived from a numerical score on an "intelligence test." Satisfactory performance on these tests—of which there are many—depends greatly on language acquisition and development. Usually, a person must be skillful at defining and using words. He or she must also be able to make connections and see distinctions between verbal concepts. Finally he or she must know the facts which the test designer believes are important to know. At the very least, almost all IQ tests measure some aspect of academic skills that are either taught in school or that predict success in school.

The information probed for in intelligence tests reflects knowledge gained from daily living in a specific and educational milieu (Gardner, 1983). IQ tests, then, are "culture biased," in spite of recurring efforts to develop "culture-free" instruments. Furthermore, the scores may change, sometimes drastically, depending upon one's experience. The search for an intelligence test fair to all members of all cultures has been unsuccessful. "Each culture and subculture encourages and fosters certain abilities and ways of behaving; and it discourages or suppresses others" (Anastasi, 1982, p. 344). Most psychologists today would agree that IQ scores are strongly influenced by social, educational, and general culture background.

Howard Gardner (1983, pp. 17–18) summarizes incisively IQ and aptitude testing in general. ". . . the IQ movement is blindly empirical. It is based simply on tests with some predictive power about success in school and, only marginally, on a theory of how the mind works." IQ testing has been primarily, if not exclusively, concerned with establishing a predictive relationship between a score and grades in school. If a score on the exam predicts with *some* accuracy how well people do in school, then it is considered by many as a "valid" and useful instrument. Most often, there is no further attempt to decipher how the mind works in obtaining that score. IQ tests, for example, rarely assess skill in assimilating new information or in solving new problems (Gardner, 1983).

The concept of "intelligence," however, is a different matter. While the term "IQ" is generally restricted to scores on an intelligence test, intelligence defies any straightforward or simple definition. It means many things to different people. Gardner (1983), for example, outlined several forms of intelligence, including musical, logical-mathematical, spatial, body-kinesthetic, and personal intelligence. He added that there are probably many others. For example, how do we account for wisdom, synthesizing ability, intuition, metaphoric capacities, humor, and good judgment (Gardner, 1986)?

It is extremely important that the distinction between IQ and intelligence be recognized. The IQ-delinquency connection refers to a correlation between a *test score* and official and self-reported delinquency. The association is not between the broader meaning of *intelligence* and delinquency, although some mistakingly make that inference. There is even little match between intelligence tests and theories of intelligence (Goodnow, 1986). The IQ score will vary depending upon the type of test used, its content, the many attributes and conditions of the testing situation, the examinee's interpretation of the reasons for the testing, and so forth. Similarly, the definitions of juvenile delinquency used by the researchers will vary. Still, even with these variations, the inverse relationship occurs. As IQ goes down, the probability of misconduct goes up, and vice versa.

What does this correlation mean? It could mean many things. As we have just pointed out, IQ scores typically are crude indices of mainstream language skills that are influenced by experiences. In general, rich experiences increase IQ scores and limited experiences decrease them (Anastasi, 1982; Garbarino and Asp, 1981). School experiences, if positive, may increase language skills, and, if negative, may freeze, or even decrease, language skills. Rosenbaum (1975) assessed the effects of educational tracking or ability grouping on intellectual development and IQ scores. The sample consisted of white, working class high school youths, a choice which eliminated the potentially confounding variables of race and social class. Rosenbaum discovered that the IQs of students who were in the lower three tracks declined, while those of students in the upper two tracks increased. In addition, the variance (or individual differences) of the upper two tracks increased but it decreased in the lower three. Good environments and enhanced opportunity to refine mental constructs seemed to raise the IQ mean and increase the variance, while less enriching environments and limited cognitive opportunity decreased the mean and variance (Garbarino and Asp, 1981). Thus, IQ tests may well be measuring—at least to some extent—educational experiences and attitudes. They also may be reflecting the influence of family lifestyles and parental attitudes.

Tulkin and Kagan (1972) interviewed and observed middle class and working class mothers at home with their first-born 10-month-old daughters. The researchers discovered that verbal behavior and general communication were far more frequent among middle class mothers. They talked and interacted with their daughters continually, whereas the working class mothers rarely did. The working class mothers in this sample indicated that it was futile to interact verbally with infants, because infants are unable to communicate verbally with others. In fact, these mothers felt that they had very little influence on the development of their child. Many reflected a belief that children are born with a set of characteristics waiting to unfold, and that environmental events have minimal influence.

Tulkin and Covitz (1975) reassessed the daughters in these groups after they entered school. Their performance on tests of mental ability and language were significantly related to the prior measures of mother-and-infant interactions. Low interactions were linked with low IQ scores. Since these girls were at a very early phase of their academic careers, this relationship apparently had been established even before the many frustrations of academic failure appeared.

IQ scores, then, seem to be influenced by parent-infant interactions and school experiences, among other things. Disruption in the home may also play a role, reducing opportunities for children to interact with parents. Ethnic or cultural background may be an important factor. If children learn to speak one language, or predominantly one language at home, and take IQ tests in another, their scores may be significantly affected. We could continue to speculate, but the point is that the significance of the IQ cannot be ascertained without knowing the relative importance of a host of other factors.

Hirschi and Hindelang postulated that IQ contributes to school failure which, in turn, contributes to delinquency. In a recent examination of this position, Menard and Morse (1984) discovered that "institutional practices" (such as tracking, promoting, and grading) contributed more to delinquency than did individual characteristics. Menard and Morse contend that IQ and academic performance are linked to delinquent behavior only because of the responses of school officials to the different IQs and the levels of academic performance. School officials may negatively label children with a low IQ. This initial labeling follows a child through his or her school career. The institutional practice of attaching a negative label and selectively denying access to desirable social roles may lead to delinquent behavior. Menard and Morse speculate that if these social reactions to low IQs could be eliminated, the relationship between IQ and delinquency may also be eliminated.

Despite the frequent sightings of significant negative correlations between IQ and delinquency, the connection is not one that of itself helps us to identify causal factors in delinquency. In fact, IQ carries too much excess baggage: It is weighted by misconceptions and misinterpretations and by a complex array of contributing factors. It may allow us to *predict* with some accuracy, but its explanatory power is limited. We can predict roughly how a group of tested students will perform in school, but we cannot with confidence say why, or even who, in the group will do well and who will not. With respect to the traditional relationship with delinquency, IQ is statistically descriptive but causally ambiguous. It "predicts" academic performance within a large margin of error, but little else.

On the other hand, the multifaceted concept of *intelligence could* be much more useful, particularly if different forms of intelligence could be taken into account. Juvenile delinquents as a group are not "unintelligent." Different types of delinquency, or delinquency under different situations, might be explained in part by the presence or absence of different *forms* of intellectual ability. It is unlikely, however, that the concept of intelligence can ever be directly measured.

COGNITIVE CONSTRAINTS AND NEUTRALIZATIONS

Under normal circumstances, we perceive, interpret, compare, and act on the basis of cognitive structures, which we will refer to as personal standards. If we do not like what we are doing, we can change our behavior, justify it, or try to stop thinking about it. We can also reward and punish ourselves for our conduct. Self-punishment is expressed as guilt or remorse following actions we consider alien to our standards. In most instances, however, we prefer self-reinforcement to self-punishment; therefore, we behave in ways to correspond to our cognitive structures. We anticipate the feelings of guilt we will experience for "bad" actions and thus restrain ourselves. Therefore, each of us develops personal standards or codes of conduct that are maintained by self-reinforcement or self-punishment, as well as by external reinforcement and punishment. Walter C. Reckless's "containment theory" addresses the balance between internal (cognitive) and external controls of behavior, and Sykes and Matza talk about psychological neutralizations of internal controls. We now turn our attention to these two theories.

Walter C. Reckless: Containment Theory

Sociologist Walter C. Reckless (1961, 1973) describes delinquent and nondelinquent behavior as "functions" of personality and social/family influences, both of which serve to "contain" the individual. This "containment theory" is based upon two sources of constraints. One source originates from within the person, a kind of self-regulatory mechanism that prevents us from acting out our impulses or desires. This source is called "inner" containment. A second source originates from outside the person and is found within the social institutions of the family, friends, church, school, and generally the community. This source, which represents informal social control, is termed "outer" containment.

Reckless assumes that strength in one source of containment compensates for weaknesses in the other. For example, a youngster with strong inner containment—which Reckless describes variously as self-concept, goal orientation, frustration tolerance, sense of responsibility, and resistance to distractions—will be prevented from engaging in delinquent behavior, even under circumstances of weak external containment. Outer containment, in order to be strong, must offer effective supervision and discipline, a reasonable set of social expectations and activities and good social role models. Similarly, if inner containment is weak, a strong outer containment will compensate and hold the adolescent in check.

Reckless acknowledges that in our mobile society, with external circumstances changing frequently, the individual is forced to rely upon internal standards more than ever. Hence, Reckless affirms, the most important prevention of delinquency in contemporary society is the development of strong inner constraints. Of greatest importance in inner containment, he tells us, is a solid self-concept, a product of favorable socialization by parents.

Reckless and Dinitz (1967) tested the role of self-concept in delinquency using a group of predominantly white boys living in high delinquency areas of Columbus, Ohio. Reckless and Dinitz found that, over a four-year period, boys with a "good" self-concept, as measured by an inventory of self-concept developed by the investigators, had significantly fewer contacts with the juvenile court system compared to boys with a poor self-concept. Reckless and Dinitz concluded that a good self-concept is ". . . indicative of a residual favorable socialization and a strong inner self, which in turn steers the individual away from bad companions and street corner society, toward middle class values, and to awareness of the possibility of upward movement in the opportunity structure" (p. 196).

Containment theory does offer a plausible explanation for some delinquent behavior. For example, it is reasonable to assume that some juveniles resist serious and even minor delinquent behavior, even given ample opportunity in a high crime area, because of strong inner containment. But why do some juveniles with strong outer containments or informal social controls, such as found in cohesive, stable families and neighborhoods, engage in delinquent behavior? According to containment theory, the strong outer constraints provided by such environments should override any factors of a weaker inner containment, and delinquency should not occur. Likewise, why do some juveniles in high delinquency areas (weak outer containment), who give every indication of also having weak inner containment (poor self-concept, lack of goals, etc.) remain uninvolved in SR or official delinquent acts?

Containment theory is also weak in operationalizing or clearly defining inner and outer containment. Reckless throws in an armory of vague terms to describe each, but direct measurement of them is nearly impossible. This may be one reason why the theory, while often cited, has drawn exceedingly little research.

Sykes and Matza: Techniques of Neutralization

The criminologists Gresham Sykes and David Matza (1957) enumerated five major strategies people use to avoid self-blame and blame from others. These are common methods used, alone or in combination, to separate or disjoin our construct systems from our action. Sykes and Matza called these personal strategies *techniques of neutralization* and applied them specifically to delinquents. They are:

- denial of injury,
- denial of the victim,
- denial of responsibility,
- condemnation of the condemners, and
- appeal to higher loyalties

Sykes and Matza believed delinquents are at least partially committed to the dominant social order and are therefore susceptible to experiencing guilt or shame when they engage in deviant acts. However, they protect themselves from these unpleasant feelings by rationalizing that their violations are acceptable.

According to Sykes and Matza, each delinquent has a preferred strategy which he or she applies across situations. A youth may excuse his act of vandalism, for example, by convincing himself (and others) that "I didn't really hurt anybody." The youth is convinced that what he did was just "a prank" or "mischief." On the other hand, he might conclude that the person whose property has been destroyed can well afford it. Both reactions describe *denial of injury*. The *denial of the victim* technique usually is expressed in the form of rightful retaliation or punishment. The victim is transformed into one deserving of injury. "He had it coming to him." Alternately, delinquents might convince themselves that their theft was from "crooked" chain stores.

Denial of responsibility involves such perceptions as "I couldn't help myself" or "I didn't mean it." Delinquents who use this strategy see themselves as billiard balls— or better yet, soccer balls—helplessly propelled or kicked from event to event. They are not actors as much as they are acted upon. *Condemnation of the condemners* includes the belief that "the cops are out to get me" or "society gave me a bum rap." These delinquents shift attention away from their own deviant acts to the motives and behavior of those who disapprove of the violation. The condemners are often hypocrites and violators of the law themselves. Finally, the delinquent using *appeal to higher loyalties* will convince him or herself, "I didn't do it for myself," or "I did it because my buddies and I are all in this together," or "My mother needed the money."

Sykes and Matza's theory is an offshoot of strain theory discussed in Chapter 4, since it assumes that society has dominant values and that these have been internalized. In fact, these values may be internalized to such an extent that the techniques of neutralization are not effective enough to shield juveniles completely from their force and from the reactions of those around them who conform to the dominant values. Therefore, many—if not most—will suffer some shame and guilt about violating the rules of the dominant social order.

In Sykes and Matza's view, learning the techniques is a crucial step; it allows the juvenile to become delinquent in the first place. He or she has accepted the validity of the dominant value system and internalized it to a large extent. He or she then rationalizes to suspend the adopted values temporarily. This viewpoint is in direct opposition to the subcultural position which argues that the delinquent rejects the values of the dominant culture and adopts and internalizes those of a particular subculture. The theory regards learning as important, but does not explain how the techniques are learned.

The Sykes and Matza position has some appeal, but it may not apply to that many situations. Moreover, it has not been tested to any great extent. Therefore, its validity as an explanation of delinquency remains unclaimed. Practicing psychologists, however, have long observed that we do use strategies of neutralization. There are also other ways by which we become disengaged from our codes of conduct. High levels of emotional arousal take our attention away from our internal mechanisms of control. When we become extremely angry, for example, we often say and do things we later regret. We feel upset, remorseful, and guilty and wish we could take back our words and actions. If we had carefully considered and evaluated the consequences of our behavior, we would probably have acted differently. But under the heat of emotion, our self-regulatory system, with all its standards and values, is sometimes held in abeyance. This is what is meant by the assertion, "We are all capable of violence," which is one reason laws are needed. Most people learn from experience to pay closer attention to their internal control mechanisms. A good percentage of delinquent behavior, especially that involving impulsive outbursts, may be partially explained by lack of maturation or mellowing.

THE SOCIETAL REACTION OR LABELING PERSPECTIVE

Cognitive constructs are the foundation of the labeling or societal reaction perspective, which is rooted in the theory of symbolic interactionism espoused by Charles Horton Cooley of the University of Michigan and George Herbert Mead and his student Herbert Blumer of the University of Chicago. Cooley (1922) introduced the concept of the "looking-glass self" to describe how one's self-concept develops. According to Cooley, we imagine ourselves as we appear in the minds of others; our evaluations of this image lead to a continuous modification of our own behavior. In this way, Cooley argued, we learn our identity from others and mold it in response to their subjective judgments.

Mead (1934) accepted Cooley's perspective but placed great emphasis on the *meanings* events and actions have for the individual. These meanings arise out of social interactions. Language, the essence of social interaction, played a crucial role in Mead's approach. It represents the shared symbols of a culture; through these shared symbols a child develops a fully human mind. The symbols allow us to think and feel like others within our culture. It is through this process that we develop our self-identities. Mead's concept of the "I" represents the spontaneous, natural, self-interested self; the "me" represents the socialized self, the self as social construct, imbued with the norms of society and the awareness of social obligations. Cooley and Mead both emphasized the interaction process: the continuing, dynamic interplay between society and the individual. This symbolic interaction was originally called "social behaviorism," in counterreaction to Watsonian psychological behaviorism.

Labeling perspectives incorporated many aspects of symbolic interactionism. The main tenet in the labeling perspective is that deviant acts alone do not make a person deviant. The main culprit is social labeling by powerful or otherwise influential agents. Persons labeled "deviant" by significant members of society gradually accept (internalize) this label as characteristic of their personality and begin to act in deviant ways.

Labeling is a "perspective" rather than a theory. The writers who originally proposed it, Edwin M. Lemert and Howard S. Becker (who coined the term labeling), advanced it to sensitize criminologists and society in general to the interactions involved in deviant behavior.

Edwin M. Lemert and Societal Reaction Theory

Edwin M. Lemert was the earliest to outline in detail the labeling perspective, which he preferred to call the "societal reaction perspective," in his book *Social Pathology* (1951). Even after others joined the labeling camp, Lemert's work continued to provide the most sophisticated and systematic statement of the labeling view (Davis, 1975).

Social Pathology was not taken seriously by criminologists and sociologists in general until ten years after its publication, however. During the 1960s, the labeling perspective gained favor under the influence of Howard S. Becker, Erving Goffman, John Kitsuse, Kai T. Erikson, and Edwin Schur. Throughout the 1960s, labeling was the *Zeitgeist* in the sociology of deviant behavior. In the 1970s it became the target of strong criticism and skepticism (Goode, 1975).

In *Social Pathology*, Lemert expressed the view that it was a mistake to take for granted the "natural" existence of deviance. Traditional theories of deviance had up to that point accepted deviance as a given and as functional (serving a purpose) in society. These traditional approaches failed to recognize that society should take some responsibility for the deviance in its midst. Lemert noted that deviance theory assumes deviance was something that existed naturally, almost like a disease, independent of social norms and labels, and that it could be conceptualized as an objective category of behavior. Lemert argued that deviance was relative; a deviation in one culture or society would not necessarily qualify as such in another or even in the same culture at another time.

Lemert proposed that researchers explain how and why laws are passed and enforced, and why police and court personnel officially process some persons but not others. He was trying to direct attention away from research focused almost exclusively on "deviance" as a static entity and toward research on how social sanctioning processes could alter definitions and categories of deviance—in other words, from explaining deviant behavior to explaining the social processes involved, as well as their consequences. From Lemert's perspective, social process systematized and prolonged deviance by altering the self-concept and the social identity of the person labeled.

Lemert distinguished between two kinds of deviant behavior, *primary* and *secondary* deviation. Primary deviation is neither identified nor punished by anyone in authority. In a sense, it is "hidden" or "secret." While the behavior violates a norm, it remains undetected and thus escapes the reactions of others. In Lemert's view, deviant behavior in society is ubiquitous and secret, since most forbidden behavior goes unobserved and unsanctioned. Not even the offender may consider the behavior representative of inner personality or self-concept. Consider Kingston, who regularly lifts tapes from the unattended music counter in a nationwide chain store and has never been apprehended. According to Lemert, Kingston may not see himself as a thief. His "violations" are really not violations at all, but occasional lapses of forgetfulness, reactions to boredom, or an adventure peripheral to his cognitive constructs, his perceptions of himself. They are, in essence, behaviors largely foreign to Kingston's "true self." Sykes and Matza, in contrast, would say that Kingston temporarily "neutralized" his own standards of conduct and that he would likely experience some guilt.

Rule breaking behavior profoundly changes the individual when he or she receives negative recognition from the outside world. Detection of Kingston's conduct by the store detective *begins* to change his self-image. The unpleasant identity of "thief" or "delinquent," even if not officially imposed by a juvenile court, prompts Kingston to defend his actions as nothing serious or not in character. "I am not a thief!" However, with continued societal reactions to the transgressions—notification of police and/or parents, contact with a court diversion program or with a juvenile court judge, Kingston gradually comes to believe that he is, in fact, a "thief." Gradually, he incorporates these "societal reactions" into his existing cognitive structure. It is at this point, according to Lemert, that he may begin to do the things and play the role that others associate with him. Kingston then enters into a pattern of additional violations of the norms, or what Lemert calls *secondary deviance*. "When a person begins to employ his deviant behavior or a role based upon it as a means of defense, attack, or adjustment to the . . . problems created by the consequent societal reaction, his deviation is secondary" (Lemert, 1951, p. 76).

There is, then, a significant difference between the experience of one who shoplifts and is not caught and one who is certified a thief. Secondary deviance affects the self-concept or inner belief system as well as the performance of social roles. Lemert stressed, however, secondary deviance does not follow from a single reaction to an individual, but rather after a long and sustained process. Kingston is a good candidate after his parents do not let him forget what happened. Like Cooley, Lemert believed we tend to see ourselves as others see us and tend to act on this self-definition. The person labeled deviant comes to see him or herself as deviant and to behave accordingly. Labeling leads to "symbolic reorganization" (or construct rearrangement). Primary deviance, which is not detected, usually does not affect one's self-concept or social roles, nor does it initiate symbolic reorganization.

Being publicly or officially labeled a deviant is socially stigmatizing, adversely affecting social relationships and opportunities. The young vandal may find her circle of friends dwindling, since parents warn their children not to associate with her. Employers rarely hire known deviants or delinquents. Thus, according to Lemert, the initial societal reactions precipitate a chain of events, perceptions, identities, and actions that call forth new interactions that reinforce the delinquent label. "Interactions" is a critical word here, because it underscores the complicated interplay of the deviance process. It transforms "deviance" from a simple cause-and-effect relationship—you steal, therefore you are a thief—to a complex process that continually feeds upon the individual's own constructs along with those of others.

Lemert believed the "societal reaction process" is affected by many factors, including age, sex, social class, race, manner of dress, and neighborhood. Each of these may influence the responses of legal authorities to the young offender, for example. The police officer who realizes a youth is the son in one of the model (and powerful) families in the community may be more likely to ignore his behavior. Youths from less powerful families, perceived as "continually breeding trouble," will not have that advantage.

In 1979, Lemert credited Howard Becker as the real initiator of the labeling perspective. "Becker's ideas of labeling took precedence over mine so far as popular acceptance and recognition were concerned. At the same time his writings seem to have been the target for more criticism than mine" (Lemert, 1983, p. 125). Lemert also admitted that he became disinterested in the societal reaction approach because ". . . it was becoming too psychological" (Lemert, 1983, p. 126). It was never developed to its full potential to show the reciprocal effects of the labeling process, Lemert said. Instead, it focused too much on the self-concept issue and not enough on the interplay with the labelers. "Without looking at this—the way the labeled persons respond, and problems created for the agents of social control by their responses—it is difficult to study changes in patterns of deviance, policy, and social control" (Lemert, 1983, p. 126). In a similar critique, Nanette Davis (1975) charged that, by focusing on the reactions of the labeled, labeling analysts essentially bypassed the entire process of social control, and, unfortunately, adopted a social psychological orientation centered on the deviant actor.

Howard S. Becker: The Stigma of Being Labeled

Lemert's observation concerning the popularity and influence of Becker's writings is probably an accurate one. Becker's book *The Outsiders* (1963) is one of the most frequently cited criminology books of the period between 1945 and 1972 (Downes and Rock, 1982). The book was the flagship for the labeling perspective throughout the 1960s. However, an event that antedated the publication of *The Outsiders* and probably contributed equally to the emergence of this new perspective was the appointment of Becker as editor of the journal *Social Problems* in August, 1960.

Becker had earned his Ph.D. in sociology at the University of Chicago, where he was exposed to, perhaps saturated with, the symbolic interaction approach of Mead, Cooley, Herbert Blumer, and others. Symbolic interaction, as noted earlier, stressed the effect of both real and imagined reactions of others upon how we act and conceive of ourselves. Becker worked his way through graduate school by performing as a jazz pianist in Chicago night clubs and taverns. (His Master's thesis was titled "The Professional Dance Musician of Chicago.") This avocation brought him into daily contact with the "deviant world" of drug addicts, prostitutes, gamblers, and others. At the same time, he helped conduct drug studies for the Chicago Institute for Juvenile Research.

Becker's first issue of *Social Problems* appeared in 1962. Over the course of the next two years, with an editor sympathetic to the labeling perspective, the journal published several influential theoretical papers on labeling. Three were especially significant: Kitsuse's "Societal Reaction to Deviant Behavior: Problems of Theory and Method" (1962); Erikson's "Notes on the Sociology of Deviance" (1962); and Kitsuse and Circourel's "A Note on the Use of Official Statistics" (1963). These are considered three of the most significant sources of the labeling movement during the 1960s (Spector, 1976). Had it not been for Becker's editorship, they might never have been published. Most manuscripts on labeling that had been published previously in *Social Problems* had been criticized vehemently, simply ignored, or rejected for publication in other journals. Criminologists were not ready to entertain the perspective and did not take it seriously. Labeling advocates, therefore, ". . . while . . . suffering disfavor from their discipline, fortuitously found a forum in the young and uncommitted journal, *Social Problems*" (Spector, 1976, p. 73).

Lemert and Becker worked independently of one another at first but eventually their respective perspectives began to merge into an approach dubbed the Neo-Chicago or West Coast School. Most of the pioneers of the perspective (Lemert excepted) were

University of Chicago graduates, and many had moved to universities in California where academic positions were plentiful.

According to Becker (1963, p. 9):

> . . . *social groups create deviance by making the rules whose infraction constitutes deviance*, and by applying those rules to particular people and labeling them as outsiders. From this point of view, deviance is *not* a quality of the act the person commits, but rather a consequence of the application by others of rules and sanctions to an "offender." The deviant is one to whom that label has successfully been applied; deviant behavior is behavior that people so label.

The term "outsiders" refers to those people who are judged deviant by others and therefore stand outside the circle of normal members of a group. Becker, more than Lemert, succeeded in moving deviance far "outside" of the individual, treating it not as a quality of the person or his acts, but as a social problem. The police, the courts, correctional and residential personnel, and welfare agencies are the principal culprits; their labeling and dehumanizing produced deviance in those they considered outside mainstream society. These stigmatizing social labels placed on the rule violator by institutional powers push the offender into additional deviant behavior, a deviant way of life, and, basically, a deviant identity.

While Lemert delineated two categories of deviants, primary and secondary, Becker (1963) outlined four:

1. those who have violated a rule and have been sanctioned, or the "pure" deviants;
2. those who have violated a rule but have escaped sanction for the violation, the so-called secret deviants; they have committed improper acts not noticed or reacted to by others;
3. those who have not violated a rule but who have been negatively sanctioned anyway; this category includes the falsely accused, such as the girl labeled a delinquent because her two best friends have a record of police contacts; and
4. those who have neither violated a rule nor been negatively sanctioned; this category represents conforming behavior.

Becker was recognizing that conforming behavior, under certain conditions may be deviant behavior, as when someone obeys orders beyond their intentions. An example would be where a subordinate takes it upon himself to do "things he thinks" his commander wants done, although the commander did not have that intention.

The most controversial type is Becker's "hidden deviant," who differed from the primary deviant described by Lemert. According to Becker, secret deviants have so labeled themselves, even though others are unaware of their behavior. Deviance comes from the realization of what would happen if they did know. For example, Becker describes the sado-masochistic fetish market that not only publishes expensive, high quality catalogs, but has a large clientele as well. While a person who is detected using fetishes for sexual pleasure is commonly labeled a "sexual deviant," the thousands of individuals who browse and purchase the items from the catalog, but who remain undetected, are examples of secret deviants.

Becker also makes the distinction between a "master status" and a "subordinate status" to emphasize that some statuses in a society override all others and have a certain priority. Race is an example. Membership in the black race may take priority over other status considerations. Regardless of whether a person is a physician, a plumber, a lawyer, a husband, or a wife, being black remains the master status for many in American society. This same "master status" identity may develop for deviants. If one received the status of "deviant" as a result of breaking rules, this self-identification may develop to be more important in one's daily life than other "subordinate" statuses combined.

Becker's approach suggests that people lack a sure knowledge of what they are and what they can accomplish. Individuals are assumed to follow almost blindly the dicta of social groups and institutions. Becker does not allow the person to resist or reject a label assigned by some social group. Individuals are social puppets; differences in deviant behavior do not occur as a result of individual choices but as a result of differential applications of the rules and labels.

Like Lemert, Becker emphasized that the labeling perspective was not a causal theory, but rather a way of looking at a general area of human activity. Furthermore, public stigmatization was neither a necessary nor a sufficient condition for an individual's commitment to a career in deviance. Although he attached a name to the process he was describing—labeling—he, like Lemert, preferred to refer to his views as an "interactionist" perspective. Interactionism, however, is usually reserved for a mutually influential actor and social environment situation, a topic we shall return to in more detail in Chapter 9. Becker's argument rested primarily with the actor being acted upon, not doing any acting. The effects are unidirectional: Social agents create rules and label the rule breaker, and the rule breaker gradually assumes the label and its accompanying behavior.

Joseph Scimecca (1977) suggested that the labeling approach, in general, is a disservice to the symbolic interactionism of George Herbert Mead because it conveys a unilateral process which omits human choice. Both Becker and Lemert concentrated almost exclusively upon the regulation of the deviant by some group. Scimecca noted that Mead's symbolic interactionism sees the individual as one who is actively engaged in trying to control his or her own destiny. Individuals may or may not accept the labels assigned or the social reactions incurred. Mead continually stressed the subjective or inner life of the actor as the source of personal social behavior. "Self," "mind," and "society" are coauthors of the human personality. To Mead, humans are not simply responsive to stimuli (as John B. Watson argued) or malleable by environmental influences (as the labeling perspective supposes), but are active, dynamic agents of their own destiny.

George Vold (1979) notes that the labeling perspective has been criticized on three additional fronts. First, it overemphasizes the importance of the official labeling process. Second, it assumes that deviants resent the deviant label. Actually, perhaps particularly in the case of juveniles, deviance may allow the person to gain status or approval from peers or even significant adults. Third, reducing the labeling process may create more crime than it eliminates, since it waters down the effect of general deterrence. This criticism assumes that most people do not commit crime because they fear the stigma which would result.

SUMMARY AND CONCLUSIONS

In this chapter we have reviewed the mental or cognitive side of the individual system and related it to several theories of delinquency. In light of the amount of recent research and theory, the mental side of the system appears to be far more palatable to American criminologists than the genetic-biological side.

Understanding the individual's construct system is highly important in explaining why a *certain* ''delinquent'' *did* certain things. This understanding is also important in trying to predict what a *certain* person will do, although this knowledge has numerous limitations in its power to predict. Theories built upon an individual system perspective are invaluable for explaining (or speculating) why a particular juvenile suddenly decided to shoot his family. These explanations, please note, are *after* the event, or *post hoc*. Theories based on individual systems also help us *estimate* how well a person will do academically, provided the person has the motivation, emotional maturity, and concentration to do the work. Individual systems can also help us estimate how a political candidate will perform in office if elected. However, since everyone operates within a social systems framework involving a vast range of co-determining factors, predictions are risky. If we could take into consideration a wider range of influences, we could be substantially more accurate in our forecasts of human behavior.

Thus, the statements and theories discussed in this chapter provide only a *partial* explanation of delinquency. Their predictive power should not be overestimated. Moreover, they can far better explain the *delinquent* than the trends, patterns, social structures, and social pressures of *delinquency*. The failure to make this distinction has created unnecessary tension between the individual or psychological perspective and the societal or sociological perspective. The grand mistake of the individual perspective is assuming that individual systems can explain patterns of delinquency. They cannot. The mistake of the societal perspective is in dismissing the potential contribution of its counterpart. Individual systems represent but one level in the interacting levels of stratification within any social phenomenon. Moral development, social learning theories, interpersonal-maturity theory, IQ measures, labeling theory, containment theory, and neutralization techniques are all basically anchored at the same level of explanation: the individual.

Criminology can best be construed as a family of related sciences focusing at different levels, accepting different tasks, and employing different methodologies. The individual level adds immeasurably to the picture, but the overall picture is a stratified one. When individual-based theories try to cut across levels by being all things to all persons for all times, they are destined to fail. Kohlberg's moral development theory and Eysenck's theory of criminality are but two examples of allegedly universal theories going bankrupt. As theories proposed at the individual level of explanation, they are more promising. One delinquent's behavior might be explained by high needs for stimulation, but it is a mistake to assume that the single factor of variations in stimulation needs accounts for all or most delinquency.

Typically, textbooks include in the discussion of delinquency theories their weaknesses and their supposedly "fatal flaws." Although the present text does this to some extent, it is more intent on emphasizing that theories are often directed at different levels. Researchers who cherish aggregate data criticize individual-based theorists and researchers for being too narrow, too reductionistic, and too psychological in their efforts to understand delinquency. Those who persist with individual explanations claim that the aggregate or macro-level approach is misguided; it will never understand delinquency and especially the delinquent without becoming more "humanistic." We must recognize that stratification of explanation is necessary in order to make substantial inroads into the prevention and control of delinquency. The point is that we can criticize endlessly without agreement or solution. It is more worthwhile to construct systems developed for specific levels of explanation. In the next chapter, we plan to move up one more rung in this ladder of explanation.

The Microsystem of the Family

8 CHAPTER

The family represents the first step in our upward climb along the social systems ladder toward broader context. The microsystem of the family is, in this book, the single most important system in the development of delinquency. The family is, after all, the principal context in which human development takes place. Throughout most of the 20th century, popular magazines concluded that parental neglect and faulty training at home were the principal causes of delinquency (Gordon, 1971). Surprisingly, however, the family has not been regarded as very important from the perspective of many criminologists, at least as evidenced by the amount of research. Traditionally, peer groups and neighborhoods have dominated the work of the sociologically oriented theorists, and individual systems have dominated that of psychologically oriented theorists. Between these two orientations there exists a void of knowledge about delinquency development, although in recent years there has been some renewed interest in the structure and process of the family and delinquency. In this chapter we will try to fill some of this void by directing attention to the "classic" investigations of the family and delinquency and then move on to recent research on family structure and family process. The terms "family structure" and "family process" will be defined later in the chapter.

James Garbarino (1982) contends that children who are exposed to social impoverishment and lack the basic psychological necessities of life are at *sociocultural risk* of becoming developmentally impaired. Garbarino is particularly concerned about deprivation in any of the following areas:

1. important relationships (as may happen when one parent is absent);

2. experiences that lead to self-esteem (as happens when children are rejected or neglected by significant people in their lives or are alienated from significant social settings, such as the school); and

3. values and experiences that contribute to socialization and the development of competence (as happens when children do not learn the value of reading or work).

Garbarino believes that children who are thus impaired are susceptible to academic, occupational, and personal failure as well as alienation from mainstream society.

Garbarino warns that it is no easy task to understand the complicated chains of events that result in a child's basic needs not being met. "It requires a multidisciplinary understanding of how the many parts of a child's life—home, neighborhood, school, government, and the world of work—all fit together" (Garbarino, 1982, p. 632). In poverty-stricken neighborhoods, for example, pressures from the street and the ubiquity of despair may far overshadow positive influences in the home (Johnstone, 1980). On the other hand, in more affluent communities, unstable family relationships may constitute the worst social experience in the child's life.

The remainder of the book looks for clues about how these influences interact with the individual systems described in Chapters 6 and 7 to provide a comprehensive, multidisciplinary picture of the juvenile delinquent. This will require familiarity with contemporary research and theory in such diverse fields as developmental psychology, sociology, and ecological criminology. This approach, as mentioned earlier, will be structured within a social systems framework, beginning with microsystems which, according to Bronfenbrenner, are the core of systems theory. As he defined them, microsystems are patterns of activities, roles, and interpersonal relations that take place within settings directly experienced by the individuals. For most children, the most prominent and influential microsystem is that of the family.

THE FAMILY, DELINQUENCY, AND RECIPROCAL INFLUENCE

After a careful review of the research literature, Walter Gove and Robert Crutchfield (1982, p. 302) concluded, "The evidence that the family plays a critical role in juvenile delinquency is one of the strongest and most frequently replicated findings among studies of deviance." Although we cannot isolate the family as the principal causal agent of juvenile delinquency, we can be quite sure that its role is significant, since the family is the context in which children spend most time and often establish their most long lasting and influential interpersonal relationships. Whatever the variations in the structure and process of the family at different times and in different places, it is after all the basic socialization group in all human societies (Yorburg, 1973). Families provide children with their initial experiences with other human beings and with their earliest definitions of themselves and the world in which they are destined to live. We must be careful, however, not to overemphasize the role played by the family. Other systems, particularly the peer system, have enormous impact on the adolescent.

It is assumed here, however, that the family is the most influential microsystem in most children's lives. Within the family context, we especially have to be mindful of the chronosystem, which produces change over time. According to Bronfenbrenner, you will recall, each life course experiences normative and non-normative (traumatic) transitions. Entering school is a normative transition, which shifts some influence away from the family to the school environment. Teachers, school officials, and peers become increasingly important to each child as his or her microsystems expand. During adolescence, peers become highly influential on one another's behavior, often more so than parents or school. These microsystems—school and peers—will be discussed in Chapter 9, along with the relationships among them—the mesosystems—that Bronfenbrenner stresses must be recognized.

A family's physical, social, and economic situation has considerable impact on the way parents carry out their parenting functions and on the nature of parent-child interactions. In addition, the family that abuses, neglects, represses, misunderstands, or is otherwise inadequate in meeting its children's needs is one desperately in need of community support systems. Some of the early sociologists of the Chicago School believed that some families could not properly socialize their children to society, because they lacked the necessary resources and social support systems. Thrasher asserted that the single most important factor determining whether a boy became delinquent was the family. Shaw and McKay considered the neighborhood—an exosystem—a crucial mediating component between the family and the larger community.

Structure and Process Variables in Family Research

The contemporary sociological and psychological literature on the relationship between the family and delinquency is voluminous but confusing. The empirical work can be roughly dichotomized into studies that examine family *structure* and those that examine family *process*, and there is some disagreement about which is more important. Studies of structure examine such variables as family size, birth order, spacing of siblings, number of natural parents living with the children, income, place of residence, and socioeconomic status. Process studies explore parent-child interactions, parenting styles, discipline, the quality of marital relationships, and the general emotional tone within the family. While we do know quite a bit about the relationship between family structure and delinquency, we know little about family process—how the family *works*—and the significance of this process to delinquent behavior.

Lawrence Rosen (1985) writes that the debate over the relative merits of structure or process in explaining delinquency represents an erroneous preoccupation with finding one major cause of delinquency. Both—structure and process—are important. An exclusive focus on structure offers a static construction that does not consider the continuous interactions through which the behavior of participants in the family system is instigated, sustained, and developed. On the other hand, exclusive focus on process ignores the possibility that much of it might be explained by structure. A family's area of residence may have a strong influence on the modes of discipline used by the parents. In a high crime area, for example, some parents will place strict controls—e.g., early curfews—

on their children's activities. Conversely, the parents' philosophy of discipline may influence their choice of neighborhood in the first place. Which is more important, structure or process? Both deserve to be examined.

To appreciate why delinquency occurs we must view the family as a complicated, dynamic system nested within other social systems. It is a complex unit varying widely in composition and cohesion from family to family as well as from culture to culture (Hartup, 1979). Moreover, the family contains constantly changing, dynamic social subsystems. A brother and sister close in age may harangue and harass each other incessantly when they are in the 5th and 6th grades; in high school, they may be one another's main source of emotional support. Examinations of both structure and process will yield the maximum information about this complex system. Our task, therefore, is to decide what family structures *and* what processes are significantly linked to juvenile delinquency.

Before probing the complexities of the family-delinquency relationship, it is important to repeat that family influences do not flow in one direction; they are apt to be multidirectional, a feature we will refer to as *reciprocal influence*. For example, while the parents affect the development of the child, the child also affects the development and growth of the parents, including their marital relationship, relationships with friends, and even level of job satisfaction. As James Snyder and Gerald Patterson (1987, p. 219) observe, "The antisocial child is a product and an architect of his environment." As we have seen, certain characteristics of family members (e.g., temperament) influence the whole family system. Reciprocal influence implies that the social environment influences an individual, and the individual, in turn, has an impact on the social environment. This reciprocal influence extends across several levels of the general social system, although one's personal effect diminishes as one encounters higher levels of the system. A child's impact on the state, for example, is obviously weaker than his or her impact on the neighborhood.

In a systems approach, the factors that influence the individual are conceptualized and measured at a number of different levels. Choosing the relevant factors and most meaningful level of analysis remains one of the most challenging problems of systems analysis. With respect to the family at the microsystem level, research has focused very heavily on the "broken home," a structural variable which, it is maintained here, is not the most relevant. Before reviewing this research, it will be instructive to critically review four of the classic studies on family variables and delinquency, the works by Sheldon and Eleanor Glueck, William and Joan McCord, F. Ivan Nye, and Travis Hirschi.

EARLY STUDIES OF FAMILY AND DELINQUENCY

The Gluecks of Harvard

Sheldon Glueck, born in Warsaw, Poland in 1896, was a Harvard Law Professor throughout most of his professional career, until his retirement in 1963. Dr. Eleanor Touroff Glueck was a research associate in criminology until her retirement in 1964.

This husband-wife team worked together for over 36 years and became widely known in American criminology as "the Gluecks of Harvard." Although they published over 14 books, their work on family factors and delinquency is the most relevant for our present purpose.

The Gluecks were studying the effectiveness of various types of "peno-correctional" treatment when, in the late 1930's, they abruptly shifted their interest to the causes of delinquency. After many years of research, they were convinced that it was impossible to treat delinquency without knowing its causes. They were critical of sociological criminologists, calling them narrow-minded, myopic, and misguided in their search for environmental causation. ". . . (A) weakness or an incompleteness of much sociologic reasoning on the causal process of crime is the assumption that the mass social stimuli to behavior, as reflected in the particular culture of a region, is alone or primarily the significant causal force" (Glueck and Glueck, 1950, p. 5).

In 1939, the Gluecks began to collect data on a sample of 500 boys incarcerated in juvenile correction institutions for serious delinquency. For comparison purposes, data were also gathered on a control group of 500 nondelinquent boys attending public schools in the area. The two all-white groups were matched in age, ethnic origin, area of residence, and IQ (as measured by the Wechsler-Bellevue intelligence test). Four kinds of data were collected:

1. sociocultural (which included family variables);
2. physical (body type and size);
3. intellectual; and
4. emotional-temperamental.

A wide variety of measures were used, including IQ tests, Rorschachs (inkblots), and personal interviews. The Gluecks also conducted interviews, observed, and took notes on the home and neighborhood. They analyzed the home environment, looking for discipline techniques, marital relationships, conduct standards, family pride, cultural refinements, recreational outlets, cohesiveness, and signs of who was the dominant parent. The results of this massive project were published in the classic monograph *Unraveling Juvenile Delinquency* (1950).

No specified theory of delinquency appeared to guide the collection of data, although the Gluecks clearly were biased in the favor of individual or dispositional variables. Correlations were their principal statistical tools. The Gluecks calculated reams of data and concluded that family factors were among the most critical in the formation of delinquency. More precisely, the following were significantly related to delinquency: the discipline of the boy by the father (whether it was overstrict or erratic, lax, firm but kindly); supervision of the boy by the mother (unsuitable, fair, suitable); affection of the father for the boy (indifferent or hostile, warm, including overprotective); affection of the mother for the boy; and family cohesion (unintegrated, some elements of cohesion, cohesive). Delinquent boys had parents whose disciplinary tactics vacillated between extremes of laxity and harshness. Parental discipline, in general, was more closely related to delinquent behavior than any other family variable.

Parents of delinquents were also seen as careless, sometimes negligent, in their supervision of their children. Moreover, a high proportion of the delinquent families were disorganized as opposed to cohesive. Family disorganization, with its attendant lack of warmth and respect for the integrity of each member, seemed to play a critical role in the development of serious delinquency. "Since the family is the first and foremost vehicle for the transmission of values of a culture to the young child, noncohesiveness of the family may leave him without ethical moorings or convey to him a confused and inconsistent cultural pattern" (Glueck and Glueck, 1950, p. 280).

The Glueck data also suggested that delinquent boys tend to come from families where fathers, mothers, and siblings had been indifferent or hostile toward them. Most of the boys were not attached to their parents and felt their parents were not concerned about their welfare. Compared to nondelinquent boys, twice as many of the delinquent boys did not look upon their fathers as acceptable symbols for emulation.

In sum, the "obvious inferiority of the families of delinquents" contributed greatly—though not exclusively—to delinquency. While the Gluecks did find a small relationship between delinquency and father's presence, family size, and the boy's ordinal position (which are all structural features), the most significant association existed between delinquency and process variables—parental discipline, maternal supervision, affection of both father and mother for the boy, and family cohesion. The Gluecks declared, however, that these features of the home environment do not act on the child in isolation. Rather, the environment interacts with his or her constitutional and personality traits to produce delinquency. Specifically, they believed that the traits of mesomorphy, restlessnesss, and impulsiveness predispose youths toward delinquency.

Soon after the publication of *Unraveling Juvenile Delinquency*, stinging criticisms of the entire project and its conclusions appeared throughout the professional literature (e.g., Rubin, 1951; Reiss, 1951a; Peterson and Becker, 1965; Hirschi and Selvin, 1967). Among the more influential was the critique by Sol Rubin (1951), who attacked the Gluecks' methodology. The study, Rubin said, did little more than compare boys who had been institutionalized on the average of seven months to boys who had not been institutionalized. Rubin argued that the Gluecks had failed to recognize the psychological and social effects of an institution on a 13-year-old boy. For example, the observed personality differences between delinquents and nondelinquents could have easily been due to the effects of institutionalization or of being labeled delinquent rather than to any inherent personality traits. A far better procedure, Rubin said, would have been to compare institutionalized delinquents with both non-institutionalized delinquents and nondelinquents so the effects of being in a house of corrections could be more properly evaluated. Non-institutionalized delinquents then might have been more similar to the nondelinquents than to delinquents in institutions.

Critics also chastised the Gluecks for making unwarranted conclusions about cause-and-effect relationships, and they excoriated them for attempting to formulate a "scientific law" on the basis of correlational analysis. According to the "Glueck Law," boys who

1. are physically mesomorphic (solid and muscular) in constitution;
2. are temperamentally restless, impulsive, extraverted, and aggressive; and
3. who come from homes displaying little understanding, affection, stability, and moral fibre were destined to become delinquents.

The Gluecks advanced this "law" tentatively and with the admonishment that it needed much more testing, but nevertheless they provoked the ire of criminologists well versed in scientific methods (e.g., Reiss, 1951a; Hirschi and Selvin, 1967). To formulate a behavioral law on the basis of crude correlations was inexcusable. The variables were poorly defined and data were based on vague personality indicators, such as responses to inkblots. Lawful relationships are assumed to have wide generalizability. In this case, the "law" could have applied to all boys who had the required combination of antecedent events, behavioral characteristics, and physical features. Could the results on these 500 white boys from specific social areas and ethnic backgrounds be valid predictors for all boys from all social areas, across all ethnic groups, and across all time? Obviously, criminologists did not think so.

To some extent, the Gluecks' disdain toward the sociological perspective may have kindled the onslaught of criticism. Albert Reiss, Jr. (1951a), for example, asserted pointedly that any criminologist well trained in the sociological perspective could detect numerous and fatal deficiencies in the Glueck study and would arrive at decidedly different conclusions. "The sociologist must also question the various assumptions regarding the inevitability of delinquency as a consequence of the person's 'physical and psychologic equipment' . . . which permits one to decide who will be a delinquent when one is six years of age. The social environment of the child from age six to sixteen is hardly so negligible a circumstance in his life history" (Reiss, 1951a, p. 117).

The criticisms directed at the Glueck project apparently were effective, for many criminology textbooks today hardly mention it except to note its flawed assumptions, design, and conclusions. Wilson and Herrnstein (1985) comment that the methodological criticisms were probably less decisive in directing criminologists away from the study than the distaste the sociological community had for the individual variables considered by the Gluecks. This conclusion fails to appreciate the crucial importance of methodological soundness in the social sciences. The Glueck project had numerous weaknesses, most of which preclude drawing conclusions from its data.

Still, the Glueck study has value and deserves to be recognized in the criminology literature. It directed attention to a possible relationship between family variables (both structure and process) and delinquency. The very process of criticism opened the way for dialogue about the merits of directing research attention to micro-level variables. Despite their flawed methodology, the Gluecks were cited heavily by researchers interested in studying the importance of family systems (e.g., Peterson and Becker (1965); F. Ivan Nye (1958); Travis Hirschi (1969)). Although the limitations of the Glueck study were well recognized, other researchers took their cue from the two and began to examine, with more methodological rigor, the role of the family in the development of delinquency. As Lawrence Rosen (1985, p. 554) notes, ". . . there is little question that their study served to reestablish the credibility of the central role of family dynamics in delinquency etiology.''

The Cambridge-Somerville Youth Project

Another classic in the family-delinquency literature is William and Joan McCord's *Origins of Crime*, published in 1959. The book represents a further examination of the Cambridge-Somerville Youth Study, a project, begun in the 1930s, ''. . . which attempted to prevent delinquency and develop character by means of friendly guidance'' (McCord, McCord, and Zola, 1959, p. vi). The project, which was launched in 1936, was conceived, initiated, and financed by Robert Clark Cabot, Professor of Social Ethics and Clinical Medicine at Harvard University. Cabot hypothesized that delinquency could be prevented if a close and caring friendship was developed between a youngster and an adult counselor. He reasoned that if intensive family and individual counseling were provided, buttressed by proper medical care, recreational facilities, and other social services, delinquency could be prevented.

The study focused on the 2000 boys, ages 6 to 12, attending schools in the factory-dominated cities of Cambridge and Somerville, Massachusetts. Six hundred and fifty boys were eventually selected for the experiment. They were divided randomly into two groups by the flip of a coin. One group, the ''experimental group,'' received treatment and social services, beginning in 1939. The other group, the ''control group,'' did not receive counseling and services. Between 1939 and 1945, counselors visited the homes of both groups twice a month, filing a comprehensive and detailed report of everything observed, including the physical conditions of the neighborhood. Unfortunately, World War II raised havoc with the project. For example, many of the counselors, social workers, and older boys in the experiment were drafted or enlisted into the armed services. When the project was terminated in 1945, only 75 boys remained. A follow-up study was launched in 1951 by Edwin Powers and Helen L. Witmer (1951), and later by William and Joan McCord (1959).

It is difficult to evaluate the ''success'' of the treatment because of the many problems the ''experiment'' faced. Possibly, Cabot's original hypothesis was never really tested. The McCords concluded that the experiment failed, despite being one of the most extensive and costly experiments tried anywhere on the prevention of delinquency. According to the McCords, the experiment ''. . . failed primarily because it did not affect the basic psychological and familial causes of crime'' (p. vi). Interestingly, 30 years after termination of the program, many of the boys remembered their counselors, often with considerable fondness (McCord, 1978). ''Were the Youth Study program to be assessed by the subjective judgment of its value as perceived by those who received its services, it would rate high marks'' (McCord, 1978, p. 288). However, none of the objective measures revealed that treatment had a significant effect on improving the lives of the boys. In fact, some of the data are quite disturbing. For instance, those who had been in the treatment program were more likely to commit further crime than those who had not received treatment. The reasons for this unexpected finding remain a mystery. Still, the project offered reams of data, and the McCords used the available records of the boys to see if they could tease out causal factors. For the researchers, delinquency was measured by official juvenile court records.

The McCords complained that sociologists for a long time had been misguided in their search for causes of delinquency, since they looked upon crime ". . . as primarily, if not entirely, a group phenomenon" (McCord, McCord, and Zola, 1959, p. 67). Gangs, subcultures, sociological factors were not the answer. Individual or psychological factors, facilitated or inhibited by family dynamics, were where the basic causes could be found.

In addition, the McCords felt their study was on more solid theoretical footing than previous investigations, because they used information gathered through multiple "observations" by psychologists, psychiatrists, and social workers. Observations consisted of sifting through the many records and written documents available on the boys. Therefore, the McCords claimed, bias was kept to a minimum. However, it is likely that these clinicians had a strong bias in favor of individual factors, and this sensitivity probably dictated their search to a great extent.

Overall, the McCords found the following:

- Intelligence was not strongly related to crime.
- Social factors (neighborhood conditions, SES) were not strongly related to crime.
- Broken homes were not strongly linked to crime.
- A child's "home atmosphere" (cohesiveness, affection, conflict) was not strongly related to crime.
- Erratic, punitive discipline was related to crime.
- The father's personality had an important effect on crime (warm fathers and passive fathers produced very few criminals).
- The mother's personality had the greatest effect on the genesis of criminality (maternal love led to low crime; maternal passivity, cruelty, absence, or neglect led to high crime).

The McCords, like the Gluecks, were critical of sociological viewpoints of crime and delinquency, and apparently relished disposing of traditional sociological theories on the basis of their data. Virtually every mainstream sociological factor—social disorganization, gangs, broken homes, cultural deviance, strain—was subtly attacked. This is probably one reason why the McCord research—like the Glueck research—has also failed to receive much positive recognition in the criminological literature.

F. Ivan Nye and the Sociology of the Family

F. Ivan Nye (1958), a sociologist at Washington State University specializing in family relations, conducted a SR study in 1955 in an effort to evaluate family characteristics associated with delinquency. The study is often cited in the criminological literature, especially in reference to the connection between parental marital happiness and delinquency. Nye and his colleagues administered several questionnaires to high schoolers (grades 9 through 12) living in three small cities (population 10,000 to 30,000) in the state of Washington. He was able to gather information from 780 predominately white students representing a cross section of the SES characteristics.

Nye correlated items on mother's employment, broken homes, family structure (birth order, family size), SES, discipline, parental appearance, parental character, and values with the 23-item SR questionnaire designed to measure delinquency. He found that girls committed only a fraction of the delinquent behavior committed by boys and attributed the difference to differential parental practices relating to boys and girls. Parents exerted more social control on girls than boys. He also found a ''U-shaped'' relationship between discipline and delinquency. Too much or too little discipline was related to delinquency, with a balance between harsh and lax discipline showing the lowest delinquency. Furthermore, identification with parents by a child is associated with low delinquency.

Nye found that mothers who worked had more delinquent children than those who stayed at home, primarily because of the limited supervision working parents provide. His most controversial finding was discussed in his chapter ''Legally and Psychologically Broken Homes'' in his book *Family Relationships and Delinquent Behavior*.

His analysis revealed a large discrepancy between the proportion of children from broken homes incarcerated in ''state training schools'' (48 percent) and the proportion who fall into the most delinquent high school group (23.6 percent). The discrepancy, Nye concluded, was probably the result of the differential treatment children from broken homes received from the police, courts, parents, and neighbors. In addition, delinquent children (still in high school) were *slightly* more likely to come from broken homes than nondelinquent high school students. Nye, however, concluded that it was not a matter of the broken home *per se* that contributed to delinquency, it was the *happiness* of the marriage that makes the difference. Unhappy homes where parents quarreled and argued were more likely to engender delinquent children than the more happy, less conflictful homes. This finding has become one of the most widely cited of the Nye study.

However, before we rush to tell parents they must not quarrel or fight—else they will produce delinquents—several points need to be made about the Nye project. First, examination of the 23-item delinquency scale reveals that it measured *very* minor juvenile ''offenses,'' some of which just about every American high school student has ''committed'' at some point during adolescence. For example, there were questions about whether the student has ever defied his or her parents' authority (to their face); ever disobeyed parents; told a lie; skipped school without a legitimate excuse; taken little things (worth less than $2); bought or drank beer, wine, or liquor. Other items inquired as to whether the respondent ever had sexual relations with persons of the opposite sex, the same sex, or gone hunting or fishing without a license, or driven a car without a driver's license or permit. More ''serious'' questions asked about running away from home, fist fights, gang fights, taking a car for a ride without owner's knowledge (including parents'), narcotic drugs, theft (over $50), and vandalism.

It is clear that most of these items do not qualify for serious juvenile offending, even if committed frequently. Nye's conclusions, then, are generally based on "common," nonserious juvenile actions, mingled in with some status offenses.

Secondly, Nye's "marital happiness" finding is predicated on a *single-item* estimate by the adolescent of the marital happiness of each parent. Furthermore, he found no relationship between another 9-item questionnaire measuring parental quarreling and delinquency for boys and only a weak relationship for girls. It is difficult to know precisely what "quarreling" and "arguing" means. Mildly acting-out adolescents may raise havoc with any stable, "happy" home, and quarrels may be a "natural" parental response to this behavior. In conclusion, Nye's finding concerning family "happiness" and delinquency should not be employed as supportive documentation for a marital discord-delinquency connection without considerable caution.

SOCIAL CONTROL THEORY

In 1969, Travis Hirschi began his well-known book *Causes of Delinquency* by evaluating the three fundamental perspectives on the causes of delinquency which were prominent at that time:

1. *strain* or motivational theories;
2. *cultural deviance* theories; and
3. *social control* or bond theories.

Hirschi examined the assumptions underlying each perspective and explained why his own form of social control theory had the most promise for explaining the phenomenon of juvenile delinquency.

Strain theory, which was introduced in Chapter 5 and will be discussed again in the next chapter, assumes that people have bought into the values promoted by American society, primarily its material goals of wealth and success. The legitimate means for reaching those goals are not universally available, however. There is, in strain theory, a crucial interaction between structure and culture, with structure represented by the institutional means and culture represented by the goals. Strain results from the fact that one wants the goals but does not have access to the acceptable means. Some persons, then, choose illegitimate means; deviance becomes the reasonable recourse. Thus, strain theory views the offender as being forced into crime by culturally induced desires that cannot be otherwise satisfied. With reference to delinquency, strain theory assumes that both delinquents and nondelinquents are bonded to the social order; deviance occurs because the road to success is blocked.

As Hirschi noted, classical strain theory is essentially a social class theory, since members of the lower class are the ones most likely to have limited access to opportunity. In most instances, strain theorists assume a strong connection between social class and delinquency. Furthermore, strain theorists rarely consider the relevance and importance of the family; parent-child relationships are not important, although in some theories the *structure* of the family plays an important role (e.g., Cohen, to be discussed in Chapter 9).

Cultural deviance theory, as expressed in the work of Edwin Sutherland, hypothesizes that delinquency represents conformity to a set of standards not accepted by a larger or more powerful society. Hirschi believes that cultural deviance theory assumes human beings are incapable of committing deviant acts that go against *all* social standards. Being easily susceptible to group influences, they must accept some set of cultural or group standards, even those in opposition to mainstream society. Therefore, the juvenile gang fills the void created by estrangement from parents and the other social institutions. According to the cultural deviance perspective, a person learns to become criminal in much the same way he or she learns anything else. Walter Reckless, discussed earlier, observed: ''There is almost every reason to admit that companionship is one of the most important, universal causes of crime and delinquency among males'' (1961, p. 311).

Control or bond theories—of which there are many—argue that delinquency occurs when the child's ties to the conventional order are weakened or broken. Control theory is very old theory. It can be traced back through Durkheim to Hobbes and to Aristotle (Downes and Rock, 1982). The fundamental assumption of control theories is detected in Nye's (1958) obervation that delinquent behavior occurs because it is not prevented (Weis and Sederstrom, 1981). In other words, when delinquency occurs, the appropriate socializing institutions have been remiss. Socialization instills internal moral controls, and societal sanctions hold the child in check. Delinquency—and deviance in general—occurs when individuals have not been adequately indoctrinated with the rules and expectations of a given society and when external social constraints are lacking.

The Drift In and Out of Delinquency

David Matza (1964), Hirschi's mentor, developed a theory that may also be considered a control theory. Matza hypothesized that adolescents—delinquent and nondelinquent alike—subscribe to conventional values and abide by the rules most of the time. However, ''The delinquent *transiently* exists in a limbo between convention and crime, responding in turn to the demands of each, flirting now with one, now the other, but postponing commitment, evading decision. Thus, he drifts between criminal and conventional action'' (Matza, 1964, p. 28). In other words, delinquents ''drift'' in and out of social controls. They *occasionally* engage in deviant or illegal behavior, not because they are driven or motivated, but because their normal attachment to conventional norms is temporarily suspended by various neutralization techniques. Further, ''The delinquent as drifter more approximates the substantial majority of juvenile delinquents who do not become adult criminals than the minority who do'' (Matza, 1964, p. 29). Most delinquents drift back into law-abiding ways as adults.

While Matza did lay some groundwork for control theory, Hirschi's *Causes of Delinquency* outlined it more clearly than it had been before. Today, control theory is largely attributed to Hirschi, and his book continues to be its most widely cited elaboration.

The Hirschi Version of Social Control

Hirschi rejected both cultural deviance and strain theories in favor of social control. Cultural deviance theory, he said, was too ambiguous and conceptually circular to be empirically falsifiable. Furthermore, any predictions from Sutherland's theory were "trivial." He found fault with strain theory because it could not clearly identify so-called strain, could not satisfactorily explain why most delinquents outgrow it, and could not explain the high incidence of delinquency that occurred outside of the lower socio-economic class. Furthermore, Hirschi found strain theory, like cultural deviance theory, incapable of being empirically falsified, because no one had been able to define operationally its major independent variables.

Hirschi set out to operationalize, then test empirically, the concepts of control theory. He proposed four basic elements of the bonding process:

1. *attachment* to parents, teachers, and peers;
2. *commitment* to conventional lines of activity, such as educational and occupational aspirations;
3. *involvement* in that conventional activity; and
4. *belief* about the legitimacy and morality of the social rules and laws.

He speculated that the elements had an additive effect: the more attachment, commitment, involvement, and belief, the more likely that the individual would be bonded to society, and consequently the less likely he or she would be to engage in delinquent activity. Furthermore, Hirschi posited that the more a person was tied or bonded to conventional society by one element, the more likely he or she would be bonded to the others.

Attachment refers to the degree of sensitivity a person has to the opinions of others, that is, the extent to which a person cares about and internalizes the wishes and expectations of other people. According to Hirschi, the most important persons within the social environment are parents, peers, and school officials, with parents the most critical. ". . . (T)he fact that delinquents are less likely than non-delinquents to be closely tied to their parents is one of the best documented findings of delinquency research" (Hirschi, 1969, p. 85). Insensitivity to what these groups think and feel is a sign of weakened or nonexistent bonds to the conventional social order.

Commitment involves the physical and emotional investment a person puts into the normative, conventional way of life. It includes such activities as studying, building up a business, saving money, acquiring a reputation of virtue and honesty, and generally doing those things encouraged and expected by conventional others. The more a person commits him or herself to these activities, the less likely that the person will engage in acts that ultimately will jeopardize his or her position in the social order. "The person becomes committed to a conventional line of action, and he is therefore committed to conformity" (Hirschi, 1969, p. 21).

Involvement refers to the *amount* of time and energy expended in the pursuit of conventional activities. According to Hirschi, a person heavily involved in conventional endeavors has neither the time nor the energy to engage in deviant behavior. "The person involved in conventional activities is tied to appointments, deadlines, working hours, plans, and the like, so the opportunity to commit deviant acts rarely arises. To the extent that he is engrossed in conventional activities, he cannot even think about deviant acts, let alone act out his inclinations" (Hirschi, 1969, p. 22). Thus, the juvenile involved in recreational, social, religious, and school endeavors has little time to engage in delinquent acts, underscoring the adage "The idle mind is the devil's workshop." In some ways, Hirschi sees delinquents as members of a leisure class, plagued with free time and characterized by ". . . a search for kicks, disdain for work, a desire for the big score, and the acceptance of aggressive toughness as proof of masculinity" (Hirschi, 1969, pp. 22–23).

Belief is the degree to which a person internalizes and accepts the common value system of the society or group. The value system includes sharing, sensitivity to the rights of others, respect for and acceptance of laws and rules, and concern for the plight of others. Traditional control theory assumed that the delinquent believed the rules, even as he or she violated them. Hirschi noted that there were two approaches to reconciling this discrepancy between believing in legitimate rules while violating them. In one approach, theorists treated "beliefs" as mere words, not internalized beliefs at all. That is, the person might have said the right things but did not really believe in the values and social goals expressed by the words. In sum, the beliefs had not been internalized. A second approach contends that the person *rationalizes* behavior, allowing him or her to violate the rule but still retain belief. Sykes and Matza (1957), discussed in Chapter 7, adopted this view, referring to this rationalizing behavior as "neutralization." Neutralization occurs after the delinquent act, freeing the person from any mental dissonance or conflict.

Hirschi disagreed with both approaches. Instead, he proposed variations in the extent to which people believe they should obey the rules of society, that beliefs in the rules are not all-or-none things. Beliefs exist on continua, ranging in degrees of conviction. Generally speaking, the less a person is committed to the rules (the weaker the bonds), the more likely he or she will violate them.

Hirschi tested his control theory in 1964, in a study of 1,300 junior high and high school boys living in an urban California county. He used data from both official and self-report sources. The boys were administered questionnaires in which they were asked about their involvement in delinquency. In addition, Hirschi included a number of questions which were designed to measure the four elements of his bond to society. For example, attachment was measured by such questions as: "Would you like to be the kind of person your father is?" Commitment was measured primarily by the importance the boys placed on grades, involvement by the amount of time they devoted to school activities, and belief by their degree of respect for police and the law.

The most striking finding of the Hirschi study was the impact of identification with the male parent. Boys who reported that they discussed their future plans and shared their thoughts and feelings with their fathers were much less likely to engage in delinquent acts than boys who reported less intimate communication. The *amount* of communication was less significant than the *closeness* or the intimacy as perceived by the boys. Hirschi discovered that, with few exceptions, as the intimacy of the communication increased, the boy was less likely to commit delinquent acts.

The Hirschi data suggested that relationship with the father was possibly the most important factor in the development of male delinquency. A close and intimate relationship between father and son was correlated with nondelinquency, regardless of the relationship with the mother. A similar finding has been reported by Alayne Yates et al. (1983). These researchers discovered that a vast majority of the 339 young male violent offenders (ages 18 to 20) they reviewed described the early relationships with their fathers as more important than the early relationships with their mothers. Interestingly, in Hirschi's study, boys whose parents themselves engaged in criminal behavior were no more likely to be delinquent than those boys whose parents were noncriminal. Hirschi explained this by speculating that all parents—criminal and noncriminal—express allegiance to the norms of conventional society, even though they may not conform to them personally.

The Hirschi survey also uncovered a complex relationship among parents, the child, the school, and peers. Boys who did poorly in school tended to lack intimate communications with parents. Hirschi disagreed with theorists who concluded that dislike for school was a source of motivation to delinquency, or that delinquency was a means of relieving frustration generated by unpleasant school experiences. Success in school, Hirschi said, depended upon how competent the boy believed himself to be. These perceptions of competence stemmed partly from the parent's perceptions of his competence as they were communicated to him. If parents communicated that the boy was competent and should do his best, then school became tolerable and even challenging. Although teachers and peers played significant roles, parental influences were paramount. In this sense, Hirschi was pointing to the important role of mesosystems—or interactions between microsystems—in the development of delinquency. We will return to this issue in Chapter 9.

In sum, attachment to parents became a central tenet in Hirschi's control theory: Strong attachment essentially precluded delinquency. Furthermore, attachment to parents was associated with other relationships, both within and away from home. Attachment to parents was often associated with attachment to peers, for example. And Hirschi found that the closer the boy was to his peers, the less delinquent he tended to be. This would not be predicted by cultural deviance theory, which suggested an inverse relationship between attachment to parents and to peers: Children unattached to parents were more likely to be influenced by those outside the family. Hirschi also found a negative relationship between ambition and delinquency. The more ambitious a boy was, the less likely he would become delinquent, a finding quite different from what would be predicted by Merton's theory of anomie and strain theory in general.

Michael J. Hindelang (1973) conducted a "quasi-replicative" study of Hirschi's survey, using both male and female adolescents in a rural New York state community. Hindelang's project was "quasi-replicative" because some of the questions were worded slightly differently, and the resouces available to Hindelang were not nearly as extensive as Hirschi's. Even so, and despite the fact that the surveys were conducted nearly ten years apart and in different parts of the country, Hindelang's results were remarkably similar to those of Hirschi's. Attachment to parents, teachers, and school officials; commitment to "adult" activities and conventional activities; involvement in school-related activities; and all the belief items produced results very similar to Hirschi's. However, Hirschi in his original study hypothesized and found the greater the peer attachment, the lower the reported delinquency. In contrast, Hindelang found the greater the peer attachment among his rural subjects, the higher the reported delinquency.

Hirschi's publication helped bring attention to family factors as strong influences on delinquency. Social control theory also proved to be formidable "oppositional" theory to strain and subculture deviance because it was not class based. It applies equally to lower, middle, or upper class delinquency. Overall, social control theory is perhaps the most heuristic theory in the contemporary literature on delinquency. But the theory does have its problems, as do all theories in the social sciences.

Hirschi's version of social control has rekindled a human nature debate. The underlying assumption of social control theory is that all humans are basically disposed toward criminality. If left unsocialized or without social controls, humans would soon rape, kill, plunder and destroy. Like Freud, Hirschi finds himself arguing that socialization and social control are the saviors of humankind. The big question left unanswered by Hirschi is: *Why* are humans this way in the first place? Is he suggesting humans are naturally biologically and genetically destructive and deviant?

While Hirschi's theory has drawn considerable research, his terms and concepts remain vague and confusing. Terms like "attachment," "commitment," and "bonding," are defined principally by responses to questionnaire items, but we remain unsure beyond the content of the items what they actually mean.

The theory is problematic with respect to peer attachment. Hirschi emphasizes that attachment to delinquent peers should have little effect on delinquency involvement. Research by Hindelang (1973) and Marvin Krohn and James Massey (1980) do not support this claim. Moreover, Wiatrowsi et al. (1981) and Krohn and Massey (1980) report that they found that a number of adolescents who committed delinquent acts did not demonstrate any broken or weakened bonds to parents. Krohn and Massey (1980) also found that the theory is better able to account for nonserious offenses than serious offenses. Still, Hirschi's theory of social control continues to be a popular and durable one in the study of delinquency.

FAMILY STRUCTURE AND DELINQUENCY

The Broken Home

Criminologists interested in the study of delinquency have given a great deal of attention to the so-called "broken home," generally defined as the family which has experienced divorce, separation, desertion, or the death of one of the parents. Although many researchers are now using the term "single- (or one-) parent family," the traditional term has predominated and will be used here as well. Later in this section, we will discuss the conceptual quagmire that results from using either "single-parent family" or "broken home," however.

Karen Wilkinson (1974) noted that the history of belief and theory about the relationship between delinquency and broken homes is characterized by periods of acceptance followed by periods of rejection. During the first 30 years of this century, it was widely accepted that broken homes led directly to delinquency. Shaw and McKay (1932), writing an influential review of the research between 1900 and 1932, summarized the thinking during that period with the comment: "It is significant only to note that the belief that the broken home is one of the most important causes of delinquency is widely accepted" (p. 514). Research by Breckinridge and Abbott (1912) reported that 44 percent of all the delinquent boys brought before the Juvenile Court of Cook County lived in homes that were broken by death of one or both parents, desertion, divorce, or separation. Healy (1915; Healy and Bronner, 1926) claimed that his delinquent samples contained anywhere between 36 and 49 percent of children from broken homes. Shideler (1918) found that over 50 percent of the delinquents he studied were from broken homes. Monahan (1957) reviewed 14 studies published between 1903 and 1933 and reported that, indeed, all of them affirmed a strong association between broken homes and delinquency.

Articles by Shaw and McKay (1931; 1932), Joanna Colcord (1932), and Katharine Lenroot (1932) marked the beginning of serious questioning of the dictum that broken homes led directly to a delinquent and criminal way of life. In their 1931 monograph, Shaw and McKay asserted that the broken home was not necessarily conducive to delinquency unless there were additional complicating factors, such as low morale, poverty, or a physically deteriorating neighborhood. The combination of these factors, not the broken home alone, would be more likely to draw children into delinquency. According to Shaw and McKay, a vast majority of the early research supporting the broken home-delinquency combination had neglected to use control groups of comparable nondelinquent youths. Moreover, the early investigations did not distinguish between homes broken because of parental conflict and those broken because of death.

Although the years 1900 through 1932 were characterized by the strong belief that a youngster from a broken home had a high probability of becoming delinquent, criminologists during the next 20 to 30 years either rejected or ignored the relationship. The British criminologist Herrmann Mannheim, after an exhaustive review of the literature on the subject, wrote (with apparent discouragement):

> No other term [the broken home] in the history of criminological thought has been so overworked, misused, and discredited as this. For many years universally proclaimed as the most obvious explanation of both juvenile delinquency and adult crime, it is now often regarded as the "black sheep" in the otherwise respectable family of criminological theories, and most writers shamefacedly turn their backs to it. (Mannheim, 1965, p. 618)

Wilkinson (1974) noted (as do Wilson and Herrnstein, 1985) that the major theories on crime and delinquency developed during this period for the most part did not include family factors as important variables. Differential social class, economic opportunities, the operations of the criminal justice system, and peer group patterns were all considered much more relevant to the search for the causes of delinquency. To Wilkinson, the neglect of family factors was inconsistent with the traditional interest of sociologists in the family. She speculated that the lack of interest in familial variables might be explained by the strong aversion of sociologically oriented criminologists to psychologically oriented explanations of behavior. Familial relationships, such as those between parent and child, were too psychological for their research tastes. In a similar manner, Gove and Crutchfield (1982) suggested that criminologists and family sociologists during those years left research on outcomes of specific family relationships on the child to developmental psychologists.

Wilson and Herrnstein (1985) attribute the lack of attention to family factors to the political climate of the 1950s and 1960s. In the 1950s Americans were worried about mob violence; in the 1960s the country's attention turned to civil rights and economic opportunity. ''Gangs, race prejudice, social class, and criminal justice were concepts that seemed close to the problem and amenable to change. By contrast, the family as a concept suffered from two defects: It was not on the public agenda and it was not clear how its practices might be altered'' (p. 216).

As we have seen, the work of F. Ivan Nye (1958) and Travis Hirschi (1969) prompted a resumed interest in sociological investigations of the relationship between delinquency and the family. Since the 1970s sociological researchers have had a particular interest in re-examining what some see as an intuitively appealing relationship between the broken home and delinquency. It would be misleading to suggest that this trend symbolizes mainstream sociological criminology, however. There continues to be resistance by criminologists to looking at the family, particularly at the processes therein.

Recent empirical assessments of the family-delinquency relationship have yielded equivocal and conflictful findings. Grinnell and Chambers (1979), using official statistics to measure delinquency, found little or no relationship between broken homes and white middle class delinquency. Gibson (1969) found no higher incidence of delinquency among London school boys from low-income broken homes than among boys from low-income intact homes. Rankin (1983) found a positive relationship between broken homes and delinquency, but only for certain offenses (e.g., runaway, truancy, auto theft) and for certain types of homes (specifically where neither natural parent was present). Hennessy et al. (1978) conducted a self-report study with middle class high school students of both sexes and found no significant relationship between broken homes and delinquent behavior.

Some research (e.g., Toby, 1957; Wadsworth, 1979) on *official* delinquency has suggested that the earlier the parental break occurs in the developmental history of the child, the greater its impact on the development of delinquency (Wells and Rankin, 1985). This is compatible with studies in child development which suggest that age at time of parental discord and separation is a relevant factor in determining the effect on the child. Similarly, the age at which the family discord and separation occurs may also have a significant impact on the development of delinquency. Older children, because they have formulated friendships with peers and have achieved some degree of personal autonomy from parents, appear to find separation less traumatic than younger children

(Kellam et al., 1982). Younger children experiencing divorce not only have fewer experiences outside the home, but also lack the cognitive and social competencies to understand and deal with the dissolution of their parents' marital relationship (Belsky et al., 1984). Child development research suggests that the coping styles of children of different ages vary as a function of their cognitive and social competencies. Young children, for example, may blame themselves for causing the separation and otherwise be unable to evaluate the divorce situation accurately (Belsky et al., 1984). The few self-report studies conducted on the topic are at odds with the official studies; the self-report research does not support this age-divorce hypothesis (e.g., Nye, 1958; Rankin, 1983).

A child's temperament also may be a factor in how he or she reacts to a divorce situation. In a study by Hetherington, Cox, and Cox (1978), children who exhibited the highest level of behavioral problems as a result of divorce or marital discord were those

1. described by their mothers as having had, during their infancies, a prevalence of fussiness or crying;
2. who adapted slowly to new situations and showed distress under those conditions; and
3. who displayed biological irregularities in sleeping, feeding, and eliminating.

Possibly, some combination of marital disharmony and individual temperament produced a high risk environment for the development of delinquency.

One of the more frequent observations is that delinquent girls come from broken homes more often than delinquent boys (Rodman and Grames, 1967), suggesting that parental discord and separation may have a greater negative impact on girls. Jackson Toby (1957) argued that this difference is due to the greater control parents maintain over girls: When separation occurs, the contrast effects (from control to much less control) have a stronger impact on girls. Most of the studies finding sex effects were based on official delinquency records, however (Wells and Rankin, 1985). Some investigators (e.g., Datesman and Scarpitti, 1975; Rankin, 1983), therefore, have suggested that the sex difference may be due to the family-related bias in official processing of female delinquents. Girls are more likely than boys to be referred to juvenile authorities and to receive official sanctions for such "ungovernable" behaviors as sexual misconduct, running away, and truancy, all of which are likely to be affected by the family situation (Wells and Rankin, 1985). Datesman and Scarpitti (1975) did find some sex differences in the effect of father absence, but the relationship is weak. Austin (1978) replicated the study with a larger sample and found support only for the hypothesis that father absence would have a stronger negative effect on white girls than white boys.

The sex differences are not universally accepted, therefore. There is some evidence that boys are more strongly affected by divorce than girls (Emery, 1982) and that family conflict is as important in male as in female delinquency (Norland et al., 1979). Self-report studies in general are less convincing about purported sex differences. Wells and Rankin (1985, p. 256) summarize the empirical research with the comment, ". . . the simple proposition that family break up has a greater negative effect on girls than on boys is too simple to be meaningful.'' They add that the broken home-delinquency relationship may itself be nothing but an artifact of official processing procedures.

In similar fashion, after reviewing the research literature, Rosen and Neilson (1982, p. 134) wrote: ''. . .(T)he concept of broken homes, no matter how it is defined or measured, has little explanatory power in terms of delinquency.'' This is a strong and absolute statement that is probably premature. Although the research findings have been inconsistent, there exists enough support for the relationship to warrant its further consideration. In the next section we will examine some of the major reasons why the research has been so equivocal. The reasons for frequent and frustrating inconsistencies are multiple. It is instructive to review them not only because they underscore the complex relationship between structure and process family variables, but also because they suggest some sense of the difficulty in finding the causes of human behavior.

Methodological Problems

Self-report and official data often are discrepant with respect to the delinquency-broken home connection. Studies relying on official statistics have reported, with some regularity, that juvenile delinquents come disproportionately from broken homes. Self-report studies, on the other hand, have yielded mixed results, sometimes finding little or no overall relationship between broken homes and admitted delinquent behavior, and other times finding a significant relationship (Gove and Crutchfield, 1982).

Michael Hindelang, Travis Hirschi, and Joseph Weis (1979) argued that the discrepancy between self-report and official statistics is illusory, because the two methods do not measure the same domain of behavior. Self-report surveys measure a large assortment of the more common and less serious forms of delinquency, whereas official statistics are slanted toward more serious offenses. It should not be assumed, therefore, that their results are contradictory; both provide valuable information of a different sort. The correlation between broken homes and serious delinquency might be high, while that between broken homes and mischievous or nonrepetitive offending might be quite low.

Richard E. Johnson (1986) suggests that the discrepancy between official and self-report studies in this area may be explained in a number of ways. Johnson surveyed 672 high school sophomores, using self-report questionnaires, in the spring of 1975. He asked the students to report *both* unreported delinquent acts they had committed (theft, vandalism, and assault) during the past year, and their officially recorded delinquent acts (nontraffic police apprehensions and juvenile court appearances). The questionnaire also sought information on family structure (e.g., number of natural parents in the home) and the quality of parent-child relationships (as reflected by a student's perceptions of his or her parents' love and concern). Johnson's results supported earlier studies using both types of data. Family structure (broken homes) was significantly associated with self-reported trouble with police, school, and juvenile court (self-reported ''official'' data). Self-reported frequencies of undetected or hidden delinquency did *not* show a relationship with broken homes.

Johnson concludes that his results are consistent with the view that police, school, and court officials discriminate on the basis of family structure alone. This is especially true in the case of girls. When officials realize that a misbehaving child is from a broken home, they may be more inclined or feel obligated to bring the child under the "protection" of the state. Thus, the oft-reported discrepancy between official and self-report delinquency *might* be due to the inclinations of authorities to process youth from broken homes (and thus officially record their misbehavior) as an intervention strategy, to protect them from further deterioration. This is the *parens patriae* philosophy in action. Although they may be well-meaning, they are giving the implicit message that broken homes are unable to socialize their children properly into mainstream society. Johnson is quick to note that this hypothesis is speculative, since he did not test it directly, and that alternative explanations could surely be advanced.

Gove and Crutchfield (1982) added a new twist to the self-report procedure and obtained results contrary to those of Johnson. Noting that almost all self-report studies collect data from the youths, Gove and Crutchfield decided to collect them from both the youths and their parents. They randomly chose households from census tracts of Chicago and interviewed a randomly selected adult in each. They were able to collect complete data on 620 families. Adults were submitted to a structured interview (questions constructed before the interview, allowing systematic analysis of the data at a later date). Juveniles of both sexes from broken homes were much more likely to be delinquent than youngsters from intact families. This was in sharp contrast to Johnson's self-report finding of no differences.

Conceptual Problems

Even more basic than the problems in methodology are the definitions used in the research on broken homes and delinquency. Most generally, "broken home" or, as some researchers prefer, "single-parent family" is defined as a household where at least one natural parent is absent because of death, desertion, divorce or separation. This definition is so broad that it is virtually meaningless for research purposes. Research clearly suggests, for example, that more serious childhood problems are present in homes broken by divorce, separation, or desertion than homes broken by death (Emery, 1982). But even if one were to concede that homes broken by death probably constitute a nonsignificant minority in any given sample, it is still not justifiable to treat separation, desertion, or divorce as part of a unitary concept. Ideally, research focused on structure should clearly delineate *how* the homes in its sample are "broken."

Even this, however, assumes that all divorces, all desertions, all separations affect families in the same way. It is for this reason that some researchers prefer to examine process variables rather than structure variables in family research.

This is not easily done. Research on the effects of divorce in general often fails to acknowledge that the legal formality of divorce usually follows long after alienation (psychological and physical) between the spouses (Lamb, 1977). There are, however, exceptions, and the research does not tell whether these exceptions are significant. Furthermore, although the stresses and strains of divorce generally occur gradually, including the psychological separation between the children and the conflictful parents, this is not invariably the case. Also, the absent parent may continue to maintain a significant relationship with both the separated spouse and the child or children, with or without a shared custody arrangement. It is also not unusual for parental conflict to continue unabated after the home has been formally "broken." Some research indicates that children of divorced parents who remain in conflict after the divorce decree are more likely to be delinquent than children from low-conflict divorces (Hetherington, Cox, and Cox, 1979). Structure research—that which focuses simply on whether the family is broken or intact—does not address these fine points.

Emery (1982) and Gove and Crutchfield (1982), concluded after extensive literature reviews that it is parental conflict rather than separation *per se* which results in delinquency. Children from broken, but conflict-free homes are less likely to be delinquent than children from conflict-ridden but "intact" homes.

To continue with definitional problems, investigators far too often have treated "intact" families as though they were a homogeneous collection. Some children live with both of their natural parents; others live in restructured nuclear families, where a stepparent has entered the family, or in "blended families," where two adults each bring offspring into the new nuclear group. Recent studies (Johnson, 1986; Dornbusch et al., 1985) suggest a strong link between the presence of a stepfather and delinquency. Stepfathers, for reasons unknown, appear to engender delinquent behavior in their stepchildren. It may be more meaningful, therefore, to classify families on the basis of whether they are "original" intact families or "restructured nuclear families."

In addition, broken homes are invariably defined from the reference point of children vis-à-vis their relationship with parents, whereas siblings and extended family members who might be living in the household (e.g., grandparents, aunts, and uncles) are ignored (Wells and Rankin, 1986). Some research is beginning to pay attention to some of these factors. Neilsen and Gerber (1979) found that brothers and sisters of chronic truants tended also to be truant. G. R. Patterson (1986), after reviewing the literature, concluded that the evidence so far suggests that siblings are similar across a considerable range of behavior, including involvement in delinquency.

Even the word "parent" is not sufficiently defined in much of the existing literature. Some researchers study only homes of biological parents, while others discount the primacy of biological ties, counting as parents any adults who effectively carry out parental tasks and perform the necessary care-giving functions (Wells and Rankin, 1986). The most common version of the broken home defines parents in biological terms (Wells and Rankin, 1986; West, 1982; Wilgosh and Paitich, 1982), but noteworthy studies have expanded the definition to include anyone considered by the children in the home as parents (e.g., Gove and Crutchfield, 1982; Matsueda, 1982; Blechman, 1982).

"Parental absence" is a condition that encompasses a wide variety of situations. The absence may be due to occupational demands, military service, hospitalization, or incarceration. It may be total or partial (e.g., shared custody, visitation privileges, correspondence), temporary or long-term, voluntary or involuntary (Wells and Rankin,

1986). Also, research rarely considers distinctions between father-absent and mother-absent homes, although the implicit assumption is that broken homes are generally father-absent households. Such variations in "absence" may have differential effects on the child's development and possible misconduct.

Not surprisingly, the concept of juvenile delinquency itself has been problematical in the broken home research. Researchers often approach the construct as a unitary one. It is more likely that, if there is any relationship, it is between broken homes (specifically defined) and different delinquent behaviors. Rankin (1983) suggests that the level of statistical significance and the direction of the correlations may depend upon the types of juvenile delinquency examined. Austin (1978) and Dentler and Monroe (1961) found no correlation between broken homes and theft, whereas Gibbons and Griswold (1957) reported one for broken homes, incorrigibility, and running away. Wilkinson (1980) found significant relationships, but only for specific types of self-reported delinquency under certain conditions. For example, the broken home seems to be more closely associated with delinquency in cultural contexts that reflect little tolerance for divorce—such as a rural area with strong traditional values. In addition, broken homes seem to be more related to certain juvenile offenses (vandalism, drug abuse, truancy) than others. "Thus, broken homes may be positively related to some delinquent acts, unrelated to others, and negatively associated with still other types of delinquency (Rankin, 1983, p. 467). Rankin himself found (1983) that three types of juvenile misconduct—running away, truancy, and auto theft—were strongly linked to broken homes in which *both* natural parents were missing. Other misconduct was not so related.

It is clear that the broken home literature is like a long-neglected fishnet whose compartments must be disentangled, perhaps mended, before it can be put to use. This is a formidable task, made even more challenging when we consider that the broken home-delinquency relationship, even with carefully defined concepts, is doubtless confounded with other structure variables, such as SES, ethnicity, income, place of residence, and educational level of parents. For example, there appears to be an inverse relationship between social class and divorce rates (Belsky, et al., 1984). Couples at the lower end of the socioeconomic ladder have the highest divorce rates, while persons in the upper middle and upper classes have significantly lower divorce rates. Separation and desertion rates are also much lower at these class levels. There is also an inverse relationship between divorce and educational level—the lower the educational level, the higher the divorce rate. Insufficient income is likely to engender strain on a marital relationship, or, conversely, a conflictful marital relationship is apt to raise havoc with the partners' ability to work at their jobs effectively.

Attention to process variables, such as the emotional tone and frustrations concomitant with the separation, death, or divorce of a spouse, is also warranted. It is possible to take into account the relative influence of any of these variables in attempting to explain delinquency. The task requires sophisticated research designs and analyses which have only recently been accessible to social scientists. In the last section of the chapter, we shall examine several studies which exemplify this approach. At this point, we will complete our discussion on family structure variables by covering the effects of family size and birth order on delinquency.

Family Size, Birth Order and Delinquency

A sizable amount of evidence suggests that both family size and birth order are linked to delinquency (Ernst and Angst, 1983). Family size refers to the number of siblings within one family. Birth order refers to the ordinal position in the birth sequence among siblings (e.g., first born, second born, last born, only born, etc.).

The Gluecks (1950) found that their delinquent group was more likely to come from a large family than their nondelinquent group. Hirschi (1969, pp. 239–240) concluded from his SR study of delinquency that: ". . . children from large families are more likely than children from small families to have committed delinquent acts." West and Farrington (1973) reported similar findings. From their literature review of mostly British studies, Cécile Ernst and Jules Angst (1983, p. 233) summarize: "Delinquents' origin from larger sibships than controls in the same social class is well established. Beyond that, it was repeatedly found that the *rate* of delinquency . . . also increases with sibship size." In their very extensive review of the research literature, Rolf Loeber and Magda Stouthamer-Loeber (1986) concluded that delinquents often come from large families. At the same time, they could not locate a single study that tried to investigate *why* this relationship exists. That is, no study that they are aware of has concentrated on the familial processes that contribute to the family-size delinquency connection.

Research further shows that if one sibling is delinquent, there is a high probability the other siblings will be also. Therefore, "delinquent families" contribute disproportionately to the delinquency rate. For example, Harriet Wilson (1975) found in her study of disadvantaged inner-city families in Britain that 16 percent of the families produced 62 percent of the delinquent children. Similarly, David Farrington and his colleagues (1975) reported that about four percent of the families from a working class neighborhood in London produced 47 percent of the convicted delinquents. Furthermore, Loeber and Stouthamer-Loeber found that siblings engaged in much the same delinquent activities—drug abuse, burglary, shoplifting, and so forth. In discussing the delinquent behavior of siblings, however, it is important to keep in mind the possibility that whole families may be unjustly "labeled" as a result of the actions of one or two of their members.

The evidence for birth order effects is also quite robust. Middle born boys are overrepresented in delinquency (Ernst and Angst, 1983; West and Farrington, 1973; Glueck and Glueck, 1950; Lees and Newson, 1954). William and Joan McCord (with I. K. Zola) (1959) also found that middle born boys were more likely to be delinquent. The McCords speculated that the middle born children tend to be forgotten during a time when the burdens of a family are most pressing. Many others have also speculated about the many possible reasons for the birth order effect, but research has yet to examine the processes through which middle born children are potentially more prone toward delinquent behavior. We also do not know from the available research whether birth order is related to serious delinquency, nonserious delinquency, or both.

Again, we have a reported significant relationship between family structure and delinquency, but little empirical evidence as to *why* it exists. Until further research focuses more on the family process involved, we can only speculate on what these connections mean. The causal chain, however, is unlikely to be as simple as: Family size (or birth order) causes delinquency. M. Wadsworth (1979), for example, found that family size appears to be most strongly associated with delinquency in disadvantaged families (measured by income and father's occupation) and only weakly with middle class families. There are likely to be *many* other contributing, co-determining variables in the equation.

FAMILY PROCESS: STYLES OF PARENTING, DISCIPLINE, AND SUPERVISION

Whereas most of the discussion thus far has centered around structure factors, we now move to family processes, particularly parental discipline and supervision. Few would deny that parents or other permanent caretakers employ a variety of strategies to guide, regulate, and control their children's behavior. Yet these strategies rarely are examined in criminology. While research on family structure is fairly extensive—albeit equivocal, as we saw in the previous section—empirical explorations of the family dynamics that might influence delinquency are sparse. This is troubling, since some criminologists who see a role for the family believe that delinquent behavior is more strongly related to family processes than to family structure (Johnson, 1980). The emotional climate of the family—reflected, for example, in parental conflict, depression, or rejection of children—is more relevant to the child's behavior than whether the home is "broken" or intact or whether there are two or five children. Although research on family structure should be encouraged, this should not be at the expense of research on process. There are numerous problems in approaching this latter type of research. How is it to be conducted? What designs can be used? Obviously, researchers cannot expect to observe family interactions within the home as anthropologists study different cultures. Although this has occasionally been done, with parental permission (e.g., Patterson, 1982), the family's right to privacy precludes extensive research of this type. Most studies focused on process use interview or questionnaire techniques. At this point, a variety of theories about possible links between family process and delinquency have been proposed, but few have been studied. Moreover, the limited research is largely confined to the effects of disciplinary styles and parental supervision on the misconduct of boys. We will examine some of these theories and studies and suggest alternate possibilities for approaching this sensitive, but very important topic.

The Baumrind Typology of Parental Styles

Diana Baumrind (1967, 1971), a researcher at the University of California, observed and interviewed parents and identified three types of child-rearing and disciplinary styles commonly used by parents: authoritarian, permissive, and authoritative. Like all typologies, hers has weaknesses, which will be discussed shortly. Nevertheless, the concepts provide a useful framework for our discussion.

According to Baumrind, parents displaying an *authoritarian* style try to shape, control, and evaluate the behavior of their children in accordance with some pre-established, absolute standard. The authoritarian household has numerous rules and regulations which must be rigidly observed, often without question or explanation. Authoritarian parents expect their children to be obedient and respectful of authority, work, tradition, and the preservation of order. Deviations and transgressions are met with punitive, forceful measures, which may or may not include corporal punishment. The authoritarian parent discourages any verbal exchanges that imply equality between parent and child; the power of the parent is explicit. Children are taught that parents and other adults in positions of authority know best, and that their words should be accepted without question.

The *permissive* parent adopts a tolerant, nonpunitive, accepting attitude toward children's behavior, including expressions of aggressive or sexual impulses. Permissive parents generally avoid asserting authority or imposing social controls or restrictions on their children's behavior. They make few demands for more mature behavior; they permit children to regulate their own behavior and make their own decisions. In this type of family, parents may see themselves as "resource persons" to be consulted if needed, but most children see no need to do this. Permissive parents allow children to set their own time schedule for eating, sleeping, watching television, leaving the home, and returning. Generally, these parents do not make it a point to encourage their children to accept the norms of society or to abide by its standards. They are, in essence, ineffective in their socializing roles.

Authoritative parents try to direct their children's activities in a rational, issue-oriented manner. There are frequent decision-making exchanges and a general spirit of open communication between parents and children. The hallmark of the authoritative family is reasoned discussion punctuated by social controls. Authoritative parents expect age-related "mature" behavior from the child, and they apply firm, consistent enforcement of family rules and standards. At the same time, they encourage independence and individuality. They listen to the child's point of view and also express their own position. Children of authoritative parents are led to see that rights and duties of parents and children are complementary.

Baumrind's typology is not without its problems. Like theories, typologies are influenced by the bias of their constructor. They represent a particular version of the world which may not be widely accepted or very helpful. Baumrind has proposed a typology that, from her perspective, and based on her data, represents in approximate form most parental disciplinary strategies. Other researchers (e.g., Hoffman and Saltzstein, 1967; Saltzstein, 1976) have proposed slightly different parental disciplinary typologies. Whether it is valid to attribute one particular style to each family is an open question. Many parents vacillate between permissiveness and authoritativeness, for example. They may allow their children to set their own eating and sleeping schedules and choose their modes of dress, but may demand extensive input into decisions related to school or work. The typology also does not take into account inconsistent parents, such as those who are generally permissive but may, for no apparent reason, erupt into anger and demand that their children abide by a newly announced rule. Nevertheless, acknowledging some weaknesses, it is useful to examine Baumrind's typology in light of the empirical research.

Parental Style and Delinquency

Baumrind used her typology to predict which parental style would lead to problem (although not necessarily delinquent) behavior in children. Her choice? The authoritarian style. Child development research tends to support this view. Children of highly authoritarian parents are often described as moody, unhappy, apprehensive, and easily annoyed. In addition, they tend to lack interpersonal skills for interacting with adults and peers (Maccoby and Martin, 1983) and tend to be rejected by "normal" peers (Hartup, 1978). In an extensive survey of parenting in Denmark and the United States, Kandel and Lessor (1972) discovered that, while authoritarian parents imposed more regulations than other parents, they were not necessarily effective in controlling their children's behavior. In both countries, children of authoritarian parents were more rebellious than children raised with other parental styles. They also had more difficulty with social interactions.

   The Kandel and Lessor study stopped short of suggesting that children of authoritarian parents were more likely to engage in *delinquent* behavior, however. Other researchers seem more ready to make that link. After an extensive review of the research literature, James Snyder and Gerald Patterson (1987) conclude that there are two parental styles which directly or indirectly contribute to delinquency. They label the two styles "enmeshed" and "lax." In the enmeshed style, parents see an unusually large number of minor behaviors as problematic, and they use ineffective, authoritarian strategies to deal with them. "These parents don't ignore even very trivial excessive behaviors. They issue more and poorer commands, use verbal threats, disapproval, and cajoling more frequently, but fail to consistently and effectively back up these verbal reprimands with nonviolent, nonphysical punishment" (Snyder and Patterson, 1987, p. 221). The ineffective use of coercive punishment sets up a reverberating pattern of family interactions ". . . which elicits, maintains, and exacerbates the aggressive behavior of all family members" (p. 221). When one family member in this coercive interaction acts aversively, other family members react the same way, escalating the exchange. Susie reacts strongly to her brother's loud music by suddenly screaming to him to turn it off. He screams back for her to "stick it." Susie bangs violently on his door. He screams louder. The father screams at both, telling them to "shut up" or else. Susie screams louder and proceeds to kick in her brother's door. She throws a vase at him, just missing. He runs after her, throwing a book. Eventually, the child sometimes "wins" this escalating confrontation when parents "give in" to demands, reinforcing this highly aversive interpersonal strategy—for example, father "orders" her brother to turn the loud music off. Thus, parents and children "teach" each other this harsh tactic works in social interactions, a pattern which soon extends to members outside the family.

Enmeshed parents also sometimes dispense authoritarian, harsh punishment, although it is inconsistent and ineffective. However, they probably do not have the energy to apply punishments to each and every behavior they perceive as problematic. Consequently, there are many instances where aversive behavior goes unpunished, such as in the preceding example. This pattern results in an intermittent, inconsistent punishment schedule that, in the long run, does little to discourage antisocial behavior.

For the most part, however, research does not *strongly* support a relationship between authoritarian parenting or harsh punishment and delinquent behavior. Surprisingly, the parental style most closely tied to delinquency is the permissive, or lax. Permissive parents have long been faulted both for lack of discipline and lack of supervision. In one of the earliest research projects examining the connection between discipline and delinquency, Healy and Bronner (1926) found that 40 percent of their sample of 4,000 delinquents came from homes where the parents failed to exert even a "minimum of good discipline." More recently, Harriet Wilson (1980) reported that parents who were lax in discipline and supervision (measured by their allowing children to roam streets without time limits and without knowing their whereabouts) were more likely to produce delinquent children, particularly in neighborhoods where delinquency rates were already high. In D. J. West's longitudinal study of London boys (1982), the researcher concluded that "poor supervision" was "one of the most important ways in which parents fail to protect their sons from delinquency" (p. 49). Poor supervision was defined as laxity in applying rules and a lack of vigilance over the child's activities and whereabouts.

As we have noted, Snyder and Patterson argue that the lax disciplinary style, like the enmeshed style, fosters delinquent behavior. In the lax style, parents are not sufficiently attuned to what constitutes problematic or antisocial behavior in their children. Consequently, they allow much of it to slip by, without disciplinary action. For a variety of reasons, they fail to recognize or accept the fact that their children are involved in deviant, antisocial, or even violent actions. They simply do not believe it is happening, or they convince themselves that there is very little they can do about it. "As a result, very few antisocial behaviors are punished. These parents, especially fathers, use punishment very infrequently, and when punishment is used, it has minimal deterrent effect" (Snyder and Patterson, 1987, p. 223).

Baumrind (1967) also suggested that parental permissiveness may have disastrous effects on children. The permissive parents in her sample displayed warmth toward their children, but their failure to provide control and structure appeared to promote impulsive and antisocial behavior in their offspring. The children exhibited very low levels of self-reliance and had great difficulty controlling their impulses. They were often in some kind of trouble with authority. Interestingly, the children also tended to be more pleasant and cheerful than the children of authoritarian parents.

As noted earlier, Baumrind's typology does not take into account inconsistency of supervision and discipline. Some parents and caretakers waver from time to time and behavior to behavior: At some times, and for some conduct, they provide no discipline or supervision, while at other times they are strict and harsh. Furthermore, their reactions are unpredictable, so the child is never sure how his or her conduct will be regarded. Craig and Glick (1963) found that

1. careless or inadequate supervision combined with
2. erratic or overstrict discipline are two of the most important factors in the development of delinquency.

Glueck and Glueck (1950) found most parents of nondelinquents treat their children in a "firm but kindly" way, while the parents of delinquents were either too harsh, too soft, or alternated unpredictably between severity and laxness. You may recall earlier in the chapter that the Gluecks have been widely criticized for their conclusions about the characteristics of delinquents. Their conclusions about parental styles, however, are more acceptable, as long as we keep in mind that they were comparing parents of institutionalized delinquents to parents of nondelinquents.

William and Joan McCord (1959, p. 154), in their well-known and comprehensive Cambridge-Somerville project, (described earlier) concluded that inconsistency, then laxity, were the parental characteristics most related to delinquency. "Relatively few boys who had been disciplined consistently in a love-oriented manner became criminal. Relatively few boys who had been disciplined in a consistently punitive manner became criminal." However, "Erratic discipline involving punitiveness was highly conducive to criminality. Boys disciplined in this manner had the highest conviction rates for every type of crime except traffic violations" (p. 155). Laxity in discipline was a very close second. Peterson and Becker (1965) noted in a summary of the research literature that mothers of delinquents were most guilty of extreme laxity, while fathers of delinquents were most likely to be excessively strict. Peterson and Becker concluded, however, that while laxity and severity of discipline may be factors in the development of delinquency, an inconsistent approach to discipline seems to be the most damaging. Nevertheless, ". . . the notion that *something* is wrong with the discipline is well established. The nature of the fault is not quite so clear . . ." (p. 83).

The Peterson-Becker statement that "the nature of the fault is not quite so clear" continues to be valid. While it appears that inconsistent discipline and careless supervision are particularly conducive to delinquency, we must be wary of oversimplification. For example, parental approaches to supervision seem to change as the children (and the parents) get older. Straus (1983) found an almost linear decline with age in parental use of physical punishment, for example. That is, parents are less inclined to discipline older children by corporal punishment than they are younger children. Similarly, the amount of time children in our society spend in direct contact with their parents or other adults decreases with the child's age (Snyder and Patterson, 1987). Finally, it is unlikely that most parents are consistent across all situations or social contexts. Major transgressions of the rules may be dealt with consistently, while the handling of minor ones may depend on the mood of the moment. Research has not examined what effect, if any, this might have on delinquent behavior. There is also unlikely to be the neat categorization in parental styles that the research assumes. As noted earlier, a parent may be authoritarian about school work ("Anything lower than a B and you don't get the car for a month! No ifs, ands, or buts, buddy!"), permissive about at-home schedules ("Around here, they eat when they're hungry and hit the sack when they're tired.") and flexible about curfews ("Past midnight? Well, it's negotiable.") Finally, the moods of children and parents affect the interchanges among them as well as the disciplinary styles.

Closely related to parental disciplinary styles is the issue of parental supervision or *monitoring*. Monitoring ". . . refers to parents' awareness of their child's peer associates, free time activities, and physical whereabouts when outside the home" (Snyder and Patterson, 1987, p. 225–226). To be effective in the control of deviant behavior, monitoring requires clear communication of the rules as well as reasonable punishment for their violation. Clear communication includes such standards as what time the child should be home from school, weekday and weekend curfews, and places that are off limits. Reasonable punishment includes restrictions or curtailment of certain privileges for clearly defined periods of time. Monitoring appears to be especially important from the ages of nine or ten through mid-adolescence, an observation that has received substantial support from longitudinal studies (Snyder and Patterson, 1987). Effective monitoring appears to be particularly critical in preventing delinquency in children from disadvantaged backgrounds (Wilson, 1980).

Although the research just cited tries to make associations between parental styles and delinquency or parental styles and other troublesome behavior, it gives only hints about what might be at issue or where we should go from here. Do parents who fail to supervise their children believe "excessive" supervision is "bad," perhaps reflecting their own childhood experiences? Are they so overwhelmed with other concerns (e.g., economic) that they simply have neither the time nor the energy to provide consistent discipline and supervision? Do they not care about their children? Would they provide different supervision if they received more support from the community? These questions should be answered, but the available research simply does not allow us to make confident inferences.

We will end the chapter by presenting several studies that have made gallant attempts to not only examine family processes but the outside influences (e.g., community) as well. This material provides a more panoramic view of the dynamic interplay of systems both within and outside the family microsystem.

PROCESS STUDIES ON FAMILY AND DELINQUENCY

The Johnstone Studies: Relationships Among Microsystems

John Johnstone (1978a, 1980) examined the simultaneous effects of environmental and family factors on different forms of delinquent behavior. Johnstone viewed delinquent behavior as the end product of three sets of forces: peer group influences, family influences, and community-norm pressures. Community-norm pressure was measured by the prevalence of poverty-level families, the unemployment rate, and the number of single-parent, female-headed households within the area where the youngsters lived. Measures of family integration, attachment to a delinquency-prone peer group, and participation in law violations were all measured by questionnaire responses by the adolescents themselves.

Johnstone's contextual analysis demonstrated that the influence of the family varied both with the type of delinquent behavior and with the community setting in which the adolescent lived. In reference to the type of delinquent behavior, there was an inverse relationship between the seriousness of the delinquency and the importance of the family to the child. When it came to serious offenses (burglary, larceny, robbery, and violence), the environment had the strongest effect. In other words, serious offenses were predicted better by characterstics of community than by characteristics of the family. Adolescent participation in serious offenses seems to be rooted in the wider social environment. On the other hand, less serious offenses (status offenses, minor drug infractions, and property violations) were more likely to be determined by characteristics of the family.

Johnstone concludes that in communities that are crowded and deteriorated and where poverty is constant and ubiquitous, the influence of the family over the adolescent appears to be minimal. In communities characterized by stability, security and safety, and moderate affluence, disrupted or conflictful family conditions can and do generate delinquency, usually of the minor variety. Thus, "Deteriorated families seem to have a stronger impact on youngsters in benign than in hostile ecological settings" (Johnstone, 1980, p. 92).

The Dornbusch Studies: Is Mother Alone Enough?

Sanford Dornbusch (1985) and his colleagues have conducted a series of important studies on the relationship between single-parent (primarily mother-present) homes and adolescent deviance or delinquency. In one study, Dornbusch explored the interrelationships among family structure, patterns of family decision-making (process), and deviant behavior. He used data from a nationwide sample of 7,514 subjects drawn from a population of 23 million, noninstitutionalized youths between the ages of 12 and 17. The sample was representative of the U.S. population for sex, race, region, population density, and population growth.

Dornbusch hypothesized that mother-only households would differ from two-parent households in their ability to control adolescents. Researchers administered questionnaires to both adolescents and their parents. They sought to ascertain to what extent parents were perceived to exert direct control over decisions concerning adolescent issues. A lack of control by parents was assumed to lead to adolescent deviance and delinquency. Measures of delinquency included number of contacts with the law, number of arrests, frequency of running away from home, truancy, and frequency of disciplinary actions by school officials.

The proportion of delinquency among mother-only households was greater than that in households with two natural parents, even when social class and income level were taken into account. This held for both males and females. However, and more important, the presence of a second adult in the mother-only households substantially *reduced* adolescent deviance. The data further suggested that the second adult could be anyone—grandmother, friend, aunt—*other than a stepfather*. Furthermore, there were sex differences in the stepfather arrangement. Male youths with stepfathers living in the home engaged in as much deviance and delinquency as those in mother-alone families, and more than those in two-parent families. On the other hand, females in stepparent families exhibited more deviance and delinquency than their male counterparts in two-parent families but *less* than females living in mother-only families. Dornbusch concludes that something about the internal processes of families with stepfathers has a stronger negative impact on male than on female adolescents. We could speculate that the stepfather encourages more control on the behavior of the daughters than on that of the sons.

In addition to these family structure variables, Dornbusch examined family decision-making processes as an index of parental control. In an earlier study (1983), he had found that family decision-making style was *partly* related to SES. Higher income families were more likely to demonstrate joint decision-making patterns. However, Dornbusch noted that in that earlier study, mother-only families comprised a high percentage of the lower SES families, confounding any conclusions about income and decision-making processes. In the 1985 study, the data continued to reveal that mother-only households showed less control over the adolescent, regardless of SES. The adolescent was making decisions independent of the mother's input. It appears that mothers, faced with the problem of controlling adolescents without another adult, are more likely to allow their children to make their own decisions. Adolescents making their own decisions, according to Dornbusch, are more likely to be deviant.

The cause-and-effect relationship between decision-making and delinquency remains very unclear, however. Parents faced with recalcitrant or delinquent youths may reduce their attempts to influence or control them. On the other hand, it may be that parents who try too hard to influence or control their adolescents may ''drive'' them to deviant behavior. The causal effect may go in either direction, most likely in both.

The Steinberg Study: Is the Family Microsystem Enough?

Laurence Steinberg (1987) concurs with some of the conclusions drawn from the Dornbusch study. In a self-report survey of 865 adolescents in Madison, Wisconsin, Steinberg discovered that those living in stepparent families were as much at risk of becoming deviant as their peers living in single-parent households. There was support for the assumption that two-natural-parent households are more effective in controlling (or produce less) deviant behavior than other forms of family structure. This was especially the case for girls of all age groups. Steinberg's data did not strongly support the ''additional adult hypothesis'' (other adults living in single-mother households diminish deviance). The hypothesis did hold for sixth grade girls, but not for boys and girls in the other age groups. According to Steinberg, there is a possible link between family structure and adolescent deviance: ''Family structure may affect adolescents' susceptibility to antisocial peer pressure, which in turn may affect their involvement in deviant or delinquent activity'' (Steinberg, 1987, p. 274).

The recent evidence suggests that children living in homes with both natural parents are significantly less likely to become involved in delinquent or deviant behavior. It does not suggest that delinquency or deviance are products of any unitary concept such as the broken home or the single-parent home, however. Researchers are just beginning to uncover the complicated interplay among the myriad of variables that influence the family system. Variations in patterns of child rearing, social support systems, reciprocal interchanges between child and parent, and the influences of siblings on one another are uncharted areas of research. Furthermore, even if a single-parent-delinquency association were clear, it would be dangerous to blame the caregiver. Individual single parents may be excellent caregivers, but as a microsystem, their household may be insufficient unless it is augmented to produce a fuller, richer range of roles, activities, and relationships for the child. Sufficient income is also a critical factor. Single-parent or broken homes with adequate finances and adequate social support systems are likely to be as effective in promoting pro-social behavior as the two-natural-parent household.

SUMMARY AND CONCLUSIONS

In this chapter we examined the principal context in which human development takes place: the family. It is apparent from the available research that the family is a major force in the development of delinquency, although *precisely* how it is is largely unknown. We summarized four ''classic'' studies that have analyzed the family-delinquency connection. The Glueck and McCord projects, while massive and extensive in their detail and data collection, have remained largely ignored in the delinquency literature. If not ignored, their significance has been downplayed. Two reasons for this were suggested. One relates to each research team's disagreement with the sociological orientation to criminology. The second relates to their heavy reliance on individual variables as explanations of delinquent behavior. The study of delinquency has been dominated by a sociological orientation, originating from the Chicago School. Thus, it is unlikely that the sociologically based researchers and theorists take kindly to the Glueck or McCord remarks and research approach.

The two ''classics'' that have made inroads into the delinquency literature and prompted greater attention to family factors were the works of F. Ivan Nye and Travis Hirschi. Hirschi especially has had an enormous impact in stimulating thinking and research centering on the many aspects of family and social control in recent years.

We then looked at family structure and its relationship to delinquency. The family structure variable receiving the most attention has been the ''broken home.'' Despite this attention, however, the empirical literature does not explain how this variable contributes directly to delinquency. We reviewed methodological and conceptual problems which provide partial answers to why the results are inconsistent and difficult to decipher. Although similar problems plague other areas of social science research, they seem especially troublesome in the family-delinquency literature.

Family structure variables *are* important. They highlight what needs to be studied, but they do not, by themselves, encourage theoretical development and cogent explanations of delinquent behavior. Investigations into family processes offer greater promise for a deeper and more systematic understanding of delinquency. Unfortunately, they are often much more difficult to conduct.

But let us not be too myopic and overemphasize family influences to the exclusion of other systems. Work by Jeffrey Fagan and Sandra Wexler (1987), for example, indicates that the role of families in the development of many violent delinquents may have been overstated in recent years. Their data imply that much of the learning for violence may occur outside the family—e.g., within peer groups, neighborhoods, and schools. Fagan and Wexler suggest that families by themselves may be powerless in mitigating well-entrenched neighborhood social processes in the development of serious delinquency. They recommend that policy makers look beyond the family to the social domain of school, peer, and community in establishing ways to prevent delinquent behavior.

The causes of delinquency continue to be elusive. This probably can be attributed in part to our tendency to look for cause at only one level of the world's stratification. We fail to see delinquency as a result of an enormous range of interacting structures and systems. We isolate partial causes, such as faulty practices in parental discipline, or deviant construct systems, or modeling, but this does not seem good enough. Our explanations are not rich enough in accounting for other factors, be they physical, biological, psychological, or sociological. To repeat a comment made by criminologist Charles F. Wellford (1987, p. 7), ". . . we must develop theories of criminal behavior that take seriously the notion that there are biophysical effects on criminal behavior, psychological effects, social effects, cultural effects or any other organized effects that we wish to identify through our specialization on the appropriate categories or levels of analysis." And as psychologists Peter T. Manicas and Paul F. Secord (1983, p. 405) write: "Identification of structures and their dynamics can only be accomplished by the *multilevel* application of imaginative theory that simultaneously guides observation, analysis, and experiment" (Italics added).

Microsystems and Mesosystems

9
CHAPTER

In this chapter we will explore the influence of two other microsystems—peers and the school—on delinquency. In addition, we will discuss the important mesosystems of family *and* peers, family *and* school, and family *and* work. In the peer and delinquency section we will introduce social network analysis, a procedure and conceptual framework that is particularly useful in analyzing the complicated world of peer influence. Social network analysis will also provide a helpful framework for examining the three mesosystems surveyed in the chapter, as well as for the ecological factors to be discussed in Chapter 11. First, we turn to the microsystem of friends and peers.

PEERS AND THEIR INFLUENCE ON DELINQUENCY

Research on peer influences on delinquent behavior has almost invariably focused on sizable juvenile groups or gangs. Virtually no one has studied delinquent or nondelinquent dyads or triads. Even research on *adult* crime partnerships is scarce. Therefore, although we should recognize that some delinquent behavior is displayed by two or three juveniles working in collusion, just as some is individual, the concentration here will be on group influences.

All intellectual paths on group delinquency originated with the pioneering efforts in Chicago of Frederick M. Thrasher, who published his observations in the well-received classic *The Gang* (Geis, 1965). At a time when psychiatrically oriented criminologists treated gang behavior as a throwback to primitive man roaming in herds, Thrasher dramatically shifted the discussion. Gang behavior, he said, was one way for youths to react to economic and social conditions. Although his colleagues at the Chicago School were drawing similar conclusions about delinquency in general, Thrasher specialized and studied only gangs. He observed that gangs emerged and thrived in the interstitial areas of cities, particularly those areas lying between adjacent commercial and residential neighborhoods. Thrasher essentially equated gangs with group delinquency, since virtually all of the gangs which he studied engaged in criminal activities. For our purposes, we will be referring in the following section only to those gangs that encourage their members to violate the law, recognizing that many may not.

In contrast to the evolutionary and Darwinian explanations of the day, Thrasher concluded that faulty social controls were at the root of gang delinquency. Specifically, the youths who violated norms had been ineffectively or weakly socialized by their families, churches, and schools. The social void created by these ineffectual social institutions prompted the youths to seek each others' company and form groups. Free of traditional social controls, youth gangs did what they wanted, subject only to the social constraints of their own subculture. Thrasher also observed that female gangs were exceedingly rare (he could locate only six that were independent of male gangs). He attributed the rarity of female gangs to the closer supervision families gave to girls.

Following Thrasher's pioneering work, interest in gang delinquency ebbed, peaked, and ebbed once again. Interest was high in the 1950s and 1960s, and several provocative theories were proposed. Since the mid-1960s, no new theory of gang delinquency has been advanced, nor has there been much research on the topic (Stafford, 1984). Thus, our knowledge in this area is limited. Mark Stafford (1984) cites two primary reasons for the lost interest. First, the study of gang delinquency has been hampered by its parochialism. Researchers and theorists have focused almost exclusively on lower class, urban boys, which has limited the scope of any potential theory of group delinquency. A notable exception is the work of Anne Campbell (1984), who studied group delinquency among girls. Second, there is considerable disagreement over the use of the word "gang." For example, what are the social boundaries of a gang? Where does it begin and where does it end? Members are not always identified, and membership often fluctuates. Furthermore, it is not clear how a gang differs from a formal group or even, in some cases, a youth organization.

A rather exasperated Walter B. Miller (1980), whose work on gang delinquency will be discussed shortly, noted also that there is no systematic procedure for identifying and characterizing different kinds of law-violating youth groups; worse, there has been little attempt to develop such a procedure. While criminologists often conclude that most delinquency is committed in groups (Miller, 1980; Hansell and Wiatrowski, 1981), we are able to obtain only very rough estimates of the amount of group delinquency in the United States or elsewhere. What little information is available has been gathered from self-report research or field observation and not from official tabulations. There is a "sense" that groups of juveniles operate together, and virtually every law enforcement official is personally familiar with the phenomenon of group delinquency, but quantifiable data are hard to find. Some of the best work on gangs in recent years has taken a *qualitative* track, such as Campbell's (1984) work, which is discussed later in the chapter.

Social Ability Versus Social Disability Models

Stephen Hansell and Michael Wiatrowski (1981) called attention to a major theoretical disagreement about the nature of delinquent group relationships. Some criminologists believe that most gang members have average social and interpersonal skills and generally belong to strong, cohesive groups. Group solidarity, close friendships, and loyalties are assumed to be features of the delinquent gang. In this sense, delinquent groups are not unlike nondelinquent groups. Other criminologists perceive delinquents as loners and social isolates with below average interpersonal skills. They are social outcasts who gravitate to other deviant and socially inept peers and form gangs. Because the members comprising them are socially inadequate, the gangs remain unstable, chaotic, disorganized bands of youths who cannot establish close, intimate relationships with one another.

Theories that view delinquent gang members as socially normal and their groups as cohesive and close-knit are *social ability models* in Hansell and Wiatrowski's terminology. Those theories that consider delinquent gang members outcasts and socially inept adolescents who make little attempt to develop cohesive groups are called *social disability models*. Examples of social ability models are the classic theories of Albert K. Cohen, Walter B. Miller, Richard Cloward and Lloyd Ohlin, and Herbert Bloch and Arthur Niederhoffer. Social disability models are best represented in the work of James Short, Jr. and Fred Strodtbeck, and more recently by Gerald Patterson. Hansell and Wiatrowski included Travis Hirschi's social control theory in this second category, but we will not discuss Hirschi in the following pages since he said little about group behavior. Hirschi did comment that many delinquents may be handicapped in cognitive skills and intellectual capacity, but he did not suggest that they were socially disabled (Hirschi, 1969, pp.132–133).

SOCIAL ABILITY MODELS

Cohen: Delinquent Boys and the Strains of the Working Class

The concepts of subculture, social class, and status deprivation are central themes in Albert K. Cohen's book on male delinquency, *Delinquent Boys: The Culture of the Gang* (1955). The book is an extensive revision of the author's doctoral dissertation, which was completed at Harvard University in 1951. Although Cohen's primary intent was to outline a general theory of subcultures, the book is most commonly regarded as a classic statement on the causation of delinquency, falling under the *strain* perspective. However, we should keep in mind that Cohen's statement refers specifically to *lower class*, *male* delinquency.

Cohen stipulated that the basic cause of lower class male delinquency rested with the very limited opportunities for lower class youths to gain access to mainstream, middle class society and their resulting strong feelings of alienation from that society. Thus, like Merton's theory, Cohen's was fundamentally a strain theory. Whereas Merton concentrated on the goal of material wealth, Cohen emphasized the importance of additional or higher status. According to Cohen, lower class youth were *ascribed* a low status by their families of origin. They then entered society and found that they were unable to *achieve* status. This occurred because boys of the lower social class had not been socialized in the manner of the dominant class and were not privy to the proper behavior needed to get ahead. Middle class parents had taught their children self-control, postponement of gratification, and effective planning for the future. They had communicated to their children that if they worked hard, were patient, and did what was expected, "good things" would come to them in the long run. Lower class children had no such advantage. Lower class boys were impulsive, hedonistic, and concerned with immediate gratification. *They* had been socialized to the tenet, "Get what you can when you can get it. Tomorrow will be too late."

Cohen believed that lower class children were at a serious disadvantage in the schools, where all children were constantly evaluted against the "middle class measuring rod" (Cohen, 1955, p. 84). This concept referred to the set of social expectations regarding the characteristics of "good children." One could meet this abstract standard only if one displayed responsibility, ambition, courtesy, and the proper control of aggression. Lower class children were unable to do this.

The low ascribed status and the inability to achieve status among both peers and adults created strain in the lower class boy. He realized that his upbringing had not emphasized order, punctuality, and time consciousness. He had learned to be easy-going and spontaneous, not to be concerned about achieving the long-term material goals desired by most of society. He had learned also to solve his problems by physical aggression and threats. Thus, the lower class boy began to feel alienated from middle class children, school officials, and other middle class adults. Eventually, he found other lower class boys who felt the same way. They formed the groups which, according to Cohen, were the essence of the delinquent subculture.

Cohen described the delinquent subculture as *nonutilitarian*, *malicious*, *negativistic*, and *versatile*. It was further characterized by *short-run hedonism* and *group autonomy*. These features differed significantly from Merton's conception of anomie. Merton, for example, assumed that lower class members stole for material gain and to try to be in tune with mainstream America; Cohen suggested that delinquent boys more often than not stole "for the hell of it." In fact, they often discarded, destroyed, or gave away stolen property. They valued the status they obtained from their fellow gang members, not material gain. This was the nonutilitarian feature of the delinquent subculture. Its members usually acted with no discernible purpose.

Delinquent subcultures, according to Cohen, were also generally "malicious." They seemed to delight in the discomfort of others—non-gang peers and adults—and enjoyed defying societal taboos. ". . . (T)here is keen delight in terrorizing 'good' children, in driving them from playgrounds and gyms for which the gang itself may have little use, and in general in making themselves obnoxious to the virtuous" (Cohen, 1955,

p. 28). Teachers often received the brunt of the malice. "There is an element of active spite and malice, contempt and ridicule, challenge and defiance, exquisitely symbolized, in an incident described to the writer by Mr. Henry D. McKay, of defecating on the teacher's desk" (Cohen, 1955, p. 28).

Cohen's term "negativistic" was closely related to maliciousness. Delinquent subcultures flouted the values and norms of mainstream society. Delinquents did things *in spite of* expectations and *against* mainstream norms. "The delinquent's conduct is right, by the standards of his subculture, precisely *because* it is wrong by the norms of the larger culture" (Cohen, 1955, p. 28). When society asserted it was improper to curse in public or spit on the street and delinquents performed these behaviors just to express their contempt for the rules, they were being "negativistic."

"Versatility," which Cohen referred to as the "spirit" of the delinquent subculture, signified the *diversity* of the antisocial behavior exhibited by the delinquent gang. Delinquents did not "specialize" in one activity. They were involved in many different irritating or illegal activities, often using ingenious strategies and devious plots.

"Short-run hedonism" underscored the lack of long-term planning, patience, or socialized ability to control the impulse of the moment, which Cohen believed characterized the delinquent subculture as well as the lower social class in general. Members of the delinquent gang typically congregated—with no specific purpose in mind—at some street corner or hang-out spot. They responded impulsively to suggestions or spontaneous events. Typically, they did not like organized or supervised recreation nor being told what to do by the adult world. They enjoyed the "fun" of the moment, without regard for the consequences. Cohen recognized that this characteristic was common for adolescents across all social classes but said ". . . it reaches its finest flower" in the delinquent gang (Cohen, 1955, pp. 30–31).

Another feature not entirely specific to the delinquent gang was its "group autonomy," which referred to intolerance of restraint from persons or institutions outside the immediate circle of gang members. According to Cohen, gang relationships were intense, showing solidarity and commitment, features which place Cohen's theory into Hansell and Wiatrowski's social ability category. Relationships with other groups tended to be indifferent, hostile, or rebellious. Cohen warned that he was not referring to an individual's autonomy from parents or other social agents, but specifically to the autonomy of the gang as a social unit. "For many of our subcultural delinquents the claims of the home are very real and very compelling. The point is that the gang is a separate, distinct and often irresistible focus of attraction, loyalty and solidarity" (Cohen, 1955, p. 31).

In Cohen's view, the frustrations inherent in status deprivation and the limited opportunity to change it within mainstream society *may* lead to the formation of the delinquent subculture with all its group dynamics and cohesiveness. Notice that the word "may" is emphasized here. This is because status frustration does not lead automatically to delinquency. Rather, Cohen maintains, juveniles plagued by status frustration are more likely to join delinquent subcultures than others.

Cohen was also a student of Edwin Sutherland. Reflecting Sutherland's differential association theory, Cohen believed that boys learned delinquent behavior from each other; they looked for "signs" or gestures of support (definitions) from their fellow group members. As those signs gradually appeared, the group became progressively committed to a set of new behaviors—a process Cohen called "mutual conversion." Merton treated the deviant act as a sudden, discontinuous change of state, a leap from a state of strain and anomie to a state of deviance (Cohen, 1965). From Cohen's perspective, deviance and delinquency developed gradually. "Human action, deviant or otherwise, is something that typically develops and grows in a tentative, groping, advancing, backtracking, sounding out process. People taste and feel their way along" (Cohen, 1980, p. 162).

In summary, Cohen explained that a large segment of delinquency was a reaction against middle class values and occurred as a function of participation in a delinquent subculture. Boys of similar circumstance formed a subculture, complete with a system of beliefs and values generated by a process of "communicative interaction." The similar circumstance—more often than not—was membership in the lower social class, where access to mainstream opportunity was severely limited. Frustrated in their attempts to gain status, lower class boys allied themselves with gangs which engaged in a wide assortment of delinquent activity. In essence, the delinquent subculture was a way of dealing with the "problems of adjustment"; it provided a criterion of status which the boys could meet and with which they were reasonably comfortable. Within the gang, with peer support, they could flout middle class values and standards. Together they could reject school and anything else representative of the middle class system.

Cohen added a surprising twist to his theory, suggesting that the rejection of middle class norms was a kind of "reaction formation." Reaction formation, a concept used in the psychological and psychiatric literature, refers to one of the defense mechanisms which humans are said to use to ward off threatening levels of anxiety. Sigmund Freud identified it as a hypothetical process which results in the person overtly stressing behaviors that are antithetical to his or her unconscious desires. The person who employs reaction formation presumably does not have to acknowledge his or her unconscious wishes. If these wishes were to come into awareness, they would cause considerable anxiety or guilt. ". . . (W)e would expect the delinquent boy who, after all, has been socialized in a society dominated by a middle-class morality and who can never quite escape the blandishments of middle-class society, to seek to maintain his safeguards against seduction" (Cohen, 1955, p. 133). Thus, reaction formation takes the form of an "irrational" and "malicious" behavior against all symbols and agents of middle class society. Cohen believed, therefore, that gang delinquents never actually repudiated conventional norms and standards. Subconsciously, they had the same goals, the same material interests, as the rest of society.

Critics often point out that one major weakness in Cohen's theory is its inability to account for middle class or female delinquency. However, in fairness to Cohen, his intentions were to explain lower class, male delinquency—nothing more. In his book, *Delinquent Boys*, he acknowledged that practically all children, regardless of social class, commit delinquencies. However, he also argued that delinquency is certainly more heavily concentrated in the working class. Viable theories of delinquency, he said, should begin there.

Although Cohen acknowledged the existence of female delinquents, he argued that their delinquency was overwhelmingly sexual in nature and not to be explained by his theory. "Stealing, 'other property offenses,' 'orneriness' and "hell raising in general are primarily practices of the male"(p. 45). Cohen believed that woman's adjustment in society was dependent upon her ability to form a satisfying relationship with a male. ". . . (A) female's station in society, the admiration, respect and property that she commands, depends to a much greater degree on the kinds of relationships she establishes with members of the opposite sex" (p.14). "Boys collect stamps, girls collect boys" (p. 142). Female delinquency, then, represented a failure on the part of the girl to fulfill her proper role. The "true" delinquent, however, was the "rogue male" (p. 140).

Walter B. Miller and Lower Class Gangs

The Harvard cultural anthropologist Walter B. Miller disagreed with Cohen's contention that delinquency was a reaction against middle class standards and values. To Miller, who also restricted his study to boys, delinquency was an adaptive effort to achieve success within the constraints of lower class membership. Based on the data he collected on delinquent gangs in the slums of Boston, Miller concluded that delinquency was little more than lower class adolescents modeling the behavior and adopting the beliefs of lower class adults. In an article published in 1958, Miller argued that the prime motivation of delinquent activity was the desire to realize the values of the lower class community itself, not a defiant response directed at the middle class.

Miller analyzed the lower class value system as an anthropologist would study a culture in East San Loa. The American lower class, according to Miller, is a long established, distinctively patterned tradition with an integrity of its own. He suggested, in fact, that it may comprise as many as four to six subcultures. About 15 percent of Americans represented a real "hard core" lower class group from which most male gang delinquency evolved.

Miller's gang theory revolved around two important structural variables which he saw as central ingredients of lower class culture:

1. female-dominated households; and
2. single-sex peer groups.

A majority of the households he studied were clearly dominated by a woman (mother, grandmother, or sibling). The male authority figure either was entirely absent from the home or appeared only sporadically; when present, he took little or no part in the care and support of the children. Furthermore, the dominant woman in the household often had a number of different partners, in or out of wedlock. Boys brought up in this female-based world, according to Miller, lacked an adequate male identity and sex role. To discover their places in the masculine world, they "hung out" and eventually became members of street corner gangs, all comprised of male adolescents seeking their proper roles. Within this gang structure, the boys would not rail against the middle class, as Cohen suggested. Instead, they emulated and modeled what males they could find in the lower class culture, including older boys in their gang. There was very little concern about middle class attainment.

Miller believed that gang delinquency was a natural product of lower class culture, which had six *focal concerns*, none of which appeared in the middle class. The lower class gave widespread attention to these concerns, which were

1. trouble;
2. toughness;
3. smartness;
4. excitement;
5. fate; and
6. autonomy.

All of these concerns were embraced by the gang and could be observed easily by field researchers.

"Trouble" referred to how much difficulty one had with the law. Miller asserted that members of the lower class assigned each other a "trouble index," indicating where someone fell along some hypothetical "trouble dimension." This index was so important that it dictated how others related to the person. If a woman's daughter was spending time with a boy, it was normal for the mother to be concerned about how much "trouble" the boy had faced in the past and was likely to face in the future. The trouble also influenced the boy's status within the gang; some gangs responded positively to a high index but others did not.

A second focal concern of the lower class was "toughness," or physical prowess, strength, endurance, and athletic skill. Miller believed that the lower class, especially lower class males, demonstrated excessive concerns about masculinity, a feature that might be attributed to the predominance of female-based households. Miller believed that excessive concern with masculinity could reflect a "compulsive reaction-formation," a term which he, like Cohen, borrowed from the currently fashionable psychology of the day.

"Smartness" designated a capacity to outsmart, outfox, outwit, dupe, or generally "con" others. Whereas the middle class emphasized intellectual ability, the lower class was concerned about the ability to outsmart others and, more generally, society. Miller contended that this trait had a long tradition in lower class culture and was demonstrated in such practices as card playing and other forms of gambling.

A fourth focal concern was the constant search for excitement and thrills. Miller believed that this search was exhibited in excessive use of alcohol, gambling of all kinds, music, and sexual adventuring. Fighting was also a feature of this need to take risks and seek danger. Gangs looking for trouble were an obvious product of this focal concern.

The last two focal concerns—fate and autonomy—referred to control over one's life. Miller posited that lower class people as a group strongly felt their lives were subject to a set of forces over which they had little control. Whatever happened was a matter of fate, and hence, any directed effort at a long-term goal was ultimately futile. They lived for the moment and took whatever came their way. On the other hand, they insisted on autonomy and resented the idea of external controls or restrictions on behavior. Lower class people said they do not like to be "pushed around," yet expected it was part of their fate.

Adolescents had two additional concerns: *belonging* and *status*. Miller described these two as "higher order concerns" because before one could "belong" or have "status" within a gang, one had to demonstrate toughness, smartness, etc. "Belonging" means a boy is "part of the club" or had in-group membership in the gang—"he hangs with us" was the terminology used by Miller. Violation of the group's code of conduct and beliefs results in exclusion. "Status" refers to the boy's ranking within the group, which is tested constantly by means of a set of status-ranking activities. One gains status within the group by demonstrating superiority in one of the six basic concerns just described.

Bloch and Niederhoffer: Psychodynamic Aspects of Gangs

In 1958, the same year that Miller published his theory in the *Journal of Social Issues*, Herbert A. Bloch, a sociologist, and Arthur Niederhoffer, a police lieutenant, published *The Gang: A Study in Adolescent Behavior*. Their approach was distinct from others in two respects: It took a decidedly "psychological" perspective, and it was not limited to lower class delinquent behavior. Adolescence is a psychological stage of development that all youths throughout the world experience. It is characterized by a role "strain" toward obtaining adult status. Bloch and Niederhoffer maintained that adolescents were constantly testing out their upcoming adult roles. If adults hampered or interfered with this, adolescents were forced to seek alternate forms of behavior, including delinquency. Parents might hamper the adolescent's development of adult roles by not allowing them to try things that they (the adolescents) perceive as adult-like behavior, including smoking, drinking, driving cars, swearing, sexual behavior, and so forth.

According to Bloch and Niederhoffer, adolescents who lacked adult support turned to gangs, which eased their transition to adult society. Gangs fulfilled the same psychological function as formalized rituals, such as puberty rites. For example, the investigators noticed that many gang members displayed tattoos or other identifying marks signifying a rite of passage or an initiation. Bloch and Niederhoffer observed that gangs were close-knit and cohesive, with an organized hierarchy of leadership and status. Thus, they argued, the gang satisfied deep-seated needs of adolescents in all cultures. Within the gang, however, delinquent behavior was encouraged and approved because this behavior was a natural offshoot of adolescent immature behavior. In fact, like Thrasher, Bloch and Niederhoffer virtually equated delinquency with gangs: Gangs almost automatically led to delinquency, and delinquent acts were usually committed by gangs.

Bloch and Niederhoffer disagreed with Cohen's descriptions of lower class gangs.

They did not believe, for example, that delinquent behavior was nonutilitarian. From their observations and experiences with gangs, they concluded that most delinquent behavior either had material value or great ''psychological utility'' in satisfying personal needs and tensions. Moreover, they found little evidence of Cohen's short-run hedonism; many gangs not only had long-range plans but also would forego immediate pleasures to reach them. Finally, many of the descriptive features of Cohen's lower class delinquency (malice, hatred, versatility, nonutility, and short-run hedonism) could be just as readily applied to middle and upper class gangs.

The authors tried to incorporate psychological theories about development which were popular at the time into their explanations of gangs and delinquency. They particularly favored psychoanalytic theory. Gangs, they said, released forces and urges that were suppressed and repressed in nongang boys. Bloch and Niederhoffer did not convince many criminologists that their perspective had merit, however. Those amenable to gang theory were attending to the work of Cohen, Miller, and soon after to the work of Cloward and Ohlin. *The Gang* has had little impact on thinking about gang delinquency.

Cloward and Ohlin: Opportunity Theory

A book that did have considerable impact was *Delinquency and Opportunity: A Theory of Delinquent Gangs*, written by Richard Cloward and Lloyd Ohlin (1960). The book—and the differential opportunity theory contained therein—developed from field studies its authors had conducted in two juvenile institutions in New York: one private (Children's Village) and the other public (Warwick). Cloward and Ohlin set out to explore the various types of delinquent subcultures which they believed existed; other subcultural theorists had acknowledged only one type. Cloward and Ohlin hypothesized that different institutional environments produced different kinds of inmate subcultures. Thus, they predicted that the social climate and structure of the public institution would elicit a significantly different subculture than the social climate and structure of the private one. Hence, the Cloward and Ohlin theory was formulated on institutionalized youngsters and generalized to community gangs. ''Thus it was a transfer of basic theoretical notions we were developing in the institutions, that we developed further and applied by analogy to the community'' (Ohlin, 1983a, p. 211).

Cloward and Ohlin, both former students of Sutherland, were impressed with theories of Durkheim and Merton as well as the ecological work of the Chicago School. The Cloward-Ohlin theory of differential opportunity incorporates concepts from each of these. It was, in fact, one of the earliest attempts to integrate theory.

Cloward and Ohlin believed that ''pressures toward the formation of delinquent subcultures originate in the marked discrepancies between culturally induced aspirations among lower-class youth and the possibilities of achieving them by legitimate means'' (Cloward and Ohlin, 1960, p. 78). Thus, they accepted Merton's position that the fundamental sociological cause of strain is blocked opportunity to achieve socially valued goals. In this sense, the Cloward-Ohlin theory is often subsumed under the strain theory perspective. They also acknowledged Merton's very helpful distinction between cultural goals and institutionalized means and the interchange between them. The means are the approved ways of reaching the desired goals. The social structure of a society establishes the patterned relationships in which individuals are involved, such as the division of social class on the basis of wealth, power, or prestige. Cloward and Ohlin theorized that individuals had differential opportunities for reaching the cultural goals, depending upon their position in the social structure as well as their abilities. Consequently, individuals experienced differential pressure toward deviance. Under some conditions, lower class youths were under great strain toward deviance, but this was not as universal as earlier theorists had maintained. "It is our view that many discontented lower-class youth do not wish to adopt a middle-class way of life or to disrupt their present associations and negotiate passage into middle-class groups. The solution they seek entails the acquisition of higher position in terms of lower-class rather than middle-class criteria" (Cloward and Ohlin, 1960, p. 92).

Cloward and Ohlin emphasized that the formation of delinquency did not follow a simple or universal pattern. Like their mentor Sutherland, they believed that delinquency was learned in the everyday interaction with others, and that the nature of that interaction varied substantially among groups. They saw, as well, strong relationships among the social environment, the economic structure, and the behavioral choices that were available. Put another way, subcultures had differential accessibility to both legitimate *and* illegitimate means of achieving higher status or positions. Not only were the legal and socially approved opportunities blocked for some, but so too were illegal opportunities. Even the illegitimate means to success were unevenly distributed. For example, some lower class neighborhoods provided greater opportunity for illegal gain than did others.

Cloward and Ohlin proposed that three general, delinquent subcultures existed. They labeled these the *criminal*, *conflict*, and *retreatist* subcultures. Each not only had its specific features but also advocated different forms of criminal behavior. Members of the criminal subculture were interested in instrumental gains, such as money that would allow them to obtain the material wealth advocated by society. Cloward and Ohlin believed that the criminal subculture depended heavily upon illegitimate success models— persons who were highly visible to lower class youth and willing to establish a relationship with them. These success models were usually older lower class youths who had obtained material goods through one of the few avenues available to them: theft, robbery, prostitution, or other instrumental crimes. Thus, whereas middle class youth had such middle class success models as lawyers, bankers, physicians, and other educated persons, lower class adolescents generally had only illegitimate models to imitate. One way to avoid a life of deprivation and frustration was to acquire the values and skills of successful "deviants."

Cloward and Ohlin noted that learning the values and skills of the criminal subculture would not ensure successful acquisition of the desired material goods, however. Individuals also needed the support of other members of the criminal subculture. They often had to have middlemen, fences, and partners, for example. Furthermore, they needed access to lawyers and bondsmen. To qualify for membership in the criminal subculture, a person had to be able to conform to the standards of the group and control undisciplined, unpredictable, or erratic behavior. Impulsive acts had no place in the pursuit of a successful criminal career. Individuals also had to prove themselves by engaging in criminal activities that would meet with the group's approval. In this social context, theft was a way of "expressing solidarity with the carriers of criminal values . . . and a way of acquiring the various concrete skills necessary before the potential criminal can gain full acceptance in the group to which he aspires" (Cloward and Ohlin, 1960, p. 309). This contrasted sharply with Cohen's belief that delinquent activity was nonutilitarian.

According to Cloward and Ohlin, not all boys could become "successful criminals." Some, because of personality features, beliefs, or physical skills, were locked out of the illegitimate avenue toward desired goals. Furthermore, reflecting the influence of the Chicago School, Cloward and Ohlin maintained that some neighborhoods were more likely to support the criminal subculture than others. Illegitimate avenues were most available in lower class neighborhoods that were integrated and organized. Youths living in lower class neighborhoods which lacked unity and cohesion—socially disorganized neighborhoods—were frustrated in their quest for both conventional and criminal opportunities.

Heightened frustration, according to Cloward and Ohlin, became the chief motivator of participation in the "conflict subculture." Youths deprived of both conventional and criminal opportunities were outcasts of both the criminal minority and the cultural majority, and their behavior reflected this frustration. The illegal activity of the conflict subculture tended to be unorganized, petty, and unprotected. Members of this subculture often endangered their own lives and the lives of others for minimal gain. They caused extensive property damage and were especially prone to "impulsive violence." Violence, in fact, was the hallmark of the conflict subculture. It was often displayed in gang warfare.

The third subculture, the retreatist, typically comprised drug users and social isolates. Their criminal activities were often individualistic. Social contacts were made only to secure sufficient drugs or money to maintain a retreatist lifestyle. Members of the retreatist subculture suffered from "double failure." Not only were they unable to participate in conventional or illegal activities, but they were also likely to alienate all others in their social world.

The general source of social strain was the same for all three subcultures: anomie produced by blocked legitimate opportunities (Pfohl, 1985). What differed was the specific channel each subculture used to adapt to its plight.

When Hansell and Wiatrowski (1981) discussed the social ability and social disability models of gang delinquency, they placed the Cloward-Ohlin theory in the former group. The criminal subculture clearly deserves this characterization, since it suggests that group solidarity and mutual assistance are needed for success. It is less clear that the conflict and retreatist subcultures have these features. Retreatists in particular would fall more convincingly into the social disability model.

SOCIAL DISABILITY MODELS

Short and Strodtbeck: The Sociology of Gangs

One of the most extensive studies ever undertaken on gang delinquency was conducted in Chicago by James F. Short, Jr., and Fred L. Strodtbeck during a three-year period (1959 to 1962). This now-classic study, published in the book, *Gang Process and Gang Delinquency* (1965), grew out of the "detached-worker" program sponsored by the YMCA of Metropolitan Chicago. Detached workers were asked to conduct systematic, detailed observations of youth gangs and monitor "the flow of events." The Short-Strodtbeck project collected data on 16 gangs, ranging in size from 16 to 68 members and totaling 598 boys. Eleven of the gangs were black, totaling 464 boys. Additional data were collected on another 12 black and 10 white gangs. Gang members were almost entirely of lower SES; Short and Strodtbeck could not locate a single middle class gang. "Gangs of middle class youngsters apparently are rare, however, despite mounting public concern over middle class delinquency" (p. 15).

While the YMCA detached-worker program of Chicago was modeled after the Cloward-Ohlin theory, Short and Strodtbeck were unable to locate the neat categories suggested by the theory. They were also unable to identify any of the group solidarity discussed by other theorists. The image of the gang as a carefree, close-knit, all-for-one-and-one-for-all group was not supported. Instead, Short and Strodtbeck found that gang members were socially *disabled* individuals alienated from mainstream society. They were, according to these researchers, social misfits. "Our gang boys failed often in schools, on the job, in conventional youth-serving agencies, and in the eyes of the law enforcement officials . . . They fail more often in each of these respects than do the non-gang boys we have studied, both middle and lower class" (Short and Strodtbeck, 1965, p. 230). Short and Strodtbeck also claimed that gang boys, compared to nongang boys, were less self-assertive, slightly more neurotic and anxious, less gregarious, and generally had few of the qualities which engender confidence and nurturant relationships with others. Overall, they lacked fundamental social or interpersonal skills. The boys also exhibited limited verbal skills and appeared to be significantly below average in cognitive development.

According to Short and Strodtbeck, the emotional atmosphere of the gangs was similar to that reported for the lower class culture, accentuated by a strong distrust of both "insiders" and "outsiders." The gangs also seemed to be socially isolated from social networks beyond immediate gang members and had limited meaningful contacts with adults.

This contrasts sharply with the work of Cohen, Miller, Bloch and Niederhoffer, and Cloward and Ohlin, all of whom had emphasized, although to different degrees, that gang delinquents were adapting to their lower class status and found some measure of support in their own peer groups. Short and Strodtbeck maintained that delinquent gang boys were *not* like other boys in "normal" groups. They were ill-equipped socially and intellectually to deal with the demands and expectations of mainstream society, and they found no succor in their gangs.

Furthermore, Short and Strodtbeck added an unfortunate racial bias to their theory. Although they included white as well as black gangs, the latter predominated. In reporting their findings, they compared the two racial groups and concluded that there were crucial differences between the two. They suggested, for example, that black communities and their youths demonstrated most of the characteristics of the lower social class described by Miller. "Negro communities provide a flow of common experiences in which young people and their elders share, and out of which delinquent behavior emerges almost imperceptibly, albeit at times dramatically" (Short and Strodtbeck, 1965, p. 114). In contrast, the white lower class communities generally became more deeply disturbed about delinquent acts and made more of an effort to curb them. This kind of conclusion, without acknowledgment that racial injustice might explain these differences, is troubling.

Patterson's Two-Stage Process

Patterson and his colleagues (Patterson, 1982; Snyder and Patterson, 1987; Patterson, Dishion, and Bank, 1984) consider delinquency to be largely a result of faulty socialization. Moreover, this faulty socialization occurs in two stages. The first stage takes place during childhood and primarily within the home setting. This stage is a consequence of inept parenting, such as the enmeshed and lax parental styles and the inadequate monitoring discussed earlier. Inept parenting fosters poor interpersonal, academic, and work skills in children. Since the child lacks the necessary skills to adapt to normal daily living conditions, he or she is likely to move into the second stage of antisocial training. The child's hostility and inadequate interpersonal approach toward others "turns people off," encouraging and accelerating rejection by others. This social and emotional rejection restricts opportunity to acquire the necessary skills to adjust or achieve in society, resulting in a kind of "catch-22." Rejected by mainstream society and closed off from adjusting within it, these youths are drawn toward other unskilled, socially disabled children. This association increases opportunity ". . . to acquire, perform, and hone antisocial behavior" (Synder and Patterson, 1987, p. 219). Consequently, antisocial and delinquent behaviors, under the watchful eyes and encouragement of other deviant peers, become more frequent, varied, and serious. Thus, the relationship between skills deficits and delinquent behavior becomes reciprocal within the context of a deviant, socially-disabled peer group.

Snyder and Patterson admonish that their two-stage model is very incomplete. It is based almost exclusively on their assessment of the development of delinquent behavior in males, and the factors and processes outlined may be substantially different for females. Furthermore, they acknowledge that we simply do not know enough about the reciprocal processes of family, parenting, and peer interactions to be confident that the model represents the complicated dynamics of delinquency development. One attempt to understand these dynamics is found in peer network analysis.

PEER NETWORK ANALYSIS

In the preceding pages, we have used Hansell and Wiatrowski's (1981) social ability-disability dichotomy as a framework for the discussion of classic theories of gang delinquency. According to the social ability model, delinquent gangs have well-developed status hierarchies characterized by closeness, friendships, and group cohesion. Members accede to the agreed-upon, shared delinquent norms rather than to those of conventional society. Social disability models postulate that youths who gravitate to delinquent gangs have not been adequately bonded to social institutions or lack appropriate social and interpersonal skills for interacting and adjusting to mainstream society. Socially disabled youngsters are simply out of social step with the rest of their ''normal'' peer group.

Hansell and Wiatrowski applied *social network analysis* to their contrasting models. This is a method of social science which will reappear in Chapter 11 with the discussion of ecological features of the macrosystem. Network analysis can be applied to all levels of systems except the individual level. In this chapter, it is applied at the microsystems level, specifically to peer relationships. For the moment, therefore, it is important that we digress on the nature of this method.

Network analysis developed in 1954 with the work of the British anthropologist John A. Barnes. Barnes was conducting an anthropological study of the Norwegian fishing village of Bremmes (population 4,600). During a year spent observing the inhabitants of this tiny island village, it became clear to Barnes that the traditional approach used by British anthropologists did not adequately capture the rich tapestry of relationships in Bremmes. Like other anthropologists, Barnes had been focusing solely on social structure, which at the time referred to group and class memberships and the amount of involvement in various social institutions.

Barnes had little trouble analyzing the fishing village according to territorially and industrially based social structure. But these aspects about the village were dry and uninteresting. The reader can easily sense this in his writing.

> The territorial arrangement of the Bremmes population is fairly stable. The same fields are cultivated year after year, and new land comes into cultivation only slowly . . . Thus for the most part the same people go on living in the same houses and cultivating the same land from year to year. (1954, p. 41)

The industrial structure of the herring fishing industry was hardly more interesting. What did begin to interest Barnes keenly were the friendships and other relationships among the villagers.

Barnes made the obvious but important observation that each resident of Bremmes had a number of friends and acquaintances and that these friends and acquaintances had other friends and acquaintances. Some of them knew one another, others did not. He called this social field of friendship ties a "network." While the term "network" has been used in various ways by scholars, Barnes reserved the term to describe the nature of the relationships and the methods by which individuals made use of personal ties of kinship and friendship. It became obvious that the richer the network, the greater the opportunity and privileges within the community.

In his 1954 article, Barnes urged his reader to imagine persons as points on a chart, joined by lines to other points. The lines represented relationships or ties, but they did not simply "connect" people, as previous scholars had suggested. Barnes was fascinated by the *characteristics* of these linkages. "Certainly," he wrote, "there are clusters of people who are more closely knit together than others . . ." (1954, p. 44). He referred to this characteristic as the "mesh" or density of the network (perhaps he was influenced by the different patterns of fishnets found throughout the village).

Other investigators became interested in Barnes's analysis and refined it, using it in different contexts to examine a variety of social situations (e.g., Bott, 1955, 1957). Gluckman (1967) studied the judicial process in a community in northern Rhodesia and discovered that the links between people may be multiple. That is, the relationships people have with one another may not be restricted to one context. In other words, people share different microsystems. Two adolescents may be siblings, be in the same class at school, be on the same baseball team, and may even be working for the same employer. Gluckman called these multiple linkages a *multiplex*, or more simply, a multi-stranded or many-stranded relationship. Relationships which have only one link, such as employer to employee, are called *uniplex*, or more simply, single-stranded relationships.

Since Barnes's original statement, the concept of network density has accrued additional properties. Bott (1957) used the word "connectedness" for a while to communicate the idea that some families are close-knit, have many relationships with one another or share a number of microsystems, and others are loose-knit. Density is commonly used to show the *degree* of connectedness, or the ratio of actual to possible relationships. Put differently, density is the number of people who know each other and exchange information within a group divided by the number of people possible to know within that particular group.

Network analysis has been applied in many disciplines, but it is used in slightly different ways in each. Within the present context, we are following the social anthropological line previously described together with the work of J. Clyde Mitchell (1969; 1979) and Claude S. Fischer and his associates (1977; 1982). In Chapter 11, we will take a slightly more sociological slant, following the lead of Marvin Krohn (1986).

J. Clyde Mitchell (1969) defined a network as a specific set of linkages among a defined set of persons. Edward Laumann (1979, p. 392) modified this definition slightly to say networks may be redefined ". . . as a set of *nodes* (e.g., persons) linked by a set of *social relationships* (i.e., Mitchell's linkages) of a specified *type*." The term "nodes" is used to signify that we can, in addition to individuals, have groups and organizations within a network. The term "linkages" is expanded to "social relationship" to accommodate larger, more complex systems than Mitchell originally intended. It is important to keep these slightly different definitions in mind. In this context, we are limiting our discussion to peer groups, but later we will expand it to include larger, more complex, aggregate systems.

Network Analysis and Delinquency

Social network analysis is *not* a theory, but only a conceptual or analytical tool which provides a framework for examining the social relations between individuals and groups. It does not offer postulates, stipulations, or hypotheses. However, network analysis *is* a powerful framework from which to derive theory, as Hansell and Wiatrowski (1981) have done. They suggest that the social disability model predicts that delinquent gangs, because they have low "cohesion," will correspondingly have low network density. Because the gang members who are socially disabled have inadequate social and inter-personal skills, their network will not, they predict, be as close-knit as comparable non-delinquent groups. Alternately, the social ability model predicts that delinquent groups will demonstrate the same degree of network density as any other comparable youth group, perhaps even greater density.

Hansell and Wiatrowski take the analysis one step further. They suggest that, since the social ability model predicts that both delinquent and nondelinquent groups have a dense pattern of relationships within their groups, we can expect that the members will likewise have multiple roles and functions with one another outside the microsystem of the gang. In fact, this is one important, but largely untested, proposition stated by Mitchell (1979). Multiplex relationships in time will become more dense. This is based on the assumption that if two people interact with a third person regularly in different social contexts, eventually they will feel obliged to extend the type of relationship they have with each other to include all three persons. On the other hand, the social disability model implies that, since delinquents are more likely to have single-stranded relationships, over time they will tend to become less dense. Thus, "we would . . . expect their relationships to be relatively compartmentalized and single-stranded rather than multiplex" (Hansell and Wiatrowski, 1981, p. 101). Single-stranded relations tend to discourage the formation of well-developed, cohesive delinquent group norms. If delinquent gangs are a collection of socially disabled adolescents, then social network analysis should reveal this through various measures.

Unfortunately, Hansell and Wiatrowski lament, present research on gang delinquency does not allow conclusions about the accuracy of these predictions. "With few exceptions, the hypotheses advanced in this paper cannot be tested with existing data on delinquent peer groups" (1981, p. 103). Current research in human development may test the Hansell-Wiatrowski hypotheses, however. Before we examine that research there are some comments that need to be made about the Hansell-Wiatrowski gallant attempt to apply network analysis to gang delinquency.

First, any strict dichotomy between social disability models and social ability models based on classic theory is problematic. It is more likely that gangs and youth groups can be better conceptualized as existing on a continuum, with social disability at one pole and social ability at the other. Few groups would fall at either end. Second, network density does not appear to work very well as a distinguishing variable of youth gangs. We can assume that members of a gang do interact with one another and do know each other reasonably well, regardless of whether we are discussing a delinquent or nondelinquent gang. Thus, the traditional measure of density—proportion of actual relationships to possible relationships within a particular group—is apt to yield the same approximate ratio, regardless of the specific gang being studied. Therefore, by itself, network density is unlikely to be powerful at distinguishing the two models. Mitchell (1979) makes the same point, "to have much utility, however, a measure of density must relate to some specified content of linkage" (p. 441). In other words, density is a crude measure which provides little information without further examination of the characteristics of the relationships.

One of the many strengths of social network analysis is that it encourages researchers to examine relationships in many different ways. For instance, it cautions that relationships differ in intimacy, frequency of contact, and duration (Fischer, 1977). Relationships may also differ in reachability, content, range and directedness (Mitchell, 1969). Hansell and Wiatrowski acknowledged the importance of frequency, reachability, and directedness to future research on gang delinquency; in the case of reachability, they suggested methods for measuring it. We will briefly review what each of these terms signifies, then illustrate how they can be applied to the study of delinquent gangs.

Intimacy can reflect many aspects, including to what extent people confide in one another, depend on one another, or consider each other close or best friends. *Frequency* refers to how often people get together. *Duration* connotes how well the tie has endured disruption and competition from other relationships (Fischer, 1977). *Reachability* refers to the extent a person may be directly and immediately contacted by another person. To take an extreme example, the President of the United States is not reachable to a vast majority of the population. The same may be said of a president of a major corporation or political or entertainment personalities.

> Reachability merely implies that every specified person can be contacted within a stated number of steps from any given starting point. If a large proportion of the people in a network can be contacted within a relatively small number of steps then the network is compact in comparison with one in which a smaller proportion may be reached in the same number of steps. (Mitchell, 1969, p. 15)

Thus, it might be interesting to discover if delinquent groups differ in "compactness" from nondelinquent groups or, put another way, whether their members are reachable. Delinquent gang members at the social disability end of the continuum probably have little influence outside their immediate circle, whereas those at the other end probably have the normal influence outside their group.

Content refers to the meanings the relationships have for the parties involved. The links between an individual and the people with whom he or she interacts have some purpose or interest which either or both of the parties recognize (Mitchell, 1969). Content may involve religious cooperation, economic necessity, kinship obligation, or simply friendship. *Intensity* refers to the degree of loyalty or commitment that exists in a relationship. ''The intensity of a link in a personal network refers to the degree to which individuals are prepared to honour obligations, or feel free to exercise the right implied in their link to some other person'' (Mitchell, 1969, p. 27). *Range* (or span) indicates the heterogeneity of the relationships a person has within his or her personal network. ''A person in contact with thirty others of widely differing social backgrounds has a wider range network than a person in contact with thirty people of the same general social background'' (Mitchell, 1969, p. 19). *Directedness* signifies the degree of reciprocity involved in a relationship. A person may choose another as her friend without having her choice reciprocated. In this instance, the relationship is one-directional.

Studies of delinquent gangs could explore each of these characteristics. It would be interesting to know, for example, what specific relational purpose gangs serve for the various youths within them (content). With respect to intensity, we are reminded that the most striking feature in most early gang theories was the degree of loyalty and commitment gang members displayed to each other. Do today's gangs or youth groups differ in intensity? Are delinquents more loyal to their comrades than nondelinquents? What about range? Do gangs at the social disability pole have a narrower range than those at the other, and how do these compare with nondelinquent groups. The two delinquency models (or, more realistically, the two poles) imply different tendencies toward directness in delinquent peer dyads. The social ability model predicts that delinquent relationships are similar to normal peer relationships, while social disability predicts less reciprocity and more instability than occur in nondelinquent dyads. Hansell and Wiatrowski suggested that reachability be measured by the number of contacts delinquents have with the outside world, beyond their immediate neighborhood. As noted earlier, gang members at the social disability end of the continuum are likely to have less influence outside their group than are gang members at the social ability end.

The foregoing discussion underlines the point that human relationships have multiple components and may be measured any number of ways. Network density and multiplexity are but two. Furthermore, gangs and groups must be identified through systematic definition and procedure that will make it clear to others how the researcher delineated the group, instead of simplifying a ''gang'' or a group of adolescents. With a clear definition of boundaries, network analysis offers considerable promise toward understanding the characteristics of youth gangs.

DEVELOPMENTAL STUDIES ON PEER RELATIONS

There exists a growing body of psychological literature with implications for the study of delinquency, particularly the relationships among delinquents and their peers. Most researchers in this area are operating on parallel tracks to sociological criminologists, and there is little indication that the disciplines may converge. In the following pages, this developmental literature is reviewed and its potential impact on the study of delinquency is assessed.

In a comprehensive review of peer relations, Willard W. Hartup (1983) reported that available research suggests that antisocial children are unpopular and tend to be excluded from peer groups. "A repertoire of friendly, prosocial, and competent social behaviors is clearly predictive of social acceptance, while devious, aversive reactions to other children enhance one's chances of social rejection" (Hartup, 1983, p. 135). Olweus (1978) found that bullies are not popular and are socially isolated. Patterson (1982) also found "hyperaggressive" children to be social isolates. M. Roff and Sells (1968), in a longitudinal study of 40,000 school children in Minnesota and Texas, reported that boys who eventually became delinquent (measured by official contact with juvenile court) were not liked or accepted by their peers. In another study, M. Roff (1975) found that the same relationship holds for girls: Later delinquency seems to increase as their peer status at school decreases. And more recent research has suggested this relationship holds for both boys and girls regardless of SES (J. D. Roff and Wirt, 1984). Conversely, children liked by peers very rarely became delinquent. Conger and Miller (1966) found that delinquents-to-be had more difficulty getting along with peers, both in individual one-to-one contacts and in group situations. They also were not liked by or accepted into peer groups. Moreover, youths who later became delinquent were considerably less interested in organized parties, school functions, or organizations. West and Farrington (1973) observed that boys judged most dishonest by their peers were more likely to become delinquent. In a recent literature review, Eleanor Maccoby (1986, p. 275) concluded: ". . . it is not participation in the boys' culture, but failure to participate in it, that is associated with certain kinds of predelinquent activity." In another extensive literature review. Jeffrey Parker and Steven Asher (1987, p. 371) conclude:

> . . . the evidence for a link between early peer-relationships disturbance and later criminality is generally very good. The . . . studies reviewed show that the backgrounds of criminals of all types show a history of aggressiveness and poor peer regard that in some cases extends as far back as the point of the child's entry into formal schooling.

In hindsight, then, relevant data in human development suggest that delinquents were less integrated into their social networks and had less developed mesosystems than their peers. This literature alone would also suggest that delinquents tend to be more "socially disabled" than their counterparts. It is unclear, however, to what types of delinquency researchers were referring, how often the delinquency was committed, or how it was measured. Most psychological research focuses on aggression and "antisocial behavior." Both terms imply acts against others, usually in a violent or harmful manner. It may be that the ostracized "antisocial" youths who so commonly appear in the psychological research are those who eventually commit violent acts against persons. Psychologists seem to be studying youths who fall closer to the social disability model, and this model may be more relevant to serious delinquency. The social ability model may pertain to the more "common," nonserious delinquency.

All of this assumes that groups or gangs are homogeneous and that pre-adolescents and adolescents are attracted and remain in youth groups whose members are very similar to them. Hartup (1983) suggests that this assumption is warranted. There is, he says, a great deal of similarity both in activities and values among members of youth groups.

Attitudes, personality traits, abilities, physical characteristics, and behavior (such as drug use), are usually held in common by members of a group. However, the three attributes that appear to be the most consistently shared by these youth groups are age, sex, and race. Behavioral and attitudinal similarities, while important, do not occur with the same consistency and strength as these three.

Denise Kandel (1986), however, admonishes that studies designed to determine which attributes draw youngsters together must consider carefully what stage of the friendship is being evaluated. Personality attributes seem to be most important in the beginning of a friendship, shared values emerge as crucial later in the relationship, and shared construct systems become the most important later on (Duck and Craig, 1978).

Why do birds of a feather flock together? Hartup suggests three reasons. First, youths *select* their groups, and they likely select groups with which they feel most compatible and comfortable. In short, they select groups whose members are like themselves. This tendency is particularly prominent during late pre-adolescence. Second, early relationships based on similarity appear to continue over time, at least until late adolescence. Third, noted similarities may perpetuate themselves. That is, in a reciprocal fashion, group members may generate and reinforce attitudinal and behavioral concordances. In short, they may socialize one another. Further, peer groups generate their own norms, applying them only to themselves, beginning around middle childhood.

In her comprehensive series of studies of adolescent friendships, Denise Kandel (1986) found that adolescents who share certain characteristics are more likely to become friends, and those who associate with each other become even more alike over time. Thus, selection and socialization *both* appear important in the process.

SEX DIFFERENCES IN GANG OR GROUP BEHAVIOR

The gang theories of Thrasher, Cohen, Miller, and Short and Strodtbeck were all formulated with boys as subjects of study. There is a general assumption in the literature that, although girls engage in delinquent behavior, they do so less frequently and that girl gangs are rare. Criminologists have spent little energy discussing this phenomenon, a noteworthy exception being Anne Campbell (1984).

Anne Campbell: Girls in the Gang

Campbell's ''girl-gang'' study was described briefly in Chapter 2 as an example of qualitative research. Her work represents one of the very few studies on youth gangs in recent years. Campbell spent six months in the early 1980s observing and talking with members of three gangs in New York City, particularly the girls. She reported her results, often in the girls' own words in her book, *The Girls in the Gang*. Although she focused on girls, she also made interesting observations about contemporary gang characteristics in general. She noted also that youth gangs are primarily an American phenomenon. While other cultures have youth groups, they lack the structure, demarcated roles, rules, and territoriality of American gangs. Nor do they have the initiation rites, the gang names, the "colors," the long-term commitment, or the specific philosophy found in American youth gangs.

The gangs she observed had a traditional pyramidal power structure, with males as the head and female members as subordinates. Gang members—both male and female—spent many hours a day in front of television sets, watching game shows, soap operas, and other depictions of American "life." The girls almost worshipped clothes and makeup, and took particular care of the clothes they had. The gang members were conservative and displayed an American-capitalistic-society-is-alright attitude, despite their failure to fit into it. Certain illegal acts, such as selling soft drugs, were not wrong, but burglary, robbery, rape, or assault generally were. When the gang was warring with another, however, their criminal activities were acceptable. Gang members claimed to keep the streets safe and the neighborhood clean. At the same time, they did not seem to mind being portrayed to the public as outlaws, rebels, tough, and persecuted.

While gang members most generally came from backgrounds of poverty, minority status, unemployment, and unfinished educations, this pattern was especially evident for female members. Campbell's girls came from homes characterized by geographic and emotional instability, a pattern more typical of girls than boys. During their childhoods, their families had moved frequently and they had attended a series of schools. Family life had been and remained stormy and unhappy, and physical violence was common. Physical aggression between parents was particularly frequent, and the girls often grew up with fears of being victims of abuse themselves. Alone and alienated, the girls had gravitated to the gang hoping to find sisters who were like them and who were willing to treat them with respect.

In sum, Campbell found the girls in the gang much like minority, poor, undereducated girls in general. She found them neither violent nor overly aggressive, nor independent. Their main reason for belonging to the gang was to have companionship and security. They had dreams, but believed that these probably would never be fulfilled in light of their current skills, education, and living arrangements. Finally, they accepted the traditional double standard approach with respect to the sexes. They believed that a man was "the boss" in a relationship, and they accepted this behavior without question with regard to the males in their lives. The roving, unfaithful nature of men was expected and tolerated. It is interesting to note, however, how the macrosystem (the society at large) influenced the values and philosophies of the microsystem of the gangs, although largely in one direction. The macrosystem, primarily through television, had a great impact on how the girls thought they should dress, think, and live.

Maccoby: Why Boys Join Gangs More Often than Girls

Eleanor Maccoby (1986) outlined several cultural reasons that may explain why boys become more involved in gang delinquency than girls. *First*, boys tend to congregate in public places. They are generally outdoors, while girls are often indoors. Boys meeting in public places—parks, playgrounds, or streetcorners—are more likely to escape adult supervision. Maccoby suggests that when girls are outdoors, they are more likely to be kept around their homes under the watchful eyes of adults. Meda Chesney-Lind (1986) suggests that this parental control factor may account for the repetitive research findings that girls are less delinquent than boys. The premise is supported by Mawby (1980), who studied self-reported delinquency in England and noted that families exerted greater control over the behavior of their daughters than over their sons.

Second, Maccoby notes that research in developmental psychology consistently reveals that boys tend to play in larger groups, while girls tend to play in groups of two's or three's. There also appears to be a qualitative difference between males and females in the nature and significance of friendships. The friendships of girls are sometimes called "intensive," while those of boys are "extensive." Specifically, girls are more likely to have one or two close "best" friends who play important roles in their lives. They seem to place greater emphasis on emotional sharing and intimacy in their friendships. On the other hand, the friendships of boys tend to be multiple and to be closely associated with group activities and group games (Bell, 1981). They develop their identities through an alliance with a gang or a group. Moreover, friendships among boys appear to be more oriented toward a shared struggle for independence from adult authority (Stokes and Levin, 1986).

Third, there tends to be more fighting in boy groups than girl groups (Maccoby and Jacklin, 1980). This appears to be more a feature of the interactive behavior of boys within social groups than any kind of individual predisposition on the part of boys to be aggressive, however. Social encounters among boys often center around issues of dominance and the formation of an order of status. The play of girls, on the other hand, tends to be oriented toward a strong convention of taking turns and compromising.

Fourth, Maccoby suggests that even the social speech of boys and girls is different and serves different functions. Summarizing the research on speech among girls, she notes that they learn to do three important things with words:

> (1) to create and maintain relationships of closeness and equality; (2) to criticize others in acceptable ways, and (3) to interpret accurately the speech of other girls. Symptomatic of these functions are the facts that girls frequently express agreement with others' ideas, let others have a turn to talk, and acknowledge what others have said when they speak; in other words, girls use speech as a means of cooperation. (Maccoby, 1986, pp. 272–273).

Boys, on the other hand, tend to use speech to

1. assert status or dominance;
2. attract and maintain an audience; and
3. assert themselves when others have the floor.

Sex differences in delinquency will be discussed again in more detail in Chapter 10. For the present, it is sufficient to note that the research suggests that boys do indeed seek the company of delinquent peers more than girls. Does this reflect the inability of parents to control their sons? Is group-joining by boys encouraged by the culture? Is it "more natural" for boys to seek out others when they are rejected by families or by society? Although we might speculate on these questions, there is very little evidence to apply. To repeat, classic criminology theories focusing on gang behavior were formulated with boys in mind, and group or gang delinquency among girls has received very little study. Although developmentalists have shed some light on intersex group behavior, it is premature to draw conclusions about gang delinquency among girls without additional research.

THE FAMILY-PEER MESOSYSTEM

Theorists often assume that delinquents are lost to their parents because of the parents' neglect, ill-treatment, unsophistication, or incompetence. To fill this void, the children find peers who are in similar circumstances. Bixenstine et al. (1976, p. 235), reflected this position when they stated:

> The clear implication is that it is not an advancing regard for and loyalty to peers that accounts for a child's growing readiness to affirm peer-sponsored antisocial behavior, but an intense disillusionment with adult veracity, strength, wisdom, importance, good will, and fairmindedness. The child is not won away from parents to children, rather he is, at least for a time, lost to parents.

Some research suggests, however, that this is a questionable assumption. Thomas Berndt (1979) concluded that the adolescent lives in two separate worlds, one for family and one for peers. Hans Sebald (1986) made a similar claim specifically with reference to middle class white adolescents. He noted that they seek parental advice in matters of finances, education, and career plans, but in making decisions about their social lives—dress, drinking, dating, drugs—adolescents overwhelmingly want to be attuned to the opinions and standards of their peers. Sebald discovered that adolescents are under considerable pressure from peers to conform to peer standards about social life, but not about other matters.

In her large-scale longitudinal survey of adolescents in New York state, Denise Kandel (1986) examined to what extent adolescent development is influenced by parents and by peers. Students from 18 public high schools were administered questionnaires in their classrooms twice during the school year. Parents of each student also received questionnaires through the mail, and approximately two-thirds returned them for analysis. Students were asked about their relationships with parents and friends. The purpose was to reconstruct social dyads and triads between and among the adolescent subjects (called the "focal adolescents"), their parents, and their peers. The dyads and triads were then examined to obtain specific information about shared values, attitudes, and characteristics. Kandel was able to establish 4,033 adolescent-parent dyads, 1,879 best-friend dyads, and 1,112 triads among the focal adolescent, best friend, and parent. In a sense, she was conducting a form of network analysis.

The most frequent attributes shared by friends were not values and attitudes but sociodemographic characteristics such as age and sex. These same sociodemographic attributes seem to be the most important among adults as well (Fischer, 1982). The next important attribute shared by adolescent friends was behavior. In other words, the adolescents were drawn to others who liked to *do* the same things, such as go to movies, play basketball, drive around, or drink. The most important shared behavior, however, was the use of illicit drugs. Kandel found that the least shared attributes were psychological factors, such as feelings of self-esteem and confidence and attitudes, including political orientation.

What of the respective influence of parents and friends on adolescent behavior? Kandel warns that the proper question to ask is not how much adolescent behavior is under the general influence of parents compared to friends. Rather, it is, "What are the areas of influence for friends and what are the areas of influence of parents?" Peers are more influential in some things, parents in others. Like Sebald, Kandel found that peers are most influential in settling issues of immediate relevance to the adolescent's life, such as whether to become involved in drugs. For issues relevant to basic values, including future plans, occupational choice, religion, and education, parents play the crucial role.

The attraction of adolescents to peers who like to *do* similar things is important, because it involves the use of illicit drugs and provides some clues on the relative importance of peers vis-à-vis parents. Two explanations of an adolescent's involvement in illicit drugs have been suggested in the literature. One argues that adolescent drug use results predominantly, if not exclusively, from peer influences. Social learning theories would predict, for example, that participation in a drug subculture and the heavy association with peer drug users will almost certainly result in heavy drug use by each member of the subculture. A second argument suggests that parental influence, not the peer group, is the most important component in drug behavior and the adolescents act primarily in accordance with family values and standards. If parents use drugs (i.e., alcohol, marijuana, cocaine, or even heavily used prescriptions drugs), the children will be likewise inclined to use drugs.

In the aforementioned study, Kandel (1984) tried to tap the relative influences of peers and parents on drug usage. She found that only 15 percent of her focal adolescents reported having used marijuana if their best friends reported never having used it. However, when best friends had used marijuana 60 times or over, 79 percent of the focal adolescents also used marijuana. This result indicates that perceived extent of marijuana use in a *peer* social network is the strongest predictor of marijuana use by adolescents. The highest rate of adolescent marijuana use (70 percent) occurred when both parents and peers admitted considerable drug use. On the other hand, the lowest rate (12 percent) occurred when neither peers nor parents admitted drug use. Kandel also found that girls were slightly more influenced by their peer relationships than boys. This comports with research that girls do not report stronger bonds to their parents than boys (Cantner, 1981). Kandel concluded that parents have a moderate influence on the adolescent in spite of peer drug usage, however. Teenagers of nondrug-using parents were somewhat *less* likely to use drugs than their peers, whereas teenagers of drug-using parents were somewhat *more* likely to do so. The same patterns occurred for adolescent drinking of alcohol.

Ronald Akers (1985), in a test of his theory of differential association-reinforcement discussed in Chapter 7, found that the extent to which individuals approved or disapproved of alcohol and marijuana use was related most strongly to the norms of their significant peers, although the norms of parents and others also played a role. When *actual* self-reported drinking and marijuana use were studied, however, the results were mixed. Parental influence was only slightly below that of peers in drinking behavior; with respect to marijuana use, the influence of peers was far above that of parents.

Richard Johnson and his associates (Johnson, Marcos, and Bahr, 1987) also found peers have considerable influence on frequency and type of drug usage. Furthermore, they conclude "It is not so much that adolescents use drugs because the drug use of their friends makes drug use seem right or safe; rather, they apparently use drugs *simply because their friends do*" (p. 336).

In summary, peers do *seem* to have the overriding influence on drug usage by adolescents, particularly in the case of nonalcoholic drugs. While it is unclear which comes first—the use of drugs and the seeking out of compatible peers or the asssociation with peers who influence drug usage—the data indicate a strong association between drug use and drug-using peers.

With respect to educational aspirations, Kandel found opposite patterns of influence. Parents were far more influential than the adolescent's best friends. In follow-up studies, however, Kandel reports there are indications that, over time, parents may have the greater effect on *both* drug use and educational aspirations. R. Jessor (1986) conducted a longitudinal study of 7th, 8th, and 9th grade boys and girls drawn from three junior high schools in a small Rocky Mountain city, beginning in 1969. He found that about 50 percent of the men who had been problem drinkers as adolescents were no longer problem drinkers as young adults. For women, the shift was even more dramatic; about 75 percent of adolescent problem drinkers were no longer so as young adults. Problem drinkers were defined as those who reported being drunk six or more times in the past year, or who had experienced significant negative consequences—such as coming to the attention of law enforcement officials—at least twice in the past year. According to Jessor, the long-term influence of parents and increased responsibilities appear to be the major determinants of changes in behavior.

The Kandel project demonstrated that interaction with parents and interaction with peers could coexist. In other words, as Berndt (1979) had observed, adolescents did seem to live in two worlds. More than half of Kandel's sample reported feeling extremely close or very close to their mothers (62 percent) and to their fathers (51 percent).

Furthermore, in an earlier study, Kandel (1978) discovered that adolescent groups differed drastically in both behavioral preferences and values, and that future considerations of gang behavior must be highly sensitive to these striking differences. Gangs were not simply groups of adolescents seeking to fill the social void in their lives; they varied widely in orientation and social network systems. However, Kandel did find that groups characterized by heavy marijuana use performed significantly less well in school (they also held more liberal political views) compared to non-marijuana-using groups.

Kandel's research highlights the interplay between the family and peers, a critical mesosystem in the development and maintenance of behavior. More research of this type and magnitude will promote better understanding of the important family-peer mesosystem in delinquent behavior. As Kandel emphasizes, we are only at a modest beginning in this endeavor.

It is instructive to consider here a recent study on drugs and adolescents, even through it does not refer specifically to peer networks. Cheryl Carpenter et al. (1988) conducted a qualitative investigation of drug use by adolescents through extensive interviews of 100 youths. The interviews were done after fieldworkers got to know the youths by spending time with them in their neighborhood. Their major data gathering strategy was "listening." They state, ". . . we undertook our study with the conviction that listening to adolescents is esssential to the study of juvenile delinquency" (p. 4). Listening, they believe, gives one a glimpse of adolescent behavior from the adolescent point of view, rather than strictly from the perspective of the adult researcher. Researchers are often isolated and unaware of how their subjects perceive the world around them and how these perceptions influence their actions. "Most studies begin with theories and employ data-gathering techniques such as experiments or surveys, which remove us from the experience and perceptions of kids" (p. 5). As Carpenter and her colleagues correctly note, few studies tell us what juveniles or juvenile delinquents do in their daily round of activity or what they think about themselves, society, or their own behavior.

Carpenter et al. learned that adolescents made a fine distinction between "selling" and "dealing" drugs. Dealing involved the sale of large quantities on a regular and predictable basis, while selling was occasional profitmaking. Drug dealers normally acquired large supplies of drugs on credit, an arrangement not available to the drug seller. A very large segment of the drug activity involved marijuana. The study found that both adolescent drug sellers and dealers tend to be drug users themselves, often heavy users. Furthermore, the main customers of drug sellers were friends, family, and acquaintances. Drug dealers, on the other hand, engaged in many more sales, sold to a wider range of persons, and sometimes sold in public places. Interestingly, neither adolescent drug dealers nor sellers were generally concerned about parental or police pressure against their selling. In fact, they thought the risk of arrest was really very small.

The investigation revealed that the most delinquent youths reported heavy alcohol and marijuana use, as well as some use of other drugs such as speed, hallucinogens, and cocaine. These findings are similar to those reported in quantitative studies (e.g., Elliott & Huizinga, 1984; Johnson & Wish, 1986). In addition, there were substantial differences in the way the youths perceived the relationship among drugs, alcohol, and crime. Basically, there was a split between those who were involved in delinquent activities and drug usage and those who were not. Nondelinquent youths perceived crime as irrational behavior or saw drugs and alcohol as related to crime because of a need for money for drugs. Delinquent youths, on the other hand, believed that crime was rational, explainable behavior and that their drug use was not an important contributing factor to their involvement in crime. They claimed that they did not commit thefts or other property crime to gain money with which to buy drugs, since the drugs they preferred were inexpensive and could be acquired with their lunch money or allowances. Rather, much of their theft happened because someone had created an opportunity, such as leaving a car unlocked or walking in the wrong neighborhood, "asking for trouble." For example, during one interview, a 17 year-old stated, ". . . (T)his guy was up on Lowell Street, down toward Underwood more, and we were walkin' by, and he, uh, parked his car and left it runnin' and went in this house; we just jumped in that sucker, and we were gone'' (p. 105). The delinquent youths in general thought that people who hide their car keys under floor mats or under the car in ''hide-a-key'' containers are stupid and deserve to have their cars or valuables stolen.

In sum, the Carpenter et al. study found that serious delinquents are usually regular and frequent users of drugs and alcohol. In addition, the relationships among drugs, alcohol, and criminal activity are complex and seem to take on a different meaning depending upon time, place, and social context. In general, serious delinquents indicated that the vast majority of their crimes were committed without concurrent substance abuse. Most delinquents said that they did not engage in property crimes to support their drug use.

THE SCHOOL AND DELINQUENCY

The school, like the family and peer group, is an important microsystem in the child's social network. Criminologists have pointed with regularity to a strong correlation between delinquency and school failure (Kelly, 1980; Schafer and Polk, 1967; Wilson and Herrnstein, 1985). Delinquents, compared to nondelinquents, have far more trouble performing adequately within the school setting. This is not surprising. What is surprising, however, is that little research has been directed at explaining this oft-cited correlation. One explanation, advanced without much empirical documentation, is that the delinquent child is intellectually handicapped or at least ill-prepared for the rigors of school. We shall refer to this as the ''student deficit hypothesis.'' Another explanation is the ''school deficit hypothesis,'' which places the blame on the shoulders of the educational system.

The student deficit hypothesis suggests that poor and minority children are especially prone to intellectual deficits. Their deficiency is presumed to arise from any number of causal factors, including faulty parenting, inadequate genes, limited intellectual capacity, cultural deprivation, and poor attitudes and motivation, or some combination of these. Whatever the reasons, the disadvantaged child enters school ill-equipped to succeed, begins to experience failure, becomes frustrated and angry, and often drops out as soon as possible. Somewhere along the line, usually before dropping out, the child begins to engage in delinquent conduct.

The evidence for disproportionate dropout rates among minorities exists, but it is not clearcut, especially across time. Between 1967 and 1976, for example, the dropout rate among black youth declined from roughly 25 percent to slightly below 20 percent (Sternberg et al., 1984). Since 1976, the rate for blacks has risen to slightly less than 25 percent, about equal to the national dropout rate in American high schools. The dropout rates for Hispanics has risen steadily from approximately 30 percent in 1974 to 40 percent in 1979 (Sternberg, et al, 1984). The rate for American Indians has ranged between 70 and 90 percent for some time. As Laurence Sternberg and his colleagues (1984) asserted, however, these rates are due primarily to the child's difficulty with the

English language and to cultural orientation, *not* to intellectual deficiency. Overall, an inability to read consistently appears to be the major problem preventing minorities from meeting educational requirements.

The tendency to drop out seems clearly related to delinquency. Potential dropouts are more likely to be involved in delinquency than their peers who eventually graduate (Elliott and Voss, 1974; Camp, 1980; Carnegie Council, 1979). Note that we are referring to *potential* dropouts here. Delbert Elliott and Harwin Voss (1974) found that youths appeared to engage in less delinquency *after* they left school than before. Elliott and Voss concluded that the school is the critical social context for the development of delinquent behavior. Academic failure and difficulty at school seem to be participating factors in delinquency—at least in boys. The pattern for girls was not as clear. To Elliott and Voss, male delinquency is primarily a response to school failure. Specifically, delinquency is a way of coping with the social stigma and loss of self-esteem associated with this failure. Furthermore, Elliott and Voss did not find that delinquents dropped out of school because they felt socially alienated and isolated. Instead, "Respondents with the highest rates of delinquency were youth who had strong commitment to peers and weak commitment to parents"(p. 205). In fact, they seemed "over-committed" to peers. If anything, school peer networks seemed to be "launching pads" for entering delinquent groups. Academic and behavioral problems may prompt individuals to seek the company of those in similar circumstances. Once the individual dropped out of school, however, both contacts with peers remaining in school and involvement in delinquency were significantly reduced. Despite these observations, the relationship between delinquency and the school remains unclear.

The "school deficit hypothesis" places the blame for school failure upon the school and many of its supporting groups. It predicts that the school system sets the stage early for a child's failure as well as for actions and reactions that often lead to delinquency. This argument was raised earlier in the context of institutional practices and IQ. Specifically, the school is said to cultivate the failure process for some children by using negative labels such as "slow learner," "disadvantaged," "special learner," or "academically handicapped," and reacting toward the child accordingly. The child assumes the label and also begins to act accordingly, as do others, including parents and peers. Once this process has begun ". . . students who fail tend to be progressively shunned and excluded by other achieving students, by individual teachers, and by the 'system as a whole' " (Schafer and Polk, 1967, p. 230). Because of this negative labeling process, the targeted children find themselves caught up in a deteriorating downward spiral. School becomes aversive and frustrating, and the child begins to violate its rules and regulations, as well as those of society.

Advocates of the school deficit hypothesis acccept that some children begin school at a disadvantage, usually because of lack of preparation, but they say it is the school system that exacerbates the condition. The school deficit position, best represented in the work of Walter Schafer and Kenneth Polk (1967, 1975), also assumes that much of the curriculum is irrelevant to the child's life. Segments of the population considered formal schooling so irrelevant that public education had to be made compulsory to assure that children would attend school.

Which better explains dropout rates, the student deficit hypothesis or the school deficit hypothesis? Before answering, we need to sidetrack a bit. In Chapter 7 we reviewed construct systems and their ramifications for perceiving the world and for acting. It was suggested that intellectual capacity can be defined in many ways and probably cannot be measured. Accordingly, dropping out of school may not reflect lack of capacity or ability, but rather *orientation* (Bernstein, 1974). Youngsters from different subcultures and different neighborhoods, who have been subjected to different family styles and have spoken different languages, are apt to have different orientations and constructs about the world and acceptable ways of acting. The anthropologist John U. Ogbu (1974) studied middle and lower class sections of Stockton, California. The "lower class" section, Burgherside, was comprised mostly of blacks and Mexican-Americans. Ogbu learned that the children of Burgherside almost universally did not feel it was important to do the best they could on exams or achievement tests in school. They did not try to get better-than-average grades. The vast majority of Burgherside children, from the elementary to the high school levels, received grades of "C" or "D" in classroom work. Very few received a single "A." The Burgherside youths wanted to get by and get school over with, and there was little attempt to maximize their scores and grades. Ogbu rejected any notion of intellectual deficit or handicap. He believed their way of seeing the world simply did not dovetail with that of middle class whites, who felt it was important to get the best grades possible.

Middle class Stocktonians were generally convinced that Burgherside parents had low expectations for their children and that it was this attitude which resulted in poor school performance. But interviews with the Burgherside parents revealed they *did* have high occupational and educational hopes for their children and *did* urge the children to do the best they could in school. Why, then, the poor performance? According to Ogbu, the Burgherside parents seemed to be giving their children double messages. While urging them to do well in school, they also communicated that they (the children) would continuously be victims of discrimination. There was an implicit message that proclaimed, "No matter how hard you work, you probably won't get ahead." Widespread and pervasive discriminatory practices would not abate. While this second message was not stated explicitly, it was often embedded in comments or stories about discriminatory practices encountered by the parents themselves or by acquaintances. Thus, part of the problem may be ascribed to parental deficit rather than a school or student deficit.

Some investigators have found that as many as 75 percent of school dropouts demonstrate intellectual or cognitive skills sufficient enough to do passing or even superior school work (Elliott et al., 1966; Garbarino and Asp, 1981). Furthermore, although some studies have reported that delinquents are plagued by learning disabilities, one literature review (Murray, 1976, p. 61) concluded that the "disparity of estimates fairly reflects the disparity of definitions, procedures, and analyses in the studies." In addition, no estimate of the incidence of learning disabilities could be satisfactorily derived from the existing research, and no study yet conducted demonstrates that the average delinquent even is more likely to suffer from learning disability than his or her nondelinquent counterpart. The evidence for a causal link between learning disability and delinquency is feeble. So, too, is the evidence for the student deficit hypothesis in general.

James Garbarino and C. Elliott Asp (1981) suggested that schools are primarily social institutions rather than cognitive ones. American schools—and this has been said many times before—are designed to socialize American youths into middle class, mainstream society. They promote and establish social networks oriented toward what middle class America thinks is important. What the school social network advocates as important, however, a vast majority of the disadvantaged, minorities, and members of various subcultures consider largely irrelevant. It is, after all, difficult for even middle class youngsters to see the relevance of precalculus in their daily or professional lives. Low socioeconomic class youngsters may find the majority of the curriculum irrelevant. It is the challenge of the school to find something to excite all children.

Wholesale indictments of the educational system are not new. There is no question that schools do manage to accommodate children from various backgrounds and subcultures, in spite of their differing life experiences, strategies for processing information, and attitudes and values. Nevertheless, some youngsters do not catch the current. They get washed ashore, often quite early in the flow of things. Intellectual capacity may have little to do with this.

At this point, the school deficit hypothesis gets more support than the student deficit hypothesis. The extent to which what happens in school contributes *directly* to delinquency is highly debatable in view of our present knowledge about the systems and processes involved, however. Also, the role played by other significant microsystems such as parents, siblings, and peers, remains ambiguous.

The School-Family Mesosystem

Bronfenbrenner (1979, 1986) has emphasized the importance of the mesosystem of the family and the school in the development of the child and his or her performance in school. The greater the frequency of contacts between family and the school, the stronger the mesosystem and the more integrated the child will be into the system.

> The available research evidence suggests that a powerful factor affecting the capacity of a child to learn in the classroom is the relationship existing between the family and the school. (Bronfenbrenner, 1986, p. 735)

Elsewhere, Garbarino and Asp conclude in much the same vein:

> The school-home mesosystem is of great developmental significance for the child. In general, we would expect enhanced development in cases where this mesosystem was characterized by a lot of interaction between parents and school personnel, where more was known to members of both settings, and where home and school communicate frequently. (Garbarino and Asp, 1981, p. 27)

In his investigation of the school system in Stockton, Ogbu (1974) found that the relationships between the Burgherside families and the school was ". . . characterized by social distance, mutual stereotyping, and lack of effective communication" (p. 159).

Communications from the school were one-way and authoritarian: The school did the communicating and parents were expected to listen. Although the school sent Burgherside families messages by way of phone calls, notes, and personal visits, parents felt they were not given opportunities to state their concerns or positions. Teachers decided when, where, why, and how they interacted with parents. Many mothers expressed a wish to establish a bi-directional link with the school, but they found school officials cold, unsympathetic, and unresponsive. Parents complained that they were made to feel ''dumb'' by school officials. This observation corroborates the one made by Schafer and Polk (1967) who report that lower income parents frequently perceive the school as hostile, cold, and alien. Unfortunately, the black and Mexican-American fathers in the Burgherside community generally thought that involvement with the school was part of the woman's role, and they made little or no attempt to contact the school.

Bronfenbrenner (1979) cited Ogbu's work as important in our understanding of the interconnections between the school, family, neighborhood, and the influence of economic conditions and community attitudes on school effectiveness. ''Moreover, he [Ogbu] looks at the nature of the processes involved in these connections rather than merely at the statistical correlations between low income, minority status, and poor school performance'' (Bronfenbrenner, 1977, p. 254). The research on the relationship between the family-school mesosystem and delinquency is virtually nonexistent. More attention to this kind of research would bring us much closer toward understanding the social system of delinquency.

FAMILY, WORK, AND DELINQUENCY

The mesosystem between family and work and its effect on delinquency also has received scant attention. Research examining it has often failed to appreciate the complexities and interplay between the relationships. Early research on the links between work and its effects on family life assumed a simplistic relationship: Maternal employment was bad for the developing child. If the mother is at work, she cannot be home rearing her children, and therefore her children will be more prone toward delinquent behavior. Conversely, parental *unemployment* was considered bad for the child (Bronfenbrenner and Crouter, 1982). A despondent, irritable, unemployed father could only add an unhealthy element to the home environment.

But research focused on maternal employment or paternal unemployment and delinquency, and which considers the labyrinth of relationships, is exceedingly rare. As just mentioned, a vast majority of the research has proceeded on a narrow path, only looking at maternal employment or maternal unemployment to see what effects they have on the delinquency rate. Rarely did studies examine the connection between paternal unemployment (or employment) and delinquency.

Glueck and Glueck (1957) reported a higher incidence of delinquency among boys of employed mothers. This pattern was especially evident if the mothers only worked ''occasionally'' or ''sporadically.'' Interestingly, the Gluecks suggested that the effect of the working mother was most damaging when the boy was physically ectomorphic and temperamentally sensitive and prone to worry. However, the Gluecks (1950, 1957) implied that an arrangement for proper supervision (such as a relative or neighbor) could neutralize any negative effects of maternal employment. Nye (1958) also found that youngsters of working mothers tended to engage in more delinquency, but the behavior was minor and the relationship was weak. In addition, he suggested that maternal employment seemed to have a more adverse effect on girls than it did on boys. Even after Nye controlled many of the background variables, such as social class, mother's education, and family size, a small relationship persisted. Nye speculated that the maternal employment-delinquency relationship was due to a loss of direct control and supervision associated with the absence of the mother. Hirschi (1969) also cited a significant link between maternal employment and SR delinquency, although it was not *highly significant*. He suggested that "physical proximity" of the mother may be a factor. More specifically, a youngster might feel less controlled if his mother worked 70 blocks away versus a situation where the mother worked only 5 blocks away. More recently, Hirschi (1983) suggests that the maternal employment-delinquency relationship might also be due to a "destruction of the nest" effect, whereby the unoccupied house may become less appealing to the adolescents, prompting them to spend more time away from home.

Some research (e.g., Bandura and Walters, 1959; Andry, 1960; Wadsworth, 1979; West and Farrington, 1973) reported no significant relationship between delinquency and the working status of the mother. Some writers (e.g., Rutter and Giller, 1984) have concluded that the relationship is unsupported and should be forgotten. However, research to date has not examined the many aspects involved, such as the type of employment, the hours worked, availability of family support systems, the children's age when mother goes to work, the children's attitude about mother working, father's support of mother's working, and so forth. One exception is the work being done by Laurence Steinberg (1986) on "latchkey children." So far, he has learned that latchkey kids without adult supervision are more prone toward minor delinquent actions than those who have some type of adult supervision, primarily because of the formers' apparent increased susceptibility to peer pressures. Even if the working parent just calls home after school, this strategy appears to have an effect on lowering delinquency rates. We do not know what effect different levels of adult supervision will have on serious delinquency, however. The research by Johnstone, discussed earlier, suggests that it would have little.

In sum, it is too early to say conclusively that no relationship exists between work and family and delinquency. Only when we begin to understand the matrix of interacting and stratified variables will we be able to advance the knowledge in this area appreciably.

INTERACTIONISM: A SUMMING UP

The most productive strategy in our quest for explaining, preventing, and treating delinquency may lie in *interactionism*. We have made reference to this concept throughout the text (in Chapter 2 it was introduced as reciprocity), and it is time its principal features be summarized. It is important to realize that interactionism is not a new approach. Its many variants were used in the first half of this century by James Mark Baldwin, George Herbert Mead, C. H. Cooley, Herbert Blumer, William James, Kurt Lewin, and John Dewey—to mention only a few. More recently, the principles of interactionism have been expressed most clearly by the Swedish psychologist, David Magnusson, and his colleagues (1981, 1983).

Interactionism refers to the continuously ongoing, bidirectional influence that goes on between systems. The most obvious illustration is the interactionism between the individual system (the person) and the microsystem (the immediate environment). Magnusson and Allen (1983, p. 370) state ''. . . the person-environment interaction process is an open system that consists of a dynamic process in which mutual influence and change are taking place continuously.'' The person influences the microsystem and the microsystem influences the person in a continuous stream of influences across time. The individual and the environment are inseparable. They form an indivisible whole or totality. Therefore, to illustrate interactionism correctly, we need more than a linear, static, two-way interaction. We need a series of ''causal loops'' connected across time (see figure 9-1). In this sense, the development of delinquency can be conceptualized as a spiral or helix.

Furthermore, ''The process of person-environment interaction is a system, as we have noted; but it must be remembered that this system is embedded within a hierarchy of other systems, some of which are at a higher, and others at a lower, level than the person-environment system itself'' (Magnusson and Allen, 1983, p. 370). Thus, the development of delinquency is best conceptualized as spirals within spirals (like funnel clouds of tornados within increasingly larger funnel clouds), each influencing the other. Moreover, the larger, more powerful, funnel clouds (e.g., macrosystems) influence the inner funnels more than the inner funnels influence the outer. To understand delinquency development adequately, ''. . . we need to know as much as possible about the degree and frequency of penetration from other systems at different levels into the systems being studied'' (Magnusson & Allen, 1983, pp. 370–371).

As we have described in this chapter, the family, school, and peer systems interact with each other, and with the larger systems (the community) and smaller systems (the person), forming a rich tapestry of mesosystems. The delinquent is not an isolated entity of deviance. The person is embedded among swirls of other systems. The delinquent is

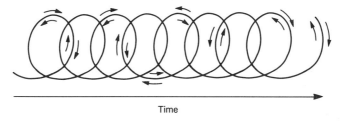

Time

Figure 9-1 Illustration of person-environment interactionism.

a totality who views the world from a certain perspective, functions as an ongoing system, and interacts with other systems.

Recently, Terence Thornberry (1987) has ably introduced interactionism to theory and research on delinquency. Thornberry asserts that contemporary theories of delinquency, specifically Hirschi's social control, Akers's social learning, and integrated models, are plagued by three fundamental limitations. First, they tend to be unidirectional in their explanations rather than reciprocal. They describe adolescents as being propelled along a single, one-way pathway. Early factors affect later ones in a single direction. Falling into the company of bad peers, for instance, presumably leads to delinquency. Second, the theories fail to recognize the important developmental changes that occur over the life course. They fail to consider that, ". . . as the developmental process unfolds, life circumstances change, developmental milestones are met (or, for some, missed), new social roles are created, and new networks of attachments and commitments emerge" (Thornberry, 1987, p. 881). Third, the theories assume uniform causal effects throughout the social structure, without considering a person's position in that structure. In so doing, they "fail to provide an understanding of the sources of initial variation in both delinquency and its presumed causes" (p. 864). Thornberry believes that youngsters from the lower class, for example, are at a decidedly greater disadvantage relative to commitment to family, school, and conventional beliefs than those from the middle class. He is arguing that contemporary theories are not sensitive to the initial systems network within which one begins life.

According to Thornberry, a viable theory of delinquency must take into consideration reciprocity, developmental changes across time, and the initial setting for a person's developmental sequence. He attempts to do all of this in his own interactional model. Two concepts are emphasized: the concept of reciprocity itself and the initial starting place to begin describing this reciprocity or interactionism. In other words, at what point should we begin describing the interactive course toward delinquency? Thornberry begins at the weakening of social controls.

His theory asserts

> . . . that the fundamental cause of delinquency lies in the weakening of social constraints over the conduct of the individual . . . The weakening of controls simply allows for a much wider array of behavior, including the continued conventional action, failure as indicated by school dropout and sporadic employment histories, alcoholism, mental illness, delinquent and criminal careers, or some combination of these outcomes. (p. 865)

Thus, weakened social controls reduce the behavioral restrictions, encouraging the individual to experiment with any variety of nondeviant and deviant behaviors. For delinquency to occur, the individual must find himself or herself in an ". . . interactive setting in which delinquency is learned, performed, and reinforced" (p. 865). In this sense, Thornberry seems to be including concepts from both control and Akers's social learning into his model. His is careful to emphasize that he is not integrating the two theories but simply engaging in "theoretical elaboration."

Thornberry focuses upon the interrelationships among six concepts:

1. attachment to parents;
2. commitment to school;
3. belief in conventional values;
4. associations with delinquent peers;
5. adoption of delinquent values; and
6. engaging in delinquent behavior.

The first three are from Hirschi's social control theory. The next two are from Akers's social learning theory. When attachment to parents, commitment to school, and belief in conventional values are strong, the person's behavior is channeled toward conventional society. When one or more of these bonds are weakened, behavioral freedom increases and the probability of delinquent involvement correspondingly increases. Involvement in delinquency, in turn, reduces the bonds to parents, school, and conventional society. Thus, while weakening of bonds initially causes engagement in delinquency, delinquency eventually becomes its own indirect cause because it influences (weakens more) the individual's bonds to family, school, and conventional beliefs. Unless this causal loop is interrupted, more delinquent involvement is likely.

Thornberry also suggests that parental influences have their greatest impact during the early formative years and that this impact decreases as the child grows older. "The family declines in relative importance while the adolescent's own world of school and peers takes on increasing significance" (p. 879). In other words, the social systems of the child change, and the networks and microsystems grow larger, more complicated, and more influential with age. This observation has the substantial support of many developmental psychologists (e.g., Bronfenbrenner, 1979; Hartup, 1983; Garbarino, 1982).

Finally, theories must consider where each person begins his or her developmental odyssey.

> . . . (Y)ouths from middle-class families, given their greater stability and economic security, are likely to start with a stronger family structure, greater stakes in conformity, and higher chances of success, and all of these factors are likely to reduce the likelihood of initial delinquent involvement. In brief, the initial values of the interactional variables are systematically related to the social class of origin. (p. 885)

Children deprived of family stability, a decent physical and comfortable environment, a caring social network, adequate nutrition and medical care, and a neighborhood where crime is held in check, begin the interactional course at a decidedly different place than others more fortunate.

This interactive model illustrates well some of the points made in this chapter and appears to hold great promise in understanding, preventing, and treating delinquency.

In the years ahead, Thornberry and his associates plan to test this theory through the Rochester Youth Development Study, described briefly in Chapter 1.

SUMMARY AND CONCLUSIONS

Principal concepts in this chapter were microsystems, mesosytems, and networks; our goal was to demonstrate how juvenile delinquency might be associated with each. A microsystem is limited to processes taking place within the individual's single, immediate setting—the family, the classroom, the peer group, the work environment. A mesosystem takes into account the joint effect of processes occurring within and between two or more settings, such as family and school, family and peers, family and work, and family and neighborhood. We discussed delinquency in relation to each. Social networks refer to the social relationships within or between groups.

Criminologists have some knowledge about delinquency in relation to each topic but still have a long way to go and much to do before arriving at a firm understanding of delinquency in present society. This conclusion is certainly not new. We have made substantial progress, however. We are beginning to recognize that multilevels of explanations are necessary, that unidirectional causes between and among social variables are often an oversimplification, that social environments are always changing, that predictions of human actions are extremely risky, and that social theories and research are developing conceptual arrangements of a stratified world rather than searching for universal truths.

The astute reader may have noted that the concepts "mesosystems" and "social networks" have much in common. Both are analytical frameworks for examining social links or associations among groups, communities, organizations, institutions, cultures, and societies. More important, however, the two are based on a similar implicit theory about human behavior. Both began strictly as analytical tools, but they now represent an implicit theoretical position: The richer (the more social strands or links, or the more developed the mesosystems) and the more varied the points (the more microsystems), the better the child's development and the less deviant the individual. In a sense, we could say that the richer and more varied the network or mesosystem, the more likely is the individual to conform to societal and cultural rules. Said differently, the more relationships a person has, and the more varied these relationships, the less likely the person is to become deviant.

This perspective at first glance seems very much in line with Hirschi's social control theory. Recall that Hirschi (1969) contended that people conform to conventional norms and expectations because they are bonded to people and social institutions. Hirschi's analysis suggests, however, that these links or associations are additive—the more links, the stronger the bond to mainstream society (Krohn, 1986). What we are saying here is somewhat different. Hirschi and other social control theorists see causation as moving in one direction, a relationship often called "asymmetrical." Social influences move in the single direction of social environment (family, social institutions) to child or adolescent. What we suggest throughout the text is that social influence is bi-directional or "symmetrical." The child or adolescent influences and selects the social environment, and the social environment at multiple levels influences and selects the child or adolescent.

Furthermore, we have also been emphasizing that the *variety* of the network or social system is crucial. Hirschi tends to focus on family influences while neglecting other microsystems, such as the peer microsystem. We are saying that an individual who has wide and varied social systems or social networks is less susceptible to pressures from any one system. For example, if an adolescent lives his formative years within a restricted microsystem (e.g., a gang) and has limited opportunity to interact with other systems, then he will be highly susceptible to influences of that peer microsystem. If that microsystem advocates deviance, and he chooses to stay within it, there is a high probability that he too will engage in delinquent or deviant actions. This hypothesis might help explain the SES relationship often reported in the criminological literature. People living under dire financial conditions in a physically deteriorating neighborhood where residents are in constant mobility are apt to have limited social networks or opportunities to interact with other systems of their own choosing. On the other hand, individuals with access to greater resouces also have a greater opportunity to interact with multiple networks or systems.

Some of the evidence reviewed in the chapter suggests that serious, violent offenders tend to be social isolates with very restricted social networks. Perhaps the unusually violent juveniles are those who are so socially ostracized that they develop their own "deviant" construct systems that do not fit with mainstream thinking. Rich and extensive personal networks and social systems will keep our construct systems in line with what others think and feel.

Higher Level Systems: The Social Structure and the Ecological Perspective

10 CHAPTER

Social structure is a difficult concept to define. Although is is one of the most frequently used concepts in sociology, it has no specific and universally accepted meaning. One common definition relates to the observation that, although societies, cultures, and social groups change members, their patterns of social relations and customs remain essentially the same over time. Thus, the phrase a "social structure" is used to mean simply a social regularity, to indicate that the social behavior is repetitive and nonrandom. Ideology, beliefs, traditions remain intact, despite births, deaths, and the coming and going of the participants. Hence, social structure describes patterns which change more slowly than the individuals who are involved in them.

Researchers measure social structure through an almost infinite number of variables, including sex, social stratification, race, income, crime rates, occupations, amount of rented housing within an area, single-family homes, ethnic origin, religion, and so forth. There does not seem to be any single, preferred measure. Different researchers use different combinations of variables. In addition, the concept may be applied to small groups, larger associations, communities, and societies.

In this chapter we begin to examine research at the macrosystem level. "The macrosystem refers to the consistency observed within a given culture or subculture in the form and content of its constituent micro-, meso-, and exosystems, as well as any belief systems or ideology underlying such consistencies" (Bronfenbrenner, 1979, p. 258). Included in the analysis of the macrosystem are, of course, social structures.

256

For the most part, the material in previous chapters pertained to lower levels of analysis, although in some instances, such as Kandel's study of New York teenagers described in the previous chapter, researchers were operating at the macro level. Ecological research, particularly that which analyzes data obtained from large samples and examines structural variables in those data, is the best example of macrosystem research. In the pages ahead, we will cover the work of researchers who examined structural variables such as social class or sex in large samples. We will also be discussing radical and conflict theories in criminology. Since these theories attribute crime and delinquency to features of society as a whole, they clearly fall within the macro level category.

THE ECOLOGICAL PERSPECTIVE AND THE RISE OF MULTIVARIATE TECHNIQUES

The ecological study of crime and delinquency developed by the Chicago School, particularly through the work of Park and Burgess and subsequently Shaw and McKay, all but ceased during World War II and the postwar years, with the exception of the ongoing Chicago Area Project. Ecological research was revitalized in the 1950s, however, probably due to two related events:

1. the development of sophisticated and promising statistical techniques; and
2. the rapid development of the computer, enabling researchers to examine very large aggregates of data rapidly and with a variety of methods.

Furthermore, criminologists by then were suspecting that successful efforts to explain delinquency would require attention to a constellation of influences at the larger, "higher levels" of explanation, such as delinquency rates in relation to SES levels of communities. Many believed that lower levels of analysis had not been either efficient or fruitful. An ecological approach appeared to provide more and better answers to the dilemmas of crime and delinquency. And now, for the first time, researchers had powerful statistical tools for probing and detecting patterns in aggregate data.

As you will recall, Shaw and McKay had amassed a wealth of materials, including plots, maps, information from interviews, and official reports, from which they had derived correlations describing the spatial relationships between delinquency and specified areas of the community. They were not the first to *describe* geographical distributions of juvenile delinquency, but apparently they were among the first to attempt a systematic analysis and explanation of these distributions. By painstakingly mapping incidents of crime, Shaw and McKay were able to demonstrate that it was distributed geographically in identifiable and consistent patterns: Crime and delinquency diminished the farther one travelled away from the center of Chicago and was especially prevalent in interstitial areas. In addition, the delinquency distribution within the city did not seem to be affected by population changes in each neighborhood. When residents moved out, they apparently did not bring their lawbreaking behaviors with them. It appeared that the criminal behaviors were adopted by the incoming population. Shaw and McKay—and other researchers—found similar patterns in some 20 other cities across the United States. They theorized that delinquency was the result of social disorganization and lack of community control generated primarily by population movement in and out of the interstitial areas, where mixtures of residents with conflicting values were attempting to adapt to a rapidly changing environment.

After publication of Shaw and McKay's work, most of the ecological research immediately following focused on identifying important links between delinquency rates and sociodemographic variables of community composition (Bursik, 1984). The strongest, most consistently emerging relationship was that between delinquency and social class. Simply put, conditions of poverty seemed to be strongly related to delinquency and even seemed to explain delinquency. This relationship between social class and delinquency became sociological dogma. It was examined and researched in combination with other variables, but it was rarely attacked.

The Lander Statistical Study

In 1954, the sociologist Bernard Lander re-examined the long-standing ecological factors which were presumed to be strongly linked to delinquency. Whereas Shaw and McKay and other researchers in their tradition had obtained straightforward correlations between two variables (e.g., class and delinquency), Lander had the advantage of contemporary statistical techniques called multivariates. Armed with these newly "rediscovered" methods, he examined the social and economic data of the 1940 U.S. Census for the city of Baltimore as well as official delinquency rates for that city between 1939 and 1942.

Lander divided the city into geographical sections and analyzed seven social variables in each to determine how they were related to delinquency. The seven variables were:

1. the median years of school completed by all persons 25 years old and over living in an area;
2. the estimated median monthly rent;
3. the percentage of persons living in homes where there were 1.51 or more persons per room (as an index of overcrowding);
4. the percentage of substandard housing (defined as homes needing major repairs and/or having no private baths);
5. the percentage of nonwhites;
6. the percentage of foreign born; and
7. the percentage of owner-occupied homes.

Lander relied on correlational methods to analyze his data. Correlation methods for determining the strength of the linear relationship between two or more variables are among the most widely used statistical techniques in the study of crime and delinquency. The term "linear relationship" means that the person applying the technique assumes the relationship between the variables of concern follow basically a straight line pattern without drastic variations or curves when plotted on a graph (See Figure 10-1). There are several strategies one may use which are built upon the fundamental concept of correlation, including regression, canonical analysis, factor analysis, path analysis, and time series analysis.

Lander first obtained *zero-order correlations*, the traditional method of analysis. A zero-order correlation merely tells how strongly one variable is related to another, without consideration of the possible influence of any other variable. A researcher might obtain a zero-order correlation of .63 between family income and the delinquency rate, for example. (A perfect correlation, which we would very rarely expect, would have a correlation coefficient of 1.00.) The .63 correlation coefficient would suggest that family income and delinquency are strongly related. It would not tell, however, whether the relationship is affected by other factors, such as overcrowding. That is, overcrowding may contribute more to delinquency than family income.

Lander's zero-order correlations revealed that all seven variables were significantly related to the rate of delinquency. He then went several steps beyond this simple analysis. He obtained *partial correlations* from the data and conducted regressions and factor analysis. Keep in mind that Lander was trying to discover the "true" causes of delinquency and believed these multivariate techniques could help.

Partial correlations allow the researcher to hold constant certain variables while the relationship between others is studied. Note that this is far more powerful than a zero-order technique, which cannot take into account the influence of other variables. When *one* variable is held constant while two others are studied, the resulting correlation coefficient is called a *first-order* partial correlation. If *two* variables are held constant while two others are studied, a *second-order* partial correlation is obtained. Lander performed a partial correlation between the delinquency rate and each of the seven social variables in turn. He held six variables constant while examining the relationship be-

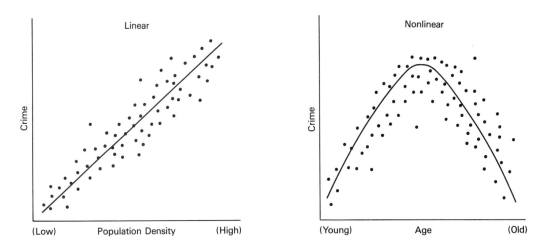

Figure 10-1 Illustration of presumably linear and nonlinear relationships.

tween delinquency and the seventh. For example, he correlated delinquency with over-crowding while holding constant the variables of rent, education, quality of housing, percent nonwhites, percent foreign born, and percent owner-occupied housing. He then did the same for the variable "rent," and so on. Lander was conducting a *sixth-order* partial correlation on each variable.

Using this method, Lander found only one significant relationship—between de-linquency rate and percentage of owner-occupied homes within the area—and that rela-tionship was very weak. Undaunted, Lander tried a combination of other strategies to discover the "true relationship" between delinquency and each of the seven variables, at times recoding variables into two or more different variables. He eventually obtained "tenth-order partial correlations" so far removed from the original meaning of the vari-ables as to render any conclusions highly questionable. Lander seemed determined to "partial" until a relatively large correlation emerged. The danger in this technique is that the investigator generally loses perspective—"partialling" until he or she loses sight of the theoretical significance and causal relationships between the variables. This is what Robert A. Gordon (1967) has referred to as the *partialling fallacy* in social science research.

After considerable analyses using the "new" statistical techniques (such as regres-sion and factor analysis), Lander thought he had discovered convincing "proof" that delinquency was more likely a result of anomie factors than economic factors. That is, he concluded that delinquency was more likely caused by the breakdown or weakening of the regulatory structure of society, as measured by home ownership and the amount of racial heterogeneity in a given area, than by economic factors, such as poverty, bad housing, overcrowding, and closeness to the center of the city. The higher the racial heterogeneity and the lower the home ownership within a particular areas, the higher the delinquency. "The factor analysis clearly demonstrates that delinquency in Baltimore is fundamentally related to the *stability* or *Anomie* of an area and is not a function of nor is it basically associated with the economic characteristics of an area" (Lander, 1954, p. 59).

Initially, other criminologists reacted ambivalently to Lander's conclusions. On the one hand, his research supported anomie theory; on the other, he was rejecting the cherished tenet that crime and social class are closely related. His challenge to the eco-logical approach in the tradition of Shaw and McKay was met by researchers who began to question his assumptions and his methods. There were two main attempts at replica-tion and re-evaluation of Lander's study, one by David Bordua in 1958 using Detroit data, and another by Roland Chilton in 1964 using Lander's and Bordua's data along with additional data gathered in Indianapolis.

Bordua included the seven social variables used by Lander plus three of his own: cash value of the dwelling units, median income, and percent of unrelated individuals living in the home (as an index of family stability). He discovered that, while owner-occupied homes continued to be negatively related to delinquency rate, the racial het-erogeneity variable lost its significance. Furthermore, in contrast to Lander's results, Bordua found that education and overcrowding (represented in Lander's economic fac-tor) were also significantly related to delinquency rate.

Chilton (1964) tried to reconcile these differences. In his study of the three cities, he reported that, for the most part, the same variables that significantly correlated with delinquency rates in the Bordua and Lander projects also correlated in his own data (he also used zero-order correlation, regression analysis, and factor analysis). However, he questioned Lander's interpretations that percent renters, racial heterogeneity, and rate of delinquency were indices of anomie. Moreover, like Bordua, Chilton found that overcrowded housing, income, percent unrelated individuals, and education were indeed related to delinquency, contradicting Lander's conclusion. Chilton qualified his own research by noting that the statistical links were not strong. Nevertheless, "Our findings suggest that delinquency still appears to be related to transiency, poor housing and economic indices; this supports the assumption of almost all sociological theories of delinquency, that delinquency in urban areas is predominately a lower class phenomenon" (Chilton, 1964, pp. 82–93). He did not interpret his data within a theoretical framework, however, leaving others to speculate about the significance of his replication. Interestingly, Chilton questioned the heavy reliance on aggregate data in the understanding of delinquency. He concluded his study by advocating that researchers examine "mental aspects" of behavior, such as—in his words—norms, goals, self-concepts, and status aspirations.

In the long run, criticisms of the Lander study were extensive and damaging. For example, Gordon (1967) questioned virtually all of Lander's assumptions, analyses, and interpretations. Rosen and Turner (1967) questioned the appropriateness of the statistics as well as Lander's interpretation of them. Thus, Lander's Baltimore study has the dubious distinction of being a model for how to make faulty conclusions on the basis of inappropriately used multivariate statistics. However, on the positive side, it succeeded in prompting criminologists to make use of these new techniques available to them, and prompted a movement toward re-examining the ecological approach of Shaw and McKay.

SOCIAL AREA ANALYSIS

At about the time the Lander study was published, Eshref Shevky and his colleagues (Shevky and Williams, 1949; Shevky and Bell, 1955) were in the process of developing an ecological research method called *social area analysis*. It was designed to measure systematically the "social structure" of any given city so it could be compared to that of other cities. The method is built around three constructs developed from the population characteristics reported in census tracts: social rank, urbanization, and segregation. These are considered by some criminologists as logical extensions of early ecological studies and as important measures of crime and delinquency. *Social rank* is measured by combinations of census variables that are related to economic status, such as occupation, education, and level of rent. Together these variables form an *index of economic status*. *Urbanization* is measured by combinations of variables relating to fertility ratio, percentage of women in the labor force, and the proportion of single-family dwelling units within a given area. The underlying assumption is that childlessness, women working, and families living in apartments are more characteristic of urban areas than rural areas. Together, these variables make up the *index of familism*. *Segregation* is measured by the ratio of other racial groups to whites or of ethnic to nonethnic groups living in a specific area. The ratio is called the *index of ethnic status*.

The procedure introduced by Shevky is important in the study of delinquency because it shifted the direction of ecological research from a strict analysis of geographical and spatial factors as found in the Shaw-McKay studies to an examination of social structural determinants of crime (Byrne and Sampson, 1986). There has been much controversy over the definitions of the three constructs, however, especially familism (Baldwin, 1979). Researchers using social area analysis typically correlate the three constructs—economic status, familism, and ethnic origin—(or others they themselves have developed) with various crime indicators and try to discover whether and how the "social structure" is related to crime and delinquency. For example: One might want to correlate index of economic status or social rank with statistics on petty larceny, hypothesizing that this crime is committed out of economic necessity.

One of the earliest studies on juvenile delinquency using social area analysis was conducted by Kenneth Polk (1957), a professor in the Department of Anthropology and Sociology at the University of California, Los Angeles. Polk analyzed census data for the city of San Diego according to the three constructs outlined by Shevky and correlated these with 1952 official delinquency data. He obtained zero-order and second-order partial correlations. Polk found a zero-order correlation of $-.24$ between the delinquency rate and economic status, a $-.21$ between delinquency rate and familism, and a .45 between delinquency and ethnic status. When partial correlations were computed, however, economic status mysteriously dropped out as a significant factor—it did not seem to play an important role in the delinquency rate, once familism and ethnic status were held constant. The Polk research did not support the earlier finding of Lander concerning "Anomie." In addition, Polk's partial correlation suggested that family status also played only a minor role in the formation of delinquency, indicating that family "disruption" or "breakdown" were insignificant factors in delinquency. The strongest partial correlation was between ethnic status and delinquency rate, indicating that blacks and Mexican-Americans were more likely to become delinquent than whites. Polk did not offer an explanation for the lack of significance of the economic and family indices. He suggested, though, that the significance of ethnic status could be due to a tendency on the part of law enforcement authorities to arrest minorities and ethnic groups.

In a subsequent paper, Polk (1967) argued strongly in favor of a Shevky schema as a suitable framework for the analysis of delinquency rates. Using 1960 official delinquency data from Portland, Oregon, Polk underscored the need to examine urban areas in a way that includes the economic, ethnic, and familism status parameters. The approach used by Lander, Bordua, and Chilton blurs the picture of urban life hopelessly through zero and higher order correlations. Polk claimed that each of the three social analytic variables contributes a unique effect to the distribution of delinquency. The highest levels of delinquency were found at the lowest levels of economic status and familism and at the highest levels of ethnic status (minority groups). According to John Baldwin (1974, 1979), however, Polk made the critical mistake of advancing conclusions about individual characteristics strictly on the basis of ecological characteristics. This is known as the *ecological fallacy*.

The ecological fallacy was first alluded to by the psychologist Edward L. Thorndike (1929), when he cautioned researchers not to assume that correlations reported for large groups are valid for making judgments about the characteristics of individuals or smaller groups. Years later, W. S. Robinson (1950) warned sociologists about this same problem. According to Robinson, the ecological fallacy is the error of assuming that relationships, or correlations, based upon group data or ecological areas will hold at the individual level. Correlations between variables measured on groups or ecological areas are not necessarily identical to correlations measured on individuals, despite the fact that those individuals may be part of the group or may live in those areas. More recently, James Acker (1987) argued cogently that the fallacy is not limited to researchers. Courts, he said, are "flirting" with committing an ecological fallacy when they condone law enforcement practices which infer that individuals living in or travelling to high crime areas are more suspicious than others.

As Acker notes, a study may report that neighborhood X has a higher crime rate than other neighborhoods in the city. It would be incorrect to assume that individuals living in the high crime sector are far more likely to be criminal than those living in other sectors. The higher crime rate might be due to a number of factors besides the general behavior of the *individuals* within that area. It might be due to a very small proportion of the residents who are committing an inordinate number of crimes. Alternately, outsiders may be coming into these neighborhoods to engage in illegal activities. Still another explanation for the high crime rate could be a policy decision on the part of local law enforcement to intensify its efforts to arrest. Any combination of factors may be contributing to the rate. Ecological data, therefore, do not allow us to make conclusions about the behavior of individuals.

Social area analysis is particularly susceptible to the ecological fallacy. Despite this limitation, this research method has produced a number of important studies which have drawn attention to some of the weaknessses in the Shaw-McKay tradition (Byrne and Sampson, 1986). As Byrne and Sampson (1986, p. 5) assert: ". . . social-area analysis has played an important role in turning the focus of areal research from a strict analysis of geographical and spatial influence to an examination of the social structural determinants of crime. Many contemporary ecological studies have incorporated this viewpoint."

SOCIAL CLASS AND DELINQUENCY

Social class has been a central focus in studies of crime and delinquency. Most pre-1960 sociological theories of delinquency included it as a crucial ingredient. Specifically, they predicted an inverse or negative relationship between social class and criminal involvement: The lower the social class, the greater the likelihood of involvement in criminal or delinquent behavior. In the mid-1950s and early 1960s, however, researchers began to question the social class-delinquency connection. Lander's study just discussed prompted some concern about the presumed relationship. It was self-report research, however, which played the major role in generating serious doubts about the assumption that delinquency and social class were so closely related. As you will discover from the material in the pages ahead, the debate over the role of social class continues.

It is important at the outset that we address a problem in terminology. As with broken home research, there is remarkable definitional inconsistency in the research on social class. Until approximately 25 years ago, theorists and researchers referred primarily to three distinct strata, defined primarily in economic terms: lower, middle, and upper classes. Hirschi (1969), however, noted that criminologists were really talking about two classes: "them" and "us." "The *class* model implict in most theories of delinquency is a peculiarly top-heavy, two-class model made up of the overwhelming majority of respectable people on the one hand and the lumpenproletariat on the other" (Hirschi, 1969, p. 71). Gradually, a new term, socioeconomic status (SES), defined by the educational, occupational, or income level of the father, mother, or both, began to replace "social class" in the literature. SES was no less problematic than social class, however, since it carried with it many different meanings, and since researchers did not agree upon how it could be measured. Consequently, researchers began to use the terms interchangeably along with status and social position. Others have criticized this approach (Thornberry and Farnworth, 1982). For consistency, we use the term social class in the pages ahead.

A series of studies by James Short and Ivan Nye (Short and Nye, 1957, 1958, and Nye and Short, 1957) have become benchmarks in criminology, not only because they firmly established the self-report method in the study of delinquency, but also because they asked crucial questions about the presumed relationship between social class and delinquency. Short and Nye compared results obtained from official statistics and from their own self-report questionnaire. Using a sample of institutionalized delinquent boys in Washington training schools, they found a strong correlation between delinquency and social class. In percentage terms, almost 50 percent of the institutionalized boys were considered members of the "lower class." Since the boys had been processed by the criminal justice system, they were assumed to represent "official" statistics. Short and Nye's finding supported previous research indicating a strong association between *official* measures of delinquency (i.e., court records, police contacts, or institutionalization) and lower class adolescents.

Short and Nye also did something nontraditional. They administered questionnaires to male and female high school students in three small western cities, asking whether they had been involved in delinquent behavior. Using this method, the researchers found little if any indication that delinquent behavior was predominately a lower class phenomenon. Rather, the Short-Nye data revealed that middle class youths reported more involvement in delinquent activity than their lower class counterparts. Taken together, the self-report and official data suggested to Short and Nye that adolescents from the lower class (as well as those from broken homes) were more likely to be committed to an institution, even though they were not necessarily more likely to be violators of cultural norms.

The Short and Nye article was controversial because it contradicted the long-standing belief that the economically disadvantaged were less law-abiding than others. Recall that the mainstream strain theories of Robert Merton, Albert K. Cohen, and Walter Miller assumed that the law was violated by individuals who were not afforded the means of getting ahead in a materialistic society. How would these theories now explain the phenomenon that youths of all social classes violated the norms of society? The results did not "fit into" culture conflict theories, either. Sutherland's differential association approach, for example, did not explain why middle class youths—presumably protected from definitions unfavorable to law violations—would nevertheless exhibit delinquent behavior. Although some criminologists had long suspected that delinquency was not the province of any particular social class, others found it alien to their thinking. When Short and Nye's study was first reported, therefore, there was considerable criticism directed at the self-report method itself, particularly its internal and external validity.

There was, however, a major weakness in Short and Nye's questionnaire: It tapped very mild behavior, much of which would not be considered delinquent at all. For example, as we noted in Chapter 1, the researchers asked such questions as, "Have you driven a car without a driver's license or permit?" or "Have you skipped school without a legitimate excuse?" "Serious" delinquency questions (of which there were very few) asked, "Have you taken things of large value (over $50) that did not belong to you?" or "Have you used or sold narcotic drugs?"

Therefore, while Short and Nye found support for a class-delinquency association in official statistics but not in self-report data, they never really asked about much serious delinquency, which is the topic of most concern to researchers. They did not ask high school students if they had burglarized a home or place of business or if they had assaulted someone. Later self-report studies were conscious of this weakness and included measures of serious or repetitive delinquency in their own questionnaires. Nevertheless, Short and Nye brought attention to the fact that self-report measures could yield a very different picture of delinquency than the official measures which had been relied upon to date.

Other researchers refined the self-report method and used it in continued tests of the link between class and delinquency, but many still did not examine serious delinquency. Self-report studies by Akers (1964), Voss (1966), Gold (1966), Hirschi (1969), and Williams and Gold (1972) all indicated there was no relationship—or at best a weak one—between class and delinquency. Only the research of Gold, however, made a conscientious effort to tap serious law-breaking behavior. Official statistics, meanwhile, continued to reflect a strong inverse relationship.

In 1979, Hindelang, Hirschi, and Weis addressed this apparent discrepancy between official and self-report data. They reanalyzed the official studies which showed a high correlation between class and delinquency and concluded that the correlations were not as great as originally assumed. Furthermore, there was, they said, only an illusion of discrepancy. Official and self-report data referred to different domains of behavior. Official statistics measured serious offenses and were valid indicators of demographic distributions of criminal behavior. Self-report measures were more likely to capture the prevalence of minor offending.

Charles Tittle and his colleagues (Tittle, Villemez, and Smith, 1978) examined 40 major studies—every one they could uncover—which included class and either adult crime or juvenile delinquency as variables in their analysis. They noted that 85 percent of these investigations focused upon juvenile delinquency, primarily among white males. The studies varied widely in methodology, data sources, methods of reporting, and statistical analyses. In spite of these limitations, Tittle and his colleagues combined data from 35 of the studies and submitted them to statistical analysis.

Contrary to general theoretical expectations and widespread popular opinion, the combined data revealed only a slight negative relationship between social class and crime-delinquency. That is, the Tittle study suggested that neither official nor self-report data supported the belief that class is closely associated with crime and delinquency. The overall correlation was $-.09$, indicating virtually no relationship. Furthermore, the correlation declined in strength from the 1940s to the 1970s, reminding us that theories are often dependent upon time, place, and culture.

Tittle and his colleagues noted that virtually every sociological theory of delinquency has class as a central ingredient, explicitly or implicitly. They challenged criminologists to recognize that the class and crime-delinquency connection may be a ''myth,'' and they recommended that all future theory building eliminate class as an explanatory variable. Note that Tittle et al. (1978) did not say that the connection does not exist, they only said it has not been empirically established (see Tittle, 1985).

John Braithwaite (1981) followed with an article in which he expressed serious doubt that the class and delinquency-crime relationship is a ''myth.'' Braithwaite criticized Tittle and his colleagues for not unearthing all of the published investigations examining class and crime or delinquency. He was able to locate 53 studies examining the relationship between official records and class, and another 47 examining the relationship between self-reported delinquency and class, substantially more than were assessed by the Tittle group. Two of Braithwaite's official studies and eight of the self-report studies were published after the Tittle search, however.

Braithwaite's survey revealed that the social class-delinquency association could not be laid to rest. Of the 53 studies using official data, 44 demonstrated that lower class juveniles have substantially higher offense rates than middle class juveniles. Of the 47 self-report studies reviewed, 18 found lower class youths reporting significantly higher levels of involvement in delinquency than middle class youths. Another seven reported ''qualified support'' for the relationship. On the other hand, 22 of the self-report surveys found no relationship, again generating confusion and doubt about the class delinquency connection.

One of the studies reviewed by Braithwaite and completed after the Tittle et al. article was conducted by Delbert S. Elliott and Suzanne S. Ageton (1980). It is important because it highlights the complexity of the social class variable. Elliott and Ageton tried to settle the debate by analyzing self-report data on 1,726 adolescents participating in the National Youth Survey. The sample was first interviewed and asked about involvement in a wide range of delinquent behavior during the one-year period 1976. The adolescents were asked only about behaviors that would be crimes if committed by adults. The interviews were repeated in 1978 for the calendar year 1977.

The youths were divided into three groups on the basis of the occupation and education of the principal wage earner of the family. The "middle class" group consisted of wage earners employed in the professional or managerial occupations and with college educations. In the "working class," wage earners were owners of small businesses, clerical workers, persons in sales, and persons in skilled manual occupations with high school educations or some college work completed. Wage earners in the "lower class" category were employed in semiskilled occupations or unskilled manual occupations. They had high school or lower levels of education.

Working class and middle class youths did not differ significantly with respect to their involvement in delinquency overall. The lower class youths, however, differed significantly from the other two groups. Overall, the Elliott-Ageton data revealed class differences in the total offenses. While the differences were not large, they were in the traditionally expected direction. Lower class youths reported higher frequencies of delinquency than either the working or middle class youths.

A number of qualifiers must be attached to this conclusion. First, the relationship seemed to depend upon the type of offense. The largest differences between lower class youths and the other two class divisions occurred in "predatory" crimes against persons, with lower class youths reporting nearly four times as many offenses as middle class youths, and one-and-one-half times as many as working class youths. Crimes against property, on the other hand, were not explained by social class. Second, further analysis by Elliott and Ageton indicated that class differences occurred only if *frequency* and *seriousness* of offending were considered. Virtually all youths reported some delinquent activity; for the vast majority, however, the offenses were neither very frequent nor very serious. That is, if the analysis focused on how many individuals committed offenses, there would be few class differences. On the other hand, when the frequency and seriousness of the offenses were taken into account, class differences emerged. *Significant* differences were found only at the high end of the frequency range. Elliott and Ageton found that lower class youths engaged in significantly *more* delinquent behaviors than either working class or middle class adolescents. The researchers then divided their data into frequency categories. In the high frequency group (those reporting more than 54 offenses), lower class adolescents reported nearly three times as many "predatory" offenses as middle class adolescents and one-and-one-half times as many as working class adolescents. Thus, the Elliott-Ageton data suggest that previous research finding no significant relationship between class and delinquency may have focused on minor delinquent activities, which tends to be what most self-report questionnaires tap. Furthermore, the research may have neglected the number of times delinquent acts were committed by particular individuals.

The class and delinquency debate has been one of the most active controversies in the criminological literature during the 1980s. As noted earlier, the research often lacks precision in terminology and methodology. Terence P. Thornberry and Margaret Farnworth (1982) faulted researchers for using the terms "social class," "social status," "social position," and "socioeconomic status" interchangeably, although they often mean different things. Thornberry and Farnworth are especially concerned about the lack of precise distinctions between "social class" and "social status." "Social class refers to major social cleavages that demarcate a relatively small number of discrete groups within society" (1982, p. 507). On the other hand, ". . . social status . . . refers to the manner in which individuals are arrayed along a continuous status hierarchy'' (p. 507). Social class, by definition, has discrete divisions or points of separation; moreover, it is generally something into which one is born. Social status is a continuous distribution of social strata without discernible divisions, and it is attained by the individual. Therefore, ''The two concepts cannot be measured in the same fashion, nor do they lend themselves to the same interpretation'' (1982, p. 507). Most empirical investigations have used occupation, education, or income as indices of social status, often in combination. But, as Thornberry and Farnworth warn us, these three measures are most likely *separate* dimensions of social status, and any analysis of the relationship of social status to delinquency must carefully take this feature into account.

In their own analysis, Thornberry and Farnworth measured social status (not social class) in three different ways:

1. position of respondent's family within a continuous status hierarchy;
2. area of residence during adolescence; and
3. the individual's own occupational, educational, and income attainment by the age of 26.

It is important to keep in mind that Thornberry and Farnworth analyzed data from the Wolfgang longitudinal study which followed over the years 9,945 males born in 1945 and residing in Philadelphia from at least the ages of 10 to 18. Thus, they were able to trace the development of a large number of subjects from early adolescence to young adulthood, obtaining data on both delinquency and adult crime.

Thornberry and Farnworth reported that none of the measures of status was ''strongly related'' to delinquent involvement for either black or white subjects, and in neither official nor self-report measures of delinquency. However, the relationship between social status and *adult* crime was more promising. There was a clear relationship between the person's own social status and his criminal activity. This relationship was significant for whites and strongly significant for blacks. More specifically, years of education completed was inversely related to

1. the self-report criminality of black respondents; and
2. the official criminality of both black and white respondents.

That is, the higher the education, the lower the tendency to offend. Furthermore, job stability was strongly related to criminal activity for both blacks and whites, although the relationship was stronger in official than in self-report measures. Level of income, however, was not related, and occupational status only weakly related.

In sum, the Thornberry and Farnworth research suggests that one's own social status appears to be the best predictor of adult criminal involvement, and that the dimension of social status most closely linked to crime is educational attainment. On the other hand, the Thornberry-Farnworth analyses did not identify any social status dimensions that were significantly related to *delinquency*.

AGE STRUCTURE AND DELINQUENCY

In 1983 Travis Hirschi and Michael Gottfredson began an article with the disarming comment that virtually no criminologist, regardless of theoretical persuasion, disagrees that crime, as generally defined, is inordinately committed by the young. They added that criminologists also generally agree that the age distribution across the life cycle has a distinct shape: There is a sharp increase in crime during adolescence, it peaks during mid to late adolescence, shows a sharp decline in the early 20s, then follows a slow but steady decline thereafter (see Figure 1-1 p. 15). This is consistently supported in aggregate data, across the sexes, geographical areas, and socioeconomic status. There are two important caveats, however. First, keep in mind the ecological fallacy: Because this distribution characterizes crime in general, it obviously does not necessarily characterize the behavior of all individuals. Second, criminologists disagree over what the crime-age relationship means, and how it can be explained. This disagreement is the subject of one of the current controversies in the field. Hirschi and Gottfredson (1983) argued that this age distribution is *invariant* (to be explained soon), a position which—to their critics— has unsettling implications for the future direction of criminal justice research and policy.

Hirschi and Gottfredson also commented that, in light of consistent support for the age distribution, age could well replace social class as the ''master variable'' of sociological theories of crime. Age seems to be emerging as the principal criterion upon which the adequacy of theories of crime and delinquency is judged. In other words, a ''good theory'' must be able to account for the consistently reported observation that involvement in crime decreases after late adolescence. Hirschi and Gottfredson noted that failure to account for this downward swing in offending has rendered some theories suspect. In similar fashion, David Greenberg (1977) argued that the delinquency theories of Miller, Cohen, and Cloward and Ohlin are defective specifically because of this oversight or inability.

The age factor has been instrumental in the increased use of the longitudinal study as the preferred method of criminological research. Cross-sectional investigations, where researchers examine several age groups only once rather than follow them over a period of years, are insensitive to age effects. Thus, many criminologists view cross-sectional approaches as flawed because they are unable to detect developmental or social trends.

To Hirschi and Gottfredson, however, this longitudinal research is unnecessary. They argue that those who use maturation or age changes as a criterion of theoretical and research adequacy are misguided, because the age effect is *invariant* across all social and cultural conditions, regardless of the offense. That is, the relationship between age and offending is the same, regardless of the country or culture being discussed, or the period in history being reviewed. The *form* of the age distribution (a rapid rise to a peak than a steady decline) occurs again and again, wherever, however, or whenever it is measured. ''If the form of the age distribution differs from time to time and from place to place, we have been unable to find evidence of this fact'' (Hirschi and Gottfredson, 1983, p. 555). Hirschi and Gottfredson further maintained that the invariance of the age and crime relationship applies across sex and race. Again, it is important to emphasize that we are talking about the *shape* of the age distribution, not about frequencies or rates of offending.

Let us be careful about what is being said here. Hirschi and Gottfredson's "invariance hypothesis" specifically reads that "the age distribution of the tendency to commit criminal acts is invariant across social and cultural conditions" (1983, p. 561, note 9). A critical phrase is "tendency to commit criminal acts." They do not say "the age distribution of crime." This point is underscored because, while crime commission is strongly related to age, there may be circumstances that prevent the commission of the criminal act itself, even though the tendency remains the same. It is, therefore, more accurate to state that the *tendency* to commit is a function of age, although "tendency" is never clearly defined. This is consistent with Hirschi's general social control theory, discussed in Chapter 8, which assumes that people would commit crimes were it not for the bonds that have been established between themselves and parents, friends, and society. Hirschi's theory does not, however explain *why* we would engage in criminal activity in the absence of social controls. Are we to assume that "tendency" is a biological drive, or a physiological motivational state toward deviance? We simply do not know.

Hirschi himself acknowledges that his theory cannot satisfactorily *explain* the age factor. Neither, of course, can any other current sociological theory of crime and delinquency. Current theories assume that correlations between age and offending can be attributed to processes inherent in the culture, society, or social experience. Hirschi and Gottfredson propose that age effects will occur across a large sample of subjects, independent of shifts in economic, political, or social events, or independent of individual developmental factors. The invariant hypothesis also implies that the traditional etiological division between juvenile and adult crime—that is, that different factors cause each—is unlikely to be useful, because the causes of crime are likely to be the same *at any age*. Therefore, although correlated with crime, age is not useful in predicting involvement in crime over the life cycle of offenders. To know that a child of 10 has committed delinquent acts is no more useful for predicting subsequent involvement than to know that a child of 15 has done so.

According to Hirschi and Gottfredson, age-related hypotheses in the prediction of delinquency are also of questionable value. Criminologists traditionally have placed great importance on the point at which an individual first engages in criminal activity. For example, the "age of onset" hypothesis predicts that the earlier the child begins to offend, the more serious and persistent the criminal career will be. David Farrington (1979) writes that boys first convicted at the earliest ages tended to become the most persistent offenders as adults. Hirschi and Gottfredson charge that researchers have often arrived at prediction models based on age of onset that are confounded with other measures. They insist that no special explanations for age of onset are needed because *all* groups share a common age-crime distribution. In other words, if a youth begins criminal activity at age 13, he or she will peak between ages 16 and 18; if the youth begins at age 8, he or she will still peak between ages 16 and 18.

Criminologist David Greenberg (1985) finds the invariance hypothesis particularly troubling in its postulation that the age-crime relationship holds regardless of the economic and social atmosphere. In an earlier publication which was criticized in the Hir-schi-Gottfredson 1983 article, Greenberg (1977) argued that the increasing level of ju-venile crime in the United States and Western countries could be explained by the "structural position" of juveniles in an advanced capitalist economy. More specifically, Greenberg challenged those who see age variations in criminality as a result of biological or psychological reactions to the physiological changes of adolescence. To Greenberg, the age-crime relationship is primarily the result of social forces within a given culture. He suggested that the detachment of adolescents from their families, along with the extensive advertising directed at them, increased their need to finance their social activi-ties. Theft and related activities helped both male and female adolescents to meet their social needs for entertainment and material goods. Greenberg saw violence, primarily a male enterprise, as a product of "masculine status anxiety." He posited that certain economic conditions evoke anxiety in males, especially males of low socioeconomic status. They fear unemployment, being without occupational status, and thus being un-able to fulfill their traditional sex role expectations. One result of this masculine status anxiety, Greenberg posits, is increased violence.

Greenberg theorized that as adolescents get older they are deterred from criminal activity by the prospect of apprehension. Social relationships, jobs, and other social benefits are too much to lose; thus, their criminal behavior decreases. According to Greenberg, this is what accounts for the age-crime relationship. In his view, the rela-tionship between age and crime will change from culture to culture, society to society, depending on the economic and political conditions. It will also change across time, as differential values are emphasized.

In his 1985 article, Greenberg not surprisingly disagrees with many of the conclu-sions drawn by Hirschi and Gottfredson. He notes that analyses based on cross-sectional and longitudinal data will generally yield different results. Hirschi and Gottfredson had based their characterization of the link between age distribution and crime exclu-sively on aggregate, age-specific, cross-sectional data and cohort rates. They challenged the heavy reliance on the longitudinal method over the cross-sectional methodology in research on the causation of delinquency. But their argument is not based on whether one method is superior to the other. Instead, they question whether the contributions to our knowledge made by longitudinal studies are really worth their cost in time, effort, and money. "This design has been oversold to criminology at high substantive and economic costs" (1983, p. 582).

Greenberg does not agree. If a time period is necessary for an effect to take place, a cross-sectional design will not be sensitive to these "time-lagged" antecedents, he remarks. Crime rates could be related to economic conditions of several years past. A design examining current economic conditions and crime, such as we find in the usual cross-sectional approach, would not detect this, since cross-sectional designs are partic-ularly insensitive to reciprocal and dynamic relationships. Longitudinal designs, on the other hand, are better suited and more easily applied, especially when the causal ordering of variables is not known. Variables measured simultaneously do not reveal the order of cause.

The Greenberg argument sounds sensible, but it does not account for the fact that the robust relationship between age and crime emerges time after time, culture after culture, society after society. Explanations for this continually emerging relationship are rarely convincing, however. Hirschi and Gottfredson imply that a biological-developmental factor emerges during early adolescent that predisposes the teenager to a tendency to be antisocial or be involved in illegal acts. Cogent evidence for this contention is lacking.

The Hirschi-Gottfredson versus Greenberg debate has captivated contemporary criminologists. Lawrence Cohen and Kenneth Land (1987) tried to shed light on the relationship between age and delinquency by analyzing changes in crime from 1946 through 1984. They studied motor vehicle theft and homicide. Their longitudinal data suggest that the age-crime relationship appears to be bidirectional as opposed to unidirectional. In other words, while age emerged as a very powerful factor (in agreement with Hirschi and Gottfredson), the age effect also appears to be modified over time by criminal opportunities, economic cycles, and imprisonment rates. This finding supports Greenberg's assertion that longitudinal studies provide crucial information, as well as his insistence on the important role of changes in society. Using four variables (age, criminal opportunity, economic cycles, and imprisonment rates), Cohen and Land constructed a model designed to predict further offending patterns. The model predicts a steady decline in motor vehicle thefts and homicides over the next two decades, because there will be a substantial drop in the teenage population. Age structure alone could predict this result. However, Cohen and Land also predict that teenage motor vehicle theft is likely to fluctuate as a result of possible changes in economic cycles and criminal opportunities (e.g., more effective theft-proofing of cars). In contrast, homicide rates, which presumably are less influenced by these structural changes, will remain stable. Cohen and Land also predict that the crime rates will not decline to the low levels reported in the 1950s, even though the age distribution of the young will be similar, because the nature of criminal opportunities will differ significantly from what they were in the 1950s. Cohen and Land obviously have faith in the longitudinal method for detecting shifts and changes in the age-crime relationship, but we will have to wait a few years before deciding whether their model has merit. They do not dispute the persistent configuration of the age distribution, however, nor is it their apparent intent to design an acid test of the age-related tendency to commit crime. Their analyses do emphasize the complexity of that relationship, including its possible bi-directional, interactional nature.

In conclusion, the controversy among criminologists is not whether the age-crime relationship is consistent, but rather whether it is invariant. If it is invariant, as Hirschi and Gottfredson claim, the value of longitudinal studies is lessened. Moreover, invariance would have important implications for policy setting, as the two have illustrated in a recent article on the merit of programs aimed at incapacitating "career criminals" (Gottfredson & Hirschi, 1986). It makes little sense, they say, to target individuals who are making a lifetime career of crime, since they are in the minority; most criminals reduce their involvement as they age.

Charles Tittle (1988) finds the debate over the respective values of longitudinal and cross-sectional data nonresolvable. He argues, ". . . whether longitudinal data are preferred over cross-sectional is something like asking whether hammers or saws are more useful to carpenters. Any overall choice between the two is likely to inhibit progress. Both are useful tools appropriate for specific jobs'' (p. 76). With regard to the age invariance hypothesis itself there is likely to be lively debate for some time to come. The interested reader is encouraged to consult recent commentary on the issue by Blumstein et al. (1988), Gottfredson and Hirschi (1988), Hagan and Palloni (1988), Tittle (1988), and Shavit and Rattner (1988).

RADICAL AND CONFLICT CRIMINOLOGY

David Greenberg's comments about delinquency, previously noted, serve as a good introduction to the radical perspective in criminology, which emerged in the early 1960s as the "new criminology." It soon splintered into diverse, sometimes overlapping schools, which were variously called "Marxist," "left-wing," "critical," and "socialist" perspectives. At the same time, the conflict school of criminology was receiving renewed attention (e.g., Vold, 1958; Dahrendorf, 1959). All of these theoretical approaches defy neat distinctions. While some were "new" compared to mainstream criminology, their foundations were not new, having appeared in the writing and ideas of Karl Marx and Frederick Engels or of earlier theorists who spoke of clashes between cultural groups. Because these theories, especially the radical, reject the role of microsystems in the etiology of crime and concentrate upon the weakness of society, they are excellent examples of the macrosystem approach to crime and delinquency.

The new criminology and the resurgence of interest in conflict theory accompanied the dramatic social upheavals of the 1960s and early 1970s. The widespread civil rights struggle, the intense protest movement against the Viet Nam War, the growing awareness that governments and corporations engaged in exploitation and illegal activity, and the impatience with the gradualism of democratic politics, all precipitated a call for new world-making. Official crime statistics were seen by many, especially by young adults, as ploys and strategies of the powerful to keep other groups under control. Criminal law and law enforcement agencies were said to represent a double standard: The underprivileged and powerless were greeted harshly, while the rich were treated leniently. Reflecting this perspective, one author succinctly titled his book "The Rich Get Richer and the Poor Get Prison" (Reiman, 1984). Some criminologists interpreted the existing theories on crime and delinquency as ". . . predicting too little bourgeois, and too much proletarian criminality" (Taylor, Walton, and Young, 1973, p. 107). The new approach, by contrast, "replaced the concept of blaming the victim with that of blaming the system" (Balkan, Bergen, and Schmidt, 1980, p. 36).

Although the work representing the new criminology is multidimensional, accommodating a variety of differing positions, we will review only the radical perspective and conflict theory, realizing that purists may wish that finer distinctions had been drawn. Keeping these two broad categories separate, however, is difficult enough. There is much ambiguity and overlap between radical and conflict perspectives, and they sometimes seem to meld. According to Thomas Bernard (1981), there are two major reasons for the confusion. First, most American radical criminologists initially considered themselves conflict theorists. In their gradual theoretical transition from conflict to radical views, they blurred the lines between them. Second, even if theorists did not move from one camp to the other, they share some of the same intellectual heritage in the writings of Marx and Engels. Each is strongly rooted in Marxist tradition and its perception of class and group conflicts within society.

Radical Criminology

Karl Marx never said much about crime, and there is some disagreement about what he did say about it. At the least, he implied that crime was the result of class conflict based on economic inequality. He also noted that crime produces occupations, such as police, judges, prosecutors, and prison guards. Moreover, it takes criminals out of the running for jobs in society.

Criminologists of the radical persuasion believe that crime is fundamentally caused by the social order and the bitter struggle between the "haves" (the rich capitalists of the ruling class) and the "have nots" (the working class). Whereas a pure Marxist perspective sees only two classes in society, that which owns the means to production (the bourgeoisie) and that employed in production (the proletariat), many contemporary radicals accept that society is divided into a number of classes and competing groups. Nevertheless, the principal conflict is between the powerful and the powerless. Some writers make note of an intermediate group which, though not possessed of power, is dependent upon the wealth derived from the ruling class for its own survival (Balkan, Berger, and Schmidt, 1980). A store manager, for example, may not himself be "rich," but he supports the economic system because it enables him to achieve a good measure of material goods.

Richard Quinney (1977), an early spokesperson for the radical position of criminology, stated that in a capitalist society the poor and the powerless are forced into crime for survival. "Nearly all crimes among the working class in capitalist society are actually a means of *survival*, an attempt to exist in a society where survival is not assured by other, collective means" (Quinney, 1977, p. 58). Others have discussed the concept of marginalization, which keeps workers never assured of employment. There is in capitalist society a surplus of workers, "an industrial reserve army of labor," that benefits the owners of the means of production and forces others to compete for jobs. This leads to a lack of self-esteem and powerlessness. Recall that Greenberg (1977), discussing juvenile delinquency, referred to consistent pressures on lower class males to fulfill society's role expectations by amassing material goods.

Criminals outside the capitalist class comprise a "lumpenproletariat." Quinney (1977) outlined two types of lumpenproletariat crimes, calling them "crimes of accommodation":

1. predatory crimes and
2. personal crimes.

Predatory crimes, those of a parasitical nature, include burglary, robbery, drug dealing, and prostitution. They are committed by a powerless class desperate to surmount the economic cruelties of capitalism. Thus, predatory crimes are easily explained by the impoverished conditions of the underemployed, the unemployed, and the unemployable (Scheingold, 1984). Personal crimes are violent and usually directed against members of the same class. They include murder, assault, and rape. Personal crimes are pursued by the powerless working class in anger and frustration at being brutalized by the conditions of capitalism. The more dehumanized their lives, the more violent the underclass will be. Radical criminologists note that these serious crimes are destructive to the proletariat; when they prey upon one another, their ability to band together is diminished, and the division between the classes is reinforced. Moreover, fear of personal victimization distracts the attention of the working class away from their oppression by the bourgeoisie (Lynch and Groves, 1986).

In addition to these predatory and personal crimes, the powerless commit a third type, primarily in direct resistance to the capitalist system. Examples are the sabotaging of industrial equipment or even political assassinations. Quinney theorized that these "defensive actions" and "crimes of resistance" by workers would eventually lead to socialist revolution.

Radical criminologists draw attention to actions of the ruling class which may not be defined as crimes according to the criminal code but which cause harm to the fabric of society. These actions are intended to protect and further the accumulation of wealth. They are divided into three categories, economic, political, and social crimes (Scheingold, 1984; Quinney, 1977). *Economic*, or "white collar" crimes, include embezzlement, price-fixing, pollution, fraud, and failure to provide workers with safe working environments or to recall dangerous products or equipment. Note that some of these are now violations of the criminal code, while others involve the rules of regulatory agencies [e.g., the Environmental Protection Agency (EPA)]. *Political* crimes center around government dishonesty or corporate cover-ups of schemes to exploit employees. *Social* crimes include sexism and racism, which are not legally defined as crimes. Even when civil measures are in place to protect individuals (e.g., laws against sexual harassment), they are often ignored by those in power.

According to the radical perspective, the most powerful members of society are the capitalists who control wealth and the methods of production. Because of their power, they are able to write their interests and values into the criminal code and into law in general. Law in this sense is the tool of the capitalist intent upon maintaining control over the worker. Since crime is a by-product of capitalism, radical criminologists believe that the only effective way of ridding society of crime is to do away with capitalism and embrace socialism. Thus, the principal task of radical criminology is to promote the overthrow of the capitalist economic system (Bernard, 1981; Lynch and Groves, 1986). In short, a *radical*—not to be equated with violent—solution is needed.

Radical criminologists do not often concentrate upon juvenile delinquency as distinct from crime in general, since both can be explained by similar factors. Greenberg (1977), however, as we noted, attributed delinquency to the structural position of adolescents and their frustration at not being able to obtain the material goods advertised by society. Balkan, Bergen, and Schmidt (1980) pointed to the role of the school in creating a special population of marginal individuals and cited research indicating that delinquency decreases when schools are not in session. This is similar to the evidence in Chapter 9 that youths may engage in more delinquency before they drop out of school than afterward. Radical criminologists suggest—as did the social ability gang delinquency theories also discussed in Chapter 9—that youths gain support and pride from being members of a group, delinquent or law-abiding. The radical approach differs from earlier perspectives, however, in that it emphasizes the class nature of official response to antisocial activity.

> . . . (W)hen lower-class and minority youths engage in these activities, adults become alarmed about the problem of juvenile gangs. Thus, although school problems and delinquency cut across all social classes, it is primarily disadvantaged youths who are arrested by the police and whose parents cannot pay attorney fees to keep them out of jail or help finance any future college education. (Balkan, Bergen, and Schmidt, 1980, p. 72)

Conflict Criminology

Conflict criminologists do not believe that ridding society of its capitalist economic system and establishing a socialist state will solve the crime problem. According to the conflict perspective, the development of divisions and conflicts among groups and participants is a natural course of events in any society, but especially in those that promote disagreement and debate. These divisions give rise to multiple patterns of values and interests. "Rich people and poor people, blacks and whites, and lawyers and police officers tend to see the world in different ways" (Scheingold, 1984, p. 19). What one group values, others do not, or not to the same degree. Stuart Scheingold put it this way:

> The underlying premise of conflict criminology is that individuals differ from one another in a variety of ways that affect the goals they choose as well as their chances of reaching those goals. People are born into different circumstances and endowed with a wide variety of talents and handicaps, and people tend to be thrown into competition for the scarce resources that society makes available. The competition goes on among individuals and among groups that band together because of things they have in common. People unite because their life chances are similar as a result of their jobs, race, or sex. (Scheingold, 1984, p. 21)

Conflict criminology differs from the radical perspective in that it considers the divisions in society normal and acceptable. Rather than perceiving society as consisting of two basic classes—the powerful and the powerless—it perceives of a pluralistic society producing conflicting interests and values. Because of this, crime is inevitable. To radical criminologists, the principal cause of crime and social conflict is the economic division between the capitalist and the worker. To conflict theorists, it is the clashing of *different* groups with *different* viewpoints, values, and ways of world-making. These interest groups vie for control and power, and in doing so they disparage the values or suppress the activities of other groups.

According to conflict criminology, criminal law and its enforcement is a major source of the conflict among groups within a society. Therefore, explanations for delinquency rates reside principally in the legal process or in how laws are defined and enforced. At any given time the law represents the values and interests of those groups who have been able to muster a majority of power (Bernard, 1981). In time, in a stable, democratic society, another group will attain power and write and enforce laws that best serve their own values and interests. The distribution of delinquency rates, then, will depend on what set of interests and values are being appropriated and promoted by a group at some point in history. The debate over whether or not status offenses should be included in the determination of delinquency is a case in point. For many years, the dominant group (e.g., lawmakers) believed that juveniles who ran away from home or were truant should come under the aegis of the criminal law. In some jurisdictions, decreases in the juvenile delinquency rate reflected a resistance on the part of those lower in the power strata (e.g., law enforcers) to carry out this policy.

Unlike their radical colleagues, conflict criminologists generally take no position on whether any specific action is socially harmful or is a violation of human rights (Bernard, 1981). Furthermore, the conflict perspective does not demand social action on the part of its adherents. "It considers only whether the action is criminalized by the official agencies of social control, and analyzes the power relationships that underlie criminalization . . . It argues only that the distribution of criminalized actions is an inverse function of the distribution of political power" (Bernard, 1981, p. 375). Crime is strictly the result of how it is defined or labeled by the interests and values of those who hold the most power at any point in time. There is nothing intrinsically "moral" or "good" about a pattern of behavior. Bernard observes that the conflict perspective is often found "unpalatable" because of this stance.

SEX AS A STRUCTURE VARIABLE IN DELINQUENCY

As early as 1842, Lambert Adolphe Jacques Quetelet, a Belgian social statistician, noted that arrest data decidedly "favored" males by a four to one margin; that is, four men were arrested for every one woman. Since that time, data have continually indicated that males commit far more crime than females. In fact, males have been so overrepresented in *violent* crimes (approximately a 9 to 1 ratio) for so long that some theorists have suggested that hormonal factors are the most logical explanation for these sex differences (Wilson and Herrnstein, 1985). Juvenile crime statistics show a similar trend, although the male to female ratio diminishes when status offenses are included in the data. Girls, in fact, appear in the runaway statistics more than boys and may be as "incorrigible" as boys, but there is no indication that they are as assaultive. With reference to the male-female differential consistently reported, John Hagan writes, "The correlation of gender with criminal and delinquent behavior was one of the few findings from the beginnings of criminological research that although questioned, never was doubted seriously'' (Hagan, 1987, p. 3). Victimization data (Hindelang, 1979), self-report data (Smith and Visher, 1980), and official data (Steffensmeier, 1978, 1980) all support sex differences in criminality.

Until the late 1960s, most explanations for these differences were based on biological or psychological assumptions about the nature of women, and this ''nature'' invariably had a negative taint (Klein, 1973). Cesare Lombroso (with W. Ferrero) (1895) wrote that women were closer than men to their atavistic origins and were not shrewd enough to commit crime. The women who did, however, were even more evil than men, because they were acting against their ''nature.'' W. I. Thomas (1923) believed that girls were more apt than boys to be *maladjusted* and thus less likely to be accused of rogue-like delinquent behavior. The ''inherent nature'' explanation was perpetuated by Otto Pollak, whose book *The Criminality of Women* was published in 1950. Pollak believed that the gap between male and female offending was an illusion, however. He suspected that women committed as much crime as men but were able to escape detection because of their devious, concealing nature. In addition, women's roles in society made it less likely that their crimes would be detected. For example, as caretakers of children they could commit assaults; as domestic workers, they could steal from their employers. These crimes would seldom be uncovered or reported. Moreover, Pollak argued that when they *were* detected, the male criminal justice system was reluctant to arrest, prosecute, or punish women.

In the mid-1970s, some researchers suggested that some sex differences in criminality would disappear primarily because of the effect of the women's movement (Simon, 1975; Adler, 1975). Others strongly disagreed with these assertions. Today, evidence suggests that the female-male ratios in offending have not changed dramatically. There continue to be gaps between male and female rates, although they are smaller for some offenses, such as drug and status offenses. Darrell Steffensmeier and Rene Hoffman Steffensmeier (1980) combined national arrest statistics with juvenile court, self-report, and field observational data to evaluate the general trends in female delinquency between 1965 and 1975. They reported that, based on these varied sources of data, there had been no increase in female violence or in the traditionally male-dominated gang-related delinquency. ''Generally, females are *not* catching up with males in the commission of violent, masculine, or serious crimes'' (Steffensmeier and Steffensmeier, 1980, p. 80). When status offenses are excluded, female delinquency rates have remained generally unchanged in most offense categories. Smith and Visher (1980), however, noted that the sex difference is smaller for youths than for adults, and suggested that this may reflect shifting sex-role ideologies, which are more salient for the young.

Coramae Mann (1984, p. 7) observes: ''In the past twenty years the arrests of females, according to official data, have not varied by more than five percentage points as a proportion of total arrests.'' This obervation holds for both juveniles and adults, and is especially the case for violent crimes, where males clearly predominate. Mann adds that any slight increases that have occurred for women and girls are almost entirely in the area of larceny-theft.

It seems clear on the basis of our present knowledge that the persistent sex differential continues, particularly for serious offenses. Moreover, this relationship holds for both adults and juveniles, provided status offenses are controlled for in the latter group. After a comprehensive review of the literature Nagel and Hagan (1983) concluded, "Female crime rates remain, in absolute terms, far below those for men" (p. 94). The next step is to explain why this differential might exist.

As we have seen, some early explanations of the gap between male and female offending rates focused on unsupported assumptions about the nature of women or upon differential treatment by the criminal justice system. Most theories of criminology, however, did not try to explain male-female differences. In fact, most theories ignored female delinquency and crime altogether. They were formulated almost entirely on the basis of data about the behavior of boys, particularly lower class boys. One explanation for this is that, since girls simply do not violate the law very much, there is no need to develop theory on such a small group. Another explanation: It was assumed that the causal factors identified for boys would apply to girls as well. Eileen Leonard (1982), however, systematically reviewed each of the major theories in criminology—with the inexplicable exception of Hirschi's social control theory—and concluded that none satisfactorily explains female crime or delinquency.

In Chapter 9, we encountered research by developmental psychologists which might shed light on sex differences in juvenile offending. Specifically, research by Eleanor Maccoby (1986) suggests that girls and boys learn different types of prosocial behavior, with girls accommodating to others more than boys. The current work of cognitive psychologists suggests that there *may* be socialized differences in the way girls and boys construct their worlds. Social learning theorists have long held that girls are "socialized" differently than boys, or taught not to be aggressive. Meda Chesney-Lind (1986), however, suggests that the sex differential may represent the greater control exerted by parents over their daughters than their sons. Other explanations have focused upon different role orientations of males and females. It is hypothesized that a masculine orientation—in either a male or female—is more likely to be associated with criminality than a feminine one. Support for this explanation is weak, however. In the following pages, we will address in more detail two additional approaches to explaining sex differences in criminal offending, the *social control* theory of Travis Hirschi (1969) introduced in Chapter 8, and John Hagan's (1986) *power-control* theory of delinquency.

Social Control Theory and the Gender Differential

To review briefly, Hirschi (1969) maintained that conformity is achieved through the crystallization of a bond between a child and society. Four elements make up that bond: belief, attachment, commitment, and involvement. The four elements usually work in some combination, and additively: The more elements involved, the stronger the bond. Hindelang (1973) and Jensen and Eve (1976) attempted to test control theory's ability to explain sex differences in delinquency. "Compared to boys, girls are typically depicted as more closely bound to conventional persons, values, and institutions, and such sex differences in attachment, commitment, involvement and belief should, according to control theory, lead to a sex-differential in delinquent behavior" (Jensen and Eve,

1976, p. 433). While social control theory assumes that both males and females have equal *tendencies* to deviate, girls are assumed to conform to societal expectations more than boys because society presumably makes a special attempt to bond girls to parents, social institutions, and values. This suggests that if an adolescent girl is to engage in delinquency, her bond to society must be weakened to a greater extent than would be necessary for an adolescent boy. Hindelang (1973) and Jensen and Eve (1976) found only mild support for the "weak-bond" premise. Other research has noted that girls do not report stronger bonds to their parents than do boys (Cantner, 1981).

Jill Rosenbaum (1987) reported on a comprehensive attempt to test social control theory's power to explain sex differences. She collected data from a self-report questionnaire administered to over 1,600 adolescents living in Seattle between 1977 and 1979. For comparison purposes, three groups of adolescents were delineated:

1. adolescents in Seattle high schools who did not have police or juvenile court records;
2. adolescents who had police records but not juvenile court records; and
3. adolescents who had both police and juvenile court records.

Rosenbaum concentrated on three different forms of delinquency: drug, property, and violent offenses. The independent variables, all measured by questionnaire items, were social class (as determined by father's occupation and education); attachment to peers; attachment to school; commitment to conventional activities; and involvement in conventional activities.

Rosenbaum found that social control theory was better at explaining the relatively minor offenses and drug violations than it was for explaining either property or violent offenses. In fact, the theory did not account for violent offenses at all. Rosenbaum believes that the theory has considerable promise as an explanation for "common delinquency," but that something other than bonding is needed to account for violence. Research by Marvin Krohn and James Massey (1980) also suggests that social control theory has the power to explain less serious delinquency for both sexes.

More relevant to our present discussion, Rosenbaum found that social control theory was better at explaining *female* than male delinquency across all offenses. This finding was especially strong for upper middle class female drug offending. Interestingly, drug use for all socioeconomic classes was associated strongly with dating. Specifically, girls who dated more often were more apt to use drugs. Furthermore, they were less attached to their parents and to school and less committed to conventional activities. Thus, Rosenbaum hypothesizes that girls whose bonds to parents and school are weak date more and also are more likely to use drugs.

She concludes, however, that social control theory leaves much delinquency unaccounted for, especially that associated with violent offenses. Furthermore, the theory does not account for sex differences in other serious offenses. However, it has some explanatory power with reference to minor juvenile offending. There is some indication, also, that it might better account for male-female differentials at the middle or upper classes than at the lower class. In sum, social control theory continues to present a viable framework to use in searching for the causes of delinquency, but it is in need of considerable elaboration.

Hagan's Power-Control Theory

John Hagan (1987) observes that although social class and sex are widely studied as correlates of delinquency, the two seldom been been studied in combination. He and his colleagues (Hagan, Simpson, and Gillis, 1987; Hagan, Gillis, and Simpson, 1985) have formulated a theory which tries to account for both the complicated relationship between social class and delinquency and the more consistent relationship between sex and delinquency. To Hagan, social class is a dimension largely dependent upon the *nature* of one's occupation. Hagan notes that some occupations are managerial in nature, while others require an individual to take orders and be under supervision most of the working day. According to Hagan, persons in jobs with authority constitute the *command class* and those with little or no authority comprise the *obey class*. "Members of the *command class* exercise authority, regardless of whether they are subject to it themselves. . . . (P)ersons in the *obey* class are subject to the authority of others and exercise none themselves" (Hagan et al., 1987, p. 795). Ralf Dahrendorf (1959), whose writings influenced Hagan's theory, stated that the term "authority" is associated with social positions or roles, and that the person in authority has legitimate power over others because of an earned or appointed position. Obviously, members of the command class are at a discernibly higher social status in the workplace than members of the obey class.

Hagan's basic premise is that authority in the workplace is related to power in the household. Before discussing this more fully, we need to review basic family "power" structures described in his theory.

Power-control theory divides families along a continuum of child-rearing styles. At the poles are two ideal types: patriarchal and egalitarian. The theory predicts that child-rearing styles (the home's power structure) are partly determined by the nature of the parent's work. Thus, the theory attempts to make cross-level inferences, considering both a microsystem (the family) and an exosystem (parent's place of work). In Hagan's words (1987, p. 788), "The theory brings together a macro-level consideration of class in the work place with a micro-level analysis of gender differences in the parental control and delinquent behavior of adolescents" (1987, p. 788).

Six variants in family structure are then identified, based upon parent's work (see Table 10-1). The *patriarchal* family is characterized by a two-parent household where the husband is employed in an authority position (manager or employer) and the wife remains in the home and assumes most of the child-rearing responsibilities. In essence, the husband is in the command class and the wife is in the obey class. Hence, the home adheres to traditional sex roles where the man is boss and the woman is subservient. This kind of home, Hagan tells us, exerts strict control over its daughters, and it is the mother who does most of the day-to-day controlling. Hagan theorizes that patriarchal

TABLE 10-1 POWER RELATIONS IN THE WORKPLACE OF PARENTS

Wife's authority in workplace	Husband's authority in workplace	
	Has Authority	Has No Authority
Has Authority	Both parents in command class (prototype of Egalitarian Household)	Husband in obey class and wife in command class
Has no Authority	Husband in command class and wife in obey class (prototype of Patriarchal Household)	Husband and Wife in obey class
Not Employed	Husband in command class and wife not employed	Husband in obey class and wife not employed

homes cultivate girls who are unwilling to take risks and reluctant to engage in forms of misconduct. They are usually prepared for a life of domestic tranquillity. Patriarchal parents believe that girls have to be watched and controlled, but that boys can be allowed to ''be boys.'' Therefore, the delinquency rate differential will be most pronounced in adolescents of patriarchal families, with boys offending at their normal (or even higher) rates but controlled girls demonstrating little delinquency.

In the egalitarian family, both parents work in authority positions outside the home. In Hagan's terms, this situation represents the high command class or highest status class. The egalitarian family prepares its daughters for professional or authority work positions. The authority the mother has in the workplace translates to an increase of control-power in the family. As mothers gain power relative to fathers, daughters gain freedom relative to sons. In these egalitarian families, there is reduced control by both parents and an increased willingness to take risks on the part of the adolescent girl. Willingness to take risks, Hagan believes, is a fundamental requirement for delinquency. The egalitarian home environment cultivates daughters who are most likely to engage in various kinds of misconduct. Hagan predicts that as women join the labor force in increasing numbers, the delinquency rates for girls should increase. Therefore, it is the egalitarian home which is most apt to close the gap between male and female offending.

The gap should be greatest in situations where the father has authority at his workplace and the mother is unemployed. It should also be wide, but slightly less so, when the father has authority and the mother works, but is in an obey class situation. The fact of working allows the mother to gain some power relative to the father, but not as much as she would were she in a high status job. In contrast, as just noted, the gap should be smallest in situations where both parents share power, such as in the ideal egalitarian household. Hagan does not attempt to make predictions for the other three household styles.

Hagan also predicts that female juvenile offending will be unusually high in mother-only homes. His reasoning behind this seemingly contradictory prediction is as follows: The primary reason for the differential offending rests with the amount of power exerted by the *father* within the home. Anything that reduces or weakens that power will allow the adolescent girl more freedom, a greater likelihood to take risk, and ultimately an increased tendency to deviate. Furthermore, the continued absence of one supervising (or controlling) parent increases the adolescent girl's freedom. Therefore, the male-female gap in delinquency will *decrease* as divorce and separation rates rise and as the number of single-parent homes *increases*.

The theory is so new that it is just beginning to be tested. However, it can be criticized on the same grounds as earlier theories which blamed women's liberation for increases in crimes committed by women—and which were discredited. We would argue, furthermore, that a home in which both parents have power should be *less* conducive to delinquency in either sons or daughters. Moreover, even if egalitarian homes encourage risk taking, boys are just as likely to do this as girls. In that sense, the delinquent behavior of both sexes would increase. If it has explanatory power, Hagan's theory would appear—like social control theory—to be most applicable to "common" or non-serious delinquency. Hagan's own research supports this observation. Craig Little (1987) believes the theory is useful for explaining sex differences in the minor, relatively frequent delinquency that is annoying but not serious. Little suggests (1987, p. 15) that Hagan's theory is actually a "structural theory of gender socialization" rather than a power-control theory of delinquency. In fact, the terms "power" and "control" are elusive, although Hagan tries to distinguish between them. He seems to reserve "control" for the relationships in the workplace and "power" for relationships of domination within the family. Still, it is difficult to understand when control in the workplace becomes power in the home and vice versa. Without more precise definition of terms, the theory will be limited by its conceptual vagueness.

Recently, Gary Hill and Maxine Atkinson (1988) addressed a key process proposed by Hagan's power-control theory. They tested the proposition that boys and girls are subjected to different parental expectations and levels of control for their behavior. In short, they wanted to find out if girls are subject to more family control than boys. Data were collected through SR surveys of approximately 3,000 youths, ages 14 to 18 years. Hill and Atkinson found that, while there was some evidence to suggest that girls were more likely the object of family control, the main differences were in the type of control rather than the degree. Boys reported more emotional support from their fathers along with rules regarding appearance (e.g., "In your home, are there any rules about the way you dress or wear your hair?"), while girls reported emotional support from mothers along with curfew rules ("In your home, are there any rules for you about weeknight curfews?"). In fact, paternal support and appearance rules were more likely to inhibit common or minor delinquency in males, while maternal support and curfew rules were more likely to curb common delinquency in females.

In summary, both Hirschi's social control theory and Hagan's power-control theory may account for male-female differences in common or minor juvenile offending. We are still at a loss, however, to explain sex differences in serious delinquency, where the gap is most pronounced. Overall, there remains a *critical* shortage of contemporary research and theory, especially on this form of female delinquency.

SUMMARY AND CONCLUSIONS

At the higher and more encompassing level of analysis introduced in this chapter, terms, concepts and debates become less concrete and more difficult to conceptualize. Take social structure, for example. "As used by sociologists, 'structure' seems to refer first to those aspects of social behavior that the investigator considers relatively enduring or persistent" (Homans, 1975, p. 53). A wide variety of "things" may be relatively enduring, however. These include social institutions with their roles and rules, or certain distributions of the population—age, sex, social class. Generally, social scientists use "social structure" to mean—in George C. Homans' words (p. 54)—"some kind of social whole" which can be divided conceptually into interdependent parts. Nevertheless, the concept remains abstract and ambiguous.

The relationship between class and delinquency is not only ambiguous but also full of controversy. Research suggests that chronic and serious juvenile offenders are more likely to come from lower class backgrounds than occasional and nonserious juvenile offenders, but explanations for this phenomenon vary widely. The relationship by no means should be interpreted as low social class *causes* delinquency. There are simply too many factors subsumed under the rubric for us to draw such dogmatic conclusions. The relationship between age and delinquency is strong and persistent, and the connection between sex and delinquency is only slightly less so. In neither case do criminologists agree on explanations or on how these relationships develop. Some believe, for example, that girls are supervised more closely than boys, while others believe that girls "think differently." Some believe youthful offenders are responding to hormonal changes, while others assert that as they get older, they have more to lose by breaking the law.

The modern ecological approach demands a wider and more sophisticated sweep of the matrix of possible factors in the development and maintenance of delinquency. Statistics and statistical techniques of enormous complexity and potential have become tools of the trade. We briefly described the fundamental zero-order correlations and partial correlations, and mentioned some other statistical methods. Path analysis is also virtually indispensable in the research for causal factors of delinquency. It was developed by Sewall Wright in 1934 as a method for analyzing the direct and indirect effects of variables believed to be causes (Pedhazur, 1982). Path analysis can be particularly useful in analyzing causal relationships among variables over a prolonged period of time. The method does *not* establish cause; it simply helps the researcher confirm or disconfirm his or her hypotheses about causal relationships. For example, a researcher might hypothesize that delinquency can be explained by class, sex, the percentage of single parent families, percentage of school dropouts, percentage of absentee landlords, and school performance. He or she creates a model or diagram representing these links on a chain of influences and then tests this model, determining both the weight and direction of each variable in relation to the others. In recent years path analysis has been refined to allow researchers to examine data across time and across levels of analysis.

All three of the empirically confirmed relationships discussed in this chapter—

delinquency and social class, age, and sex—illustrate the importance of studying social structure. Clearly, social structure variables are invaluable benchmarks for focusing research attention. However, social structure by itself is not enough. If we concentrate at only one level of analysis, we will lose sight of the underlying processes and interplay of systems. Both the interactionist approach discussed in Chapter 9 (Thornberry, 1987) and John Hagan's power-control theory (1987), try to account for these processes, and each is likely to stimulate research and lively discussion.

Higher Level Systems: Community Networks and Processes

11 CHAPTER

Network analysis was developed primarily as a strategy for examining the nature of relationships within a group. At the end of Chapter 9, however, we noted that an implicit theory is at the root of the analysis itself; the more extensive and varied one's personal networks, the greater the commitment toward the conventional thinking of the total social network. Put another way, the more extensive and varied one's associations, the greater the pressure to abide by the social network's expectations. It is important not to forget, however, that we often select and to some extent influence our personal networks.

Network analysis—both as an analytic strategy and as a theory—can serve as a bridge between different levels of explanations. This chapter will illustrate this, beginning with the work of Marvin D. Krohn, who has refined network analysis and, in the process, made more explicit its theoretical potential. We will also examine how Krohn applies his modification specifically to delinquency. Next, we will discuss the neighborhood and community as macrosystems and review current research focusing on the *processes* of these higher systems. Within this context, we include some discussions of chronosystems. We conclude the chapter with a brief sketch of comparative criminology, a field that studies the broadest macrosystem. For illustration purposes, we will concentrate on Japan, because it exemplifies an industralized, modern society with an exceedingly low crime rate (compared to the United States) and a complex system of social networks and community involvement.

KROHN'S REFINEMENT AND APPLICATION OF NETWORK ANALYSIS THEORY

Marvin D. Krohn (1986) has proposed a promising theory of delinquency with considerable potential for explaining it across neighborhoods, cultures, and even nations. Called *network analysis theory*, it has its roots in the work of Georg Simmel (1922) and, generally, cultural anthropology.

Krohn's version of network theory, though not one which seeks integration, incorporates observations made by both Hirschi and Sutherland. Krohn agrees with Hirschi that an adolescent's belief in and conformity to conventional norms is dependent upon his or her attachment to people and institutions. The Hirschi theory suggests that these links are additive: The more links the adolescent has, the stronger will be the bonds to conventional society. If the links are weakened or broken, the adolescent is released from constraints, and this increases the chances that he or she will slip into delinquency. Krohn notes that while Hirschi's theory has received modest empirical support (e.g., Hindelang, 1973; Krohn and Massey, 1980; Krohn et al., 1983; Wiatrowski et al., 1981), it clearly does not adequately explain the causes of delinquency. The *interactions* adolescents have with their peers, families, and the community at large are also crucial. Thus, Krohn accepts the contentions of Sutherland that behavior is learned through associations with significant others in the social environment.

Four concepts are at the root of network theory: *social network*, *personal network*, *multiplexity*, and *density*. Social network refers to sets of *groups* or *organizations* linked by the web of social relationships, such as friendships or memberships. It describes the structure and relationships among aggregates of people. As such, it has many of the features found in Bronfenbrenner's exosystems and macrosystems. Personal network refers specifically to the *participant* and the links that he or she has with other people. In many ways, this level is similar to the individual system, microsystems, and mesosystems. Personal networks refer to those social relationships experienced by a participant, whereas social networks refers to a *set* of social relationships among social groups and organizations. A simple strategy for determining a personal network is to ask a person to list all the units or individuals to which he or she is "linked," or associated. Identification of a social network, on the other hand, would require asking randomly selected samples of participants to list the units or individuals to which they are linked. Any number of ways may be employed to construct the social network—surveys, interviews, observations.

Network multiplexity refers to the number of contexts (microsystems) in which the *same* people interact jointly. For example, the extent to which people go to school together, work together, go to church together, party together, or even live in the same neighborhood, reflects network multiplexity. As we discussed in Chapter 9, multiplexity of social relationships fosters consistency in behavior and individual conformity. A person who interacts with the same people in different settings (microsystems) knows that the way he or she acts in one will affect how others expect him or her to behave in another. "Thus, multiplexity in social relationships is likely to constrain the individual's behavior" (Krohn, 1986, p. 83).

Inappropriate behavior in one microsystem may have adverse effects on participation in another, however. Becoming drunk, hostile, and offensive at the office party may have adverse consequences for the individual when promotion time comes and may even extend to his or her standing in the community or within the local church group or social club. For the gang member, betraying friends under pressure is apt to promote dire consequences within the microsystem of the gang.

Krohn hypothesizes that the greater the number of contexts (such as family, church, schools, clubs, or other activities) in which there is network multiplexity, the lower the probability of delinquent behavior. In other words, youths who participate together in a number of conventional activities are less likely to engage in serious, antisocial delinquency. He observes that Hirschi's theory is restrictive because it concentrates primarily on the degree of adolescent attachment to parents. Krohn's network theory expands the explanation beyond the family context. In fact, he suggests that the concept of multiplexity can be extended to describe relationships at even higher levels of social aggregation, such as among neighborhoods, cities, and society as a whole (all relationships which he calls "social units"). "In general, social units with higher levels of multiplexity will constrain behavior more than those with less multiplexity" (Krohn, 1986, p. 84). Put another way, those neighborhoods whose residents demonstrate high levels of multiplexity will show lower rates of delinquency. Homogeneous neighborhoods where the members have similar values and participate in activities together, such as we might find in ethnic neighborhoods, should show low rates of delinquency, compared to more heterogeneous neighborhoods. Multiplexity may also help explain the lower rates of delinquency in countries like Japan and Switzerland.

Network density refers to the extent to which individuals in a particular social network (or social system) are connected by direct relationships or ties, or the extent to which they know and interact with one another directly. Density answers the question, "How well do the inhabitants of a particular neighborhood know one another and talk to one another?" It does not refer simply to the *number* of contacts within a certain social group. Network density is usually measured as the *ratio* of actual social ties in a network to the maximum number of possible ties. A social network reaches maximum density when everyone knows one another, such as we might find in a small town. In this case, the behavior of each town member is potentially subject to the reactions of *all* town members. Under these conditions of maximum network density, the behavior of all the members will be under close scrutiny and maximum constraint. Therefore, we would expect the delinquency rate in isolated rural towns to be very low because of the very high network density.

Moreover, "There is a possibility that personal network density and social network density interact to produce different behavioral outcomes in different contexts" (Krohn, 1986, p. 85). That is, high density networks at one ". . . level of aggregation may inhibit the formation of social networks at a larger aggregate" (p. 85). Put differently, density at one level of a system may inhibit the formation of dense social networks at higher levels. If a group of people know one another well and are close interpersonally, they may see themselves as self-sufficient, with little need to develop networks beyond their circle of friends and relatives. They may even view outside systems as infringements upon their own network. While behavior within their group may be constrained, the group's behavior in the larger context of other systems may not be so constrained. Hence, a group of boys who develop a network may feel little need or social pressure to constrain their behavior to the expectations of a larger network, such as the school environment or the community.

It is clear from the available ecological research that the rate of crime and delinquency in urban areas is significantly greater than the rate in suburban or rural areas (Krohn et al., 1984; Lylerly and Skipper, 1981; Toby, 1979). Krohn suggests that this may be due to population density, an important structural component of a community or neighborhood. He hypothesizes that as *population* density increases, *network* density will decrease. Remember that network density is measured by the *ratio* of the number of people members of a social area know and interact with, over the number of the *potential* people to know and interact with within that area. As population density increases, the number of potential contacts also increases. Since it is not likely that the individual will interact with everyone, however, network density in a high population area is apt to be low. Krohn assumes—logically—that there is a limit to the number of people with whom a person can maintain social relationships. Since *network density* increases constraints on behavior, it follows that as population increases, the rate of delinquent behavior will increase.

Both self-report and official data indicate a positive relationship between population density and both crime and delinquency. However, it is also clear that this relationship will hold up only to a certain point. At that point further increases in population will not affect the already high delinquency rate. As the population density of an area goes up, delinquency rates will correspondingly go up in a linear fashion. It is expected that the delinquency rate will reach a saturation point so further increases in population density will have little effect on the rate (Roncek, 1975).

A large population also provides for the expression of widely diverse interests. This increases the number of contexts or systems around which social networks can be developed. As the number of potential contexts increases in a given area, the proportion of social relationships that are multiplex will decrease. Thus, Krohn hypothesizes that as the diversity of interests and potential contexts increases, it follows that delinquency will also increase.

A number of other predictions can be made from network theory. There is some evidence to suggest that people who live in houses are more likely to have local social relationships than people who live in apartments (Fischer et al., 1977). This is especially true for multiple family units, where it becomes difficult to know a high ratio of one's neighbors. "Therefore, I would expect there to be a lower social network density and multiplexity in communities having a high proportion of multiple-family housing and, hence, a higher rate of delinquent behavior" (Krohn, 1986, p. 87).

A high rate of residential mobility also changes the complexion of an area, as we have seen from the pioneer work of Shaw and McKay and others. When residents move often, it is difficult for members of the community to get to know one another or to establish social networks. Therefore, we can expect that areas of considerable residential turnover will have high rates of delinquency. Countries with low levels of residential mobility—e.g., Switzerland—can be expected to show low levels of delinquency (Clinard, 1978).

Krohn further reminds us that limited financial resources make it difficult for individuals of lower SES to participate in volunteer and other community-oriented organizations (e.g., parent-teacher organizations, church groups, family activities) within their locale. There may be many reasons for this, including a need to work longer hours, work nights, or feelings of not being accepted by the community. For this reason, lower SES families will be less involved in microsystems within which to develop multiplex relations than middle or upper SES groups. Krohn also supposes that lower SES juveniles are less likely to participate in extracurricular activities than their middle and upper SES peers. Thus, the social networks of lower SES juveniles are apt to be less extensive (multiplex). The range of constraints on their behavior will be limited and the probability of delinquent involvement increased.

ROLE RELATIONSHIP THEORY

In 1976 Paul C. Friday and Jerald Hage launched a theory that has interesting parallels to network theory and, to some extent, systems theory in general. Friday and Hage's *role relationship theory* may be applied across cultures and across levels of explanation. It posits that to understand delinquency, we must consider five "patterns of role relationships" which play a key role in the socialization and integration of youth into society. To avoid confusion and to coordinate Friday and Hage's theory with the theme of this chapter, we will refer to "patterns of role relationships" as "social networks."

The five social networks, then, are:

1. kin relations, including the extended family;
2. community or neighborhood;
3. school;
4. work; and
5. peers not otherwise included in the four other networks.

Friday and Hage postulated that delinquency depends on the extent to which a person is enmeshed into these five social networks. The more enmeshed, the lower the probability of delinquent behavior. Friday and Hage see the five social networks as interconnected, in somewhat the same way Bronfenbrenner talks about mesosystems. The stronger the links among the social network systems, the lower the delinquency and general tendency to deviate from society's norms. Therefore, it is not so much a matter of whether a youth lives in a ghetto or has unemployed parents, but rather how well that youth is worked into the social network of a society.

Two other concepts are crucial in the Friday-Hage model: the *number* of relationships and the "intimacy" of those relationships. A person may have a large number of relationships within a single network or a large number within different networks. Role relationship theory implies that many relationships within different networks—network diversity—are likely to ward off delinquency. The more diverse the youth's contacts with family, school, work, peers, and community, the less the likelihood of deviance. In this sense, role relationship theory emphasizes the interrelationships and interactions across all five networks rather than just one, as many traditional theories of delinquency have done. For example, Hirschi has focused upon the importance of the family, school, and peers. Role relationship theory expands the network into other areas, across different levels of network systems. Furthermore, it stresses the frequency of interactions (behaviors), rather than abstract attitudes and beliefs.

"Intimacy" in Friday and Hage's theory refers to the nature or quality of the relationships. In other words, what matters is not simply the number of relationships or passing acquaintances a youth has within the five networks, but rather the closeness or significance of those relationships.

> The general hypothesis then becomes that *if youth have intimate role relationships in all five areas or kinds, they are much less likely to engage in youth crime.* Or, to put this more dynamically, as the intimacy declines both within certain areas and across all of them, the youth is less integrated into society and more likely to be involved in various kinds of crime. (Friday and Hage, 1976, p. 350)

Like Krohn's network analysis theory, role relationship theory suggests that integration into the family, the school, work, friendship circles, and the community constrain toward conformity. The more socially isolated and unintegrated the youth, the greater the tendency toward deviation. Delinquency, then, arises among youths who are alienated because of being outside much of the social system.

Friday and Hage attributed increases in delinquency in many countries throughout the world to industrialization. Growing needs for skilled and educated workers restrict opportunities for many adolescents, particularly those youths who drop out of school, to become integrated into society. Friday and Hage contended that many youths of today are precluded from integration into society by virtue of their age, talents, and skills. Feeling alienated and cut off from social networks, they gravitate to youth gangs who become a barrier for further opportunities and interactions with other networks.

Industrialization also encourages residential mobility, with skilled, trained, or professional workers constantly on the move to better and different jobs. High residential mobility undercuts neighborhood stability, an important ingredient for informal control of deviant or delinquent activity. Residential mobility also diminishes the chances for community members to develop meaningful and extensive networks within the community.

Although the Friday-Hage model did not draw much interest nor generate research testing, this seeming lack of interest should not be interpreted as evidence of poor theory. Research and scholarly interest also depend on the inclinations of the criminology community at the time a theory is formulated. Stephen Cole (1975) wrote that ". . . the acceptance or rejection of a theory is not primarily dependent on empirical evidence. It is dependent on the way the theory fits in with the other interests of the community of scientists and the ability of the theory to fulfill what might be called its 'functional requirements' '' (Cole, 1975, p. 212).

It may be time for theories or hypotheses that advance arguments which can be applied across levels of explanations. These theories may well receive increased attention by criminologists in the years ahead. This is not to advocate integration of the wide assortment of theories of delinquency proposed over the past 50 years. On the contrary, it is important to keep in mind that each theory is a statement about how one or more persons view the world. Theories are constructions seen from different perspectives and construct systems and built upon different assumptions. These ways of viewing the world would be difficult, if not impossible, to integrate without distorting or damaging the original statements. On the other hand, Krohn and Friday and Hage have made provocative and heuristic proposals from a different perspective than those of traditional theories of criminology. They are offered here as frameworks for the research which will be reviewed in the remainder of this chapter.

NEIGHBORHOOD AND COMMUNITY SYSTEMS

In recent years there has been a resurgence of interest in the role of the neighborhood or the community in preventing and controlling criminal activity (e.g., *Communities and Crime* edited by Albert J. Reiss, Jr. and Michael Tonry; *Social Ecology of Crime* edited by James M. Byrne and Robert J. Sampson). Traditionally, ecological studies examined geographic or demographic correlates of delinquency at one point in time and did not consider the dynamic processes underlying such distributions (Bursik and Webb, 1982). Thus, important differences between static and process factors were lost in the interpretation of empirical results. According to Bursik and Webb (1982) if such cross-sectional data are to be used as a basis of generalization, researchers must at least be mindful of the ever-changing processes within the community before drawing conclusions. Note that this is similar to the current controversy discussed in Chapter 10 regarding longitudinal and cross-sectional studies using age as an independent variable. Just as many criminologists believe longitudinal research is essential when individual level variables are studied, many also believe longitudinal procedures are necessary when examining macrolevel variables. Communities "age" and change, they deteriorate or are gentrified, industries move in and they fold. Each of these processes has an effect on crime and delinquency.

To underscore this point, Bursik and Webb analyzed the changes in male delinquency rates in relation to changes in ecological processes. Four demographic variables were examined in 74 areas of Chicago which corresponded roughly to areas studied by Shaw and McKay. The researchers examined data from the census years 1940, 1950, 1960, and 1970. The variables were

1. population;
2. percentage of foreign-born whites;

3. percentage of nonwhites; and

4. levels of household density (the percentage of households with over one person per room).

Delinquency was measured by the number of referrals to the Chicago Juvenile Court per 1000 males between the ages of 10 and 17.

In their analysis of changes from 1940 to 1950, Bursik and Webb discovered that ecological change was not related to changes in delinquency rates. This was consistent with the repeated finding of the Shaw-McKay investigations that delinquency was confined to specified areas and was not affected by the coming and going of their inhabitants. This finding had prompted Shaw and McKay to formulate their "cultural transmission hypothesis," which states that delinquent values are passed on among the children in specified neighborhoods, even if populations within the area are constantly coming and going.

Bursik and Webb's analysis of the changes between 1950 and 1960, and again between 1960 and 1970, seriously questioned the cultural transmission hypothesis, however. During those decades, the stability of the neighborhoods (social networks) strongly correlated with the rates of delinquency. When neighborhoods were stable, as defined by low residential mobility, the delinquency rates dropped correspondingly. The Bursik-Webb results suggest that until the social networks and informal social support systems are crystallized, we can expect high rates of delinquency within a neighborhood. Bursik and Webb, in effect, suggest that when social networks are stable, delinquency will be dramatically reduced.

The results of the Bursik and Webb analysis should keep us mindful of two things. First, Shaw and McKay worked within a specific historical context and based their interpretation on a model of ecological processes that has changed substantially over the past three or four decades. Based on the nature of their data, they may have been justified in making their conclusions. Second, cross-sectional studies cannot capture the dynamic changes of neighborhoods or communities. Static structural analysis is very helpful for evaluating the characteristics of a particular community at a specific point in time. Conclusions based on these data must consider chronosystems and the likely impact of change on all components of the social system. Currently, many criminologists are turning to "time series analysis," a research method which specifically enables them to take into account these changes over time. Monitoring trends and ecological changes across time allows investigators to draw better diagrams of the multicausal flow of events associated with any phenomenon, including delinquency.

Neighborhood Changes: Chronosystems

Most neighborhoods are fairly stable social systems for a period of years (Skogan, 1986). Although they are always changing, they do so very slowly unless change is triggered by an unexpected series of events which propels the neighborhood into demographic and

economic flux and instability. While numerous events can trigger neighborhood instability, Wesley Skogan (1986) identifies four factors that have major influence:

1. disinvestment;
2. demolition and construction;
3. demagoguery; and
4. deindustrialization.

The quality and appearance of a neighborhood depends partly on the decisions of
landlords and homeowners to repair and maintain their property. When homeowners do
not invest time or money, physical deterioration begins to set in. Once this happens,
other powerful and influential interests (such as mortgaging institutions and insurance
companies) lose faith in an area, which serves as a warning to others that the neighborhood is "going." This process describes *disinvestment*.

Even before the pioneering studies of Shaw and McKay neighborhood physical
deterioration was linked to crime and delinquency. Physical deterioration communicates
that residents feel helpless, ineffective, or simply do not care. Overgrown or cluttered
vacant lots, littered streets, stripped and abandoned cars, and boarded up buildings, are
all closely associated with high crime in urban settings. In these same neighborhoods,
bands of teenagers, public drunkenness, street prostitution, open gambling, and drug use
soon become prevalent. "Just as unrepaired broken windows in buildings may signal
that nobody cares and lead to additional vandalism and damage, so untended disorderly
behavior (drunks, gangs, prostitutes, pan handling, remarks to passers-by) may also
communicate that nobody cares . . . and thus lead to increasingly aggressive criminal
and dangerous predatory behavior" (Kelling, 1987, p. 93).

It is a common belief that crime causes deterioration: Many criminologists believe
it is the other way around. Richard Taub and his colleagues noted that the relationship
is not unidirectional and that other factors may be more relevant. "(T)he presence of
deterioration and crime together does not necessarily mean that one caused the other.
Nor does it mean that causal relations only go one way. Deterioration could either cause
crime or create the conditions that allow crime to flourish. Arson by property owners is
one dramatic example" (Taub et al., 1984, p. 1).

The quality of a neighborhood is also strongly affected by land use patterns. Skogan (1986) notes that freeways built during the 1950s tore through the hearts of low
income, minority neighborhoods where land was cheaper and easier to pry loose from
owners. These road networks were extremely destructive to neighborhoods and their
sense of community. They not only consumed land, but they also created rigid boundaries between communities, dramatically decreased land values, and lowered the overall
appeal and attractiveness of neighborhoods. This is what Skogan means by *demolition
and construction*. Another example is the tearing down of older homes in favor of high
rise, low-income apartment complexes. While the original intentions may have been
laudable, they were short-sighted. They had unintended consequences of de-stabilizing
neighborhoods and destroying whatever social networks had existed therein. There is

clearly nothing well-meaning, however, in the appropriation of neighborhoods by investors and the subsequent displacement of the residents without any provision for alternative housing. In any event, high rise, impersonal buildings that jam low-income residents together and isolate them from the streets below do little to cultivate closeness and concern for the neighborhood.

Albert J. Reiss, Jr. (1986) also notes how federal legislation, the administration of federal programs, and judicial decisions can adversely affect the physical, moral, and social order of communities. "These changes often are incremental, and their cumulative effects can ultimately destroy the integrity of communities as viable collectivities to control the behavior of their inhabitants" (Reiss, 1986, p. 20). As an illustration, Reiss describes the redevelopment process in Boston's West End, a project which virtually eliminated the village as a viable social system. ". . . (C)ommunities have a delicate balance of moral and social integration that rarely survives rapid change," he notes (Reiss, 1986, p. 20).

Anthony Bottoms and Paul Wiles (1986) scrutinize the important process of how residents get into a residential area in the first place, a point often neglected by ecologically oriented criminologists. Bottoms and Wiles, basing their conclusions on a study of British public housing communities, found that national housing plans and policies can have dramatic effects on an area's crime statistics. These policies may help to maintain the stability of crime rates in particular communities, increase the rate, or even reduce the rate. More specifically, these British researchers were interested in how the allocation and housing policies of the local public housing authority can affect the crime rates within certain areas of the community. They found that similar housing areas, even when matched for social class, ethnic origin, age, sex, household size, and education level, showed differential rates of crime. One factor which led to these differential rates was how the assignment of the housing was made by the local housing authorities. In Britain, public rental housing is controlled and assigned by local authorities within the community. The housing differs in desirability and often has waiting lists. Desirability is partly dictated by the crime rate. Areas with high crime rates are highly undesirable. In fact, waiting lists are excellent barometers of the desirability of the housing. The more people on the lists and the longer the wait, the more desirable the location. On the other hand, certain families and potential residents with a variety of "social problems" are desperate for housing and cannot wait—even though rents between desirable and undesirable locations may be the same. Bottoms and Wiles found that local housing authorities often assigned housing on the basis of ability to wait as well as the nature of the family's "social problems." A common practice of the housing authority was to "dump" renters with social problems and a known propensity toward crime into specific areas, a procedure that contributed directly to differential crime rates between the public estates.

The Bottoms-Wiles study is important because it underscores the need to understand the process—how residents got there in the first place—in differential crime rates within geographical areas. A strictly social structure analysis, on the other hand, would have revealed a differential crime rate in relation to a geographical area but would not have provided answers as to why this occurred. Bottoms and Wiles conclude with ". . .

if indeed it is obvious that to study the criminality of a particular area we need to know something about how the residents got there in the first place, we can only say that most criminologists have shown a remarkable lack of interest in the details of the process'' (p. 151).

Similarly, R. J. Bursik, Jr. (1987) suggests that political dynamics can affect the delinquency rate in a community. He offers the example of the politically planned construction of a new public housing project in Chicago, which immediately affected the residential stability of local neighborhoods. The project introduced a new source of instability into the neighborhood that essentially decreased the community's ability to regulate itself. Specifically, the construction of public housing itself appeared to be enough to set off a chain of events which dramatically accelerated the instability of the neighborhood, resulting in an increase in the rate of delinquency.

Social networks and informal support systems are crucial to the prevention of crime and delinquency, a point to which we will return in Chapter 12. Delinquency is encouraged by low levels of surveillance and supervision by concerned adults. In stable neighborhoods, residents supervise activities of youths, watch over one another's property, and challenge those who seem to be ''up to no good'' (Skogan, 1986). They offer a sense of security and peace of mind for the parent, feelings that translate into a more relaxed and positive stance toward the task of child rearing. This aspect appears to be especially important for the poor who are trapped in their surroundings. The more affluent can escape to another neighborhood or purchase whatever resources or support systems may be necessary.

Skogan's concept of *demagoguery* refers to the process whereby unscrupulous real estate agents or other vested-interest parties frighten residents into leaving an area in order to gain substantial profits. This is similar to, but more subtle than, the outright appropriation of neighborhoods just alluded to. Usually, the scare tactics center around crime and racial threats. Real estate agents have been known to frighten residents into selling their homes at reduced prices by planting rumors of increasing crime or a potential influx of ethnic groups, a practice known as ''block busting'' (Goodwin, 1979). Homes are resold at inflated prices to those desperate for housing. Even Shaw and McKay in their early work made reference to these tactics, noting that ''social disorganization'' reflected concerted efforts at market manipulation by entrepreneurs trying to reap quick profits at the expense of residents (Bursik, 1986a).

Playing upon fear of crime is certainly an effective tactic. Second-hand information, even if it conflicts with official reports of crime, can increase fear that may accelerate neighborhood decline (Skogan, 1986). It is well known that people make extensive use of information gathered second-hand through social networks, especially in tight-knit communities. If this network perceives and communicates to its members that crime is rampant, this information may have a stronger impact on resident decisions that officially reported crime and victimization rates (Greenberg, 1985). Fear encourages some residents, especially those more educated and in the higher income brackets, to move out. Those less fortunate, or those who do not wish to relocate, often withdraw physically and psychologically from the community life. Fearful people stay at home more often and become discouraged about anything being done to curb the "crime problem." They avoid contact with others they do not know and avoid monitoring the neighborhood.

Deindustrialization refers to the loss of jobs and the general economic decline of an area, which affect both the industry and people living there. Crime-plagued urban neighborhoods have considerable concentrations of unemployment and poverty (McGahey, 1986). On the other hand, low-crime neighborhoods, are characterized by stable, relatively affluent households, willing and able to maintain their homes and neighborhoods (McGahey, 1986). Furthermore, the economic status of the neighborhood is very much dependent on a higher social system—the metropolitan and national economies. Jobs, income, and social status depend on the state of the national and local economy as well as on how much corporations and businesses are willing to invest in the community.

All four factors, Skogan reminds us, are typically dependent on the decisions of persons in positions of political and financial power. "They reflect the interests of banks, manufacturing firms, government agencies, and others with large economic and political stakes in what they do" (Skogan, 1986, p. 207).

Phases of Neighborhood Deterioration

Leo Schuerman and Solomon Kobrin (1986) likewise note that ecological research has continually shown a link between severely declining urban neighborhoods and rates of delinquency. They too conclude that deteriorated residential areas generally have the highest crime and delinquency rates. These researchers were more interested in discovering the *processes* neighborhoods follow in evolving into high-crime areas, however. Using a "developmental model," they analyzed longitudinal data spanning a 20-year period (1950 to 1970) in Los Angeles County's highest crime areas. Their data consisted of census figures and official crime rates. In addition, Schuerman and Kobrin measured community structure through four basic social structural dimensions:

1. land use;
2. population composition;
3. SES; and
4. subculture.

Land use measures included such factors as the concentration and distribution of single- and multiple-family dwellings, industrial and commercial parcels, and traffic-generating establishments (such as offices, restaurants, and shopping centers). Population composition measures included size and density of neighborhood populations, residential mobility, and household composition (number of parents, number of children, etc.). SES measures consisted of occupation, unemployment, education, and housing conditions. Subculture variables involved indicators of the ethnic makeup of the neighborhood.

The data suggested that in the initial stage of neighborhood change, land use and population composition are the early signs of impending change in neighborhood crime levels. Once in the initial stage, land use shows a shift from single toward multiple dwellings combined with rising numbers of commercial establishments. Eventually, in the more advanced stages of neighborhood decay, there is a gradual trend toward "abandonment" of the area where properties are sought by very few home buyers, renters, or investors. The population composition variables then shift toward higher population density, increased mobility, and an increase in broken family units and unattached individuals. These trends proceed at an increasing rate, eventually to a point where the social and cultural character of a neighborhood is qualitatively altered.

During the later stages of neighborhood deterioration, SES and subculture changes become more prominent. The Schuerman and Kobrin data indicate that high crime areas evolve from initial ecological physical decay to social and cultural decay at the advanced stages of neighborhood deterioration. During the later stages, there is a sizable decrease in professional and skilled occupational groups and in the educational level of the population, and an increase in unskilled laborers, unemployed persons, and overcrowded and deteriorated housing. The data also showed decline in the white and Hispanic population, but no change in the black population. Thus, at the advanced stage of deterioration, the neighborhood is characterized by instability, a breakdown in social controls, and an increase in normative ambiguity.

In Schuerman and Kobrin's study, changes in the crime rate paralleled the SES and subcultural changes recently described. Neighborhood crimes increased steadily through the physical changes, changes in population composition, changes in SES characteristics, and changes in prevailing normative controls. Schuerman and Kobrin identified three distinct phases of neighborhood changes in crime rates. In the *emerging* stage, neighborhoods once relatively free of crime began to exhibit moderate crime rates. In the *transitional* stage, crime increased from a moderate to high level. The *enduring* stage was characterized by persistent, ongoing high crime rates over long periods of time. In this stage, property was abandoned, the populations became increasingly unemployed and discouraged, and there was little social control over deviant behavior beyond token police patrols.

Schuerman and Kobrin also examined the *velocity* of these neighborhood changes. They discovered that speed of change was crucial in the process. The greater the velocity of structural change in the neighborhood, the more precipitous the rise in crime rates. Crime rates radically increased with rapid changes in SES and subcultural variables.

The researchers suggest that neighborhoods characterized by high levels of crime and delinquency over a period of several decades may be considered "lost" for purposes of effective crime reduction. In other words, some neighborhoods are so infested with crime that crime reduction strategies are futile. Schuerman and Kobrin suggest that police resources, police planning, and other forms of formal social control and social services be directed at communities in the emerging and transition stages of crime infiltration, since there is hope that the eventual slide into persistently high crime rates may be avoided.

Neighborhood Social Control and Family Structure

Families and communities are mutually connected, and to the extent that families are disrupted, we can expect communities to be similarly disrupted. It is important to note here that we are not speaking only of the traditional nuclear family of parents and children, but rather of the nuclear group that comprises a household. As we have seen, delinquency most often occurs in neighborhoods or communities where informal social controls are reduced or absent. This is not to deny that youths living in stable neighborhoods commit crime. Explanations for the phenomenon of delinquency among youths of higher SES levels are more likely to be found at the individual or microsystem level, however. Keep in mind that in this chapter we are discussing macrosystems and concentrating upon theories and data that transcend the boundaries of a youth's very personal situation.

Surveillance and supervision by parents and concerned adults are the principal means for informal control and prevention. If parents are in marital conflict or unsupported in caregiving, their ability to monitor the activities of their own children, let alone those of others, is seriously hampered. More often than not single parents are forced to work outside the home, frequently for extended work days, and must leave adolescents unsupervised, sometimes for long periods of time. Accordingly, communities that have extended clusters of single-parent homes, especially with low incomes, should have higher rates of delinquency. Robert J. Sampson has made some attempts to test this hypothesis.

Sampson (1986) postulates that widespread marital and family disruption concentrated in certain neighborhoods is linked to the crime and delinquency rates of those areas, even when racial composition, poverty, or income are controlled. As noted previously, family disruption (divorce, family conflict, separation) often has the effect of removing family members from active participation in their community and reducing informal social controls. Sampson hypothesizes that communities with high concentrations of family disruption have low rates of participation in voluntary organizations and local affairs. A high level of family disruption, he notes, "interferes with the individual and collective efforts of families to link youth to the wider society through institutional means such as schools, religion, and sports" (1986, p. 278). In other words, single-parent and/or conflictful families develop fewer networks which would link their children to mainstream institutions and society in general.

Conflictful families may be less able to supervise their children as well as others in the neighborhood. In neighborhoods characterized by stable, intact families, children are generally supervised, watched, and even reprimanded by adults besides their own parents. Furthermore, neighbors take note of strangers, question them, watch over each others' property, and often intervene in local disturbances. This adult surveillance, supervision, and intervention is apt to have a substantial effect on the delinquency rate of a particular area.

Sampson tested his hypotheses by examining robbery and homicide rates in 171 American cities with populations over 100,000. Because the number of juvenile offenders involved in homicide was too small to suggest meaningful inferences, he focused on juvenile robbery. Family disruption was defined in two ways:

1. proportion of intact black and white families within a given area (with "intact" defined as married couple families); and
2. the divorce rate within that targeted area.

He examined a wide range of variables, including neighborhood instability, income heterogeneity, percent nonwhite, percent living alone, and percent over age 65. Sampson concluded that, "Of all city characteristics . . . family structure clearly has the strongest effects on juvenile robbery offending for both sexes" (Sampson, 1986, p. 298). Unfortunately, Sampson did not take direct measures of informal controls, such as parental and adult supervision of children, adolescents, and groups. Still, his project brings us one step closer toward understanding the complicated and bi-directional effects of family and neighborhood structure. Sampson's research suggests that families can alter the delinquency characteristics of the neighborhood, and the neighborhood, in turn, can affect the security and well-being of the family.

A similar argument was advanced by Marcus Felson and Lawrence Cohen (1980; Felson, 1986), who emphasized the importance of guardianship and adult supervision in preventing delinquency within the community. They suggested that the quality and extent of this supervision has been eroded by the changing structure of modern American society. The primary lifestyle of most Americans today—not just single-parent families—requires that family members be separated from one another and from their homes for extended periods of time. This reduces the amount of supervision over both households and juveniles. The home is unattended for long hours, increasing its chances of being burglarized or vandalized. Youngsters are left with idle time to pursue delinquent activities. Thus, neighborhood family structure is an important community level factor in explaining offender rates and victimization risk. Of course, theories such as the foregoing assume that when opportunity lurks, budding delinquents rise to the occasion, a supposition that would be challenged by other theories of delinquency.

In summary, this section sampled some of the contemporary work being done on higher level process and structure factors as potential causes of delinquency. This work illustrates how macrosystem or social structure findings can be used as a foundation for pursuing process variables. We now shift our attention to an even higher level of analysis—the international level.

COMPARATIVE CRIMINOLOGY: THE INTERNATIONAL MACROSYSTEM

In this section we will review the largest social system, that involving different nations of the world. Obviously, this international macrosystem is an unwieldy mix of cultures, values, customs, and languages. Comparative criminology ". . . seeks to locate commonalities and differences in patterns of criminality and crime among divergent economic, political, social, or cultural systems'' (Johnson and Barak-Glantz, 1983, p. 7). Based on our current limited knowledge, efforts to make international comparisons, articulate differences, or even to speculate must be guarded. Most research on delinquency has been conducted in the United States, Canada, and Great Britain. A fair amount of research has been conducted in Japan and more recently in Israel. In general, however, we know pathetically little about delinquency in most parts of the world.

One of the major reasons for our ignorance is that comparative criminology, as a systematic field of study, did not really exist until the late 1950s and 1960s (Beirne, 1983). Some researchers and commentators (e.g., Tarde in *La Criminalité Comparée* in 1902) certainly gave some recognition to cultural differences in the study of crime and delinquency, but *systematic* investigation did not begin until the last half of the 20th century. Among the earliest books on comparative criminology were Hermann Mannheim's *Comparative Criminology* (1965), Wolfgang and Ferracuti's *The Subculture of Violence* (1967), and Cavan and Cavan's *Delinquency and Crime: Cross-cultural Perspectives* (1968). However, as pointed out by Piers Beirne (1983), these early books were only marginally comparative and provide "only the preparatory spirit of cross-cultural investigation" (p. 21).

It is debatable to what extent international comparisons can be made, or even are feasible. Just within the last decade or so, Graeme Newman (1977) and Paul Friday (1973) both noted that a labyrinth of methodological problems were just beginning to be acknowledged. Beyond the obvious ones—such as difficulty obtaining comparable data—there are major differences in how members of varying countries or cultures view the world; we all have different construct systems. As noted by Joseph Scott and Fhad Al-Thakeb (1980, p. 45), ". . . crime statistics are the result of decisions and action taken by persons in a social system which defines, classifies, and records certain behavior as criminal. The process is therefore crucially affected by the subjective attitudes of individuals and how they define and interpret behavior as criminal." Having a language in common makes the task of comparative criminology much easier, of course, but even then there are obstacles. The United States and Canada, to note just one example, differ substantially in their methods of crime reporting, making comparisons of official statistics in the two countries downright hazardous.

Most comparative research to date has been conducted by American criminologists testing American versions of the world (e.g., anomie, differential association, subcultural, and social control theories) on other nations. As Roland Robertson and Laurie Taylor (1973) noted, the overpowering conceptual edifice of American criminology, coupled with the international prestige of its theorists, have dominated the world scene in the study of crime and delinquency throughout most of the twentieth century. There is danger in this, if we assume that American versions of crime and its causes can be applied universally. ". . . (S)ocieties have their own histories, characteristics, and perceptions of the significance of criminality" (Johnson and Barak-Glantz, 1983). It is no surprise, therefore, that American theories of delinquency have not fared well in other countries and societies. In fact, most attempts at comparative study with classic American criminological theory as a basis of explanation have not been successful. (See Beirne, 1983, note 5.)

In an incisive and thoughtful essay, Piers Beirne (1983) outlined three approaches to comparative criminology:

1. the method of agreement;
2. the method of difference; and
3. methodological relativism.

The method of agreement assumes that there are basic, underlying commonalities in delinquent behavior, no matter what culture or nation is being discussed, and that these commonalities can be integrated into one master theory. "The primary aim of the method of agreement is to identify a commonality among as many possible empirical cases of crime" (Beirne, 1983, p. 24). Furthermore, the more abstract the theory, the greater its generality from culture to culture, society to society. Pushing abstraction to its ultimate extreme, we can conclude that all societies have a delinquency problem. But there is a price to high abstraction in theory. It may become so abstract that while it is highly "cross-cultural," it also is "virtually impervious to empirical test" (Campbell, 1962, p. 45).

According to Beirne, the best illustrations of the method of agreement are Clinard and Abbott's *Crime in Developing Countries* (1973), Gurr, Grabosky, and Hula's *The Politics of Crime and Conflict* (1977), and Shelly's *Crime and Modernization* (1981). All three focus on broad, abstract societal features that are assumed to explain crime. Shelly, for example, argued that "modernization provides the best theoretical explanation of the evolution of criminality in the last two hundred years" (Beirne, 1983, p. 25). Modernization was believed to override all cultural, economic, or political factors. Since modernization has universal application as an explanation of crime, Shelly believed it could be used as a rallying point for international comparisons of crime and delinquency data.

The method of difference focuses on the empirical data that are unexplained by the method of agreement. "The inexplicable cases encountered in investigations of the method of agreement automatically become the domain of the method of difference" (Beirne, 1983, p. 27). Illustrations of this method are Clinard's *Cities with Little Crime* (1978) and Herbert's *The Geography of Urban Crime* (1982). Clinard, for example, saw Switzerland as an "exception" to common viewpoints that urbanization and crime go together. He noted that, while the country has a high degree of affluence, industrialization, and urbanization, it has an exceedingly low crime rate (even though it also has one of the highest rates of firearm ownership in the world). Clinard compared Switzerland's low crime rate to Sweden's high crime rate, since the two countries share certain features, including democracy. There are, however, two major differences. First, Sweden is a centralized democracy which tends to inhibit citizen initiative and responsibility, whereas Switzerland's system of government encourages citizens to participate in decisions affecting their lives. Secondly, Switzerland's urbanization has been a very gradual process; the country does not have extremely large cities, nor does it have slums. In contrast, urbanization in Sweden has resulted in large cities with heavy population densities and widespread slums. Clinard concluded, therefore, that crime and delinquency were caused by the particular ecology of cities and the degree of political centralization. Clinard is convinced that the way the Swiss handle the crime problem should be adopted by the United States and other high crime, industrialized countries.

The third approach to comparative criminology, methodological relativism, arises from sensitivity to cultural diversity. "'. . . (T)he major obstacle to the construction of cross-cultural generalizations is the impossibility of precise equivalence of action and meaning in different cultures" (Beirne, 1983, p. 29). Relativism encourages some cross-cultural generalizations, but it remains sensitive to cultural diversity. It advocates "the larger view" while recognizing "the cultural-bond view." Whereas the other two methods are mutually exclusive, methodological relativism searches for both similarities and differences.

This third approach encourages researchers to consider carefully the instruments and techniques used in their work. They must be conscious of the fact that they are alien observers in an alien culture. As Beirne correctly noted, "Research instruments can never occupy a neutral position between observer and observed; they are conceptual products and always operate through and with concepts." Conceptual fits between measures and observations between countries present an extremely difficult challenge, one that requires much attention if comparative criminology is to be a meaningful enterprise. As Robertson and Taylor noted:

> When we begin to unpack such terms as fraud, sexual offenses and larceny, we find that they do not refer to a clearly identified, readily circumscribed behaviour. They are not sociological categories with pretensions to universality but rather legal and statistical categories which reflect historical and contemporary attitudes toward particular behaviour in their titles—fraud, embezzlement, grand larceny, dangerous driving—and their differentiation—misdemeanors and felonies, indictable and non-indictable. (1973, pp. 32–33)

In many ways, the classification and legal definition of juvenile offenders tell us more about the social system in which they are embedded than about the offenders themselves. Valid comparisons of societies require more than a knowledge of crime rates. The research instruments of international statistics *by themselves* are meaningless. Comparative criminology requires comparisons of societal policies, the practices of the police and others who carry them out, the tolerance levels of the citizens for deviant behavior, and more important, appreciation of the cultural matrix with all its social relationships.

Methodological relativism also encourages researchers to try to understand differences in language and construct systems before initiating a comparative research endeavor. Concepts cannot be overly culture-bound, but must have transcultural application. Robertson and Taylor (1973) referred to this as the need to have "anthropological distance." The most effective way of grasping deviance and crime among different cultures is to remove oneself from the context of immediate familiarity. When researchers observe a social phenomenon or identify a problem, the very words and concepts they use to comprehend it strongly color what they perceive. This is true of all research, not simply comparative research. Although researchers cannot eliminate conceptual bias, they can at least be sensitive to it and take it into careful consideration in any formulation of their theory or in preparing, gathering, and interpreting their data. A society must be seen in its own terms before any comparative work can be advanced. Robertson and Taylor used Albert Cohen's research to illustrate this point. Cohen's delinquents were not just "deviants." "They [were] necessarily working class, American educational failures; these are the characteristics which give meaning to their behavior" (Robertson and Taylor, 1973, p. 37). When we consider Cohen's delinquents in this culturally specific way, we find that his concepts are not immediately transferable to other cultures. The same may be said of such culturally specific concepts as "social disorganization," "subculture," and "opportunity structure."

According to Beirne, each of the three methods—agreement, difference, relativism—has its own unique problems. The method of agreement, in its insistence on finding broad generalizations, overlooks significant or subtle differences and cultural variations among societies. The method of difference is exceedingly narrow in focus, comparing aspects of one particular culture to another. Usually, those using this method try to generalize to other societies or cultures. Methodological relativism is extremely complex; it requires some rearrangement of measurements and concepts and may leave discernible cultural variations without theoretical explanation. Beirne appears to favor methodological relativism as the most effective approach in comparative criminology.

With these admonishments in mind, we will propose a rudimentary comparison of delinquency in two countries, Japan and the United States, within a systems framework. In other words, we will suggest how information about delinquency may be rearranged within a systems perspective, while respecting cultural variations.

Crime and Delinquency in Japan

Japan has the lowest crime rate among industrialized nations of the world; furthermore, *overall* incidents of crime have declined since 1955. Japan has a population of about 120 million, crowded into 140 million square miles of mountainous islands. In 1982, the country recorded only 1.5 million non-traffic penal code violations and 130,000 non-traffic statutory offenses, which are about equivalent to a misdemeanor (Araki, 1985). In comparison, in the same year the state of California, with a population of only 25 million, recorded 1.8 million felonies and 700,000 non-traffic misdemeanors. California in 1982 had an estimated 600,000 more serious offenses than the entire country of Japan. More specifically, Japan recorded 2,231 robberies, 2,399 rapes, 1,764 homicides. Correspondingly, California had 91,988 robberies, 12,529 rapes, and 2,778 homicides. In reference to drug offenses, Japan recorded 38,000 cases, almost all involving the use of stimulants (especially toluene or organic solvents, such as plastic glue), while California recorded 150,000 drug offenses and another 230,000 incidents of public drunkenness. As in the United States, crime rates in Japan are higher in urban than in rural areas (Tokoro, 1983).

While overall adult crime rates have declined in Japan, juvenile rates have shown a moderate increase during the past decade, especially among junior high school students (Kashiwagi, 1986). The delinquency rate is still extremely low compared to other industrialized nations. Still, the increase has generated some concern among Japanese officials. Robert Christopher (1983) suggests that this is because Japan is such an orderly society that even a small, marginal increase in delinquency is seen as cause for alarm.

The court system of Japan is comprised of 570 summary courts, 50 family courts, eight high courts, and one supreme court (Araki, 1985). The family court has jurisdiction over all juvenile cases as well as adult offenses which involve the violation of laws protecting the welfare of juveniles. Japan recognizes three legal categories of delinquents: juvenile offenders, law-breaking children, and delinquent offenders (Suzuki, 1981). Juvenile offenders are youths between the ages of 14 and 20 who have violated the criminal code. Law-breaking children are youths below the age of criminal responsibility (14 years) who have committed acts considered criminal if committed by an adult. Delinquent offenders are similar to status offenders: They are persons under age 20 who demonstrate persistent disobedience to reasonable dictates of their parents or guardians. In Japan, age 20 marks the entry into adulthood. Most of the concern is directed at the moderate increase in "juvenile offenders," although very few of their offenses are of a violent nature. In recent years, the violence or assaultive behavior that has occurred has often been directed at school officials or teachers. Criminologists speculate that this hostility may be a result of the persistent and pervasive overemphasis on academic achievement, complicated by very intense competition among students. Most of the increase in nonviolent delinquency is due to shoplifting and the theft of bicycles and motor bicycles (Suzuki, 1981).

The Japanese delinquency problem is minuscule compared with that of the United States, although we should guard against overstating the scope of the problem in this country. Why is delinquency so uncommon in Japan? The answer may lie in the social fabric and a close social network system which assures that Japanese youth will conform to the norms. Consider the following remarks about the country by scholars:

> . . . a tightly knit social system leaves many tied down by heavy burdens of duty and obligation, or uncomfortably constrained by rules of social conformity. (Reischauer, 1978, pp. 230–231)

> The threat of exclusion from the community, not the severity of formal punishment, is the basis of conformity. An individual's sense of well-being, indeed his very identity, depends on his place within groups—family, workplace, school, neighborhood, and nation. (Bayley, 1976, p. 155)

> Japan is rightly characterized as a society with a high degree of social solidarity whether it be within a household, a division of a company, a union, a department of a university, or a social or religious organization. (Rosch, 1987, p. 257)

Rosch notes that when village life has been destroyed by modernization, the Japanese try to create "pseudo-villages" to maintain a sense of comfort through the traditional dense, multiplex social networks. George DeVos (1980) found that commitments among the Japanese people were intertwined with occupational and social networks. Peer pressures from family, school, work, colleagues, and neighbors are apparently intense. Years ago, criminologists Harry Barnes and Hegley Teeters (1945) concluded that the Japanese are a law-abiding nation because of their strong family and community ties. Many forms of self-assertion are strongly discouraged and considerable emphasis is placed on the sacrifice of personal needs for the collective benefit of the group (Wagatsuma and Rosett, 1986). ". . . (M)aintenance of harmonious and smooth interpersonal relations, interdependence, and mutual trust are of utmost importance" (Wagatsuma and Rosett, 1986, p. 465).

Another relevant factor in Japanese society is the lack of residential mobility. DeVos (1980) conducted a field study of the Arakawa ward of metropolitan Tokyo and emerged with two striking observations. First, the population was extremely stable. The Japanese community remained stable over extended periods of time, often across many generations. In contrast to the rapid mobility in the United States, "one is more apt to die in the area in which one was born" (DeVos, 1980, p. 140). "Even in newer communities, residents assume they will become permanent" (p. 142). DeVos found that, because of this quality of permanence, the Japanese take great pride in their neighborhoods, keeping them in good repair.

Second, DeVos found that extensive social networking existed throughout the Japanese community. Not only did a majority of the residents remain in one place throughout their lives, but most also participated in various volunteer organizations both within and outside the local community. The social networks, DeVos found, were part of their cultural tradition. Furthermore, some of the organizations were directly related to the formal and informal supervision of problem children. For example, there were 56,000 probation officers in Japan at one point, but only 500 were full-time professionals (Ross and Benson, 1979). The remainder were private citizens who volunteered their services. Another 36,500 volunteered as guidance workers who offered counseling to both children and parents (Suzuki, 1981).

The relationship between police and citizen is positive, strong, and encouraged. Police maintain thousands of small substations (called Koban) in the community and encourage visitors on a 24-hour basis (Tokoro, 1983). Japanese citizens also participate in local crime prevention associations which patrol their own districts and protect areas where crime is most likely to occur (Ross and Benson, 1979). Furthermore, over 80 private organizations run various facilities for juvenile delinquents. Interestingly, Japan has a 400-year-old tradition as a society without weapons (Ross and Benson, 1979). Registration of any firearms, knives, or swords is mandatory. Citizens simply are not allowed to own handguns.

We can speculate that some changes have occurred since these observations were made. In a recent article, for example, Joel Rosch (1987) notes that Japan is becoming an increasingly mobile society. Whether this new mobility will affect delinquency, as mobility arguably does in the United States, remains to be seen. Still, we must wonder about the possibility of a strong relationship between dense and multiplex social networks and the low rates of crime and delinquency. The two certainly coexist. Whether there is cause and effect is a question worth pursuing.

The explanation for low delinquency in Japan is unlikely to be that simple, however. The country represents a homogeneous culture with a long-formulated tradition and history. Even if it were possible for another country to emulate Japan's elaborate social networks, and even if that country wanted to do that, there would not necessarily be a significant drop in delinquency. Personal construct systems, family relationships, government policies and regulations, and other components of social systems also would need to be adjusted. In other words, some attention to all system levels is appropriate. It is important to note also, however, that Japan's own system of social networks faces a challenge from those who may resist the traditional and opt instead for personal status and geographical and economic mobility.

SUMMARY AND CONCLUSIONS

Social network theory and processes at the macrosystem level were the major topics of this chapter. We also included a brief glance at the highest social macrosystem—comparative criminology or international viewpoints of crime and delinquency.

We began with the important contribution of Krohn in his proposal for a network analysis theory of delinquency that allows investigators to bridge all levels of the social system. Krohn's theory maintains that chracterics of social networks determine the amount of constraint placed on people. "With decreasing constraint, the probability of behavior that does not fall within the acceptable parameters of the network increases" (Krohn, 1986, p. 89). One thing we must be careful about in this context is not to conceive of the influence as being only in one direction, from social networks to individual. The individual is not usually an inactive, passive recipient, but an active, influencing participant in any causal ordering.

While Krohn's discussion is limited to the micro and macro levels of analysis, a social system approach encourages us to view the worlds of delinquency as multistratified ones. A social system orientation presumes finer gradients of social influence rather than simply an individual versus the environment perspective. Furthermore, a social systems perspective underscores the continual mutual influence of the systems at all levels. The model argues that one level cannot be meaningfully understood without the other. Delinquency as a social phenomenon cannot be meaningfully understood without careful consideration of family, peers, siblings, school, neighborhood, the chronosystem, and the national cultural environment within which all these systems are embedded. Understanding of an individual delinquent requires an examination of his or her construct system as well as an appreciation of other higher level systems of influence. Even the national or state policy about health care or employment may play a key role.

This is not to say that we need to understand every aspect of all the systems to work with delinquency or the delinquent. Rather, we must be ever mindful of the complex of influences that work within any social behavior, and decision-making should not be dictated by a simplistic version of cause-and-effect. Tearing down the slums, by itself, will not necessarily change the crime rate in that area. Research concentrating at one level of analysis should be open to other influences rather than making firm conclusions based on a restricted focus. Social causes are reciprocal and multiple.

The enormous complexity of the delinquency problem should not be discouraging. The complicated picture we have painted is the result of scientific progress. Criminologists are becoming more cautious in their statements about delinquency and its causes, the research strategies and methods are more sophisticated, and the research is more encompassing in the number of variables analyzed. It seems the more we know about crime and delinquency, the less sure we are about what we do know. But this is the sign of progress and increasing knowledge.

Prevention and Control of Delinquency

12 CHAPTER

In this concluding chapter, we consider two broad alternative strategies for dealing with delinquency. On the one hand, we can try to prevent delinquency by a variety of methods, including both formal and informal measures; on the other, we can concentrate upon controlling it effectively after it has occurred, again by both formal and informal means. The ideal strategy combines the two approaches, but realistically, one will dominate. Joseph Weis and John Sederstrom (1981) reserve the term ''control'' to refer to treatment and punishment *after* entrance into the juvenile justice system and ''prevention'' to refer to an action taken to preclude or correct illegal behavior *before* entrance into the system. Although it is not altogether clear what constitutes ''entrance into'' the system, we will proceed cautiously with this dichotomy, since it is helpful in organizing the material ahead.

Prevention strategies require extensive knowledge about social systems. They are exemplified by proposals with such diverse emphases as developing social support systems, changing educational policies, or altering the structure of society. Control strategies emphasize the need to punish criminal activity or to change the offender. Control strategies often, but not invariably, require knowledge about individual offenders. Typical control strategies include court diversion programs, incarceration, psychological treatment, and vocational rehabilitation, often used in combination. Obviously, there is overlap. One provides treatment, for example, with the hope and premise that individuals will not offend in the future. In that sense, the control strategy of treatment is also preventive. A neighborhood watch program may prevent crime, but it is also instrumental in having offenders caught and punished.

It is important to note that both prevention and control may be formal or informal. Formal control mechanisms rely heavily on written rules or laws and on the prescribed punishments for breaking these rules and laws. The police, the courts, and correctional agencies are social institutions designed to maintain formal control. Informal control, on the other hand, is based more on custom, norms, social expectations and common agreement (Greenberg, Rohe, and Williams, 1985a). The sanctions applied to rule violators may involve verbal reprimands, rejection, embarrassment, warnings, or threats. "Informal social control depends on the existence of cohesive social groups, the strength of which depends upon the amount of social interaction, similarity of residents on socioeconomic attitudinal dimensions, physical and visual proximity, and group size" (Greenberg, Rohe, and Williams, 1985a, p. 7).

This informal control is often virtually indistinguishable from informal prevention. For example, an individual begins to realize that he or she will be punished for deviating from expected behavior and therefore may resist engaging in norm violations. A neighborhood or social group can create an atmosphere in which rule violations are not tolerated. According to Greensberg et al. (1985a), informal social control should be viewed as a continuum from primary peer group pressures to the activities of neighborhood organizations (See Table 12-1). When informal control is not present or ceases to be effective, formal control is needed.

Prevention, especially formal prevention, is a slow, gradual process, and its discernible effects are rarely immediate; embarking on prevention strategies requires risk and a major leap of faith. It requires the cooperation, commitment, and action of large segments of the population. Control, formal or informal, appears to move more rapidly, because it brings relatively immediate action—harsh words, community ostracism, detention, or referral to a drug treatment center.

FORMAL PREVENTION AND CONTROL OF DELINQUENCY

In 1974, Congress passed the *Juvenile Justice and Delinquency Prevention Act* (JJDPA). As the statute's name suggests, its philosophy was preventive. In effect, however, it became at least as controlling as preventive. Thus, it is actually illustrative of both formal prevention and formal control. This landmark federal statute altered the course

TABLE 12-1 FORMS OF SOCIAL CONTROL*

Formal		Informal	
Police and courts enforce official laws	Neighborhood organization pressure to conform to norms	Informal ad hoc group pressure to conform to norms	Individual or peer group pressure to conform to norms

*Source: Greenberg, Rohe, and Williams, 1985a, p. 5.

of juvenile justice more than any other *legislative* action since the passage in 1899 of the Chicago Juvenile Court Act. It has precipitated what Frank Hellum (1979) called "the second revolution" in juvenile justice. For that reason, we will use the JJDPA to illustrate both strengths and weaknesses of formal methods of prevention and control. It is important to note, however, that we are focusing upon a legislative rather than a *judicial* action. The juvenile justice system was changed dramatically in the 1960s as a result of a series of U.S. Supreme Court decisions. In the early 1980s, other decisions related to the detention and care of juveniles were announced. These judicial actions were discussed in Chapter 3 and will not be reconsidered here. It should be recognized, however, that judicial decisions have a great deal to do with preventing and controlling delinquency, both in obvious and not so obvious ways. When a court invalidates a particular treatment method or limits the number of days a juvenile may be kept in detention, the connection to delinquency prevention and control is obvious. In a more subtle way, custody, educational, and even zoning decisions may affect individual or community delinquency.

Juvenile Justice and Delinquency Prevention Act of 1974

The federal government was only minimally involved in the prevention or control of delinquency prior to the late 1940s. The Children's Bureau, established in 1912, represented the extent of its leadership. With respect to delinquency, this agency limited itself to keeping voluntarily submitted data on the activity of juvenile courts. Shortly after World War II, however, the public perceived delinquency as an increasingly serious problem. In response to this concern, the Interdepartmental Committee on Children and Youth was established in 1948. Its primary function was to develop better relationships among existing federal agencies totally or peripherally concerned with youth. It had no power or funds to advise or assist state or local governments in their attempts to prevent or control delinquency.

In early 1961, as an outgrowth of the White House Conference on Children and Youth, the President's Commission on Juvenile Delinquency and Youth Crime was established. The Commission was able to recommend and secure enactment of the Juvenile Delinquency and Youth Offenses Control Act of 1961 and its amendments of 1964 and 1965. This statute authorized the Secretary of Health, Education, and Welfare (HEW) to provide grants to state, local, and private agencies to conduct various projects in search of improved methods for the prevention and control of juvenile delinquency. The Control Act of 1961 was replaced by the broader (and better financed) Juvenile Prevention and Control Act of 1968. In 1971, the Control Act of 1968 was superseded by the Juvenile Delinquency Prevention Act (JDPA), designed to provide grants to support community-based juvenile delinquency prevention programs. The ultimate result of this bureaucratic leap-frogging (see Table 12-2) was the historic Juvenile Justice and Delinquency Prevention Act (JJDPA) of 1974, the focus of our attention.

The 1974 statute contained a broad mandate for reform and qualifies as the most comprehensive federal juvenile justice legislation ever enacted (Krisberg, et al., 1986). It was signed into law reluctantly by President Gerald Ford, following almost six years

TABLE 12-2 SUMMARY OF FEDERAL GOVERNMENT ACTIVITY IN JUVENILE JUSTICE

Year	Event
1912	Children's Bureau created by Act of Congress. The Act directed the Bureau to investigate and report on all matters pertaining to the welfare of children and child life among all classes of people, and especially to investigate the questions of infant mortality, the birth rate, orphanages, juvenile courts, desertion, dangerous occupations, accidents, and diseases of children, employment, and legislation affecting children.
1948	Interdepartmental Committee on Children and Youth established. Its purpose was to develop closer relationships among federal agencies concerned with children and youth.
1950	The Midcentury White House Conference on Children and Youth met in Washington, D.C. The Conference considered methods to strengthen juvenile courts and the development of juvenile police services and studied prevention and treatment services of social agencies, police, courts, institutions, and after-care agencies.
1961	President's Committee on Juvenile Delinquency and Youth Crime established. It recommended enactment of the Juvenile Delinquency and Youth Offenses Control Act of 1961.
1961	Juvenile Delinquency and Youth Offenses Control Act of 1961 enacted. It had a three-year authorization for the purpose of demonstrating new methods of delinquency prevention and control.
1964	Juvenile Delinquency and Youth Offenses Control Act extended to carry out a special demonstration project in Washington D.C. The Act was subsequently extended through the fiscal year 1967.
1968	Juvenile Delinquency Prevention and Control Act of 1968 enacted. This Act assigned to HEW responsibility for developing a national approach to the problems of juvenile delinquency. States were to prepare and implement comprehensive juvenile delinquency plans and, upon approval, receive federal funds to carry out prevention, rehabilitation, training, and research programs.
1968	Omnibus Crime Control and Safe Streets Act of 1968 enacted. This Act provided block grants to states to improve and strengthen law enforcement. While not specifically mentioning juvenile delinquency, this Act's broad crime control and prevention mandate authorized funding of delinquency control and prevention programs.
1971	Juvenile Delinquency Prevention and Control Act extended for one year. The Interdepartmental Council to coordinate all federal juvenile delinquency programs was established by this Act.
1971	Omnibus Crime Control and Safe Streets Act amended. The definition of law enforcement was amended to include programs related to prevention, control, and reduction of juvenile delinquency. Grants were authorized for community-based juvenile delinquency prevention and correctional programs.
1972	Juvenile Delinquency Prevention Act enacted. This Act was an extension of the Juvenile Delinquency Prevention and Control Act of 1971. Under the Act, HEW was to fund preventive programs outside the juvenile justice system. Efforts to combat delinquency within the juvenile justice system were to be assisted through the Omnibus Crime Control and Safe Streets Act by the Law Enforcement Assistance Administration.
1973	Omnibus Crime Control and Safe Streets Act amended. The Act now specifically required that there be a juvenile delinquency component to the comprehensive state plan for the improvement of law enforcement and criminal justice.

TABLE 12-2   *(cont.)*

Year	Event
1974	Juvenile Justice and Delinquency Prevention Act of 1974 enacted. This Act provides, for the first time, a unified national program to deal with juvenile delinquency prevention and control within the context of the total law enforcement and criminal justice effort.
1977	JJDPA of 1974 amended by President Carter.
1980	JJDPA of 1974 amended.
1984	Comprehensive Crime Control Act enacted.

of exhaustive study by the Senate Subcommittee to Investigate Juvenile Delinquency. Although the Ford administration—and the Nixon administration it replaced—opposed the legislation, the JJDPA had broad-based support from juvenile justice and child welfare professionals, public interest groups, and Congress itself (Krisberg, et al., 1986). It passed in the House of Representatives by a vote of 329 to 20 and received only one dissenting vote in the Senate. The statute boosted efforts at juvenile justice reform already in progress at the state level and stimulated nationwide reforms. It was intended to deinstitutionalize status offenders (e.g., ''incorrigibles,'' truants, runaways); provide additional funds to localities to improve delinquency prevention programs; establish a federal assistance program to deal with the problems of runaway youth; and insure that juveniles would not be detained in the same facilities as adults.

The JJDPA also created a Juvenile Justice and Delinquency Prevention Administration within the Law Enforcement Assistance Administration (LEAA) of the Department of Justice, called the Office of Juvenile Justice and Prevention of Delinquency (OJJPD). (Although the LEAA is now defunct, OJJPD remains in place.) It had four major functions:

1. information collection and dissemination;
2. research and evaluation;
3. development and review of standards; and
4. training through National Training Institutes.

Also established were an independent Runaway Youth Program to be administered by HEW (an acronym for the Department of Health, Education, and Welfare, now defunct), and a National Institute of Corrections within the Justice Department.

At the time Congress debated the statute, the public was hearing consistently through the media that over one million children per year run away from home, that they leave at younger ages than before (over 40 percent between the ages of 11 and 14) and that many resorted to illegal activities to support themselves or their drug habits. Moreover, the runaway problem seemed to be primarily a white, middle class phenomenon involving girls, many of whom turned to prostitution. There were few reliable data available to support or refute these media proclamations. It would be foolhardy to suggest, however, that the country had no runaway problem.

The Runaway Youth Act authorized the Secretary of the then HEW to provide assistance to local groups to operate *temporary* shelter care programs in areas where runaways tended to congregate. Runaways would be provided with a place to stay and immediate assistance, such as medical care and counseling. Although they were to be encouraged to contact their families, they were not to be forced to do so. The statute also authorized funds to conduct research on the scope and nature of the runaway problem and the characteristics of children who left their homes. Congress wished to determine the age, sex, and socioeconomic background of runaway children as well as the places from which and to which they ran and the relationship between running away and other behavior.

A major goal of the JJDPA overall was the *deinstitutionalization* of status offenders and, if at all possible, all nonserious delinquents. Some members of Congress felt that none but the most serious offenders should be incarcerated, but as it turned out only status offenders were protected from institutionalization.

The federal government traditionally has preferred to leave the subject of juvenile crime to the states. This policy is made explicit in the recent overhaul of federal statutes pertaining to crime, the Comprehensive Crime Control Act of 1984. Nevertheless, the federal government did and continues to maintain control over state practices by making receipt of federal funds contingent upon meeting the provisions of the JJDPA. Therefore, if a state received federal funds for its delinquency-related programs, it was mandated to deinstitutionalize status offenders. The JJDPA also strongly encouraged the development of alternatives to incarceration for dealing with delinquent youth (Krisberg and Schwartz, 1983).

As used in the statute, deinstitutionalization included both "decarceration" and diversion to noninstitutional programs or nonpunitive facilities. Deinstitutionalization did not mean that juvenile status offenders could not be placed in group homes or residential treatment programs, however. They simply could not be placed in institutions operated by correctional officials. They were to be diverted "from" juvenile justice processing "to" alternative services and treatment facilities (Hellum, 1979). Since these facilities could be residential, some status offenders were in effect still confined, though not incarcerated. It was a question of size and punishment: Large institutions and punitive environments were to be avoided. Proponents of the JJDPA assumed that juveniles, due to their age and experience, are less culpable than adult offenders and more amenable to treatment and rehabilitation, both of which are difficult if not impossible to achieve in punitive or coercive institutional settings (Smith et al., 1980). This was based on the time-honored observations of the nature of institutions and the powerful effects of peers. Institutions were believed to encourage brutality and the inhumane treatment of juveniles. Furthermore, the presence of inmate social systems which created resistance and recalcitrance among inmates (Smith et al., 1980) precluded effective programs. It was believed that deinstitutionalization would bypass these group systems.

The JJDPA of 1974 was amended in 1977 to provide greater flexibility relative to the requirement that status offenders be deinstitutionalized. Congress now was responding to alleged increases in school violence and vandalism and the need to encourage private support for delinquency prevention programs (e.g., from business and charitable organizations). The statute was amended once again in 1980, this time to mandate the removal of juveniles from adult jails and lock ups. While the JJDPA of 1974 called for the *separation* of juveniles from adults in jails and lock ups, the amendment of 1980 explicitly *prohibited* states receiving federal funds from detaining or confining juveniles in the same facility with adults who were charged with or convicted of a crime. State legislatures appeared to be slow in developing statutes that clearly spelled out the need for separation, and Congress sought to put ''more teeth'' into the Act.

Aftermath of the JJDPA: The Shift Toward Punishment

Over the past decade, a ''get-tough'' approach toward adult and juvenile crime has dominated public policy. Lloyd Ohlin (1983a) observed that growing fear of crime and increasing demands for repressive action, such as more punitive sentencing, was very high throughout the mid to late 1970s. Frank Hellum (1979) identified a twofold orientation and philosophy toward juvenile justice which emerged during the mid to late 1970s. On the one hand, a ''velvet glove'' was to be extended to noncriminal, status offenders in the form of restrictions on confinement. On the other, there was an emerging ''iron-fisted,'' punitive approach to nonstatus offenders. There were calls for remanding juveniles to adult criminal courts or for demanding accountability akin to that demanded of adults, including the imposition of fines or imprisonment.

This ''iron-fisted'' philosophy was specifically directed at the violent and repetitive offender, whom the JJDPA of 1974 (and its amendments of 1977) seemed to ignore. The overall, primary mission of the JJDPA was to strengthen the ties of ''common delinquents'' to their families, school, and work (Galvin and Blake, 1984). It sought to develop a strong and comprehensive national policy on *prevention*. The common, nonserious, or status offender constituted about 95 percent of the total delinquent population, and the serious offender made up the residual 5 percent. These approximate figures continue to be representative, with serious delinquency hovering between 5 and 10 percent. It is important to note, however, that the figures refer to individuals, not to crime, a distinction which will be discussed soon. When the JJDPA was being debated, it seemed more important to respond to the greatest percentage of the juvenile problem. Nevertheless, those who supported the JJDPA hoped that the policies it advocated would affect serious delinquency as well.

Beginning in 1981, the Reagan Administration instituted an agenda that changed the direction of national policy from one of prevention to one of control. The target was the serious or repetitive offender, the youth who committed persistent violent acts. The White House announced that it wished to prevent the victimization of children, reduce school violence, support the nuclear family and traditional values, compensate the victims of juvenile crime, and restore the concept of ''accountability'' or just deserts to the juvenile justice system. There was indication that even status offenders might not escape the iron fist. In a report by the National Advisory Committee for Juvenile Justice and Delinquency Prevention (1984), it was recommended that grants to states to accomplish the deinstitutionalization of status offenders not be renewed.

Those who agreed with the shift in attention pointed out that not only is 80 percent of serious juvenile crime committed by less than 10 percent of juvenile offenders, but also that a third of all serious crime is committed by juveniles. Furthermore, some juvenile offenders were allegedly committing as many as 150 to 200 felonies per year, much like their adult counterparts. Juvenile justice policies, then, must be directed at identifying and incapacitating these serious, violent, chronic offenders.

The Reagan administration further believed that for too long the juvenile justice system had been overly concerned with protecting the juvenile offender at the expense of society and the victim. Traditionally, juvenile courts since 1899 had emphasized what was in the best interest of the offending child rather than what was in the best interest of society and the child's victim. It was time to change all that. Recommendations and procedures for restitution were advanced. Restitution, the requirement that an offender make amends to the victim, meant for the most part that offenders should pay back their victims monetarily what they had stolen or destroyed.

According to this approach, the philosophy reflected in the JJDPA of 1974 was all wrong. The Administrator of the Office of Juvenile Justice and Delinquency Prevention commented, "To a great extent, the system has been based on the Rousseauian notion that people are born good, but corrupted by institutions" (Regnery, 1986, p. 49). Delinquents now would be considered as having rational choice; they were no longer at the mercy of forces beyond their control. They must take the consequences of their behavior, and courts must hold them accountable. Furthermore, while the intent behind the JJDPA was to have the federal government provide leadership, it was now to encourage states and local communities to solve their delinquency problems in their own way.

The administration also argued that the underlying cause of delinquency was the erosion of traditional values and the disruption of the family structure, as reflected by the number of broken homes, the high incidence of child abuse and neglect, the fact that some 1.5 million children a year apparently ran away from home, and the recorded annual 7 million births out of wedlock. This observation seems to contradict the iron-fisted approach, however. If children are delinquent *because* they have been abused or neglected, their individual choices have been restricted by social conditions beyond their control. To be consistent, one would call for an assessment of the conditions which lead to delinquency and meaningful intervention before delinquency occurs; in other words, we still need a strategy of formal prevention, which is what the original JJDPA was intended to promote, rather than a strategy of control.

While this policy shift at the national level was occurring, however, states were in the process of complying with the JJDPA and its amendments. At the time the law was passed, it was estimated that 40 percent of all institutionalized children under the control of the juvenile justice system were status offenders or dependent and neglected youths. They were juveniles who had done nothing that could be considered a violation of the criminal code. Most states thus began to alter their laws to comport with the federal statute, particularly insofar as it mandated the deinstitutionalizatic offenders (DSO). Some removed status offender categories from their statutes enu.

The philosophy behind DSO was commendable, but the practice brought numerous unanticipated consequences, primarily because most states did not wish to relinquish their authority over status offenders. Therefore, they placed themselves in the difficult position of finding nonsecure placements and devising new methods of enforcing compliance with court-ordered treatment, services, and out-of-home placements. This resulted in the 1980 Amendment to the JJDPA which allowed the confinement of a status offender in a juvenile correctional institution if he or she violated a court order. More significantly, DSO, as well as the JJDPA in general, widened the net of control over the juvenile population. That is, although the number of status offenders decreased and many states looked for alternatives to incarceration for minor offenders, the number of youths placed on probation or in other supervisory programs expanded considerably. As we will note shortly, there is disagreement about whether this net-widening effect is beneficial.

The three most frequent strategies adopted by states to deinstitutionalize status offenders and seek alternatives to incarceration were decarceration, divestiture, and diversion. We will describe each one briefly, then concentrate upon juvenile diversion, which has been widely lauded as well as criticized.

Decarceration, Divestiture, and Diversion

Jurisdictions employing the decarceration strategy treat status offenders in much the same way as they did before the JJDPA was passed. Status offenders are brought before the juvenile court and a petition is filed alleging that the child is delinquent or, as is now more common, a "child in need of supervision" (CHINS) (or, alternatively, PINS, MINS, JINS—person, minor, juvenile). A hearing follows and, if the facts outlined in the petition are upheld, the youth is given a disposition by the court. This can include probation or an out-of-home placement in a nonsecure facility. Alternately or concurrently, the child may be required to enroll in specified programs.

States which have adopted a divestiture strategy essentially have relinquished their authority over youths who have committed no criminal offense. Status offenses no longer appear in their juvenile statutes. Juvenile courts cannot consider petitions, detain, adjudicate, or dispose of youths on the basis of behavior which previously was identified as a status offense.

The diversion strategy antedated the JJDPA of 1974. It has been used in some format, officially or unofficially, for many years, at least as far back as the turn of the century. The Chicago Juvenile Court Act of 1899, in fact, was a type of diversion program in itself, since it sought to "divert" the child from the authority of the adult criminal justice system. Today, official diversion programs, for adults as well as for juveniles, steer certain offenders (usually minor first-time offenders) away from the courts. The 1967 President's Commission on Law Enforcement and the Administration of Justice offered diversion programs their first official support, and the JJDPA of 1974 highlighted and sustained them.

Juvenile diversion can be defined in various ways, but it at least involves the substitution of a temporary alternative to continued processing by the judicial system. It may be used for status offenders as well as other youthful offenders. Diversion programs vary widely in both structure and effectiveness. They range from setting up individualized plans and closely supervising the individuals to simply referring them to appropriate programs within the community. As Steven Lab (1988, p. 131) states: "Diversion appears to provide whatever the individual agencies deem appropriate. There does not appear to be any coherent, underlying direction for all diversion programs."

Two of the more popular diversion programs in recent years have been the Juvenile Awareness Program (also known as Scared Straight) and the Wilderness Program (also known as Outward Bound) (Lab, 1988). The Juvenile Awareness Program began at Rahway State Prison in New Jersey. Youths who were feared to be candidates for future criminality were taken in groups into a maximum security prison for an emotionally grueling 2-hour session with inmates. The inmates (generally "lifers") told of their own disrupted backgrounds and preached about the cruelties of prison life. The program was direct and simple. It tried to frighten a youth headed for trouble into realizing where his or her deviant actions would eventually lead. The original program—which attracted widespread media attention—claimed an 80–90% success rate. Variants of the program were quickly experimented with by 38 states (O'Donnell, et al., 1987). Despite its immediate popularity, however, evaluations of the program have generally concluded that it is not an effective procedure for reducing recidivism (O'Donnell et al., 1987; Buckner & Chesney-Lind, 1983; Finckenauer, 1979, 1982).

The purpose of the Wilderness Program is to teach youths how to be self-reliant, interdependent, and confident of their own abilities (Lab, 1988). High risk youths are removed from their familiar home environments and placed in situations where they must learn to deal with basic needs and problems associated with survival in the wilderness. Camping, hiking and living off the land for a considerable amount of time are required activities. While the philosophy behind Wilderness Programs has been well received in the literature, very little carefully designed research has examined their effects on delinquency.

Theoretically, diversion should involve less intervention in a youth's life by the criminal justice system than either probation and parole, particularly since the decision to divert is usually made without an adversary process and before a youth has been found guilty of any criminal behavior. In reality, however, depending on the state and jurisdiction, diversion often falls somewhere between regular probation and incarceration. Presumably, it gives a greater measure of guidance than is traditionally associated with probation, but it may also exert much more control over a youth's activities. Moreover, although diversion technically limits official processing, it does so by diffusing official contact over a wider area, creating a risk of subtly, yet continually, involving the individual with the juvenile or criminal justice system. Although individual and family counseling constitutes the major form of diversion intervention (Lab, 1988), the threat of additional involvement by the criminal justice system, if this counseling is ineffective, is an ever present reality. It is important to note that the persons accepted for diversion have not been found guilty of any criminal offense, but are merely alleged to have broken the law.

Diversion can be instigated at any stage of police or judicial processing. Its success depends greatly, however, on the support of the police, the prosecutor, courts, the diversion board itself, and other relevant agencies. One vocal critic of diversion, Malcolm Feeley (1983), finds unacceptable the power given to the public prosecutor with reference to adult diversion programs. The defense attorney, if there is one, has little input into the decision to divert. Alleged offenders often are persuaded to opt for the diversion program without fully understanding its implications; often, they never see a defense attorney. Youths are often diverted from the courts in the same way; although they become part of the program voluntarily, critics question the extent to which their consent is informed. Sometimes failure to participate ''voluntarily'' can result in stronger punishment administered through the juvenile justice system, including confinement or detention.

Although there have been studies assessing individual diversion programs, the variances in program approaches allow diversion as a general strategy to elude empirical assessment. Arnold Binder and Gilbert Geis (1984) make interesting observations on the basis of their scan of the available research. They suggest that ''. . . characterizations of diversion tend to follow a disciplinary party line: Psychologists are prone to regard diversion as a decent enterprise, lawyers to list merits and demerits, and sociologists to derogate diversion as, at best, foolhardy and, at worst, diabolic'' (p. 309). According to Binder and Geis, sociologists line up in virtually unbroken ranks in opposition to diversion programs, but *without* the benefit of convincing empirical documentation of their failure. They charge that opponents generate emotional reactions against diversion, rather than logical, scientific data. Many critics believe, for example, that diversion ''widens the net'' over youth, restricting their freedom. Binder and Geis argue that sociologists have used the term ''widening the net'' pejoratively, with the intention of evoking negative emotional responses from their audience. ''. . . (It) conjures up visions of a mesh net that is thrown over thrashing victims, incapacitating them, as they flail about, desperately seeking to avoid captivity'' (Binder and Geis, 1984, p. 315). Binder and Geis also argue that critics of diversion fail to provide empirical research in support of their claims or to offer compelling documentation of what would happen to youths not diverted from the system. Without diversion, some youths could eventually go deep into the system, ending in long-term confinement. This is, of course, highly speculative, and is itself lacking in documentation.

According to Binder and Geis, other critics of diversion reflect the labeling perspective, with its strong condemnatory tone and its use of terms such as ''dramatization of evil,'' ''secondary deviance,'' ''moral entrepreneurs,'' and ''outsiders.'' Diversion is said to label the child who might otherwise escape this kind of stigmatization. Feeley (1983) notes, ironically, that the original impetus for diversion was rooted in the labeling approach, since it was believed that individuals would escape the stigma associated with formal court processing. Binder and Geis assert there is no cogent evidence that the label affixed to a youth by the diversion process will have the lasting impact on peers and family that repeat offending and more formalized juvenile justice processing would have. This assumes again, of course, that youths not diverted will continue their illegal behavior. Binder and Geis's literature review suggests, however, that there is no evidence that the child's self-concept will suffer irreparable damage from diversion.

At this point, critics and supporters seem to have equally valid claims. While Binder and Geis emphasize that the arguments against diversion are weak in science and strong in rhetoric, we must keep in mind the fact that, overall, diversion has not been well evaluated. Diversion programs have multiple formats and are replete with discretion; furthermore, their long-term effects are unknown. Feeley (1983) argues persuasively that numerous adult diversion efforts were dismal failures. Binder and Geis note that, "Among those redirected [juveniles], at least some would benefit from such services as employment counseling, family counseling, a requirement of restitution, a relationship with a Big Brother or a Big Sister, substance abuse education, or even psychotherapy" (1984, p. 326). Important questions remain unanswered, however. What percentage do benefit and what happens to those who do not? Are the effects upon the latter neutral or harmful? To what extent is it possible to identify, prior to diversion, those who will and will not benefit? Can they be identified prior to being diverted? At present, there seems to be no one diversion strategy that has been shown to be successful wherever tried. What is needed is careful study of those diversion programs which remain in existence and identification of the characteristics of those juveniles who benefit from them.

The Swing Back to Getting Tough

As we have noted, considerable effort was made during the 1970s to remove status offenders from institutions and shift policy regarding juvenile offending toward prevention. Now, however, there have been increasing calls for returning runaways, truants, and other troubled youth back to juvenile court jurisdiction (Krisberg, 1986). This signals a shift back to control as a major objective. Critics of the deinstitutionalization strategy now argue that the anticipated network of alternatives never materialized and that many troubled youths are now left without the help and supervision they need. It is important to note that status offenders in general do not usually become serious or violent offenders (Schneider, 1984). *Chronic* status offenders, however, are at some risk for committing misdemeanors and more serious offenses down the line. It is this knowledge which leads many critics to argue that states should continue their efforts to supervise runaways or "incorrigibles."

Current data reveal that, although the number of juvenile arrests is dropping, the juvenile justice system has become more formal, restrictive, and more oriented toward punishment (Krisberg, et al., 1986). For example, juvenile reform legislation in many states now calls for mandatory and determinate sentencing of juveniles, greater access to juvenile records, and a lowering of the upper age of juvenile jurisdiction (Ohlin, 1983b). In recent years, a considerable amount of juvenile justice legislation, both state and Federal, has facilitated the transfer of serious juvenile offenders to adult criminal courts. This process, "waiver of jurisdiction," may take the form of "certification," "transfer," or "remand" (see Hamparian et al., 1982, for a comprehensive review).

There are two avenues for transferring juvenile offenders to the adult criminal justice process (Feld, 1981). The most common, the *judicial waiver* of jurisdiction, involves case by case decisions by the court on a youth's dangerousness or potential for treatment. *Legislative waivers* are laws mandating that juveniles accused of certain serious offenses be tried in the adult criminal court. Both waivers are intended to see that juveniles considered threats to public safety are subjected to the more punitive adult system, where defendants are held accountable for their actions. The "waiver of jurisdiction" is an extremely consequential action, one that ". . . strips individuals of the allegedly protective status of 'juvenile' and subjects them to the punitive force of the adult criminal justice system" (Bortner, 1986, p. 53).

Under the Comprehensive Crime Control Act of 1984, the minimum age at which juveniles can be prosecuted under *federal* law has been lowered from 16 to 15. They may be prosecuted for any felony involving violence or for certain drug offenses. Furthermore, transfer is mandatory, if the government requests it, for youths who repeat serious crimes. As noted earlier, however, the federal government prefers not to deal with juvenile offenders and not infrequently waives its own jurisdiction to the states.

Over half the *states* have responded to current trends in juvenile justice reform by enacting legislation designed to process serious juvenile offenders in adult courts. Some of the statutes outrightly exclude certain offenses from juvenile court jurisdiction; others make it easier to process juvenile offenders in adult courts; while still others lower the age at which judges may consider a judicial waiver, e.g., from 16 to 14. In addition, a number of states have attempted to stiffen juvenile court penalties for serious juvenile offenders by mandating minimum terms of incarceration or enacting sentencing guidelines which include juvenile offending. Researchers are beginning to evaluate the impact of these harsher policies.

The evidence on the effectiveness of "waiver of jurisdiction" for serious delinquents is mixed. M. A. Bortner (1986) found that only about 30 percent of a sample of 214 "serious" delinquents transferred to adult courts received postconviction incarceration. Slightly over half (55%) of these transferees had been charged with felonies against persons; the remainder were charged with property felonies or drug offenses. This challenges the contention that only the most dangerous juveniles are waived to adult criminal courts. On the other hand, Rudman et al. (1986) studied 117 *violent* youths transferred to adult criminal courts in Boston, Newark, Phoenix, and Memphis. They found that over 90 percent of the transferred violent youth were convicted, that criminal court sanctions were more severe than we would expect from juvenile court, and that 90 percent of those convicted were incarcerated—72.6% in prisons, 17.7% in jails.

Juvenile Correctional Facilities

Obtaining statistics on the precise number of juveniles incarcerated is a challenge. In 1880, there were 53 juvenile public facilities in 23 states and the District of Columbia

(Cahalan, 1986). By 1910, the number had risen to 100, by 1923 to 145. In 1979, there were an estimated 2,551 public and private facilities in the United States which housed juveniles committed to their care. The population of public facilities is diverse, often including status and more serious offenders and sometimes sheltering youths in need of protection who have not been accused of committing any offenses. Moreover, many status offenders and substance abusers are cared for in private institutions whose primary function is to treat emotionally troubled youths. The state pays the cost, but the care-giving role is transferred to the private facility.

Census data reveal that overall, the youth population in the United States over the past 15 years has decreased. Correspondingly, so have the number of juvenile arrests and the number of admissions to juvenile correctional facilities. On the other hand, data also show that juvenile correctional facilities of all types now hold more youths than at anytime since the early 1970s, and that these facilities are increasingly crowded and understaffed (Krisberg et al., 1986). It appears, therefore, that juveniles are now held *longer* in these facilities than at any time previously (Krisberg et al., 1986). In addition, data are beginning to show that a growing disproportionate number of minorities (black, Hispanic, Mexican-American, and native American) are being detained in these juvenile facilities. Furthermore, a two-tiered juvenile correctional system is beginning to develop between private and public facilities (Krisberg et al., 1987). Minorities make up over 50 percent of all juveniles confined at any one time in *public* correctional facilities, while whites make up over 65 percent of the juveniles housed in *private* facilities.

The public-private distinction is one way of categorizing juvenile correctional institutions. Another is to consider whether they have "open" or "institutional" environments. Facilities differ in the amount of community access they provide and in in-house restrictions. Some are long-term facilities for persons whose behavior does not necessitate the strict physical confinement of a training school, such as a ranch, forestry camp, or farm. Others may be short-term facilities that provide temporary care in a physically restrictive environment for juveniles in custody pending court dispositions, awaiting transfer to another institution, or for juveniles adjudicated delinquent but awaiting further decision. The latter, called "detention centers," are maximum security facilities which are far more secure and restrictive than other juvenile correctional facilities (Krisberg et al., 1986). An estimated 9,000 youths nationwide are in adult prisons and 12,000 are in "end-of-the-line" juvenile institutions: long-term, secure institutional facilities for serious offenders.

The JJDPA clearly has been instrumental in deinstitutionalizing status offenders, however. Nationwide, the number of juveniles committed to or detained in public correctional facilities for status offenses has declined substantially since 1973 (Schneider, 1984). According to *Children in Custody*, the number of status offenders in public correctional institutions rose from just over 4,500 in 1973 (the first year these data were kept) to a high of 4,916 in 1977. The numbers dropped considerably in 1979 and continued to decline until 1985. As of February 1, 1985, 2,293 status offenders (1,096 males, 1,197 females) were held in public facilities.

Not all of these status offenders are held in secure institutions. Many are in camps, ranches, or group homes. However, since the 1980 amendment permitting the incarceration of juvenile status offenders who violate court orders, there has been a slight increase in the number of offenders confined in secure facilities. In addition, there has been a decrease in short-term detention and an increase in long-term detention.

While the number of status offenders in public facilities has declined, however, the number in private facilities has increased markedly. Since the private facilities usually are group homes or similar nonsecure, open settings, it may appear that there is little cause for alarm. Increasing privatization in corrections, however, could mean that more status offenders will be turned over to those who operate secure, closed institutions. This is a trend which should be watched very carefully.

There is growing evidence, also, that juveniles in detention centers and other public correctional facilities are kept under increasingly more harsh conditions of confinement (Krisberg et al., 1986). Public facilities are deteriorating, overcrowded, understaffed, and beginning to take on the character of adult jails. As noted earlier, the overall number of juveniles confined in these correctional facilities, particularly minority youths, has increased.

Violent Youth Crime: Prevention or Control?

Violent, repetitive juvenile offending remains unabated and epitomizes pervasive public concern about serious juvenile crime. We must emphasize, however, that only five to ten percent of all juvenile offenders fall under this category. Nevertheless, their crimes in raw numbers are substantial.

As a rule, chronic violent offenders, juvenile or adult, do not seem to respond to rehabilitation, which we define here as intervention designed to change an offender's behavior or situation and presumably prevent him or her from offending in the future. Although a variety of rehabilitative strategies have been attempted, their effectiveness has not been promising where the violent youth offender is concerned. Such strategies are extremely difficult to evaluate, however. Like diversion, rehabilitation programs are packaged in an infinite number of ways, are often implemented inconsistently, and are evaluated haphazardly or not at all. Diversion itself, in fact, can be considered one form of rehabilitation.

Steven Lab and John Whitehead (1988) surveyed the professional literature on juvenile correctional treatment between 1975 and 1984. As we might expect, the studies surveyed used a wide array of subjects, interventions, and outcome measures. Lab and Whitehead's measure of success was the effect of the treatment on recidivism. Unfortunately, no distinction was made between violent offenders and nonviolent offenders. The authors found that at least half of the studies reported negative or no impact on recidivism. On the other hand, those treatment programs that reported success were often based on "dubious, subjective evaluations" (Lab & Whitehead, 1988, p. 60). Interestingly, the treatment programs that seemed to hold the greatest promise were diversion programs, particularly those formally administered by the criminal justice system (e.g., court diversion programs).

Other reviews by Quay (1987b), Gottschalk et al. (1987), Garrett (1985), and Gendreau and Ross (1987) indicate that certain types of rehabilitation strategies do have positive effects on reducing the recidivism rates of delinquents. Moreover, approaches that are community based, rely on extensive social support systems, and use well-trained counselors seem to have the best results (Gendreau and Ross, 1987; Davidson et al., 1987). The positive results, however, are almost invariably achieved with nonviolent offenders.

Even if a violent, repetitive offender is willing and able to change and rehabilitation appears to have been achieved, the youth generally returns to the social systems from whence he or she came. Youths discharged from institutions usually go back to the same home, the same neighborhood, the same community, the same peer network, and the same systems which teach, encourage, and support the same deviant behaviors. In the following section, we will consider to what extent informal methods might both prevent and control future offending.

INFORMAL PREVENTION AND CONTROL OF DELINQUENCY

We began this chapter by noting that we are using *control* to refer to actions taken *after* a youth has committed an offense and *prevention* to refer to actions taken to preclude deviant behavior. Both prevention and control incorporate wide-ranging and sometimes overlapping measures, and both can be formal or informal in nature. Up until this point, we have focused upon formal prevention and control. For the remainder of the chapter, we will discuss informal approaches, focusing primarily on organized programs which can be and have been tried in the small community or neighborhood setting. Such organized measures fall close to the formal end of the Greenberg continuum mentioned earlier (Table 12-1).

It has been noted that in recent years informal social control has been given back to the community (Weis and Sederstrom, 1981; Greenberg et al., 1985b). "Social control" in this sense encompasses both prevention and control as we have been using those terms. Agents of the criminal justice system, be they police officers, prosecutors, criminal court judges, or prison officials, cannot be expected to prevent and control crime without cooperation from the public. This is not to suggest that citizens must assume the power to punish, but rather that they can and must share responsibility in creating environments which are neither conductive to nor tolerant of criminal activity. Furthermore, it is suggested here that agents of the criminal justice system, particularly the front-line police officer, have an important place in this informal network of prevention and control.

Since the early work of the Chicago School, delinquency rates have been reported to be higher in urban, low-income neighborhoods characterized by physical deterioration, rented housing, social disorganization, and population mobility. James Q. Wilson (1975, 1983) argues that what is lacking in high crime areas is a "sense of community," which is more likely to exist in small towns than cities. "Small towns and suburbs, because they are socially more homogeneous than large cities and because local self-government can be used to reinforce informal neighborhood sanctions, apparently make the creation and maintenance of a proper sense of community easier" (1975, p. 28).

Wilson's critics note that those who live in high crime areas are often unable to pay the high taxes and exert the influence which results in better police protection.

Both arguments have merit. However, it is not unreasonable to expect that a lack of informal measures will be linked to rates of delinquency in any neighborhood or community, affluent or not. The direction of the "causal flow" is not entirely clear, but it is surely more complex than we would like. At a minimum, it is likely bi-directional: Social and individual factors play substantial roles in producing delinquency, while criminal and delinquent behavior in turn produce fear, anxiety, feelings of helplessness, and social disorganization. Realistically, however, the absence of informal measures probably hurts low income communities far more than it does those higher in the economic strata.

It is assumed here that the establishment and maintenance of informal measures in neighborhoods and communities help reduce delinquency rates, partly by constraining delinquent behavior (prevention) and partly by responding to it effectively early on (control). This is most likely to occur in close-knit, cohesive, and dense networks. Network theorists also contend that the *multiplexity* of social relationships fosters consistency and conformity in behavior (Krohn, 1986). If an individual interacts with the same people in different social contexts, it is most likely that the same constraining pressures operate across situations. Thus, neighbors who do things together within a variety of contexts, such as going to ballgames, having parties, and working together, will exert considerable control over each other's actions. Krohn (1986, p. 84) asserts, "If our focus is on delinquency rates within a specified geographical area, then it follows that those areas characterized by higher levels of multiplexity in the social relationships of their residents will have lower rates of delinquent behavior." Informal social control is cultivated by frequency as well as multiplicity of social contacts. In addition, frequency and multiplexity of contacts usually depend on some perceived similarity between the participants, such as we saw in peer group networks.

These hypotheses would suggest that social network intervention may be a promising approach to the problem of delinquency. Clifford O'Donnell et al. (1987) warn, however, that we must be careful about the effect of network intervention on peer relationships. While effective programs should cultivate *prosocial* social networks, they should, at the same time, discourage *antisocial* peer networks.

> Regardless of the nature of the intervention program, if contact with peers who are engaged in delinquent activities is increased, the effect of the intervention on delinquency will be diminished . . . What is needed are more interventions that specifically alter the social networks of youths to reduce contact with delinquent peers and increase prosocial relationships. (O'Donnell, Manos, & Chesney-Lind, 1987, p. 261)

Direct empirical evidence of the effectiveness of social networking is lacking at this point, but we can gather supportive clues from the sociodemographic characteristics of neighborhoods and their relationships to delinquency. Informal social control may be reflected in the pride and care exhibited in a neighborhood. Property maintenance is certainly one indicator. Conversely, a lack of informal social control is indicated by the amount of nuisance crime or incivilities in the neighborhood. "Nuisances or incivilities refer to vandalism, litter, abandoned buildings, graffiti, public drunkenness, harassment of passersby by teens and drunks, prostitution, open sale or use of drugs, and the like" (Greenberg et al., 1985a, p. 12). These indicators suggest a sign of decay of informal measures of prevention and control and may reflect an inability of residents to enforce conventional standards of public order. It is important to note, however, that informal measures are unlikely to operate well in isolation. The nuisances just mentioned also may reflect the failure of absentee landlords to maintain their property adequately or of police to enforce the law.

The neighborhood literature reviewed by Stephanie Greenberg and her colleagues (1985a, 1985b) implies that emotional attachment to the neighborhood, perceived control and responsibility over what happens there, the expressed willingness of a resident to intervene in a criminal event, and the belief that others in the neighborhood would also intervene are linked to low crime and delinquency rates. On the other hand, high crime rates are found consistently in neighborhoods characterized by low economic status, a high proportion of minorities, ethnic and class heterogeneity, residential mobility, and a high ratio of teens to adults. While we do not conclude that social networking and informal social controls are the only reasons—or even the major reasons—for the differences, they undoubtedly play a significant part.

Informal social measures should reduce the rate of delinquency, at least nonserious delinquency, substantially. Close-knit and cohesive neighborhoods will be less tolerant of deviant behaviors within the confines of that geographical area. Attempts to attack the delinquency problem, therefore, require that neighborhoods develop informal measures for prevention and control. This suggestion is not new. It has been tried—as far back as the Chicago Area Project—with mixed success and considerable difficulty.

Joseph Weis and John Sederstrom (1981) carefully evaluated a variety of community efforts at delinquency prevention and control. They concluded that virtually all showed ambiguous, mixed, or negative results if success was measured through reduced rates of official delinquency (Weis and Sederstrom, 1981). Broad, all-encompassing federal programs on delinquency prevention fared no better, however. Weis and Sederstrom suggest that this is because they were implemented without rigorous study and careful development. ". . . (R)ecent Federal prevention efforts appear to lack the conceptual foundation, clear prevention focus, and commitment to rigorous research that are necessary to generate the knowledge required for effective delinquency prevention" (Weis and Sederstrom, 1981, p. 3). Clearly, there remains a strong need for enthusiastic commitment to research and development on delinquency prevention, particularly at the neighborhood and community levels.

Community Surveillance

We noted previously that agents of the criminal justice system, particularly law enforcement officers, have an important role to play in informal efforts to prevent and control delinquency. It will certainly be argued that a police or probation officer better represents the formal side of the formal-informal dichotomy. In general, this is correct. However, we suggest that, given the wide discretion exercised and the wide range of activity which "policing" involves, much of what the law enforcement officer does is informal in nature. The police officer who gives a pep talk to the 11-year-old caught dropping an open beer can is exercising informal control. Her partner, meeting with local high school students to hear their views and answer their questions about drugs, can be said to be preventing delinquency—informally.

Recent literature on policing suggests that strategies which keep the law enforcement officer physically closer to the community and in a better position to communicate with citizens encourage citizen participation in crime control efforts. Lawrence Sherman (1987) has reviewed and assessed a variety of these strategies which are often discussed under the rubric "community policing." They include such varied approaches as opening police storefront centers, holding meetings to assess citizen needs, distributing newsletters, and organizing neighborhood clean-up efforts. Research evaluating these efforts generally focuses on what impact these community policing strategies have on fear of crime or reporting victimization to police. Sherman reports mixed results. There appears to be greater success when the strategies do not depend upon extensive citizen participation, however. According to Sherman, there is indication that such citizen involvement increases fear of crime and leaves citizens with an exaggerated perception of the crime problem in the community. In a study of 6 Atlanta neighborhoods, Greenberg et al. (1982) discovered that worry about crime increased as more information was exchanged. Sherman notes, however, that programs involving citizens may not work because police themselves may not be supportive. In some communities, for example, citizens may believe that they can handle crime better than the police, or that the police budget has grown out of hand. "It is therefore no surprise that many police unions are suspicious of citizen-involvement programs" (Sherman, 1987, p. 374).

One popular crime control strategy involving citizens which has received considerable attention in the literature and which underscores the complexity of initiating local efforts is the neighborhood watch program. Typically, residents of a specified area meet in small groups to share information about local crime and delinquency problems, exchange crime prevention tips, and make plans both to supervise the neighborhood and report criminal activities (Rosenbaum, 1987). Lab (1988) estimates that 20,000 communities comprising 5 million people are involved in either neighborhood watch or citizen patrols. The watch programs may be organized by the police or by members of the community, but to be successful a program requires the cooperation of both. The assumption is that contacts and social interactions will strengthen informal social controls, enhance community solidarity, and ultimately reduce crime and delinquency. At the very least, it is hoped that neighborhood watch will improve the collective surveillance of a neighborhood and increase the probability that residents will call the police when they detect strange happenings or criminal actions. Neighborhood watch programs also are intended to decrease the fear of crime among the local residents and increase their confidence in their ability to cope with crime in their immediate environment.

Dennis P. Rosenbaum (1987) has both reviewed the neighborhood watch literature and conducted his own research on the topic. According to Rosenbaum, there is widespread public belief that neighborhood watches can be successfully implemented *any-*

where or *anytime*. This belief, he argues, is without foundation. Neighborhood watches initiated in middle class, culturally homogeneous neighborhoods have been reasonably successful experiments in community participation and have reduced some crimes, *at least in the short haul*. They have not, however, been successful in lower income, culturally heterogeneous neighborhoods. Studies have consistently shown that participation in voluntary organizations is largely a middle class phenomenon (Rosenbaum, 1987; Roehl and Cook (1984); Shernock (1986); Wandersman, Jakubs and Giamartino, 1981). The typical profile of the neighborhood watch participant is a well-educated, middle income, married homeowner with children. Such a person prefers to live in neighborhoods characterized by a shared set of norms, where given public behaviors are approved or disapproved. Furthermore, even without neighborhood watch, informal measures for prevention and control appear to occur naturally and effectively in middle income neighborhoods characterized by single-family home ownership, shared norms and values, and low residential mobility, where the average household has been stable and in place for at least five years.

On a more positive note, Steven Lab (1988) commends the neighborhood watch program for its ability to reduce certain types of crime and delinquency, particularly property offenses such as burglary or larceny. Moreover, this reduction in crime was verified both through official crime records and victimization surveys. Lab also cites research evidence that indicates a substantial reduction in fear of crime by residents once the neighborhood watch program is implemented. Overall, the watch program cultivates an increased communal atmosphere and a sense of togetherness.

Rosenbaum (1987) concludes, however, that neighborhood watches are not suitable strategies for all neighborhoods, and particularly not for low income, heterogeneous neighborhoods whose residents hold conflicting views, subscribe to different norms, and display varied family styles. He notes also that local government plays a critical role in starting and sustaining community-based programs and that cooperative police involvement is essential. Others have noted that even when there is widespread participation in neighborhood watches, the passage of time often reduces the interest (Lindsay and McGillis, 1986).

Still others have offered a number of explanations for the difficulty of maintaining citizen participation. It is suggested that residents of low income, culturally heterogeneous, urban neighborhoods tend to be more suspicious of each other and the formal institutions of social control (Greenberg et al., 1985b). In such neighborhoods, there are pervasive beliefs that police are dishonest, politicians are corrupt, and the government is uncaring. Although the specific targets of suspicion may vary, distrust is widespread and persistent. Thus, attempts by the local police or community agencies to organize meetings to plan neighborhood watches are most likely to be met with distrust and disinterest. Organizers in the Minnesota Community Crime Prevention Program (described in Rosenbaum, 1987), for example, found that participation by culturally diverse and low SES neighborhoods was disappointingly low, despite intensive efforts to persuade residents to attend the meetings.

There is some evidence that residents of lower income neighborhoods are far *more* likely than those of more affluent neighborhoods to call police, particularly for the resolution of interpersonal disputes. M. P. Baumgartner (1985) found that members of the lower or working class were more likely than those of the middle class to call police and to use criminal and administrative law agencies to settle conflicts with family members, friends, and neighbors. Some research (e.g., Crenson, 1978) indicates that the structure of the neighborhood network is an important consideration. Loose-knit neighborhoods, where many residents do not know one another, are more likely to call police than close-knit neighborhoods, where residents rely much more on informal social controls. Donald Black (1976) observed that as societies become larger and more complex, informal sources of social control are weakened and are replaced by heavy reliance on more formal controls. This suggests that as neighborhoods become more impersonal, people are less likely to take responsibility for preventing or controlling crime and delinquency and more likely to rely on official or formal agents.

Boggs (1971) cited data from a statewide survey in Missouri suggesting that rural residents, suburbanites, and central city residents had distinct orientations toward formal and informal control of neighborhood crime and delinquency. Those in rural areas were more likely to believe that informal measures were responsible for neighborhood safety. They tended to rely less on the police. Interestingly, they did not take personal precautions to avoid becoming victimized, believing them to be unnecessary. This may be explained by the presence of dense social networks usually found in rural regions. Suburbanites and central city residents, on the other hand, depended on three sources of protection from crime and delinquency: informal controls, the police, and individual precautions.

Residents of lower income, culturally diverse neighborhoods are said to share fewer common norms and values, which makes it difficult to obtain a consensus about how to deal with the local delinquency problem. Rosenbaum (1987) noted, for example, that when residents of culturally diverse, multi-ethnic neighborhoods attend neighborhood watch meetings, the discussions are often heated and counterproductive because the residents hold conflicting views about the causes, nature, and appropriate responses to the delinquency problems. In some cases, such meetings engendered more animosity and distrust than existed before the meeting.

Stephanie Greenberg et al. (1985b) argue that the conflicting values and discordant norms and value orientations of the low income, multi-ethnic neighborhoods result from the lack of geographical choice most of the residents have in regard to living arrangements. They have limited resources and are forced to find inexpensive housing without regard for the social composition of the neighborhood. Families with greater resources are able to *select* neighborhoods which are compatible with their values and lifestyles. Lower income families do not have that luxury. In other words, because the people of higher incomes have choices of residential locations, they tend to live in homogeneous neighborhoods, where residents already share many assumptions about appropriate public behavior, upkeep of property, and control of children.

Residents of low income neighborhoods also tend to feel less in control over what happens in their area and perceive their personal impact on the local crime and delinquency problems to be minimal, if not nonexistent (Greenberg et al., 1985b). The lower the sense of control over what happens in one's neighborhood, the higher the fear of crime and delinquency. Available research indicates that fear of crime tends to be highest in low income, multi-ethnic, multi-cultural neighborhoods (Greenberg et al., 1985a). Moreover, as Rosenbaum (1987) noted, this fear can be exacerbated when residents articulate their own perceived fears, personal victimizations, and other crime incidents. Recall that Greenberg et al. (1982) discovered that worry about crime increased as more information was exchanged among residents of 6 Atlanta neighborhoods.

It appears that those low income neighborhoods which do develop strong informal social control tend to be characterized by the dominance of one ethnic group, which—while perhaps not the majority—takes it upon itself to exert social control through churches, schools, and families (Greenberg et al., 1985b). This group is much more likely to exert its influence at the most informal end of the social control continuum (Table 12-1). That is, rather than organize or participate in programs such as neighborhood watch, residents express individual and group disapproval of behavior which falls outside expected norms. More important, they may prevent delinquency by communicating before the fact that antisocial behavior will not be tolerated. Neighborhoods or communities with such a high degree of homogeneity are the exception rather than the rule, however.

In sum, much of the research assessing citizen participation in preventing and controlling crime and delinquency, especially in high crime neighborhoods, is not encouraging. However, the literature often misses a very important point, and in some respects, reflects an unfortunate philosophy. Even if not so intended, the impression given is that residents of lower class neighborhoods are less competent and cooperative, and that some ephemeral organizer (presumably in the form of an official of government) must take the helm. We would argue, however, that the perceived failures of many community programs may be due to insensitivity on the part of organizers to the needs of the residents. Often, successful community efforts are not possible unless they are initiated and maintained by the residents themselves. Since these citizen efforts generally require official support both in the form of financial investment and allocation of resources, there is an understandable temptation for government officials or outside community activists to play a heavy hand.

This problem was well recognized in early literature on community organizing, but seems to be ignored in the studies just discussed. Stephen Rose (1972) wrote a powerful indictment of the local and state governments which coopted the community action programs so prevalent in the 1960s and appropriated funds for management purposes which were really intended for the direct benefit of the poor. James Cunningham and Milton Kotler (1983) assessed a variety of neighborhood programs nationwide and offered invaluable suggestions for making such programs viable. Building successful neighborhood organizations, they noted, requires dedication to a wide range of tasks, including identifying community leaders, developing communication, leadership, and negotiation skills, learning how to deal with groups outside the neighborhood, raising funds, and building power. The process is not simple, but it is worth the effort, as successful organizations illustrate. Often, ''crime watching'' becomes part of the function of a more generalized neighborhood group. In sum, we should be careful about accepting the conclusions of neighborhood watch and other research which indicates that these programs do not generally work at low social class levels, without attending to the reasons.

Furthermore, we have used brute simplification in this section in distinguishing between low income and middle income neighborhoods, primarily because the available research does the same. It must be acknowledged, however, that population distributions are not only determined by income, but also by health, age, family style, occupation, marital status, presence of children, and, unfortunately, race and religion. "Childless professional couples tend to prefer central locations with access to entertainment; parents on limited incomes look for single-family houses with backyards, usually finding them in distant surburbs; and elderly pensioners are so constrained by their poverty that they must often settle for small apartments in dangerous neighborhoods" (Fischer, 1982, p. 26). In some communities, however, the elderly are just as constrained by the need to live near public transportation and health care facilities as by their income. In others, potential homeowners regardless of their income level, are driven away because they are of a different race or ethnic background. The success of such projects as neighborhood watches, therefore, requires not only knowledge of the population, but also of the relationships with groups outside the neighborhood. It requires, also, some appreciation of the micro- and mesosystems of the residents. Future efforts at evaluating informal programs of prevention and control would do well to pay some attention to these factors.

A SUMMING UP

In this text we have tried to present the literature on juvenile delinquency comprehensively, accurately, and within a historical framework. Theories of delinquency, we have argued, cannot be appreciated if they are separated from the economic, political, and sociocultural backdrop against which they develop. Merton's strain theory was formulated in the late 1930s, still in the aftershock of the Great Depression. The theory may have been a viable one at the time, but it appears less so in the current social climate, although others will certainly disagree. On the other hand, recent research and theory-building, though contemporary, does not necessarily add appreciably to knowledge about juvenile delinquency. We have followed the social, scientific, legislative, and judicial recognition of delinquency along a historical course to encourage readers both to assess the relative merits of what has been tried and what is being tried now and to speculate about future efforts to approach the problem of delinquency efficiently and creatively.

In addition to noting the substantial influence of the historical context on explanations of delinquency, we also have admonished that data are collected and theories formulated within the constraints of belief. All theorists enter the research design and data collection process with assumptions that affect their methodology and sensitize them to interpretations of the data which fit their own theoretical perspectives. We are all caught within the framework of our assumptions, our experiences, even our language. Knowledge of any kind is a construction of the human mind, and that mind is itself constructed within a social and cultural context.

Subjectivity is inevitable, but it does not render research invalid. There are, however, rules of science which must be followed to minimize it. For example, terms, concepts, and methodology must be defined clearly enough for others to comprehend and to challenge. Researchers should be encouraged to state explicitly their assumptions, rather than leave others to deduce them. Statistical analyses must be appropriate to the task. Researchers should be free, however, to interpret the data and posit about their theoretical implications within their own construct systems, without fearing disparagement from others.

Students of criminology often ask, "What is the best explanation for delinquency?" or "Which theorist makes the most sense?" Others, more pragmatic and action oriented, want to know, "How will these theories help us to control or prevent delinquency?" There is simply no right or wrong answer to any of these questions, no single best theory, no single best direction for social policy. Theories are merely tools for thought, valid insofar as they are illuminating and worth citing as long as they are thought provoking. They are not, however, complete or absolute answers. Although in our opinion, a social systems approach is best suited for understanding delinquent behavior and for formulating social policy, others have and will have different suggestions.

If we pretend that there is one truth, one reality, and one answer to social problems, we will likely feel defeated about the extent to which we can contribute toward an understanding of delinquency. A conceptual odyssey through the theories and empirical data is apt to end with the traveler feeling confused, dissatisfied, and disillusioned about the incomplete and imperfect models of reality concerning the delinquency problem.

The overall mission of the book, in addition to familiarizing readers with the study of juvenile delinquency, has been to cultivate flexibility and encourage readers to see the world from multiple perspectives. This is not to say that we should avoid choosing a theoretical position. It is to say that we should construct our position with tolerance and remain open to other points of view.

Have criminologists made progress in the study of delinquency? Without a doubt. Much of it has been in the direction of understanding science and how it contributes to the study of delinquency. Criminologists have recognized and become more tolerant of the complexity involved in the crime problems. Increasingly, they have come to realize that single, immediate causes are elusive, and their research models have tried to accommodate this knowledge. Refinements and modifications of earlier theories have been less grandiose and conclusive and more specific and tentative. Most criminologists realize that individual behavior is part of a continuously ongoing, bi-directional process with multiple, dynamic influences; predictions, especially long-term predictions, are risky. It may well be that theories focusing on "causal loops" provide the best explanations of the many processes impinging upon human behavior. In addition, it is becoming increasingly acknowledged that the study of juvenile delinquency can be revitalized by contacts with the methods, concepts, and knowledge of other disciplines, including economics, anthropology, and political science.

Having said this, we are still ill at ease and haunted by the remarks of R. Kirkland Schwitzgebel (1977, p. 139): "I have arrived reluctantly at last at the conclusion that some people are mean, and a few people are repeatedly mean." How does one explain the repeatedly violent, serious juvenile offender? Is this offender a victim of what anthropologist Loren Eiseley (1970) has termed "restive ghosts"? "We know that within our heads there still exists an irrational restive ghost that can whisper disastrous messages into the ear of reason" (p. 154). Are we victims of our evolutionary, genetic past, some of us more genetically programmed to violence than others? We think not. We are social beings, partly influenced by biology, but more the victims and influencers of our social environments.

We have suggested that analyses and theoretical developments that recognize different levels from the individual system to the macrosystems will lead us further along toward a more complete understanding of delinquency. At the aggregate level of explanation, serious delinquents do not necessarily engage in their behavior for the same reasons as they did 100 years ago. Furthermore, at the individual level, each delinquent engages in antisocial actions for different reasons and within different contexts. Serious delinquents are products of a series of events along the life course that we are just beginning to understand within our own historical context. The statement that some people are mean, or repetitively mean, while correct, is unsatisfactory. It needs to be supplemented with the statement that society can and must continue its efforts to prevent "mean-ness" as much as possible. Criminologists have made progress, but the field is eager for imaginative theoretical development and research, particularly on the problems associated with the serious delinquent.

References

ACKER, J. R. (1987). Social sciences and the criminal law: The Fourth Amendment, probable cause, and reasonable suspicion. *Criminal Law Bulletin, 23*, 49–79.

ADLER, F. (1975). *Sisters in crime.* New York: McGraw-Hill.

AGETON, S. S. (1983). The dynamics of female delinquency, 1976–1980. *Criminology, 21*, 555–584.

AGNEW, R. (1987). On "testing structural strain theories." *Journal of Research in Crime and Delinquency, 24*, 281–286.

AKERS, R. L. (1964). Socio-economic status and delinquent behavior: A retest. *Journal of Research in Crime and Delinquency, 1*, 38–46.

AKERS, R. L. (1977). *Deviant behavior: A social learning approach.* (2nd ed.). Belmont, CA: Wadsworth.

AKERS, R. L. (1985). *Deviant behavior: A social learning approach.* (3rd. ed.). Belmont, CA: Wadsworth.

ALLEN, F. A. (1964). *The borderland of criminal justice.* Chicago: University of Chicago Press.

ALLPORT, G. (1961). *Pattern and growth in personality.* New York: Holt, Rinehart and Winston.

ANASTASI, A. (1982). *Psychological testing.* (5th ed.). New York: Macmillan.

ANDRY, R. G. (1960). *Delinquency and parental pathology.* London: Metheuth.

APPLEGATE, J. L., BURLESON, B.R., BURKE, J. A., DELIA, J. G., & KLINE, S. L. (1985). Reflection-enhancing parental communication. In I. E. Sigel (Ed.), *Parental belief systems.* Hillsdale, NJ: Lawrence Erlbaum Associates.

Araki, N. (1985). The flow of criminal cases in the Japanese criminal justice system. *Crime and Delinquency, 31*, 601–629.

Austin, R. L. (1978). Race, father-absence, and female delinquency. *Criminology, 15*, 487–504.

Baldwin, J. (1974). Social area analysis and studies of delinquency. *Social Science Researcher, 3*, 151–168.

Baldwin, J. (1979). Ecological and areal studies in Great Britain and the United States. In N. Morris & M. Tonry (Eds.), *Crime and justice: An annual review of research.* Chicago: University of Chicago Press.

Baldwin, J. M. (1894). *Mental development in the child and the race.* New York: Macmillan.

Baldwin, J. M. (1897). *Social and ethical interpretations in mental development: A study in social psychology.* New York: Macmillan.

Balkan, S., Berger, R., & Schmidt, J. (1980). *Crime and deviance in America.* Belmont, CA: Wadsworth.

Bandura, A. (1973). Social learning theory of aggression. In J. F. Knutson (Ed.), *The control of aggression.* Chicago: Aldine.

Bandura, A. (1977). *Social learning theory.* Englewood Cliffs, NJ: Prentice-Hall.

Bandura, A. (1978). The self-system in reciprocal determinism. *American Psychologist, 33*, 344–358.

Bandura, A. (1983). Psychological mechanisms of aggression. In R. G. Geen & E. I. Donnerstein (Eds.), *Aggression: Theoretical and empirical reviews*, Vol. 1. New York: Academic Press.

Bandura, A., & Huston, A. C. (1961). Identification as a process of incidental learning. *Journal of Abnormal and Social Psychology, 63*, 311–318.

Bandura, A., Ross, D., & Ross, S. (1963). Vicarious reinforcement and imitative learning. *Journal of Abnormal and Social Psychology, 67*, 601–607.

Bandura, A., & Walters, R. H. (1959). *Adolescent aggression.* New York: Ronald.

Bandura, A., & Walters, R. H. (1963). *Social learning and personality development.* New York: Holt, Rinehart.

Barnes, H. E., & Teeters, N. K. (1945). *New horizons in criminology.* New York: Prentice-Hall.

Barnes, J. A. (1954). Class and communities in a Norwegian island parish. *Human Relations, 7*, 39–58.

Bartol, C. R., & Bartol, A. M. (1986). *Criminal behavior: A psychosocial approach.* (2nd ed.). Englewood Cliffs, NJ: Prentice-Hall.

Bates, J. E. (1980). The concept of difficult temperament. *Merrill-Palmer Quarterly, 26*, 299–319.

Baumgartner, M. P. (1985). Law and the middle class: Evidence from a suburban town. *Law and Human Behavior, 9*, 3–24.

Baumrind, D. (1967). Authoritarian vs. authoritative parental control. *Adolescence, 3*, 255–272.

Baumrind, D. (1971). Current patterns of parental authority. *Developmental Psychology Monographs, 4*, 1–103.

Bayley, D. H. (1976). *Forces of order.* Berkeley, CA: University of California Press.

Becker, H. S. (1963). *Outsiders: Studies in the sociology of deviance.* New York: Free Press.

BEIRNE, P. (1983). Generalization and its discontents: The comparative study of crime. In I. L. Barak-Glantz & E. H. Johnson (Eds.), *Comparative criminology*. Beverly Hills, CA: Sage.

BEIRNE, P. (1987). Between classicism and positivism: Crime and penality in the writings of Gabriel Tarde. *Criminology*, *25*, 785–819.

BELL, R. R. (1981). *Worlds of friendship*. Beverly Hills, CA: Sage.

BELSKY, J., LERNER, R. M., & SPANIER, G. B. (1984). *The child in the family*. New York: Random House.

BEM, D. J., & ALLEN, A. (1974). On predicting some of the people some of the time: The search for cross-situational consistencies in behavior. *Psychological Review*, *81*, 506–520.

BENDIX, R. (1963). Concepts and generalizations in comparative sociological studies. *American Sociological Review*, *28*, 532–542.

BENNETT, J. (1981). *Oral history and delinquency: The rhetoric of criminology*. Chicago: University of Chicago Press.

BERNARD, T. J. (1981). The distinction between conflict and radical criminology. *Journal of Criminal Law and Criminology*, *72*, 362–379.

BERNARD, T. J. (1987a). Testing structural strain theories. *Journal of Research in Crime and Delinquency*, *24*, 262–280.

BERNARD, T. J. (1987b). Repy to Agnew. *Journal of Research in Crime and Delinquency*, *24*, 287–290.

BERNDT, T. (1979). Developmental changes in conformity to peers and parents. *Developmental Psychology*, *15*, 608–616.

BERNSTEIN, B. (1974). *Class, codes, and control: Theoretical studies towards a sociology of language: Vol. 1.* (revised ed.). New York: Schocken.

BERTALANFFY, L. VON. (1968). *General system theory*. New York: George Braziller.

BIJOU, S. W., & BAER, D. M. (1961). *Child development*. New York: Appleton-Century-Crofts.

BILESA, D. (1971). Birth order and delinquency. *Australian Psychologist*, *6*, 189–193.

BINDER, A., & GEIS, G. (1984). *Ad Populum* argumentation in criminology: Juvenile diversion as rhetoric. *Crime and Delinquency*, *30*, 309–333.

BIXENSTINE, V. E., DESORTE, M. S., & BIXENSTINE, B. A. (1976). Conformity to peer-sponsored misconduct at four grade levels. *Developmental psychology*, *12*, 226–236.

BLACK, D. (1976). *The behavior of law*. New York: Academic Press.

BLALOCK, H. M., JR., (1969). *Theory construction*. Englewood Cliffs, NJ: Prentice-Hall.

BLALOCK, H. M., JR., (1970). *An introduction to social research*. Englewood Cliffs, NJ: Prentice-Hall.

BLECHMAN, E. A. (1982). Are children with one parent at psychological risk? A methodological review. *Journal of Marriage and the Family*, *44*, 179–195.

BLOCK, H. A., & NIEDERHOFFER, A. (1958). *The Gang: A study in adolescent behavior*. New York: Philosophical Library.

BLUMSTEIN, A., COHEN, J., & FARRINGTON, D. P. (1988). Criminal career research: Its value for criminology. *Criminology*, *26*, 1–36.

BOGGS, S. (1971). Formal and informal crime control: An exploratory study of urban, suburban and rural orientation. *Sociological Quarterly*, *12*, 319–327.

BORDUA, D. J. (1958). Juvenile delinquency and anomie. *Social Problems*, *6*, 230–238.

BORTNER, M. A. (1986). Traditional rhetoric, organizational realities: Remand of juveniles to adult court. *Crime and Delinquency, 32,* 53–73.

BOTT, E. (1955). Urban families: Conjugal roles and social networks. *Human Relations, 8,* 345–385.

BOTT, E. (1957). *Family and social network.* London: Tavistock.

BOTTOMS, A. E., & WILES, P. (1986). Housing tenure and residential community crime careers in Britain. In A. G. Reiss, Jr., & M. Tonry (Eds.), *Communities and crime.* Chicago: University of Chicago Press.

BOX, S., & HALE, C. (1984). Liberation/emancipation, economic marginalization, or less chivalry. *Criminology, 22,* 473–497.

BRAITHWAITE, J. (1981). The myth of class and criminality reconsidered. *American Sociological Review, 46,* 36–57.

BRECKINRIDGE, S., & ABBOTT, E. (1912). *The delinquent child and the home.* New York: Russell Sage Foundation.

BRONFENBRENNER, U. (1979). *The ecology of human development: Experiment by nature and design.* Cambridge, MA: Harvard University Press.

BRONFENBRENNER, U. (1986a). Ecology of the family as a context for human development: Research perspectives. *Developmental Psychology, 22,* 723–742.

BRONFENBRENNER, U. (1986b). Recent advances in research on the ecology of human development. In R. K. Silbereisen, K. Eyferth, & G. Rudinger (Eds.), *Development as action in context.* Berlin: Springer-Verlag.

BRONFENBRENNER, U., & CROUTER, A. C. (1982). Work and Family through time and space. In S. B. Kamerman & C. D. Hayes (Eds.), *Families that work: Children in a changing world.* Washington, DC: National Academy Press.

BRONFENBRENNER, U., & CROUTER, A. C. (1983). The evolution of environmental models in developmental research. In P. H. Mussen (Ed.), *Handbook of Child Psychology: Vol. 1.* New York: Wiley.

BRONOWSKI, J. *The common sense of science.* Cambridge, MA: Harvard University Press, 1978.

BROUGHTON, J. M. (1981). The genetic psychology of James Mark Baldwin. *American Psychologist, 36,* 396–407.

BRUNER, J. S. (1986). *Actual minds, possible worlds.* Cambridge, MA: Harvard University Press.

BUCKLEY, W. (1967). *Sociology and modern systems theory.* Englewood Cliffs, NJ: Prentice-Hall.

BUCKNER, J. C. & CHESNEY-LIND, M. (1983). Dramatic cures for juvenile crime: An evaluation of a prisoner-run delinquency prevention program. *Criminal Justice and Behavior, 10,* 227–247.

BURGESS, E. W. (1923). The study of the delinquent as a person. *American Journal of Sociology, 28,* 657–680.

BURGESS, E. W., & BOGUE, D. J. (1967). The delinquency research of Clifford R. Shaw and Henry D. McKay and associates. In E. W. Burgess & D. J. Bogue (Eds.), *Urban Sociology.* Chicago: University of Chicago Press.

BURGESS, R. L. & AKERS, R. L. (1966). A differential association-reinforcement theory of criminal behavior. *Social Problems, 14,* 128–147.

BURKETT, S. R., & WARREN, B. O. (1987). Religiosity, peer associations, and adolescent marijuana use: A panel study of underlying causal structures. *Criminology*, *25*, 109–132.

BURSIK, R. J., JR., (1984). Urban dynamics and ecological studies of delinquency. *Social Forces*, *63*, 393–413.

BURSIK, R. J., JR., (1986a). Ecological stability and the dynamics of delinquency. In A. J. Reiss, Jr. & M. Tonry (Eds.), *Communities and crime*. Chicago: University of Chicago Press.

BURSIK, R. J., JR., (1986b). Delinquency rates as sources of ecological change. In J. M. Byrne & R. J. Sampson (Eds.), *The social ecology of crime*. New York: Springer-Verlag.

BURSIK, R. J., JR., (1987). *Political decision-making and ecological models of delinquency: Conflict and consensus*. The Albany Conference: Theoretical Integration in the Study of Deviance and Crime. May 7–8.

BURSIK, R. J., JR., & WEBB, J. (1982). Community change and patterns of delinquency. *American Journal of Sociology*, *88*, 24–43.

BURT, C. (1929). *The young delinquent*. New York: Appleton.

BURTON, R. V. (1963). Generality of honesty reconsidered. *Psychological Review*, *70*, 481–499.

BURTON, R. V. (1976). Honesty and dishonesty. In T. Lickona (Ed.), *Moral development and behavior*. New York: Holt, Rinehart and Winston.

BUSS, A. H., & PLOMIN, R. (1975). *A temperament theory of personality development*. New York: Wiley.

BUSS, A. H., & PLOMIN, R. (1984). *Temperament: Early developing personality traits*. Hillsdale, NY: Erlbaum.

BYRNE, J. M., & SAMPSON, R. J. (1986). Key issues in the social ecology of crime. In J. M. Byrne & R. J. Sampson (Eds.), *The Social ecology of crime*. New York: Springer-Verlag.

CAHALAN, M. W. (1986). *Historical corrections statistics in the United States, 1850–1984*. Rockville, MD: Westat.

CAIRNS, R. B. (1983). The emergence of developmental psychology. In P. H. Mussen (Ed.), *Handbook of Child Psychology: Vol. 1*. (4th ed.). New York: Wiley.

CAMP, C. (1980). *School dropouts*. Sacramento, CA: Assembly Office of Research, California.

CAMPAGNA, A. F., & HARTER, S. (1975). Moral judgment in sociopathic and normal children. *Journal of Personality and Social Psychology*, *31*, 199–205.

CAMPBELL, A. (1962). Recent developments in survey studies of potential behavior. In A. Ranney (Ed.), *Essays on the behavioral study of politics*. Urbana, IL: University of Illinois Press.

CAMPBELL, A. (1984). *The girls in the gang*. Oxford: Basil Blackwell.

CAMPBELL, D. T., & STANLEY, J. C. (1966). *Experimental and quasi-experimental designs for research*. Chicago: Rand McNally.

CAMPOS, J. J., BARRETT, K. C., LAMB, M. E., GOLDSMITH, H. H., & STENBERG, C. (1983). Socioemotional development. In P. H. Mussen (Ed.), *Handbook of Child Psychology: Vol. 4*. (4th ed.). New York: Wiley.

CANTNER, R. (1981). *Family correlates of male and female delinquency*. Boulder, CO: Behavioral Institute.

CAREY, J. T. (1975). *Sociology and public affairs: The Chicago school*. Beverly Hills, CA: Sage.

CARNEGIE COUNCIL ON POLICY STUDIES IN HIGHER EDUCATION. (1979). *Giving youth a better chance: Options for education, work and serivce*. San Francisco: Jossey-Bass.

CARPENTER, C., GLASSNER, B., JOHNSON, B. D., & LOUGHLIN, J. (1988). *Kids, drugs, and crime.* Lexington, MA: Lexington Books.

CARR, E. H. (1962). *What is history?* New York: Knopf.

CASPI, A., ELDER, G. H., JR., & BEM, D. J. (1987). Moving against the world: Life course patterns of explosive children. *Developmental Psychology, 23,* 308-313.

CAVAN, R. S., & CAVAN, J. J. (1968). *Delinquency and crime: Cross-cultural perspectives.* Philadelphia: Lippincott.

CHESNEY-LIND, M. (1986). Women and Crime. *Signs, 12,* (pages unnumbered).

CHILTON, R. J. (1964). Continuity in delinquency area research: A comparison of studies for Baltimore, Detroit, and Indianapolis. *American Sociological Review, 29,* 71-83.

CHRISTOPHER, R. C. (1983). *The Japanese mind: the Goliath explained.* New York: Simon & Schuster.

CLECKLEY, H. (1976). *The mask of sanity.* Saint Louis: C. V. Mosby.

CLINARD, M. (1978). *Cities with little crime: The case of Switzerland.* New York: Cambridge University Press.

CLINARD, M. B., & ABBOTT, D. J. (1973). *Crime in developing countries: A comparative perspective.* New York: Wiley.

CLOWARD, R. A., & OHLIN, L. E. (1960). *Delinquency and opportunity: A theory of delinquent groups.* Glencoe, IL: Free Press.

COHEN, A. K. (1955). *Delinquent boys: The culture of the gang.* Glencoe, IL: The Free Press.

COHEN, A. K. (1965). The sociology of the deviant act: Anomie theory and beyond. *American Sociological Review, 30,* 5-14.

COHEN, A. K. (1980). The sociology of the deviant act: Anomie and beyond. In S. H. Traub & C. B. Little (Eds.), *Theories of deviance.* (3rd ed.). Itasca, IL: Peacock.

COHEN, A. K. (1983). Interview with Albert K. Cohen. June 1, 1979. In J. H. Laub, *Criminology in the making: An oral history.* Boston: Northeastern University Press.

COHEN, B. (1981). Reporting crime: The limits of statistical and field data. In A. S. Blumberg (Ed.), *Current perspectives on criminal behavior.* (2nd ed.). New York: Knopf.

COHEN, L. E. & LAND, K. C. (1987). Age structure and crime: Symmetry versus asymmetry and the projection of crime rates through the 1990's. *American Sociological Review, 52,* 170-183.

COGAN, N. H. (1970). Juvenile law before and after the entrance of ''parens patriae.'' *South Carolina Law Review, 22,* 147-181.

COLBY, A., KOHLBERG, L., GIBBS, J., & LIEBERMANN, M. (1983). A longitudinal study of moral judgment. *Monographs of the Society for Research in Child Development, 48,* (Nos. 1-2, Serial No. 200).

COLCORD, J. C. (1932). Discussion of ''Are broken homes a causative factor in juvenile delinquency?'' *Social Forces, 10,* 525-527.

COLE, S. (1975). The growth of scientific knowledge: Theories of deviance as a case study. In L. A. Coser (Ed.), *The idea of social structure: Papers in honor of Robert K. Merton.* New York: Harcourt, Brace, Jovanovich.

CONGER, J. J., & MILLER, W. C. (1966). *Personality, social class and delinquency.* New York: Wiley.

COOK, T. D., & CAMPBELL, D. T. (1979). *Quasi-experimentation: Design and analysis issues for field setting.* Boston: Houghton-Mifflin.

COOLEY, C. H. (1922). *Human nature and the social order.* Glencoe, IL: The Free Press.

CORNELL, D. G., BENEDEK, E. P., & BENEDEK, D. M. (1987). Juvenile homicide: Prior adjustment and a proposed typology. *American Journal of Orthopsychiatry, 57,* 383–393.

CORTES, J. B., & GATTI, F. M. (1972). *Delinquency and crime: A biopsychological approach.* New York: Seminar Press.

CRAIG, M. M., & GLICK, S. J. (1963). Ten years' experience with the Glueck social prediction table. *Crime and Delinquency, 9,* 249–251.

CRENSON, M. A. (1978). Social networks and political processes in urban neighborhoods. *American Journal of Political Science, 22,* 578–594.

CRESSEY, D. R. (1960). The theory of differential association: An introduction. *Social Problems, 8,* 2–5.

CRESSEY, D. R. (1983). Interview with Donald R. Cressey, March 20, 1979. In J. H. Laub (Ed.), *Criminology in the making: An oral history.* Boston: Northeastern University Press.

CROMWELL, P. F., JR., KILLINGER, G. C., KERPER, H. B., & WALKER, C. (1985). *Probation and parole in the criminal justice system.* (2nd ed.). St. Paul, MN: West Publishing.

CROWE, R. R. (1974). An adoptive study of antisocial personality. *Archives of General Psychiatry, 31,* 785–791.

CUNNINGHAM, J. V., & KOTLER, M. (1983). *Building neighborhood organizations.* Notre Dame, IN: University of Notre Dame Press.

CURTIS, G. B. (1976). The checkered career of parens patriae: The state as parent or tyrant? *DePaul Law Review, 25,* 895–915.

DAHLSTROM, W. G. (1985). The development of psychological testing. In G. A. Kimble & K. Schlesinger (Eds.), *Topics in the history of psychology: Vol. 2.* Hillsdale, NJ: Lawrence Erlbaum.

DAHRENDORF, R. (1959). *Class and class conflict in industrial society.* Stanford, CA: Stanford University Press.

DALGARD, O. S., & KRINGLEN, E. (1976). A Norwegian twin study of criminality. *British Journal of Criminology, 16,* 213–232.

DATESMAN, S. K., & SCARPITTI, F. R. (1975). Female delinquency and broken homes: A reassessment. *Criminology, 13,* 33–54.

DAVIDSON, W. S., REDNER, R., BLAKELY, C., MITCHELL, C., & EMSHOFF, J. (1987). Diversion of juvenile offenders: An experimental comparison. *Journal of Consulting and Clinical Psychology, 55,* 68–75.

DAVIS, N. J. (1975). *Sociological constructions of deviance.* Dubuque, IA: Wm. C. Brown.

DELORTO, T. E., & CULLEN, F. T. (1985). The impact of moral development on delinquent involvement. *International Journal of Comparative and Applied Criminal Justice, 9,* 128–139.

DENTLER, R., & MONROE, L. (1961). Social correlates of adolescent theft. *American Sociological Review, 26,* 733–743.

DEVOS, G. (1980). Delinquency and minority status: A psychocultural perspective. In. G. R. Newman (Ed.), *Crime and Deviance.* Beverly Hills, CA: Sage.

DORNBUSCH, S. M. (1983). *Social class, race and sex differences in family influence upon adolescent decision making.* Paper presented at the meeting of the Pacific Sociological Association, San Jose, CA.

DORNBUSCH, S. M., CARLSMITH, J. M., BUSCHWALL, S. J., RITTER, P. L., LEIDERMAN, H., HASTORF, C., & GROSS, R. T. (1985). Single parents, extended households, and the control of adolescents. *Child Development, 56,* 326–341.

DOUGLAS, J. W. B., ROSS, J. M., & SIMPSON, H. R. (1968). *All our future.* London: Peter Davies.

DOWNES, D., & ROCK, P. (1982). *Understanding deviance.* Oxford: Clarendon Press.

DUCK, S. W., & CRAIG, G. (1978). Personality similarity and the development of friendship: A longitudinal study. *British Journal of Social and Clinical Psychology, 17,* 237–242.

DUGDALE, R. L. (1877). *The "Jukes".* New York: G. P. Putman.

DYSON, F. (1988). *Infinite in all directions.* New York: Harper & Row.

EINSTEIN, A. (1949). *The world as I see it.* New York: Philosophical Library.

EISELEY, L. (1970). *The invisible pyramid.* New York: Charles Scribner.

EISENBERG, N., & LENNON, R. (1983). Sex differences in empathy and related capacities. *Psychological Bulletin, 94,* 100–131.

ELLIOTT, D. S. (1985). The assumption that theories can be combined with increased explanatory power: Theoretical integrations. In R. F. Meier (Ed.), *Theoretical methods in criminology.* Beverly Hills, CA: Sage.

ELLIOTT, D. S. & AGETON, S. S. (1980). Reconciling race and class differences in self-reported and official estimates of delinquency. *American Sociological Review, 45,* 95–110.

ELLIOTT, D. S., AGETON, S. S., & CANTER, R. J. (1979). An integrated theoretical perspective on delinquent behavior. *Journal of Research in Crime and Delinquency, 16,* 3–27.

ELLIOTT, D. S., DUNFORD, T. W., & HUIZINGA, D. (1987). The identification and prediction of career offenders utilizing self-reported and official data. In J. D. Burchard & S. N. Burchard (Eds.), *Prevention of delinquent behavior.* Newbury Park, CA: Sage.

ELLIOTT, D. S., & HUIZINGA, D. (1983). Social class and delinquent behavior in a national youth panel. *Criminology, 21,* 149–177.

ELLIOTT, D. S., & HUIZINGA, D. (1984). *The relationship between delinquent behavior and ADM [Alcohol, Drug, and Mental Health] problems.* Boulder, CO: Behavioral Research Institute.

ELLIOTT, D. S., & VOSS, H. L. (1974). *Delinquency and dropout.* Lexington, MA: Lexington Books.

ELLIOTT, D. S., VOSS, H. L., & WENDLING, A. (1966). Capable dropouts and the social milieu of the high school. *Journal of Educational Research, 60,* 180–186.

ELLIOTT, M. A., & MERRILL, F. E. (1934). *Social disorganization.* New York: Harper & Brothers.

ELLWOOD, C. A. (1901). The theory of imitation in social psychology. *American Journal of Sociology, 6,* 721–744.

EMERY, R. E. (1982). Interparental conflict and the children of discord and divorce. *Psychological Bulletin, 92,* 310–330.

EMPEY, L. T. (1982). *American delinquency.* Homewood, IL: Dorsey Press.

EPPS, P., & PARNELL, R. W. (1952). Physique and temperament of women delinquents compared with women undergraduates. *British Journal of Medical Psychology, 25,* 249–255.

ERIKSON, K. T. (1962). Notes on the sociology of deviance. *Social Problems, 9,* 307–314.

ERNST, C., & ANGST, J. (1983). *Birth order: Its influence on personality.* Berlin: Springer-Verlag.

EYSENCK, H. J. (1977). *Crime and personality.* (2nd ed.). London: Routledge and Kegan Paul.

EYSENCK, H. J. (1983). Personality, conditioning, and antisocial behavior. In W. S. Laufer & J. M. Day (Eds.), *Personality theory, moral development, and criminal behavior.* Lexington, MA: Lexington Books.

EYSENCK, H. J. (1984). Crime and personality. In D. J. Miller, D. E. Blackman and A. J. Chapman (Eds.), *Psychology and law.* Chichester, England, Wiley.

FAGAN, J., & WEXLER, S. (1987). Family origins of violent delinquents. *Criminology, 25,* 643–669.

FANCHER, R. E. (1987). Henry Goddard and the Kallikak family photographs. *American Psychologist, 42,* 585–590.

FARIS, R. E. L. (1967). *Chicago sociology: 1920–1932.* San Francisco: Chandler.

FARRINGTON, D. P., BIRON, L., & LEBLANC, M. (1982). Personality and delinquency in London and Montreal. In J. Gunn & D. P. Farrington (Eds.), *Abnormal offenders, delinquency, and the criminal justice system.* Chichester, England: Wiley.

FARRINGTON, D. P., GUNDRY, G., & WEST, D. J. (1975). The familial transmission of criminality. *Medicine, Science and the Law, 15,* 177–186.

FARRINGTON, D. P., OHLIN, L. E. & WILSON, J. Q. (1986). *Understanding and controlling crime.* New York: Springer-Verlag.

FEDERAL BUREAU OF INVESTIGATION. (1987). *Uniform crime reports.* Washington, DC: U.S. Government Printing Office.

FEELEY, M. M. (1983). *Court reform on trial: Why simple solutions fail.* New York: Basic Books.

FELD, B. C. (1981). Legislative policies toward the serious juvenile offender. *Crime and Delinquency, 27,* 497–521.

FELSON, M. (1986). Linking criminal choices, routine activities, informal social control, and criminal outcomes. In R. Clarke & D. Cornish (Eds.), *The reasoning criminal.* New York: Springer-Verlag.

FELSON, M., & COHEN, L. E. (1980). Human ecology and crime: A routine activity approach. *Human Ecology, 8,* 389–406.

FERNALD, W. (1919). A state program for the care of the mentally defective. *Mental Hygiene, 3,* 556–574.

FEYERABEND, P. (1970). Consolations for the specialist. In I. Lakatos & A. Musgrave (Eds.), *Criticism and the growth of knowledge.* Cambridge: Cambridge University Press.

FILSTEAD, W. J. (1970). *Qualitative methodology: First hand involvement in the social world.* Chicago: Markham.

FINCKENAUER, J. O. (1979). Scared crooked. *Psychology Today, 13,* 6–13.

FINCKENAUER, J. O. (1982). *Scared straight! and the panacea phenomena.* Englewood Cliffs, NJ: Prentice-Hall.

FINESTONE, H. (1976a). The delinquent and society: The Shaw and McKay tradition. In J. F. Short, Jr. (Ed.), *Delinquency, crime and society.* Chicago: University of Chicago Press.

FINESTONE, H. (1976b). *Victims of change: Juvenile delinquents in American society.* Westport, CT: Greenwood Press.

FINK, A. E. (1938). *Causes of crime: Biological theories in the United States 1800–1915.* Philadelphia: University of Pennsylvania Press.

FISCHER, C. S., JACKSON, R. M., STUEVE, C. A., GERSAU, K., JONES, L. M., & BALDASSARE, M. (1977). *Networks and places.* New York: Free Press.

FISCHER, C. S. (1982). *To dwell among friends: Personal networks in town and city.* Chicago: University of Chicago Press.

FOX, S. J. (1970). Juvenile justice reform: An historical perspective. *Stanford Law Review, 22,* 1187–1239.

FRIDAY, P. C. (1973). Problems in comparative criminology: Comments on the feasibility and implications of research. *International Journal of Criminology and Penology, 1,* 151–160.

FRIDAY, P. C. (1980). International review of youth crime and delinquency. In G. R. Newman (Ed.), *Crime and deviance: A comparative perspective.* Beverly Hills, CA: Sage.

FRIDAY, P. C. (1983). Patterns of role relationships and crime. In S. Giora Shoham (Ed.), *The many faces of crime and deviance.* New York: Sheridan House.

FRIDAY, P. C., & HAGE, J. (1976). Youth crime in postindustrial societies: An integrated perspective. *Criminology, 14,* 347–368.

FRIDAY, P. C., & STEWART, V. L. (1977). Youth crime and juvenile justice. *International perspectives.* New York: Praeger.

GALVIN, J., & BLAKE, G. F. (1984). Youth policy and juvenile justice reforms. *Crime and Delinquency, 30,* 339–346.

GARDNER, H. (1983). *Frames of mind: The theory of multiple intelligences.* New York: Basic Books.

GARDNER, H. (1986). The waning of intelligence tests. In R. J. Sternberg & D. K. Detterman (Eds.), *What is intelligence?* Norwood, NJ: Ablex.

GARBARINO, J. (1976). A preliminary study of some ecological correlates of child abuse: The impact of socioeconomic stress of mothers. *Child Development, 47,* 178–185.

GARBARINO, J. (1982). Sociocultural risk: Dangers to competence. In C. B. Kopp & J. B. Krakow (Eds.), *The child: Development in a social context.* Reading, MA: Addison-Wesley.

GARBARINO, J., & ASP, C. E. (1981). *Successful schools and competent students.* Lexington, MA: Lexington Books.

GARRETT, C. J. (1985). Effects of residential treatment on adjudicated delinquents: A meta-analysis. *Journal of Research in Crime and Delinquency, 22,* 287–308.

GEIS, G. (1965). *Juvenile gangs.* Washington, DC: U.S. Government Printing Office.

GEIS, G. (1982). The *Jack-Roller*: The appeal, the person, and the impact. In J. Snodgrass (Ed.), *The Jack-roller at seventy.* Lexington, MA: Lexington Books.

GENDREAU, P., & ROSS, R. R. (1987). Revivification of rehabilitation: Evidence from the 1980s. *Justice Quarterly, 4,* 349–407.

GERGEN, K. J. (1973). Social psychology as history. *Journal of Personality and Social Psychology, 26,* 309–320.

GERGEN, K. J. (1978). Toward generative theory. *Journal of Personality and Social Psychology, 36,* 1344–1360.

GERWITZ, J. L. (1961). A learning analysis of the effects of normal stimulation, privation, and deprivation on the acquisition of social motivation and attachment. In B. M. Foss (Ed.), *Determinants of infant behavior.* New York: Wiley.

GIBBENS, T. C. N. (1963). *Psychiatric studies of borstal lads.* London: Oxford University Press.

GIBBONS, D. C. (1986). Juvenile Delinquency: Can social science find a cure? *Crime and Delinquency*, 32, 186–204.

GIBBONS, D. & GRISWOLD, M. (1957). Sex differences among juvenile court referrals. *Sociology and Social Research*, *42*, 106–110.

GIBSON, H. B. (1969). Early delinquency in relation to broken homes. *Journal of Child Psychology and Psychiatry*, *10*, 195–204.

GILLIGAN, C. (1977). In a different voice: Women's conceptions of self and morality. *Harvard Educational Review*, *47*, 481–517.

GILLIGAN, C. (1982). *In a different voice.* Cambridge, MA: Harvard University Press.

GLUCKMAN, M. (1967). *The judicial process among the Barotse of Northern Rhodesia.* Manchester, England: Manchester University Press.

GLUECK, S., & GLUECK, E. T. (1930). *Five hundred criminal careers.* New York: Knopf.

GLUECK, S., & GLUECK, E. T. (1934). *One thousand juvenile delinquents.* Cambridge, MA: Harvard University Press.

GLUECK, S., & GLUECK, E. T. (1937). *Later criminal careers.* New York: Commonwealth Fund.

GLUECK, S., & GLUECK, E. T. (1940). *Juvenile delinquents grow up.* New York: Commonwealth Fund.

GLUECK, S., & GLUECK, E. T. (1943). *Criminal careers in retrospect.* New York: Commonwealth Fund.

GLUECK, S., & GLUECK, E. T. (1950). *Unraveling juvenile delinquency.* Cambridge, MA: Harvard University Press.

GLUECK, S., & GLUECK, E. T. (1956). *Physique and delinquency.* New York: Harper and Brothers.

GLUECK, S., & GLUECK, E. T. (1957). Working mothers and delinquency. *Mental Hygiene*, *41*, 327–352.

GLUECK, S., & GLUECK, E. T. (1968). *Delinquents and nondelinquents in perspective.* Cambridge, MA: Harvard University Press.

GODDARD, H. H. (1913). The Binet tests in relation to immigration. *Journal of Psycho-asthemics*, *18*, 105–107.

GODDARD, H. H. (1914). *Feeble-mindedness: Its causes and consequences.* New York: Macmillan.

GODDARD, H. H. (1917). Mental tests and the immigrant. *Journal of Delinquency*, *2*, 243–277.

GOLD, M. (1966). Undetected delinquent behavior. *Journal of Research in Crime and Delinquency*, *3*, 27–46.

GOLD, M. (1987). Social ecology. In H. C. Quay (Ed.), *Handbook of juvenile delinquency.* New York: Wiley.

GOLDSMITH, H. H., BUSS, A. H., PLOMIN, R., ROTHBART, M. K., THOMAS, A., CHESS, S., HINDE, R. A., & McCALL, R. B. (1987). Roundtable: What is temperament? Four Approaches. *Child Development*, *58*, 505–529.

GOLDSMITH, H. H., & CAMPOS, J. J. (1982). Toward a theory of infant temperament. In R. N. Emde & R. J. Harmon (Eds.), *The development of attachment and affiliative systems.* New York: Plenum.

GOODE, E. (1975). On behalf of the labeling theory. *Social Problems*, *22*, 570–583.

GOODMAN, N. (1978). *Ways of worldmaking.* Indianapolis, IN: Hackett.

GOODNOW, J. J. (1988). The socialization of intelligence. In M. Perlmutter (Ed.), *Perspectives on intellectual development.* Hillsdale, NJ: Lawrence Erlbaum Associates.

GOODWIN, C. (1979). *The Oak Park strategy: Community control of racial change.* Chicago: University of Chicago Press.

GORDON, M. (1971). *Juvenile delinquency in the American novel, 1905-1965.* Bowling Green, OH: Bowling Green University Popular Press.

GORDON, R. A. (1967). Issues in the ecological study of delinquency. *American Sociological Review, 32,* 927-944.

GOTTFREDSON, M., & HIRSCHI, T. (1986). The true value of Lambda would appear to be zero: An essay on career criminals, criminal careers, selective incapacitation, short studies and related topics. *Criminology, 24,* 213-234.

GOTTFREDSON, M., & HIRSCHI, T. (1987). The methodological adequacy of longitudinal research on crime. *Criminology, 25,* 581-614.

GOTTFREDSON, M., & HIRSCHI, T. (1988). Science, public policy, and the career paradigm. *Criminology, 26,* 37-56.

GOULD, S. J. (1981). *The mismeasure of man.* New York: Norton.

GOVE, W., & CRUTCHFIELD, R. D. (1982). The family and delinquency. *The Sociological Quarterly, 23,* 301-319.

GREENBERG, D. F. (1977). Delinquency and the age structure of society. *Contemporary Crises, 1,* 189-224.

GREENBERG, D. F. (1985). Age, crime and social explanation. *American Journal of Sociology, 91,* 1-21.

GREENBERG, S. W., ROHE, W. M., & WILLIAMS, J. R. (1982). *Safe and secure neighborhoods: Physical characteristics and informal territorial control in high and low crime neighborhoods.* Washington, DC: U. S. Government Printing Office.

GREENBERG, S. W., ROHE, W. M., & WILLIAMS, J. R. (1985a). *Informal citizen action and crime prevention at the neighborhood level.* Washington, DC: U. S. Government Printing Office.

GREENBERG, S. W., & ROHE, W. M., & WILLIAMS, J. R. (1985b). *Informal citizen action and crime prevention at the neighborhood level: Executive summary.* Washington, DC: U. S. Government Printing Office.

GRINNELL, R. M., & CHAMBERS, C. A. (1979). Broken homes and middle class delinquency. *Criminology, 17,* 395-400.

GURR, T. R., GRABOSKY, P. N., & HULA, R. C. (1977). *The politics of crime and conflict.* Beverly Hills, CA: Sage.

HAAN, N. (1978). Two moralities in action contexts: Relationships to thought, ego regulation, and development. *Journal of Personality and Social Psychology, 36,* 286-305.

HAGAN, J. (1982). *Research methods in criminal justice and criminology.* New York: MacMillan.

HAGAN, J. (1985). Toward a structural theory of crime, race, and gender: The Canadian case. *Crime and Delinquency, 31,* 129-146.

HAGAN, J. (1987). Micro and macro-structure of delinquency causation and power-control theory of gender and delinquency. *Albany conference on theoretical integration in the study of deviance and crime.* State University of New York at Albany, May 7-8.

HAGAN, J., GILLIS, A. R., & SIMPSON, J. (1985). The class structure of gender and delinquency: Toward a power-control theory of common delinquent behavior. *American Journal of Sociology, 90*, 1151–1160.

HAGAN, J., & PALLONI, A. (1988). Crimes as social events in the life course: Reconceiving a criminological controversy. *Criminology, 26*, 87–100.

HAGAN, J., SIMPSON, J., & GILLIS, A. R. (1987). Class in the household: A power-control theory of gender and delinquency. *American Journal of Sociology, 92*, 788–816.

HAMPARIAN, D. M., ESTEP, L. K., MUNTEAN, S. M., PRIESTINO, R. R., SWISHER, R. G., WALLACE, P. L., & WHITE, J. L. (1982). *Youth in adult courts: Between two worlds.* Washington, DC: U. S. Government Printing Office.

HAMPARIAN, D. M., SCHUSTER, R., DINITZ, S., & CONRAD, J. D. (1978). *The violent few.* Lexington, MA: Lexington Books.

HANSELL, S. & WIATROWSKI, M. D. (1981). Competing conceptions of delinquent peer relations. In G. F. Jensen (Ed.) *Sociology of Delinquency: Current Issues.* Beverly Hills, CA: Sage.

HARRIS, P. W. (1988). The interpersonal maturity level classification system: I-level. *Criminal Justice and Behavior, 15*, 58–77.

HARTUP, W. W (1978). Children and their friends. In H. McCurk (Ed.), *Issues in childhood social development.* London: Methuen.

HARTUP, W. W. (1979). The social world of childhood. *American Psychologist, 34*, 944–950.

HARTUP, W. W. (1983). Peer relations. In P. H. Mussen (Ed.), *Handbook of child psychology: Vol. 4.* (4th ed.). New York: Wiley.

HARVEY, L. (1987). The nature of 'schools' in the sociology of knowledge: The case of the 'Chicago School.' *The Sociological Review, 35*, 245–278.

HATHAWAY, S. R., & MONACHESI, E. D. (1957). The personalities of pre-delinquent boys. *Journal of Criminal Law, Criminology, and Police Science, 48*, 149–163.

HATHAWAY, S. R., & MONACHESI, E. D. (1963). *Adolescent personality and behavior.* Minneapolis, MN: University of Minnesota Press.

HAZARD, G. C., Jr. (1976). The jurisprudence of juvenile deviance. In M. K. Rosenheim (Ed.), *Pursuing justice for the child.* Chicago: University of Chicago Press.

HEALY, W. (1915). *The individual delinquent.* Boston: Little, Brown.

HEALY, W. (1925). The Psychology of the situation: A fundamental for understanding and treatment of delinquency and crime. In *The child, the clinic and the court.* New York: Johnson Reprint Corporation.

HEALY, W., & BRONNER, A. F. (1916). Youthful offenders: A comparative study of two groups, each of 1,000 young recidivists. *American Journal of Sociology, 22*, 38–52.

HEALY, W., & BRONNER, A. F. (1926). *Delinquents and criminals: Their making and unmaking.* New York: Macmillan.

HEALY, W. & BRONNER, A. F. (1936). *New Light on delinquency and its treatment.* New Haven, CT: Yale University Press.

HEALY, W., BRONNER, A. F., & BOWERS, A. M. (1930). *The structure and meaning of psychoanalysis.* New York: Alfred A. Knopf.

HELLUM, F. (1979). Juvenile justice: The second revolution. *Crime and Delinquency, 25*, 299–317.

HENNESSY, M., RICHARDS, P. J., & BERK, R. A. (1978). Broken homes and middle class delinquency: A reassessment. *Criminology, 15*, 505–528.

HERBERT, D. (1982). *The geography of urban crime.* London: Longman.

HETHERINGTON, E. M., COX, M., & COX, R. (1978). The development of children in mother headed families. In H. Hoffman & D. Reiss (Eds.), *The American family: Dying or developing?* New York: Plenum.

HETHERINGTON, E. M., COX, M., & COX, R. (1979). Family interaction and the social emotional cognitive development of children following divorce. In V. Vaughn & T. Brazelton (Eds.), *The family: Setting priorities.* New York: Science and Medicine.

HEWITT, L. E., & JENKINS, R. L. (1946). *Fundamental patterns of maladjustment: The dynamics of their origin.* Springfield, IL: State of Illinois.

HILL, G. D., & ATKINSON, M. (1988). Gender, familial control, and delinquency. *Criminology, 26*, 127–149.

HINDELANG, M. J. (1971). Age, sex and versatility of delinquency involvement. *Social Problems, 18*, 522–535.

HINDELANG, M. J. (1973). Causes of Delinquency: A partial replication and extension. *Social Problems, 20*, 471–487.

HINDELANG, M. J. (1979). Sex differences in criminal activity. *Social Problems, 27*, 143–156.

HINDELANG, M. J., HIRSCHI, T., & WEIS, J. G. (1981). *Measuring delinquency.* Beverly Hills, CA: Sage.

HIRSCHI, T. (1969). *Causes of Delinquency.* Berkeley, CA: University of California Press.

HIRSCHI, T. (1983). Crime and family policy. *Journal of Contemporary Studies*, Winter, 3–16.

HIRSCHI, T. (1987). Exploring alternatives to integrated theory. *Albany conference on theoretical integration in the study of deviance and crime.* State University of New York at Albany, May 7–8.

HIRSCHI, T., & GOTTFREDSON, M. (1983). Age and the explanation of crime. *American Journal of Sociology, 89*, 552–584.

HIRSCHI, T., & HINDELANG, M. J. (1977). Intelligence and delinquency. *American Sociological Review, 42*, 571–587.

HIRSCHI, T., & HINDELANG, M. J. (1978). Reply to Ronald L. Simons. *American Sociological Review, 43*, 610–613.

HIRSCHI, T., & SELVIN, H. C. (1967). *Delinquency research: An appraisal of analytical methods.* New York: The Free Press.

HOFFMAN, M. L. (1977). Sex differences in empathy and related behaviors. *Psychological Bulletin, 84*, 712–722.

HOFFMAN, M. L., & SALTZSTEIN, H. D. (1967). Parent discipline and the child's moral development. *Journal of Personality and Social Psychology, 5*, 45–57.

HOGAN, R., & JONES, W. H. (1983). A role-theoretical model of criminal conduct. In W. S. Laufer & J. M. Day (Eds.), *Personality theory, moral development and criminal behavior.* Lexington, MA: Lexington Books.

HOLSTEIN, C. B. (1976). Irreversible, stepwise sequence in the development of moral judgment: A longitudinal study of males and females. *Child Development, 47*, 51–61.

HOMANS, G. C. (1975). What do we mean by social "structure"? In P. M. Blau (Ed.), *Approaches to the study of social structure.* New York: The Free Press.

HUDGINS, W., & PRENTICE, N. M. (1973). Moral judgments in delinquent and nondelinquent adolescents and their mothers. *Journal of Abnormal Psychology, 82,* 145-152.

HUIZINGA, D., & ELLIOTT, D. S. (1987). Juvenile offender: Prevalence, offender incidence, and arrest rates by race. *Crime and Delinquency, 33,* 206-223.

HUTCHINGS, B., & MEDNICK, S. A. (1977). Criminality in adoptees and their adoptive and biological parents: A pilot study. In S. A. Mednick & K. A. Christiansen (Eds.), *Biological bases of criminal behavior.* New York: Gardner Press.

JARVIK, L. F., KLODIN, V., & MATSUYAMA, S. S. (1973). Human aggression and the extra Y chromosome. *American Psychologist, 28,* 674–682.

JENCKS, C. (1987). Genes and crime. *New York Review of Books, 34,* 33-41.

JENKINS, R. L., & GLICKMAN, S. (1974). Patterns of personality organization among delinquents. *The Nervous Child, 6,* 329–339.

JENNINGS, W. S., KILKENNY, R., & KOHLBERG, L. (1983). Moral development theory and practice for youthful and adult offenders. In W. S. Laufer & J. M. Day (Eds.) *Personality theory, moral development, and criminal behavior.* Lexington, MA: Lexington Books.

JENSEN, G. J., & EVE, R. (1976). Sex differences in delinquency. *Criminology, 13,* 427–448.

JESNESS, C. F. (1987). Early identification of delinquent-prone children: An overview. In J. D. Burchard & S. N. Burchard (Eds.), *Prevention of delinquent behavior.* Newbury Park, CA: Sage.

JESNESS, C. F. (1988). The Jesness inventory classification system. *Criminal Justice and Behavior, 15,* 78–92.

JESSOR, R. (1986). Adolescent problem drinking: Psychosocial aspect and developmental outcomes. In R. K. Silbereisen, K. Eyferth, & G. Rudinger (Eds.), *Development as action in context.* Berlin: Springer-Verlag.

JOHNSON, B. D., & WISH, E. (Eds.). (1986). *Crime rates among drug abusing offenders.* New York: Interdisciplinary Research Center.

JOHNSON, E. H., & BARAK-GLANTZ, I. L. (1983). Introduction, In I. L. Barak- Glantz & E. H. Johnson (Eds.), *Comparative criminology.* Beverly Hills, CA: Sage.

Johnson, R. E. (1979). *Juvenile delinquency and its origins.* Cambridge: Cambridge University Press.

Johnson, R. E. (1980). Social class and delinquent behavior. *Criminology, 18,* 86–93.

JOHNSON, R. E. (1986). Family structure and delinquency: General patterns and gender differences. *Criminology, 24,* 64–80.

JOHNSON, R. E., MARCOS, A. C., & BAHR, S. J. (1987). The role of peers in the complex etiology of adolescent drug use. *Criminology, 25,* 323–340.

JOHNSTONE, J. W. C. (1978). Juvenile delinquency and the family: A contextual interpretation. *Youth and Society, 9,* 299–313.

JOHNSTONE, J. W. C. (1980). Delinquency and the changing American family. In D. Schichor & D. H. Kelly (Eds.), *Critical issues in juvenile delinquency.* Lexington, MA: Lexington Books.

JURKOVIC, G. J., & PRENTICE, N. M. (1977). Relation of moral and cognitive development to dimensions of juvenile delinquency. *Journal of Abnormal Psychology, 86,* 414–420.

KANDEL, D. B. (1984). Marijuana users in young adulthood. *Archives of General Psychiatry, 41,* 200–209.

KANDEL, D. B. (1986). Process of peer influences in adolescence. In R. K. Silbereisen, K. Eyferth, & G. Rudinger (Eds.), *Development as action in context*. Berlin: Springer-Verlag.

KANDEL, D. B., & LESSER, G. S. (1972). *Youth in two worlds*. San Francisco: Jossey-Bass.

KELLAM, S. G., ADAMS, R. G., BROWN, H. C., & ENSMINGER, M. E. (1982). The long term evolution of the family structure of teenage and older mothers. *Journal of Marriage and the Family, 44*, 539–554.

KELLAM, S. G., BRANCH, T. D., BROWN, C. H., & RUSSELL, G. (1981). Why teenagers come for treatment: A ten year prospective epidemiological study in Woodlawn. *Journal of the American Academy of Child Psychiatry, 20*, 477–495.

KELLING, G. L. (1987). A taste for order: The community and police. *Crime and Delinquency, 33*, 90–102.

KELLY, G. A. (1963). *A theory of personality: The psychology of personal constructs*. New York: Norton.

KELLY, D. H. (1980). The educational experience and evolving delinquent careers: A neglected institutional link. In D. Schichor & D. H. Kelly (Eds.), *Critical issues in juvenile delinquency*. Lexington, MA: Lexington Books.

KELVES, D. J. (1984). Annals of Eugenics II. *The New Yorker*, October, *15*, 52–125.

KENRICK, D. T., & SPRINGFIELD, D. O. (1980). Personality traits and the eye of the beholder: Crossing some traditional philosophical boundaries in the search for consistency in all of the people. *Psychological Review, 87*, 88–104.

KING, C. H. (1975). The ego and the integration of violence in homicidal youth. *American Journal of Orthopsychiatry, 45*, 134–144.

KITSUSE, J. I. (1962). Societal reaction to deviant behavior: Problems of theory and method. *Social Problems, 9*, 247–256.

KITSUSE, J. I. & CICOUREL, A. V. (1963). A note on the use of official statistics. *Social Problems, 11*, 131–139.

KITTRIE, N. N. (1971). *The right to be different: Deviance and enforced therapy*. Baltimore: Johns Hopkins University Press.

KLEIN, D. (1973). The etiology of female crime. *Issues in Criminology, 8*, 3–30.

KOBRIN, S. (1959). The Chicago area project—A 25 year assessment. *The Annals of the American Academy of Political and Social Science, 322*, 19–29.

KOBRIN, S. (1982). The uses of the life-history document for the development of delinquency theory. In J. Snodgrass (Ed.), *The Jack-roller at seventy*. Lexington, MA: Lexington Books.

Kohlberg, L. (1969). Stage and sequence: The cognitive developmental approach to socialization. In D. A. Goslin (Ed.), *Handbook of socialization theory and research*. Chicago: Rand-McNally.

KOHLBERG, L. (1976). Moral stages and moralization: The cognitive developmental approach. In T. Lickona (Ed.), *Moral development and behavior*, New York: Holt, Rinehart and Winston.

KOHLBERG, L. (1977). The child as a moral philosopher. In CRM, *Readings in developmental psychology today*, New York: Random House.

KOHLBERG, L., & FREUNDLICH, D. (1973). Moral judgment in youthful offenders. In L. Kohlberg & E. Turiel (Eds.), *Moralization, the cognitive development approach*. New York: Holt, Rinehart and Winston.

KOHN, M. L. (1977). *Class and conformity: A study in values*. (2nd ed.). Chicago: University of Chicago Press.

KORNHAUSER, R. R. (1978). *Social sources of delinquency: An appraisal of analytic models*. Chicago: University of Chicago Press.

KRISBERG, B. (1986). Introduction. *Crime and Delinquency, 32*, 3–4.

KRISBERG, B., & SCHWARTZ, I. (1983). Rethinking juvenile justice. *Crime and Delinquency, 29*, 333–364.

KRISBERG, B., SCHWARTZ, I., FISHMAN, G., ELSIKOVITZ, Z., GUTTMAN, E., & KAREN, J. (1987). The incarceration of minority youth. *Crime and Delinquency, 33*, 173–205.

KRISBERG, B., SCHWARTZ, I. M., LITSKY, P., & AUSTIN, J. (1986). The watershed of juvenile justice reform. *Crime and Delinquency, 32*, 5–38.

KROHN, M. D. (1986). The web of conformity: A network approach to the explanation of delinquent behavior. *Social Problems, 33*, 81–93.

KROHN, M.D., KANZA-KADUCE, L., & AKERS, R. L. (1984). Community context and theories of deviant behavior: An examination of social learning and social bonding theories. *Sociological Quarterly, 25*, 353–371.

KROHN, M. D., & MASSEY, J. L. (1980). Social control and delinquent behavior: An examination of the elements of the social bond. *Sociological Quarterly, 21*, 529–544.

KROHN, M. D., MASSEY, J. L., SKINNER, W. F., & LAVER, R. (1983). Social bonding theory and adolescent cigarette smoking: A longitudinal analysis. *Journal of Health and Social Behavior, 24*, 337–349.

KRUTTSCHNITT, C. (1982). Women, crime and dependency. *Criminology, 19*, 495–513.

KUHN, T. S. (1970). *The structure of scientific revolutions*. (2nd ed.). Chicago: University of Chicago Press.

KURTZ, L. R. (1984). *Evaluating Chicago sociology: A guide to the literatue with an annotated bibliography*. Chicago: University of Chicago Press.

LAB, S. P. (1988). *Crime prevention: Approaches, practices and evaluations*. Cincinnati, OH: Anderson Publishing.

LAB, S. P., & WHITEHEAD, J. T. (1988). An analysis of juvenile delinquency correctional treatment. *Crime and Delinquency, 34*, 60–83.

LAKATOS, I. (1970). Falsification and the methodology of scientific research programmes. In I. Lakatos & A. Musgrave (Eds.), *Criticism and the growth of knowledge*. Cambridge: Cambridge University Press.

LAMB, M. E. (1977). The effects of divorce on children's personality development. *Journal of Divorce, 2*, 163–174.

LANDER, B. (1954). *Towards an understanding of juvenile delinquency*. New York: Columbia University Press.

LANGE, J. (1928). *Crime as destiny*. London: George Allen and Unwin.

LANGNER, T. S., GERSTEN, J. C., & EISENBERG, J. G. (1977). The epidemiology of mental disorders in children: Implications for community psychiatry. In G. Serban (Ed.), *New trends of psychiatry in the community*. Cambridge, MA: Ballinger.

LATANE, B., & DARLEY, J. M. (1970). *The unresponsive bystander: Why doesn't he help?* New York: Appleton-Century-Crofts.

Laub, J. H. (1983). Trends in serious juvenile crime. *Criminal Justice and Behavior*, *10*, 485–506.

Laumann, E. O. (1979). Network analysis in large social systems: Some theoretical and methodological problems. In P. W. Holland & S. Leinhardt (Eds.), *Perspectives on social network research*. New York: Academic Press.

Lees, J. P., & Newson, L. J. (1954). Family or sibship position of some aspects of juvenile delinquency. *British Journal of Delinquency*, *5*, 46–55.

Lefkowitz, M. M., Eron, L. D., Walder, L. O., & Huesmann, L. R. (1977). *Growing up to be violent*. New York: Pergamon.

Lemert, E. M. (1951) *Social pathology*. New York: McGraw-Hill.

Lemert, E. M. (1983). Interview with E. M. Lemert, March 16, 1979. In J. H. Laub (Ed.), *Criminology in the making*: *An oral history*. Boston: Northeastern University Press.

Lenroot, K. R. (1932). Discussion of "Are broken homes a causative factor in juvenile delinquency?" *Social Forces*, *10*, 527–529.

Leonard, E. B. (1982). *Women, crime, and society*. New York: Longman.

Lindesmith, A., & Levin, Y. (1937). The Lombrosian myth in criminology. *American Journal of Sociology*, *42*, 653–671.

Lindsay, B., & McGillis, D. (1986). Citywide community crime prevention: An assessment of the Seattle program. In D. P. Rosenbaum (Ed.), *Community crime prevention*: *Does it work?* Beverly Hills, CA: Sage.

Linn, J. W. (1935). *Jane Addams*. New York: Appleton-Century.

Little, C. B. (1987). Strategies for cross-level theorizing: Comments on the Meier and Hagan papers. *Albany conference on theoretical integration in the study of deviance and crime*. State University of New York at Albany, May 7–8.

Loeber, R., & Stouthamer-Loeber, M. (1986). Family factors as correlates and predictors of juvenile conduct problems and delinquency. In M. Tonry & N. Morris (Eds.), *Crime and Justice*: *Vol. 7*. Chicago: University of Chicago Press.

Lombardo, P. A. (1985). Three generations, no imbeciles: New light on *Buck v. Bell*. *New York University Law Review*, *60*, 30–62.

Lombroso, C., & Ferrero, W. (1895). *The female offender*. London: Fisher Unwin.

Lou, H. H. (1927). *Juvenile courts in the United States*. New York: Arno.

Lylerly, R. R., & Skipper, J. K., Jr. (1981). Differential rates of rural-urban delinquency: A social control approach. *Criminology*, *19*, 385–399.

Lynch, M. J., & Groves, W. B. (1986). *A primer in radical criminology*. Albany, NY: Harrow & Heston.

McCall, R. B. (1981). Nature-Nurture and the two realms of development: A proposed integration with respect to mental development. *Child Development*, *52*, 1–12.

McCandless, B. R., Persons, W. S., & Roberts, A. (1972). Perceived opportunity, delinquency, race and body build among delinquent youth. *Journal of Consulting and Clinical Psychology*, *38*, 281–287.

McCord, J. (1978). A thirty-year follow up of treatment effects. *American Psychologist*, *33*, 284–289.

McCord, J. (1986). Instigation and insulation: How families affect antisocial behavior. In D. Olweus, J. Block, & M. Radke-Yarrow (Eds.), *Development of antisocial and prosocial behavior*. Orlando, FL: Academic Press.

McCord, W. & McCord, J., & Zola, I. K. (1959). *Origins of crime: A new evaluation of the Cambridge-Somerville study*. New York: Columbia University Press.

Maccoby, E. E. (1986). Social groupings in childhood. In D. Olweus, J. Block, & M. Radke-Yarrow (Eds.), *Development of antisocial and prosocial behavior*. Orlando, FL: Academic Press.

Maccoby, E. E., & Jacklin, C. N. (1980). Sex difference in aggression: A rejoinder and reprise. *Child Development*, *51*, 964–980.

Maccoby, E. E., & Martin, J. A. (1983). Socialization in the context of the family: Parent-child interaction. In P. H. Mussen (Ed.), *Handbook of child psychology: Vol. 4*. New York: Wiley.

McGahey, R. M. (1986). Economic conditions, neighborhood organization, and urban crime. In A. J. Reiss, Jr. & M. Tonry (Eds.), *Communities and crime*. Chicago: University of Chicago Press.

Magnusson, D. (1981). *Toward a psychology of situations: An interactional perspective*. Hillsdale, NJ: Lawrence Erlbaum.

Magnusson, D., & Allen, V. L. (1983). Implications and applications of an interactional perspective for human development. In D. Magnusson & V. L. Allen (Eds.), *Human development: An interactional perspective*. New York: Academic Press.

Manicas, P. T., & Secord, P. F. (1983). Implications for psychology of the new philosophy of science. *American Psychologist*, *38*, 399–413.

Mann, C. R. (1984). *Female crime and delinquency*. University, AL: University of Alabama Press.

Mannheim, H. (1965). *Comparative criminology*. Boston: Houghton Mifflin.

Maslow, A. H. (1954). *Motivation and personality*. New York: Harper.

Matsueda, R. (1982). Testing control theory and differential association: A causal modeling approach. *American Sociological Review*, *47*, 489-504.

Matza, D. (1964). *Delinquency and drift*. New York: Wiley.

Matza, D. (1969). *Becoming deviant*. Englewood Cliffs, NJ: Prentice-Hall.

Mawby, R. (1980). Sex and crime. *British Journal of Sociology*, *31*, 525–543.

Mead, G. H. (1934). *Mind, self and society*. Chicago: University of Chicago Press.

Mednick, S. A. (1977). A biosocial theory of the learning of law-abiding behavior. In S. A. Mednick & K. O. Christiansen (Eds.), *Biosocial bases of criminal behavior*. New York: Gardner.

Mednick, S. A., Moffitt, T., Gabrielli, W., & Hutchings, B. (1986). Genetic factors in criminal behavior: A review. In D. Olweus, J. Block, & M. Radke-Yarrow (Eds.), *Development of antisocial and prosocial behavior*. Orlando, FL: Academic Press.

Metzer, H. (1967). Contributions to the history of psychology: VI. Dr. William Healy — 1869 to 1963 — The man in his time. *Psychological Reports*, *20*, 1028-1030.

Menard, S., & Morse, B. J. (1984). A structuralist critique of the IQ-delinquency hypothesis: Theory and evidence. *American Journal of Sociology*, *89*, 1347-1378.

MENNEL, R. M. (1983). Attitudes and policies toward juvenile delinquency in the United States: A historiographical review. In M. Tonry & N. Morris (Eds.), *Crime and justice: Annual review of research: Vol. 4.* Chicago: University of Chicago Press.

MERTON, R. K. (1938). Social structure and anomie. *American Sociological Review, 3*, 672–682.

MERTON, R. K. (1949). *Social theory and social structure.* Glencoe, IL: The Free Press.

MERTON, R. K. (1957). *Social theory and social structure.* (Revised ed.). New York: The Free Press.

MILLER, W. B. (1958). Lower Class culture as a generating milieu of gang delinquency. *Journal of Social Issues, 14,* 5-19.

MILLER, W. B. (1980). Gangs, groups, and serious youth crime. In D. Schichor & D. H. Kelly (Eds.), *Critical issues in juvenile delinquency.* Lexington, MA: Lexington Books.

MINUCHIN, P. P., & SHAPIRO, E. K. (1983). The school as a context for social development. In P. H. Mussen (Ed.), *Handbook of Child Psychology: Vol. 4.* New York: Wiley.

MISCHEL, W. (1968). *Personality and assessment.* New York: Wiley.

MISCHEL, W., & PEAKE, P. K. (1982). Beyond déjà vu in the search for cross-sectional consistency. *Psychological Review, 89,* 730–755.

MITCHELL, J. C. (Ed.), (1969). *Social networks in urban situations.* Manchester, England: Manchester University Press.

MITCHELL, J. C. (1979). Networks, algorithms, and analysis. In P. W. Holland & S. Leinhardt (Eds.), *Perspectives on social network research.* New York: Academic Press.

MONACHESI, E. D. (1936). Trends in criminological research in Italy. *American Sociological Review, 1,* 396–406.

MONAHAN, T. P. (1957). Family status and the delinquent child: A reappraisal and some new findings. *Social Forces, 35,* 250–258.

MONTEMAYOR, R. (1978). Men and their bodies: The relationships between body types and behavior. *Journal of Social Issues, 34,* 48–64.

MORASH, M. A. (1981). Cognitive development theory. *Criminology, 19,* 360–371.

MORASH, M. A. (1983). An explanation of juvenile delinquency: The integration of moral reasoning theory and sociological knowledge. In W. S. Laufer & J. M. Day (Eds.), *Personality theory, moral development, and criminal behavior.* Lexington, MA: Lexington Books.

MORRIS, T. P. (1957). *The criminal area: A study in social ecology.* London: Routledge and Kegan Paul.

MOULDS, E. F. (1980). Chivalry and paternalism: Disparities of treatment in the criminal justice system. In S. Datesman & F. Scarpitti, (Eds.), *Women, crime and justice.* New York: Oxford University press.

MOWRER, O. H. (1950). *Learning theory and personality dynamics.* New York: Ronald.

MOWRER, O. H. (1960). *Learning theory and behavior.* New York: Wiley.

MURRAY, C. (1976). *The link between learning disabilities and juvenile delinquency: Current theory and knowledge. Executive Summary.* Washington, DC: U. S. Government Printing Office.

NAGEL, I. H., & HAGAN, J. (1983). Gender and Crime: Offense patterns and criminal court sanctions. In M. Tonry & N. Morris (Eds.), *Crime and Justice: An annual review of research: Vol. 4.* Chicago: University of Chicago Press.

NAPOLI, D. S (1981). *Architects of adjustment: The history of the psychological profession in the United States*. Port Washington, NY: Kennikat Press.

NETTLER, G. (1984). *Explaining crime*. (3rd ed.). New York: McGraw-Hill.

NEWMAN, G. R. (1977). Problems of method in comparative criminology. *International Journal of Comparative and Applied Criminal Justice, 1,* 17-31.

NIELSEN, A., & GERBER, D. (1979). Psychological aspects of truancy in early adolescence. *Adolescence, 41,* 313-326.

NORLAND, S., SHOVER, N., THORNTON, W., & JAMES, J. (1979). Intrafamily conflict and delinquency. *Pacific Sociological Review, 22,* 233-237.

NYE, F. I. (1958). *Family relationships and delinquent behavior*. New York: Wiley.

NYE, F. I., & SHORT, J. F., Jr. (1957). Scaling delinquent behavior. *American Sociological Review, 22,* 326-331.

O'DONNELL, C. R., MANOS, M. J., & CHESNEY-LIND, M. (1987). Diversion and neighborhood delinquency programs in open settings: A social network interpretation. In E. K. Morris & C. J. Braukmann (Eds.), *Behavioral approaches to crime and delinquency*. New York: Plenum.

OGBU, J. U. (1974). *The next generation: An ethnography of education in an urban neighborhood*. New York: Academic.

OHLIN, L. E. (1983a). Interview with Lloyd E. Ohlin, June 22, 1979. In J. H. Laub, *Criminology in the making: An oral history*. Boston: Northeastern University Press.

OHLIN, L. E. (1983b). The future of juvenile delinquency policy and research. *Crime and Delinquency, 29,* 463-472.

OLWEUS, D. (1978). *Aggression in the schools*. New York: Wiley.

OLWEUS, D. (1980). Familial and temperamental determinants of aggressive behavior in adolescent boys: A causal analysis. *Developmental Psychology, 16,* 644-660.

PALMER, T. (1974). The California Youth Authority. *Federal Probation, 38,* 3-14.

PARK, R. E., & MILLER, H. A. (1921). *Old world traits transplanted*. New York: Harper & Brothers.

PARKER, J. G., & ASHER, S. R. (1987). Peer relations and later personal adjustment: Are low-accepted children at risk? *Psychological Bulletin, 102,* 357-389.

PARSON, T. (1951). *The social system*. Glencoe, IL: The Free Press.

PASSINGHAM, R. E. (1972). Crime and personality: A review of Eysenck's theory. In V. D. Nebylitsyn & J. A. Gray (Eds.), *Biological bases of individual behavior*. New York: Academic.

PATTERSON, G. R. (1982). *Coercive family process*. Eugene, OR: Castalia Press.

PATTERSON, G. R. (1986). The contribution of siblings to training for fighting: A microsocial analysis. In D. Olweus, J. Block, & M. Radke-Yarrow (Eds.), *Development of antisocial and prosocial behavior*. Orlando, FL: Academic Press.

PATTERSON, G. R., & DISHION, T. J. (1985). Contributions of families and peers to delinquency. *Criminology, 23,* 63-79.

PATTERSON, G. R., DISHION, T. J., & BANK, L. (1984). Family interaction: A process model of deviance training. *Aggressive Behavior, 10,* 253-267.

PATTERSON, G. R., & STOUTHAMER-LOEBER, M. (1984). The correlation of family management practices and delinquency. *Child development, 55,* 1299-1307.

PEARSON, F., & WEINER, N. A. (1985). Toward an integration of criminological theories. *Journal of Criminal Law and Criminology, 76,* 116-150.

PEDHAZUR, E. J. (1982). *Multiple regression in behavioral research*. (2nd ed.). New York: Holt, Rinehart and Winston.

PEIRCE, B. K. (1969/1869). *A half century with juvenile delinquents*. Montclair, NJ: Patterson Smith.

PEIRCE, C. S. (1955). *Philosophical writings*. New York: Dover.

PETERSON, D. R., & BECKER, W. S. (1965). Family interaction and delinquency. In H. C. Quay (Ed.), *Juvenile delinquency: Research and theory*. Princeton, NJ: Van Nostrand.

PFOHL, S. J. (1985). *Images of deviance and social control: A sociological history*. New York: McGraw-Hill.

PHARES, E. J. (1972). Applications to psychopathology. In J. B. Rotter, J. E. Chance, & E. J. Phares (Eds.), *Applications of a social learning theory of personality*. New York: Holt, Rinehart and Winston.

PLATT, A. M. (1969a). *The child savers*. Chicago: University of Chicago Press.

PLATT, A. M. (1969b). The rise of the child saving movement: A study in social policy and correctional reform. *The Annals*, *381*, 21–38.

POLK, K. (1957). Juvenile delinquency and social areas. *Social Problems*, *5*, 214–217.

POLK, K. (1967). Urban social areas and delinquency. *Social Problems*, *14*, 320–325.

POLLAK, O. (1950). *The criminality of women*. New York: A. S. Barnes.

POPPER, K. R. (1968). *The logic of scientific discovery*. New York: Harper and Row.

POWERS, E., & Witmer, H. (1951). *An experiment in the prevention of delinquency*. New York: Columbia University Press.

PRICE, W. H., & WHATMORE, P. B. (1967). Behaviour disorders and patterns of crime among XYY males identified at a maximum security hospital. *British Medical Journal*, *1*, 533-536.

PULKKINEN, L. (1986). The role of impulse control in the development of antisocial and prosocial behavior. In D. Olweus, J. Block, & M. Radke-Yarrow (Eds.), *Development of antisocial and prosocial behavior*. Orlando, FL: Academic Press.

QUAY, H. C. (1987a). Patterns of delinquent behavior. In H. C. Quay (Ed.), *Handbook of juvenile delinquency*. New York: Wiley.

QUAY, H. C. (1987b). Institutional treatment. In H. C. Quay (Ed.), *Handbook of juvenile delinquency*. New York: Wiley.

QUETELET, L. A. (1842). *A treatise on man and the development of his faculties*. Gainesville, FL: Scholars Facsimiles and Reprints.

QUINNEY, R. (1977). *Class, state, and crime: On the theory and practice of criminal justice*. New York: Longman.

RANKIN, J. H. (1983). The family context of delinquency. *Social Problems*, *30*, 466–479.

RECKLESS, W. C. (1961). *The crime problem*. (2nd ed.). New York: Appleton-Century-Crofts.

RECKLESS, W. C. (1973). *The crime problem*. (5th ed.). New York: Appleton-Century-Crofts.

RECKLESS, W. C., & DINITZ, S. (1967). Pioneering with self-concept as a vulnerability factor in delinquency, *Journal of Criminal Law, Criminology and Police Science*, *63*, 515–523.

REGNERY, A. S. (1986). A federal perspective on juvenile justice reform. *Crime and Delinquency*, *32*, 39–51.

REICHENBACH, H. (1947). *Elements of symbolic logic*. New York: Macmillan.

REIMAN, J. (1984). *The rich get richer and the poor get prison*. New York: Wiley.

REISCHAUER, E. O. (1978). *The Japanese*. Cambridge, MA: Harvard University Press.

REISS, A. J., JR. (1951a). Unraveling juvenile delinquency: An appraisal of the research methods. *American Journal of Sociology, 52*, 115–120.

REISS, A. J., JR. (1951b). Delinquency as the failure of personal and social controls. *American Sociological Review, 16*, 197–207.

REISS, A. J., JR. (1986). Why are communities important in understanding crime? In A. J. Reiss, Jr. & M. Tonry (Eds.), *Communities and crime*. Chicago: University of Chicago Press.

REISS, A. J., & RHODES, A. L. (1961). The distribution of juvenile delinquency in the social class structure. *American Sociological Review, 26*, 720–732.

REST, J. R. (1979). *Revised manual for the defining issues test: An objective test of moral judgment development*. Minneapolis, MN: Moral Research Projects.

ROBERTSON, R., & TAYLOR, L. (1973). *Deviance, crime and socio-legal control: Comparative perspectives*. London: Martin Robertson.

ROBINSON, W. S. (1950). Ecological correlations and the behavior of individuals. *American Sociological Review, 15*, 351–357.

RODHAM, H. (1973). Children under the law. *Harvard Education Review, 43*, 493–497.

RODMAN, H., & GRAMS, P. (1967). Juvenile delinquency and the family: A review and discussion. *Task force report: Juvenile delinquency and youth crime*. Washington, DC: U. S. Printing Office.

ROEHL, J. A., & COOK, R. F. (1984). *Evaluation of the urban crime prevention program: Executive summary*. Washington, DC: National Institute of Justice.

ROFF, J. D., & WIRT, D. (1984). Childhood aggression and social adjustment as antecedents of delinquency. *Journal of Abnormal Child Psychology, 12*, 111–126.

ROFF, M. (1975). Juvenile delinquency in girls: A study of a recent sample. In R. D. Wirt, G. Winokur, & M. Roff (Eds.), *Life history research in psychopathology: Vol. 4*. Minneapolis, MN: University of Minnesota Press.

ROFF, M., & SELLS, S. B. (1968). Juvenile delinquency in relation to peer acceptance-rejection and socioeconomic status. *Psychology in the Schools, 5*, 3–18.

RONCEK, D. W. (1975). Density and crime. *American Behavioral Scientist, 18*, 843–860.

ROSCH, J. (1987). Institutionalizing mediation: The evolution of the Civil Liberties Bureau in Japan. *Law and Society Review, 21*, 243–266.

ROSE, S. M. (1972). *Betrayal of the poor*. Cambridge, MA: Schenkman Publishing Company.

ROSEN, L. (1985). Family and delinquency: Structure or function. *Criminology, 23*, 553–573.

ROSEN, L., & NEILSON, K. (1982). Broken homes and delinquency. In L. Savitz & N. Johnson (Eds.), *Contemporary Criminology*. New York: Wiley.

ROSEN, L. & TURNER, S. H. (1967). An evaluation of the Lander approach to ecology of delinquency. *Social Problems, 15*, 189–200.

ROSENBAUM, D. P. (1987). The theory and research behind neighborhood watch: Is it a sound fear and crime reduction strategy? *Crime and Delinquency, 33*, 103–134.

ROSENBAUM, J. L. (1975). The stratification of socialization processes. *American Sociological Review, 40*, 42–54.

ROSENBAUM, J. L. (1987). Social control, gender, and delinquency: An analysis of drug, property, and violent offenders. *Justice Quarterly, 4*, 117–132.

ROSNOW, R. L. (1978). The prophetic vision of Giambattista Vico: Implications for the state of social psychological theory. *Journal of Personality and Social Psychology, 36,* 1322–1331.

ROSS, R. A., & BENSON, G. C. S. (1979). Criminal justice from East to West. *Crime and delinquency, 25,* 76–86.

ROTHBART, M. K. (1986). Longitudinal observation of infant temperament. *Developmental Psychology, 22,* 356–365.

ROTHBART, M. K., & DERRYBERRY, D. (1982). Emotion, attention and temperament. In M. E. Lamb & A. L. Brown (Eds.), *Advances in developmental psychology: Vol. 1.* Hillsdale, NJ: Erlbaum.

ROTHMAN, D. J. (1980). *Conscience and convenience.* Boston: Little, Brown.

ROWE, D. C., & OSGOOD, D. W. (1984). Heredity and sociological theories of delinquency: A reconsideration. *American Sociological Review, 49,* 526–540.

RUBIN, S. (1951). *Unraveling juvenile delinquency.* Illusions in a research project using matched pairs. *American Journal of Sociology, 52,* 107–114.

RUDMAN, C., HARDSTONE, E., FAGAN, J., & MOORE, M. (1986). Violent youth in adult court: Process and punishment. *Crime and Delinquency, 32,* 75–96.

RUTTER, M., & GILLER, H. (1984). *Juvenile Delinquency: Trends and perspectives.* New York: Gilford Press.

RYERSON, E. (1978). *The best-laid plans.* New York: Hill and Wang.

SALTZSTEIN, H. D. (1976). Social influence and moral development. In T. Lickona (Ed.), *Moral development and behavior: Theory, research, and social issues.* New York: Holt, Rinehart, and Winston.

SAMPSON, E. E. (1978). Scientific paradigms and social values: Wanted—a scientific revolution. *Journal of Personality and Social Psychology, 36,* 1322–1343.

SAMPSON, R. J. (1986). Crime in cities: The effects of formal and informal social control. In A. J. Reiss, Jr., & M. Tonry (Eds.), *Communities and crime.* Chicago: University of Chicago Press.

SAPIR, E. (1921). *Language.* New York: Harcourt, Brace and World.

SCARR, S., & MCCARTNEY, K. (1983). How people make their own environments: A theory of genotype-environment effects. *Child Development, 54,* 424–435.

SCHAFER, W. E., & POLK, K. (1967). Delinquency and the schools. *Task force report: Juvenile delinquency and youth crime.* Washington, DC: U. S. Government Printing Office.

SCHEINGOLD, S. A. (1984). *The politics of law and order.* New York: Longman.

SCHICHOR, D. (1983). Historical and current trends in American juvenile justice. *Juvenile and Family Court Journal, 34,* 61–75.

SCHLOSSMAN, S. L. (1977). *Love and the American Delinquent.* Chicago. University of Chicago Press.

SCHLOSSMAN, S. & SEDLAK, M. (1983). The Chicago area project revisited. *Crime and Delinquency, 29,* 398–462.

SCHNEIDER, A. L. (1984). Divesting status offenses from juvenile court jurisdiction. *Crime and Delinquency, 30,* 347–370.

SCHUERMAN, L., & KOBRIN, S. (1986). Community careers in crime. In A. J. Reiss, Jr., & M. Tonry (Ed.), *Communities and crime.* Chicago: University of Chicago Press.

SCHUESSLER, K. (Ed.) (1973). *Edwin H. Sutherland: On analyzing crime.* Chicago: University of Chicago Press.

SCHWARTZ, H., & JACOBS, J. (1979). *Qualitative sociology: A method to the madness.* New York: The Free Press.

SCHWITZGEBEL, R. K. (1977). Professional accountability in the treatment and release of dangerous persons. In B. D. Sales (Ed.), *The criminal justice system: Vol. 1.* New York: Plenum.

SCIMECCA, J. A. (1977). Labeling theory and personal construct theory. *Journal of Criminal Law and Criminology, 68,* 652–659.

SCOTT, J. E., & AL-THAKEB, F. (1980). Perceptions of deviance cross-culturally. In G. R. Newman (Ed.), *Crime and deviance: A comparative perspective.* Beverly Hills, CA: Sage.

SCOTT, J. E., & AL-THAKEB, F. (1980). Perceptions of deviance cross-culturally. In G. R. Newman (Ed.), *Crime and deviance: A comparative perspective.* Beverly Hills, CA: Sage.

SEBALD, H. (1986). Adolescents' shifting orientations toward parents and peers: A curvilinear trend over recent decades. *Journal of Marriage and the Family, 48,* 5–13.

SHAVIT, Y., & RATTNER, A. (1988). Age, crime, and the early life course. *American Journal of Sociology, 93,* 1457–1470.

SHAW, C. R., & McKAY, H. D. (1931). Social factors in juvenile delinquency. In *Report on the causes of crime: Vol. 2.* Washington, D. C.: National Commission on Law Observance and Enforcement.

SHAW, C. R., & McKAY, H. D. (1932). Are broken homes a causative factor in juvenile delinquency? *Social Forces, 10,* 514–533.

SHAW, C. R., & McKAY, H. D. (1942). *Juvenile delinquency and urban areas.* Chicago: University of Chicago Press.

SHAW, C. R., & McKAY, H. D. (1969). *Juvenile delinquency and urban areas.* (Revised ed.). Chicago: University of Chicago Press.

SHELLEY, L. I. (1981). *Crime and modernization: The impact of industrialization and urbanization on crime.* Carbondale, IL: Southern Illinois University Press.

SHERMAN, L. N. (1986). Policing communities: What works? In A. J. Reiss, Jr., & M. Tonry (Eds.), *Communities and crime.* Chicago: University of Chicago Press.

SHERNOCK, S. R. (1986). A profile of the citizen crime prevention activist. *Journal of Criminal Justice, 14,* 211–228.

SHEVKY, E., & BELL, W. (1955). *Social area analysis: Theory, illustrative application and computational procedures.* Stanford, CA: Stanford University Press.

SHEVKY, E., & WILLIAMS, M. (1949). *The social areas of Los Angeles: Analysis and typology.* Berkeley, CA: University of California Press.

SHIDELER, E. H. (1918). Family disintegration and the delinquent boy in the United States. *Journal of Criminal Law, Criminology, and Police Science, 261,* 21–37.

SHORT, J. F., JR., (1979). On the etiology of delinquent behavior. *Journal of Research on Crime and Delinquency, 16,* 28–33.

SHORT, J. F., JR., (1982). Life history, autobiography, and the life cycle. In J. Snodgrass (Ed.), *The Jack-roller at seventy.* Lexington, MA: Lexington Books.

SHORT, J. F., JR., (1987). Exploring integration of theoretical levels of explanation: Notes on juvenile delinquency. *Albany conference on theoretical integration in the study of deviance and crime.* State University of New York at Albany, May 7–8.

SHORT, J. F., JR., & NYE, I. F. (1957). Reported behavior as a criterion of deviant behavior. *Social Problems*, *5*, 205-213.

SHORT, J. F., JR., & NYE, I. F. (1958). Extent of unrecorded juvenile delinquency: Tentative conclusions. *Journal of Criminal Law, Criminology and Police Science*, *49*, 296-302.

SHORT, J. F. JR., & STRODTBECK, F. L. (1965). *Group process and gang delinquency.* Chicago: University of Chicago Press.

SHORTLAND, R. L., & GOODSTEIN, L. F. (1984). The role of bystanders in crime control. *Journal of Social Issues*, *40*, 9-26.

SILVERMAN, D. (1985). *Qualitative methodology and sociology: Describing the social world.* Hants, England: Gower.

SIMMEL, G. (1922). *Conflict and the web of group affiliation.* New York: The Free Press.

SIMMEL, G. (1950). *The sociology of Georg Simmel.* Kurt H. Wolff (Ed.). New York: The Free Press.

SIMON, R. (1975). *Women and crime.* Lexington, MA: Lexington Books.

SIMONS, R. L. (1978). The meaning of the IQ-delinquency relationship. *American Sociological Review*, *43*, 268-270.

SKOGAN, L. W. (1986). Fear of crime and neighborhood change. In A. J. Reiss, Jr., & M. Tonry (Eds.), *Communities and crime.* Chicago: University of Chicago Press.

SMITH, C. P., & ALEXANDER, P. S. (1980). *A national assessment of serious juvenile crime and the juvenile justice system: The need for a rational response: Vol. 1. Summary.* Washington, DC: U. S. Government Printing Office.

SMITH, C. P., ALEXANDER, P. S., KEMP, G. L., & LEMERT, E. N. (1980). *The national assessment of serious juvenile crime and the juvenile justice system: The need for a rational response: Vol. 3.* Washington, DC: U. S. Government Printing Office.

SMITH, D., & VISHER, C. (1980). Sex and involvement in deviance/crime: A quantitative review of the empirical literature. *American Sociological Review*, *45*, 691-701.

SNAREY, J. R., & VAILLANT, G. E. (1985). How lower and working class youth become middle-class adults: The association between ego defense mechanisms and upward social mobility. *Child Development*, *56*, 899-910.

SNODGRASS, J. (1982). *The Jack-roller at seventy.* Lexington, MA: Lexington Books.

SNODGRASS, J. (1984). William Healy (1869-1963): Pioneer child psychiatrist and criminologist. *Journal of the History of the Behavioral Sciences*, *20*, 332-339.

SNYDER, J., & PATTERSON, G. (1987). Family interaction and delinquent behavior. In H. C. Quay (Ed.), *Handbook of juvenile delinquency.* New York: Wiley.

SPECTOR, M. (1976). Labeling theory in *Social Problems:* A young journal launches a new theory. *Social Problems*, *24*, 69-75.

SPIVACK, G., & CIANCI, N. (1987). High-risk early behavior patterns and later delinquency. In J. D. Burchard & S. N. Burchard (Eds.), *Prevention of delinquent behavior.* Newbury Park, CA: Sage.

STAFFORD, M. (1984). Gang delinquency. In R. F. Meier (Ed.), *Major forms of crime.* Beverly Hills, CA: Sage.

STEINBERG, L. (1986). Latchkey children and susceptibility to peer pressure: An ecological analysis. *Developmental Psychology*, *22*, 443-439.

STEINBERG, L. (1987). Single parents, stepparents, and the susceptibility of adolescents to anti-social peer pressure. *Child Development, 58,* 269–275.

STEFFENSMEIER, D. (1978). Crime and the contemporary woman: An analysis of changing levels of female property crime, 1969–1975. *Social Forces, 57,* 566–584.

STEFFENSMEIER, D. (1980). Sex differences in patterns of adult crimes 1965–1977: A review and assessment. *Social Forces, 58,* 1080–1108.

STEFFENSMEIER, D. J., & STEFFENSMEIER, R. H. (1980). Trends in female delinquency. *Criminology, 18,* 62–85.

STERNBERG, L., BLINDE, P. L., & CHAN, K. S. (1984). Dropping out among language minority youth. *Review of Educational Research, 54,* 113–132.

STOKES, J. & LEVIN, I. (1986). Gender differences in predicting loneliness from social network characteristics. *Journal of Personality and Social Psychology, 51,* 1069–1074.

STRAUS, M. A. (1983). Ordinary violence, child abuse, and wife beating: What do they have in common? In D. Finkelhor, R. J. Gelles, G. T. Hotaling, & M. A. Straus (Eds.), *The dark side of families.* Beverly Hills, CA: Sage.

SULLIVAN, C. E., GRANT, M. Q., & GRANT, J. K. (1957). The development of interpersonal maturity: Applications to delinquency. *Psychiatry, 20,* 272–282.

SUTHERLAND, E. H. (1931). Mental deficiency and crime. In K. Young (Ed.), *Social attitudes.* New York: Henry Holt.

SUTHERLAND, E. H. (1939). *Criminology.* (3rd ed.). Philadelphia: Lippincott.

SUTHERLAND, E. H. (1956a). Varieties of delinquent youth. In A. Cohen, A. Lindesmith, & K. Schuesser, (Eds.), *The Sutherland Papers.* Bloomington, IN: Indiana University Press.

SUTHERLAND, E. H. (1956b). Critique of theory—1944. In A. Cohen, A. Lindesmith, & K. Schuessler (Eds.), *The Sutherland papers.* Bloomington, IN: Indiana University Press.

SUTHERLAND, E. H., & CRESSEY, D. R. (1974). *Criminology.* (9th ed.). Philadelphia: Lippincott.

SUTTON, J. R. (1985). The juvenile court and social welfare: Dynamics of progressive reform. *Law and Society Review, 19,* 107–146.

SUZUKI, Y. (1981). Japan. In L. L. Stewart (Ed.), *Justice and troubled children around the world: Vol. 3.* New York: New York University Press.

SYKES, G. M., & MATZA, D. (1957). Techniques of neutralization: A theory of delinquency. *American Sociological Review, 22,* 664–670.

TANNENBAUM, F. (1938). *Crime and the community.* Boston: Ginn.

TAPPAN, P. W. (1949). *Juvenile delinquency.* New York: McGraw-Hill.

TARDE, G. (1897/1969). Criminal youth. In T. N. Clark (Ed.), *On communication and social influence.* Chicago: University of Chicago Press.

TARDE, G. (1902). *La criminalité comparée.* Paris: Felix Alcan.

TAUB, R. P., TAYLOR, D. G., & DUNHAM, J. D. (1984). *Paths of neighborhood change: Race and crime in urban America.* Chicago: University of Chicago Press.

TAYLOR, I., WALTON, P., & YOUNG, J. (1973). *The new criminology: For a social theory of deviance.* New York: Harper & Row.

TERMAN, L. M. (1916). *The measurement of intelligence.* Boston: Houghton Mifflin.

THOMAS, A., & CHESS, S. (1977). *Temperament and development.* New York: Brunner/Mazel.

THOMAS, A., CHESS, S., & BIRCH, H. G. (1968). *Temperament and behavior disorders in children.* New York: New York University Press.

THOMAS, W. I. (1923). *The unadjusted girl.* Boston: Little, Brown.

THOMAS, W. I. (1931). *The unadjusted girl.* (Revised ed.). Boston: Little, Brown.

THOMAS, W. I., & THOMAS, D. S. (1928). *The child in America.* New York: Knopf.

THOMAS, W. I., & ZNANIECKI, F. (1927). *The polish peasant in Europe and America.* New York: Knopf.

THORNBERRY, T. P. (1987). Toward an interactional theory of delinquency. *Criminology, 25,* 863–891.

THORNBERRY, T. P., & FARNWORTH, M. (1982). Social correlates of criminal involvement: Further evidence on the relationship between social status and criminal behavior. *American Sociological Review, 47,* 505–518.

THORNDIKE, E. L. (1929). On the fallacy of imputing the correlations found for groups to the individuals on smaller groups composing them. *American Journal of Psychology, 15,* 351–357.

THRASHER, F. M. (1927). *The gang: A study of 1,313 gangs in Chicago.* Chicago: University of Chicago Press.

TITTLE, C. R. (1985). A plea for open minds, one more time: Response to Nettler. *Social Forces, 63,* 1078–1080.

TITTLE, C. R. (1988). Two empirical regularities (maybe) in search of an explanation: Commentary on the age/crime debate. *Criminology, 26,* 75–86.

TITTLE, C. R., VILLEMEZ, W. J., & SMITH, D. A. (1978). The myth of social class and criminality: An assessment of the empirical evidence. *American Sociological Review, 43,* 643–656.

TOBY, J. (1957). The differential impact of family disorganization. *American Sociological Review, 22,* 505–512.

TOBY, J. (1979). Delinquency in cross-cultural perspective. In L. T. Empey (Ed.), *Juvenile Justice: The progressive legacy and current reform.* Charlottesville, VA: University of Virginia Press.

TOENNIES, F. (1957). *Community and society.* New York: Harper Torchbooks.

TOENNIES, F. (1971). The place of birth of criminals in Schleswig-Holstein. In W. J. Cahnman & R. Heberk (Eds.), *On sociology: Pure, applied, and empirical.* Chicago: University of Chicago Press.

TOKORO, K. (1983). Japan. In E. H. Johnson (Ed.), *International handbook of contemporary development in criminology.* Westport, CT: Greenwood Press.

TONRY, M. & MORRIS, N. (Eds.) (1983). Introduction. *Crime and justice: An annual review of research.* Chicago: University of Chicago Press.

TOULMAN, S. (1961). *Foresight and understanding: An inquiry into aims of science.* New York: Harper.

TOWN, C. H. (1913). Mental types of juvenile delinquents, considered in relation to treatment. *Journal of Criminal Law and Criminology, 46,* 83–89.

TRASLER, G. (1987). Biogenetic factors. In H. C. Quay (Ed.), *Handbook of juvenile delinquency.* New York: Wiley.

TULKIN, S. R., & COVITZ, F. E. (1975). *Mother-infant interaction and intellectual functioning at age six.* Paper presented at the meeting for the Society for Research in Child Development, Denver.

TULKIN, S. R. & KAGAN, J. (1972). Mother-child interactions in the first year of life. *Child Development, 43,* 31–41.

United States Bureau of The Census (1978). *State and local probation and parole systems.* Washington, DC: U. S. Government Printing Office.

United States Bureau of the Census (1987). *Statistical abstracts of the United States 1987.* Washington, DC: U. S. Government Printing Office.

U. S. Department of Justice (1983). *Report to the nation on crime and justice: The data.* Washington, DC: U. S. Government Printing Office.

VOLD, G. B. (1951). Edwin Hardin Sutherland: Sociological Criminologist. *American Sociological Review, 16,* 3–9.

VOLD, G. B. (1958). *Theoretical criminology.* New York: Oxford University Press.

VOLD, G. B. (1979). *Theoretical criminology.* (2nd ed.). New York: Oxford University Press.

VOSS, H. L. (1966). Socioeconomic status and reported delinquent behavior. *Social Problems, 13,* 314–324.

WADSWORTH, M. E. J. (1975). Delinquency in a national sample of children. *British Journal of Criminology, 15,* 167–174.

WADSWORTH, M. E. J. (1979). *Roots of delinquency: Infancy, adolescence and crime.* Oxford: Martin Robinson.

WAGATSUMA, H., & ROSETT, A. (1986). The implications of apology: Law and culture in Japan and the U.S. *Law and Society Review, 20,* 461–498.

WALKER, N. (1968). *Crime and punishment in Britain.* Edinburgh: Edinburgh University Press.

WANDERSMAN, A., JAKUBS, J. F., & GIAMARTINO, G. A. (1981). Participation in block organizations. *Journal of Community Action, 1,* 40–47.

WARREN, M. Q. (1969). The case for differential treatment of delinquents. *Annals of the American Academy of Political Science, 381,* 47–59.

WARREN, M. Q. (1983). Applications of interpersonal maturity theory to offender populations. In W. S. Laufer & J. M. Day (Eds.), *Personality theory, moral development, and criminal behavior.* Lexington, MA: Lexington Books.

WEIS, J. G. & SEDERSTROM, J. (1981). *The prevention of serious delinquency: What to do?* Washington, DC: Center for Law and Justice.

WELLFORD, C. F. (1987). Towards an integrated theory of criminal behavior. *Albany conference on theoretical integration in the study of deviance and crime.* The State University of New York at Albany, May 7–8.

WELLS, L. E., & RANKIN, J. H. (1985). Broken homes and juvenile delinquency: An empirical review. *Criminal Justice Abstracts, 17,* 249–272.

WELLS, L. E., & RANKIN, J. H. (1986). The broken homes model of delinquency: Analytic issues. *Journal of Research in Crime and Delinquency, 23,* 68–93.

WERNER, E. E. (1987). Vulnerability and resiliency in children at risk for delinquency: A longitudinal study from birth to young adulthood. In J. D. Burchard & S. N. Burchard (Eds.), *Prevention of delinquency.* Newbury Park, CA: Sage.

WERNER, E. E., BIERMAN, J. M., & FRENCH, F. E. (1971). *The children of Kauai: A longitudinal study from the prenatal period to age ten.* Honolulu: University of Hawaii Press.

WERNER, E. E., & SMITH, R. S. (1977). *Kauai's children come of age.* Honolulu: University of Hawaii Press.

WERNER, E. E., & SMITH, R. S. (1982). *Vulnerable, but invincible: A longitudinal study of resilient children and youth.* New York: McGraw-Hill.

WERNER, H. (1957). The concept of development from a comparative and organismic point of view. In D. B. Harris (Ed.), *The concept of development.* Minneapolis, MN: University of Minnesota Press.

WEST, D. J. (1982). *Delinquency: Its roots, careers and prospects.* Cambridge, MA: Harvard University Press.

WEST, D. J., & FARRINGTON, D. P. (1973). *Who becomes delinquent?* London: Heinemann Educational.

WEST, D. J., & FARRINGTON, D. P. (1977). *The delinquent way of life.* London: Heinemann.

WHORF, B. L. (1956). Science and linguistics. In J. B. Carroll (Ed.), *Language, thought, and reality: Selected writings of Benjamin Lee Whorf.* Cambridge, MA: M.I.T. Press.

WIATROWSKI, M. D., GRISWOLD, D., & ROBERTS, M. K. (1981). Social control theory and delinquency. *American Sociological Review, 46,* 525–541.

WILGOSH, L., & PAITICH, D. (1982). Ratings of parent behaviors for delinquents from two-parent and single-parent homes. *International Journal of Social Psychiatry, 28,* 141–143.

WILKES, D. (1974). The new federalism in criminal procedure: State court evasion of the Burger Court. *Kentucky Law Journal, 62,* 421.

WILKINSON, K. (1974). The broken family and juvenile delinquency: Scientific explanation or ideology? *Social Problems, 21,* 736–739.

WILKINSON, K. (1980). The broken home and delinquent behavior: An alternative interpretation of contradictory findings. In T. Hirschi and M. Gottfredson (Eds.), *Understanding Crime.* Beverly Hills, CA: Sage.

WILLIAMS, J. R., & GOLD, M. (1972). From delinquent behavior to official delinquency. *Social Problems, 20,* 209–229.

WILSON, H. (1974). Parenting in poverty. *British Journal of Social Work, 4,* 241–254.

WILSON, H. (1975). Juvenile delinquency, parent criminality and social handicap. *British Journal of Criminality, 15,* 241–250.

WILSON, H. (1980). Parental supervision: A neglected aspect of delinquency. *British Journal of Criminology, 20,* 203–235.

WILSON, J. Q. (1975). *Thinking about crime.* New York: Vintage Books.

WILSON, J. Q., & HERRNSTEIN, R. J. (1985). *Crime and human nature.* New York: Simon and Schuster.

WOLFGANG, M. E. (1983). Delinquency in two birth cohorts. *American Behavioral Scientist, 27,* 75–86.

WOLFGANG, M. E., & FERRACUTI, F. (1967). *The subculture of violence.* London: Tavistock.

WOLFGANG, M. E., FIGLIO, R. M., & SELLIN, T. (1972). *Delinquency in a birth cohort.* Chicago: University of Chicago Press.

YATES, A., BEUTLER, L. E., & CRAGO, M. (1983). Characteristics of young, violent offenders. *Journal of Psychiatry and Law, 11,* 137–149.

YORBURG, B. (1973). *The changing family.* New York: Columbia University Press.

ZELENY, L. D. (1933). Feeble-mindedness and criminal conduct. *American Journal of Sociology, 38,* 564–576.

ZILLMAN, D. (1979). *Hostility and aggression.* Hillsdale, NJ: Erlbaum.

ZILLMAN, D. (1983). Arousal and aggression. In R. G. Geen & E. I. Donnerstein (Eds.), *Aggression: Theoretical and empirical reviews: Vol. 1.* New York: Academic Press.

Subject Index

Name Index